GCHQ

By the same author

British Intelligence, Strategy and the Cold War, 1945–51 (editor)

*Intelligence, Defence and Diplomacy: British Policy in the
Post-War World* (editor, with M.F. Hopkins)

Espionage, Security and Intelligence in Britain, 1945–70 (editor)

*Intelligence and the War Against Japan: Britain, America and the
Politics of Secret Service*

The Clandestine Cold War in Asia, 1945–65 (editor, with
G. Rawnsley and M.Y. Rawnsley)

*The Hidden Hand: Britain, America and Cold War Secret
Intelligence*

Secret Intelligence: A Reader (with Christopher Andrew and
Wesley K. Wark)

RICHARD J. ALDRICH

GCHQ

The Uncensored Story of Britain's
Most Secret Intelligence Agency

Harper
Press

HarperPress
An imprint of HarperCollins*Publishers*
77–85 Fulham Palace Road,
Hammersmith, London W6 8JB
www.harpercollins.co.uk

Published by HarperPress in 2010

1

A catalogue record for this book is available from the British Library

HB ISBN 13 978-0-00-727847-3
HB ISBN 10 0-00-727847-0
TPB ISBN 13 978-0-00-731265-8
TPB ISBN 10 0-00-731265-2

Set in Meridien by Palimpsest Book Production Limited,
Falkirk, Stirlingshire

Printed and bound in Great Britain by Clays Ltd, St Ives plc

Mixed Sources
Product group from well-managed
forests and other controlled sources
www.fsc.org Cert no. SW-COC-001806
© 1996 Forest Stewardship Council

FSC is a non-profit international organisation established to promote the
responsible management of the world's forests. Products carrying the FSC
label are independently certified to assure consumers that they come
from forests that are managed to meet the social, economic and
ecological needs of present and future generations.

Find out more about HarperCollins and the environment at
www.harpercollins.co.uk/green

For Libby
(for the dark night-time)

CONTENTS

THE 1960s
SPACE, SPY SHIPS AND SCANDALS

THE 1970s
TURBULENCE AND TERROR

THE 1980s
INTO THE THATCHER ERA

AFTER 1989
GCHQ GOES GLOBAL

ILLUSTRATIONS

Alastair Denniston. *(US National Archives and Records Administration)*
Edward Travis. *(US National Archives and Records Administration)*
Voice interception during the Second World War. *(US National Archives and Records Administration)*
Arlington Hall, where Venona was broken. *(US National Archives and Records Administration)*
UKUSA meeting in the early 1950s. *(US National Archives and Records Administration)*
Russian radio equipment captured in Korea, 1951. *(US National Archives and Records Administration)*
President Sukarno of Indonesia, whose *'Konfrontasi'* was defeated with the help of British sigint. *(US National Archives and Records Administration)*
British phone-tapping equipment from the 1950s. *(US National Archives and Records Administration)*
George Blake. *(Imperial War Museum)*
Tony Beasley. *(By permission of Tony Beasley)*
HMS *Turpin*. *(Royal Submarines Museum)*
A Russian sigint 'trawler' in the North Sea. *(UK National Archives)*
The cypher room of Britain's Embassy in Peking after it was overrun by 'protesters' in 1967. *(UK National Archives)*
Clive Loehnis. *(National Portrait Gallery, London)*
Commander Robert 'Fred' Stannard. *(Imperial War Museum)*
The *Blue Peter* team admire Britain's first Skynet communications satellite in November 1969. *(UK National Archives)*

Sigint operators at RAF Chicksands in Bedfordshire listen in to the Soviet Air Force. *(US National Archives and Records Administration)*

Benhall, one of the two GCHQ sites at Cheltenham in the 1970s. *(Gloucester Citizen)*

USS *Oxford*, one of America's spy ships. *(US National Archives and Records Administration)*

US President Richard Nixon and CIA Director Richard Helms. *(US National Archives and Records Administration)*

An American SR-71 Blackbird spy plane at RAF Mildenhall, October 1973. *(US National Archives and Records Administration)*

Bodies of some of the kidnappers after the shoot-out at Kizildere in March 1972. *(By permission of Batu Erkan)*

The Mayor's house at Kizildere after the siege. *(By permission of Batu Erkan)*

HMS *Endurance* during the Falklands War. *(US National Archives and Records Administration)*

HMS *Conqueror* after sinking the *General Belgrano*. *(Imperial War Museum)*

Geoffrey Prime. *(Imperial War Museum)*

Benson Buffham. *(US National Archives and Records Administration)*

GCHQ protesters in Cheltenham in 1984 after the trade union ban. *(Gloucester Citizen)*

An 'Odette' intercept unit during the Gulf War in 1991. *(MoD/Royal Signals Museum)*

John Scarlett and Sir David Omand. *(Getty Images)*

'The Doughnut'. *(© Topfoto)*

Sigint and Comsec Locations in the UK

1 Adastral Park, Martlesham Heath, Suffolk, BT Research Laboratories, 1975–
2 Beaumanor/Garats Hay, Leic., post–war Army sigint base & Special Projects Agency, 1945–94
3 Bletchley Park; this remained a sigint training site after the war until 1985
4 Boddington, Glos, (RAF) military communications unit working with GCHQ
5 Bower, Bowermadden near Wick, listening station, closed 1975
6 Brawdy, Haverfordwest, Wales, 14 Signals Regiment (electronic warfare)
7 Brora, Sutherland, listening station, closed 1984
8 Capenhurst Tower, Cheshire, intercepting telephone traffic to Ireland, 1990–98
9 Cheadle, Staffs, (RAF) listening station, closed 1996
10 Cheltenham (Oakley and Benhall); GCHQ moved to the twin sites between 1952 and 1954
11 Chicksands, Beds, NSA/USAF until 1994, then UK Defence Intelligence & Security Centre
12 Cricklade, Wilts, GCHQ experimental radio station
13 Culmhead, Somerset, GCHQ Central Training School, replacing Bletchley, 1985–94
14 Digby, Lincs, main centre for RAF ground sigint and now UK joint services sigint centre
15 Edzell, Brechin, US Navy/NSA site, 1960–96
16 HMS Flowerdown, near Winchester, listening station, closed 1977
17 Gilnahirk, Belfast, listening station, closed 1978
18 Hanslope Park, near Milton Keynes, Diplomatic Wireless Service and DTMS
19 Hawklaw, (Cupar) Fife, listening station, closed 1988
20 Hereford, 264 Signal Squadron supporting 22 SAS
21 Irton Moor, Scarborough, listening station, now GCHQ Scarborough
22 Island Hill, Comber, Northern Ireland, closed 1977
23 Ivy Farm, Knockholt Pound, Kent, listening station
24 Kirknewton, near Edinburgh, US listening station, closed 1966
25 Menwith Hill, near Harrogate, US Army listening station, taken over by NSA 1963
26 HMS Mercury, near Petersfield, naval signals centre, 1941–93
27 Morwenstow, now GCHQ Bude, focused on satellite communications, 1969–
28 Oakhanger, (RAF) control centre for Skynet since 1967
29 Royal Radar Establishment, Malvern, from 1953, later Defence Research Agency
30 Waddington, Lincs, (RAF) Nimrod R1s of 51 Squadron since 1995
31 Watton, Norfolk, (RAF) Central Signals Establishment, 192 Squadron 1945–63
32 Whaddon Manor, Bucks, outstation of Bletchley Park, closed 1946
33 Wyton, Cambridgeshire, (RAF) Comets and Nimrod R1s of 51 Squadron, 1963–95
34 **London**
   Chester Road, Borehamwood, (GCHQ/SIS) factory making radio microphones in the 1950s
   Chesterfield Street W1, London office for GCHQ in the late 1940s
   Dollis Hill, North London, Post Office Research Station, 1921–75
   Eastcote, Harrow; GCHQ moved here in 1946 and some comsec staff remained after 1952
   Empress State Building, Earl's Court, listening station, 1962–94
   London Processing Group, St Dunstan's Hill, City of London, moved to Cheltenham 1975
   Northwood Hills, small post–war GCHQ site; Permanent Joint HQ since 1996
   Palmer St W1, LCSA headquarters until 1969; also GCHQ's London office

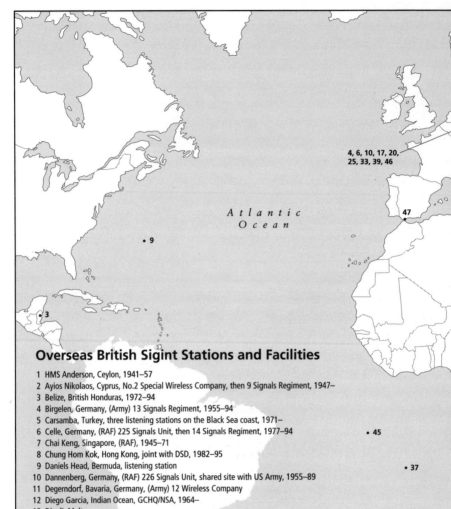

15, 44

11 •

4, 6, 10, 17, 20,
25, 33, 39, 46

14,

*Atlantic
Ocean*

• 9

47

• 3

• 45

• 37

31

Overseas British Sigint Stations and Facilities

1 HMS Anderson, Ceylon, 1941–57
2 Ayios Nikolaos, Cyprus, No.2 Special Wireless Company, then 9 Signals Regiment, 1947–
3 Belize, British Honduras, 1972–94
4 Birgelen, Germany, (Army) 13 Signals Regiment, 1955–94
5 Carsamba, Turkey, three listening stations on the Black Sea coast, 1971–
6 Celle, Germany, (RAF) 225 Signals Unit, then 14 Signals Regiment, 1977–94
7 Chai Keng, Singapore, (RAF), 1945–71
8 Chung Hom Kok, Hong Kong, joint with DSD, 1982–95
9 Daniels Head, Bermuda, listening station
10 Dannenberg, Germany, (RAF) 226 Signals Unit, shared site with US Army, 1955–89
11 Degerndorf, Bavaria, Germany, (Army) 12 Wireless Company
12 Diego Garcia, Indian Ocean, GCHQ/NSA, 1964–
13 Dingli, Malta
14 Frohnleiten, near Graz, Austria, 3 Wireless Squadron, 1945–47
15 Gatow, Berlin, (RAF) 26 Signals Unit, 1945–89
16 Geraldton, Australia, replaced joint GCHQ–DSD sites in Hong Kong, 1995–
17 Gluckstadt, Hamburg, Germany, 1 Special Wireless Regiment, 1946–50
18 Graz, Austria, 12 Wireless Squadron, 1947–55
19 Habbaniya, Iraq, (RAF) 123 Signals Unit, 1945–57
20 Hambruhen, Germany, (RAF) 291 Signals Unit, 1952–58
21 Heliopolis, Egypt, 1941–46
22 Khormaksar, Aden, (RAF)
23 Kranji, Singapore, (RAF), 1945–74
24 Labuan, British North Borneo, (RAF) 606 Signal Troop, later 266 Signal Squadron, 1963–66

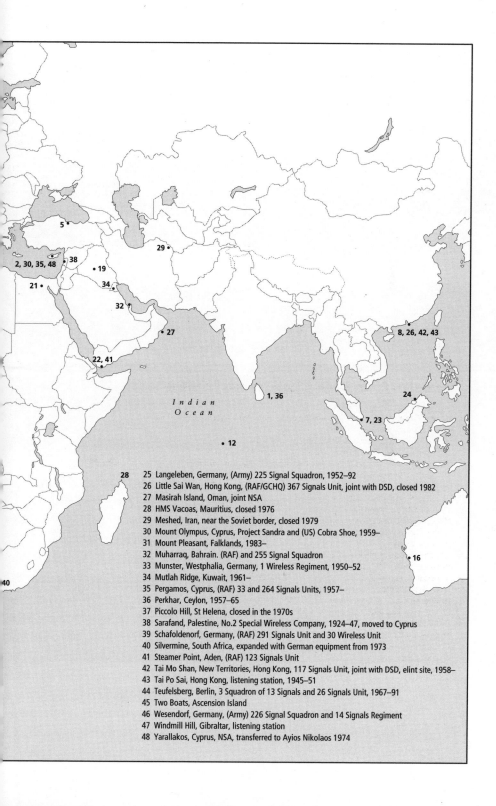

5 ·

29 ·

2, 30, 35, 48 · 38
· 19
21 ·
34 ·
32 ·

· 27

22, 41 ·

8, 26, 42, 43 ·

1, 36 ·

24 ·

Indian Ocean

7, 23 ·

· 12

28

· 16

40

25 Langeleben, Germany, (Army) 225 Signal Squadron, 1952–92
26 Little Sai Wan, Hong Kong, (RAF/GCHQ) 367 Signals Unit, joint with DSD, closed 1982
27 Masirah Island, Oman, joint NSA
28 HMS Vacoas, Mauritius, closed 1976
29 Meshed, Iran, near the Soviet border, closed 1979
30 Mount Olympus, Cyprus, Project Sandra and (US) Cobra Shoe, 1959–
31 Mount Pleasant, Falklands, 1983–
32 Muharraq, Bahrain. (RAF) and 255 Signal Squadron
33 Munster, Westphalia, Germany, 1 Wireless Regiment, 1950–52
34 Mutlah Ridge, Kuwait, 1961–
35 Pergamos, Cyprus, (RAF) 33 and 264 Signals Units, 1957–
36 Perkhar, Ceylon, 1957–65
37 Piccolo Hill, St Helena, closed in the 1970s
38 Sarafand, Palestine, No.2 Special Wireless Company, 1924–47, moved to Cyprus
39 Schafoldenorf, Germany, (RAF) 291 Signals Unit and 30 Wireless Unit
40 Silvermine, South Africa, expanded with German equipment from 1973
41 Steamer Point, Aden, (RAF) 123 Signals Unit
42 Tai Mo Shan, New Territories, Hong Kong, 117 Signals Unit, joint with DSD, elint site, 1958–
43 Tai Po Sai, Hong Kong, listening station, 1945–51
44 Teufelsberg, Berlin, 3 Squadron of 13 Signals and 26 Signals Unit, 1967–91
45 Two Boats, Ascension Island
46 Wesendorf, Germany, (Army) 226 Signal Squadron and 14 Signals Regiment
47 Windmill Hill, Gibraltar, listening station
48 Yarallakos, Cyprus, NSA, transferred to Ayios Nikolaos 1974

Note on Terminology

On 1 November 1919, Britain created the Government Code and Cypher School, or 'GC&CS', the nation's first integrated code-making and code-breaking unit. The term GC&CS remained in widespread use until the end of the Second World War.

By contrast, Government Communications Headquarters, or 'GCHQ', is a term of uncertain origin. Originally developed as a cover name for Bletchley Park in late 1939, it competed for usage with several other designations, including 'BP', 'Station X' and indeed 'GC&CS'. However, the Government Code and Cypher School remained the formal title of the whole organisation in wartime. During 1946, GC&CS re-designated itself the 'London Signals Intelligence Centre' when the staff of Bletchley Park decamped to a new site at Eastcote near Uxbridge, although GCHQ remained in widespread use as a cover name. On 1 November 1948, as Britain's code-breakers began to investigate a further move away from London to Cheltenham, the term GCHQ was formally adopted and has remained in use ever since.

'Code-breaker' is also a troublesome phrase. Codes are usually considered to be words substituted for others, often chosen somewhat at random. Typically, the military operations that constituted D-Day in 1944 were code-named 'Overlord'. By contrast, systems of communication where letters and numbers are substituted in an organised pattern, either by machine or by hand, are referred to as cyphers. Yet the term code-breaker is so frequently applied to the people who worked at Bletchley Park and at GCHQ that this book follows common usage.

The constantly changing names of the Soviet intelligence and security services are especially vexing and so, despite the inescapable anachronisms, the Soviet civilian intelligence service is referred to as 'KGB' until 1989, while the military intelligence service is denoted as 'GRU'. In Britain, the Security Service is denoted here by the commonly known term 'MI5' and its sister organisation, the Secret Intelligence Service or MI6, is referred to as 'SIS'. Ships' and submarines' names are italicised, e.g. HMS *Turpin*. Onshore naval bases and training establishments, e.g. HMS Anderson, are not italicised.

Abbreviations

A-2	US Air Force Intelligence
ASA	Army Security Agency [American]
ASIO	Australian Security Intelligence Organisation
BDS	British Defence Staff, Washington
BfV	West German security service
BJ	'Blue jacket' file for signals intelligence or an individual intercept
Blue Book	Weekly digest of comint material for the PM
BND	Bundesnachrichtendienst – foreign intelligence service of West Germany
Brixmis	British Military Mission to the HQ Soviet Army in East Germany
BRUSA	Anglo–American signals intelligence agreement, 1943
'C'	Chief of the British Secret Intelligence Service (SIS)
CESD	Communications-Electronics Security Department, succeeded by CESG
CESG	Communications-Electronics Security Group
CIA	Central Intelligence Agency [American]
comint	Communications intelligence
comsec	Communications security
CSE	Communications Security Establishment [Canadian]
CSU	Civil Service Union
CX	Prefix for a report originating with SIS
DIS	Defence Intelligence Staff

DMSI	Director of Management and Support for Intelligence in DIS
DSD	Defence Signals Department [Australian], formerly DSB
DWS	Diplomatic Wireless Service
elint	Electronic intelligence
FBI	Federal Bureau of Investigation [American]
GC&CS	Government Code and Cypher School
GCHQ	Government Communications Headquarters
GRU	Soviet Military Intelligence
GTAC	Government Technical Assistance Centre, established in 2000 – later NTAC
IRSIG	Instructions and Regulations concerning the Security of Signals Intelligence [Allied]
JIC	Joint Intelligence Committee
JSRU	Joint Speech Research Unit
JSSU	Joint Services Signals Unit, combined sigint collection units
KGB	Russian secret service
LCSA	London Communications Security Agency, until 1963
LCSA	London Communications-Electronics Security Agency, until 1965
LPG	London Processing Group
MI5	Security Service
MI6	Secret Intelligence Service (also SIS)
MiG	Mikoyan – Soviet fighter aircraft
MoD	Ministry of Defence
MTI	Methods to Improve, sequential five-year sigint programmes at GCHQ
NATO	North Atlantic Treaty Organisation
NSA	National Security Agency [American]
NTAC	National Technical Assistance Centre, previously GTAC
PHP	Post-Hostilities Planning Committee

PSIS	Permanent Secretaries' Committee on the Intelligence Services
SAS	Special Air Service
SBS	Special Boat Service
SDECE	French intelligence service
Sigdasys	An allied operational sigint distribution system in Germany in the 1980s
sigint	Signals intelligence
SIS	Secret Intelligence Service (also MI6)
SOE	Special Operations Executive
SUSLO	Special United States Liaison Officer based in Britain
TICOM	Target Intelligence Committee dealing with signals intelligence
UKUSA	UK–USA signals intelligence agreements
VHF	Very High Frequency
Y	Wireless interception, usually low-level
Y Section	SIS unit undertaking interception activities
Y Service	Signals interception arms of the three services

Introduction

GCHQ – The Last Secret?

GCHQ has been by far the most valuable source of intelligence for the British Government ever since it began operating at Bletchley during the last war. British skills in interception and code-breaking are unique and highly valued by our allies. GCHQ has been a key element in our relationship with the United States for more than forty years.

Denis Healey, House of Commons, 27 February 1984[1]

'GCHQ' is the last great British secret. For more than half a century, Government Communications Headquarters – the successor to the famous wartime code-breaking organisation at Bletchley Park – has been the nation's largest and yet most elusive intelligence service. During all of this period it has commanded more staff than the Security Service (MI5) and the Secret Intelligence Service (SIS) combined, and has enjoyed the lion's share of Britain's secret service budget. GCHQ's product, known as signals intelligence or 'sigint', constituted the majority of the secret information available to political decision-makers during the Cold War. Since then, it has become yet more significant in an increasingly 'wired' world. GCHQ now plays a leading role in shaping Britain's secret state, and in the summer of 2003 it relocated to a spectacular new headquarters that constituted the single largest construction project in Europe. Today, it is more important than ever – yet we know almost nothing about it.[2]

By contrast, the wartime work of Bletchley Park is widely celebrated. The importance of decrypted German communications – known as 'the Ultra secret' – to Britain's victory over the Axis is universally recognised. Winston Churchill's wartime addiction to his daily supply of 'Ultra' intelligence, derived from supposedly impenetrable German cypher machines such as 'Enigma', is legendary. The mathematical triumphs of brilliant

figures such as Alan Turing are a central part of the story of
Allied success in the Second World War. The astonishing achievement of signals intelligence allowed Allied prime ministers and
presidents to see into the minds of their Axis enemies. Thanks
to 'sigint' we too can now read about the futile attempts of
Japanese leaders to seek a favourable armistice in August 1945,
even as the last screws were being tightened on the atomic
bombs destined for Hiroshima and Nagasaki.[3]

However, shortly after VJ-Day, something rather odd happens.
In the words of Christopher Andrew, the world's leading intelligence historian, we are confronted with the sudden disappearance of signals intelligence from the historical landscape.
This is an extraordinary omission which, according to Andrew,
has 'seriously distorted the study of the Cold War'.[4] Intelligence
services were at the forefront of the Cold War, yet most accounts
of international relations after 1945 stubbornly refuse to recognise even the existence of the code-breakers who actually constituted the largest part of this apparatus.[5] Nor did this amazing
cloak of historical invisibility stop with the end of the Cold War.
In 2004, following the furore over the role of intelligence in
justifying the invasion of Iraq, Lord Butler, a former Cabinet
Secretary, was appointed to undertake an inquiry into 'British
Intelligence and Weapons of Mass Destruction'. Butler's report
into the workings of the secret agencies was unprecedented in
its depth and detail. However, GCHQ is mentioned only once,
in the list of abbreviations, where we are told that the acronym
stands for 'Government Communications Headquarters'.[6] This
is all we learn, for in the subsequent 260 pages the term GCHQ
is in fact never used, and the organisation is never discussed.
The subject is simply too secret.

Sigint was not simply a Second World War phenomenon.
Throughout the twentieth century, Britain's code-breakers
continually supplied Downing Street with the most precious
jewels of British intelligence, discreetly delivered in what
became known as the 'Blue Book'. Nicholas Henderson,

formerly Britain's Ambassador to Washington, explains: 'All Prime Ministers love intelligence, because it's a sort of weapon . . .The intelligence reports used to arrive in special little boxes, and it gave them a belief that they had a direct line to something that no other ordinary departments have.' It was partly for this reason that British Prime Ministers 'never minded spending money on intelligence'. Signals intelligence also matters to political leaders because it allows them to hear the authentic voices of their enemies. Although Winston Churchill was the most famous recipient of such material, his predecessor, Neville Chamberlain, was also offered some remarkable insights into the mind of Adolf Hitler. In 1939, shortly after the Munich appeasement, Chamberlain was given an intelligence report which showed that Hitler habitually referred to him in private as *der alter Arschloch*', or 'the old arsehole'. Understandably, this revelation 'had a profound effect on Chamberlain'.[7]

However, constant exposure to secrets derived from the world of code-breaking, bugging and other kinds of secret listening has the capacity to induce paranoia. Harold Wilson regularly dragged his Private Secretary, Bernard Donoughue, into the bathrooms and toilets of Downing Street. Only there, with the taps turned on full and water sloshing noisily in the basins, did he feel immune to the threat of bugs.[8] A top priority for Britain's technical security specialists during the Wilson years was the installation of the latest scrambler phones at the Prime Minister's holiday home in the Scilly Isles, so he could speak to Whitehall without fear of interception. Doubtless, Wilson would have been delighted to learn that some of his opponents felt equally oppressed by electronic surveillance. When Ian Smith, the Rhodesian leader, visited London in late 1965 he insisted on having some of the more sensitive conversations with his delegation in the ladies' lavatory, convinced that this was the one location where British intelligence would not have dared to plant microphones.[9]

Secret listening terrified friend and foe alike. Harold Macmillan recalled the almost unbearable sense of oppression he felt on his visit to Moscow to see the Soviet leader, Nikita Khrushchev, in 1959. His delegation feared that British codes were compromised, and they were unable to talk freely, even outside in the open air, because of constant technical surveillance. He would have been fascinated to learn that, at the very same moment, Khrushchev and his immediate circle also felt increasingly anxious about KGB microphones, to the extent that they dared not speak freely, even amongst themselves in their own capital.[10] In June 1966, to his immense fury, President Tito of Yugoslavia discovered that he was being bugged by his own security chief. 'Concealed microphones have been installed everywhere,' he exclaimed angrily to a friend: 'Even my bedroom!'[11]

The supreme example of the way in which eavesdropping could have political consequences was the Watergate scandal, which gradually brought about the downfall of President Richard Nixon between April 1973 and July 1974. Nixon had used a team of former CIA operatives known as 'The Plumbers' to burgle and bug premises used by the Democratic Party. Not everyone was shocked. In 1973, Britain's Prime Minister, Edward Heath, made a visit to China. Mao Tse-tung asked him, 'What is all this Nixon nonsense about?' Heath asked what he meant by 'nonsense'. Mao replied: 'Well, they say he bugged his opponents, don't they? But we all bug our opponents, don't we, and everybody knows it? So what is all this fuss about?'[12] Others took bugging in their stride. When Tony Blair visited India in October 2001, his security team found two bugs in his bedroom, and reported that 'they wouldn't be able to remove them without drilling the wall'. Blair 'decided against making a fuss', and quietly moved to another room.[13]

Eavesdropping and code-breaking are certainly nothing new. Even in medieval times the crowned heads of Europe had recourse to secretive 'black chambers' where encyphered letters from diplomats were intercepted, opened and decoded in order to produce intelligence. However, the modern-day GCHQ owes its origins to the arrival of the radio and the enormous impact of science upon methods of fighting during the Second World War. It was the struggle against Hitler that revolutionised the importance of intelligence from encyphered radio messages. Blitzkrieg and surprise attack were the hallmarks of a new style of warfare that arrived in the late 1930s. The sheer speed of war now meant that secrets smuggled under the coat collar of a traditional human spy were no longer of much use to commanders. The code-breakers of Bletchley Park were the perfect answer, offering intelligence in 'real time' from intercepted enemy signals. In some cases, messages sent from Hitler to Rommel in the Western Desert were decoded and arrived on Churchill's desk before they were read by their intended recipient. Soon, Bletchley Park presided over machine-based espionage on an industrial scale.

With the onset of the Cold War, 'sigint', as it had become known, seemed equally important for a dangerous new era of nuclear confrontation. Atomic weapons and equivalent breakthroughs in biological and chemical warfare, together with ballistic rockets such as the V2, against which there was no defence, were the new currency of conflict. World leaders were required to comprehend strange new threats and the accompanying possibility of devastating surprise attack – which Lord Tedder, the British Chief of the Air Staff, called a potential 'nuclear Pearl Harbor'. The precarious world of early warning, deterrence and 'targeting' had arrived. Military chiefs demanded better intelligence, and concluded that global sigint coverage was indispensable to the Western allies. By the mid-1950s, Britain's code-breakers had abandoned their nissen huts at Bletchley Park for new accommodation in Cheltenham, the distinctive radomes and satellite dishes of which became an integral part of the Cold War landscape.[14]

Ironically, the story of GCHQ after it entered 'peacetime' in 1945 is very much about military operations, and even war. Britain's vast sigint programme was managed by GCHQ, but run in cooperation with the armed services, which used their bases, ships and aircraft to collect the raw enemy signals. As this book reveals, GCHQ sat at the centre of a spider's web that consisted of many other hidden organisations, both civil and military, which helped it collect signals intelligence. Many of its stories intertwine closely with Britain's long legacy of small wars and guerrilla conflicts in locations such as Korea, Malaya, Borneo, Aden and the Falklands. GCHQ's operations also involved hair-raising confrontations with the Russians. Britain ran secret submarine spy missions designed to gather signals intelligence from the Russian fleet. Specially converted submarines entered the protected harbours of the Russian Navy and rose precariously beneath cruisers to within six feet of their electronic quarry. Submarines that were sent on sigint missions – known to their anxious crews as 'Dodgies' or 'Mystery Trips' – were detected off Murmansk and pursued by Russian destroyers with depth charges. GCHQ's ocean-going activities have been a well-kept secret, but some British submariners still bear the scars of this secret signals war in the far north.

Code-breaking is sometimes depicted as highly technical – more 'Billion Dollar Brain' than James Bond – and therefore perhaps a little dull. But much of the GCHQ story involves dramatic incidents experienced by individual sigint operators in forward locations, including in submarines and aircraft. However it was done, gathering sigint almost always involved a three-stage process. First, someone had to listen in to and record the inter-cepted message. Throughout the Cold War this person was often the Godforsaken GCHQ 'operator' who sat for eight hours at a time in front of a rack radio made by Racal. With headphones on and the volume turned up to 'max' he or she endured the freezing cold of the German winter and the unbearable heat of the Iraqi summer. Once the message was captured it was passed back to Cheltenham for processing. If it was in code, it might be given to X Division, a section staffed by 'boffins' with vast computers whose power far outstripped that available to ordin-ary scientists. Finally, intelligence analysts would try to compose the resulting material into useful summaries. Stamped with an excruciatingly high security classification, it was then circulated to Cabinet Ministers, defence chiefs and senior policy-makers. Often, only a few hours after they had been read by the 'high-ups', the summaries were whisked away in 'burn-bags' and consigned to vast incinerators to protect their secrecy.

GCHQ is also synonymous with the mysterious international network known as 'Echelon', run by British and American intelligence. Echelon is the world's largest information 'vacuum cleaner', drawing in huge amounts of communications – an estimated five billion intercepts every day. Yet much of what we have come to believe about this network is wrong.[15] The Anglo–American sigint relationship is often portrayed as a cosy affair of affable, pipe-smoking professor types. In fact, the politics of intelligence was often opportunistic and harsh. Secretly, the British and Americans worked together to read the traffic of their own minor allies, including France and West Germany. Even at the top, relations between the two main partners, Britain and the United States, could turn nasty and involved sharp disagreements.

What bound Britain and America together in the world of signals intelligence was realism, not romanticism. Anglo–American intelligence cooperation was about trading 'terrain for technology'. America had its own vast code-breaking organisation, the National Security Agency (NSA), with infinitely more resources than the British. However, the American code-breakers needed remote outposts in Britain's 'residual empire' at which to base their listening stations, and they rewarded GCHQ handsomely with access to remarkable technology. Some locations, such as Cyprus, were so important to the collection of sigint that UKUSA actually helped to shape the international politics of the region. In 1974, faced with a financial crisis, the British government formally decided to withdraw from its bases in Cyprus in order to save money. Within days, Washington told London that this decision was not acceptable and they must stay. The reason was simple. The sigint bases that allowed America to listen in to the Middle East were quite indispensable. In 2009, more than thirty years after the British government's decision to withdraw from Cyprus, the sigint bases are still there, and have grown considerably in size.

Cold War espionage activity enjoyed a high profile. British defectors such as Guy Burgess and Donald Maclean hit the headlines in the 1950s. The 1960s opened with the shooting down of the American U-2 spy plane piloted by Gary Powers, the CIA's fiasco at the Bay of Pigs and the Profumo affair. Yet GCHQ managed to avoid the glare of unwelcome publicity until the last decade of the Cold War. Its journey from the shadows into the spotlight only began in 1976, when the radical journalist Duncan Campbell revealed its intelligence operations on Cyprus in an article in *Time Out* magazine. This led to the infamous 'ABC trial', at which Campbell and his associates were prosecuted under the Official Secrets Act. Thereafter, GCHQ's hopes to return to obscurity were dashed by the Geoffrey Prime affair in 1982. Prime, who revealed the innermost working of America's latest multi-billion-dollar sigint satellite programme to the Soviets, was one of the most damaging moles ever recruited from inside British intelligence. Just as the Prime case subsided, any hopes of a return to anonymity were obliterated by Margaret Thatcher's controversial decision to ban trade unions at GCHQ.

Expensive technical agencies such as GCHQ and America's NSA were obvious targets for cuts at the end of the Cold War. At the same time, both agencies were struggling to cope with the pace of the global information-technology revolution, that had made access to high-grade encryption easy for the private individual. All this, together with the exponential growth in internet traffic, threatened to make the work of GCHQ and NSA impossibly difficult. Soon the world was sending several million emails a second, and not even the great sigint leviathans could read them all. The days of the super-secret sigint agencies seemed numbered. However, in the 1990s Britain's prominent role in the wars in Bosnia and then Kosovo reminded government that the need for sigint is perennial. In these Byzantine conflicts, the radio experts at Cheltenham were never quite sure which of the many different former Yugoslavian factions their various friends and allies were supporting.

Bitter conflicts such as Bosnia helped to convince Whitehall and Westminster that GCHQ was worth new investment. In 1996, under the direction of Sir David Omand, GCHQ began to develop plans for a remarkable new intelligence headquarters that quickly became known as 'the Doughnut' owing to its circular design. The intention was to bring all the staff together under one roof for the first time. Absorbing no less than fifteen miles of carpet and several hundred miles of fibre-optic cabling, 'the Doughnut' constituted the largest secret intelligence headquarters outside the United States. However, by the time it was completed in 2003, it was already too small. GCHQ had by then undergone a crash expansion following the 9/11 terrorist attacks. Its employees, now numbering more than 5,200, were soon 'hot-desking'. A shanty town of subsidiary buildings is already springing up around the new headquarters.

Today, in somewhat cramped circumstances, GCHQ struggles with some of the most difficult issues of the twenty-first century. Not only is it the leading edge of Britain's struggle against al Qaeda, it is also involved in fundamental issues of freedom and privacy that will shape the future of our society. Over the last decade, Britain has engaged with global e-commerce and finance more enthusiastically than perhaps any other country in the world. Our porous electronic borders present their own enormous problems. Globalisation, and in particular the global communications revolution, has brought many benefits, but it has also allowed miscreants to communicate and organise anonymously. The need for GCHQ to monitor both terrorists and organised crime means that the distinction between domestic and foreign communications has less meaning than it once had. GCHQ used to be a wholly outward-looking foreign intelligence service, but this is no longer the case.

Who will rule the internet? Will ordinary citizens be allowed genuinely confidential communication? Would ID cards erode our privacy or extend our security? These are some of the questions that GCHQ ponders daily at the beginning of the second decade of the twenty-first century. Britain is already one of the most watched societies in the world, and some would argue that it is now addicted to surveillance. In 2008, Britain announced a £12 billion project to modernise the interception of telephone calls and email. The following year GCHQ announced a remarkable project entitled 'Mastering the Internet' that collects the details of Britain's communications and internet traffic for security purposes. Even Britain's Director of Public Prosecutions thought things had gone too far. Tasked with taking the lead on technological aspects of intelligence, GCHQ now finds itself at the centre of controversies that are of immense public importance. Accordingly, the time is ripe to trace GCHQ's long and secretive journey from the nissen huts of Bletchley Park – via the Cold War – towards what now looks increasingly like a Brave New World.

THE 1940s

BLETCHLEY PARK
AND BEYOND

1

Schooldays

'How wonderful!' I said. 'Do you mean we're overhearing Portsmouth ships trying to talk to each other – that we're eavesdropping across half South England?'
   'Just that.'

Rudyard Kipling, 'Wireless', 1904[1]

In December 1902, Guglielmo Marconi made history by sending the first wireless radio message across the Atlantic. Remarkably, only two years later, Rudyard Kipling foretold the possibility of exploiting such radio messages to gather intelligence. In 1904 he published a short story entitled 'Wireless' that focused on intercepting communications sent from Morse equipment on board Royal Navy ships off the Isle of Wight. Kipling is thought of as a quintessentially late-Victorian author, but here he looks to the future, more in the manner of H.G. Wells, as his characters fret over technical matters such as induction and radio frequencies. To the readers of this fictional first instance of radio interception, the process seemed utterly magical. The Morse instrument 'ticked furiously', and one of the listening party observes that it reminds him of a séance, with 'odds and ends of messages coming out of nowhere'. His companion retorts that spiritualists and mediums 'are all impostors', whereas these naval messages that they are eavesdropping on are the real thing.[2]

Kipling's 'Wireless' is the first public discussion of the secret business of signals intelligence, or 'sigint'. The magical process of extracting information from the ether would be one of the twentieth century's most closely guarded secrets. Initially, producing 'sigint' only required equipment that would allow a third party to eavesdrop on a conversation broadcast by a radio transmitter using 'wireless telegraphy', but as this possibility became more widely known, communicators often resorted to using cyphers to keep their messages private. Thereafter, producing sigint usually required skilled listeners to capture the message and then a team of code-breakers to unscramble it. If the message was sent by cable rather than wireless, the listening-in process could be no less difficult than the code-breaking, or 'decyphering'.

What did Britain's code-breakers make of Kipling's public airing of their black arts? The simple answer is that there were none to ask. Indeed, there had been no British code-breakers for more than fifty years. In the distant past, Britain had possessed a 'black chamber' in which skilled 'cryptanalysts' had broken the codes contained in diplomatic correspondence and private letters. These arcane skills resided in the 'Secret Department' of the Post Office. However, in 1847 this was exposed in a scandalous episode when the House of Commons heard that the Home Secretary had ordered the interception of the private correspondence of the heroic Italian nationalist in exile, Giuseppe Mazzini. Shocked Members of Parliament ordered an inquiry, leading to the closure of the 'Secret Department', just as the telegraph initiated what we now understand as a Victorian communications revolution. By 1904, Britain had been without a code-breaking centre for more than half a century.[3]

The immediate origins of MI5 and its sister service SIS (often known as MI6) can be traced to scares about German espionage in 1909. But British code-breaking was not revived until the very eve of the First World War. On 2 August 1914 the British Army set up a secret code-breaking section called MI1b. Soon, specialist Army units at various locations in Europe and the Middle East were busy intercepting German radio communications. One of the largest sites was the intercept station in Mesopotamia. In December 1916 the military code-breakers of MI1b were given a fabulous Christmas present when the drunken chief of the German signals organisation in the Middle East sent all his Radio Operators a seasonal greeting using the same obvious formula in no fewer than six different codes. Up until that point the British had only been able to read one of these codes, but with these clues they could read all six. In the First World War, the Second World War and again in the Cold War, poor discipline by the human operators often proved to be the great weakness in otherwise impregnable cypher systems.[4]

The Royal Navy code-breakers, who had established themselves in the Admiralty's 'Room 40', achieved even greater success. Famously, they broke the 'Zimmermann Telegram', a message sent from the German Foreign Minister, Arthur Zimmermann, suggesting an alliance between Germany and Mexico against the United States. As an inducement, Mexico was to be offered the return of her lost territories in Texas, New Mexico and Arizona. These revelations, made public in March 1917, were central in bringing the United States into the First World War on the side of Britain and France. The American entry into the war, together with a tightening blockade, persuaded Germany to seek an armistice the following year. The code-breakers of Room 40 celebrated with champagne. There are few more significant examples of the direct impact of code-breaking upon international relations.[5]

In 1919 the British government's Secret Service Committee, chaired by Lord Curzon, the rather formidable Foreign Secretary, recommended that a unified peacetime code-breaking agency should be created. This involved the difficult merger of two quite separate organisations. The head of the Army code-breakers, Major Malcolm Hay, was awkward and argumentative, while his naval equivalent, Commander Alastair Denniston, proved to be suave and diplomatic. Denniston secured the job as chief of a new combined code-breaking organisation, which initially consisted of around two dozen intelligence officers and a similar number of clerical staff, and found himself installed in splendid accommodation at Watergate House in The Strand, next to the Savoy Hotel. Formed on 1 November 1919, the new organisation was given the name 'Government Code and Cypher School', or GC&CS, which was not inappropriate, since the leading code-breakers devoted a great deal of time to the patient training of new initiates.[6] Both during the First World War and in the interwar period about half the staff of GC&CS and its predecessors were women, mostly in the clerical grades.

Almost immediately, GC&CS adopted a disingenuous description of its duties that would remain in place until the 1980s. Publicly, its functions were described as merely defensive; in other words, it was to assist in the provision and protection of codes and cyphers used by government departments. However, its more secret duty was to give priority to offensive activity, namely attacking the cypher communications used by foreign powers. GC&CS gradually shifted its focus to diplomatic traffic, and at the suggestion of Lord Curzon it was transferred to the control of the Foreign Office. It seemed natural that within the Foreign Office structure it should be placed under the supervision of Britain's traditional overseas intelligence service, SIS, which recruited human spies. But a subliminal naval influence remained. The talented Chief of SIS, Mansfield Cumming (known within the organisation as 'C', the name by which the head of SIS would continue to be called), was a former naval officer. Cumming died in harness in 1923 and was succeeded by another sailor, the former head of Naval Intelligence, Hugh 'Quex' Sinclair. Naval intelligence and naval signals officers continued to exercise a profound influence on GC&CS and its successors as late as the 1970s.

The means by which Britain collected its intelligence was changing. During the First World War, much of its intelligence work had involved overhearing military wireless messages by means of receiving stations scattered around Europe, the Mediterranean and the Middle East. The shift to diplomatic traffic meant undertaking more work on encyphered diplomatic telegrams sent by cable. Each country had teams of code clerks who carefully encyphered diplomatic messages before they were sent by telegram using a worldwide network of cables. Although government cable censorship had officially ended in 1918, a private arrangement meant that all the commercial cable companies secretly handed over their traffic to GC&CS for copying. Most of the foreign embassies in London used cable companies to send their encyphered messages, and British dominance of international telecommunications networks meant that many of the world's messages travelled over British cables at some point. Private companies such as Standard Cable & Wireless Ltd were almost an integral part of the worldwide British sigint system. This secret state–private network remained hidden until it was exposed by the journalist Chapman Pincher in February 1967 in the *Daily Mail* under the headline 'Cable Vetting Sensation'.[7]

In 1925 both SIS and GC&CS were moved into Sinclair's new secret service headquarters at Broadway Buildings, opposite St James's Park tube station, which its occupants thought 'more dingy than sinister'. The walls of the corridors were painted dark brown to a height of about four feet from the floor, and the ancient lifts moved between the many storeys with a slow clatter. The code-breakers were given the third floor. From here, the sigint product, which consisted of the verbatim text (or sometimes summaries) of the messages of foreign governments was distributed around Whitehall in files with special blue jackets that became known as 'BJs'. GC&CS worked on the cyphers of many countries in the interwar period, including those of France, the United States and Japan, since they all shed light on international affairs; but the most important were those of Russia.[8]

Both MI5 and SIS, together with intelligence officers from the three armed services, were obsessed with the threat from Bolshevik Russia in the interwar period. GC&CS followed suit. There were good reasons for making Moscow the pre-eminent target. Bolshevik agents were actively seeking to subvert the British Empire, and sigint produced operational intelligence that could be used to thwart these plots. Alastair Denniston enjoyed a major advantage, having recruited Ernst Fetterlein, the Tsar's leading code-breaker, when he fled Russia after the Revolution of 1917, and in the 1920s GC&CS was successfully reading Soviet diplomatic cyphers. Several times during that decade the British government directly accused the Soviets of underhand activities in London, making use of these intercepts and referring to them openly. In 1923, for example, Lord Curzon publicly quoted Soviet messages intercepted by GC&CS stations in India. The Soviets responded by changing their cyphers, but Fetterlein simply broke them again.[9]

However, in May 1927, a year after the General Strike, a disastrous row erupted over secret support from Moscow for the strikers and the distribution of subversive propaganda in Britain. A veritable centre for Soviet subversion was being run under the cover of its Trade Mission, located in the Arcos building in Moorgate. The building was raided on 12 May, but advance warning allowed the Soviets to destroy most of the incriminating material. The Prime Minister, Stanley Baldwin, was embarrassed. He ardently desired to break off relations with Moscow, but having failed to garner any incriminating evidence from the Arcos raid, he turned to the priceless intercepts provided by GC&CS. To the dismay of the code-breakers, Baldwin and his Foreign Secretary, Neville Chamberlain, read out four decyphered Soviet telegrams in Parliament in order to make their case. Alastair Denniston was especially bitter about this flagrant compromise of GC&CS secrets.[10]

Henceforth, the Soviets changed their cyphers and deployed more secure systems for communications with diplomatic and commercial missions overseas, including their intelligence stations. They now used the 'one-time pad' for their more important communications. The one-time pad was a breakthrough system created by an American army officer, Major Joseph Mauborgne, during the First World War and widely adopted by other powers. It involved using a sheet of random numbers to encypher a message. Each letter in the message was given a number. Each number was then added to another from a stream of random numbers taken from a sheet on the one-time pad. The result was a sheet of text that consisted simply of groups of five numbers, one after another. Recipients could decode the message if they possessed the same sheet from the same one-time pad. If that sheet was used only once – hence the name – and for a single message, the lack of repetition prevented decryption. In short, the code was unbreakable. The disadvantage was that it was slow and cumbersome, and therefore it was reserved for high-grade secrets. Moreover, vast numbers of pads with lists of random numbers were required. No country, not even the security-obsessed Soviet Union, could send all its communications by this means.[11]

Nevertheless, after 1927, few Soviet diplomatic messages were being read by GC&CS. The only high-grade Soviet traffic that was decyphered were the messages of the Comintern, the part of the Soviet Communist Party that dealt with relations with Communist parties overseas. This effort was led by John Tiltman, a brilliant major from the Indian Army who had been running a small but successful interception effort in north India during the 1920s. In 1929 he was brought back to London to lead an expanded operation against Comintern communications (which were code-named 'Mask'). This allowed the British government to learn of the secret subsidies paid by Moscow to the Communist Party of Great Britain and its newspaper, the *Daily Worker*. It also contributed to important successes against major Comintern agents in imperial outposts and international centres such as Singapore and Shanghai.[12]

Faced with the real threat of active subversion throughout the British Empire by the Comintern, GC&CS paid limited attention to military matters or the rise of the Axis until the mid-1930s. Germany, Italy and Japan were a remarkably low priority. Admittedly, a small naval section of GC&CS had been set up in 1925, and its most important work was done overseas by naval officers like Eric Nave, based in Hong Kong. From here they had ample practice at following military operations, because of the extensive fighting in Manchuria during the 1930s. Italy's attack on Abyssinia in 1936 provided a new target for British code-breakers in the Middle East, located at sites such as

Habbaniya in Iraq and Sarafand in Palestine. Remarkably, and despite the growing importance of air power, GC&CS only developed an RAF section in 1936, under Josh Cooper, a young and talented code-breaker who had joined the organisation a decade earlier with a First in Russian from King's College London.[13]

Cyphers were important to the Axis military powers. One-time pads were slow and cumbersome. Moreover, they were out of step with the emerging new methods of warfare. Blitzkrieg, for example, required armoured forces to move forward at lightning speed, coordinating their activities with artillery and air support. So the pressure was on to find a way of making the growing volume of military radio traffic unintelligible to the enemy. Most developed countries turned to cypher machines to make their immense volumes of traffic secure.[14] Complex cypher machines had been pioneered by banks and businesses – banks had long used fairly simple cyphers to keep commercial matters secret. In the 1920s, the German military adapted a Dutch invention to produce the Enigma cypher machine as an alternative to laborious hand cyphers. In fact, the first Enigma machines were sold commercially, and were widely used by banks and businesses. Enigma was what we now recognise as a 'commercial off-the-shelf solution' to a difficult military problem.[15]

The Enigma machine itself looked like an early typewriter in a square wooden box, but with a keyboard set out in alphabetical order rather than the traditional 'QWERTY' arrangement. As each letter key was depressed a set of lights that corresponded to the alphabet lit up, seemingly at random. The innovation was the rotors, which looked like fat metal wheels, embedded in the top of the machine. These rotated and scrambled the message in a highly unpredictable way. There were initially three – later four – rotors, with twenty-six positions relating to the letters of the alphabet. These moved round in a stepping motion that generated a cypher with an enormous number of possibilities. Moreover the complex nature of the rotation caused subtle changes in the stream of material, creating substantial headaches for any would-be code-breaker. The Germans were not alone in developing cypher machines. The British and Americans developed similar devices, respectively called the Typex and Sigaba.[16]

Critical to the breaking of Enigma was assistance from the secret services of France and Poland. French intelligence employed a lugubrious German agent called Hans Schmidt, who worked in the German military cypher department. Fond of the finer things in life, which the French secret service supplied to him in abundance, Schmidt divulged many technical documents about Enigma, including messages in both clear and encyphered text. He was later betrayed, and would commit suicide using cyanide procured for him by his daughter. By 1938 these secrets were being shared with the British through 'Biffy' Dunderdale, the SIS station chief in Paris. However, when the French gave the British material on German Air Force communications a further secret was accidentally revealed, namely that the French were also working on Enigma in collaboration with the Poles. In January 1939 Alastair Denniston took two of his top code-breakers, Hugh Foss and Dilly Knox, to Paris to meet their French and Polish opposite numbers. Eventually they discovered that the Poles had completely reconstructed the German version of the Enigma machine.[17]

Remarkably, by 1938 the Polish code-breakers were able to read the majority of German Army Enigma messages. The Polish breakthrough had been to train professional mathematicians to help them, together with the use of a primitive processor called the 'bomba' or 'bombe' – so named because of the alarming ticking noise it made – to find the rotor settings. One of their first 'bombes' was a weird contraption that consisted of no fewer than six Enigma-type machines wired together to provide rapid processing of possible solutions. Polish resources were limited, and by late 1938 new advances in the Enigma machine were running ahead of the ability of the Poles to do their calculations. But the precious secrets that the Poles taught the British were enough to continue the unravelling of Enigma. The timing was an extraordinary stroke of luck, since the talented Polish cypher bureau was within two months of being broken up by the coordinated German–Soviet invasion of Poland in the autumn of 1939. Before the Polish secret service was forced to flee Warsaw, its agents had achieved the remarkable feat of stealing several examples of the military Enigma machine from the German factory where they were made.

In the late 1930s, Britain lived in the shadow of the aerial bomber. Following the tragic fate of the Spanish town of Guernica in the spring of 1937, the presumption was that the first few days of the approaching war with Germany would bring untold destruction from the air, levelling the cities of Europe. By the Munich Crisis of 1938, Whitehall had begun to make emergency preparations. Admiral Hugh Sinclair, the Chief of SIS, was busy looking for alternative wartime accommodation away from London for both SIS and GC&CS. He soon settled on a country house, Bletchley Park, near Milton Keynes in Buckinghamshire, as an ideal location for the code-breakers. Much has been made of Bletchley Park's proximity to Oxford and Cambridge, but in fact the availability of good trunk cable communications was the dominant consideration. Bureaucratic bickering now erupted. Although GC&CS was run by the Foreign Office, its relocation was considered to be war contingency planning, so the diplomats insisted that the military pay the bill. Predictably, the War Office insisted that GC&CS was nothing to do with it, and emergency relocation for Britain's most valuable wartime asset stalled. In the end, Hugh Sinclair bought Bletchley Park with his own money, paying over £7,500 (more than £330,000 at today's prices). This remarkable act of generosity allowed the first wave of evacuated staff to arrive at Bletchley on 15 August 1939. Sinclair's largesse did not stop there. He acquired a top chef from London to provide food to the code-breakers in a restaurant in the main hall, complete with full waitress service.[18]

The emphasis at Bletchley Park was distinctly military. The

main body of GC&CS was initially broken up into Naval, Military and Air Sections and allocated to the ground floor of the main house, while SIS was given the top floor, indicating that it still ruled the roost. On the periphery, an ever-growing collection of numbered wooden huts – including the famous Hut Three and Hut Six – were being constructed. Particular activities were associated with each hut: typically, the core of the Enigma problem was worked on in Hut Six, while its exploitation for intelligence purposes was undertaken in Hut Three. One former code-breaker recalls that the main house was soon 'too small for more than a handful of top brass and their immediate acolytes'. So Bletchley Park's considerable garden, with its rosebeds and delightful maze, gradually disappeared beneath the expanding penumbra of temporary structures.[19] The shadow of the bomber even reached out to Bletchley Park. The radio transmission infrastructure involved elaborate aerials which had the potential to give away the site's location from the air. Accordingly, Bletchley Park's own radio station was moved to nearby Whaddon Hall. As the operation gained momentum, other nearby premises were absorbed. Elmers School, a neighbouring boys' boarding establishment, was requisitioned for the GC&CS Diplomatic Sections.

Bletchley Park was Admiral Sir Hugh Sinclair's last bequest to Britain's sigint community. Through the early autumn of 1939 it was clear that he was terminally ill with cancer. His deputy and heir apparent, Stewart Menzies, was not regarded as a great brain, and indeed despised intellectuals. Sir Alexander Cadogan, the Permanent Under-Secretary at the Foreign Office, vigorously resisted the idea that Menzies might succeed Sinclair, and argued for someone from outside SIS to shake the organisation up. Senior SIS officers, however, did not want 'a new broom at this critical stage'.[20] Cadogan noted in his diary, 'I am not satisfied that Menzies is the man,' but Menzies did have a crude talent for furthering his own ambitions, which he soon demonstrated. On Sunday, 5 November he came to see Cadogan bearing the sad news of the death of Sinclair the previous day.

Cadogan noted that he 'gave me a sealed letter from "C" recommending him (M[enzies]) as successor'.[21] Lord Halifax, the Foreign Secretary, pressed for Menzies, who was finally accepted as the new Chief on 28 November.[22]

The arrival of Menzies was a problem for Bletchley Park because the code-breakers were still subordinate to SIS. Under Menzies the administration of SIS was 'chaotic', and its headquarters was in 'a state of upheaval' throughout 1940.[23] Cadogan maintained his view that Menzies was a mentally disorganised intriguer who devoted more time to protecting the interests of SIS than to serious intelligence-collection. Typically, in March 1941, after Cadogan had met Menzies and the Directors of Intelligence of the three armed services, he recorded in his diary: '"C" as usual, a bad advocate on his own behalf. He babbles and wanders, and gives the impression he is putting up a smoke-screen of words and trying to put his questioners off the track.'[24] Cadogan longed to see a thorough overhaul of SIS, which he regarded as an organisational basket-case. However, as the war dragged on, he had less and less time for the politics of intelligence.[25] Quite understandably, SIS wanted to keep all code-breaking under its wing, since it was a form of foreign intelligence-gathering. Menzies was also adamant that he should retain personal control over Ultra.[26] If possible, he preferred to take this material to Churchill personally, basking in its reflected glory. But he did not know how to manage Bletchley Park, and as a result it was under-resourced.[27] In the words of one SIS contemporary, Menzies regarded anything to do with personnel or administration as 'dirty work', and would go to considerable lengths to avoid it.[28]

Bletchley Park may have been chaotic, but it was a creative and innovative chaos that allowed the code-breakers to make a fresh start in the Buckinghamshire countryside.[29] The head of GC&CS, Alastair Denniston, spent the autumn of 1939 making detailed war preparations. His task was to find new cryptographers to fill out the ranks of Bletchley Park. His valuable contacts with the Poles and their success with the 'bombe' had led him to realise that he not only needed more code-breakers, he also needed mathematically-inclined individuals. Most of the current inhabitants of GC&CS were linguists with a penchant for Latin and Greek. He now needed people who loved maths and machines, and in September 1939 he was actively scouring the high tables of Oxbridge colleges for talent. The brilliant new mathematicians he recruited included Gordon Welchman from Trinity College, Cambridge, who would run the heart of the code-breaking operations in Hut Six. He brought with him Stuart Milner-Barry from the same college, who was the chess correspondent of *The Times* and who eventually took over as head of Hut Six. In turn, Milner-Barry brought fellow members of the British chess team, Hugh Alexander and Harry Golombek, to Bletchley.[30]

These arrivals came not a moment too soon. Hitler's attack on Poland had tipped Europe into all-out conflict, and Bletchley Park was now a fully operational war station. The pressure was on to make progress against Enigma. The most brilliant mind engaged in this task was Alan Mathison Turing, who made an early and important contribution. Despite understanding the abstract problems of Enigma some months into the war, GC&CS was having difficulty in breaking any real Enigma messages, and was not delivering much product. To have examples of the machine was not enough, since the security of the messages it sent depended on the 'key', in other words the settings of the machine, which changed each day. Turing was sent to see the remnants of the Polish code-breaking team, now residing near Paris, to try to work out what the British were doing wrong. The Poles explained that the British had failed to think through the way in which the wiring was attached to the rotors of the Enigma machine.

In early 1940, with this further helpful shove from its allies, Bletchley Park began breaking substantial amounts of Enigma traffic. There were many different Enigma cyphers, and to distinguish them, they were colour-coded. In February 1940, Bletchley Park began breaking 'Red', which was an invaluable system used for liaison between the German Army and the Luftwaffe. Periodically, a change to a German cypher system would cause the British code-breakers to lose it for a while, and quite often recovering it depended on second-guessing the lazy habits of the operators. German overconfidence in the improved Enigma machine led to basic mistakes that greatly simplified the task of those whose objective was to tease out the rotor setting for each day.[31]

By early 1941, the flow of material from the breaking of Enigma was impressive. The intelligence from Bletchley Park was circulated on a very select basis, and was marked with the code word 'Ultra' to denote the extremely high level of security attached to the material. Menzies showcased his triumph by taking senior figures from Whitehall on day trips to Bletchley Park. On 11 January it was the turn of Alexander Cadogan. He noted in his diary:

*

Cold but thawing. Had a rush at the FO till 11, when I left with Menzies for Bletchley. Got there about 12.30. Very Interesting – I should like to spend a week there so as to try and understand it. A charming young Cambridge professor of geometry – Welshman [Gordon Welchman] – did his best with me. A good show, I think.[32]

*

Others soon made the pilgrimage to the strange mock-Tudor mansion surrounded by temporary huts. On 6 September 1941 Winston Churchill himself, now Prime Minister, stood on a pile of bricks left by some workmen alongside Hut Six and gave an impromptu speech – delivered with deep emotion – about the value of Bletchley Park to the war effort.[33]

Unbeknown to Churchill, Bletchley Park was in deep crisis. This was partly due to its rapid growth, and partly to the uncertain institutional boundaries that were evolving almost daily. The situation was exacerbated by a complex relationship with the 'Y services', the lower-order radio intercept organisations run by the Army, Navy and Air Force that fed Bletchley with captured traffic. Meanwhile the three armed services were themselves vying for increased control over who received the output from GC&CS. This was precisely the kind of complex organisational puzzle that Menzies was ill-equipped to deal with. Matters reached a head in the autumn of 1941, forcing Menzies to appoint a Joint Committee of Control, which included members of both SIS and GC&CS. However, as the historian Philip Davies observes, 'Like so many of Menzies' administrative initiatives, the committee proved unequal to the task.'[34] There was also a general resources problem. Having made significant inroads into German Enigma traffic, there were simply not enough staff at Bletchley Park to process the vast torrents of accessible German communications. Neither Alastair Denniston nor his deputy, Edward Travis, had the pull in Whitehall to overcome the shortage.[35]

Churchill was not ignorant of this state of affairs for long. Recalling the Prime Minister's kind words during his recent visit, the code-breakers resolved to go straight to the top. On 21 October 1941, four of the most brilliant minds at Bletchley Park, Hugh Alexander, Stuart Milner-Barry, Alan Turing and Gordon Welchman, wrote directly to Churchill to beg for more resources, explaining that their work was so secret that it was hard to explain their requirements to those who controlled personnel.[36] So secret was their missive that Milner-Barry took the train to London and delivered it personally to 10 Downing Street. Churchill was shocked by these revelations, and demanded 'Action This Day'. He ordered his military assistant, General Hastings 'Pug' Ismay, to ensure that GC&CS had everything it needed, and to report that this had been done.[37] As a result, Bletchley Park underwent a further expansion, and more importantly a major reorganisation.[38]

GC&CS was now divided into two distinct parts, civil and military. The end of the Blitz meant that the civil side, which dealt with economic and diplomatic traffic, could be sent back to London with relative safety. It took up residence in Berkeley Street, partly because the work of attacking diplomatic codes often had to be coordinated with discreet telephone taps on the foreign embassies in London. The military side remained at Bletchley Park. This did not resolve the heated arguments about who controlled the spoils of GC&CS, but it did address the immediate accommodation problems, and created two organisations of a more manageable size. Menzies retained his post as overall Director, but was a notably absentee landlord. Alastair Denniston was sent to London as Deputy Director (Civil), while his talented deputy, Commander Edward Travis, remained at Bletchley as Deputy Director (Services).[39] Travis was now the rising star.[40]

British code-breaking in the early years of the war was not just about the German military secrets revealed through Enigma. Even harder to break than the Enigma machine had been a German teleprinter on-line cypher machine known as 'Tunny', used by the German High Command to produce 'Fish' messages. On-line cypher machines were especially challenging because they were automatic, and sent a continuous stream of text, much of it dummy material, sometimes offering no obvious start or end points to each message. This went some way to eliminating another weakness of the Enigma machine – its operators, who were prone to human error. To address the problem of 'Tunny', the British later built 'Colossus', one of the earliest general-purpose electronic machines, and perhaps the first device that might be described as a 'computer'. Conceived by Professor Max Newman and then developed by Tommy Flowers from the British Post Office research facility at Dollis Hill, this was one of the supreme technical achievements of the war.[41]

The achievements of the civil side of GC&CS have often been neglected. By 1940 it was analysing not only the diplomatic codes and cyphers of the Axis powers, but also those of more than twenty other countries. These included the Soviet Union, which did not enter the war until it was attacked by Germany on 22 June 1941. The diplomatic communications of quarrelsome allies such as the Free French, or important neutrals such as the Turks and the Spanish, proved as interesting and as useful as those of Germany. Moreover, the traffic of Germany's allies, such as Japan, could shed a penetrating light on the mindset of Berlin. Throughout 1941 Hitler held regular meetings with Baron Oshima, the Japanese Ambassador in Berlin, often referred to as 'Hitler's Japanese confidant'. Japan had its own complex cypher, known as 'Magic', produced by a machine called 'Purple', and Oshima used it to send detailed accounts of his long conversations with Hitler to Tokyo. 'Magic' had been broken by the Americans, and early Anglo–American cooperation on code-breaking ensured that all this was being read in London. Remarkably, Berkeley Street was also working on the cyphers of the United States, which did not join the war until the Japanese attack on Pearl Harbor on 7 December 1941.[42]

The dramatic events of 1941 transformed the course of the Second World War. Although the Battle of Britain had staved off the possibility of a German invasion, by the summer of 1941 Britain had been fighting for almost two years without a major victory. Therefore, Hitler's bizarre decision to invade Russia in June 1941, which required the legions of the Wehrmacht to turn east, provided a welcome breathing space. After Japan's attack on Pearl Harbor, Britain, the United States and Russia found themselves ranged together against the Axis in what was soon called the 'Grand Alliance'. Welcome as this was, a genuine *world* war created new dilemmas for the denizens of Bletchley Park, who now confronted the ticklish issue of large-scale Allied cooperation in the business of code-breaking.

2

Friends and Allies

. . . there is no better analogy than the schoolboy with his stamp collection.

GC&CS, discussing intelligence cooperation
with the Russians in 1943[1]

The most secret aspect of Bletchley Park's wartime work was its dealings with friends and allies. Many have pondered whether the British attacked Soviet codes and cyphers during the Second World War. The official history of British intelligence insists that Churchill ordered this activity to stop in June 1941, following Hitler's invasion of the Soviet Union, since Moscow had suddenly become an ally.[2] However, it is now clear that this is quite untrue. At the end of October 1941, intelligence chiefs were actually discussing the expansion of the sigint organisation in India, which was then dealing with 'material from Russian, Persian and Afghan sources'. Remarkably, it was not yet working on German traffic.[3] Moreover, in January 1942, and again in early 1943, the British and the Americans were discussing the mutual exchange of intercepted material from 'Slavic nations'.[4] Soviet cyphers had been the core business for Britain's interwar code-breakers, and work on this material never stopped completely during the Second World War.

To understand why, we must cast our minds back to the approach of the war. During the 1930s, GC&CS continued to follow the traffic of the Comintern even after other Soviet systems were lost. This revealed persistent efforts to subvert the British Empire in locations such as India, Malaya and Hong Kong. Indeed, the Soviet Union appeared to be in league with

Germany after the Nazi–Soviet Pact of August 1939. It is often forgotten that Poland was invaded by Germany and the Soviet Union *together*. For a nightmare period between August 1939 and June 1941, many suspected that Germany, Italy, Japan and the Soviet Union would act in uneasy concert, dividing the spoils of the world between them. This was precisely the plan that Germany's Foreign Minister, Baron Joachim von Ribbentrop, was trying to press upon his irascible master. However, in the end Adolf Hitler's racist outlook could not tolerate the idea of alliance with the Slavic peoples, and he had always declared his desire for '*Lebensraum*' in the east.[5]

Throughout this dangerous period, before Hitler and Stalin turned upon each other, the Soviet Union remained a key intelligence target. SIS even organised a secret squadron to conduct aerial reconnaissance of possible bombing targets deep inside southern Russia, notably the oilfields. GC&CS developed close relations with code-breakers in the Baltic states who were also working on Soviet codes. A month after the outbreak of war with Germany, Clive Loehnis, a naval officer at GC&CS (who would become Director of GCHQ in the 1960s), told Alastair Denniston that additional premises were needed to cope with the increase in the interception of Soviet military traffic, so new buildings were erected at Scarborough.[6] With the military chiefs keen to 'get cracking on Russian traffic', Denniston began a unique and profitable experiment. In 1939 GC&CS sent a party of British sigint operators to Sweden to work secretly out of the British Embassy in Stockholm, where there was better radio reception from Russia. The creation of this forward listening station was fortuitous, since Stalin embarked on the Winter War against Finland in November 1939, and GC&CS enjoyed a front-seat view of the whole proceedings.[7]

John Tiltman remained the key figure in the effort against Soviet communications. A colonel in the King's Own Scottish Borderers, he was noted for his smart uniform, which included tartan trews. However, as the war progressed he came under the influence of the spirit of Bletchley Park, and was often seen in a baggy pullover and green corduroy slacks.[8] One of his first duties was to visit Helsinki to conclude a deal with the talented Finnish code-breakers. Britain funded the expansion of the Finnish cryptographic bureau, and supplied it with the latest equipment in return for material on the Soviets. In March 1940, after imposing a series of humiliating defeats on the Soviets, the Finns signed the Moscow Peace Treaty, ceding about a tenth of their territory.[9] The sigint deal with the British was unaffected, and indeed in September 1940 its scope was expanded during a visit by Admiral Godfrey, the Director of Naval Intelligence. According to an internal GC&CS history written after the war, 'The Finns had agreed to supply us with copies of all their intercepts and cryptographic successes, provided that we did the same.' Preceding the agreement with the Americans by more than a year, this was perhaps Britain's first comprehensive sigint alliance.[10]

By March 1940, the interception of Soviet traffic was big business. For the first time, collection began in the Middle East, at Sarafand in Palestine, although it was still sent to India for analysis. Soviet traffic was also being taken at Ismailia in Egypt and Dingli in Malta. Meanwhile, in Hong Kong, other British sigint operators were also listening to the Soviets before they packed up their equipment to move to Singapore in anticipation of a Japanese attack. The surge of Soviet traffic meant changes were required at GC&CS, where an inter-service Soviet section was created to work in close conjunction on naval, military, air, diplomatic and commercial material. After the fall of France in the summer of 1940, evacuated French cryptographers joined the effort on Soviet traffic at GC&CS. A Polish section, based at Stanmore on the northern fringes of London, soon discovered that it was able to listen in to Soviet traffic as far away as Ukraine.[11]

Ultra had provided Bletchley Park with an intimate picture of the build-up of German forces in the east, prior to their attack on the Soviet Union. As early as January 1941 it was clear that Hitler's vast armies were being moved eastwards in preparation for some grand project. Yet even with the evidence of many

German divisions massing in the east, Whitehall refused to believe that Hitler was mad enough to deliberately opt for war on two fronts. Like Stalin himself, the British Chiefs of Staff believed that this was more likely to be a prelude to a German ultimatum, a bluff in which Hitler would demand the cession of some further territory in Eastern Europe. Throughout early 1941, Stalin believed that all war warnings were self-serving efforts at deception by the West, which sought to provoke a war between Germany and the Soviet Union. Stalin has frequently been ridiculed for ignoring the warning signs of the impending attack, but despite the benefits of Ultra, it was only the month before the fateful date of 22 June 1941 that British intelligence chiefs realised what was about to occur.[12]

Hitler's decision to turn east was a fabulous stroke of luck for Britain. At a time when its forces were struggling, this was a most welcome redirection of the main German war effort. Taken together with Pearl Harbor at the end of the year, it is right to regard 1941 as nothing less than the fulcrum of the war. However, Bletchley Park now faced a new problem. Should it pass sensitive intelligence derived from Ultra to the new Soviet ally, which had been a dedicated enemy of Britain since 1917? The idea that two of Britain's adversaries were about to fight to the death filled most military intelligence officers with ill-disguised glee. Many argued that passing sigint to the Soviets was pointless, since few expected them to hold out later than 1942. Others insisted that not even Ultra could penetrate the fog of self-deception with which Stalin had surrounded himself.[13]

In the event, Bletchley Park did develop a precarious sigint liaison with the Soviets. When the British Chiefs of Staff despatched a military mission to Moscow, the code-breakers decided to work through it to find out what the Soviets were doing. They began cautiously, asking about 'low-grade material only', notably German Air Force three-letter tactical codes. They intended to send an officer from Bletchley, and in the long term even hoped to persuade the Soviets to accept a British Y unit, or forward listening station, that would intercept German tactical messages on their front. In late 1941 the Soviets agreed to a visit from Squadron Leader G.R. Scott-Farnie, who worked on Britain's Y interception system in the Middle East.[14]

Scott-Farnie gave the Soviets a good deal of information on low-grade German Air Force systems, but quickly came up against a different culture of intelligence exchange.[15] The Soviets adored captured documents, and did not attach much credence to any information that was not supported by such evidence. Once the game of document exchange began, Scott-Farnie discovered that the Soviet approach 'was precisely that of a horse dealer who enjoys the poste and riposte of a bargain, and they looked at the exchange of documents on an eye for an eye basis'.[16]

Bletchley now had to decide whether to follow up the Scott-Farnie Mission. Alastair Denniston was 'full of hesitation because of the continued Soviet retreat before the German onslaught', but the intelligence directorates of Britain's three armed services thought it worthwhile. Josh Cooper, who had reviewed the exchanged material, concluded that the Soviets were 'absolute beginners' in their work on the German Air Force, but thought they should be shown the RAF Y stations at Kingsdown in Kent and Cheadle in Cheshire to point them in the right direction. If the Soviets were impressed, he added, they might allow a British Y unit to be sent to the Soviet Union.[17] In the end, Edward Crankshaw, an Army Y Service officer, was sent out, armed with more barter material in the form of documents. This was to be 'swapped' with the Soviet interceptors, since Bletchley Park thought 'there is no better analogy than the schoolboy with his stamp collection'. By the spring of 1942 Crankshaw was established in the Soviet Union, and was trading his wares.[18] However, the greatest success in the Soviet Union was achieved by the Royal Navy. It was running supply convoys to the Russian port of Murmansk, and this justified the setting up of a radio station at the nearby town of Polyarnoe. A small naval Y intercept party was soon attached to it, and began co-operating with the Soviets on low-level German naval communications. This kept going until December 1944, and yielded good material on subjects such as the movements of the German battleship *Tirpitz* in northern waters.[19]

The main worry about giving Ultra to the Soviets was the insecurity of their own cyphers – in 1942, Bletchley Park was increasingly aware of the German ability to read a great deal of Soviet operational military traffic in the field. Frederick Winterbotham, who worked on sigint distribution, argued that Moscow simply had to be told about the weak security of its cyphers. However, Winterbotham's colleagues insisted that it was 'impossible' to tell the Soviets, even though he had 'invented a good cover story' to explain how they knew.[20] The secret truth was that Bletchley Park was collecting second-hand sigint. The Germans were sending their own sigint from the Eastern Front back to Berlin using an Enigma key code-named 'Mustard', which in turn was being read by the British. Although much of the sigint obtained from the Soviets was operational, the British also noted that 'first grade traffic can be read – at least in part' by the Germans. Some of the German successes had stemmed from a Soviet codebook, 'OKK–5', known to have been captured by the Finns and given to the Germans. While the British had struggled to break these codes in the 1930s, the Germans were having more success.[21] On 16 June 1942, Nigel de Grey, the Deputy Director at Bletchley Park, stepped in and settled the argument. He noted that Edward Crankshaw, the GC&CS liaison with the Soviets, would soon be returning from Moscow for another visit. He would be ordered to give the Soviets the details of their compromised cyphers and 'the methods of reading'. This decision probably reflected the fact that, against all predictions, the Soviet forces were hanging on impressively and looked as if they were going to be in the war for some time to come.[22]

In August 1942, Crankshaw briefed the Soviets on their appalling lack of security, typified by their alarming tendency to use low-grade cyphers for high-grade secrets.[23] There was abundant evidence of this in German Air Force Enigma, but Crankshaw only hinted at it by 'somewhat tenuous means'. Predictably, the

Soviets would not accept his warnings because 'direct evidence was not forthcoming'. Depressed, he went back to Bletchley Park in February 1943, never to return to Moscow. He joined the staff at Bletchley Park and tried to keep the relationship going at a distance, 'but the temperature was falling'. The Director, Commander Edward Travis, was only willing to allow the relationship to continue 'if it is a solid gain for us'. The Polyarnoe naval listening station continued to function, but with the Soviets turning the tide on the Eastern Front they seemed to feel no need for further cooperation, and other contacts 'petered out'.[24] On 9 February 1944, London discussed the possibility of a visit to Britain by Soviet cypher experts and decided against it.[25]

Bletchley Park's heated debate on what information to give to the Soviets was academic. All along, one of the KGB's top agents, John Cairncross, had been working at Bletchley. Although Cairncross studied at Cambridge in the early 1930s, he was not recruited by Anthony Blunt, one of the key KGB talent scouts there, who found him both quarrelsome and arrogant. Instead, after Cairncross joined the Foreign Office in 1936, he was persuaded to work for Soviet intelligence by James Klugman, a prominent British Communist, who later served in the wartime Special Operations Executive. Although Cairncross was fearsomely intelligent, his difficult personality ensured that he was always being moved on. At the outbreak of the war with Germany he was sent to the Cabinet Office to work for the Cabinet Secretary, Lord Hankey. There he saw some of the early British thinking on the development of the atomic bomb. In 1941 he was moved to Bletchley Park, labouring in Hut Three on the Luftwaffe order of battle. His moment of triumph came in early 1943 when he was able to warn his KGB controller of the impending German armoured offensive at Kursk. Code-named 'Operation Citadel', this was the last great German push on the Eastern Front. It proved to be the largest tank battle of the Second World War, and the information provided by Cairncross proved to be important in launching an early attack upon the German tactical air force, much of which was destroyed on the ground. Stalin later awarded him the Order of the Red Banner in recognition of his achievement.[26]

Soon after Kursk, Cairncross moved again. He now returned to London and ended up in Section V, the counter-intelligence section of SIS, working alongside Kim Philby. Although he worked with Philby, Guy Burgess and indeed Donald Maclean, Cairncross was unaware of their common allegiance to Moscow, and believed he was the sole high-grade KGB agent in Whitehall. Bizarrely, he was caught in 1951 because of an official note in his handwriting found in the flat of Guy Burgess after Burgess had fled to Moscow with Maclean. Cairncross had given Burgess this quite innocently in the course of official business, without knowing he was a fellow spy. Once the note was found, Cairncross was followed, and MI5 surveillance believed they had caught him trying to meet with his KGB controller. Without hard evidence he could not be prosecuted, and he was merely asked to resign. Ironically, the Ultra material that Cairncross passed to the KGB was taken more seriously by Moscow precisely because it was stolen. Had the British handed it willingly to their ally, Stalin's suspicious mind would almost certainly have devalued it.[27]

Cairncross was not the only KGB agent with access to Ultra. In late 1942, Anthony Blunt, another high-grade Soviet agent, was designated one of the two MI5 liaison officers who worked closely with Bletchley Park.[28] Anxiety about KGB agents and subversion was yet another reason that the British kept working on Soviet traffic. Monitoring stations, notably the Metropolitan Police intercept station at Denmark Hill in south London, reported an upswing in traffic between Moscow and secret agents in Britain. There was also a British field unit, called the Radio Security Service, that hunted for illegal agent radio transmissions, and it told the same story, although the agent traffic could not be broken.[29] John Croft, who worked at the GC&CS diplomatic code-breaking centre at Berkeley Street in London, was one of those who soldiered on with Soviet material. Croft was engaged on wartime Comintern traffic in Europe, known as 'Iscot', which could be read. Although circulated only to a very select group of individuals within Whitehall, this material mostly revealed a dutiful Soviet struggle against their shared enemy, Nazi Germany. There is no indication that this material was exchanged with Washington.[30]

Early British cooperation with the American code-breakers was also tentative. Again, the obstacle was obsessive security. Security problems existed on several different levels. The British and the Americans had cooperated on sigint during the First World War, but this had bequeathed a legacy of doubt and anxiety, even distrust. In November 1940, when reviving sigint cooperation with the Americans was discussed, Alastair Denniston was quick to point out that after the First World War the 'notorious' American code-breaker Herbert O. Yardley had published a tell-all book about his experiences. The very name 'Yardley' caused a shudder in British code-breaking circles. Yardley was now working for the Canadians, and GC&CS insisted that they sack him summarily before they were allowed to join the wartime sigint club.[31] Indeed, the Canadians were told that other agencies 'would not touch Yardley with a ten foot pole'.[32]

The British, and especially Sir Stewart Menzies, the Chief of SIS, were frosty towards the Americans, and regarded them as fundamentally insecure. By contrast, the Americans generously opted to share the secret of their spectacular code-breaking success against the Japanese 'Magic' diplomatic cypher with the British as early as January 1941, even handing over precious examples of their copies of the Japanese cypher machine. The British were 'flabbergasted'. They did not expect the Americans to 'simply walk in and plonk down their most secret cryptanalytical machine'.[33] Yet the British remained reticent, and did not initially reciprocate fully with their knowledge of Enigma. The jibe about American insecurity had a certain irony, since the British chose to send one of the priceless American copies of the 'Purple' machine out to their naval base at Singapore shortly before it fell to the Japanese. The machine was delivered by ship just as the Japanese invasion of Malaya began, and disappeared into the chaos of battle. To this day its fate is unknown.[34]

Collaboration with Washington was also hard because American sigint was a house divided. Although William Friedman, the US Army's best cryptologist, was busy advocating sigint cooperation with the British in early 1940, the US Navy's chief code-breaker, Commander Laurance Safford, was adamantly set against working with allies. But after pressure from President Franklin D. Roosevelt the Navy had been won round, and the Americans sent a team of technical experts to Britain in early 1941. Known as the 'Sinkov Mission', they spent several weeks touring Bletchley Park and visiting outlying intercept stations. The British were willing to receive them because they knew the main focus of American attention was Japan. At this stage the British were keen to keep discussions focused on Japan, because this allowed them to hide the extent of their knowledge of the German Enigma system. Both Sir Stewart Menzies and Sir Alexander Cadogan were adamant that the Ultra secret would not be shared with the Americans.[35] Laurance Safford later represented the first Anglo–American exchanges of late 1940 and early 1941 as a one-way street in which the Americans handed over their precious 'Magic' material on Japan but got nothing in return. In fact this is far from the case. Prescott Currier, one of the Americans who came to Bletchley in early 1941, recalled: 'All of us were permitted to come and go freely and to visit and talk with anyone in any area that interested us.'[36] Later that year, a select circle of American code-breakers were also given more details about Enigma.[37]

The hottest issue was the distribution of sigint to the policy-makers. In late May 1941, Brigadier Raymond Lee, the American Military Attaché in London, conveyed an American request for comprehensive intelligence exchange in the Far East. There followed painfully slow and complex discussions about who would get sigint with what levels of security: 'The whole thing has been so tangled up,' he complained.[38] Sigint was also very confused in Washington. Unlike Britain's GC&CS, American signals intelligence was less centrally organised, resulting in great rivalry between the armed services.[39] Because the American wartime sigint organisation was divided between the Army and the Navy, one of the great problems for the British was cooperating with one without upsetting the other. Famously, the Americans solved the tussle over who would decrypt Japanese codes by agreeing that the Army would decode the material on the even days of the month, and the Navy on the odd days. A more ludicrous system for the division of labour would have been hard to devise.[40]

GC&CS might have been more centralised than the Americans, but it had less money. Expanded cooperation with America on Japan allowed GC&CS to shed some difficult code-breaking tasks. High-grade Japanese Army cyphers had proved impenetrable for a decade. By 1941, Bletchley Park was too busy with the European war, while its Far Eastern code-breakers were struggling to cope with the mass of material on Japanese espionage derived from low-level consular intercepts in South-East Asia. On 22 August 1941, Anglo–American cooperation lifted this task from their shoulders. During talks in Washington, Alastair Denniston persuaded the US Army that it should 'take over investigation of Japanese main army cipher soon as priority commitment'. Shortly after, Captain Geoffrey Stevens from Singapore travelled to Washington carrying all the British material on the Japanese main army cypher.[41] The British were glad to see the back of it. At the end of the war approximately 2,500 Americans would still be working on this one Japanese cypher to no avail.

All the while, Britain was also decyphering some American traffic. Amongst the decrypts selected for the personal perusal of Winston Churchill were those of many Allied and neutral countries. GC&CS was clearly working successfully on the American diplomatic code 'Grey' until December 1941.[42] Remarkably, there was no embarrassment about this. In June 1941, while discussing comprehensive sharing of Far East intelligence, the British asked the US Military Attaché, General Raymond Lee, for his opinion on the security of American cyphers. This was the conduit through which sigint would pass between London and Washington. Lee replied tartly that the GC&CS already knew a great deal about this matter. He recorded in his diary:

*

The talk then turned again on the question of security. They wanted to know whether my despatches went by radio or cable and were relieved to hear that they went by cable, and were further relieved to hear that we have a direct wire straight into the War Department. However, I pointed out that this wire was subject to interception by their people here in England [GC&CS] and I had no doubt they had taken our messages and attempted to decipher them.

*

He added that it was now very much in the interests of GC&CS to be honest about the security of American cypher systems, 'because the stuff that is going over it is more vital to them than to us'. Lee's frank exchange with the British underlines one of the hidden benefits of cooperation between the Allied code-breakers. Once they began to share their most precious assets, 'Magic' and then eventually Ultra, improved communications security became paramount. London and Washington now had a vested interest in the impenetrability of each other's messages. After all, if GC&CS could break American codes, then so, perhaps, could the Germans.[43]

Churchill eventually wrote to Roosevelt and owned up to British work on American diplomatic codes. 'From the moment we became allies,' he explained, 'I gave instructions that this work should cease. However, danger of our enemies having achieved a measure of success cannot, I am advised, be dismissed.' In fact, it is unlikely that all work on American traffic ceased. In areas such as the Middle East, Britain had a considerable incentive to continue to work on American commercial traffic, much of which was in commercial code or plain text. Indeed, a close reading of Churchill's assurance to Roosevelt suggests that it might have related to diplomatic traffic only.[44] Some GC&CS staff recall work on the traffic of American commercial attachés throughout the war, although as yet no documents have been released.[45] Predictably, clear traffic from American oil companies was being intercepted in 1944 as they began to look for new markets in Europe.[46]

For this very reason, the US Army and Navy were agreed that nothing should be passed to the British about American code-making procedures, such as the Sigaba cypher machine. General George Marshall, the US Army Chief of Staff, specifically forbade any such exchange in September 1940.[47] Anxiety about protecting national cypher systems persisted through the war on both sides of the Atlantic. In February 1945 Britain's newly formed Cypher Policy Board debated a proposal by its Secretary, Captain Edmund Wilson, for 'free and complete interchange' with the Americans on cypher machine development, together with scrambler phones and secure speech.[48] This horrified both Edward Bridges, the Cabinet Secretary, and Sir Stewart Menzies, Chief of SIS, and the idea was rejected. Cooperation on communications security would focus on machines specially designed for combined use.[49]

The gradual collapse of the British monopoly over Ultra intelligence paved the way for closer Anglo–American sigint cooperation. As we have seen, Bletchley's initial idea for wartime cooperation was that the Americans would continue their pre-war focus on Japanese traffic; meanwhile the British would handle the work on Enigma, dispensing its product to the Americans as they saw fit. Although they had informed the Americans about Enigma in 1941, some precise details of processing had been withheld. Bletchley was determined to prevent the Americans working on Enigma in parallel, even though the Battle of the Atlantic gave Washington a legitimate need for Ultra intelligence. However, once the German Navy introduced an improved Enigma machine with four rotors, the British could not produce enough 'bombes' to deal with the increased number of tests required to break it.[50] In September 1942, Joseph Wenger, who led the US Navy code-breakers, proposed spending $2 million to acquire no fewer than 230 four-wheel 'bombes'. This was ten times the number available to Bletchley. John Tiltman, Britain's Soviet code specialist, realised that American sigint was beginning to operate on an industrial scale, and that for Bletchley Park the game of 'Ultra monopoly' was surely up.[51]

In September 1942, Edward Travis and the head of Bletchley Park's Naval Section, Frank Birch, travelled to Washington and concluded the 'Holden Agreement', which established full and integrated collaboration on German naval traffic, including Enigma. This was a key part of the emerging Anglo–American sigint relationship, and a constituent part of the secret alliance which still exists to this day.[52] Travis's hand was strengthened by the remarkable fact that the US Navy breathed not a word about the Holden Agreement to the US Army. The British therefore persisted in their hopes of keeping control over the processing of Ultra material derived from Luftwaffe and German Army traffic. Nigel de Grey, the Deputy Director of Bletchley Park, was apoplectic at the possibility of the Americans being allowed to duplicate further British work on Enigma. However, a US Army code-breaker based at Bletchley, Colonel Telford Taylor, suggested a tactful way forward. He advised his superiors in Washington that all they needed for the time being was a small 'foothold' in the work on Enigma, which would allow them to gain experience. More level-headed organisational types at Bletchley Park, such as Gordon Welchman, could see that the ability of the Americans to procure unlimited numbers of bombes was crucial, adding, 'We certainly need help.'[53] The result was the BRUSA agreement, a further crucial landmark in the construction of the Anglo–American sigint relationship. On 17 May 1943, Bletchley agreed to American participation in work on German Army and Air Force traffic. A second Holden Agreement on naval sigint followed in 1944. These treaties were of enormous importance, and paved the way for more ambitious post-war sigint alliances.

The exigencies of war had broken Britain's cryptographic monopoly on Ultra. However, Ultra was a military system, representing the core work of Bletchley Park. There is no evidence that Britain and the United States concluded an overarching treaty on diplomatic or commercial sigint, the material that GC&CS worked on at Berkeley Street. In 1942, Alastair Denniston, who had been moved sideways to manage diplomatic sigint, arranged for cooperation on a number of specific countries such as Italy, France, Spain, Portugal, Japan and, of course, Germany. However, this was done on an ad hoc basis. There was no diplomatic BRUSA agreement. It seems that the Americans were not intercepting and working on a range of materials that would have prompted a wider deal. Typically, Denniston told John Tiltman, with evident relief, 'They do no work on any of the Near Eastern governments.'[54]

Denniston's main point of contact in the United States was William Friedman and the US Army code-breakers, who dominated American work on diplomatic systems. The Americans were keen to cooperate, since up until 1941 the US Army had been intensely focused on the diplomatic cyphers of Japan. In 1940 the Americans lost access to Japan's diplomatic cypher, and it was only recovered as the result of a prodigious effort by a team under Frank Rowlett. By contrast, British code-breakers were working on the diplomatic cyphers of some twenty-six different countries.[55] Therefore, when the Americans offered access to 'Magic', the British reciprocated with a wide range of diplomatic material, including high-grade Italian systems. Then, in March 1942, John Tiltman visited Washington and brought with him Spanish and Vichy French cyphers. Given the arrival of American forces in the Mediterranean, this was valuable material. By 1944 the Americans had received more material from the British on diplomatic cyphers used by the Greeks, Hungarians, Iranians and Iraqis. However, the processing went on behind a curtain. Denniston asked at one point, 'Do they actually work on the stuff which we send them, or do they simply put it in their library?' Diplomatic cyphers from countries that the British considered to be client states, such as Egypt, were withheld.[56]

Sharing diplomatic product caused some embarrassing problems. Foreign diplomats in London or Washington often reported their conversations with British officials in the messages they sent home. The British sometimes did not want the Americans to 'listen in' on these conversations, since they might involve 'disparaging remarks about American policy or officials'. Therefore, they developed a special reserved series called 'Res', that contained material that was not to be given to the Americans. This was not an effective solution, because, as Alexander Cadogan, the senior official at the Foreign Office, explained to Stewart Menzies, the Americans would often obtain and break some of the same traffic themselves, and so would 'become suspicious'. By the spring of 1944 the Americans clearly knew about 'Res', and pressed the British to abandon the practice. However, Cadogan refused, since the war was drawing to an end, and the antagonistic politics of post-war settlements were looming.[57]

The Americans nurtured their own anxieties. Would Anglo–American sigint cooperation continue after the war? As early as 1942, Colonel Alfred McCormack, one of the more important visitors to Bletchley, warned his superiors in Washington that the British were 'very realistic people', and so would 'certainly at some time – possibly while the war is still on – resume work on United States communications'.[58] However, continued convergence of Anglo–American sigint was ensured by early fears of the Soviet Union, which were visible as early as 1942. Senior officers on both sides of the Atlantic, including Field Marshal Lord Alanbrooke and General Douglas MacArthur, were of one mind on the 'Russia problem'. On 31 July 1942, Geoffrey Stevens, a code-breaker from GC&CS, went out to Arlington Hall, the US Army's code-breakers' centre in Washington. One of the subjects he discussed there was the Soviet Union, and he was fascinated to learn that the Americans were intercepting all the Soviet traffic in and out of Washington. They were also collecting Soviet traffic elsewhere, for example between Moscow and the Soviet Embassy in Tokyo. He reported that the Americans 'do nothing about it at the moment' by way of decryption, since they were so pressed for code-breaking capacity against the Axis. However, sooner or later, he added, 'They will inevitably try and break this since they do not trust the Soviets further than they could throw a steam-roller.'[59] Much as Stevens predicted, the Americans began a Soviet Group in February 1943. Meanwhile, the British moved their own existing Soviet team from Ryder Street in London to larger premises at

Sloane Square in late 1944.[60] Although the two allies were still working in isolation on the 'Russia problem', the foundation of future collaboration was already emerging.

Anxiety about the Soviet Union increased markedly during early 1944. By April the Red Army was pushing into eastern Hungary, and this filled Moscow with a newfound confidence. Stalin's determination to impose a Communist government on Poland was already evident, and pointed to future trouble. Some British diplomats in the Foreign Office remained hopeful about the possibility of post-war cooperation with the Soviet Union, but their military colleagues did not share their optimism. Indeed, the main future strategic planning body in Whitehall, the Post Hostilities Planning Committee, which was shared between the diplomats and the military, tore itself apart over this issue. The Foreign Secretary Anthony Eden had to step in in late 1944, and banned the further circulation of its papers. One staff officer lamented that there were to be 'no more games of Russian scandal'. Russia was now a forbidden subject, and between late 1944 and early 1946 Britain's main body of intelligence analysts, the Joint Intelligence Committee (JIC), did everything it could to avoid discussing the dreaded subject of the Soviet Union.[61]

Accordingly, it was only in June 1945 that the American code-breakers formally proposed to the British that they co-operate against the Soviet Union, giving the overall programme the code name 'Bourbon'. The formal Anglo–American collaboration on the wider 'Russian problem' was so incredibly secret that it was not written down, and amounted to a simple hand-shake between Group Captain Eric Jones, the British sigint liaison officer in Washington, and a senior American naval officer in June 1945. Meanwhile, all eyes were on the Allied reoccupation of Europe and the remarkable sigint prizes that were even now being recovered from the smouldering ruins of the Third Reich.[62]

Every War Must Have an End

*On 26th August one of the [German] operators from Army Group,
South Ukraine . . . suddenly broke into violent remarks about
Hitler, using the peculiarly foul language in which the Germans
delight. The operator at Supreme Army Command tried to shut
him up in equally filthy language. This interchange lasted for
about ten minutes . . .*

*The incident is only noteworthy as a possible indication of the
way things are going.*

Nigel de Grey, Deputy Director at Bletchley Park,
to Sir Stewart Menzies, 14 September 1944[1]

By the autumn of 1944 the Second World War was ending and
the Cold War had, to all intents and purposes, already begun.
In the east, the German Army was collapsing fast, and by
September Soviet forces were at the borders of Prussia. A month
later, American forces had entered Germany from the west,
capturing the ancient town of Aachen. While much bitter
fighting lay ahead, the minds of officials in London, Washington
and Moscow were increasingly focused on the post-war settlement. Wartime relations with Russia had never been easy.
Stalin's intense and unwavering suspicion was underlined by
the fact that, throughout the war, he had refused to leave Soviet-
controlled territory to meet Churchill and Roosevelt. Harsh
Soviet behaviour in newly occupied areas like Poland already
pointed to post-war confrontation and rivalry, and all eyes were
on the advance into Germany.

Britain and the United States were gearing up for piratical
raids on the headquarters and laboratories of a collapsing Third
Reich, and Axis sigint material was the treasure that was most
actively sought. A joint Anglo–American planning group began
consulting with Bletchley Park about what material it wished
to scoop from an occupied Germany. By early 1945, Intelligence

Assault Units were moving into Germany alongside the fighting elements of Allied formations, looking for all kinds of top-secret German experimental weapons. Bletchley Park despatched its own Target Intelligence Committee teams, known as 'TICOM teams', made up of a mixture of British and American personnel, to seek out cryptographic equipment and sigint personnel from Germany. The whole TICOM programme was run on what Commander Edward Travis called 'an entirely inter-allied' basis.[2]

Suddenly, boffins in glasses and cardigans found themselves turned into amateur commandos. Whisked away to a quarry near Bletchley, those selected for this task were given a short course in the use of sub-machine guns and hand grenades. They began on the Thompson sub-machine gun, but soon found the lighter Sten gun to be an easier weapon to handle. None of them performed well, but nevertheless they were soon on their way to Hitler's 'Alpine Lair' at Berchtesgaden. Major Edward Rushworth, one of the senior British officers from Hut Three, led a TICOM team of a dozen officers, accompanied by Selmer Norland, an American stationed at Bletchley Park. They arrived at the major German headquarters at Augsburg on 8 May, VE-Day. Augsburg had been home to the famous German 'Fish', or Geheimschreiber, the encyphered teleprinter which Bletchley had eventually defeated with the mighty 'Colossus' computer. Sadly, all these beautiful machines, lovingly manufactured by Lorenz, had been smashed and the cypher wheels had gone. The dejected team surveyed the debris. However, a day later their spirits rebounded when they gleefully recovered a single intact late-model 'Fish' from a town on the Austrian border.[3]

On 12 May 1945 they reached Hitler's Alpine retreat. The Führer's accommodation had been heavily bombed, but a hundred feet below ground was a maze of bunkers and tunnels to explore, including an emergency power station and a complete telephone exchange. No more cypher machines seemed to be in evidence, and the mission was tailing off when, as a last task, Rushworth set off for nearby Rosenheim on the Austrian border, to question a cryptographer who had been working for the

German High Command (OKW). While they were there, a group of other German prisoners sent a message asking to speak to the 'proper people'. This team had served in the OKW headquarters sigint units and now revealed that, terrified of the rapid Soviet advance, they had buried their equipment under the pavement in front of their headquarters. Called 'OKW-Chi', they had successfully broken what was referred to as 'Russian Fish'. This was an encrypted Soviet military teleprinter that achieved an early version of packet switching, breaking each message into nine different parts and routing it along separate channels, before reassembling it. The Germans had already worked out that their code-breaking triumph would have post-war value, and hoped to sell themselves on as a complete team.[4]

They were not disappointed. By 23 May they had been encouraged to unearth and set up their equipment, allowing them to resume decrypting Soviet command traffic. The Bletchley team were in awe of this vast technical display, which was eventually packaged up again in over a hundred boxes and chests. The eight tons of equipment and the complete German staff were loaded onto five lorries, which then wound their way slowly through a devastated Germany towards Bletchley. They arrived on 6 June 1945, and the equipment was set up and tested at the nearby radio station of Wavendon Manor.[5] The German team was later employed intercepting Soviet encyphered teleprinter traffic which the British code-named 'Caviar', and although the messages were mostly about administration rather than policy or strategy, they provided rare insights into the daily activities of Soviet armed forces in post-war Europe.[6] More treasures followed, and ultimately a further five tons of documents pertaining to Soviet codes and cyphers would arrive. In mid-June, Edward Travis asked Russell Dudley-Smith, a senior Bletchley Park officer, to try to establish some priority in exploiting the mountain of material now pouring in, but little did they know that they would still be working on this material in 1951.[7] One-of-a-kind equipment stayed in Britain, while any duplicates were shipped to America.[8]

Yet another important haul was brought in by Colonel Paul Neff, an American who headed TICOM Team 6. This group included William Bundy, later US Assistant Secretary of State under President Lyndon B. Johnson, and Geoffrey Stevens from Bletchley Park. In April 1945 they pushed into southern Germany at Magdeburg, near Leipzig, and took control of a castle at Burgscheidungen which had recently been the head-quarters of a code-breaking unit of the German Foreign Ministry called the Balkanabteilung, whose tasks had largely focused on Soviet and Balkan traffic. The fourteen staff and their docu-ments were flown to Britain and taken to Bletchley Park. Burgscheidungen was in an area that would later be designated as part of the Soviet Zone, so Neff destroyed all traces of the German code-breakers' presence before departing.[9]

The British caught Generalmajor Klemme, the Senior Commander of Radio Intelligence for the Luftwaffe, at the Husum-Milstedt intercept station on 19 May 1945. At first he was taken to Neumuenster Prison, but from there he was brought to Britain, and worked with the Allies on sigint in Germany until 10 March 1948, when he was considered to have been drained of all he knew about Soviet communications. On 1 May 1945, Major Oeljeschaeger and Major Beulmann from the Berlin Cryptographic Centre, which had been based in a stable block of the Marstall-Neues Palais at Potsdam, had fled in the direction of Hitler's complex at Berchtesgaden. A few days later, with the Allies closing in, they stopped at Viehoff to burn all the records of Branch 3, and they fell into Allied hands on 22 May near Munich. On 5 July they were flown to Britain and placed in a special camp. They were surprised to be welcomed by their Branch Chief, Lt Colonel Friedrich, who had been captured before them. By June 1945 the British and Americans had scooped up most of the senior Luftwaffe sigint officers whose traffic they had listened to assiduously for much of the war.[10]

The TICOM teams were competing with the Soviets, who were also swooping on German cryptographic assets. To their surprise, Bletchley Park discovered that the Soviets had taken over some German Enigma-based communications nets and Fish teleprinters, and had begun using them for their own purposes. However, initial hopes of a post-war dividend from the breaking of these machines were quickly dashed. Roy Jenkins, who was then working at Bletchley Park, recalls this odd interlude in May 1945:

*

When the Russians got to Berlin they took over the Fish machines in the War Ministry, somewhat changed the settings, and proceeded to use them for sending signals traffic to Belgrade and other capitals in their new empire. We continued to do the intercepts and played around with trying to break the messages. We never succeeded. I think it was a combination of the new settings being more secure (which raises the question of how much the Russians had found out about our previous success) and the edge of tension having gone off our effort.

*

Elsewhere, Allied recovery teams regularly overran German sigint operations that were still chattering away, producing decrypts of mid-level Soviet Army Group traffic.[11]

The timing of raids on German sigint centres was a precarious matter. If they were captured too early there was a risk that this would cut off a flow of valuable material that Bletchley was intercepting, or else would alert the Germans to the fact that the British knew more about their cyphers than was desirable. London was especially anxious to avoid freelance raiding activities that might be counter-productive. As early as May 1944 the London Signals Intelligence Board, the supreme governing board which met monthly to set overall British sigint policy, learned that some independently-minded British intelligence officers in the Middle East were planning to use the Special Operations Executive to raid enemy signals intelligence centres in the Balkans. Sir Stewart Menzies, who chaired the board, warned them sternly that operations against such centres were 'highly undesirable', and that action should 'on no account be undertaken' without prior personal authority from him.'[12]

Bletchley's corporate takeover of the Axis sigint effort was not limited to Germany. There were even greater TICOM dividends in occupied Italy.[13] Many countries competed for the services of the talented Italian cryptanalysts. After the Italian surrender in 1943, some eighty Italian code-breakers under Major Barbieri continued to work for the Germans at a station near Brescia in northern Italy. At the end of the war in Europe they were at last interrogated in Rome, and proved to have a large quantity of material, including photocopies of the codebooks of Turkey, Romania, Ecuador and Bolivia. They had also reconstructed some of the codebooks from France, Switzerland and the Vatican, and had smaller amounts of British and American traffic. During the spring of 1945 Barbieri's unit had been concentrating on French diplomatic traffic, 'a large number being messages to Paris either from Bonnet [French Ambassador] in New York or from Catroux [French Ambassador] in Moscow'. This traffic offered insights into subjects as diverse as Soviet–Yugoslav relations, Soviet policy in Germany, French economic negotiations with the United States and French plans for exploiting the Saar coal mines in Germany.[14]

With British encouragement, this precocious Italian unit worked on into the post-war period, without deviating from its French target. The diplomatic unit at Berkeley Street was already doing extensive work on Britain's European allies, regarding them as either insecure or untrustworthy, or both. Much of this suspicion stemmed from a sense of indignation at their behaviour in 1940. In November 1944, Churchill wrote to Eden: 'The Belgians are extremely weak, and their behaviour before the war was shocking. The Dutch were entirely selfish and fought only when attacked, and then for a few hours . . .' General de Gaulle's Free French government in exile, as other historians have shown, came in for especially close attention from the code-breakers during the war, and this continued into 1946.

During the important diplomatic conferences that marked the end of the war, Jimmy Byrnes, the new American Secretary of State, was apparently more eager to see decrypted French material than anything else, concerned that Paris was likely to be working with Moscow.[15] French traffic from Moscow was of great interest to London because the former French Air Minister, Pierre Cot, had indeed begun a special diplomatic mission to Moscow to examine the possibility of cooperating against Germany in post-war Europe.[16]

French traffic provided the British and Americans with a fabulous window on the diplomacy of Western Europe.[17] Indeed, in mid-1946 half the US Army code-breakers' end product was based on intercepting French communications.[18] Alarmingly, the French still seemed keen to develop a close relationship with Stalin.[19] The traffic from French Embassies in Eastern Europe proved especially interesting. Typically, an intercept from the French Embassy in Tirana gave detailed information on the balance of power in the Albanian Cabinet and the waning power of the pro-Moscow elements, and intercepted French intelligence traffic sometimes offered information about the KGB.[20] With the work on Soviet codes still gaining momentum, the chatter of other countries that were talking to Moscow provided insights into their thinking. On 13 August 1945, Edward Travis sent Joseph Wenger, the senior American naval code-breaker, a long missive about cooperation on post-war French and Dutch systems, and explained British plans 'to increase the effort here, especially on French', adding that British plans to focus on Paris 'are going into effect at an early date'. French, Spanish, Portuguese and Latin American traffic was soon consolidated into a single group under Josh Cooper.[21]

Major Barbieri was proud of the work of his Italian code-breakers against the French, but he pressed for more staff. So many of the best cryptographers, he complained, had been captured by the French in North Africa, adding, 'the French are now employing them in their own service!' Nevertheless, the British concluded that the Italians were 'doing remarkably well with the limited reserves at their disposal'.[22] By mid-1946 they were giving them new tasks, including Soviet traffic which came from military cypher machines at division level code-named 'Taper'. British liaison officers with the Italians were working closely with code-breakers in Britain on the identification of new Taper groups. Senior Italian sigint officers knew that Taper traffic 'which had been taken with so much depth and continuity for the past month' was Soviet in origin, but many of their underlings were in a state of blissful ignorance about what they were collecting and who the ultimate customer was.[23]

The efforts of TICOM were not exclusively directed towards raiding priceless sigint secrets from the Germans, the Italians and the Japanese. They were also concerned with protecting Britain's own secret communications. Until late 1943, Bletchley Park regarded weak security as a problem restricted to Britain's allies. But the ability to read German messages had revealed a number of unexpected security nightmares for the Allies. Ultra had shown Britain's code-breakers that the Germans could read many of the codes of the Allies, such as those of the Soviets and the Free French. In Asia, terrible cypher security and serious human agent penetration ensured that Chinese codes were effectively an open book to the Japanese, even though Tokyo's code-breakers were mediocre. Accordingly, keeping Britain's secrets safe meant keeping them away from many of her allies, whose communications were being read by friend and foe alike.[24]

By the autumn of 1943 the security situation looked much worse. The Italians had now capitulated, and captured Italian code-breakers revealed their successes against British codes. Captain Edmund Wilson, who helped to look after cypher security at Bletchley Park, held prolonged 'conversations' with Commander Cianchi, head of the Italian Cryptographic Bureau in Rome, and his staff during late 1943. Wilson explained that he could hardly call them 'interrogations', since Cianchi had given all of Italy's secret information so happily and freely. Wilson said that 'very valuable information' on the breaking of British naval cyphers had been obtained, and that Britain was 'extremely fortunate' to have the cooperation of its former opponents. He pressed his colleagues to be 'very careful indeed in the use they made of the information' from these sources.[25]

The TICOM raids into Germany later confirmed that British naval cypher security had been especially weak. B-Dienst, the German naval sigint service, had been reading British naval codes and cyphers easily at the start of the war. In early 1940 this had allowed it to read British plans for the Narvik raid in Norway, contributing to Germany's success in repulsing that action. In 1942, the Dieppe raid had also been given away to the enemy before it took place due to poor cypher security. Incredibly, the Germans had been given a full five days to prepare for this 'surprise attack'. Allied troops – mostly Canadians – paid for this dearly in the slaughter that followed. B-Dienst achieved the height of its success against Atlantic convoy traffic in 1943, allowing alterations of convoy routes to be radioed to U-boat commanders within a few hours.[26]

The autumn of 1943 saw a long-overdue inquiry into the security of British cyphers, carried out by Brigadier Chitty, who began by visiting Bletchley Park. His findings did not make for comfortable reading. 'It is true,' he reported, 'that of the fourteen sections working at B.P. [Bletchley Park] one is named Security of Allied Communications. From a total staff of some six thousand, however, the part-time services of only one man (Dudley-Smith) plus two or three girls, are spared to equip this section.' At a higher level there was a supervising body called the Cypher Security Committee, supposedly chaired by Sir Stewart Menzies, but this had not attracted Menzies' interest. Moreover, it lacked the power to compel Whitehall departments to change any practices that they thought lax. Chitty had done a spot check of twelve departments around Whitehall, and found that few were taking cypher security seriously. Britain needed a decent operational security section at Bletchley Park, and a proper supervisory board with teeth.[27]

No cypher system, Chitty warned, was unbreakable. Britain's

most sensitive material was sent by one-time pads, which were, in his opinion, 'unassailable' if used correctly. Yet he reminded his superiors that Bletchley was making a 'most successful daily attack' on the one-time pads of other countries, 'which reach us in a steady stream by Photography, Theft, and the sifting of Embassy waste-paper baskets'. The majority of London government traffic went by Typex machine, the British equivalent of Enigma. This was much better than Enigma, but Chitty asserted that its security had never really been tested. Again, much depended on the diligence of the operators:

*

One of the most instructive lessons I learnt from the [Government Code and Cypher] School was the fact that the Hagelin machine used by several nations including the Americans, affords in practice a widely different degree of security in different hands. Whereas this machine, as used by the Swedes and the Finns, has so far been virtually unbreakable, in the hands of the Italians who are normally very good cryptographers, we have for a long time been able to read it with ease. This was entirely due to the increasing idleness of the Italian operators and their persistent disregard of the numerous security rules which have been laid down for them.

*

For routine traffic the Foreign Office used more elderly hand cyphers, and the services made use of field cyphers in their lower formations. Quite rightly, these were thought to be even less secure.[28]

By March 1944, no less a figure than Winston Churchill himself was calling for a shake-up. A new supervisory outfit was created, called the Cypher Policy Board. Although Menzies was in the chair, Edward Travis from GC&CS, together with the Secretary of the War Cabinet and a representative of the Chiefs of Staff were also there to keep a stern eye on him. This top-level representation underlined a deep anxiety about cypher security. A new Deputy Director of GC&CS, known as the

Communications Security Adviser, was also to be appointed, who would serve as the Secretary of the Cypher Policy Board. In reality, this person, Captain Edmund Wilson, was the new broom.[29] After the war, Wilson was replaced by Commander T.R.W. Burton-Miller, who operated from a new headquarters at 10 Chesterfield Street W1, conveniently close to both MI5 and SIS.[30] Soon they had extended their authority over the design and production of all British cypher machines, with Gordon Welchman their chief technical adviser.[31]

During 1944, Bletchley Park offered an impressive technical solution to worries about cypher security. It fielded a new and rather superior cypher machine called 'Rockex I' that produced what was effectively automated one-time pad traffic. Instead of using tiresome tear-off sheets from a one-time pad that had to be processed by hand, it used code tape, which carried the same information. This was initially used for messages between Bletchley Park and its sigint collaborators in Washington and Ottawa, together with the SIS wartime office in New York. A new version called 'Rockex II' was already being developed by the British. The machine was originally intended for the Special Communications Units that disseminated Ultra to Allied commanders in the field, but after the war it became a main-stream British cypher machine, and was still being used by smaller embassies in the 1970s.[32]

The super-secret Rockex cypher machine also had another purpose. From 1944, it provided extra security for the communications network of Britain's SIS agents around the world. With assistance from Bletchley Park, wartime SIS had been able to develop an effective long-range wireless network to support its overseas stations and agents in the field. Known as SIS Section VIII, this was run by Brigadier Richard Gambier-Parry from two country houses not far from Bletchley, at Whaddon Hall and Hanslope Park. These locations not only provided a wireless network for SIS, they also built covert radio sets hidden in suit-cases used by British agents and fitted out vehicles for the Special Liaison Units that supplied sigint to overseas commands such as Montgomery's Eighth Army. In addition, Hanslope Park had provided a base for a unit called the Radio Security Service, under Ted Maltby, that had used mobile detection vans to track the radio transmissions of enemy agents hiding in wartime Britain. SIS was a small organisation with small volumes of radio traffic, and up until 1944 it had been comfortable sending its traffic by slow but highly secure one-time pads. The Rockex machine allowed it to take a leap forward.[33]

By 1944, SIS's Section VIII had expanded considerably and was taking on new customers. With its new Rockex machines, it was carrying some traffic for Bletchley Park, typically from Canada, together with secret messages for the Special Operations Executive which conducted sabotage. The Foreign Office was now looking at this efficient radio network with growing interest, and at the end of the war SIS Section VIII was simply coopted to form the backbone of a new Foreign Office communications system called the Diplomatic Wireless Service. Gambier-Parry became the first Foreign Office Director of Communications. As early as 1943 some embassies, such as that in Cairo, had been switching over to 'experimental use of official wireless' by making use of local SIS facilities.[34] Although diplomatic wireless was technically banned by international diplomatic convention, in practice cable communications had frequently been disrupted during the war, and wireless had crept into widespread use as an alternative.[35]

The gradual development of the Diplomatic Wireless Service at Hanslope Park during 1944 and 1945 was another critical building block in the creation of the modern British sigint community. Alongside the military sigint collection stations in locations such as Ceylon, the Diplomatic Wireless Service, or 'DWS', doubled as a secret monitoring service working from within British Embassies and High Commissions. The first permanent undercover sigint station was set up at Ankara in 1943. DWS staff numbered close to a thousand, and about half its time was devoted to secret collection on behalf of the British code-breakers. Over the years it produced important results from locations as far afield as Moscow and Luanda because of its ability to collect short-range transmissions.

In August 1945 the Second World War finally drew to a close. Winston Churchill was of the view that Bletchley Park was the deciding factor in the defeat of the Fascist powers: in 1945 he apparently told King George VI that Ultra had effectively won the war.[36] Robert Harris, author of the novel *Enigma* (1995), rightly points out that most of the major combatants had military forces that were superior to those of Britain, not least in their weapons technology. Bletchley Park was the one place where we enjoyed a crucial world lead.[37] Harry Hinsley, a junior figure at Bletchley Park, but later the official historian who produced a magisterial study of intelligence during the Second World War, has famously asserted that Ultra shortened the war by several years, saving countless lives on all sides. Without Ultra, he states, 'Overlord would have had to be delayed until 1946'.[38] Andreas Hillgruber, the distinguished German historian of Hitler's strategy agrees, adding that as a result the Soviets might well have advanced much further west.[39]

Yet others, including the British historian Paul Kennedy, have argued that the Second World War was largely a battle of material production, and that once America and Russia were both pitted against the Axis, their industrial might made the outcome only a matter of time – epitomised by the use of the atomic bomb in August 1945. In reality, the debate about the overall value of Bletchley Park has a troubling 'What if?' quality. Inevitably, we are encouraged to ponder the alternative universe of 'no Ultra'. Ralph Bennett, like Harry Hinsley a Bletchley Park veteran turned historian, has expressed impatience with such counter-factual speculations, regarding them as a parlour game. He has argued that the absence of Ultra would have forced the faster development of other forms of intelligence, such as aerial reconnaissance.[40] Peter Calvocoressi, another distinguished historian who spent the war at Bletchley Park, has dismissed Hinsley's assertions as 'silly'.[41]

Some propositions can however be advanced with confidence. Ultra and other kinds of sigint contributed hugely to the outcome of the Battle of Britain. The breaking of naval Enigma changed the course of the Battle of the Atlantic, allowing the Admiralty to direct convoys away from concentrations of U-boats and bringing the level of ship losses down to a bearable, although still frightening, level. This in turn allowed a breathing space for more successful anti-submarine warfare techniques to be developed which would finally turn the tide in the battle against the U-boat in 1943. Ultra also contributed greatly to the British naval victories at the Battle of Cape Matapan (March 1941) and the Battle of North Cape (December 1943). Parallel code-breaking work by the Americans in the Pacific allowed the dramatic interception of the aircraft carrying the brilliant Admiral Yamamoto, architect of Pearl Harbor, which sounded the death knell for Japanese naval forces in the Pacific. It is impossible to understand the war at sea without comprehending the contribution of Ultra in the west and the breaking of a range of Japanese cypher systems in the east. Appropriately, it fell to a naval officer, Commander Edward Travis, to pilot Bletchley Park as it sailed forward into the post-war era.

Even in the spring of 1945, final victory in Europe had loomed like the end of an interminable school year – with the distant summer holidays already beckoning. Bletchley Park, with its nearby dormitories and improvised tennis courts, had looked rather like a vast boarding school waiting for the end of term. Post-war worries were not troubling many of the brilliant minds there. Instead, for the most part they were yearning for an end to war and a return to peacetime activities. The majority of Bletchley's wartime residents were exhausted from years of gruelling hard work. The intellectual pressure had been enormous, and some had suffered nervous breakdowns: Jean Thompson, a Wren who worked at one of the outstations, recalls that they routinely referred to Bletchley Park as the 'Nut House'.[42] Most code-breakers greeted the end of the war with relief, returning to their former activities in ivy-covered colleges, libraries and museums. However, a minority had been bitten by the intelligence bug. They understood the fundamental importance of what they had been doing for the future of international affairs, and would stay on.

Those who remained at Bletchley Park were also thinking of 'escape' – but in a different sense. For them, the end of the war did not so much offer an opportunity of personal freedom, but more the possibility of liberation for the GC&CS. Their remarkable achievements over the last five years suggested that GC&CS might cease to exist under the cloying direction of Britain's traditional overseas secret service, SIS, where the senior staff were often failed cavalry officers recruited in White's or Boodle's. Instead, GC&CS might hope to become an intelligence agency in its own right, perhaps one of a new and different kind. Indeed, its rising status was already signalled by a gradual change in everyday usage from terms like 'GC&CS' and 'BP' to the rather grander cover name of 'Government Communications Headquarters', or 'GCHQ', which had been in intermittent use since early 1940.[43]

Bletchley Park had already taken some important strides towards becoming a fully-fledged intelligence service. Peter Calvocoressi, one of its distinguished wartime denizens, recalls that in its pre-war incarnation the Government Code and Cypher School was exactly what its name implied, 'and no more'. It made up codes for use by the British government, and broke the codes of other nations. But at Bletchley Park, and especially under Gordon Welchman in Hut Six, code-breaking was gradually married to an intelligence process to provide a sophisticated system for sigint exploitation. No less importantly, Bletchley also designed a means for the secure and rapid distribution of sigint to essential customers, even in distant theatres such as South-East Asia. The sheer pressure of wartime exigency forced rapid and logical developments that might otherwise have taken decades.[44]

Another massive achievement was that Bletchley Park and

its diplomatic equivalent at Berkeley Street in London were properly 'integrated', mixing up staff from the three armed services and civilians. This was immediately obvious to any visitor from the curious blend of uniform and civilian dress, often in exotic combinations. Occasionally a visiting Admiral or General would fulminate to see members of his service dressed in colourful pullovers, and demand that they return to full uniform. However, the top brass on day trips from Whitehall were little more than a temporary nuisance. During the 1940s a sigint service which mixed up civilians and personnel from the armed services was quite remarkable. It would take the Americans until the early 1950s to achieve an integrated organisation that mirrored Bletchley. In Nazi Germany as Calvocoressi recalls, the situation had been even worse, for there 'six or seven different cryptographic establishments fought each other almost as venomously as they fought the enemy'.[45]

In the social anthropology of intelligence, sigint was emerging as the dominant tribe. 'The Ultra community at BP saw itself as – perhaps was – an elite within an elite,' recalled one codebreaker. Material gathered by other kinds of intelligence agencies was merely 'Top Secret', but sigint material was compartmentalised as 'Top Secret-Ultra'. The ability to impose draconian security on its product would be a hallmark of a fully-fledged sigint organisation, and dominated its relations with its friends and allies in the code-breaking world. This security obsession also extended to people. The security rule at Bletchley Park was 'Once in, never out.' In other words, once people had worked in sigint, there was a reluctance to allow them to move to other areas of war work, and they were effectively 'captive' for the duration of the war.

Dominance was partly about size. By the end of the war, over ten thousand people were labouring under Bletchley's direction. The expanded bombe effort alone led to the creation of five further outstations as far away as Stanmore and Eastcote on the outskirts of London. Working alongside GC&CS were

the listening units of the armed forces, known as the Y services. Although these fed high-grade material to Bletchley Park,
they also worked on low-grade material for their own purposes.
Often considered 'poor relations', they derived their intelligence
either from listening in to low-level tactical communications
that were not encrypted, including clear voice traffic, or by
simply analysing the flow of traffic. Analysing the patterns of
radio traffic, including volume and direction, even without
breaking the codes, could reveal a great deal of information
about the enemy, and GC&CS worked closely with the armed
services to develop what were known as the 'Y stations'. Bill
Millward, who continued to serve long after the war, recalls
that Bletchley Park's relationship to the Y services was to become
'a sort of university of signals intelligence, developing techniques which all might share'.[46] The Y services had been largely
responsible for deducing the enemy 'order of battle', the structure, strength and location of the units of the German armed
forces. The Navy ran intercept sites at Scarborough and
Winchester. The Army ran a site at Fort Bridgelands near
Chatham, and later opened a station at Beaumanor Hall near
Loughborough in Leicestershire. The RAF were located at
Cheadle in Cheshire, and developed a large new site at
Chicksands near Baldock in Bedfordshire. Many of these locations would continue as sigint sites after August 1945.[47] All of
them were symptomatic of an industrial revolution in secret
intelligence: both Bletchley Park and the outstations operated
like factories, with three gruelling shifts each day.

At a deeper level, there had also been a social revolution in
British intelligence. Brilliant individuals who only a year before
had been members of international chess teams or wrestling
with obscure mathematical problems in Cambridge colleges,
were now focused on intelligence. Remorselessly logical, they
could see that Bletchley Park was the intelligence machine of
the future. Moreover, they were outsiders, with no sense of
bureaucratic anxiety and no fear of the 'Establishment'. They
fearlessly articulated what to them was self-evident. GC&CS,

once a small school of code-breakers working in the service of SIS, had now vastly outgrown its parent organisation. Gladwyn Jebb, one of a number of rising British diplomats who were temporarily attached to intelligence duties during the war, noticed this dramatic change. The organisations like Bletchley Park had been forced to recruit widely from industry and the universities to fill their ranks, so they had forward-looking staff who brought with them modern organisational techniques.[48] Jebb complained that SIS had 'too much of what I would call the "false beard" mentality . . . more especially amongst those who have been in the show for a very long time'. The world had moved on, he argued: 'The idea of a deeply mysterious "Master Spy", sitting in some unknown office and directing an army of anonymous agents, is as outdated as it is romantic.'[49]

The Americans had also opened the eyes of GC&CS to what was technologically possible. Although hobbled by the bitter Army–Navy divide, Washington nevertheless threw vast scientific resources at sigint. On their visits across the Atlantic, a core of determined individuals from Bletchley were able to glimpse what the future might hold. In 1944 a small group of talented British code-breakers began the long-range planning that would turn wartime Bletchley Park – with its chess players and crossword puzzlers – into Britain's premier post-war secret service, with a strong sense of identity, a large budget and predatory designs on other agencies. Three key figures were instrumental in this: Gordon Welchman, the man behind Bletchley Park's intelligence processing centre; Harry Hinsley, who would serve as the 'sherpa' for the Anglo–American–Commonwealth sigint summits after 1945; and Edward Crankshaw, who had handled wartime sigint discussions with the Soviets. Hugh Foss joined them on his return from a posting in Washington.[50]

On 15 September 1944, only weeks after the liberation of Paris, this planning group began to consider GC&CS's post-war future. It was led by Gordon Welchman, who was Assistant Director for Mechanisation, and had also been responsible for Hut Six, where Enigma was broken. Some of the exciting ideas the group advanced for the future of GC&CS grew largely out of the Hut Six experience. It called for a more centralised 'Foreign Intelligence Office' as part of a coherent national intelligence organisation, and for a comprehensive body dealing with all forms of sigint, together with a modern signals security organisation with the latest communications engineering. This, the group believed, could become a truly modern 'Intelligence Centre' governing all types of interception activities.[51]

Welchman's group was tough-minded. There were, it argued, few people in GC&CS with real ability in general planning and strategic coordination. They observed, 'it would be difficult to count as many as a dozen'. This talent should not be wasted on the final year of the war against Japan. Instead, as soon as the war in Europe was over, 'as many as possible of the few potential planners should be set to work in the direction of our three immediate objectives, instead of devoting more of their time to Japanese problems'. GC&CS should not lose touch with developments in the field of Japanese sigint problems, since there were interesting things to learn in this sphere. However, it should merely extract technical benefits from the Japanese War, rather than expend resources upon it. British commanders in Burma, like Field Marshal Bill Slim, realised that they were now a low priority for the intelligence services, and complained bitterly about it.[52]

GC&CS realised that speed was of the essence. It was 'imperative to make an approach to the present Prime Minister at the earliest possible moment'. Any successor to Churchill, it reasoned, however sympathetic, could not have a real appreciation of 'the fruits of intelligence in this war', or Churchill's keen appreciation of the importance of tight security. In Churchill it had a heavyweight advocate, and it feared a return to the pre-war situation of under-recognition of what sigint could achieve; even now, the true scale of its wartime output was known to only a very few in high places. Moreover, the really talented sigint planners were newcomers, and would soon be recalled to their pre-war occupations unless some positive action was taken to retain them. Quite simply, this came down to cash. GC&CS had to have the status to secure 'a sufficiently liberal supply of money to enable it to attract men of first rate ability', particularly engineers and electronics experts. It was also aware that it would have to give equal weight to all types of intelligence about foreign countries, 'including scientific, commercial and economic matters'. This was a tacit reference to the targeting of friendly states.[53]

In January 1945, the torch of post-war planning passed to William F. Clarke. Clarke, who had served continuously in code-breaking from 1916, warned that the 'enormous power wielded by the Treasury' might soon be brought to bear on GC&CS. As had happened in 1919, work on military cyphers might cease in favour of concentration on diplomatic material only. This, he insisted, could be 'disastrous', because the resulting damage to ongoing cryptographic research might mean that in the event of a sudden future conflict, enemy military traffic would prove inaccessible. Even more problematic was the challenge of building up the prestige of GC&CS. Its very secrecy was its worst enemy, ensuring that many in elevated government circles did not know its true value. There was also the 'potential danger' of a Labour government coming to power, since the interwar Labour government had found many aspects of the secret state to be repellent.

Clarke also paused to consider the emerging United Nations. Allowing himself some momentary Utopian thoughts, he observed that if the new organisation took the step of abolishing all code and cypher communications, this action 'would contribute more to a permanent peace than any other'. However, he conceded that this 'is probably the counsel of perfection', and was highly improbable. Instead, he predicted that energetic code-making and code-breaking would persist into the post-war world. On the matter of who would control the British code-breakers, he felt that in the past neither the Admiralty nor the Foreign Office had been satisfactory. The current system of control by SIS also brought with it 'certain disadvantages'. Clarke vigorously asserted that GC&CS should break free, not only of SIS but also of the Foreign Office. Instead it should be a separate organisation under either the Chiefs of Staff or the Cabinet Office, and should be regarded as a wholly separate third secret service.[54]

As late as October 1944, some senior figures at Bletchley were still arguing for reabsorption by SIS. John Tiltman, the Soviet specialist, argued that the code-breakers should be 'closely fused with S.I.S. under the Director General [Sir Stewart Menzies] as the one and only Intelligence producing service'.[55] However, the stock of Menzies was continuing to fall among senior figures in Whitehall. In January 1945, the Chairman of the JIC, Victor Cavendish Bentinck, concocted his own influential vision of 'the intelligence machine'. He suggested that GC&CS should remain under the overall direction of 'C', but at the same time it would be a separate organisation and 'not a part of SIS'. It would boast its own budget alongside the other secret services as part of the Secret Vote, Britain's quaintly titled intelligence budget.[56] It was thus Commander Edward Travis, not Menzies, who determined the final shape of GC&CS shortly after VJ-Day. Although peace had arrived, Travis's mind was already focused on possible future conflict with the Soviets. Recalling the earliest days of the last war, he observed, 'When information was most urgently required, very little was forthcoming.' The next war was likely to be of shorter duration, with little time for mobilisation. In such a conflict the British would have to fight with what they had. It was essential that continuity be maintained, and that rapid expansion was possible on the eve of war.

Exactly when the post-war term 'GCHQ' came into common usage is a matter of dispute. It was first used as a cover name to confuse workmen dropping off furniture at the Bletchley Park site as early as the end of 1939.[57] By 1946, although technically still merely a cover name, it was used more and more widely to denote Britain's code-breakers. Travis decided that the new post-war GCHQ would be divided into five groups run by his key subordinates.[58] To cover its multifarious tasks, he hoped to have a thousand civilians plus a hundred military staff at a new sigint centre located somewhere near to the policy-makers in London. By contrast, the outlying Y stations would be manned by about five thousand additional personnel, of whom only a few would be civilians. GCHQ's own core staff fell rapidly from an end-of-war strength of 8,902 to a projected 1,010 for 1946.[59] Despite the dramatic drop in numbers, Travis concluded that the post-war deal he had struck with the Treasury was 'on the whole most satisfactory'. For him it was about quality rather than quantity. A few days before Christmas 1945 he explained: 'The war proved beyond doubt that the more difficult aspects of our work call for staff of the highest calibre, the successes by the Professors and Dons among our temporary staff, especially perhaps the high grade mathematicians, put that beyond doubt.' He wanted suitable conditions with which to attract these sorts of people, although he knew this would be difficult.[60] Captain Edmund Wilson, Travis's Principal Establishment Officer, echoed this view, arguing that of the 260 officers to be kept on in their post-war establishment, some two hundred of them must have not only initiative but also 'first class brains'.[61]

Where would GCHQ's new centre be? What it craved was a site in central London, next to the policy-makers, but even with the post-war demobilisation of many government departments, nothing suitable could be found. The solution was what John Betjeman would immortalise as 'Metroland'. GCHQ moved to the outer fringes of north-west London, close to Harrow and Pinner. The precise location was Eastcote, which had been used as a wartime outstation of Bletchley Park. It was also close to Dollis Hill, where the laboratories of the Post Office Research Department had built the remarkable 'Colossus' computer. Together with Stanmore, Eastcote was one of two large outstations built in 1943 to accommodate the ever-expanding number of bombes that were being used to cope with the flood of Enigma traffic. However, while it provided reasonable single-storey buildings that were superior to the huts of Bletchley, the overall site was regarded as cramped and unattractive. In June 1946, William Bodsworth, a British code-breaker, returned from a period in America to the cold and rain of an English summer to take over GCHQ's Soviet section. He found his first sight of Eastcote 'frankly shattering'. Expecting 'a nice old country house', instead he found it to be 'more cheerless than any of the temporary buildings I have seen in this racket either here or abroad'.[62]

Those who were leaving Bletchley for good and returning to civilian occupations were given the security warning of their lives. Edward Travis issued a 'Special Order' to everyone in GCHQ. He began by thanking them all for their admirable achievements and the substantial contribution they had made to the winning of the war. He then moved quickly on to the matter of maintaining secrecy, even after the end of hostilities. 'At some future time we may be called upon again to use the same methods. It is therefore as vital as ever not to relax from the high standards of security that we have hitherto maintained. The temptation to "own up" to our friends and families as to what our war work has been is a very real and natural one. It must be resisted absolutely.'[63] However, in the Far East, the secret of 'Magic', the breaking of Japanese diplomatic codes, was already out. When Bruce Keith, commander of the vast British sigint station located at HMS Anderson in Ceylon, tried to outline Travis's tight security measures, some of his subordinates openly laughed at him and observed that 'the Americans had spilled the beans in the paper the other day'.[64]

The move from Bletchley to Eastcote was undertaken during early 1946 in four main parties. The first was the priority group, and included the Soviet and East European Division; the last arrived in April 1946.[65] Staff turning up in leafy Pinner in search of lodgings were allowed to refer to their place of work as 'GCHQ', but they were told firmly that any reference to 'signals intelligence' was forbidden.[66] Between 1945 and 1948 the term 'GCHQ' was used interchangeably with both 'London Signals Intelligence Centre' and 'Station X'.[67]

Bletchley Park was now an empty shell in the Bedfordshire

countryside. Barbara Abernethy, who had worked as Denniston's personal assistant, recalls: 'We just closed down the huts, put all the files away and sent them down to Eastcote. I was the last person left at Bletchley Park. I locked the gate and took the key down to Eastcote. That was it.'[68] Much of the machinery was broken up, including examples of the mighty 'Colossus' computational machine. However, Professor Max Newman, who had been central to its development, managed to secure two 'Colossus' machines for his new computing department at Manchester University. These were transported by the Ministry of War Transport at the price of thirty-four shillings a ton. Newman offered to send a junior university lecturer down 'to sit on the van' to make sure that the precious machines were not damaged in transit.[69] In fact, this was not quite the end of Bletchley Park's active life in sigint, since GCHQ continued to use it for training courses as late as the 1960s.

The intention behind GCHQ's post-war move to London was to service the centres of power in British government. Accordingly, in the autumn of 1945 Travis took the opportunity to look at how the sigint product – the 'blue jackets' or 'BJs'– circulated around Whitehall. The Foreign Office was a big customer, receiving three sets of BJs daily. One set stayed with Ernest Bevin, the new Foreign Secretary and his war-weary Permanent Under-Secretary, Cadogan, 'for their immediate information'. Another went to the Services Liaison Department, which worked closely with the JIC. The third went to the main departments. Virtually everyone in the operational core of the Foreign Office habitually saw BJs, but they were always kept separate from other documents in special boxes which were locked up overnight.[70]

In MI5, the ritual of sigint security was closely observed. Distribution was presided over by the redoubtable 'Mrs Arbuthnot', who recorded everything meticulously in her log. Security of BJs seems to have been at its most lax inside SIS, where batches of them circulated around sections for as long as six weeks before being returned. Nor were they properly logged. GCHQ noted that, quite uniquely, inside SIS BJs were never treated as requiring special security measures, and indeed in some cases had 'found their way into the General Office for filing'. This broke the cardinal rule that sigint was never to mix with ordinary paperwork.[71]

The first major international crisis of the Cold War era was not long in coming. In June 1948, the Soviets decided to block road and railway access to the western sectors of Berlin, which were controlled by the British, the French and the Americans. The Berlin Blockade was defeated by a massive airlift of some four thousand tons of supplies a day. Hidden amongst the innumerable supply flights heading to Berlin were anonymous but highly secret aircraft collecting sigint for GCHQ, which provided some of the best intelligence during the crisis. Even before the crisis ended in May 1949, GCHQ had already been working hard on the 'Russian problem' for almost five years. The early onset of the Cold War had not only provided GCHQ with new targets, but had helped to perpetuate the wartime alliance between British code-breakers and their counterparts in allied countries. This, as we shall see, was fundamental to the postwar success of GCHQ.

4

The KGB and the Venona Project

*... Paul [Guy Burgess], and Yan [Anthony Blunt] consider that
the situation is serious.*
Message from the KGB station in London to Moscow,
February 1950[1]

The 'Venona Project' was possibly the most astounding code-breaking effort of the early Cold War.[2] Employing perhaps no more than a hundred people, it exploited a weakness in KGB communications and decoded some of the messages sent by Soviet intelligence. As a result, it revealed key Soviet agents and illuminated the unexpectedly vast scope and scale of KGB espionage in the West during the 1940s. This material was so significant that even though no new messages were collected after 1948, British and American code-breakers continued to work on the residue until October 1980. Initiated by the Americans, Venona collected new partners – first the British, and later the Australians, the Canadians, the Dutch and even the 'neutral' Swedes. It is justly famous for revealing some of the 'giants' of Russian espionage, including Klaus Fuchs and Donald Maclean, but the vast pool of messages that remain unsolved is also significant. Even now, it points unambiguously to many other cases yet to be resolved.

Anxiety about the compromise of sigint secrets was always central to the code-breaking profession. Back in 1927, Prime Minister Stanley Baldwin's infamous exposure of the reading of Soviet high-grade systems in the House of Commons had taught a whole generation of interwar code-breakers the price of careless talk. Thereafter, anxiety about the Ultra secret persuaded more than ten thousand people to keep their wartime vow of silence for decades. However, Venona introduced an even greater level of paranoia, since it hinted at the possibility of hundreds of Soviet agents active inside the governments of the West, some in high positions. For this reason it is unlikely that Venona was ever made known to President Roosevelt, and it was three years before his successor, Harry Truman, was let into the secret. Clement Attlee, Britain's first post-war leader, was not told until a major security case made it unavoidable in late 1947.[3] Nevertheless, the Venona project was compromised by several Soviet agents within five years of its initiation. This did not entirely negate its value, since the Soviets could not prevent the West from continuing work on the immense volume of KGB messages that had already been collected during the 1940s, patiently revealing the names of important agents. In the late 1950s, for example, GCHQ suddenly began to have success with Soviet Naval Intelligence messages, having used a new analytic technique.[4]

The extreme secrecy of the Venona project was its Achilles heel. Although the material often pointed to the identity of Soviet spies in the West, for security reasons it could not be shown to those arrested to persuade them to confess; still less could it be produced in court. Any sensible defence lawyer would seek to probe the nature of Venona, not only exposing its fragmentary nature, but also revealing sensitive secrets about sigint. Therefore, once spies had been identified by Venona, they had to be either caught red-handed meeting with their KGB controller, or successfully interrogated and broken. The result was a game of cat and mouse in which the mouse sometimes got away. In 1951, Donald Maclean, Guy Burgess and John Cairncross were among those who escaped by a whisker. Remarkably, Theodore Hall, an American Communist spy within the atomic programme, also brassed it out, despite close interrogation, escaping what would almost certainly have been death in the electric chair.[5] By contrast, in 1950 the atom spy Klaus Fuchs succumbed to repeated and patient questioning by MI5 after his arrest. He told his interrogators that he 'supposed he would be shot', and was pleasantly surprised when he wasn't.[6]

Venona revealed the security-minded nature of the Soviets. Much of their traffic was encrypted using a one-time pad system. This was time-consuming and slow, but they were willing to put in vast effort to protect their communications. This required huge volumes of tear-off pads with sheet after sheet of random numbers. The difficulty of generating thousands of sheets of truly random numbers should not be underestimated, and no one is clear how the Soviets made them. One individual has recalled a room full of women simply shouting out any number that came into their heads, but this seems improbable. Others have described devices not unlike lottery machines, with numbered balls. Whatever system was used, the logistical difficulties of generating many thousands of one-time pads and distributing them proved too much for wartime Russia.[7] Some time in early 1942, with Moscow on the verge of evacuation and much of Soviet industry badly dislocated, operators began to run out of pads. The KGB department that printed them committed the fatal error of reprinting twenty-five thousand pages. This made a small proportion of the messages, which should have been unbreakable, vulnerable to cryptanalysis. Far worse, they were sent to KGB units as well as to military and diplomatic users.[8]

The Venona project that exploited this mistake began in Washington. The Americans had collected Soviet messages during the war, but they lacked time to work on them. On 1 February 1943 the US Army's code-breaking service, called the Signals Intelligence Service, began a modest effort to see if it could exploit Soviet diplomatic communications. The telegrams had been collected at Arlington Hall, in Virginia, a former girls' school which was commandeered by the Army as its main code-breaking centre. Interest increased dramatically when it was discovered that some of the streams of traffic related to espionage. In October 1943 a young code-breaker, Lieutenant Richard Hallock, a Signal Corps reserve officer who had been a peacetime archaeologist at the University of Chicago, was looking at Soviet commercial traffic when he realised that the Soviets had committed a terrible error and were reusing their pads. This was an astonishing discovery, and thereafter Venona slowly began to unravel some of the KGB's most precious secrets.[9]

The US Army's head of signals intelligence, Carter W. Clarke, was the main enthusiast for Venona. Clarke was a tough, impatient, hard-drinking individual who many regarded as uncouth, but he was also a lateral thinker. Like many military intelligence chiefs in both Britain and the United States, he nurtured a deep-seated distrust of the Soviets, asserting bluntly: 'They're your friends today and they're your enemies tomorrow, and when they're on your side find out as much as you can about them because you can't when they become your enemy.'[10] The US Navy code-breakers also began work on Soviet traffic in the summer of 1943. The fact that by the autumn of 1944 the two rival armed services were both referring to all Soviet radio intercepts by the same code name of 'Rattan' suggests a directive from a high level. The following year the code name was changed to 'Bourbon'.[11]

By 1944, another talented young American code-breaker, Meredith Gardner, was busy making the first breaks into KGB traffic and even some from Soviet military intelligence (GRU). Other code-breakers were now drafted in to help. One of them was Cecil Phillips, a chemistry student who was sent to Arlington Hall in June 1943, initially to work on Japanese naval messages. In May 1944 he was switched to Soviet diplomatic traffic. He quickly realised the scale of duplication, and made a number of progressions that led to wider breaks in the cypher system used by the KGB.

However, substantial activity had to await the end of the war with Japan, when larger numbers of staff could be transferred to work on 'the Russian problem'.[12] Some of the Soviet messages were double-encrypted, and so represented a fantastic level of difficulty. Nevertheless, on 20 December 1946 Gardner decrypted a KGB message listing the names of scientists who had been working on the wartime development of the atomic bomb at Los Alamos, known as the 'Manhattan Project'. In spring 1947 he deciphered a message that showed that the Soviets were being given highly classified material from inside the US War

Department.[13] KGB agents were rarely referred to by their real names in the messages. The British spy Donald Maclean, for example, was 'Homer' or 'Gomer'. Accordingly, their identities had to be figured out from their activities and from what material they were providing to the Soviets.[14]

Early accounts of Venona suggested that the first breaks were achieved as a result of the recovery of a partly burned Soviet codebook found in Finland and sold to America's wartime intelligence agency, the Office of Strategic Services. Stories have long circulated about how American diplomats insisted that protocol required that it be returned to the Soviets. In fact, up until 1952, the progress made on Venona was probably driven by the pure sweat of mathematics, and represented a remarkable intellectual achievement. A little help was gained by intercepting Japanese traffic that contained Soviet material purchased from the Finns in 1944. The Finns had not been reading high-grade traffic, but had learned enough to be able to sort messages into homogeneous groups, the first stage of a cryptanalytical attack.[15] It was only in 1953 that the American team realised that one of the KGB systems it was working on related to a Soviet codebook that had been in their possession since 1945. At the end of the war TICOM Team 6, led by Lieutenant Colonel Paul Neff, had seized a copy of a partially burned Soviet codebook while exploring the German sigint centre at Burgscheidungen. The Germans had themselves seized the codebook from the Soviet Consulate in Petsamo in Finland during June 1941.[16]

The big shock was revelations about espionage within the Manhattan Project. This immediately raised the question of how the material might be employed for counter-espionage. Liaison was established with Robert Lamphere of the FBI's Intelligence Division, which had responsibility for maintaining physical surveillance on Soviet espionage activities. Venona was of immense help to the FBI, but it was not a one-way street. Occasionally the Bureau undertook burglaries of Soviet premises and photographed Soviet documents. Over the next decade, attempts were made to match material from these 'black bag jobs' with Venona material, but sadly there were few connections. Nevertheless, Lamphere ensured a coordinated exploitation system with the code-breakers.[17]

Meredith Gardner recalls that tight security for Venona only crept in slowly. In the beginning, everyone in the branch where it was being worked on was potentially privy to it, and 'no special treatment was given'. This was partly because crypt-analysts had to support each other by discussing problems, since systems were often related to each other. There were people who genuinely needed to know, and there were also 'mere busy-bodies who perhaps considered themselves consultants at large for all'. The Army intelligence liaison man, Howard Barkley, heard that 'there was something interesting going on' and came for a look, even though he had not been formally indoctrinated. Knowledge of Venona 'might have been picked up almost anywhere' in the branch at Arlington.[18]

Yet Venona was 'so sensational' that eventually something unusual had to be done on the security front. The focus was less on restricting the knowledge that it existed than on tightly control-ling the contents of the messages. However, counter-intelligence is a messy business. What the US Army code-breakers needed in order to identify the spies was background material from other government departments – so they were forced to work closely with a gradually expanding circle of people scattered across Washington. Typically, seven copies of one Venona message, issued on 30 August 1947 and entitled 'Cover Names in Diplomatic Traffic', were circulated. One went to GCHQ through its liaison, Colonel Patrick Marr-Johnson. The US Army code-breakers noted that the British surrounded the material with 'rigid safeguards'. Two copies went to the heads of Army and Navy code-breaking. Four went to mainstream Army Intelligence, Naval Intelligence and FBI. The State Department was also an important collabo-rator. Given that informal secondary briefing must have taken place, this means that perhaps as many as thirty people may have been given information from one circulated Venona message.[19] By contrast, an understanding on Venona was only reached with the CIA in September 1948, and detailed cooperation on active cases did not occur until 1952. Remarkably, this was six years after the American code-breakers had fully indoctrinated the British at GCHQ.[20]

It was the TICOM raids of early 1945 into Nazi Germany that had forced the British and the Americans to reveal their respective hands on the 'Russian problem'. TICOM was an Anglo–American project, and no one could disguise the fact that material on German code-breaking successes against the Soviet Union was one of its top priorities. TICOM led to some of the greatest successes of the early Cold War. During the autumn of 1945 some of its best results were coming from a Soviet encyphered teleprinter system code-named 'Caviar' which was almost certainly being broken with the help of the German team recovered by Rushworth and Norland on their foray into Germany. No less important was the breaking of a number of Soviet military machine cyphers that were not dissimilar to the Enigma machine, or its widely used Swedish equivalent, the 'Hagelin' machine. GCHQ code-named these machines the 'Poets Systems'. The first success was with an encoded Soviet teletype system code-named 'Coleridge' that gave great administrative detail relating to the Red Army in Eastern Europe. Carefully combined with material from more basic techniques such as radio direction-finding, it provided a superbly detailed picture of the Soviet Army in Europe. Thereafter, a team of GCHQ cryptanalysts led by Gerry Morgan working with an American naval team helped to decrypt another Soviet system called 'Longfellow'. Some of the best successes against Soviet machines were the product of the brilliant mind of Hugh Alexander, combined with the enormous computer power provided by GCHQ's American allies. In the Far East, Soviet naval codes were beginning to yield, but immediately after the war, 'Coleridge' and 'Longfellow' were the most important Soviet systems being exploited by the West.[21]

Britain was told about the embryonic Venona project as early as August 1945, and thereafter John Tiltman, head of the Cryptographic Group at Eastcote, was kept informed of progress.[22] However, full cooperation came a little later. The young American code-breaker Cecil Phillips spent six months at GCHQ's new location at Eastcote collaborating with Philip Howse. They focused on Soviet traffic that had been collected in Australia by monitoring Moscow's Embassy in Canberra. More senior figures such as John Tiltman did not give them much attention, since Phillips and Howse initially thought much of the traffic to be low-level consular material. In 1947 GCHQ received a further briefing, this time from Meredith Gardner, the key American analyst of the Venona messages. However, GCHQ did not set up a proper Venona office at Eastcote until December 1947, sparked by the recognition that the Australian material was actually KGB traffic.[23] Eastcote was itself in a state of permanent revolution, with sections being constantly reformed and merged, to the extent that the 'rumblings of reorganisation' drew comment from figures like Joseph Wenger, Washington's senior naval code-breaker.[24] The rumblings were the sounds of growth. From an establishment of just over a thousand in December 1945, GCHQ was nudging three thousand staff by 1948, and was already looking for new premises to accommodate its swelling numbers.[25]

The British had also collected plenty of interesting wartime KGB traffic. As early as June 1943, Alastair Denniston had met Colonel Ted Maltby of the Radio Security Service, together with Roger Hollis and John Curry of MI5, to discuss 'the interception of certain apparently illicit transmissions from this country which have been "DF-ed" to the Soviet Embassy'. ('DF' referred to the technique of radio direction-finding by triangulating between several aerials, sometimes mounted on detector vans.) These messages had attracted interest because they had nothing in common with the old Comintern style of transmissions, and it was noted that they might well be KGB traffic as they showed 'great technical skill'. Collecting this material stretched Britain's interceptor resources, since the traffic had lasted for eight hours solid in every twenty-four-hour period. Meanwhile, it was also searching for an illegal Comintern radio station in Wimbledon, using a disguised Ford Thames van with direction-finding equipment and security personnel in civilian clothes.[26]

By 1948, the Venona teams at GCHQ and Arlington Hall were small but extremely integrated. Although the British employed a different code name for Venona, calling it 'Bride', they adopted a standard procedure for the translations. The British cell was superintended by William Bodsworth, one of the initial team that began studying Enigma in 1937.[27] Like so many interwar code-breakers, Bodsworth was a linguist, not a mathematician, having read Spanish at Cambridge. Cheerful and possessed of a gentle humour, he was dubbed 'Snow White' because of his mop of white hair. Bodsworth's team undertook much of the laborious task of trying to reconstruct the Soviet codebooks. The seven dwarfs supplied almost enough nicknames for the Venona teams: by the end of 1950, the number of people at Eastcote working on 'Bride' remained at less than ten. For the Americans, British input was essential both to the efforts to track down the identity of figures like 'Homer' and to obtaining background material to allow the analysis of the KGB's Canberra messages.[28]

It is almost certain that the first person to alert the Soviets to the existence of the Venona project in any detail was a KGB agent named William Weisband. Born in the Soviet Union in 1908, Voldya Weisband had emigrated with his family to the United States in the 1920s. In 1940 he had changed his name to William, and had registered at the American University in Washington DC. By 1942 he was serving as a lieutenant in a US Army code-breaking unit in the Middle East. He was posted back to Arlington Hall in July 1944, and was soon working in the Soviet section. Weisband had in fact been a KGB agent since 1934, and he certainly displayed all the traits of a classic agent. Gregarious and popular, he had friends throughout what was now called the Army Security Agency, and charmed the senior officers. His reputation as a problem-solver allowed him wide access within the Soviet section, and Meredith Gardner actually recalls him looking at a list of names derived from Venona material in late 1946. Weisband was not himself identified by Venona, but seeing the messages decrypted must had made him feel queasy, since his name – or at least his code name 'Zhora'

– was certainly buried in traffic somewhere. In 1948 the Soviets summarised Weisband's reports that had been fed back to KGB headquarters in Moscow. They contained worrying news:

*

For one year, a large amount of very valuable documentary material concerning the work of the Americans on deciphering Soviet cyphers, intercepting and analysing open-radio correspondence of Soviet Institutions was received . . . On the basis of Weisband material, our state security organs carried out a number of defensive measures, resulting in the reduced efficiency of the American deciphering service. This has led to a considerable current reduction in the amount of deciphering and analysis by the Americans.[29]

*

In May 1950 Weisband was named by another agent who had been revealed by Venona and interrogated by the FBI. Although Weisband was questioned, there was insufficient evidence to charge him. There was also a fear that a court case would advertise the work of signals intelligence to other countries, which might then take steps to upgrade their communications. He was never prosecuted for espionage.[30]

Yet Weisband caused immense damage to Western code-breaking. On Friday, 29 October 1948 the Soviets implemented a massive change in all their communications security procedures. American code-breakers referred to this fateful event as 'Black Friday'. Many Soviet radio nets moved over to one-time pads, which henceforth were not reused. Much of the procedural material that had been sent 'in clear', or unencrypted, between operators running medium-grade Army, Navy, Air Force and Police systems, was now encrypted for the first time. Operator chatter was banned. In the space of twenty-four hours, most Soviet systems from which the West had been deriving intelligence were lost.[31] This affected the 'Poets Systems' which the British and Americans had been reading successfully as a result of their raids into Germany in 1945.[32] This was the most serious British intelligence loss of the early Cold War.

For the British, Venona was full of irony. As a joint programme with the Americans it symbolised the highest level of trust. However, its subsequent revelations damaged the most important parts of the transatlantic relationship, including agreements on code-breaking and atomic cooperation. This was because in early 1950 Venona uncovered Klaus Fuchs, who had come to Los Alamos as part of the British contribution to the Manhattan Programme, but was in fact an agent for the KGB. Venona also raised serious doubts about the possibility of Anglo–American–Commonwealth sigint and defence cooperation because of the number of KGB agents identified in Australia. Directly or indirectly, Venona also exposed four of the KGB's top agents inside the British establishment: Kim Philby, Donald Maclean, Guy Burgess and John Cairncross. The main problem for the KGB was that it did not know how many of its previous messages had been broken by the Venona project, and which of its agents had been exposed. This made it hard for it to warn specific agents. Venona also contributed to Soviet paranoia about double agents who might be planting disinformation. The KGB's strange tendency not to wholly trust even its best sources, including the SIS officer Kim Philby, was one manifestation of this.[33]

In August 1949 Philby returned from a posting in Istanbul to London. He was preparing to take over from Peter Dwyer as SIS liaison officer with the CIA in Washington, and was briefed by Sir Stewart Menzies, Chief of SIS, together with two of his senior officers, James Easton and Maurice Oldfield. Oldfield, whose responsibility was counter-intelligence, explained Venona to him in detail. Philby's blood probably ran cold as Oldfield observed that they had broken about 10 per cent of the KGB's Washington–Moscow telegrams and were now searching for a British diplomat working for the KGB and code-named 'Homer'.[34] Philby immediately requested a conference with his KGB controller, Yuri Modin. The KGB station in the Soviet Embassy in London reported the crisis that now confronted them:

*

Stanley [Philby] asked to communicate that the Americans and the British had constructed a deciphering machine which in one day does 'the work of a thousand people in a thousand years'. Work on deciphering is facilitated by three factors: (1) A one-time pad used twice; (2) our cipher resembles the cipher of our trade organisation in the USA; (3) a half-burnt codebook has been found in Finland and passed to the British and used to decrypt our communications. They will succeed within the next twelve months. The Charles [Klaus Fuchs] case has shown the counter-intelligence service the importance of knowing the past of civil servants . . . Stanley, Paul [Guy Burgess], and Yan [Anthony Blunt] consider that the situation is serious.[35]

*

Yuri Modin recalls that Venona 'hung over us like the sword of Damocles'.[36] Nevertheless, he and Philby agreed gloomily that in the short term there was nothing they could do, 'only wait and behave with extreme care and caution'.[37] Arriving in Washington in November 1949, Philby was offered a ringside seat on Venona. He was given Venona summaries by the GCHQ liaison officer in Washington, and was actually taken to Arlington and briefed on the project in detail several times.[38] Incredibly, in July 1950 he put in a successful request for GCHQ to give him an extra copy of any Venona-related material it was sending to the Americans in Washington, so he could peruse it at leisure. In any other circumstances this would have been an espionage triumph, but it caused Philby no joy. The arrests at this time of Julius and Ethel Rosenberg, perhaps the most famous figures ever to be charged with espionage for the Soviet Union, cannot have calmed his nerves.[39]

Understandably, the Americans had initially refused to show the British the KGB Washington–Moscow traffic.[40] This delayed the search for the Foreign Office spy code-named 'Homer', who eventually turned out to be Donald Maclean. In 1947, the earliest period of good code recovery, analysts knew that several messages from late March 1944 began with a stock preamble and greeting. Such standard openings were a gift for code-breakers. In this case it read: 'To the 8th section. Material "G".' The Eighth section was thought to receive political intelligence, and short breaks in other KGB messages showed that the material concerned Britain's Ambassador in Washington, Sir Archibald Clark Kerr. By December 1948, further work by Philip Howse revealed that it seemed to originate from telegrams sent by Churchill. In January 1949, after a month of frantic night-time digging in the registry of the Foreign Office (a daytime search would have alerted the regular diplomatic staff), the originals were found. The circle of suspects was gradually narrowing. The final breakthrough came in August 1950, when the Americans recovered two short stretches of material that referred to 'Homer' being entrusted with decyphering a telegram from 'Boar' [Churchill] to 'Captain' [Roosevelt]. This pointed directly to someone in Britain's wartime Washington Embassy, and the finger of suspicion began to circle over the heads of a very few people. Further work on the messages suggested that 'Homer' was married. However, it was only on 30 March 1951 that the code-breakers were sure that 'G' and 'Homer' were the same. This information placed him in New York in June 1944.[41]

At this moment, Philby knew that Maclean had been identified. However, he also knew that MI5 would have to gather traditional evidence against him to support an arrest, so a window of opportunity existed. Philby's friend and fellow Soviet agent, the diplomat Guy Burgess, was being sent home from Washington in disgrace after an especially embarrassing drunken episode, and Philby used him to pass a message to Yuri Modin, their KGB controller in London. On Friday, 25 May 1951, Burgess and Maclean fled from Britain on a ferry to St Malo. It was a narrow escape: MI5 had planned to confront Maclean when he turned up for work the following Monday. Once in France, a KGB contact handed them false papers which ensured that they could travel in relative safety across Europe towards Moscow. The false papers were essential, since by now every security service in Europe was looking for them. Inevitably, suspicion also fell on Philby, not least because Burgess had been lodging with him in Washington, but there was no hard evidence. Philby was recalled and forced into retirement, but no other action was taken against him.[42]

Venona also had ramifications in the British Commonwealth. In July 1947, Field Marshal Montgomery, now Chief of the Imperial General Staff, had held a meeting with Australia's Minister for External Affairs, Dr H.V. Evatt, about joint weapons development in Australia. Montgomery noted that 'good security precautions are very necessary' because of the appearance in Australia of a spy who was connected to the Igor Gouzenkou case, in which a defecting KGB cypher clerk had revealed a major spy ring in Ottawa in 1946. But in November and December 1947 Venona revealed that despite enhanced security precautions, sensitive documents were regularly leaking from Canberra to the KGB.[43] These revelations soon made their way to the highest level. On 27 January 1948, Admiral Roscoe Hillenkoeter, Director of the CIA, warned President Truman: 'Indications have appeared that there is a leak in high government circles in Australia, to Russia.' He explained that MI5 was engaged in expansive undercover investigations to determine just where the leakages were.[44] Highly sensitive material had been passed to the KGB from the Department of External Affairs in Canberra. The Soviets considered it to be spectacular stuff, for it included copies of the 'explosive' future strategy papers drafted by the British Post Hostilities Planning Committee, or 'PHP'. This was bare-faced anti-Soviet planning material, prepared with the encouragement of the British Chiefs of Staff, that had already resulted in rows in Whitehall. Anthony Eden, then Foreign Secretary, had banned its circulation abroad in late 1944, but by then it was too late, and the volatile PHP reports had already made their way via Canberra to Moscow.[45] The KGB chief in Australia considered the PHP papers to be such an important coup that he asked Moscow for permission to send them by cypher rather than courier. This was a bad mistake, for the two lengthy papers, 'Security in the Western Mediterranean and the Eastern Atlantic' and 'Security of India and the Indian Ocean', provided the code-breakers with a vast word-for-word 'crib' to get into other Soviet traffic.[46] Partly because it was relatively easy to identify which documents had been taken in Australia, the KGB Moscow–Canberra cables proved to be the most successful part of the Venona operation. Remarkably, by early 1948 so much progress had been made that GCHQ was virtually reading the messages in real time.[47]

London did not regard the Australians as competent enough to handle this security crisis. In February 1948 Sir Percy Sillitoe, the head of MI5, was despatched to Australia. With him came Roger Hollis, head of MI5's C Division (later himself wrongly accused of working for the KGB), concerned with protective security and background checks, and another senior security officer, Roger Hemblys-Scales. With Courtney Young, MI5's resident Security Liaison Officer in Australia, they persuaded the Prime Minister, Ben Chifley and Defence Minister, Frederick Shedden, to permit vigorous investigations. In July, following further discussions with British Prime Minister Clement Attlee, the Australians accepted British proposals for the creation of an Australian equivalent of MI5 later known as the Australian Security Intelligence Organisation (ASIO).[48] Sillitoe returned to London, but Hollis and Hemblys-Scales remained in Australia to set up ASIO and work on the list of Venona suspects, which numbered twelve.

Thereafter, ASIO was almost entirely focused on what it called 'The Case'. Tracing documents quoted in KGB traffic indicated likely suspects, including a typist, Frances Bernie, who helped to run a Communist youth league and who worked personally for Dr Evatt, the Minister for External Affairs. It also pointed to two Australian diplomats with Communist leanings, Ian Milner and Jim Hill. Hollis and Courtney Young did not tell the Australians that the names came from intercepts, but the nature of the material led some of the more experienced ASIO hands to suspect sigint as the key source. Some of the suspects were referred to by code names rather than real names, and their identities could only be deduced by careful circumstantial guesswork. Milner and Hill, who were identified positively, refused

to 'come over'. William Skardon, MI5's most experienced interrogator, made a soft approach to Hill when he visited London
in 1950, trying to persuade him to 'be sensible' and 'make a
clean breast of it', but Hill denied everything.[49]

The 'Venona Twelve' kept ASIO's staff of close to two hundred
busy well into the 1950s. Each new suspect opened a world of
further associates and contacts who required separate examination. The task was difficult, since the Communist Party of Australia
had long expected to be banned, and had built up a substantial
underground organisation. Not unlike the Communist Party of
India, seasoned by years of security attention, it had also achieved
some infiltration of the police. Even the infiltration of ASIO seemed
a possibility. ASIO's staff worked around the clock watching and
bugging the flats of suspect Soviet diplomats in Canberra. Each
visitor was tailed and investigated. ASIO's staff were learning the
hardest lesson of counter-espionage and counter-subversion:
working security cases really diligently only manufactured more
leads and opened more cases.[50] Almost a quarter of the Venona
messages relating to Canberra still remain classified, presumably
because they relate to KGB agents not pursued or prosecuted.[51]

The British and Australians were not alone in suffering KGB
penetration. Although headlines about Klaus Fuchs and Donald
Maclean generated anxiety about Britain amongst the American
elite, those on the inside knew Washington had its fair share of
Soviet agents. Venona uncovered spies in the State Department,
the Treasury, even in the White House. They included Harry
Dexter White, a senior Treasury official, and Laughlin Currie,
who had been a personal assistant to Franklin D. Roosevelt. This
was not particularly surprising, since the vast influx of academics
and scientists moving into government work during wartime
had inevitably included some Communist Party sympathisers.
The Office of Strategic Services, forerunner of the CIA, which
had recruited heavily from the East Coast academic establishment, harboured perhaps a dozen people working for the Soviets.

Venona had profound implications for the development of
the security state in America, Britain, Canada and Australia.

Just at the moment when the public were anxious to throw off the claustrophobic constraints of wartime security, officials were confronted with irrefutable evidence of a massive programme of Soviet espionage. Selling strong security measures in the late 1940s was an uphill task. This was nowhere more true than in Australia. The creation of ASIO by a Labor Prime Minister, Ben Chifley, was a remarkable development. Like the British Labour Party, its Australian counterpart had historically been sceptical about surveillance, associating it with right-wing anti-union activities. In Britain too, Venona led indirectly to the introduction of detailed personal background checks, or 'positive vetting', for officials. British civil servants resisted the idea, but it was increasingly clear that without it, Anglo–American strategic cooperation on matters like atomic energy was likely to end.[52]

Venona represents a documentary source of high value, and has helped to resolve some of the most bitterly contested Cold War espionage cases. These include the famously controversial cases of the atomic scientist Julius Rosenberg and the diplomat Alger Hiss, who were both active espionage agents for the Soviets. In these important cases, Venona offers us what Nigel West has rightly called 'a glimpse of the unvarnished truth'.[53] At the same time, much of the Venona material is rather fragmentary, and in 1995 it was further obfuscated by the lamentable decision of the British and American governments to blank out some names on grounds of potential political embarrassment. Some KGB code names for individuals were re-used and given to more than one person. Moreover, it is possible that a minority of the people who appear in the Venona cables did not knowingly have a relationship with Soviet intelligence officers, or were identified as possible targets for future recruitment, but were never actually recruited. The tendency of some intelligence officers to exaggerate their triumphs has also to be borne in mind. In short, Venona has provided us with fabulous revelations, but the full story awaits the moment when historians access the files of the KGB and Soviet military intelligence, or GRU, in Moscow. That will not happen for a long time yet.

UKUSA – Creating the Global Sigint Alliance

Much discussion about 100 per cent cooperation with the USA about SIGINT. Decided that less than 100 per cent cooperation was not worth having.
Admiral Andrew Cunningham, Chief of the Naval Staff,
21 November 1945[1]

One of the most important legacies of the Second World War was the creation of the vast global signals intelligence alliance known as 'UKUSA'. The signing of the UKUSA intelligence treaty between Britain, the United States, Canada, Australia and New Zealand has long been regarded as marking the birth of a secretive leviathan, a global multilateral alliance that has grown to embrace numerous countries and to command almost unlimited intelligence power. Its origins are often traced to a single landmark treaty between Britain, the United States and the Commonwealth deemed to be concluded in 1948. Indeed, the highly classified UKUSA treaty is widely considered to be nothing less than the linchpin of the West's post-war intelligence system. UKUSA supposedly created a cosy Anglo-Saxon club sharing everything in the super-secret realm of sigint.

Remarkably, there is in fact no singular UKUSA 'treaty' of 1948, and none of the above assertions is true. Instead, UKUSA is less an alliance than a complex network of different alliances built up from many different overlapping agreements. It is the sum of a curious agglomeration of many understandings that were mostly between two countries only, that accumulated over more than two decades.[2] Britain and the United States concluded the main agreements in 1943 and 1946, together with a further convention in 1948. According to the historian

Peter Hennessy they are still in force, and as recently as August 2006, some sixty years on, the authorities deemed them so sensitive that, after anxious deliberation, they announced that they could not be released.[3] Further agreements were added – and continue to be added – creating a complex spider's web of cooperation. However, each agreement has its limits, and all parties have withheld sigint material from each other. In short, there is no common pooling of material. Moreover, relations between the various parties have often been tense, and latterly Washington has threatened some adherents, including Britain, Australia and New Zealand, with suspension or exclusion. If UKUSA is an alliance, its members are only 'allies of a kind'.[4]

It is also wrong to think of UKUSA as exclusively concerned with sigint. It is, rather, a sigint and *security* network. Security agreements on physical control of the sigint product and on protecting the security of communications were perhaps the most important aspects of the UKUSA network. Sigint reports on particular subjects were rigidly compartmentalised and given 'Codeword' status, ensuring that they could only be seen by people cleared to see that series, and making them effectively 'above Top Secret'. Venona is the best-known example of such a Codeword. Much of this obsessive secrecy was codified in a biblical tome entitled 'International Regulations on Sigint', or 'IRSIG', which had reached its third edition by 1967.[5] UKUSA was also about secretly undermining the communications security of other states, even neutrals and allies. Communications security, or 'comsec', is perhaps even more sensitive than sigint. The efforts of the UKUSA powers to control it have been among the darkest secrets of alliance politics in Western Europe. In short, the realm of sigint alliances is profoundly realist – at times even paranoid – with operators 'taking what they can get'. While UKUSA might appear from the outside to represent a single powerful intelligence colossus, on the inside it was anything but unified.

The best example of allies spying on allies is provided by

Finland. The end of the Second World War had not turned out well for the Finns, since their Russian enemy had returned to the Baltic in overwhelming strength. Anticipating the arrival of the Russians, the talented Finnish code-breakers decamped en masse to Sweden, complete with their relatives, equipment and support staff. There they began a veritable car-boot sale of their cryptographic wares, including the results of sixteen years of continuous work against Russian systems. The beauty of selling codes is that the same items can be sold many times over. Predictably, the Finns paid their ground rent by assisting the Swedish equivalent of Bletchley Park, the Förvarets Radioanstalt, or FRA. In the last days of the war they also sold complete Russian codebooks to the American wartime intelligence agency, the Office of Strategic Services, to Britain's SIS and also to the Japanese. They also sold the Americans the details of the British codes they had broken, and work they had completed against some US State Department cyphers. The Americans were eager customers. This episode – known as the 'Stella Polaris' case because of its northern origins – underlines the duplicitous nature of friendships in the realm of code-breaking.[6]

In the autumn of 1945, even while the Stella Polaris case was 'live', President Roosevelt's successor, Harry S. Truman, was engaged in the abolition of the Office of Strategic Services. Two years later its remnants would be revived to become the Central Intelligence Agency, but for now many of its intelligence officers were dispersed and its agents paid off. By contrast, Truman regarded sigint as indispensable, and secretly gave permission for the American code-breaking agencies to work on into the post-war period and 'to continue collaboration in the field of communication intelligence between the United States Army and Navy and the British'.[7] All major countries desired the maximum world coverage. On 19 November 1945, Admiral Andrew Cunningham, Britain's senior naval commander, attended a critical meeting of the British Chiefs of Staff. There was 'Much discussion about 100 per cent cooperation with the USA about Sigint,' he recorded, adding that they 'Decided that less than 100 per cent was not worth having.' In Ottawa, George Glazebrook, a senior Canadian diplomat, recommended to the Canadian Joint Intelligence Committee that Canada enhance her independent sigint effort in order to stake a claim in this secretive emerging cooperative system. 'It is paramount,' he insisted, 'that Canada should make an adequate contribution to the general pool.'[8]

Yet a 'general pool' was not what emerged. Moreover, the way ahead was strewn with obstacles and tortuous negotiations. The complex package of agreements, letters and memoranda of understanding was not completed until 1953. In this process, Britain derived considerable benefit from her dominance over her Commonwealth partners and her imperial bases. GCHQ's approach was to align her Commonwealth affiliates to create a critical mass before entering negotiations with the Americans. The story of Britain's sigint relations with Australia illustrates this well. In March 1945, with the end of the European war looming, Edward Travis set off from Bletchley Park on a veritable world sigint tour. The possibility of transforming wartime cooperative arrangements into a post-war sigint alliance was already in his mind.[9] En route, he and his party visited major sigint centres at Heliopolis in Egypt and HMS Anderson in Ceylon. They arrived in Melbourne in early April, and spent time with the Australian code-breaking organisation there, called the Central Bureau. On 17 April they departed for New Zealand and then moved on to Hawaii, San Francisco and finally Washington. By the time they reached Hawaii they were running low on funds, and had to beg a cash advance from the Foreign Office before they could proceed further. At each stop, the possibility of continued post-war cooperation was gently raised.[10]

Relations with the Australians were somewhat awkward. Typically, London had reluctantly agreed that Sir Frederick Shedden, the new Australian Defence Minister, could be indoctrinated into the secrets of sigint, but only so he could use his power to prevent a reduction of Australian spending on intelligence. There had also been alleged leaks about intelligence in

Canberra, and in September 1945 there were momentary doubts as to whether any cooperation with Australia on sigint would be authorised.[11] Indeed, by December 1945 a 'dangerous position' had developed, with the Australians seeming to want to go it alone with their own system; what was worse, there were rival elements within the Australian armed services. British liaison officers warned, 'If we are not prompt to give a lead there may even be 3 or 4 rival shows in Australia with no hope of proper security.' During the war, material collected in Australia and the Far East had often been sent back to Britain for analysis. However, there was now a possibility that the Australians might end up 'insisting on full exploitation in Australia'. This was a situation that British code-breakers wanted to avoid at all costs, since final exploitation was power, and they wished to keep their Commonwealth associates in a subordinate position.[12]

The crucial moment in the creation of the global sigint alliance occurred on 22 February 1946, when Britain opened a two-week Commonwealth conference for 'Signals Intelligence Authorities'. This gave them critical mass prior to concluding a deal with the Americans the following month. The attendance of Australia and Canada was a foregone conclusion, and given the significant contribution that New Zealand had made during the war to naval sigint, there were hopes that she would also join in.[13] The conference was also attended by senior officers from GCHQ's regional centres. Bruce Keith, the commander of HMS Anderson, the massive sigint collection station in Ceylon, was there, accompanied by his deputy, Teddy Poulden.[14] At this conference Australia offered sixty-five operating teams, amounting to 417 personnel, from the three armed services as its contribution to a new global sigint network.[15] Australia was persuaded to set up a British-style Joint Intelligence Committee and, most importantly, a unitary Signals Intelligence Centre along the lines of GCHQ, which was given the cover name Defence Signals Branch.[16]

The big issue was the choice of the director of Australian sigint.

The Australians fielded four candidates, all experienced wartime intelligence officers. However, Travis told them bluntly that it would be a British officer. Some Australians were affronted, but on balance Travis's decision was probably correct, since it ensured that Australia would have good access to British sigint. Travis's choice was Teddy Poulden, who had spent the last two years of the war as deputy to Bruce Keith, the commander of HMS Anderson, on Ceylon.[17] Poulden took over in April 1947, commanding a staff of around two hundred, about twenty of whom were GCHQ personnel on secondment. Although senior Australian sigint officers resented the fact that Poulden had his own private cypher for communicating with Travis, he was broadly considered to have done a good job. In the early 1950s he was succeeded by an Australian, Ralph Thompson, who remained in the position until 1978, making him easily the longest-serving Western sigint chief.[18] In January 1947 a further Commonwealth sigint conference was held in London, and the Chifley government gave final approval for the integration of Australian sigint into UKUSA at the end of the year.[19] However, this was delayed by the security concerns raised by Venona, so there was little sigint contact between Australia and the United States until 1949.[20]

Canada's sigint organisation under the long-serving Lieutenant Colonel Edward Drake suffered similar 'colonial' treatment. Although Drake was a Canadian, his deputy was the stalwart British code-breaker and expert on Russian systems Geoffrey Stevens, who arrived to take up his post in Ottawa in March 1946. A few weeks later, on 13 April, the Canadian Prime Minister Mackenzie King authorised the consolidation of a number of wartime organisations into a small post-war unit of about a hundred staff known as the Communications Branch of the National Research Council (CBNRC). A number of senior posts were filled by staff seconded by GCHQ, prompting locals to observe that CBNRC stood for 'Communications Branch – No Room for Canadians'. By the late 1940s Drake had resolved to offset this British oligopoly by developing better relations with the US Army code-breakers.[21]

The two-week sigint conference that GCHQ had convened with the Commonwealth partners in February 1946 was a vital prelude to business with the Americans the following month.[22] Indeed, the Australians and Canadians had given GCHQ permission to negotiate on their behalf.[23] On 6 March, William Friedman, one of the US Army's most senior code-breakers, arrived in London to complete a revised version of the previous wartime agreements between Britain and the United States. The main section of the agreement which followed this policy conference between the principals was only four pages long; however, a UK–USA Technical Conference followed in June 1946 which added many annexes and appendices. Much of this new material was about attempting to agree on security procedures for handling sigint.[24] The terms of the 1946 agreement are still highly secret. Both parties agreed to 'pool their knowledge of foreign comint organizations', and that in any future negotiations with other parties 'every effort should be made to avoid disclosure of US/UK collaboration in the COMINT field'.[25] Joseph Wenger, the head of America's naval code-breakers, accepted that the 1946 conference had only dealt with generalities, and this had generated 'some criticism'. Nevertheless, his priority was to 'set up the framework and establish the will to make it work', so in his view it was a great success, and 'laid the foundation of a very fruitful and important partnership'.[26]

For GCHQ, liaison with allies was all-important to its new status as a proper intelligence agency in its own right. By the spring of 1946, Edward Travis was operating with two deputies at Eastcote. Nigel de Grey was the senior deputy, and had responsibility for operational coordination between the five main groups at GCHQ, together with recruitment, training and security. Following the important allied sigint conferences of February and March 1946, Travis added a second deputy, a naval officer called Captain Edward Hastings who had much wartime experience of working with Canada. His responsibilities included liaison with the US, the Commonwealth and India, together with managing GCHQ's overseas collection stations.[27]

GCHQ's strategy for cooperation with the Americans was to rapidly reorientate its collection towards Russia. Typically, the vast Forest Moor wireless station near Harrogate in Yorkshire, with an aerial farm of some ten square miles, was switched from collecting German traffic from the Eastern Front to Russian traffic as soon as the war drew to an end. British field units in Germany, Austria and Italy joined the suborned Italians in collecting Russian military traffic. The re-established sigint stations in Singapore and Hong Kong also focused on Russian traffic, with the latter specialising in KGB messages. All this made Britain an attractive partner for the United States.[28] The core of Anglo–American cooperation was a 'relentless attack' on the wartime generation of Russian cyphers. Figures like John Tiltman and Hugh Alexander provided the code-breaking expertise, while the Americans provided most of the processing capability.[29]

All the three American armed services were routinely circulated with GCHQ finished product on Russia. A key instrument was the 'Comintsum', a digest of the latest 'hot' material which made its way around comint-cleared centres. London would send twenty copies of this sort of document to Washington on a regular basis, with two copies going to US Air Force intelligence, two to US Army intelligence and so forth.[30] On Russian military targets at least, the British and Americans operated smoothly as one machine. A very high priority was given to joint planning for the use of nuclear weapons in any future war. As early as 28 April 1948, General Charles Cabell, head of US Air Force intelligence, reviewed the intelligence arrangements in support of the current emergency atomic strike plan 'Operation Halfmoon'. 'At the present time,' he noted with satisfaction, 'there is complete interchange of communications intelligence information between the cognizant United States and British agencies. It is not believed that the present arrangements . . . could be improved.'[31] This was cemented by a further Anglo–American agreement on communications intelligence signed in June 1948.

However, the sharing of material on other parts of the world remained selective, reflecting the political tensions of the moment. In 1948, even while the UKUSA alliance was gradually being drawn together, Britain and America were at loggerheads over Palestine and the emerging state of Israel. There was anxiety in London about sharing intelligence on the Middle East with the Americans. On 15 February 1948, Britain's Joint Intelligence Committee discussed the problem of circulating its own reports, which included material from SIS and GCHQ, to the newly formed CIA. Although British intelligence representatives in Washington were not aware of a specific 'pro-Zionist bloc in the Central Intelligence Agency', nevertheless they asserted that 'Jewish sympathisers were no doubt included in its establishment', and complained that there had been leaks. William Hayter, the Chair of the JIC, insisted that its material on Palestine should be shown in the first instance only to the Director of Central Intelligence in person. He added that 'It should be explained to him that if he could not guarantee that they would not fall into pro-Zionist hands, then he could not be left with them.' Even so, it was decided to withhold more sensitive recent reports on Palestine from the Americans.[32] Meanwhile, 'Operation Gold', run by US Navy intelligence, was intercepting the cable traffic of Jewish arms smugglers, but this was not being shared with Britain, or indeed acted upon.[33]

American links with the Commonwealth parties were also hesitant. The Americans were slow to do business with the Canadians. They worried about how much GCHQ had told the Canadians about Anglo–American agreements, and suspected that GCHQ was secretly giving Ottawa some American sigint.[34] During the 1948 discussions of possible CAN–USA sigint agreements, it became clear that the US Communications Intelligence Board was anxious to prevent an information free-for-all. It preferred to hand material to the Canadians on a 'need to know' basis, and was anxious to prevent a proliferation of sigint liaison officers.[35] Meanwhile, somewhat foolishly, Canada resisted the all-important standardisation of security procedures that was a foundation stone of the BRUSA agreement, so negotiations were 'very difficult', dragging on until 1953.[36] The Americans were even more wary of sigint cooperation with the Australians due to the KGB spy cases uncovered by Venona in the late 1940s. This, in turn, retarded the joint sigint effort against the newly formed People's Republic of China from 1949. In late 1953, the advent of a Liberal (i.e. conservative) government in Australia triggered a full resumption of cooperation, formalised at a tripartite sigint conference between the Americans, British and Australians. New Zealand also came in as fifth partner. It was only at this point that the name 'UKUSA' was adopted at GCHQ's request.[37]

The most prickly area of alliance relations was the business of cypher security, which protected the secrecy of diplomatic communications. Foolishly perhaps, at a meeting in London in May 1947, the British launched an audacious bid to persuade the Americans to share the innermost secrets on matters of their code-making. The discussion revolved around the replacement of the Combined Cypher Machine, which had been developed for inter-allied communications during the war, but was now thought obsolete and vulnerable. The British were also keen to replace their own national machine, the Typex, but were desperately short of money as a result of post-war austerity, and argued that for reasons of economy any new cypher machines should be capable of inter-allied use, and proposed joint research and development with the Americans.[38] The Americans were startled: it had been a cardinal principle never to share the secrets of their unique and highly prized Sigaba machine. Hoping to overcome this psychological barrier, the British revealed that they were in fact already knowledgeable about Sigaba. They not only described its inner workings 'quite accurately', but confessed that they had 'incorporated its principles in a radiotele-type machine for their own use'. Hoping that they had pushed the Sigaba obstacle aside, the British then made their pitch. They claimed that they had developed an approach to cypher machines that was 'new and revolutionary', and 'superior to the Sigaba principle'. They were happy to share this with the Americans, and perhaps make use of it in joint machines that might be developed for both national and allied use.

Far from being reassured, the Americans were horrified. Discussion had to be 'temporarily discontinued' while they withdrew to confer amongst themselves. The US Army could see no objection to releasing the Sigaba principle for use in a combined allied machine, since the British had clearly unravelled it. However, the US Navy offered 'serious objections', and used their veto. Thus the British were told that Sigaba had to be completely eliminated from the discussions. At this point they revealed their 'new and revolutionary idea' for future cypher machines, only to find that their American colleagues sneered at it and dismissed it as 'impractical' on engineering grounds. The two sides parted without agreement.[39]

While GCHQ was overawed by the scale of American sigint resources, matters looked quite different from Washington. With the Second World War now over, and an economising Republican Congress controlling the federal purse-strings, resources for American comint interception activities were remarkably tight. This contributed to American under-preparedness prior to the Korean War. It also enforced a division of labour between GCHQ and the Americans, and prevented American sigint from expanding its activities in Europe in the way it had hoped. In 1949, US Army Security Agency interception units in Europe were still passing much of their product to GCHQ for analysis, rather than back to Washington. Moreover, GCHQ retained primary responsibility for areas such as Eastern Europe, the Near East and Africa.[40] Because of this division of labour, the late 1940s saw the gradual development of American and British spheres of influence. In Scandinavia, for example, relations with Norway were an American responsibility, while those with the Swedes belonged to GCHQ, although this demarcation was not always strictly adhered to.[41] GCHQ enjoyed the additional benefits of the panoply of bases provided by Britain's imperial and post-imperial presence. Although the Empire was shrinking, the very process of retreat and the euphoria of independence often rendered the new successor states willing to grant limited base facilities to the departing British. These 'communications relay facilities' may have seemed innocuous, but in fact many countries were unwitting hosts to important GCHQ collection sites.[42]

The outbreak of the Korean War early on the morning of Sunday, 25 June 1950 took Britain and the United States by complete surprise. Although they had comint units in locations such as Hong Kong and Japan, their main focus was Russian traffic, and their sigint capabilities against North Korea were non-existent. The NSA official history notes that there was 'no person or group of persons working on the North Korean problem', and even had they done so, they had 'no Korean linguists, no Korean dictionaries and no typewriters'. Although the CIA had picked up what might be called 'rumours of war' from human agents, there was no high-profile attack warning delivered to policy-makers. During the first few weeks of the war, the Americans and their South Korean allies suffered serious reverses and were almost overrun. Sigint helped the Americans to beat back the attacks on their rapidly shrinking perimeter by providing excellent tactical intelligence, but they blundered again by missing the entry of the Chinese into the war in October 1950.[43]

The Korean War resulted in a headlong expansion of American sigint. More than two thousand additional staff were recruited, and more than $5 million of additional spending on comint and comsec was authorised within weeks of the war commencing.[44] The outbreak of the war also meant crash expansion in Asia. The Americans informed London of their 'urgent need' for a US Air Force sigint unit to be deployed to Hong Kong, and other sites were quickly developed on Taiwan in an attempt to remedy the yawning intelligence gap in East Asia.[45]

Korea had another important impact. With new employees flooding into the training wing at Nebraska Avenue in central

Washington DC, the Americans soon had a vast backlog of people requiring security clearance before they could begin work. By the end of 1950, more than a third of sigint employees were 'uncleared'. It was then discovered that since 1948 the CIA had been using the polygraph, or lie detector test, initially only to screen people who had access to sigint, although its use was soon extended to all CIA employees. By May 1951 it had been adopted for all American code-breakers, and polygraph examiners were testing 'from seven in the morning till eleven at night' to clear the backlog. Polygraphs soon became an embedded part of American sigint culture, but were not introduced at Britain's GCHQ.[46]

The Korean War was of enormous importance for GCHQ because it fundamentally reshaped the American sigint community. There had been several failed attempts to create a single unified American sigint organisation along the lines of GCHQ.[47] The war broke the logjam. In 1952, President Truman suddenly insisted on the creation of a strong central body called the National Security Agency, or 'NSA', under General Ralph Canine. The armed services fought a desperate rearguard action: in August 1952, General Samford of US Air Force intelligence denounced Truman's desire for 'strong central control' as nothing short of a 'major error'. However, Truman's mind was made up, and in November he signed the order for the reshaping of American comint.[48] NSA was given unambiguous control over comint in a historic document called NSCID-9.[49] This brought about a reduction in, but not the elimination of, what the leading historian of NSA has called 'the fractious and seemingly never-ending internecine warfare' between the American service comint organisations. The British were immensely relieved. In the background, figures like Edward Travis had been quietly urging inter-service unity on their American collaborators since the summer of 1945.[50]

The creation of NSA also had physical consequences. Up until this point there had been a plan to relocate the headquarters of American sigint to Fort Knox, near Louisville in Kentucky.

However, it was now realised that the need for high-grade communications circuits and for civilian workers made this impossible. The policy-makers, who were the consumers of their intelligence 'product' in Washington, also protested about the move, rightly anticipating that it would mean a worse sigint service. They insisted that the new headquarters be within a twenty-five-mile radius of the Washington area.[51] On 3 November 1952, Fort Meade on the northern edge of Washington's Beltway was designated the likely new headquarters for NSA under a secret programme entitled 'Project K'. Over the next five years this location would become the headquarters of the world's largest, most expensive and most secretive intelligence agency.[52]

Britain's GCHQ had made precisely the opposite decision. In 1952 it moved away from its suburban site at Eastcote on the perimeter of London to a comparatively distant location at Cheltenham in Gloucestershire. Although GCHQ had only finished the move to Eastcote in June 1946, by April 1947 it was already looking for a new home. This was partly because of the physical limitations of the Eastcote site, and also because Travis realised that in any future war there would not be time to relocate to a safe place like Bletchley, away from Soviet bombing. Several possibilities were considered, and in October 1947 GCHQ scouts had found promising twin sites at Oakley Farm and Benhall Farm, near Cheltenham, which were occupied by the Ministry of Pensions. These single-storey temporary office complexes had been built in 1940, initially for the possible evacuation of government from London during the Blitz. After 1942 they were used for the logistical organisation of the US Army in Europe. The wartime presence of the Americans was the key, since it had left a helpful legacy of improved trunk cable communications.[53]

An alternative explanation for the choice of Cheltenham is offered by Professor R.V. Jones, one of the famous architects of the 'Wizard War' which deployed British science against Nazi Germany. Jones served as scientific adviser to GCHQ in the early

1950s, and recalls that the scout who initially found the Cheltenham site was Claude Daubney, one of the senior GCHQ staff who liaised with the Y Units of the armed services, and who spent much of his time in Whitehall. Daubney was a typical RAF officer of the thirties, handsome and 'heavily moustached'. His main relaxation was betting on horseraces, and he argued endlessly with Jones about the theoretical possibility of beating the bookmakers. He 'deliberately chose Cheltenham, as he told me, so that he could combine visits from his London office to GCHQ with attendance at Cheltenham races'.[54] Others support the idea that GCHQ was attracted to Cheltenham by its proximity to the racecourse.[55] Whatever the truth of the matter, the course would serve as an occasional helicopter landing pad for future visits by British Foreign Secretaries.[56] The move from Eastcote took place between 1952 and 1954, but the rapid growth of GCHQ during the Korean War meant space was tight even at the new location. This contributed to the decision to constitute comsec as a separate organisation called the London Communications Security Agency. Its staff either moved to central London offices in Palmer Street, or stayed at Eastcote.[57]

In its move to Cheltenham, GCHQ created a unique intelligence town. It brought with it Bletchley Park's formidable reputation for secrecy. Within a decade almost everyone in Cheltenham had a family member or friends who worked at GCHQ, but nobody talked about what they did. The town welcomed the 'Foreign Office types' with open arms, and GCHQ was soon contributing an enormous amount to its intellectual and artistic life, quite apart from being its biggest employer. The GCHQ staff were also sporty, providing most of the players in the Foreign Office football team that won the Civil Service Football Cup in 1952. This could present some peculiar problems. When local reporters covered matches in Cheltenham, they were told they could name the goal-scorers of the visitors, but not of the local team. Reporting these games tested their copywriting skills to the very limit.[58]

*   *   *

The previous ten years had been a formative decade for GCHQ. By 1944, the code-breakers of Bletchley Park had made themselves Britain's premier intelligence service. Out of the chaotic brilliance housed in a few wooden huts in the Buckinghamshire countryside came one of Britain's most forward-looking and innovative organisations. Another crucial legacy of the late 1940s was the agreements with the United States and the Commonwealth that laid the foundations of UKUSA, a worldwide sigint alliance, agreements that are still in force today. Anxiety about Moscow had been a driving force behind these agreements, and even before the Second World War was properly over, the Western allies had been paying increased attention to Soviet cyphers. Despite the triumphs of Venona, and the uncovering of key KGB agents like Klaus Fuchs and Donald Maclean, Moscow's higher-level communications remained mostly unbreakable after 1948. Accordingly, GCHQ and its partners were already searching for new kinds of intelligence-gathering to use against the Soviet Union, opening up a whole new vista in the electronic war.[59]

THE 1950s

FIGHTING THE
ELECTRONIC WAR

'Elint' and the Soviet Nuclear Target

Our intelligence about Soviet development of atomic weapons is very scanty.
Joint Intelligence Committee, 29 October 1947[1]

In late August 1949, Lavrentii Beria, chief of the KGB, arrived at a small settlement on the steppes of Kazakhstan, not far from the city of Semipalatinsk. Here, Soviet scientists were hard at work in a set of temporary laboratories, intently focused on what they obliquely called 'The Article'. They were referring to the Soviet Union's first atomic bomb, now situated precariously on top of a scaffolding tower fifty miles away. Houses, locomotives, buses and even tanks, together with some unfortunate farm animals, had been placed close to the weapon to gauge the effects of an explosion. The Soviet Union's chief nuclear scientist, Igor Kurchatov, gave the command to detonate, and a small but incredibly bright light appeared at the top of the tower. Suddenly it became a white fireball. A blast wave swept out, clearing everything in its path, as the explosion itself rapidly turned into a chaotic mix of orange, red and black. A dark mushroom cloud, five miles high, formed over the test site. Back in the laboratories, the scientists were jubilant and kissed each other on the foreheads. A month later, nineteen key figures from the nuclear programme, including a German scientist, were made Heroes of Socialist Labour. Beria is reported to have used the same list of names that identified those who would have been shot immediately had the test failed.[2]

In the event, it was Western intelligence that had failed. Soviet progress towards a nuclear weapon had been a top intelligence target. The predictions of Britain's Joint Intelligence Committee, the highest authority for analysis, had actually become steadily less accurate. By 1949, when the test took place, Britain's top intelligence analysts were arguing that the probable date of the first Soviet test would be mid-1953. They were adrift by no less than four years. The CIA was no more accurate, and had similarly told President Truman that mid-1953 was the most likely date. Shocked by the surprise atomic test, Britain and America now redoubled their intelligence effort in the field of Soviet strategic weapons.[3] Throughout the Cold War, the key target for GCHQ would remain Soviet nuclear weaponry. This included not only the atomic bomb programme, but work on ballistic missiles, bombers and other means of delivery. The Chiefs of Staff were worried by Britain's relative vulnerability to nuclear attack, and wanted intelligence forecasts on this crucial issue. In their list of 'sigint targets' for 1948, the JIC exhorted Britain's code-breakers to focus their efforts on this area, together with parallel strategic threats such as chemical and biological weapons.[4] Other Soviet activities, including KGB espionage and diplomatic initiatives, only constituted GCHQ's second and third priorities.

But ever since the massive revision of Soviet cypher procedure on 'Black Friday' in 1948, GCHQ had been having a hard time with its main target. The one-time pads employed for the highest-grade Soviet messages were now being correctly used, and so could not be broken, and machine cypher procedure on systems like Taper, effectively a Soviet military version of Enigma, had also been tightened up. Moreover, Moscow and its satellites enjoyed common borders and so often used landlines instead of wireless transmissions, which could not be easily intercepted. All this eventually prompted the British to follow the Soviets down the path of more extensive physical bugging of diplomatic premises in the mid-1950s.[5]

GCHQ was nevertheless providing Whitehall with large quantities of useful material on lower-priority issues. It continued its long tradition of attacking the communications of smaller states like France, Turkey and Egypt. The JIC had also asked it to look at subjects such as Arab nationalism and the relations of Arab states with Britain and the USA, and the attitude of France, Italy and the Arab states to the future of North Africa, especially Libya. Because of the ongoing insurgency in Palestine, GCHQ was also urged to focus on the Zionist movement, including its various intelligence services. All of these proved more accessible than Soviet traffic.[6] The diplomatic traffic of smaller states also provided an excellent window on the Soviets. Conversations between Soviet diplomats and the officials of these countries were often captured in telegrams sent from Moscow that could be read with ease. In 1946 Alan Stripp, a British code-breaker who had spent the war working on Japanese codes, found himself redeployed to the Iranian border. Throughout the Azerbaijan crisis of that year, when the Soviet Union appeared to be behind a potential breakaway state in northern Iran, he worked on Iranian and Afghan communications.[7] This sigint revealed the scale of Soviet activities and ambitions in the region, helping to trigger robust counter-pressure by President Truman.[8]

How the main target lists for sigint were drawn up was of central importance. In theory, they were created by the JIC. However, much of the preliminary work was undertaken by more shadowy committees working under the London Signals Intelligence Board, Britain's supreme sigint authority. These enjoyed strong military input. When diplomats complained that political and colonial subjects were not getting enough attention, they did not get an enthusiastic response. Many felt that undue weight was being given to defence priorities, and to nuclear warfare in particular. The overwhelming emphasis given to defence had profound implications for the shape of British sigint. It accelerated the development of a revolutionary new kind of sigint that focused on equipment and military formations.[9]

During the Second World War, Bletchley Park's primary

emphasis had been the interception of communications signals for intelligence purposes. However, as the war progressed, there was growing interest in another kind of sigint that was derived from intercepting electronic signals, such as radar, which had been developed during the Second World War. A related field of interest was the growing use of radio waves to create missile guidance systems. Examining these enemy radio signals was known as electronic intelligence, or 'elint'. Elint revealed a great deal about enemy weapons, and was also essential for conducting 'radio warfare', which involved jamming enemy signals and radar. The first example of this had been the successful efforts of Professor R.V. Jones to divert the beams used to guide the German bombers attacking London. These techniques were refined during the war against Japan. An elaborate elint unit was set up within Mountbatten's South-East Asia Command under the improbable cover name of the 'Noise Investigation Bureau'. In the summer of 1945, elint-equipped aircraft called 'ferrets' patrolled the night skies over Rangoon listening to Japanese radar.[10] Elint and radio countermeasures, conducted jointly by GCHQ and special units of the RAF, were a massive growth area after 1945, partly because they were so closely linked to strategic weapons. One great advantage of elint was that it rarely required the reading of complex enemy codes.[11] Increasingly, the business of signals intelligence would consist of two branches, the familiar one of communications intelligence or 'comint' and the new one of elint.

Britain had excelled in the use of both comint and elint during the Battle of Britain, and later in bombing raids over Germany. One of the architects of this system was Arthur 'Bill' Bonsall, who would become Director of GCHQ in 1973.[12] This success had made a deep impression on American intelligence officers in Europe, who felt admiration and not a little envy.[13] In early February 1945, the US Army Air Force held a conference of all senior air intelligence officers (A-2s) across Europe, at which 'every A-2 expressed his disappointment at our utter dependence on the R.A.F.' in sigint matters. The US Ninth Air Force had deployed some very effective converted Flying Fortresses as airborne listening stations, but the British had controlled the flow of strategic sigint. The lesson was clear. Colonel Robert D. Hughes, Director of Intelligence for the Ninth Air Force, told Washington that he wanted his own air sigint units with control over sigint policy and sigint research: 'We feel that you should demand, and organize under your control, for peace as well as war, an organization similar to that of the R.A.F. . . . Unlike other highly technical forms of intelligence, in which our American Air Forces have shared, we have continued to depend entirely on the R.A.F. for this level of work in "Y".'[14]

Elint formed one of the closest parts of the Anglo–American sigint relationship during the immediate post-war period because it focused on the Soviet military target. Exchange on elint was not initially linked to the Allied sigint agreements reached at the end of the war, but in 1948 it was being brought within the growing body of Western intelligence pacts that formed UKUSA. GCHQ approached Washington with a proposal to 'extend the present British–US Comint collaboration to include countermeasures, intercept activities and intelligence' in the field of elint. This meant coordinated patterns of 'ferret' flights – effectively a division of labour – with the resulting intelligence being swapped 'via Comint channels'.[15] By the 1950s, GCHQ had achieved control over elint in Britain, and so was managing relations with all the various American outfits in this field. This had meant redrawing GCHQ's charter to include not only comint but also elint, something which had not pleased everyone. R.V. Jones, who was Director of Scientific Intelligence at the Ministry of Defence in the early 1950s, strongly resented losing this part of his empire; the benefits of having all activities superintended by GCHQ were nevertheless overwhelming.[16]

Anglo–American sharing was important, because elint was an expensive business. Many of the target Soviet signals were short-range and could only be collected from 'ferrets', which were effectively flying intelligence stations. Initially, the RAF was ahead in this new field. By 1947 a fleet of specially equipped

Lancaster and Lincoln aircraft patrolled the East German border, monitoring Soviet air activity. This was complemented by ground stations at locations such as RAF Gatow in Berlin listening to basic low-level Soviet voice traffic. British 'ferrets' made adventurous forays over the Baltic in June 1948 and the Black Sea in September 1948. Remarkably, they were soon crossing Iran to reach the Caspian Sea, thus flying perilous missions close to the very heart of the Soviet Union.[17] On the ground, a British undercover team was also operating in northern Iran, monitoring Soviet radar in the Caucasus as well as Soviet missile tests at Kasputin Yar on the edge of the Caspian. The team conducting this work were posing as archaeologists, a favourite British cover for all sorts of intelligence work. Once a week they drove from the Iranian border with the Soviet Union to the British Embassy in Tehran to deliver their precious tapes.[18]

Early Western elint efforts in the air were spurred on by the knowledge that the Soviets had launched their own secret 'ferret' programme. In April 1948 an American radar station in Germany reported that it was being probed by 'ferret' aircraft, and in November a Soviet plane circled a US radar station at Hokkaido in Japan collecting signals for an hour, and then escaped without interception due to bad weather. Defectors also brought tantalising snippets. In May 1948 Baclav Cukr, General Secretary of the Czech Air Force Association, escaped to the West bringing knowledge of a group of Dakota-like planes at Zote airfield outside Prague. These mysterious aircraft were kept under constant guard in special hangars, and had 'several special antennae on the outside', a sure sign that they were elint collectors.[19]

During the war the vested interests of many different RAF commands had made it difficult to create a single coherent elint organisation.[20] Post-war rationalisation allowed the fusion of these elements. RAF Watton in Norfolk was selected as the new home of elint, and collected the remnants of many wartime units into 100 Countermeasures Group.[21] The result was a weird menagerie of aircraft which were one-off flying laboratories adapted for various special tasks. The mainstays were twenty ageing Handley Page Halifax bombers. There were also B-17 Flying Fortresses, Lancasters, Mosquitoes and Avro Ansons, together with an Airspeed Oxford and a Percival Proctor. The unit at Watton soon received some new Avro Lincolns, effectively updated Lancasters. All were stuffed with unique items of electronic listening equipment and primitive wire recorders for collecting voice traffic.

Christened the Central Signals Establishment, or 'CSE', Watton boasted a Signals Research Squadron, a dedicated sigint unit known as Monitoring Squadron and a Radio Countermeasures Squadron. The Avro Lincolns were the best aircraft available, and they were given over to radio countermeasures and radar jamming, since they would have to work closely with RAF bomber formations in any future war with the Soviet Union. The Lincolns would soon be fitted with the revolutionary new carcinotron, or 'backward wave oscillator', in effect an electronic gun that produced powerful microwaves of the same frequencies used by radar, giving them enormous onboard jamming power. By contrast, some of the other airframes used for listening were antique. However, it was a venerable Halifax from Monitoring Squadron that was despatched on sigint collection duty over the Soviet Zone of Germany during the early stages of the Berlin Blockade in 1948. This was the first sign of a possible 'hot war' between East and West, and GCHQ decided it was time to share the lessons of sigint more widely. For the first time lectures on radio countermeasures and tactical sigint were given to officers passing through the RAF Staff College at Bracknell. A handbook on tactical sigint was prepared for all staff officers, albeit no mention was made of the mysterious 'Ultra'.[22]

In 1951 the monitoring aircraft were rechristened 192 Squadron, and worked ever more closely with GCHQ. Meanwhile the radio countermeasures and jamming unit was rebranded as 199 Squadron. The RAF received four Boeing RB-29 'Washington' aircraft, which were really American B-29

Superfortresses modified for listening. Their vast internal space allowed additional sigint equipment to be fitted by the sigint ground engineers at RAF Watton, who were known as the Special Radio Installation Flight, or 'SRIF'. In 1953 two English Electric Canberras were acquired and refitted for secret sigint operations by SRIF. Their standard duty was flights along the borders of the Warsaw Pact, alternating with longer visits to the Baltic and the Mediterranean. Training of special operators was undertaken on slow but reliable Vickers Varsity aircraft.[23]

Beneath the sea, an even more sensitive sigint programme was under way. Much of what London and Washington knew about the Soviet Navy had been derived from captured German intelligence material harvested from Berlin in 1945, or from what the British had gleaned directly from their surprisingly good relations with the Soviet Navy during the war. However, this information was now outdated. The US Navy decided to send two submarines into the Bering Sea to test the possibility of undertaking listening operations off the major Arctic ports used by the Soviets. These successful pilot operations were limited to an investigation of the area using sonar. A much more ambitious mission was then attempted. This was a proper sigint collection operation, designed to scoop the signals that emanated from regular Soviet missile tests in the Barents Sea.[24]

In the summer of 1949 the US Navy picked its latest submarines for this mission, the USS *Cochino* and the USS *Tusk*. They had been built at the end of the war, and in 1948 they were modified to bring them up to U-boat standards and fitted with the latest snorkels. This allowed them to run submerged for long periods on diesel power, venting their exhaust to the surface. They had also been streamlined and fitted with the fastest available propulsion systems. The specialist elint equipment for capturing missile control signals, or 'telemetry', was installed by British sigint technicians at Portsmouth. The submarine chosen for fitting was the *Cochino*, under Commander Rafael Benitez. The name 'Cochino' was supposed to denote a species of trigger fish, but in Spanish it simply meant 'The Pig'. Preparations were masterminded by Harris M. Austin from the US Naval Security Group and civilian sigint engineers. Additional aerials, known as 'ears', were fitted to the tailfin. The elaborate listening technology required the drilling of small holes for wires in the submarine's pressure hull, which weakened it and did not best please the crew. Trials were held along the British coast in July 1949. In August the *Cochino*, escorted by three other submarines, including the *Tusk*, headed for Arctic waters. In the Barents Sea, the *Cochino* separated and sat off the coast hoping to collect the high-frequency signals that indicated a missile test, but found nothing of great interest. After a few days of lurking, it headed back to a rendezvous with the *Tusk*.[25]

However, disaster now struck. Four hundred miles north of the Arctic Circle the *Cochino* ran into a severe storm. Water poured in through a malfunctioning snorkel and a serious battery fire developed, burning for fourteen hours and producing large volumes of dangerous hydrogen. Some of the crew battled the fire using breathing equipment, but after a series of explosions they staggered back and admitted defeat. One crew member recalls: 'They formed a grotesque aspect with their faces and hair burned. The skin was falling from their hands.'[26] Commander Benitez and his seventy-eight crew decided to abandon ship just after midnight. Despite a rescue by the *Tusk*, seven men were lost to the stormy seas off the Norwegian coast. Six of these fatalities were brave rescuers from the *Tusk* who were equipped with faulty survival suits, while the seventh was civilian signals intelligence expert Robert W. Philo from the *Cochino*. Commander Benitez was the last man to make the treacherous crossing – effected by a swaying plank – between the two vessels. By the time the *Tusk* pulled clear the *Cochino* was already half-submerged. 'With a final burst of spray she disappeared from sight,' plunging into 950 feet of water. The *Tusk* took the casualties, many with severe burns, to Hammerfest in Norway, from where they were flown to London.[27] These were the first casualties in one of the most secretive and dangerous areas of Cold War signals intelligence activity. However, London and Washington were not deterred. By the early 1950s, British and American sigint submarines were regular visitors to the headquarters of the Soviet fleet.[28]

Elint flights over the open sea were also sensitive and risky. On 8 April 1950 a US Navy elint aircraft, a PBY-42 Privateer, launched from Bremerhaven in northern Germany, was shot down while trying to identify new Soviet missile bases along the Baltic coast. The crew of four, who had named their aircraft the *Turbulent Turtle*, all perished. The Soviets later salvaged the Privateer's elint equipment from the waters of the Baltic, and were in no doubt about the nature of the mission. Further missions were postponed.[29] Within a month of the shootdown of the Privateer, General Omar Bradley, then Chairman of the US Joint Chiefs of Staff, set out the case for resuming the flights, insisting that the intelligence they gathered was of the 'utmost importance'. President Truman finally agreed to a resumption when told that US aircraft close to Soviet-controlled territory would be armed 'and instructed to shoot in self-defense'. Truman minuted, 'Good sense, it seems to me.' The President's green light was received on 6 June 1950, but after the outbreak of the Korean War later that month the flights were suspended for another few weeks due to 'current hyper-tension and fear of further shoot-downs'. By the end of 1950, regular operations with RB-50Gs, 'special mission' elint aircraft adapted from an upgraded Superfortress bomber, were operating out of RAF Lakenheath airbase in East Anglia.[30]

Norway was an early partner in all types of sigint operations. In 1952, Rear Admiral Anthony Buzzard, Britain's Director of Naval Intelligence, paid a secretive visit to Norway. His requests were so sensitive that only handwritten notes were taken at the meetings. Buzzard asked for permission to launch special reconnaissance flights from Norway into Russian airspace using the RAF's new Canberra aircraft, and also to run elint flights conducted within Norwegian airspace. However, the fate of the USS *Cochino* and then of the American Privateer had alerted the

Norwegians to elint operations as a potential flashpoint, and they were cautious. Only permission for the latter flights within Norwegian airspace was granted.[31] By the mid-1950s the Norwegian Defence Intelligence Staff was beginning to experiment with the use of commercial trawlers as platforms for intelligence-gathering in the Barents Sea. Initially these were used for photographic reconnaissance, but they were gradually expanded to involve sigint monitoring. A 'cover' shipping company, Egerfangst, was established to run these operations, and its first vessel, the *Eger*, was in operation by 1956 using equipment supplied by the American NSA.[32]

Although the most important sigint collected at short range came through perilous operations by air and sea, the British and Americans also boasted vast armies of land-based listeners crouching over their radio sets in wooden huts, often in inhospitable locations. Tactical sigint in peacetime presented a problem, since there was not much for Y service sigint to listen to. Yet on the first day of any future war with Russia – and war, if it came, was expected to come suddenly – the RAF would be required to reconstitute its vast legions of secret listeners.[33] In the event, the three services kept a large inter-service intercept formation in place, using personnel who were doing National Service. During peacetime they were lent to GCHQ, and spent much of their time collecting a wide range of signals, including diplomatic and commercial traffic. One RAF sigint officer observed, 'Our only function is to receive the stuff in its cryptic form – a purely mechanical process – and pass it on to the body whose job it is to break it down.'[34] By 1950 a system was in place whereby all those beginning National Service were asked if they would volunteer to learn Russian. The huge numbers of personnel who were trained up guaranteed a vast pool of tactical sigint operators who could be recalled on the eve of war, although GCHQ worried about how to hide the scale of the operation. This had profound consequences for the balance of power within post-war British sigint. It ensured that while the overall British sigint programme was coordinated by GCHQ, it was in fact provided by a complex alliance of GCHQ and the three armed services. This secret pact suited everyone – except for the Treasury, which struggled to track sigint spending, hidden as it was under a welter of misleading headings and cover organisations.[35]

The outbreak of the Korean War on 25 June 1950 triggered a massive expansion of the riskier and more dangerous short-range operations to collect all types of sigint, including elint. Tensions were high, because the strategic planners believed that the outbreak of global war was not far away. Hitherto the Americans had been dependent on the British to cover much of north-west Europe, but now Americans began to arrive in numbers and their listening stations sprouted all over Britain, often disguised as RAF stations. In 1952 the 47th Radio Squadron of the US Air Force Security Service arrived at Kirknewton airbase in Scotland, from where it could monitor shipping off the Kola Peninsula. In October that year Squadron Leader J.R. Mitchell became the first dedicated 'Liaison Officer for GCHQ' on elint in Washington.[36]

The accelerated pace of operations paid dividends. By 1952 elint experts in London and Washington had achieved a comprehensive picture of the Soviet Air Force. This had not required the breaking of Soviet codes. Instead, most of it was achieved through a mixture of elint or direction-finding, which simply meant using triangulation to locate specific Soviet units. GCHQ also listened in on clear voice traffic used by Soviet air-defence controllers giving instructions to fighters. There were large gaps in both Soviet air warning and coastal radar, which were mapped carefully. Anti-aircraft radar around Moscow was examined with special attention. Elint experts had been able to follow air-defence exercises in which the Soviets had used tiny strips of aluminium foil dropped from aircraft, known as 'chaff', as a radio countermeasure to fool radar operators into thinking large numbers of aircraft were airborne. Some of the more sophisticated Soviet work was thought to have been carried out by German experts captured by the Russians after 1945. Korea itself had proved to be a bonanza, with new Soviet radio equipment being captured, including direction-finding equipment which showed 'marked improvement in design and construction'.[37]

Success in the exciting new field of elint offset some recent disappointments. GCHQ and its American partners had not yet recovered the medium-grade Soviet cyphers lost during the infamous 'Black Friday' of October 1948. They had not detected the advent of the first Soviet atom bomb, nor had they anticipated the outbreak of the Korean War. However, the elint effort against the Soviet Air Force, which also involved direction-finding and traffic analysis, was one of the key areas in which GCHQ could claim outstanding achievement in the first postwar decade – and it was sustained.

There was an especially secret reason why GCHQ and NSA examined the operational anatomy of the Soviet 'nuclear bear' so minutely. During the early 1950s, target intelligence officers in London and Washington had been busy exchanging sensitive data on 'the mission of blunting the Russian atomic offensive'. This meant planning early counter-force attacks against Soviet nuclear forces, especially bombers, in the hope of destroying them on the ground in Eastern Europe before they could be used in a future war. GCHQ had given particular attention to this matter because of the vulnerability of Britain, and the Americans were impressed by the progress London had made on it. GCHQ and the RAF's secret units had amassed 'a significant amount of evaluated intelligence, particularly in the special intelligence field, which would be of the greatest value' if war broke out.[38]

American officers considered that 'vigorous efforts should be taken immediately to ensure rapid development of a joint research program to insure maximum exploitation of the British resources'. In short, it was not just the raw elint that the British had collected, but their sophisticated analysis of it that allowed it to be turned into high-quality finished intelligence, a legacy of the skills garnered during Bletchley Park's Hut Three operation.

Most of the airfields and the operational procedures for the Soviet Union's nuclear air force in the European theatre had been mapped by 1952.[39] In June of that year a team from the US Air Force Security Service centre at Brooks Field, led by Major Hill, visited GCHQ and one of its outstations at Knockholt in Kent to further converge their activities in this area. Hill also wanted to discuss the creation of new 'ground-based electronic intercept stations' in Europe. Korea had greatly accelerated preparations for a 'hot war', and GCHQ's elint success on Soviet air defences helped it to justify budget increases.[40]

Throughout 1951 and 1952, global war often seemed imminent. Communist China had entered the Korean War in 1951, and numerous Soviet advisers were busy assisting the North Korean forces. Soviet and American pilots were actually fighting each other in the skies of East Asia. Although the public were never told, sigint made this fact clear to the secret listeners. In this increasingly fevered atmosphere, improved intelligence was given a high priority. On 22 January 1952 the British Chiefs of Staff met the Permanent Under-Secretary of the Foreign Office to review plans for accelerating intelligence. GCHQ was given a large tranche of new money over five years under the heading 'Methods to Improve'. Its extensive shopping list included larger computers and 'high speed analytical equipment' for renewed attacks on high-grade Soviet communications. These were given the highest priority, and government research and supply elements were instructed accordingly. GCHQ and the Admiralty were beginning a new programme to build better receivers for ground-based and seaborne 'Technical Search Operations' which were critical to elint. Again, much of this was about targeting, and the Chiefs of Staff continually reiterated the 'very great importance' of speeding up technical development in these areas.[41] By November 1952, British defence chiefs wanted increased expenditure on intelligence, and were unanimous that in the short term the emphasis should be on sigint.[42]

Late 1952 was an exciting time for GCHQ. Equipped with a

larger budget, staff had begun to move to their new headquarters at the twin sites in Cheltenham. It also had a new
Director, Wing Commander Eric Jones. Given the rise of airborne
sigint, it was appropriate that an RAF officer should have
succeeded Edward Travis, who had been increasingly ill during
the late 1940s with lumbago.[43] Jones was a Bletchley Park
veteran who had proved himself while in charge of the critically important Hut Three. Bill Millward, another long-serving
GCHQ veteran, recalls that at first glance 'his qualifications for
the post were not apparent'. He had spent the 1930s as a cloth
merchant in Macclesfield. However, he was a quick learner, a
natural diplomat and a man of obvious principle.[44] He had proved
an excellent liaison officer in Washington towards the end of
the war, and after the 'happy outcome' of the BRUSA conference of 1946 he had decided to 'stay in the racket'.[45] This was
good for GCHQ, since Jones proved to be a leader who inspired
instinctive trust. In late 1952 he was busy filling the three
hundred extra staff posts recently authorised. GCHQ had already
proposed an additional increment of a further 366 staff, and
was going from strength to strength.[46]

In the late summer and the autumn of 1952, senior GCHQ
officers like John Somerville had been pressing defence scientists and intelligence chiefs to join them in planning the future
expansion of airborne sigint.[47] Good results were being obtained,
and GCHQ was making the most of the facilities at its disposal,
but there were just not enough 'ferret' flights, and the elint-
collection effort needed 'more equipment, personnel, aircraft
and ships'.[48] The RAF was using its three RB-29 Washingtons,
which were big enough for the increasingly complex equipment
required.[49] It was a Washington that had captured the first
recordings of 'Scan Odd', the new airborne radar which equipped
Soviet fighters. However, the RAF's Washingtons were slow and
vulnerable compared to the upgraded American variant, which
could reach 400 mph, as fast as a wartime fighter.[50] British elint
specialists longed to enter the jet age with the military version
of the de Havilland Comet, but there seemed to be no hope of

getting this desirable aircraft. Part of the problem was that 192 Squadron was not seen as a front-line fighting unit, tended to be overlooked and was continually moved between commands over the next two decades.[51] There was also an acute shortage of staff at GCHQ qualified in the rarefied field of elint analysis, which was made worse by the upheaval of the move to Cheltenham.[52]

The required extra momentum came from the Americans. Washington pressed the British for more spending and more effort at a major US/UK elint conference in December 1952.[53] Accordingly, in 1953, Britain's elint specialists acquired more small specialist Canberra jet aircraft, and a year later, after much discussion, the Treasury reluctantly approved the purchase of three much-prized de Havilland Comet C2s, a modified version of Britain's first jet airliner. Until now, all of the sigint aircraft had been rough-and-ready adaptations. The Comet C2 was Britain's first dedicated airborne sigint platform designed from scratch. In the spring of 1957 the first C2 arrived at CSE Watton and was placed in the hands of SRIF, the RAF's secret team of sigint engineers, who were based in No.3 Hangar. Their task was to cram a whole mini-sigint ground station into the cramped interior of an airliner. For George Baillie, the Principal Scientific Officer at Watton, this was the most complex task his team would ever undertake. Equipping the three Comets was extremely expensive and time-consuming. It was therefore with complete horror that they discovered a fire in No.4 Hangar in the early hours of the morning of 3 June 1959. One plane was completely destroyed, leaving CSE with only two Comets to fulfil the many missions requested by GCHQ. The Treasury boggled at the cost of the unscheduled replacement of the third aircraft, and it was two years before GCHQ's Deputy Director Joe Hooper persuaded it to find the money.[54]

In America, the new NSA was now responsible for communications intelligence or 'comint', the most important area of signals collection and code-breaking. However, battles over elint stretched on into the 1960s. Even ten years after the creation of

NSA, American officials envied the more centralised British model, which placed GCHQ in charge of both fields of sigint activity.[55] In 1953 the British approached the Americans to suggest a combined organisation for planning electronic warfare and radio countermeasures. The problem for the Americans was that they would first have to settle their bitter inter-service disputes, which was proving near impossible.[56] Notwithstanding this, the two nations managed to get together for a major US/UK Electronic Warfare Conference every two years.[57] The GCHQ approach made sense, because it was becoming harder to distinguish between signals that carried communications and other types of electronic signals. The Americans noted wistfully that this 'has been recognised by the British, who have placed all electronic search and reconnaissance under the control of COMINT authorities' – in other words, under GCHQ. In the US, control over these matters remained fiercely contested as late as the Vietnam War.[58]

By 1953, elint was considered so valuable that more aggressive British operations were being authorised. These included clandestine operations on the ground. GCHQ had manufactured a new short-range elint reception and analysis kit, code-named 'Deaf Aid', that looked like a suitcase. SIS was sending agents into the Eastern Bloc with these sets – the results are still classified. The Joint Intelligence Committee decided that the equipment would also be secretly deployed in diplomatic posts inside the Eastern Bloc alongside the covert comint stations operated by the Diplomatic Wireless Service.[59] By February 1954 experimental versions were also being deployed on the ground by the British Military Mission, or 'Brixmis', effectively a team of roving military attachés in East Germany.[60] GCHQ was settled into its new accommodation by January 1954, allowing it to work with the Ministry of Defence's Directorate of Scientific Intelligence on the much-needed expansion of T Division, the analytical unit at Cheltenham which made sense of elint once it was collected.[61]

All these new intelligence activities meant risk. In October 1952 A.V. Alexander, the Defence Secretary, and Anthony Eden, the Foreign Secretary, had been chewing over the delicate question of who should approve the expanding programme of 'ferret' flights and perilous submarine missions around the edge of the Soviet Union. They agreed that the buck should be passed upwards to Downing Street, and a process developed whereby a list of proposed secret sigint missions was regularly sent to Prime Minister Winston Churchill. Rather disingenuously, Alexander told Churchill that Britain had in the past, in cooperation with the Americans, 'carried out one or two flights with special aircraft near Soviet territory with the intention of "sniffing" at Russian transmissions'. In reality, a veritable fleet of elint aircraft had been buzzing around the perimeter of the Soviet Union for more than five years. Churchill was assured that they kept at least thirty miles from the Soviet coastline. Alexander continued:

*

The aircraft are almost certain to be picked up by Russian radar. In fact we shall be disappointed if they are not, for that is the whole object of the operations. But since the flights will take place at the darkest period of the month, and the Russians do not (as far as we know) possess airborne radar, the risks of actual interception are small.

*

In other words, if the intelligence operations against Soviet air defences were to succeed, they had to actually create alerts and prompt the Soviets to launch their fighters, as it was precisely these procedures that GCHQ wanted to listen in to. Alexander added that a key purpose in undertaking these operations was 'making our own contribution to the Anglo–American intelligence pool from which we will expect valuable returns in kind'.[62] What would happen if a secret British spy plane crashed inside the Soviet Union, or if a submarine was caught inside a Soviet harbour? So far the GCHQ's clandestine collection programmes had been remarkably free of incidents, but this enviable record was not to last for much longer.[63]

The Voyages of HMS Turpin

Depth charging continued for longer than I care to remember . . .

Tony Beasley, HMS *Turpin*, off the Soviet coast,
March 1955[1]

By early 1953 the Americans had lost a submarine and an aircraft during perilous short-range sigint missions. Their human losses were already in double figures. By contrast, the British were increasingly confident, having flown many missions without incident. The lumbering RB-29 Washington aircraft of the RAF's 192 Squadron regularly flew their routes around the Baltic, and were often 'intercepted' by Soviet fighters, but were never fired upon. This may have been because the British used a small number of experienced and specialised units for forward sigint collection who were dedicated to covert missions, working under the direction of GCHQ. Equally it could have been sheer good luck. However, in 1953 that luck was to change.

The first serious British 'flap' was the loss of an RAF Avro Lincoln on 12 March 1953. The Lincoln was effectively an improved version of the Lancaster bomber that had entered service just as the Second World War ended. It saw active service against insurgents in Malaya and Kenya during the 1950s, and although it remained Britain's heavy bomber until the arrival of the first V-bombers in 1955, a number were transferred to intelligence duties. Some were allocated to 199 Squadron, the radio warfare unit that operated out of RAF Watton. Armed with a powerful carcinotron, they were capable of a formidable barrage of jamming, and were often called on to disrupt the sigint-gathering activities of Soviet spy trawlers around the coast of Britain.[2] The RAF also boasted a Radar Reconnaissance Flight of Lincolns that took 'radar pictures' of important landmarks denoting routes to key bombing targets. Some of the more precarious Anglo–American overflights of the Soviet Union during 1952 and 1954 were effectively engaged in an intelligence-mapping exercise for bombing missions that might be directed against Moscow and Kiev.[3]

The RAF Lincoln lost on 12 March 1953 was not directly involved in radio warfare or special duties. It was merely on exercise, and wandered out of one of the defined twenty-mile air corridors over the Soviet Zone between West Germany and Berlin. However, as we have seen, British and American exercises were often designed to trigger an alert so that Soviet air-defence systems could be listened in on. The frequent efforts to get their defences to 'light up' ensured that the Soviets were often on high alert, and were inclined to fire at anything that came into their territory. Accordingly, all RAF flying near the Soviet Zone of Germany involved an element of risk. This was underlined by a Polish pilot who chose to defect to the West on 5 March 1953, and landed his Soviet-built MiG-15 jet fighter in Denmark. He confirmed that MiG pilots were 'under orders to shoot down an aircraft if it refuses to obey signals to land, even if it does not open fire'.[4]

On the morning of 12 March 1953, two Lincolns took off from the Central Gunnery School at Leconfield in Yorkshire. This was a routine training flight that involved an exercise with NATO partners and took place every fortnight, heading out over Germany on a simulated mission of about six hours. The first aircraft, 'H' (RF503), was under the command of Flight Sergeant Denham, and carried the Director of the Gunnery School, Squadron Leader Frank Doran. En route to Germany, as part of the exercise, Denham's aircraft was 'intercepted' by Thunderjets of the Dutch Air Force, Belgian Meteors and RAF Vampires. Unusually, as they approached Kassel, still well inside the British Zone, they were surprised to see two Soviet MiG-15s underneath them. The MiGs conducted a number of mock attacks, but did not open fire. Their activity was recorded on the cine cameras that were attached to the gun turrets of the Lincoln for training purposes. The anxious crew turned north and then headed back to their base in Yorkshire.

The second Lincoln, 'C' (RF531), under the command of Flight Sergeant Peter Dunnell, was following along the same track, two hours behind. It also carried an important passenger, Squadron Leader Harold Fitz, who had just taken over as Commanding Officer of 3 Squadron and who had come along for the ride as co-pilot. Just after 1 p.m., near the air corridor that stretched across the Soviet Zone from Hamburg to Berlin, two more MiG-15s appeared. This time they opened fire. Although the Lincoln had strayed some way into the Soviet Zone, by the time it was fired on the crew had realised their error and retraced their steps. They were now just west of the River Elbe, inside the British Zone. The firing took place over the village of Bleckede, where ammunition belts from the MiGs were later recovered. The Lincoln entered a steep dive, still pursued by the MiGs, and broke up, with the main fuselage landing in a wood near Boizenburg, just inside the Soviet Zone on the eastern bank of the Elbe. Other parts of the aircraft, including the starboard wing, came down on Luneburg Heath, a British military exercise area fifteen miles south of Hamburg.[5]

Of the seven crew, four were found dead inside the wreckage. Three of the crew had managed to bail out, but one parachute failed to open. The other two crew members seemed to parachute successfully, but several shocked German witnesses testified that one of the Soviet MiGs swooped low and strafed them with cannon fire. Wilma Muller, one of the witnesses, testified that one of the crew had a 'perforated parachute' as a result of being fired upon. Both crew members whose parachutes had opened died of terrible wounds shortly after landing.[6]

The RAF concluded that the Lincoln had gone off course and strayed into Soviet airspace shortly after it entered the air corridor to Berlin. However, it was obvious that its intention was to head up one of the three twenty-mile-wide air corridors that connected the three sectors of Germany occupied by the West to Berlin. While the Soviets insisted that the British crew had fired first, it was soon proved beyond doubt that the Lincoln had been unarmed, since much of the firing mechanism from its turret guns was routinely removed on training sorties. However, the Foreign Office resisted the idea of pressing hard for compensation because inspection of the wreckage showed that the Lincoln was actually carrying some ammunition, even though it was unlikely that it had fired. 'We might have to admit that the aircraft accidentally penetrated the Soviet Zone of Germany,' it noted. Nevertheless, it was confident that, from where the cases from the Soviet cannon shells fell, the MiGs had downed the Lincoln over the British Zone.[7]

British Members of Parliament were outraged. They pressed for compensation from the Soviets for the crew's families, and were told by the Minister of State for Foreign Affairs, Selwyn Lloyd, that the British High Commissioner in Germany had been ordered to 'demand' adequate payment. Churchill was clearly animated about the matter, but behind the scenes officials were soft-pedalling.[8] High-level instructions were given to British representatives to 'avoid post-mortems', and instead to focus on talks that would avoid a repetition of the incident.[9] Three months after the event, Foreign Office officials urged, 'We should be in no hurry to do anything,' and were anxious to prevent the public from learning that the Soviets had refused compensation from the outset.[10] The bodies of the seven crew members who had fallen in the Soviet Zone were returned to RAF Celle, and eventually to their families.[11]

While the Lincoln had not been on an intelligence flight, its progress was being carefully tracked by a British sigint unit on the ground at RAF Scharfoldendorf in the British Zone of Germany. The unit carefully transcribed the conversation between the MiG pilots and the Soviet ground controllers, which were 'in clear' voice communications. This sigint report was soon on the desk of the Prime Minister, and the unit received praise for catching the Soviets 'red-handed'. The report made it clear that the Lincoln was shot down in cold blood, and led to Churchill's bitter comments on the 'wanton attack' in the House of Commons.[12] It also helped to confirm that before turning around and retracing its steps, the Lincoln had in fact penetrated Soviet airspace 'fairly deeply'.[13] Later, the families of the crew members asked why Churchill was so certain about the exact pattern of events, but of course the sigint aspect of his information could not be revealed to them.[14] Churchill ordered that in future all flights over Germany, including training flights, would not only carry ammunition but would also fly with guns 'loaded and cocked'. In 1955 his successor, Anthony Eden, still required all training aircraft to carry ammunition when over Germany.[15]

An agreement with the Soviets on air incidents was badly needed. As air historians have noted, the first half of 1953 was a period of high tension in Western Europe. Only a few days before the Lincoln incident, an American F-84 Thunderjet had been shot down by a MiG. A week later a British European Airways Viking airliner was strafed by MiGs while travelling down the Berlin Air Corridor, but managed to limp home. A fortnight after that an American bomber was attacked by MiG-15s over Germany, but repelled them with vigorous cannon fire. In the Far East, where the Korean War was drawing to a close, things were even worse. On 27 July, a few hours before the final armistice came into effect, an American F-86F Sabre pilot shot down a civilian Aeroflot Il-12 airliner, killing all twenty-one persons on board. The Americans and the Soviets engaged in a protracted argument as to whether the airliner was over North Korea or China when it was shot down. No one could disguise the fact that the debris came down in China.[16] Two days later, presumably in retaliation, the Soviets downed a US Air Force RB-50G Superfortress sigint reconnaissance aircraft near Vladivostok, with the loss of seventeen of the eighteen crew.[17] The RB-50G was a much faster version of the RB-29 Washingtons flown by the RAF's 192 Squadron, but it had still not been able to escape. All

NATO aircraft flying near the Inner German Border were now operating on a fully-armed 'fire back' basis.[18]

Discussions between the four occupying powers over the RAF Lincoln did not go well. In 1945 the Allies had agreed that there would be three air corridors stretching from different points in the Western Zones of Germany across the Soviet Zone to Berlin, which was itself divided between the four powers. Sensibly, the Soviets suggested replacing the complex and confusing system of three different air corridors with a single wider corridor or 'funnel'. The Allies refused, because although this solution would have been safer, each of the three corridors passed over a subject of 'intelligence interest'. Sir Ivone Kirkpatrick, who represented the British, explained to officials in London:

*

The crux of the matter is really how much importance we attach to the intelligence interest. The Americans are at present very strong on this (they are particularly anxious to retain ability to watch the Fulda Gap), and have suggested to us privately that we are not attaching sufficient importance to intelligence interest in the Northern Corridor.

*

Negotiations were made more complex by the fact that the French, who also had a sector in Berlin, were 'obviously' not told about the intelligence issues during the negotiations.[19] The Americans later explained that the retention of the southern corridor was 'an absolutely vital requirement' for them, since what they needed above all was early warning of any concentration of forces signalling an impending Soviet attack. As well as the regular sigint flights that travelled down the corridors, the Americans were now using special aircraft equipped for lateral photography, claiming that the photographs were so good you could 'see a golf ball on a tee at 40 miles'.[20] The Americans were 'entirely rigid' on intelligence interests being paramount. Accordingly, the negotiations foundered, and the existing system, with its three corridors, remained largely unchanged.[21]

The RAF sigint units based at CSE Watton were especially lucky not to lose any aircraft in this mini air-war. In 1954 a Gloster Meteor from 527 Squadron, which claimed to be on a 'radio calibration mission', strayed over the border into East Germany. This seems to have been due to a navigational error. The crew were oblivious to their mistake, but soon realised they were running short of fuel, and opted to land at the next visible airfield. The pilot, Sergeant Don Coleman, and his navigator, Sergeant Mike Thomson, stepped out onto the tarmac and – to their horror – realised that the approaching troops had red stars on their caps. The Soviets spent several weeks inspecting the aircraft before it was returned to the RAF. The incident earned Coleman the unwelcome nickname 'Dan Dare'.

The following year, another Gloster Meteor on a 'radio calibration flight' from Watton arrived unannounced in East Germany. Again the pilots had run out fuel, but this time they could not find a runway, and opted for a belly landing in a field. After a suitable delay for technical inspection of the radio warfare equipment on board, the Meteor was again returned by the Soviets. On the night of 26 June 1955 there was a much more serious incident, when a radio countermeasures Lincoln (WD132) from 199 Squadron exercising over West Germany collided with a USAF F-86D Sabre jet fighter. The Lincoln crashed seven miles north of Bitburg, and all the crew were lost.[22]

Early incidents like these mostly occurred in northern Europe. However, Turkey and the Black Sea were also of enormous intelligence importance because of the presence of rocket-testing sites in the southern Soviet Union around the Caucasus. As early as September 1950, Britain's Technical Radio Interception Committee was directing a series of flights against Soviet radar targets on the Black Sea.[23] The sought-after prize was elint from Soviet guided missiles being tested at Kapustin Yar. In 1954, trials had been held in Turkey to see if ground stations could intercept the signals, but the equipment was not sensitive enough, and in any case it was hard to collect signals during the early stages of rocket flight, since they were blocked by hills near the launch site. The only option was to get closer to the take-off sites and to monitor from altitude, which meant flights over the Black Sea or the Caspian Sea. The most desperate option was perilous missions by SIS's Technical Collection Service, with human spies furnished with specially equipped suitcases, rather like the suitcase radios carried by wartime resistance workers, which were something of a liability, since close inspection would have revealed their true purpose.[24] This was the unit that also specialised in gathering intelligence on the Soviet atomic programme.[25]

The nearest miss probably occurred in 1955, when the RAF's 192 Squadron identified the first MiG-15 with airborne radar by flying directly at the Soviet border in an area near the Caspian Sea. However, the slow-flying RB-29 Washington only narrowly escaped being shot down, and returned peppered with holes. The Squadron Commander, Group Captain Norman Hoad, was awarded an Air Force Cross for the discovery of this new Soviet airborne radar.[26] Was the risk worth it? As a result of this incident, in mid-December 1955 some members of the Joint Intelligence Committee began to challenge the remorseless collection of elint on Soviet air-defence capabilities. To some it seemed both expensive and dangerous. However, Eric Jones, the Director of GCHQ, argued that in the realm of sigint it was possible neither to dart about from one subject to another, nor to concentrate on one only. He reminded them that it was the extremely thorough, if tedious, collection of 'order of battle' intelligence that had allowed them to pick up specialist guided weapons activity that was of extreme interest to all three services, revealing new Soviet missile developments. While this was true, one might argue that Jones was bound to defend 'order of battle' activity for institutional reasons. Struggling against high-grade Soviet cyphers that could not be broken, this was the best product he could squeeze out from the other available electronic sources. Moreover, it reflected GCHQ's secret deal with the armed services, which wanted sigint to have a strong focus on assisting military operations. The RAF shared the costs of airborne collection, and as Jones remarked, more than half of GCHQ's work was now in support of defence activity.²⁷

Britain's most dangerous and dramatic Cold War sigint operations remain largely unknown. Some of the most perilous missions were not in the air along the Inner German Border, but at sea. During the early 1950s, GCHQ and the Royal Navy had developed a joint programme for the concerted monitoring of Soviet signals around Murmansk and other important naval bases within the Arctic Circle. This involved sending submarines into Soviet territorial waters, and in some cases actually inside Soviet harbours. The Red Fleet knew these activities were taking place, and often responded with depth charges, making such secret missions breathtakingly dangerous.

The most important figures on these missions were the 'sparkers'. These were radio communications operators who had been sent to the Royal Navy's Signals School, located at the naval station HMS Mercury near Petersfield in Hampshire, for special training in sigint listening. Here, a secret unit called the Radio Warfare Special Branch cooperated with GCHQ and planned the naval dimension of Britain's sigint operations. Its task was not only to record Soviet voice traffic and telegraphy, but also to listen out for elint, including transmission from new Soviet radars on high frequencies such as 'S band' and 'X band'. In May 1953, ten new recruits passed through the basic radio course at Mercury and then, to their abundant horror, were told that they had 'volunteered' for duty on submarines. The Royal Navy had only recently lost the submarines HMS *Truculent* and HMS *Affray* in tragic accidents, so submarines were not a particularly popular assignment at the time. One of the more thoughtful individuals on this basic radio course, Tony Beasley, managed to dodge immediate deployment to submarines by volunteering for a sigint course with 'Special Branch' that included a long period ashore learning Russian at HMS Pucklechurch.

By 1954, Beasley had managed to join the elite ranks of the Radio Warfare personnel, which had its own heavily guarded compound on the northern edge of HMS Mercury. Here he was first instructed in Soviet communication procedures in preparation for his language course. Although HMS Mercury was far from the Soviet Union, radio signals bounced off the ionosphere at night, so transmissions from as far afield as Baku and Tbilisi could be heard comfortably. Towards the end of the ten-week 'special course' Beasley began to study the arcane subject of Soviet radars and guidance systems, which constituted elint collection. He had found his forte in the mysterious world of electronic signatures and wavebands, and accordingly he was diverted away from the Russian course at HMS Pucklechurch to become more of an elint specialist. Soon he was serving on fishery-protection vessels, including HMS *Truelove*, *Mariner* and *Pickle*. Operating out of Norwegian harbours such as Tromsø, their fishery duties gave them a legitimate reason to be close to Soviet exercises in northern waters, allowing them to sit listening at their leisure, often using their own personal monitoring equipment which they put together 'Heath Robinson style'.

Late in 1954, Beasley and three of his comrades found themselves back at HMS Mercury, where they had been called in to see the head of the Radio Warfare Special Branch, Lieutenant Commander Harry Selby-Bennett. As experienced elint and comint operators, they had been selected for 'special duties'. They were told to write six weeks' worth of letters that would be posted to their families at intervals, but were given no information about where they were going, or even what they might do. Arriving at Portsmouth with their kitbags, they were transferred to a motor launch, still none the wiser about their mysterious task or their destination. One of the four suggested it might be a submarine, but the other three laughed out loud at the idea, since none of them had been through the stringent obligatory three-month submarine course at nearby Gosport, which included passing through the famous hundred-foot salt-water escape tower. Moments later they pulled alongside the vessel on which they were to serve for many months.

'Never in a million years were we expecting a submarine,' recalls Beasley. 'We just could not believe it . . . Standing together like clockwork soldiers we were ushered towards the escape hatch, just forward of the conning tower and told to drop our holdalls down the steep ladder and follow. Time was of the essence.' Their escort, Leading Seaman 'Snowy' Snow, was horrified to discover that none of his new charges had been trained for submarines, and regarded them as a danger to themselves and the rest of the crew. One of Beasley's three fellow sparkers called out: 'What's the name of this iron coffin?' The answer came back, 'HMS *Turpin*.'[28]

HMS *Turpin* was a Group 3 T-class submarine which entered service at the end of the Second World War. In 1945 the Allies were aware that their submarine technology was well behind that of the German U-boats, especially Hitler's legendary late-model Type-21s. The Group 1 and Group 2 submarines that had been built earlier in the war were scrapped, but like the ill-fated USS *Cochino*, the *Turpin* and seven other Group 3 T-class submarines were sent for what was termed 'Super-T Conversion', essentially an interim measure before new classes of submarine came on stream. Crucially, the later Group 3 submarines were of welded rather than riveted construction, making them more streamlined than their predecessors. Their hulls were now lengthened to accommodate more electronic equipment, in some cases a sigint listening room, together with additional electric motors and new batteries. The deck gun was removed and the conning tower replaced with a more modern design that enclosed the periscopes and masts. The radar and sonar were improved. All eight boats could now achieve a speed of over eighteen knots, giving them an excellent chance of evading any Soviet hunters.[29]

Tony Beasley and his three 'Telegraphist Special' comrades were treated to a tour of the *Turpin*. Snowy explained that, together with all the recent conversions to bring it up to the standard of the most advanced German U-boats, extra rib supports had been fitted to the pressure hull so that it could exceed its formal safety depth in case of an emergency. As the sparkers toured the submarine, their place in the operational jigsaw gradually became clear. Of the eight submarines that had been converted to Super-T specification, the *Turpin* and the *Totem* had been stripped of some of their radar and echo-sounding equipment, and had instead been fitted out with the most up-to-date sigint collection technology. The sigint receivers were attached to the snorkel and the aft periscope, and the wires trailed everywhere. The sigint operators had their own listening room near to the boat's operations centre.

Questions as to where they were going were met with blank looks. Only the Commander, John Coote, knew their destination, and he was keeping his mouth firmly shut. Before departure, the *Turpin* received its final blessing when a harbour tug came out and painted over the serial number on the conning tower and spot-welded shut the escape hatches. This was because of the danger of ramming by a Soviet destroyer, which would rupture the hatches. With the escape hatches welded shut, all the escape apparatus was useless, so it had been removed, making space for more stores for the long journey ahead. The mission was code-named 'Operation Tartan', and the destination was the exercise area of the Soviet Northern Fleet on the Kola Inlet and the Rybachi Peninsula, deep inside the Arctic Circle.

During early March 1955 the crew endured a long journey north. Once they were within the Arctic Circle the sigint monitors began their work. Beasley's colleagues monitored comint while he listened for 'X band' and 'S band' radar. While doing this, to his surprise he detected an unusual short-range radar known as 'Q band'. GCHQ had warned him before departure that anything that was transmitted on 'Q band' would have a range of no more than two and a half miles. The signal faded and then returned much stronger. Beasley realised they were being rammed, and despite being new to submarines, instinctively shouted out the command to crash dive. This was a perilous business with the periscope and the snorkel still raised. Water began pouring into the control room through the snorkel. The periscope was quickly lowered, and its handles, that weighed close to a ton, hit Beasley, sending him crashing across the control room and inflicting a debilitating lifelong neck injury. The *Turpin* levelled off at 120 feet below the surface. The extremely cold water made sonar unreliable at any depth, and Soviet ships came and went for the next few hours, searching energetically, but without finding their quarry. Glad to have evaded the submarine hunters, Commander Coote waited for them to depart and then set a course for home.[30]

Back in London, the Admiralty Signals Division was doing what it could to protect the secrecy of its submarine missions. One of the activities it undertook was a communications security survey of the radio transmission from HMS *Totem*, *Turpin*'s sister ship, while she was on an identical mission off the Soviet coast code-named 'Operation Defiant'. The results were not good. The Signals Division warned the Director of Naval Intelligence that the KGB's listeners, the Soviet equivalent of GCHQ, might well pick up 'unusual very secret traffic on a home station submarine broadcast' continuing over a number of weeks, and might also notice that *Totem* was absent from the normal exercise areas. In future, it suggested that a suitable cover plan with 'dummy communications' be thought up. This dummy traffic would have to run on a long-term basis if special submarine operations were to continue to be carried out at short notice without the Soviets identifying what was going on.[31]

Tony Beasley's next mission to the Arctic Circle, 'Operation Sanjak', was yet more eventful. In July 1955 HMS *Turpin* had been loitering off the Soviet coast for over two weeks, but was experiencing problems with its elint equipment. Reception was good while the submarine was stationary, but not when it was in motion. They moved to the western edge of their patrol area so they could surface and see what was wrong. After a perilous climb up the submarine fin in a rolling sea, the problem, which proved to be a cross-threaded aerial, was resolved and *Turpin* submerged once more to complete the last few days of her patrol. The elint profiles of several radars from their intercept target list had already been collected, and with only two days to go they picked up an unusual contact. Commander Coote decided to chase this contact to the edge of their permitted area, moving closer to the coast than was allowed under their strict operating rules. Suddenly, Beasley intercepted an 'X band' radar very close to them, and picked up a contact dead ahead. The *Turpin* crash dived immediately.

All four sigint operators now reported multiple contacts. They were under attack. The warning was superfluous, since the propellers of several ships were quite audible as they passed directly over the submarine. Then came the horrible sounds of splashes. These were depth charges. Beasley recalls:

*

The first depth charge exploded way under our depth of 120 feet, followed by others, from different directions. A rather loud 'clunk' on our forward casing was followed by an enormous explosion which shook the boat, followed by others at a greater depth. Another depth charge exploded close above us rocking the boat much as before . . . Depth charging continued for longer than I care to remember.

*

Commander Coote took the submarine deeper and deeper, levelling off at their safety limit of 280 feet. Here they felt relatively secure, and decided not to move, relying on the cold water to render the Soviet sonar ineffective. However, they were painfully conscious that they were drifting in a strong current towards an area marked on their chart as being a probable Soviet mine-field.

As they drifted away from the action the depth charges fell further and further away from their position. In the control room everyone sat in silence, wondering what was next. Further shocks were not long in coming. They heard strange rasping sounds running down the side of the hull, followed by a 'twang' as if a wire had been caught and had then come free. Some thought the noises were caused by pieces of ice, but they then realised they had entered the minefield, and that it was the hawsers that attached the mines to the sea bed to keep them from floating away that were scraping the *Turpin*'s sides. It was high time to cease drifting, set a course and pull away.

After a long run south they surfaced off the coast of Norway, and the crew inspected the damage. The periscopes and snorkel were grotesquely bent and completely unusable. Indeed, *Turpin* had been stripped of a large part of its extremities by the multiple blasts of the depth charges. Guardrails, aerials, the sensors and much of the tail fin had also been blown away. Most dramatically, the starboard outer casing had been torn apart, leaving a thirty-foot gash which in one place was three feet deep. However, the diesel engines were undamaged, and they headed for home, albeit with rather uncertain steering. Having lost their aerials, they could not communicate. Eventually they found a trawler out from Kingston-upon-Hull which relayed a message, allowing a rendezvous with a submarine depot ship, HMS *Maidstone*, which provided much-needed supplies of food and fresh water.

Returning to HMS Mercury, they were given a week's leave. The four sparkers were then debriefed in person by Lieutenant Commander Harry Selby-Bennett, the Controller of naval sigint operations. After being briefly congratulated on a successful mission, they were told to their surprise that for reasons of 'continuity' of monitoring the Soviet transmissions they were about to board HMS *Totem* for a mission that would last another eight weeks. Understandably perhaps, Tony Beasley had now had his fill of submarines, which he had never volunteered for. Eventually he transferred to the Provost Branch, the Royal Navy's police service, to complete his naval service of sixteen years.[32]

Until 1956, Cabinet Ministers remained blissfully unaware of Britain's intelligence 'incidents', including the two perilous missions of HMS *Turpin* in 1955. As a result the British remained more relaxed about forward operations than their American counterparts. By contrast the American intelligence community strained on a tight leash held by the State Department, and indeed President Eisenhower himself. However, all that was about to change. In April 1956 a single strange episode in Portsmouth harbour ensured that the situation was quickly reversed. Thereafter, growing hesitancy in Whitehall shifted the momentum in the world of sigint special operations away from Britain towards the United States. The turning point was the infamous 'Buster' Crabb incident. This offered Cabinet Ministers a first-hand glimpse of the sheer scale of political embarrassment that could be generated by bungled surveillance operations.

In April 1956 the Soviet cruiser *Ordjoninkidze* carried the Soviet Premier, Nikolai Bulganin, and Nikita Khrushchev, leader of the Soviet Communist Party, on a goodwill visit to Britain. Despite some robust exchanges between the Soviets and Anthony Eden, Churchill's successor as Prime Minister, the visit went well, and the Soviet delegation departed on 27 April 1956. However, even as it left the press had begun to speculate about the mysterious disappearance of a British naval diver, Commander Lionel 'Buster' Crabb RNVR, in the vicinity of the visiting Soviet cruiser. Fourteen months later, in June 1957, a headless and handless body in a diving suit was recovered from the sea near Pilsey Island in the English Channel. Over the years, lurid tales of possible KGB abduction or beheading have circulated. However, newly released intelligence files show that Crabb was almost certainly killed by being drawn through the ship's propellers. Churning the propellers at intervals was a standard defence against inquisitive divers whose presence was regularly suspected during such visits.

Buster Crabb had been the lead man on 'Operation Claret', an attempt by SIS to gain intelligence from the underwater inspection of the cruiser. He was one of the Royal Navy's most experienced divers, and despite being demobbed in 1948 he was often recalled to help with difficult dives, including rescue work on submarines lost in accidents. Even at this early stage of the Cold War, such secret operations required political approval. But in this instance the system had broken down. The SIS officer who was tasked with securing the clearance for Operation Claret had suffered a family bereavement and had left the office before it had been obtained. His colleagues presumed that the green light had been given, but in fact it had not. The first rule of intelligence management – having political clearance – had been broken, and the cost for the whole British intelligence community was high.[33]

What mattered to Eden was the public furore and the humiliation he suffered in the House of Commons. Not only had SIS bungled an unapproved mission, it also failed to cover its tracks. Despite the clumsy efforts of the local Special Branch to hide the evidence, including ripping out pages from the register of the hotel where Crabb had stayed, the press was soon on the trail. Journalists quickly established that this was an SIS mission, and that no ministerial authority had been given. Hugh Gaitskell, the leader of the opposition, enjoyed taunting his opponent on the issue. Eden was furious and decided to take disciplinary action, telling the Ministers concerned to order their staff to cooperate fully with the ensuing investigation. This process cast a long shadow over all the intelligence agencies, and ushered in an era of closer political control over special operations of every kind.[34]

The head of the inquiry, Sir Edward Bridges, a somewhat nineteenth-century figure, employed the JIC to help him ferret out all aspects of the Crabb incident. As a former Cabinet Secretary, Bridges identified 'certain questions' of a broader nature. While intrusive intelligence operations clearly had a capacity to cause international repercussions, the systems for their authorisation were unclear.[35] Bridges recommended a broader inquiry reviewing all of Britain's strategic intelligence and surveillance activities, and assessing 'the balance between military intelligence on the one hand, and civil intelligence and political risks on the other'. Eden gave this job to Sir Norman Brook, the current Cabinet Secretary, working with Patrick Dean, Chairman of the JIC.[36] This review had immediate consequences for intelligence. In April 1956, coinciding with Khrushchev's visit to Britain, some of the first examples of the CIA's high-flying U-2 spy planes had arrived at RAF Lakenheath. These aircraft were mostly known for their work with high-altitude photography, but some of their missions were also sigint-orientated. Eden now decided that this, and a host of other special operations, had to stop, and the U-2s were sent to alternative bases in Germany.[37]

Eden's angry response had some unintended benefits. In 1952 Sir Stewart Menzies, Chief of SIS, had retired and was replaced by General Sir John Sinclair. The mediocre Sinclair had previously been Director of Military Intelligence, and while he was more competent than his predecessor, he was not a moderniser. He was now fired as a result of the Crabb incident; after the multiple inquiries he was pleased to go, and confessed to a friend in the sigint community that things were 'getting too hot for me'. In the summer of 1956 Eden plumped for Sir Dick White, hitherto the Director General of MI5, as the new Chief of SIS.

White was a man of enormous energy, and a forward thinker. Together with his SIS staff officer, Harry 'Shergy' Shergold, he set about dragging SIS kicking and screaming into the mid-twentieth century. For the first time in almost two decades the organisation had an effective manager at the top, and it now developed into a really effective service.[38] White's arrival also marked the formal end of SIS influence over sigint. Sinclair was the last Chief of SIS to chair the London Signals Intelligence Board, Britain's highest sigint authority; this duty passed to Eric Jones, the Director of GCHQ.[39]

Eden's review was bad news for sigint special operations. As we have seen, no less secret than the spy flights were the submarine missions. These were now being conducted by the British and the Americans on the basis of mutual exchange, swapping product for product. However, Eden's anger at the Buster Crabb incident meant that British submarine operations were cancelled. British officers in Washington spoke of their embarrassment that their half of the transatlantic deal could not be delivered on, warning that British efforts would soon be eclipsed by American submarine commanders in the Atlantic, who were pushing ahead 'so as not to be outdone by the Pacific submariners'. Like Bletchley Park and Enigma a decade before, British Naval Intelligence wanted to keep its dominant position in the game of European submarine sigint. It urged not only that the programme be restored, but that it be followed by 'a bigger and better operation'.[40]

As predicted, by the end of 1956 the US Navy was indeed beginning its own independent sigint operations off Murmansk. Initially the American Office of Naval Intelligence had decided that the British were not even to be informed. However, they eventually realised that it would be foolhardy not to draw on the more extensive British experience of similar operations in these waters. Commander John Coote, who had been on the Murmansk run several times with the *Turpin*, and had joined the Americans on the USS *Stickleback* in the Pacific, was called in to brief the first American crew. This was on the understanding that he told no other British naval officers in Washington. These new American submarine intelligence operations off Murmansk had been triggered by two factors. First, the cancellation of British operations. Second, and ironically, the US Navy had used the reports of previous British intelligence operations in the region to persuade the State Department that 'the risks of detection are negligible'. Admiral Robert Elkins, the senior British naval officer in Washington, warned First Sea Lord Admiral Mountbatten that British intelligence prestige, which was currently high, would soon suffer 'unless we resume these activities ourselves'.[41]

In 1957 a new Prime Minister, Harold Macmillan, came to the rescue. Intrusive operations using British aircraft, ships and submarines for sigint and photography were gradually resumed. Between 1956 and 1960, twenty U-2 aircraft were involved in overflights, often from British bases. Some of these even used British pilots. Most of the deep-penetration flights were launched from Adana in Turkey, staging through Pakistan, and six RAF pilots were based there. By 1957, Britain's elite Super-T submarines were gradually emerging from under the shadow of the Crabb incident, and were back in action on their perilous runs against the Soviet Northern Fleet.

In September 1957, HMS *Taciturn* took its turn to head north on what were routinely eight-week secret patrols. Most of the files relating to these highly secret missions remain closed. However, fortunately for us this 'mystery trip' was recorded by Michael Hurley, a young submariner, in what was undoubtedly an illegal personal diary. Setting sail from Portsmouth on 4 September, Commander Morris J. O'Connor chose not to tell his crew about the nature of the voyage until they were under way. Two days later, the crew were briefed. They were 'going to snoop on the Russian Fleet exercises' in the Arctic, and if they were detected it would be 'very unpleasant and most dangerous'. O'Connor explained that they would be running submerged most of the time, and would keep radio silence. On their return they were to say nothing of their mission, 'not even to wives and mothers', since this would be 'a wartime patrol'. After practising against a convenient British anti-submarine exercise off the Scottish coast, they took on more supplies at Greenock naval base in western Scotland and headed for the Arctic Circle. Extra personnel had come on board to assist with the listening, necessitating 'hot bunking' and meaning that water was in short supply.[42]

On 24 September they were able to get quite close to a Soviet submarine, and were able to record its signature over a period of more than an hour. Listening was undertaken by a special team led by Lieutenant Commander George Lucas, a fluent Russian-speaker whom Hurley described as 'fat, foreign looking with a slight accent'. However, the following day it was clear that they had been sighted, since 'a large number of aircraft plus two or three destroyers searched for us'. O'Connor had strict written orders that in such circumstance the *Taciturn* should turn back and head for home. Aircraft continued to search for them as they made their way south. On 3 October they reached the safety of Faslane naval base on the west coast of Scotland, and 'a package', presumably the sigint recordings, was 'whisked off to Prestwick airport' and flown to the United States for analysis.[43]

Michael Hurley was back on special operations six months later, with a further trip into Arctic waters. With much the same crew and the obligatory 'special team' on board they sailed down the Clyde and into open water on 13 March 1958. The extra personnel on board meant that water supply was again a problem. The special passengers consisted of the familiar Commander Lucas, who turned out to be Polish, together with a 'boffin' from the Underwater Development Establishment called Dr Newman and an American officer called Lieutenant Block. There were also two further communications intelligence specialists, including a Canadian. The routine was now familiar, diving deep by day and attempting to 'snort' by night, although this was often interrupted by Soviet aircraft. Snow storms provided ideal cover for the use of the snorkel. The very cold exterior water temperature meant that icy drops of condensation continually fell on the crew. The American officer took his turn at watches, and his distinctive voice on the Tannoy was a source of amusement. Dr Newman spent much of his time in the special sound room located in the *Taciturn*'s expanded hull, working on sigint collection.[44]

On 28 March they moved in close to the Soviet coast, and began to encounter more signals traffic. The next day, they 'got some good recordings' and managed to take some film footage of peculiar 'bullet shaped' aircraft that they did not recognise, and thought were possibly prototypes. On 2 April Hurley noted in his diary that they were well inside an inlet, with land less than a mile away all around. He could see Soviet radar installations silhouetted on the coast, and wrote, 'We are actually at the entrance to a harbour.'[45] If they were discovered here, there was little chance of escape, and Hurley realised that this was perilous work indeed.[46] By 3 April they had moved away from the coast and were in open water at periscope depth, busy making good recordings of two destroyers, a Skory class and a Kola class, together with some escorts, which were exercising. Hurley records what happened next:

*

Then suddenly out of the sun astern another Skory appeared coming towards us. We went down to 120ft. On Husk [a listening system] we could hear him coming as the sound of his engines grew louder. We went to Diving Stations and Defence State One (just in case), she passed right overhead like an express train went on a little then made a sharp turn and came back towards us again. As she did so she dropped three charges which seemed of course very loud . . .

*

The *Taciturn* went deep, down to 220 feet, and the Soviet ship moved away. Remarkably, a little later they came up and began recording the same vessels, although at a safer distance from both their quarry and the shore.[47] By 16 April they were on their way home. A week later they surfaced for the first time in thirty-four days. The *Taciturn* reached Faslane naval base four days later, to be greeted by a visibly relieved head of submarine operations. Radio silence meant that for two months no one knew the fate of submarines on these missions.[48]

By the late 1950s the Super-Ts, once the most advanced boats the Navy could field, were suffering the wear and tear from long patrols. Commanders would now refer to 'a shaky old T-boat'. *Turpin*, for example, had an elderly diesel engine for surface propulsion, in this case taken from another submarine, which had already seen twelve thousand hours of service. In 1957, while on an operation in the Atlantic, the main engine gave up the ghost and the *Turpin* suffered the indignity of being towed by an Admiralty tug for some five thousand miles.

Although the T-boats were no longer safe for perilous operations against the Soviets, the elderly *Turpin* was re-engined and sent on further Arctic intelligence missions under the command of Alfie Roake. The first set off on 21 October 1959, and the second, launched on 6 February 1960, set a record for snorkelling without surfacing of forty-two days.[49] On the second mission there were a number of 'close encounters'. One of these was thought to be with a Soviet torpedo, but fired at long range, allowing the *Turpin* to evade it by going deep and combing the tracks. Their closest call was being pursued by a flotilla of six Soviet destroyers, which they escaped by diving to a remarkable 425 feet, well below their safety depth. Engineers later told Roake that his hull would have collapsed like an eggshell at 470 feet, and that they had a lucky escape.[50]

Alfie Roake's last mission into Soviet waters was launched in the spring of 1960. By now he was very conscious that the elderly Super-Ts were 'nowhere near' American standards. A new decade beckoned with the promise of the quieter and more reliable 'O' class submarines, and eventually nuclear vessels. Just like the Super-T class, some of these new boats were modified for a special intelligence role and would be despatched on further hazardous missions inside the Arctic Circle.[51]

Sigint in the Sun – GCHQ's Overseas Empire

... with 'Sigint' locking onto targets with pinpoint accuracy, our military ached to have a go.

Tim Hardy, Special Branch, Sarawak, April 1964[1]

In the 1950s, GCHQ's top priorities were warning of an impending war with Russia, and gathering intelligence on Moscow's growing nuclear arsenal. However, on a day-to-day basis, the Middle East, Africa and Asia were the regions where sigint made a tangible difference. Since the end of the Second World War, Britain had been involved in a prolonged 'escape from empire', retreating from her colonies and hoping to replace them with a vibrant Commonwealth of newly independent states. The reality was more complex, since many of these countries contained elements that were keen to evict the British faster than they wished to go. Some hosted guerrilla groups sympathetic to Moscow, others were divided communities that faced a troubled journey towards independence. The result was that Britain was involved in an endless litany of small wars that stretched from the dusty deserts of Yemen to the steamy jungles of Borneo. Because these were often guerrilla wars, finding the enemy could be the main challenge, and here sigint was in its element. Moreover, right across Asia and Africa, cyphers were less secure than those of countries like Russia, so GCHQ could also read plenty of high-grade diplomatic traffic.

Although sigint helped to smooth the end of Britain's empire, GCHQ itself did not always want empire to come to an end. Because the 1950s and 1960s were an era when a great deal of communications was sent over long distances using high-frequency radio, GCHQ depended on the remnants of empire to provide a global network of ground stations to collect these signals. Indeed, Britain's imperial real estate was one of the key contributions to UKUSA, and was of particular assistance to the United States. Accordingly, in many colonies there were defence and intelligence bases that Britain wished to retain, prompting officials to drag their feet over independence. Elsewhere, the British attempted to persuade post-independence governments to permit some bases to remain.[2]

Throughout the 1950s Britain fought one of the most protracted colonial struggles of the post-war era, the Malayan Emergency. The enemy were a hardened band of Communist guerrillas who had been Britain's uneasy allies against the Japanese during the war. The military forces of the Malayan Communist Party, or 'MCP', led by Ching Peng, operated from refuges in the dense jungle. Britain did not initially recognise the seriousness of the Emergency in Malaya, allowing it to get out of hand. However, in October 1951 the MCP succeeded in assassinating Sir Henry Gurney, the British High Commissioner. Thereafter, striking back at the guerrillas and eliminating Ching Peng became a near-obsession for the security authorities in London. When Oliver Lyttelton, the Colonial Secretary, returned to London to report on Gurney's assassination he promised the Cabinet that he would form special teams 'aimed at certain individuals'. These were effectively killer squads, and he gave a firm assurance that they would 'hunt down individual men from Communist higher formations through their families, properties, sweethearts etc.'.[3]

Locating the guerrilla headquarters in Malaya was easier said than done. In 1950 a sigint-equipped Lancaster from the RAF's 192 Squadron was sent out to help in the hunt for the insurgents by tracking their radio communications. Later, undercover agents planted batteries with excessively high power on the guerrillas to damage their radios. When they were repaired, the workshops the guerrillas used were bribed to secretly modify the sets to give out a stronger signal. This gave the opportunity for sigint to achieve a direction-finding fix on the main guerrilla bases. Bombers from the RAF and the Royal Australian Air Force were standing by, and lightning raids were carried out on the deemed location of the signals. Avro Lincoln bombers dropped thousands of tons of bombs into the dense jungle at likely guerrilla locations. Their pilots were always impressed by the resilience of the jungle: their largest bombs vanished into the triple-canopied green foliage below them, and from the aircraft little impact was visible. It is not known how successful these operations were, but Ching Peng, the most important prize, certainly eluded them.[4]

In January 1952, Sir Gerald Templer arrived as the new High Commissioner in Malaya. Templer possessed the authority and charisma necessary to create a unified government machine and to implement an effective counter-insurgency strategy. Although famed for his emphasis on 'hearts and minds', he also sorted out intelligence, creating a coherent structure in which the army, the police and the civil authorities were forced to share intelligence. All this was done with his customary fiery language – he was quite incapable of uttering a sentence without a cussword in it.[5]

Despite Templer's forceful direction, intelligence did not improve overnight. An important intelligence issue that was never quite resolved was the question of who was actually behind the insurgency. The Colonial Office and the Special Branch officers of the Malayan Police preferred to interpret the Emergency as a wicked plot initiated by Stalin or else Mao, while the British diplomats tended to see it more as a local anti-colonial uprising. During the mid-1950s GCHQ began to intercept what it believed to be wireless traffic between the MCP guerrilla leadership and the Chinese Communist Party in Peking. The Special Branch presented this intelligence to senior British officials in Kuala Lumpur with some delight as evidence of its theory of external direction, but only in a summarised form. Diplomats in Kuala Lumpur were sceptical, and asked to see the full transcripts of the transmissions. A major altercation followed, with the diplomats accusing the Special Branch of bending the evidence, while the policemen accused the diplomats of a lack of trust. The issue of exactly how close the MCP was to Peking was never resolved.[6]

GCHQ's most important outpost in Asia was Hong Kong. China was the venue of one of Britain's early Cold War code-breaking triumphs. Between March 1943 and July 1947 GCHQ was able to read the high-grade Russian cypher traffic passing between Moscow and its mission at the headquarters of Mao Tse-tung's People's Liberation Army in Yunnan. This was a highly secret programme, and GCHQ only began passing material to the Americans in March 1946. The decision not to share until this point may have reflected anxieties about the strong differences within the American administration about China policy, but it is noticeable that the spring of 1946 also marks the advent of the revised BRUSA agreement.[7] Exactly how this breakthrough was achieved when many other Russian high-grade cypher systems remained immune to attack is still a mystery. However, SIS had placed a rather eccentric officer called Michael Lindsay at Mao's headquarters in Yunnan, where he was assisting the Chinese Communist communications team as their 'principal radio adviser'. This may eventually prove to be part of the story.[8]

The British colony of Hong Kong was of special value to the United States. This reflected the fact that, after the end of the Chinese Civil War that brought Mao Tse-tung to power in 1949, the United States did not even have an embassy in mainland China. 'Hong Kong became an American watchtower on China,' recalls Jack Smith, who looked after the Far East in the CIA's Office of National Estimates.[9] GCHQ joined with the Americans and the equivalent Australian organisation, Defence Signals Branch, to develop the facilities in Hong Kong. Washington received the full intercept output of Hong Kong, but with the onset of the Korean War demands for intelligence went up sharply, and Washington considered that combined US–UK intercept facilities in the Far East were 'far short of requirements'.[10]

In July 1952 the US Communications Intelligence Board persuaded its British opposite numbers of the 'urgent need' to send an additional eight-hundred-strong US Air Force sigint unit to Hong Kong to join the hard-pressed British and Australians. However, this was vetoed by the Governor of Hong Kong, Sir Alexander Grantham, who detested the way in which his territory had become host to a myriad of espionage activities.[11] Once the Chinese had intervened in the Korean War, an attack on Hong Kong by China was always a possibility. Therefore GCHQ negotiated emergency facilities at Okinawa in Japan for the British and Australian sigint personnel working there.[12]

Even in 1955, the United States was still negotiating for new sites in Asia. Sigint sites were not small or discreet, often requiring vast acres of wireless masts known as 'aerial farms' to capture signals of interest. In Taiwan, American officials had run into trouble securing a 335-acre site near Nan-Szu-Pu airfield where they had plans to locate hundreds of personnel from the Army Security Agency.[13] With repeated clashes between the United States and Communist China over the Taiwan Straits in the late 1950s, the British government reviewed the future of Hong Kong, which seemed exposed, and pondered the short-term value of the continued British presence in the colony. Much turned on the mysteries of the UKUSA alliance, the Anglo–American–Commonwealth sigint pact of cooperation, since Hong Kong hosted British, Australian and American eavesdroppers.[14] Alongside the GCHQ activities there were also vast British and American programmes in Hong Kong for running agents and interviewing defectors from mainland China. During the 1950s and 1960s, both the State Department and the Pentagon considered Hong Kong to be the single most important British overseas territory from the point of view of intelligence-gathering.[15]

In order to stimulate more defectors from China to Hong Kong, Britain launched 'Operation Debenture' in 1954. This was a covert radio project and constituted 'the first UK operations of any magnitude for the penetration of Mainland China'.

The aim was to provide an undercover broadcasting station that would increase the desire for contacts with the West amongst the Chinese middle classes, and increase defections across the border into Hong Kong. The emphasis was on the 'purely "intelligence" angle', and the defectors were needed because SIS human agent coverage of China was weak. The original intention had been to place this 'black station' in Hong Kong, but it was eventually located in Singapore, hidden at one of the military bases.[16]

The main GCHQ sigint stations in Hong Kong were on the coast at Little Sai Wan and the curiously-named outpost known as 'Batty's Belvedere'. The contribution of Australia's Defence Signals Branch was important, since Australia had identified China as its top sigint target, followed by Indonesia and then Vietnam.[17] During the late 1950s the commander of the sigint station was an Australian called Ken Sly, and originally it was staffed by airmen from the RAF's 367 Signals Unit.[18] A constant flow of National Servicemen had learnt Chinese at RAF Wythall near Birmingham and later at RAF North Luffenham in Leicestershire, but by 1957 the increasing use of civilians with qualifications in the language was reducing this considerable training requirement. There was also a separate cohort of Vietnamese linguists.[19] Civilianisation brought unexpected security problems, since civilians could not be used for some of the menial duties carried out by service personnel. GCHQ tried to address this problem by employing deaf and dumb locals in the more sensitive locations on the sites.[20]

Ken Sly was well aware of the attentions of Chinese intelligence. One of the locally employed Chinese, Wal Bin Chang, showed a propensity for taking photographs of groups on social occasions, and 'also took care to photograph each one of us separately'. Moreover, he tended to volunteer for extra duties at unsociable hours. He was eventually captured on the border trying to cross over into Communist China with a number of documents, including a description of the personal habits of every NCO and officer at the base. He had been entertaining some of them in 'girlie bars', and admitted that he had persuaded one of the officers to sleep with his wife, adding: 'In this way I will be able to obtain much more information of value to our side.' The officer in question was swiftly discharged. Military staff at overseas listening stations working for GCHQ were a continual target for this sort of honey-trap.[21] Ken Sly was eventually replaced by a civilian with the rank of Senior Linguist Officer, and moved on to serve in Australia and then with GCHQ at Cheltenham.[22]

In both Hong Kong and Cyprus, the British were experimenting with intelligence-gathering radar. At Hong Kong the main site was located three thousand feet up the precipitous cliffs of Tai Mo Shan in the New Territories. Operated jointly by the RAF's 117 Signals Unit and the Australians, it peered out into Chinese airspace, and its main purpose was 'to provide intelligence information for the UK, USA and Australia'.[23] Western aircraft regularly intruded over the border to generate an elint response from Chinese defences.[24] The site was constructed with great difficulty in 1957 and was operated continuously into the 1980s. By a heroic effort, cranes and lorries had moved materials up to the summit by means of what was little more than a jeep track. During construction a tenton crane had been lost over the edge, but fortunately the RAF driver leapt clear before the vehicle disappeared over the cliff. Later, the RAF Regiment, known as the 'Rock Apes', who guarded the base, lost two Land Rovers over the cliff. This prompted a local humorist to erect a sign at the base of the uphill trail that warned: 'Beware of Falling Rocks'.[25]

GCHQ does not seem to have broken much high-grade Chinese traffic; nevertheless, there were intelligence success stories. One of the most important was the prediction of the detonation of China's first nuclear weapon in 1964. Like all such programmes, China's efforts to acquire a nuclear weapon required a vast technical and industrial effort, therefore imagery from overflights together with relatively low-level signals gave a good indication of progress. Archie Potts, the UK's Deputy

Director of Atomic Energy Intelligence, noted that for about five years the British had been aware of an important secret programme controlled by 'a special ministry'. Plant construction had begun in 1958, with an elaborate effort to produce uranium ore. The Chinese had also ceased their public complaints about superpowers with nuclear weapons. All this prefaced China's first nuclear test.[26]

Although NSA viewed Hong Kong as Britain's single most valuable overseas sigint station, GCHQ placed more emphasis on the Middle East. Immediately after the war, Britain had numerous interception stations. The most important was at Heliopolis in Egypt, which boasted many civilian operators and took in much of the region's diplomatic traffic. The Army ran a large intercept station at Sarafand in Palestine, while the RAF ran a similar installation at RAF Habbaniya in Iraq. There were undercover listening stations buried within embassies and consulates in countries such as Turkey. By the 1950s Britain had also developed covert sites in northern Iran that were focused on Russia. However, the British Empire in the Middle East consisted of very few formal colonies and had long been an agglomeration of mandates, shaky treaty relationships and uncertain base rights granted by royalist regimes. Egypt, which had achieved independence in 1935, was especially anxious to divest itself of the disfiguring presence of British bases. Accordingly, British sigint gradually fell back towards its last proper colonial foothold in the region, the island of Cyprus.

Cyprus was increasingly the home for every kind of secret radio activity in the Middle East. This included not only Britain's sigint assets but also the monitoring sites of the CIA's Foreign Broadcast Information Service, which listened in to news broadcasts around the world. In addition, Cyprus offered a safe haven for Britain's overt and covert propaganda broadcasting in the region. This mushroomed during the premiership of Anthony Eden, who nurtured a special hatred of Egypt's nationalist leader General Gamal Abdel Nasser, whom he viewed as a dangerous dictator. Eden urged a reduction of British radio propaganda directed at the Soviets in favour of targeting Nasser.[27] As early as 1954 he insisted that a new broadcasting station in Aden covering Iraq and Syria was to receive 'first priority', since Nasser's radio station, The Voice of Egypt, was busily pouring out its own vitriolic message.[28] Britain's main radio weapon against Nasser was the SIS-owned station in Cyprus, Sharq el-Adna. 'Sharq' had originated as a wartime British propaganda radio station that had been taken over by SIS in 1948, and been evacuated from Palestine to the safety of Cyprus. It was soon thought to be the most popular station in the region.[29] SIS was working with John Rennie, the head of Britain's Information Research Department, to accelerate four other radio projects in the Middle East, including a secretive 'black station' that was being developed at two other sites on Cyprus with a transmitter that could reach as far as Aden.[30]

On 29 October 1956 Eden launched 'Operation Musketeer', a surprise attack to capture the Suez Canal, which Nasser had recently nationalised. Sigint and radio warfare had an important part to play. Arrangements were made for the force commanders to receive a range of key intelligence materials from national sources, including photo-reconnaissance cover and 'all CX [SIS] reports on Egypt', as well as material from 'special sources', a somewhat coy cover name for sigint. GCHQ attached liaison officers to the main Army, Navy and RAF commanders, and detailed instructions were generated to provide cover for the 'protection of SIGINT material'.[31] Most of the sigint coverage came from 2 Wireless Regiment at Ayios Nikolaos near Famagusta in eastern Cyprus, with additional help from listeners at Dingli on Malta. While the coverage was good, the radio channels available to push this material forward to field commanders were often choked. In addition, a small tactical 'Y' intercept unit was being prepared to accompany the land force from Cyprus to the landings in Egypt, and was eventually based at Port Said.[32]

The British not only had to hide the invasion preparations

from the Egyptians, but also from the Americans. Britain had engaged in an elaborate plot with the French and the Israelis which hid the real reasons for the intervention by presenting it as the arrival of a so-called 'peace-keeping' force for the disputed Suez Canal Zone. Eisenhower and his Secretary of State John Foster Dulles were astonished by Anglo–French–Israeli collusion over Suez. In the autumn of 1956 Washington's eyes were elsewhere, distracted by the uprising in Hungary, while in the Middle East its focus was on the possible break-up of Jordan and the likelihood of Israeli and Arab attempts to divide the spoils. American U-2 flights out of Turkey detected an Israeli mobilisation, but this was interpreted by some as part of Israeli ambitions on the West Bank. Allen Dulles, the Director of CIA, was tracking reports of an imminent coup in Syria.

Nevertheless, the ability of the British to hide 'Operation Musketeer' from NSA raises some interesting questions. What were American sigint liaison officers doing? During the Suez invasion there was a US Sixth Fleet exercise off Crete, yet American Naval intelligence conceded frankly that it had 'no warning of British intentions'.[33] Much of the story can be explained by NSA's obsessive focus on Russia, with the vast majority of its assets in locations such as Turkey looking north-wards to the missile-testing stations of the Caucasus. Meanwhile NSA depended on GCHQ for much of its coverage of the Middle East. Moreover, the crisis occurred just as the American code-breakers were moving to their new building at Fort Meade. The failure to spot the Suez Crisis had a significant effect on NSA, triggering a post-mortem and the creation of new divisions based on country or geographical lines.[34]

The British deliberately blanked their American allies. In a neat piece of choreography, the British Ambassador to Washington was replaced at this moment, with the new man being sent across the Atlantic by passenger liner. He was thus in mid-ocean when the Suez Crisis broke, and could not be accused of having deceived the Americans. In Tel Aviv, the British and French Military Attachés were told to give their

American counterpart a wide berth.[35] However, the American Military Attaché realised something was up when his civilian driver, a reservist in the Israeli Army who had only one arm, one leg and was blind in one eye, was suddenly recalled to duty. His American employer deduced – quite correctly – that if his driver was being mobilised it could only mean one thing: imminent war.[36]

The sharpest Americans knew something was afoot. On 12 September 1956 Robert Amory, Deputy Director for Intelligence at the CIA, set up a highly secret joint group from the CIA, NSA, the State Department and military intelligence to watch the Middle East round the clock.[37] Its main source of information was an expansion of the U-2 spy plane operations from Wiesbaden covering the Middle East. The CIA's own U-2 official history claims that this allowed them to predict the attack on Egypt three days before it took place.[38] This is probably an exaggeration: the U-2 evidence of growing forces on the ground was not precise enough to make such a forecast. Allen Dulles, the Director of the CIA, told Eisenhower he believed the Israelis were about to attack Jordan. Eisenhower attached special significance to NSA reports of an increase in signals traffic between Tel Aviv and Paris.[39] Almost certainly from sigint, the Americans had also picked up news of a secret meeting between the British Foreign Secretary, Selwyn Lloyd, and the French in Paris on or about 15 October. This was the very sensitive meeting that sealed the deal over the Suez invasion. Allen Dulles recalls: 'I remember I had a long talk with Foster [Dulles] about what this might mean in view of the fact that we were not otherwise informed about it.'[40] But Eisenhower personally dismissed the significance of the military build-up on Cyprus, refusing to believe that Britain would be 'stupid enough to be dragged into this'. Remarkably, six weeks after the invasion of Suez, many in the CIA were still uncertain whether the British had colluded directly with the Israelis.[41] Both NSA and the CIA had also failed to predict the Russian invasion of Hungary, so 1956 was not their best year.[42]

Deliberate American pressure on the pound eventually forced Britain's ignominious withdrawal from Suez, and contributed to Eden's sudden resignation in January 1957. Eden's foreign policy may have failed, but the intelligence support he received had been excellent. In the wake of Suez, Selwyn Lloyd wrote to Eric Jones, the Director of GCHQ, congratulating him on the torrents of Middle East intelligence that sigint had provided during the crisis, particularly after the seizure of the canal. 'I have observed the volume of material which has been produced by G.C.H.Q. relating to all the countries in the Middle East area,' he wrote, suggesting that the traffic of many countries was being read, and added: 'I am writing to let you know how valuable we have found this material and how much I appreciate the hard work and skill involved in its production.' Jones passed on these congratulations to units such as the Army's 2 Wireless Regiment on Cyprus and the RAF's 192 Squadron.[43] There had also been shipborne signals interception by the Royal Navy. The RAF airborne signals element was especially important during the invasion. The ageing RB-29 Washingtons had been despatched from Watton to map the characteristics of Egyptian anti-aircraft defence. This included the habit of shutting down air-defence radar routinely just after midday – a priceless piece of information.[44]

At a higher level, GCHQ read much of Cairo's diplomatic traffic with key embassies in the region during the mid-1950s, such as those in Amman and Damascus.[45] It also read traffic with Egypt's London Embassy.[46] No less importantly, GCHQ stepped up its watch on the Soviets. On 15 November 1956, Britain's leaders were reassured that there was 'still no evidence from signals intelligence sources of any large-scale Soviet preparations to intervene by force in the Middle East'.[47] However, there had been problems. Some of the newly civilianised sigint sites had complained about working round the clock during the crisis, causing managers to wonder about the wisdom of non-military intercept operations.[48]

*   *   *

Despite GCHQ's operational success, the Suez Crisis left a problematic legacy. It led directly to the eviction of GCHQ from some of its more valuable real estate in the Middle East and the Indian Ocean. In December 1956 GCHQ was just opening a large and well-equipped secret sigint station covering the Indian Ocean at Perkar on Ceylon, which had been constructed at a cost of close to £2 million. The Ceylonese government had wanted to free up access to the old sigint site at HMS Anderson for redevelopment. The purpose of the GCHQ site at Perkar was hidden from the Ceylonese, requiring the British to generate a cover story. Much debate had taken place in London over whether to let the Ceylonese Prime Minister, Solomon Bandaranaike, in on the real function of the station. GCHQ decided against candour, fearing 'leakage'.[49] British officials had always been convinced that 'the real purpose could be easily disguised'.[50]

Endless effort had gone into the Perkar site. By 1955 it had been upgraded to monitor signals traffic from 'all bearings', and boasted a vast aerial farm that covered more than four hundred acres.[51] Yet the Suez operation effectively destroyed this expensive new facility almost as soon as it was completed. The Ceylonese were incensed at Eden's imperial escapade, and believed the British had refuelled ships in Ceylon en route to the invasion of Egypt. They now demanded a schedule for the removal of all foreign bases, without exception. The Treasury was aghast, stating that even a brief visit to Ceylon 'brings home the complexity of these installations' and 'their vital importance'. Officials came up with the preposterous idea of using service personnel in civilian clothes in the hope of assuaging the Ceylonese.[52] Bandaranaike stamped his foot, insisting that all the British, however attired, had to go. A compromise was agreed: 'The GCHQ station can be given up entirely, but we should like to keep it in operation for five years.' Ultimately, Britain had lost the best site in the Indian Ocean.[53]

GCHQ felt the reverberations of Suez elsewhere. In Iraq, Britain enjoyed a good relationship with the ruler King Faisal. As a result, the British had been allowed to retain a number of bases. One of these was RAF Habbaniya, not far from Baghdad. Superficially this looked like so many military aerodromes in the Middle East, but in fact it housed 123 Signals Squadron, later 276 Signals Squadron, which ran a large sigint monitoring station. Airborne sigint flights from Habbaniya crossed into Iran, and then loitered over the Caspian Sea. However, as a result of Suez, Faisal's political situation deteriorated rapidly, with uprisings in the cities of Najaf and Hayy. Iraq's membership of the Baghdad Pact, a British-managed military alliance, only exacerbated popular hatred of the regime. Then, in the summer of 1958, Faisal's ally, King Hussein of Jordan, asked for military assistance during a growing crisis in the Lebanon. The Iraqi Army put together an expeditionary force, but in the early hours of 14 July 1958 the assembled column turned against its own supreme commander, marched right into Baghdad and carried out a coup. Revolutionary officers arrived at the Royal Palace at 8 o'clock in the morning and ordered the King, his immediate family and his personal servants into the courtyard. They were politely asked to turn away from their captors, whereupon they were machine-gunned. Most died instantly, but Faisal survived a few hours. Fortunately, GCHQ intercepts of Egyptian diplomatic traffic gave precise information about Nasser's parallel plots against the King of neighbouring Jordan a few days later, prompting timely British support for the beleaguered monarch.[54]

However, Britain's time in Iraq was now up, and the final departure from RAF Habbaniya was anything but orderly. The vast base had quickly been occupied by the Iraqi Fourth Armoured Division, and the British had even been denied access to their own signals installations and aerial farms. Most of the RAF's 276 Signals Unit were evacuated to temporary tented accommodation on Cyprus, where they continued their interception work amid terrible conditions. Three hundred personnel remained at Habbaniya, presiding over the residual technical facilities and stores. They were continually provoked by Iraqi forces, and it was not unusual for them to 'end up in the Iraqi guard room'. Although much of the radio equipment had been removed, the remnants included specialist signals vehicles, machine tools and fuel, together with the entire contents of a nearby RAF hospital.[55] The plan was for a massive 'end of empire' garage sale. Items from Habbaniya were offered to the new Ba'athist government. The Iraqi Army took the heavy weapons, explosives and ammunition, but were warned soberly that some of these were in 'a dangerous or doubtful condition'. What materials the Iraqi government did not want were then sold publicly. However, in the revolutionary climate, the ensuing auction was pure bedlam. Such was the shouting and violence that the petrified auctioneer tried to sell off the entire stock of the base as one lot. Another sale, of vehicles, was sabotaged by the appearance of a small but violent nationalist mob whose members held 'a rope noose . . . menacingly over the head of anybody who attempted to purchase' anything. The end of the British Empire is often portrayed as a serene process, but in the Middle East its passing was neither orderly nor pleasant.[56]

Cyprus was now a vast GCHQ refugee camp, holding sigint personnel who had made their exodus from the listening stations at Sarafand in Palestine, Heliopolis in Egypt, and now Habbaniya. Over a thousand found themselves in a tented encampment at RAF Pergamos.[57] A special signals unit was already at the forty-three-acre site, which was dominated by aerials, but the refugees from Habbaniya represented a further unscheduled expansion.[58] Pergamos and the Army station run by 2 Wireless Regiment (soon renamed 9 Signals Regiment) at Ayios Nikolaos now constituted the key sigint stations in the region, with over a thousand personnel. Further west, there was a British sigint station at Dingli on Malta with 230 staff, and a few dozen on Ascension Island and at Gibraltar; but Cyprus was the leviathan.[59] Negotiations over the exact extent of the Sovereign Base Areas on Cyprus were ongoing, but at least for the time being, relations with the island's authorities were relatively cordial.[60] The negotiations reached a climax in 1959. The British delegation, led by Julian Amery, Under-Secretary of State for the Colonies, started with an extravagant bid for four hundred square miles of territory, and eventually settled for ninety-nine square miles.[61] By this time the aerials and antennae of the largest sigint base on Cyprus, Ayios Nikolaos, had begun to encroach on the municipal area of Famagusta itself. The ruler of Cyprus, Archbishop Makarios, protested, and GCHQ agreed that it could retreat a little without serious damage to its operations.[62]

The main problem for GCHQ was that the two Cyprus Sovereign Base Areas were increasingly expensive to run. This partly reflected an ongoing insurgency by a guerrilla force known as EOKA, which wanted unification or *'enosis'* with Greece. Matters were made worse by the intense divisions between the Greek and Turkish communities on Cyprus. As a result, the security of the two sigint stations required a minimum land force garrison, including a heavy RAF presence. GCHQ's extensive aerial farms were also vulnerable to sabotage. However, once the Chiefs of Staff had accepted that the major bases 'must be retained because of the SIGINT facilities', other things followed. Typically, the RAF decided to keep its main regional stockpile of nuclear weapons, code-named 'Tuxedo', at Dhekelia. In other words, while the Cyprus garrison was not there solely for sigint, it was the sigint facilities that made it irreplaceable.[63] The periodic outbreaks of inter-communal strife on Cyprus led to questions from the Prime Minister, Sir Alec Douglas-Home, who asked in December 1963 whether Britain really needed bases there. Peter Thorneycroft, the Defence Secretary, responded with an unqualified yes, explaining that Cyprus 'houses most important SIGINT stations and it also provided a base from which special reconnaissance flights are carried out'. Thorneycroft said that while most of the other activities could be relocated, intelligence was the sticking point, since it was 'not considered that SIGINT facilities could be adequately replaced elsewhere'.[64]

The impact of GCHQ's work in the Middle East is best illustrated by the Yemen Civil War. This conflict had its origins in a coup by the leader of Yemen's republican faction, Abdullah as-Sallal, who overthrew the newly crowned Imam al-Badr in

1962. However, the Imam escaped and the royalist faction was soon receiving support from Saudi Arabia and, more covertly, from Britain, Jordan and Israel. Predictably, the republicans were supported by General Nasser, with perhaps seventy thousand Egyptian 'volunteers'. King Hussein of Jordan pressed London to intervene on behalf of the Imam, and an elaborate mercenary operation was developed, using both SIS and the SAS. Sigint not only gave a detailed picture of Egyptian troop deployments, but also revealed tensions between republican ministers and the Chief of Staff of the Egyptian armed forces. The British reportedly found breaking the codes of Egyptian forces in the field 'a bit of fun', and also had no difficulty in reading higher-level diplomatic traffic. GCHQ intercepts seem to have been important in October 1962, informing the JIC, and later the Cabinet, about the morale of the Egyptian troops. The Governor of neighbouring Aden, Sir Charles Johnstone, had suggested that this was low, but intercepts showed quite the reverse. This prefigured a long struggle with the Egyptian proxies which dragged on until 1970.[65]

The most decisive role played by sigint was during the 'Confrontation' between Indonesia and the British-backed Federation of Malaysia during the early 1960s. In fact the 'Confrontation' was an undeclared war which involved troops from Britain, Australia and New Zealand. President Sukarno of Indonesia had decided that Britain's creation of the Federation of Malaysia in 1962, which included parts of the island of Borneo, was an attempt to maintain a colonial presence by stealth and should be resisted. The first shots were fired in December 1962, when the Indonesian government attempted a coup against the Sultan of Brunei, an independent pro-British state on the island of Borneo. The Indonesians used a proxy force to try to capture the Sultan, and also attempted to seize Brunei's oilfields. The revolt was suppressed using Gurkhas flown in from Singapore, but it was a close-run thing. Had the Gurkhas arrived an hour later, the Sultan might have been captured and forced to abdicate. The Gurkhas had been slow in arriving because a British staff officer who loved paperwork had been laboriously recording the name of each man as he boarded the aircraft. Eventually, 'an angry Brigadier threw the movement papers onto the tarmac' and the rescue finally got under way.[66]

In early 1963, President Sukarno announced that he would step up the pace and pursue a policy of 'Konfrontasi' with Malaysia. By April, two thousand Indonesian 'volunteers', many of whom were commandos, were infiltrating into the neighbouring British colonies of Sarawak and Sabah in northern Borneo, and were soon clashing with units of Gurkhas. Buoyed up by their success, Indonesian troops actually attempted to raid the mainland of Malaysia in 1964. At this point the British government deployed the SAS, later assisted by similar special force units from Australia and New Zealand. By 1964 there were over ten thousand British and Commonwealth troops in Borneo. British soldiers were being awarded medals in a secret war that remained undeclared.[67]

Sigint assisted this clandestine conflict directly and decisively. Most importantly, it was used in a revolutionary new way in conjunction with special forces. In April 1964 the British commander in Borneo, General Walter Walker, was given permission to begin highly secret 'Claret' operations. These were counter-infiltrations across the border into the Indonesian territory of Kalimantan in southern Borneo, designed to take the war to the enemy. British forces were initially given permission to cross over the thousand-mile-long border into Kalimantan to a distance of three thousand yards. By 1965 this had been extended to twenty thousand yards.[68] Locating the enemy was the main challenge, and tactical sigint was used to provide accurate direction-finding on the elusive Indonesian jungle camps. Sigint operators would listen in to the Indonesian traffic to see if the Claret patrols had been picked up. On one occasion the operators listened in to the Indonesians as they prepared to ambush a Claret patrol, and were able to warn the intended victims, who then scooted back over the border. Tim Hardy, a Special Branch officer, recalls that the local British sigint teams had no difficulty intercepting Indonesian field pack radios, which were of Second World War vintage. Moreover, they used old-fashioned crystals to set the frequency, and 'in defiance of all military rules, these never changed'. As a result Indonesian field communications were an open book, and sigint was 'locking onto targets with pinpoint accuracy'. Hardy met SAS patrols coming back over the border accompanied by local Iban native trackers who carried 'gory trophy heads'.[69]

From February 1965 onwards the British troops engaged in little other than Claret special operations. Brigadier Bill Cheyne, the Director of Operations in Borneo, declared that 'CLARET operations so weakened the Indonesian resolve to fight that only their very best troops ventured into Sarawak latterly.' The number of incursions fell so dramatically by late 1965 – they became 'as rare as snakebite' – that it was a major event when one occurred. Cheyne considered the use of tactical sigint vital, and for security reasons even the special forces were not told of this secretive source. Instead, there were stories of human agent operations and 'other sources of intelligence to shelter behind'.[70] The top brass knew about it though, and Walter Walker, the British Commander in Chief, constantly praised the ability of sigint to pinpoint the enemy: 'Nine times out of ten we knew his every move and we brought him to battle long before he had reached a point from which he could mortar a village, let alone a town.'[71]

Britain had developed an extensive sigint station in Singapore, run jointly with Australia. However, much of the sigint effort during the Confrontation was undertaken locally by 651 Signals Troop, staffed by personnel on special detachment from 13 Signals Regiment, the main British Army sigint unit in Germany. They worked closely with 693 Signals Troop from Royal Australian Signals. Mixed units moved freely between bases at Singapore, Labuan and Kuching. Signals intelligence functioned at several levels. The main support to Claret operations came from local radio direction-finding and voice interception. Telephone tapping on the Indonesian side of the border was also very productive. Meanwhile, higher-level Indonesian diplomatic traffic was also being read in Singapore and at GCHQ at Cheltenham.[72] The result was 'high-grade intelligence that contributed significantly to the successful outcome of the conflict'.[73] Because of Australian worries about the disputed territory of West Irian, Indonesia remained Australia's main signals intelligence priority through the 1960s, even higher than Vietnam.[74]

By March 1965 the British government was asking how long the Confrontation would last. The Joint Intelligence Committee Far East, which included Brian Tovey from GCHQ, did its best to answer this. Sigint was a helpful indicator, since it showed that Sukarno was deploying large-scale units of the Indonesian Army's strategic reserve to Kalimantan, and further units seemed to be moving to Sumatra. All this suggested that Sukarno was not yet finished. Negotiations were getting nowhere, and the only serious rebellion inside Indonesia, on the island of Celebes, had suffered a setback. Sukarno was known to be ill, and optimistic officials hoped his death might be followed by an internal struggle between the Army and the Indonesian Communist Party. The intelligence from SIS was that 'Sukarno may die at any time. Without an operation he is unlikely to last more than a year.' In fact the Indonesian Premier seemed to be in alarmingly rude health, and the British Ambassador in Jakarta was sceptical about 'secret sources' on this subject.[75] Although there had been an abortive coup in September 1965, Sukarno was still clinging on, and by the end of the year the British Chiefs of Staff were considering serious military escalation, including much deeper Claret operations and commando raids into Sumatra.[76] The British effort now developed a significant naval component, with no less than a third of the entire British fleet deployed off Sumatra, often operating openly in Indonesian waters. Once again, signals intercepts were a crucial element in the naval campaign.[77]

Konfrontasi ended after Sukarno was replaced by General Suharto in 1966. Cheyne argued that this change was partly prompted by British military successes: 'Sukarno would not have been deposed except for his military failures in Borneo.' He added that once Sukarno had been overthrown, the Claret operations enabled Malaysia to negotiate from strength. Overall, he concluded, it was 'a brilliantly successful story'.[78]

For much of this period a stream of high-grade diplomatic sigint from Indonesia passed across the British Prime Minister Harold Wilson's desk, providing an accurate barometer of the thinking in the Indonesian capital of Jakarta.[79] For Denis Healey, Britain's Secretary for Defence, it was especially satisfying. On 30 May 1965 he had a conversation with the American Defense Secretary, Robert McNamara, and explained that Britain could not disengage from its commitments east of Suez until the Confrontation came to an end. McNamara had replied gloomily, 'It will not end.' But he was wrong.[80]

Although the Indonesians did not rumble the secret of sigint, they knew something was badly wrong. Senior officers believed that the British had some sort of special radar equipment that could track their patrols, and this was not a bad guess.[81] The success of sigint in Borneo offered a longer-term legacy. The British and Australians had developed a new kind of sigint that interfaced directly with special forces in real time. In 1966, when Australia sent a Task Force to Vietnam, this was accompanied by a similar signals intelligence unit.[82] The same tactics were deployed by Britain in Northern Ireland in the 1970s. This approach has since become more commonplace, with the Americans taking it to a new level with the elite Intelligence Support Activity created in the 1980s, which was mostly deployed against terrorists. Britain's new Special Reconnaissance Regiment, formed in 2004, continues the tradition with its units of 'suitcase men' who undertake short-range sigint, fully integrated with tactical operations. Few remember that the SAS–sigint partnership in the jungles of Borneo was its first proving ground.[83]

Blake, Bugs and the Berlin Tunnel

*. . . you cannot speak in the residences, town or country, put at
our disposal. Every room is 'wired'. You cannot speak in a car,
or train, or even outside the house if it be a small compound
or garden. There is a danger of the apparatus picking up what
you say.*
Harold Macmillan, diary of his official visit to Moscow,
February–March 1959[1]

Signals intelligence was delivering effective support to British
policy in the Third World during the 1950s and 1960s. The new
realm of elint was busy measuring radars and rockets around
the perimeter of the Soviet Union. However, GCHQ had stalled
badly against high-grade Soviet cyphers, the most prestigious
target. William Weisband's treachery in the 1940s had inflicted
severe damage on almost all available streams of Soviet communication. In 1952 GCHQ had been given a substantial tranche
of extra money to accelerate its work. Much of this had been
thrown at the 'Russian problem' in the hope of returning to
the glory days of Ultra, but the work went slowly. The code-
breakers were left grubbing their way through low-grade Soviet
administrative systems in the hope of picking up fragments of
useful information, or else reading Soviet intentions reflected
in the traffic of other countries that Moscow was conversing
with. Alternative routes to sigint on the Soviet Union were
badly needed.

This was a direct spur for the now famous tunnel operations
under Vienna and Berlin launched by Britain's SIS in partnership with the CIA. The CIA's own secret history of the Berlin
tunnel operation makes it clear that these schemes were a direct
response to the calamitous loss of sigint on Black Friday. 'As
early as 1948,' it noted, 'Intelligence Officers became interested

in the benefits to be derived from tapping Soviet and Satellite landlines on a scale not previously considered necessary. The loss of certain sources during this period created gaps in our intelligence coverage which were particularly unfortunate during this period of Cold War escalation.' By tapping into telephone lines, the West hoped to pick up sensitive voice traffic that the Soviets were not troubling to encrypt, because unlike messages sent by radio transmitter, underground landlines were thought to be inaccessible and therefore secure.[2]

The idea of tapping phone lines in Vienna and Berlin mirrored existing activities by the KGB. As early as October 1946, the British Control Commission in Germany had reviewed the twenty-two 'secrephones' or scrambler phones installed in Berlin for communication with the British Zone of Germany, and had found them wanting. The encypherment provided by the scrambler was weak, and with the telephone lines passing through the Soviet Zone, they were presumed to be tapped. Even within the British Zone, the military had been anxious about allowing Germans who worked in telephone exchanges to have access to military telephone directories, since this would give them a 'comprehensive guide to the most profitable extensions on which to listen in'. Only specially screened Germans were put to work in the telephone exchanges.[3]

Poor telephone security had the potential to blow high-grade British cyphers. For example, it had long been known that the direct telephone line between the British element of the Allied Commission for Austria and London was monitored by the Soviets, and in early February 1948 British intelligence had discovered that they were 'strengthening their interception arrangements'. The problem was that although officials in the British headquarters in Vienna were given continual security warnings, the officials they were talking to in London were less diligent. Frequently, telephone conversations were about agreeing the final text of a document, which was then sent by telegram in a high-grade cypher. For the Soviet code-breakers this was a gift, since they now had both the encyphered text and the clear text.[4] By 4 August 1949, John Bruce Lockhart, the head of SIS in Germany, was confident that the Soviets had '100% coverage of the telephone lines between Berlin and the Western Zones'.[5]

Predictably, SIS had already launched its own offensive activities. The first operation took place in Austria, which like Germany was under four-power occupation. In late 1948 an SIS officer at the Vienna station, Peter Lunn, happened to notice that the main telephone cables running under the British sector went out towards a major headquarters in the Soviet Zone. A twenty-foot tunnel code-named 'Conflict' was soon dug from a British police post to the underground cable, and an engineer was brought in from the Post Office Research Station at Dollis Hill to attach a tapping device. SIS was reluctant to tell the Foreign Office what it was doing, and so only informed the local Foreign Office Head of Mission, Harold Caccia. Conveniently, Caccia had recently been Chairman of the JIC, and so was favourably disposed. 'Conflict' was so successful that two other tunnels were dug, code-named 'Sugar' and 'Lord'. One reached out from the basement of a British-run jewellery store, the other from a villa in the suburbs of Vienna occupied by a British Army officer and his wife.[6]

The volume of illicit recordings and intercepts from these three tunnels was so great that SIS's Section N, which handled telephone transcripts from routine taps on foreign embassy telephones, was overwhelmed. SIS had to set up an entirely new section called 'Section Y' at 2 Carlton Gardens, just off Pall Mall, staffed partly by former East European exiles and with units for transcription, translation and analysis.[7] SIS was now desperate for Russian linguists, and brought together a motley crew. Some were retired British officers, going back as far as the Boer War. There were many émigré Poles, including a dashing cavalry officer with an eyepatch, and plenty of White Russians. They were joined by recent trainees in Russian, but the latter struggled with the language of the intercepts, which was not only very colloquial, but filled with obscenities. The lexicon that was eventually produced to assist the newcomers was classified 'Top Secret Obscene'.[8]

In 1953 Peter Lunn was chosen to head the vast SIS station in Berlin, housed in the splendid Olympic Stadium. Unsurprisingly, he soon decided to repeat his Viennese activities. This time full Foreign Office clearance was easy to obtain because of the flow of wonderful material already coming from Vienna. In contrast to Vienna, the Americans were invited in at the outset of the Berlin operation. This was partly because of a desire to share costs, but also because of the existence of an ideal building close to the Soviet telephone cables, located in the American sector.[9] The whole operation was a tightly compartmentalised Anglo–American affair. Few officers in the huge CIA or SIS stations in Berlin knew of the tunnel's existence, although back in London a CIA officer was made deputy head of Section Y, which specifically looked after the tunnel.[10] Berlin was a superb place to collect Soviet comint. Its phone lines carried communications not only to Moscow, but also Warsaw and Bucharest. Although the operation was complex, the underlying hope was that once in place, it might go on undisturbed for a long time.

SIS agents in the East Berlin Post Office provided maps of the locations of the cables, and in February 1954 digging began in earnest. Vitally important was the installation of the taps themselves, which consisted of heavy metal clips. This involved freezing the lines to prevent the interference being detected in the East, a ticklish phase that was again carried out by a special Dollis Hill Post Office research team. Finally, at the end of February 1955, the Berlin tunnel was operational. Elaborate anti-humidity barriers had to be erected to prevent damp affecting the electronics. The CIA maintained a small local unit for on-the-spot monitoring of circuits for the protection of the project and also to provide items of 'hot' intelligence for Berlin.[11]

The overall 'take' from the Berlin tunnel was vast, and far exceeded the capacity of any local monitoring. Some twenty-eight telegraphic circuits and 121 voice circuits were being monitored at any one time. Voice traffic was recorded on fifty thousand reels of magnetic tape, amounting to twenty-five tons of material. At the peak of operation the voice processing centre at Chester Terrace, overlooking Regent's Park in London, employed 317 people, and eventually 368,000 conversations were transcribed. The teletype processing centre employed a further 350 people. For each day of the tunnel's operation the output was four thousand feet of teletype messages. Western intelligence services considered it to be a key source of early warning of attack. There was excellent material on Khrushchev's denunciation of Stalin in 1956, and tantalising information about Soviet efforts to process uranium for their nuclear programme.[12] Several hundred officers of the KGB and of their sister service, the GRU or Soviet military intelligence, were also identified. The tunnel was exposed by the Soviets on 21 April 1956, little more than a year after its activation, as a result of the treachery of George Blake, an SIS officer working for the Soviets. Nevertheless, the processing of the vast haul of intelligence material the West had already captured went on until 30 September 1958.[13]

These gloomy subterranean activities shine a surprisingly bright light on the intelligence services of both East and West. In particular they illuminate a jealous rivalry. Some CIA officers have suggested that the British initially decided not to tell the Americans about their early tunnel operation in Vienna, and that SIS only came clean when the Americans arrived at the idea independently, forcing the British to reveal their own solo operation. Later, it has been claimed, the Americans failed to admit to the British that they could read certain types of the traffic taken from Berlin, using a technique called 'Tempest', which allowed them to hear the faint echoes of plain text as messages were tapped out on keyboards – although this story is unverified. What is quite clear is that while data was freely shared, its sheer volume sometimes defeated analysis. The quantity of traffic was immense. Overall, forty thousand hours of telephone conversations were recorded, and six million hours of teletype traffic were taken. Entire buildings full of translators battled to stay ahead of the wave, but inevitably fell behind.[14]

Astoundingly, this was partly because the CIA decided it would rather fall behind than work with its main rival, NSA. The CIA did not tell NSA about the Berlin tunnel. Indeed, it was running an entire rival sigint unit called 'Staff D' in parallel with its compatriots at Fort Meade, led by a code-breaker they had poached called Frank Rowlett.[15] NSA's Director, General Ralph Canine, first found out about the Berlin tunnel by reading of its exposure by the Soviets on the front page of the *New York Times* in late April 1956. He literally shouted with anger when he realised the extent of the CIA intrusion into what he considered to be NSA turf. The two chiefs, Allen Dulles and Canine, nurtured an intense personal dislike, and the bitterness between NSA and the CIA lasted for years.[16] Even in the 1970s the CIA still had numerous rival intercept operations spread around the world.[17]

Another person who was angered when the tunnel hit the headlines in April 1956 was the Berlin SIS Chief, Peter Lunn. The Western press hailed the tunnel as a brilliant intelligence success, and heaped praise on the CIA. Neither the Soviets nor the American newspapers mentioned the British, despite the fact that the tunnel was packed with their equipment. This was too much for Lunn, who assembled the whole staff of the Berlin SIS station and recounted the story from beginning to end.[18] Everybody seemed to love the so-called 'espionage tunnel'. In East Berlin, British officials reported, it had been 'turned into a major tourist attraction and scarcely a day passes without a delegation of one sort or another being conducted through it'.[19] In private, they noted, the Soviets admired the craftsmanship and the quality of the equipment.[20]

The Berlin tunnel is perhaps the most controversial intelligence operation of the 1950s. Much of the controversy stems from the fact that on 22 October 1953, even before its construction began, George Blake, an SIS officer working for the KGB as a double agent, was part of a team briefed about the planned tunnel. Blake had been captured by the North Koreans in 1950, and was recruited during his incarceration. On his release he had returned to duty and had been sent to work for Section Y, which was undertaking the tunnel operation. In early 1954 he handed over the complete plans of the tunnel to his KGB controller during a rendezvous on the top deck of a London bus. Yet, incredibly, despite this leak, the tunnel was still a success, and gathered good intelligence. The KGB had to allow the operation to continue uninterrupted in order to protect Blake's cover as a top 'agent in place'.[21] For the same reason, the KGB did not warn Eastern Bloc officials who were routing communications through Berlin. This included the GRU, which was responsible for Soviet Army intelligence operations. It decided that the tap would be endured for a year, and then 'accidentally' discovered in April 1956. In the meantime it passed out general security warnings to bureaucrats about using telephones, but to the KGB's dismay, most officials ignored them.[22] On the night of 21–22 April 1956, engineers in the East pretended to bump into the tunnel while repairing damage caused by heavy rain. Clearly there were other tunnels of this sort: recently declassified CIA documents reveal that in September 1953 'similar operations' (in the plural) were being 'conducted elsewhere'. Eventually, audacious operations of this kind were carried out by the West underneath Moscow itself.[23]

The KGB's selfish behaviour towards the GRU during the Berlin tunnel episode mirrored the attitude of the CIA towards NSA. Protection of its own security and its own sources was paramount. Unusually, in the Berlin tunnel episode, both sides could claim victory. The KGB successfully protected Blake until he was exposed by a Polish intelligence officer working for the Americans in 1959, while the West gained enormous quantities of data about its Eastern Bloc military opponents. Both sides were offered some reassurance against the possibility that its enemies were planning a surprise attack. In that sense at least, Cold War intelligence was neither fruitless nor necessarily a cause of increased tensions. Collectively, these operations calmed everyone's fears, and their most substantial benefits might be measured through greater stability and the perpetuation of an uneasy peace.[24]

Oddly, the Blake case seems to have helped, not harmed, Anglo–American intelligence relations, owing to the sensitive way it was handled by the Director of the CIA, Allen Dulles. On his retirement in September 1961, Dick White, the Chief of SIS, thanked Dulles for his generous attitude, saying: 'This was never more manifest than in your recent handling of the Blake case. I only hope that you yourself realise what a splendid impression you made upon us all by your magnanimity and understanding of our difficulties.' There were, White noted, many other incidents in which Dulles' intervention had 'restored trust and confidence between us'.[25] In fact, by this time the horrors of the Blake case had been overshadowed by the defection of William H. Martin and Bernon F. Mitchell, two American NSA civilians who turned up in the Soviet Union in August 1960. Mitchell was a distinctly odd person who had once admitted to sexually experimenting with dogs and chickens, but had still been allowed to pass his NSA vetting. After their defection, GCHQ was informed and the usual damage assessments were set in train. Although Martin and Mitchell blew a number of GCHQ's operations, and talked about them publicly at a Moscow press conference, the British reaction was muted. There was general relief that, for once, the defectors were not British-employed.[26]

The Berlin tunnel was part of a general explosion of bugging and telephone tapping in the 1950s. Both SIS and the KGB saw this as a way to get around the problem of highly secure encryption and listen in to the enemy. The Soviets led the way on bugging because of their long history of listening in on Western diplomatic premises in Moscow.[27] In July 1950 the Air Attaché at the British Embassy in Moscow was testing a wireless receiver when he heard the voice of the Naval Attaché, who was in a nearby room, broadcasting loud and clear. Despite a painstaking search, no bug could be found. The general opinion was that Russian employees within the Embassy had quickly removed it. Now the hunt was on, and the 'sweepers' who searched for bugs were busy all over Moscow. In January 1952 a microphone was found in the American Embassy. Then in September of the same year an American sweeper heard the voice of George Kennan, the American Ambassador, being transmitted, but no one could find the offending bug. Painstaking work with a British detector eventually located it.[28] Its sophistication stunned Western observers: it was a resonating device that required no external power supply, and so could remain in operation indefinitely. Consisting of a metal chamber about ten inches long, it transmitted when bombarded with microwaves from a nearby building and was hidden in a wooden model of the Great Seal of the United States which was on display in Kennan's office and which had been given to him by the Soviets as a present. In order to persuade the Soviets to activate the device, Kennan pretended to dictate a telegram, which enabled the sweepers to home in on it. Kennan recalls that he felt 'acutely conscious of the unseen presence'.[29]

The discovery of this microwave bug triggered alarm in London. On 9 October 1952 Churchill urged MI5 and SIS to 'take all necessary action', and told A.V. Alexander, his Defence Secretary, that the episode was 'most important' as it showed 'how far the Soviets have got in this complex sphere'. He ordered an active programme of research into both defensive security measures and offensive bugging techniques for Britain's own use. In the short term, MI5 busied itself protecting certain key rooms in Whitehall. Meanwhile, Sir Frederick Brundrett, the Chief Scientific Adviser at the Ministry of Defence, was asked to coordinate technical investigations into bugging possibilities for SIS, particularly with new transistor-based devices. Since the original find of an advanced Soviet bug in Britain's Moscow Embassy in 1950, three different scientists in Britain had already 'developed miniature devices which would transmit voices in the room in which they are. All the devices are different in principle from that discovered in Moscow.' It was now necessary to move from laboratory prototypes into the field, for Ministers in London called for 'devices suitable for offensive action by ourselves'.[30] By July 1954, Brundrett's group had four prototype bugs ready for field trials by SIS operatives.[31]

Why were the new audio bugs being rushed ahead, when the familiar and reliable techniques of telephone tapping had been around for years? One of the reasons is that Soviet telephone security discipline was good. George Blake illustrates this well with his recollections of the efforts of the SIS Y Section to tap Soviet and Chinese telephones during the Geneva Peace Conference of May 1954. This important conference sought a settlement to the wars in Korea and Vietnam, and set up the International Control Commission on Vietnam, consisting of observers from India, Poland and Canada. SIS sent a team to Geneva headed by Blake, with two translators, who worked with the enthusiastic support of the Swiss security service. They were set up in the suburbs of Geneva with two recording machines and a few desks. However, it was soon clear that no hot tips were going to reach Anthony Eden, the British Foreign Secretary, and his negotiating team: 'The Staff of the Communist delegations observed strict telephone security. They never discussed anything with even a remote bearing on their position and tactics at the negotiating table, or gave any inkling of what concessions they were prepared to make.' If such information was going to be scooped it was only going to happen when diplomats thought they were at a safe distance from a phone, which they had been trained to look upon as akin to a venomous serpent.[32]

The Y Section excursion to Geneva was far from valueless. SIS was amazed to see how the Soviet and Chinese Communist delegations dealt with each other on the basis of complete equality. No less interesting were the family conversations of the famously stern and unbending Soviet Foreign Minister, Vyacheslav Molotov. To the surprise of the secret listeners, Molotov enjoyed long and patient chats with his six-year-old grandson, who recounted his daily school activities. One evening Mrs Molotov complained that her best friend's son was having difficulty getting a place at Moscow University. 'Could he ring the rector and arrange it? Rather grudgingly, Molotov consented.'[33] One wonders if, at this point, Blake ever paused to reflect that the Soviet Communist system that he admired and the British system were really not so very different. SIS gathered plenty of such 'social intelligence', since Blake recalls that during the mid-1950s his unit also bugged Polish diplomatic premises in Brussels, the Soviet Embassy in Copenhagen, the Bulgarian Embassy in London and numerous locations in Cairo.[34]

The Soviets got some of their own back in late February 1959, when Prime Minister Harold Macmillan made an official visit to Moscow. He recorded his main impressions in his diary, noting for example that 'Mr Khrushchev is the <u>absolute</u> ruler of Russia and completely controls the situation.' He then added:

*

The second impression – dominating everything else – was the strange experience of being surrounded by friends and advisers . . . and yet being practically unable to communicate with them at all, by word or writing, except in one room in the Embassy in conditions of great discomfort, inside a plastic tent with a gramophone record playing continuously. This is because you cannot speak in the residences, town or country, put at our disposal. Every room is 'wired'. You cannot speak in a car, or train, or even outside the house if it be a small compound or garden. There is a danger of the apparatus picking up what you say.

*

Even in the British Embassy, Macmillan continued, the Soviet methods were so good and so unobtrusive that there could be 'no security'. He observed that diplomats who remained in Moscow a long time either gradually came to disregard the problem or became 'very irritable and nervy'. He concluded that no British Ambassador should endure this post for more than three years.[35]

Bugs and telephone taps were also being found by the Americans with increasing frequency. In early 1956, regular sweeping picked up bugs in the offices of the US Ambassadors in Tel Aviv and Belgrade. Something more troubling was found in the conference room at the headquarters of US Europe Command, the main forum where American plans for the defence of Europe were discussed. Sweepers were picking up sound emanations that suggested the room was compromised, but could not find any bugs. Then they checked the telephones in the headquarters. To their dismay, the first fourteen they examined 'were found to be equipped with jumper circuits which kept the telephones alive when the receivers remained in their cradles'. In other words, even when the telephones were not in use, they operated as active microphones, hoovering up all the sounds in their vicinity.[36] By 1960 more than a hundred devices had been found in American diplomatic premises in the Eastern Bloc. The response was to construct 'clean rooms', often containing an inner room made of Perspex, which was supposedly bug-proof.[37]

When Jackie Kennedy, the wife of the American President, met the Soviet leader Nikita Khrushchev during the Vienna Summit of 1961, they chatted amiably about the recent Soviet space programme and the emerging 'space race'. At this early stage, animals rather than humans were being sent into orbit. Khrushchev revealed that Strelka, a dog the Soviets had recently sent into space and returned safely to earth, had just produced puppies. Half-jokingly, Mrs Kennedy asked if she might have one of the puppies for her daughter Caroline. Some weeks later a puppy, called Pushinka (Fluffy), duly arrived at the White House, together with a photograph album of Moscow and a gold tea-set. The security men insisted on checking the puppy very thoroughly indeed, for fear that it had been implanted with miniature listening devices.[38] This seeming paranoia was not entirely without foundation. In May 1964, sensitive new equipment enabled the Americans to find bugs in almost every room in their Moscow Embassy, except for the specially constructed 'clean room'.[39]

*   *   *

Improbably, the sharp end of British bugging technology was the sleepy suburb of Borehamwood. Tucked away amongst the mock-Tudor dwellings of north London was a most peculiar Foreign Office factory employing four hundred people. The location was the small Chester Road Industrial Estate. Few of the local residents knew what happened here; they were only conscious of a twelve-foot-high barbed wire fence patrolled by aggressive Alsatian dogs.[40] In the mid-1950s the site was run by Lieutenant Colonel Robert Hornby, who had been chief engineer for a commercial radio company, Philco, before the war, and then head of the technical side of SIS's wartime Section VIII radio unit at Whaddon Hall.[41] The secret factory had been acquired on a lease taken out privately by Brigadier Gambier-Parry, who had transformed SIS's Section VIII into the Diplomatic Wireless Service, and was financed through private bank accounts.[42] Even Edward Bridges, one of the denizens of the British secret state, regarded this as 'a pretty queer sort of set-up'.[43] Although it was formally known as 'Department B', the intelligence officers who frequented the discreet factory at 4 Chester Road knew it simply as the 'bug shop'. Their work tended to reflect world events. The build-up to the Suez Crisis had resulted in a high demand for bugs, and in October 1956 officials noted, 'This year the Factory has been kept fully occupied because in addition to the forecast programme of production it has had many short term demands on it arising out of the political crisis in the Middle East.' To keep a steady flow of work they had also put in bids for outside work, such as development contracts for specialist comsec equipment required by the London Communications Security Agency.[44]

British eavesdropping received a boost in June 1957, when Dick White successfully pressed the Chiefs of Staff to assist with an accelerated programme of bugging Soviet premises. 'Orthodox methods of obtaining intelligence were particularly ineffective against totalitarian states,' he explained, because it was so hard to run human agents in these countries, 'and consequently some new method of "breaking through" was essential.' On the defensive side there was also the danger of falling behind the Soviets.

Roger Hollis, the Director General of MI5, was enthusiastic to make progress in this area, and noted that the costs would be modest compared to the possible gain. Much of the staff for this new effort would come from the Royal Naval Scientific Service, which worked closely with GCHQ.[45] By the summer of 1958, as a result of all this activity, the 'bug shop' at Borehamwood was undergoing further expansion.[46]

Offensive bugging brought SIS many scoops during the 1950s. However, bugging also presented a huge defensive problem, and by the late 1950s Britain was overwhelmed. The main defence force was the Foreign Office Technical Maintenance Service at Hanslope Park just outside Milton Keynes. This was the headquarters of a unit of sweepers who prowled around Britain's embassies searching for bugs, using electronic scanners that looked like brooms connected to a suitcase. However, the Soviets were 'devoting considerable scientific resources to developing new devices', and these could only be found with increased effort. Hitherto, only high-risk locations had been swept, but after the Suez Crisis it was felt that embassies in the Middle East and Africa needed more attention. By January 1957, bugs were turning up everywhere. 'Listening devices have been found in our Embassy in Spain, and there is evidence,' it was noted, 'that devices may have been planted on us in Sweden.' Moreover, Britain was receiving increasing requests to help allied governments with whom it was sharing sensitive material.[47]

SIS's knowledge of Soviet bugs came not only from physical examples, but also from the interrogation of German scientists who had been employed on bugging projects in Russia, and had excellent knowledge of the most advanced methods of electronic surveillance.[48] Embassies were the new front line in a bizarre battle that involved every conceivable kind of technical device. Here SIS and GCHQ were now working alongside other covert British groups whose activities still remain mysterious.[49]

10

Embassy Wars

This file shows the covert activities of the DWS [Diplomatic Wireless Service] which must not be revealed ...

D.H. Jones, Treasury, weeder's note on file[1]

In early April 1952 an off-duty MI5 'watcher' was alighting from a bus not far from London's Oxford Street when he spotted a regular surveillance target. This was Pavel Kuznetsov, notionally a 'Second Secretary' at the Soviet Embassy in Kensington, but in fact well known to be an intelligence officer. Whether he was KGB or GRU, MI5 was not sure. It had mounted routine surveillance on him, but his tradecraft was good and he often gave the watchers the slip. Today, confident he was not being tailed, he was in animated conversation with an unknown British person. The MI5 watcher duly followed discreetly and reported all he had seen. Soon a major surveillance operation on Kuznetsov was launched. The British were about to receive a very direct warning of how keen Moscow was to penetrate their cyphers.

MI5 employed over a hundred 'watchers', who mostly supported its counter-espionage branch – known as B Division. Their task was to follow Soviet intelligence officers as they moved around London in what was often an elaborate game of cat and mouse. A key objective was to identify the British people the KGB contacted, in the certain knowledge that some of them would be engaged in espionage. Accordingly, on 25 April 1952, a team of MI5 watchers were waiting for Pavel Kuznetsov as he left his house. A lengthy pursuit developed. Kuznetsov was obviously going to great lengths to 'dry-clean' himself of any surveillance.

His greatest ally was the familiar red Routemaster bus: his preferred technique was to stand on the open platform at the back of the bus, allowing him to jump on and off unexpectedly, putting the MI5 team through their paces. The watchers noted that it would have been 'sheer folly' to board the same buses as Kuznetsov, so they followed standard MI5 procedure and tried to use taxis, but on this day there were none to be found. Nevertheless, they followed Kuznetsov as he traced a circuitous journey through the West End, using four different buses and eventually heading out through Hammersmith towards Kew Gardens.

All morning, Kuznetsov was ahead of them. MI5 took the bus after his to Mortlake, but the experienced KGB field officer had outwitted them. Dispirited after frantically searching the streets, they moved on, again by bus, with little hope of finding their elusive target. To their amazement, as they passed through Richmond, Kuznetsov boarded their bus. The jubilant watchers recounted: 'He came aboard and sat not very far away panting and breathing heavily . . . shaking off his pursuers was indeed most strenuous work.' He got off at Marble Hill Park in Twickenham. After a period of calculated inactivity reading the newspaper on a park bench to watch out for pursuers, he made various 'excursions into back streets' before boarding yet another bus to Kingston-upon-Thames in Surrey. Here he finally met with a nervous-looking figure outside the Century-Elite cinema in Kingston High Street. The British man was in his twenties, with a pinched face, dressed in a mackintosh and distinctive yellow socks. The pair went for a meal in the café of Bentalls department store. Afterwards they walked to a secluded part of Canbury Gardens, where they would be able to see anyone who approached, and so felt safe enough to exchange information. The unknown man produced a large sheet of paper from his inside pocket, and Kutznetsov took detailed notes for an hour and a half. Whenever a passer-by approached they put their papers away. Kuznetsov's MI5 followers were still watching.[2]

When the clandestine meeting in Kingston finished, MI5's task had only just begun. The crucial part of the operation was to follow Kuznetsov's unknown British contact, to identify who was passing information to the KGB. The man had no street-craft, and was easily tailed to an address in Elborough Street at Earlsfield in Wandsworth. MI5 kept watch, and also engaged in letter interception. The contact was soon revealed to be William Marshall, a Radio Operator for the Diplomatic Wireless Service (DWS), the radio network at Hanslope Park that the Foreign Office had inherited from SIS at the end of the war.[3] Although Marshall had only joined the DWS in November 1948, he had undertaken some interesting work. Having been trained in the Royal Signals immediately after the war, he did eight months of duty at Hanslope and was then sent to the British Embassy in Cairo. SIS had just moved its offices, including its transmitters, from the Cairo Embassy to the military headquarters at Ismailia. Because SIS was short of Radio Operators, DWS lent it three of its people, including Marshall. His next posting was the British Embassy in Moscow, where he spent a year between December 1950 and December 1951.[4]

Marshall had almost certainly been recruited by the KGB during his sojourn in Moscow. The Security Department of the Foreign Office, run by William Carey-Foster, began to make background enquiries. Carey-Foster asked British diplomats in Moscow for information, asking whether there was anything odd about Marshall. One of the diplomats there offered a frank and revealing reply:

*

Marshall was a perfect example of the type who should not be sent here. He was an introvert, anti-social to a degree I have never seen before. At staff cocktail parties he would be found in a corner behind a screen, if he turned up at all, or in some other obscure spot. He was most difficult to draw into conversation, and he had a meanness which it would be difficult to surpass. If asked to give a cigarette to a colleague, he would ask for a cigarette back the following day.

*

His main interests were embroidery and documentary films. Although there were doubts about his mental state, his managers did not have security concerns about him until his very last day in Moscow, when, having completed the DWS Radio Operator's standard tour of twelve months, he was being sent home by the evening train via Leningrad. He was relieved of his duties in order to pack, but went missing for most of the day. It transpired that he spent the entire day in Moscow. When challenged about what he had been doing, he answered evasively.[5]

One of MI5's worries was that Marshall might have gleaned sensitive information about intelligence and security activities that were under way at Britain's Moscow Embassy. However, Lambert Titchner, one of the diplomats there, thought it unlikely that he had picked up anything about the recent KGB bugging of the British Naval Attaché's office. Most importantly, the diplomats did not think he knew anything about the offensive sigint work DWS conducted from the Moscow Embassy on behalf of GCHQ, which was referred to coyly as 'the watch on high-frequency wave-lengths'. This was partly because they had judged him to be of low intelligence, and uninformed about secret matters generally. This proved to be a miscalculation.[6]

It turned out that Marshall was in London on leave visiting his parents in Southwell. Having returned from his tour in Moscow, he was working on a routine radio watch at Hanslope. Like most operators he was living in a DWS hostel at Bletchley Park which housed about seventy staff. The canteen and the hostel were used by both normal DWS Radio Operators and SIS operators.

MI5 met Brigadier Richard Gambier-Parry, the head of DWS, and made arrangements to search Marshall's room at the hostel and to receive notification of when he had enough time off to meet his KGB contacts. On 19 May 1952, MI5 tried to watch a further rendezvous between him and Kuznetsov when they met for lunch in a pub called the Dog and Fox in Wimbledon village. Kuznetsov was 'very much on the alert' for watchers, engaging in his usual counter-surveillance antics of running hard for buses and scrambling aboard, making him hard to tail.[7]

There were other attempted meetings around south-west London at which MI5 thought Kuznetsov was even more aware of surveillance. Marshall was also developing his fieldcraft, and on one occasion he artfully evaded his MI5 tail by boarding an underground train at Euston, then jumping off just as the doors closed.[8] MI5 had to accept that the pair had probably managed several meetings they were unaware of, and wondered what secrets Marshall was handing over.

On 10 June it was decided to arrest the pair at their next meeting, in the hope that they would be in possession of compromising documents, which would make a prosecution easier.[9] The next day, Anthony Simkin from MI5 spoke with Colonel Ted Maltby, the deputy head of DWS at Hanslope Park. They knew Marshall was about to go on a few days' leave in London, and Simkin asked if the DWS could 'put out a document that would appeal to Marshall'. As bait, they chose a booklet giving new DWS frequencies and call signs.[10] On 13 June Marshall and Kuznetsov were arrested by Chief Inspector Hughes of the Special Branch as they met in a park in Wandsworth. They were taken to Wandsworth Police Station, and there was delight all round as they proved to be carrying a wealth of incriminating material, including the deliberately proffered frequencies booklet. Kuznetsov was supposed to enjoy diplomatic immunity, but in their excitement the police did not listen to his protests and put him in a cell to cool off.

On 15 June, Dick White went in person to Chartwell, Winston Churchill's private residence, to brief him about the case. The Prime Minister was recovering from illness, and received White in his pyjamas, sitting up in bed. White emphasised that this was not an isolated case, and that MI5 knew the Soviets had been 'very active in regard to British personnel in our Mission in Moscow'. He explained that when Kuznetsov was arrested he was found to be carrying a notebook 'in which were entered the index numbers of the cars used by our shadowing organisation', which the MI5 watchers believed showed his status as a 'professional espionage agent'.[11]

The incriminating paperwork was vital. Although Marshall was grilled by William Skardon, MI5's best interrogator, he did not give much away. He was certainly not going to confess. Proving that he had had meetings with Soviet agents was one thing, but producing hard evidence of espionage was the key. When MI5 shared their information with the Americans, they immediately asked the right question: namely, what evidence did the British have that could be produced in court? MI5 was pretty confident that the cypher material Marshall had been caught with would be enough, but it was busy hunting for more. The results of its enquiries were suggesting that Marshall was attracted to Communism even before he went to Moscow. A search of his room at Bletchley Park had produced Communist literature, including a copy of *From Trotsky to Tito* by James Klugman, a leading Cambridge Marxist and friend of Anthony Blunt.[12] The head of the Foreign Office Security Department, William Carey-Foster, had been casually strolling around Bletchley asking questions. Remarkably, he had discovered that when Marshall was first working at Hanslope Park in 1948 he used to buy the *Daily Worker*, the newspaper of the British Communist Party, every day from Turner's newsagents in the village, which was close to his lodgings at Bletchley Park. Apparently he confidentially arranged with the staff in the newsagents for the paper 'to be handed to him in such a way that his colleagues would not become aware of his interest'.[13]

Further surprises awaited MI5. On 20 June it held a meeting with Brigadier Gambier-Parry of DWS at Leconfield House, the MI5 headquarters in London, to discuss protecting sensitive information during the coming court case. Some of the papers found in Marshall's possession at the time of his arrest referred to especially secret SIS radio links used to contact its Moscow station. The assembled company were amazed by this, since Marshall should not have been able to come across such things in the course of his duties. Gambier-Parry was accompanied by Army sigint officers who explained that they were liaising closely with Eric Jones, the new Director of GCHQ. They were very concerned that Marshall's defence material in court might make 'reference to techniques such as those used by G.C.H.Q.', and explained that during his time in the Royal Signals between 1946 and 1948 he was 'engaged in the Middle East on "intercept duties" '. Jones urged that every effort be made to prevent this coming out in court. Remarkably, up until this point GCHQ had chosen to tell MI5 absolutely nothing about Marshall's earlier work on sigint.[14] A few days later, Foreign Secretary Anthony Eden tried to assure Churchill that Marshall was not important, omitting any mention of the fact that he had been a sigint operator.[15]

Security officials now began to probe Britain's Moscow Embassy. Clearly already sympathetic towards Communism when he arrived in Moscow in 1950, it seems Marshall had become enamoured of Nina Michailovna Gredjeva, a Russian domestic who waited tables in the Junior Mess in the Moscow Embassy, where he ate. MI5 already knew of this woman, who was considered attractive and had been instrumental in an attempt made by the Soviets to subvert another member of the DWS in Moscow, Leonard Douglas Ker, who eventually blew the whistle and notified his superiors.[16] It was widely assumed that she was a KGB 'swallow', an agent who specialised in using her personal charms to recruit foreign diplomatic officials. In any case, MI5 concluded that Soviet intelligence would have had 'numerous opportunities to earmark, approach and recruit Marshall during his tour in Moscow'.[17] Contrary to the assertions of senior diplomats that Marshall was a loner, in fact he appeared to have had a close circle of like-minded friends in Moscow, including Jack Howarth, the Chancery Messenger, and Anthony Hibberson, another Radio Operator.[18] Hibberson later told MI5 that he was aware that Marshall 'had an unusually large number of books on sex matters in his possession'; indeed he had been grateful to borrow some himself. However, he felt obliged to make the firm assertion that he 'did not consider that Marshall was a practising pervert of any kind', and did not feel that this had any bearing on the case.[19]

In June 1952 Marshall was tried at the Old Bailey. His plea

of guilty ensured that there was no exposure of embarrassing sigint secrets, and the grateful authorities sentenced him to a lenient five years' imprisonment.[20]

The Marshall case underlines the fact that the Soviets were almost certainly aware of the British practice of using DWS operators as an extended arm of GCHQ to undertake short-range monitoring of communications from embassies.[21] Unsurprisingly, the KGB was busy doing the same thing in London. Remarkably, one of Moscow's most valuable sigint assets in post-war Europe was not small or hidden, but was clear for all to see. During the Second World War, permission had been given for the Soviet TASS News Agency to construct a 'radio monitoring station' on the northern fringes of London. This occupied 13 Oakleigh Park North, Whetstone, only a stone's throw away from the Foreign Office 'bug shop' in nearby Borehamwood. The station, with its substantial aerial farm, was still in operation in July 1951. Moreover, as a TASS Agency site it enjoyed full diplomatic immunity.[22] Incredibly, Britain had provided the Soviets with a large sigint site from which they could conduct, with complete immunity, the illicit study of radio systems, including those connected with the air defence of London. From Whetstone they could capture far more traffic than from the Soviet Embassy in the centre of London.

John Slessor, the Chief of the Air Staff, was especially agitated, and declared that Britain was 'gratuitously presenting our potential enemy with . . . information which he could not obtain from any number of spies'. Slessor wanted the station closed down, but the Foreign Office and MI5 could not agree on how much evidence of illicit activity they had, or what legal action could be taken. Elint and radio warfare units from RAF Watton had been used to jam the station during a major RAF air exercise in the summer of 1951. 'It is absolutely fantastic,' Slessor fulminated, that 'we should continue to present the Soviets on a plate with the opportunity of learning such vital defence secrets.'[23] Remarkably, Sir Percy Sillitoe, the Director of MI5, had discovered that some of the twenty-nine staff labouring away at the monitoring station were British nationals employed by the Soviets.[24]

In early August 1951 the Cabinet Defence Committee bit the bullet and decided that the station had to go. The Soviets resisted, arguing that they had been given a special dispensation to run it by none other than King George VI in 1941. Diplomats found it more than a little amusing that Russian Communists should fall back on arguments derived from royal prerogative. The Permanent Under-Secretary's department that superintended intelligence affairs in the Foreign Office finally decided that protocol and law were no longer an impediment, and that the important thing was to shut the station down.[25] Firm orders to depart were issued to the Soviets at the end of August, but they dragged their heels, only winding up their operations in September when threatened with 'forcible action'.[26] However, they also had a residence in Ealing, and worries about 'forward interception' by the KGB from this site continued into the late 1950s.[27]

West London was also the site of a new organisation created to protect British cyphers. When GCHQ moved to Cheltenham in late 1952, much of the technical business of cypher security remained at Eastcote. Fearsome rows developed with the armed services, which complained about delays in the production of cypher equipment and scrambler phones, as well as their poor quality. T.R.W. Burton-Miller, who was in charge of communications security, had done his best to achieve good relations with the military. However, in 1953 many felt it was better to make a fresh start by creating a completely new service, the London Communications Security Agency (LCSA). This decision to separate communications security and sigint was controversial, but it was backed by the new GCHQ Director, Eric Jones, and one of his key subordinates, Joe Hooper.[28]

LCSA was effectively Britain's fourth secret service, the technical security equivalent of MI5. Its main task was to develop new and very secure cypher machines to produce better codes in the hope of thwarting the Soviet sigint services. Although it existed for nearly two decades, almost nothing is known about it. Its first chief was Major General William Penney, who had been Mountbatten's Director of Intelligence in South-East Asia. Penney was familiar with sigint, but was definitely an outsider. While the technical staff for communications security remained at Eastcote and nearby Northwood Hills, Penney and his senior officers moved into new premises at 8 Palmer Street, which doubled as GCHQ's London office. Palmer Street was close to one of the oldest underground stations in London, St James's Park, and to many of the embassies. Indeed, the warren of tunnels from the ancient station that ran under the LCSA building soon gave rise to stories of secret passages and hidden basement facilities.[29]

At obscure locations such as Palmer Street and Hanslope Park, communications security experts were at the forefront of secret battles between the embassies. DWS was both an offensive and a defensive organisation, and was admired for what officials called its 'buccaneering' spirit.[30] As the Marshall case had revealed, many of its operators acted as forward collectors for GCHQ, and one of its larger post-war stations, in Stockholm, was often referred to as a GCHQ site.[31] In fact, DWS combined a multitude of curious tasks that were at the gritty interface of technical and human espionage or counter-espionage. By 1952 they shared accommodation with the sweepers at Hanslope Park. The old manor house was now surrounded by an unsightly penumbra consisting of forty nissen huts and concrete bunkers on each side of the drive leading up to the main building. There were acres of wireless masts, serving both SIS and the radio nets for the mainstream Foreign Office. All sorts of interesting things went on there. A visiting MI5 officer noted that the outlying huts and bunkers were a research and development centre for many secret devices. 'Those near the manor and to one side of it are used for research into offensive and defensive microphone techniques. Several near the end of the drive are used for the construction, testing and development of M.I.6 agent sets.'[32]

'Buccaneering' was the right term for this kind of work. In the late 1950s and early 1960s, a new task for Britain's communications security experts was protecting embassy code rooms against piratical raids by the enemy. The most sophisticated plot was launched by the KGB in Moscow in the autumn of 1964, when a low-frequency radio beam was used to induce a malfunction in a teleprinter in the code room of the British Embassy, causing a small fire.[33] Roderic Braithwaite, one of Britain's most senior intelligence officials, recalls that within minutes the building was 'surrounded by alleged Soviet firemen'; however, it was 'pretty obvious that some of these people were not firemen at all'. They were in fact bugging technicians from the KGB's sigint department, the highly secret Eighth Directorate. The Ambassador, Humphrey Trevelyan, was called out of a performance by the visiting English National Opera at a Moscow theatre.[34] He arrived at the Embassy to discover that the valiant British code-room staff had barricaded the door and were successfully fighting off the 'furious' KGB firemen, while others tried to extinguish the fire. One of the KGB officers recalls that it was 'a real Mexican stand-off'. Privately, the KGB sigint team were enormously impressed by this dedication to duty, and one of them later declared that it was a wonderful display of 'British stiff upper lip'. When the code room was rebuilt all the materials, including the bricks and concrete, were brought out from Britain, sealed and guarded in diplomatic trucks.[35]

There were even more serious problems for British diplomats in Mao Tse-tung's China. The country was undergoing a vast political convulsion known as the 'Cultural Revolution', a frenzy of extreme – almost anarchic – activity by radical student groups and self-appointed 'Red Guards'. In August 1967 they began attacking and ransacking diplomatic premises, including the British Embassy in Peking. Percy Cradock, the Ambassador, remembers the mob banging on the Embassy windows shouting

'Kill! Kill!' At one point the whole Embassy staff thought they were going to be burned with petrol, but in the event they were merely pulled out of the building and beaten. 'I was swept along by the mob,' recounts Cradock, 'and beaten mainly about the shoulders and back.' After they were released the staff were able to destroy classified papers that had survived in one of the strong rooms. The Foreign Office security specialists had provided them with 'a remarkable chemical compound' in the form of a powder that apparently only needed to be scattered on the files and left for a period in order to reduce them to ashes. They followed the instructions on the tin, and retreated to a safe distance:

*

Unfortunately when we returned we found the files neatly charred around the edges, rather like funeral stationery, but still perfectly legible. And there was a side effect of which we had not been warned: powerful tenacious fumes had been generated, turning the strong-room into an effective gas-chamber.[36]

*

The files were eventually taken out and burned by hand. However, the staff had been unable to protect the Embassy Communications Centre, which contained cypher machines and materials. Only the generators survived intact.[37] Mingled in with the revolutionary mob was a specialist team of Chinese code experts. An SIS officer stationed in Peking at the time recalls: 'They knew exactly what they were looking for.'[38] Communications security experts in London later confirmed the Chinese success, lamenting that they had acquired a Rockex, one of Britain's top-grade post-war cypher machines.[39]

Following this attack, Britain routed its classified telegram traffic to Peking through the nearby French Embassy. Although the French were 'simply splendid', the duty cypher clerks at the Quai d'Orsay in Paris struggled with the high volume of daily traffic. The British also recognised that the French were 'scared stiff of a leak', which might trigger Chinese revolutionary action against their Embassy in Peking. British Embassy staff in Paris, who were part of the new conduit for telegrams to London, took the precaution of never mentioning the matter on the telephone line between Paris and London, even though '(as far as we know) only the French authorities are likely to have tapped it'. The real problem was *which* Frenchmen knew about the back-channel arrangement. It turned out that even the President had not been told, so the French diplomats were 'apprehensive of the resentment as much of General de Gaulle as of Chairman Mao'.[40]

The Americans had suffered a similar code-room raid in Taiwan ten years before. There had been a riot outside their Embassy in Taipei, which had been penetrated. Cryptographic material had been taken after 'the walls of the code room were broken through with sledgehammers'. Some one hundred rotors for cypher machines were also taken, although many were later recovered from the Embassy grounds after the intruders fled. No one had believed that the Embassy code room would be penetrated until it was too late to destroy the cryptographic equipment. While the cypher team claimed that they had locked the safe containing the crucial rotors, the evidence indicated that in fact they had not done so, since the safe was open but showed no sign of damage.[41]

All new buildings, whether embassies abroad or intelligence headquarters at home, were now a massive communications security headache for both the British and the Americans.[42] When SIS moved from Broadway Buildings near St James's Park to its new tower-block site at Century House in Westminster Road in 1966, about a quarter of the refurbishment costs were for communications security work, including soundproofing and double windows.[43] Even worse was the problem of new embassy buildings in Communist countries. The gradual thawing of the Cold War in the 1960s, followed by a process of 'détente', led to the British recognition of East Germany. All of a sudden there was a need to develop a new British Embassy in East Berlin.

From the outset it was assumed that this building would be a major target for the East German Intelligence Service, which was known to use the most sophisticated technical devices.[44]

James Reeve, the Ambassador Designate, was given the task of locating a suitable building for the new embassy, his choice governed largely by communications security anxieties. Accommodation was in short supply in East Berlin, and to his dismay the only premises that would fit the bill were an apartment block fronted by a rather garish shop selling ladies' lingerie. Reeve feared that the placing of one of Her Majesty's Embassies over such an establishment 'would doubtless attract amused comment if not criticism'. Nevertheless, security ruled all, and work on converting the upper floors of the building into an embassy went ahead. Reeve recalls:

*

While this preparatory building work was underway, we had no doubt that various pieces of spying equipment such as fibre optics and listening devices were also being installed. Our own installation of physical security and alarm systems at the Embassy, as well as the construction of an inner-casing sound-insulated conference room, were undertaken by direct British labour with the material brought across from West Berlin.

*

The shell of the specially insulated conference room required several tons of cement. Reeve hoped fervently that the administrators of the building had given the correct load-bearing figures for the floors, 'or otherwise the lingerie shop below would be in for a surprise'.[45]

A team of nine technicians had made their way from Hanslope Park to the construction site in East Berlin.[46] Months of hard work lay ahead. Dealing with the bugging threat was the major task, and the first stage was for all the old communications wiring to be stripped out of the building from the second floor up.[47] They then created a temporary room that was impervious to radio waves, called a 'Belling Lee', to shield their cypher equipment, before building a more permanent shielded cypher room. They also installed a 'cocktail noise'-generating system to block surveillance devices, and supervised the construction of the secure conference facility, which they called the 'speech safe room'.[48] After the ransacking of the cypher room in the Peking Embassy in 1967, they worried that the building might be quickly overrun by an orchestrated riot, so they provided cypher-equipment destruction kits.[49] Despite all these elaborate precautions, James Reeve recalls that there were still moments during his tour of service in Berlin that reminded him of what he delicately called 'the need for circumspection in office conversation'. One day he was about to head out to a meeting at the East German Ministry of Foreign Affairs. At the very last moment he decided to take an expanded delegation of five colleagues, rather than the previously announced team of three. When they arrived, a tray with five coffee cups was already waiting for them.[50]

Embassy wars – a feverish battle with bugs and telephone taps – were a dominant theme that connected the 1950s and the 1960s. Over a period of twenty years, diplomatic missions ceased to be elegant salons peacefully advancing their nations' interests and were gradually transformed into technical fortresses from which espionage was both launched and repelled. Ironically, as the Cold War moved from a period of intense hostility, symbolised by figures such as Stalin, towards the possibility of détente under a new generation of leaders such as Khrushchev, the increased diplomatic interaction between East and West only offered yet more possibilities for electronic espionage.

Other important changes were now visible. In the 1950s, GCHQ's Director Eric Jones had enjoyed tremendous success in the new field of elint, often as the result of daring operations that pushed submarines and aircraft to their very limit. In the 1960s his successor, Clive Loehnis, faced new challenges. Aircraft and submarines were still important, but looked increasingly vulnerable. Meanwhile, computers and satellites were coming to the fore as the new wonder weapons of high-tech espionage. GCHQ's partners in America were running a billion-dollar business, and the code-breakers of Cheltenham were anxiously wondering how they would manage to keep up.

THE 1960s

SPACE, SPY SHIPS
AND SCANDALS

Harold Macmillan – Shootdowns, Cyphers and Spending

It seems to me these things may become very dangerous.
Prime Minister Harold Macmillan to Foreign Secretary
Alec Douglas-Home, 1 August 1960[1]

At 8 o'clock on the morning of 1 May 1960, Captain Igor Mentyukov was standing quietly at a bus stop in the small town of Perm, two hundred miles north of Sverdlovsk in central Russia. Mentyukov was a top fighter pilot – but there was no flying scheduled today, since this was May Day, a major holiday for all the Soviet people. Quite unexpectedly, one of the ground crew from the nearby airbase rushed up and told him to report for immediate action. An American U-2 spy plane was even now heading in their direction, and the orders from Soviet Air Defence Command were to shoot it down. Minutes later, arriving breathless alongside a Sukhoi SU-9 fighter, the latest model to enter service, Mentyukov was dismayed to discover that it was unarmed. His commander explained apologetically that there had not been time to load any ammunition or missiles. Moscow was now insisting that he take off immediately in civilian clothes and ram the intruder. 'Take care of my wife and mother,' he muttered glumly in the last moments before take-off.[2]

His target was a CIA U-2 spy plane, piloted by Gary Powers. The U-2 was effectively a rocket-powered glider that was capable of cruising at over seventy thousand feet, making it immune to air defences, and was used to collect both photography and sigint over Russia. The U-2 had entered service in 1956, and its pilots had flown more than twenty successful missions; however, Soviet technology was catching up. Mentyukov's new SU-9 fighter engaged afterburners from the moment of take-off, turning it into a veritable rocket. When he finished his momentous climb he was very close to Powers, but his high speed caused him to overshoot. Somewhat relieved to find that he was already perilously low on fuel, he was excused the more demanding part of his mission and was ordered back to base.[3]

About ten minutes later, Powers came within range of a Soviet surface-to-air missile battery. Three missiles were launched. One missed its target, the second destroyed a hapless Soviet MiG-19 that was speeding towards the intruder, but the third exploded just under the U-2, badly damaging its tail and sending it into a spin. Powers made an inelegant exit from the doomed aircraft, failed to press the self-destruct mechanism that would have destroyed its cameras, and was saved by his parachute, which deployed automatically. Later that day the Soviet leader, Nikita Khrushchev, was delighted to discover that not only was the U-2 largely intact, but its pilot had been captured alive. President Eisenhower was unaware of this, and blundered by offering the public a preposterous cover story about a weather research mission – which was soon revealed to be a sham.[4]

The U-2 overflight programme, which had included six British RAF pilots, was intimately connected to sigint. Not only did the aircraft collect sigint as well as imagery, but most of the targets they were probing had been initially found by sigint. Moreover, Soviet efforts to shoot them down revealed a wealth of detail about Russian air defences, which were closely monitored. Sigint showed that Moscow's command and control system was poor, radar coverage was patchy and fighter reaction times were slow. With each U-2 flight dozens of fighters scrambled to try to shoot the aircraft down, often revealing hitherto unknown units and fighter bases. All this had encouraged confidence about the invulnerability of the high-flying U-2. Indeed, NSA staff who listened in to Soviet radars and fighter controllers during the Gary Powers flight argued that he had

Commander Alastair Denniston, the first head of GC&CS.

Commander Edward Travis, GCHQ's first post-war director.

Voice interception during the Second World War, which saw intelligence operations on an industrial scale.

Arlington Hall, where Venona was broken. The majority of those working on sigint were women.

One of the key UKUSA meetings in the early 1950s. In the front row, starting third from left, are Clive Loehnis, Joseph Wenger, D. Edwards, John Tiltman and Edward Drake. In the back row, second from left is Louis Tordella, and next to him, in glasses, is Arthur Bonsall. Also in glasses, third from the right in the back row, is Bill Millward.

Russian radio equipment captured
by sigint teams in Korea, 1951.

President Sukarno of Indonesia (right), whose '*Konfrontasi*'
with Malaysia was defeated with the help of British sigint and
'Claret' operations by the SAS and other elite units.

British phone-tapping
equipment from the 1950s.

George Blake, whose team
listened in to Molotov in
1954 and who blew the
Berlin tunnel.

Tony Beasley (second from right), the sigint specialist on board HMS *Turpin*.

HMS *Turpin* undergoing part of her Super-T modifications as a secret sigint collector.

*U H/F or V H/F D/F (?)

*V H/F D/F (?)   8 BRICK SQUARE AND BRICK ROUND FITTINGS

M/F D/F LOOPS

NEPTUNE RAD.

*''BASKET TYPE FITTING (could contain antennae tuning
units or associated equipment for U H/F · V H/F D/F arrays.
could also be associated with intercept equipment, as it
adds nothing to lookout efficiency.)

NOTE: FIRST TIME THESE THREE
ITTINGS HAVE BEEN SEEN IN SHIPS.)

An aerial reconnaissance
photo of a Russian sigint
'trawler' in the North Sea.

The cypher room of Britain's Embassy in
Peking after it was overrun by 'protesters'
in 1967. The agents of Chinese intelligence
made off with a Rockex cypher machine.

Clive Loehnis, who negotiated the awkward 'free licensing' issue with NSA in 1964. Photograph by Walter Bird.

Commander Robert 'Fred' Stannard, Director of LCSA and then CESD, 1957–69.

only been shot down because, quite inexplicably, he was flying at only thirty-five thousand feet and was heading in the wrong direction (British intelligence sources seem to confirm this story).[5] In late June 1960 the CIA's Director, Allen Dulles, confided to a friend that he was sure Powers 'was not shot down at normal altitude', but later the CIA and NSA fell into a bitter dispute over exactly how the U-2 had been intercepted by the Soviets.[6]

The Gary Powers shootdown triggered a major diplomatic confrontation between Moscow, Washington and London. The incident encapsulated many of the wider international trends of the 1960s. During the decade there were major flashpoints such as the Cuban Missile Crisis in 1962 and the Soviet invasion of Czechoslovakia in 1968. There were also serious confrontations in the Third World, the largest being the Vietnam War, which kept the temperature at boiling point. Although engaged in an arms race, East and West had achieved nuclear parity, signalled by the deployment of Soviet missiles which could reach the American homeland. In theory at least, all-out confrontation now seemed to be a remote possibility because of nuclear deterrence. Intelligence had an important part to play in the unfolding drama. On the face of it, constant intelligence monitoring, including sigint and imagery, exercised a stabilising influence on world affairs, reassuring both sides that no sneak attack was imminent and making arms control more feasible. However, the operations that gathered the intelligence, such as the Gary Powers flight, involved an element of risk and provocation. For both the British and the Americans, risk calculation became an increasingly important part of managing intelligence operations. In turn, this sense of risk helped to drive one of the most important developments of the decade, the first tentative efforts at the collection of intelligence from the safety of satellites in space.

Two months after the U-2 shootdown, with the controversy still raging, an American RB-47H ferret aircraft was shot down by Soviet MiGs over the naval airbases of the Kola Peninsula, close to where British submarines regularly conducted surveil-lance. Only two of the five crewmen survived. This was the first close reconnaissance mission the West had risked after the loss of the U-2. Although less publicised than the Gary Powers episode, this calamity reverberated more strongly for Britain, since the plane had been launched from RAF Brize Norton in Oxfordshire. American and Norwegian sigint stations had tracked it, but disputed its course, plotting it thirty miles and twenty-three miles respectively from the Soviet coast. The crew had received orders not to go closer than fifty miles. The Soviet coastal limit was twelve miles, but at aircraft speeds the margin for error was small.[7] The two crew members who survived, having been rescued by a Russian trawler, confirmed to their Soviet captors that they had left Brize Norton at 10 a.m. on 1 July, but told them little else.[8]

Prime Minister Harold Macmillan was exceedingly bitter about the Powers shootdown, because it contributed to the collapse of the impending East–West summit in Paris. Macmillan had worked hard to encourage this meeting, and reportedly exclaimed that 'the Pentagon is blowing up the Summit Conference'.[9] Macmillan noted in his diary that the Americans had committed 'a great folly'. He expressed personal disap-pointment with Gary Powers, who 'did not poison himself (as ordered) but has been taken prisoner (with his poison needle in his pocket!)'. He lamented that the Soviets had captured the aircraft, the cameras, the photographs and the pilot, adding: 'God knows what he will say when he is tortured!'[10]

Russia exploited the incident to the full, threatening coun-tries such as Britain and Japan, which hosted the reconnais-sance flights. On 30 May the Soviet Minister of Defence, Rodion Malinovsky, warned that 'crushing blows by rocket forces will be dealt to the bases from which they take off'. On 3 June these threats were repeated by Nikita Khrushchev himself to a packed press conference. In London, the Joint Intelligence Committee concluded that these threats were a bluff. Nevertheless they induced extreme caution on the part of Harold Macmillan.[11]

Two weeks later, Patrick Reilly, the British Ambassador in Moscow, tried to smooth matters by telling the Soviet Foreign Minister, Andrei Gromyko, how distressed London was at the negative impact on East–West relations. Gromyko, who was in an 'ugly mood', replied in 'unusually discourteous language', declaring that Russia 'knew the true facts' about the secret missions.[12]

London, Washington and Moscow engaged in a ritual argument about the exact position of the RB-47 when it was shot down over the sea. The Americans stated that it never came closer than forty-eight miles to Soviet airspace. Moscow claimed that the plane was 'specially equipped for espionage operations', and was definitely shot down over Soviet territorial waters. The problem for the Americans was that only a month previously, their cover story about the Gary Powers U-2 being a weather research aircraft had quickly been exposed as a tissue of lies, prompting a humiliating climbdown by President Eisenhower. Gary Powers himself was subjected to a show trial in front of the world's media, and the Soviets promised that the two surviving members of the RB-47 crew would soon be 'brought before the court and tried with the full rigour of the Soviet law'.[13]

Harold Macmillan was clearly rattled. On 12 July he told Eisenhower that the whole question of using UK bases for reconnaissance flights would have to be looked at, and suggested that 'Your and our intelligence authorities should conduct a joint review about the system and conditions under which these flights are conducted.' Macmillan felt that this was particularly important, as the Soviets had announced that they were going to adopt 'a policy of shooting down any aircraft, wherever it may be, on the grounds that it is conducting reconnaissance or is in an area from which they prefer to exclude foreign aircraft'. Macmillan wanted this review to take place as soon as possible. Although he told Eisenhower that the RB-47 incident had increased the 'sense of solidarity between us', in reality it had also heightened the sense of risk regarding the whole business of sigint surveillance from any platform.[14]

Andrei Gromyko took the opportunity to highlight the issue of the intense surveillance of Soviet vessels in international waters. He complained to Western diplomats, including Patrick Reilly, about the 'provocative buzzing of Soviet ships' by American aircraft on the high seas, and asserted that this was happening on all the oceans of the world, with even civilian research ships being subjected to the practice. 'The buzzing of Soviet ships by American planes is done, as a rule, at mast-top altitude in the dangerous proximity of Soviet ships, often involving dives down on the ships, simulated bomb and torpedo release movements, the dropping of various moving objects and incendiary devices . . . as well as other impermissible actions.' Gromyko claimed that there had been 250 such incidents in the first five months of 1960.[15] The truth of these assertions remains unknown, but there were clearly some cowboy incidents, and even NSA's own official historian of the Cold War has admitted that, broadly speaking, reconnaissance 'exacerbated an already touchy situation'.[16]

In Britain, clearance procedures for sigint flights were already stringent, having been tightened up after the Buster Crabb incident in 1956. David Ormsby Gore, the Minister of State for Foreign Affairs, asked his officials, 'Surely the RAF undertake no flights which entail some risk of incident unless the operation has been cleared by a Foreign Office Minister of State or by the Permanent Under-Secretary?' Peter Wilkinson, head of the Permanent Under-Secretary's Department, confirmed that this was correct. What happened, he explained, was that the RAF submitted a programme of 'special flights' for the Prime Minister's approval six months in advance. Closer to the time, each day flight had to receive additional clearance from the Foreign Secretary, while night flights, which were thought less risky, were cleared by the Permanent Under-Secretary. This procedure included American reconnaissance missions from British bases.[17]

Harold Macmillan absolutely hated the public fuss caused by spy scandals and espionage incidents. Accordingly, he took a deep personal interest in these matters.[18] On 1 August 1960 he asked his Foreign Secretary to conduct an inquiry into ' "buzzing" in all its forms'. He was not referring to operations like the U-2 mission, which he considered to be clearly illegal. Instead he meant 'things which are within the law but no doubt disagreeable to the victims . . . It seems to me these things may become very dangerous.'[19] Unusually, Macmillan insisted on a series of special meetings for key Cabinet Ministers with the Chairman of the JIC, Sir Hugh Stephenson, in attendance. The rules for British sigint flights were firmed up, but the problem was what to do about the Americans. Against his instincts, Macmillan admitted that there was no benefit in raising the matter in the dying days of the Eisenhower administration.[20]

In Britain, the twin shootdowns of 1960 had a similar impact to the Buster Crabb affair four years before. This time they served to crush a plan for increased airborne surveillance of the Soviet fleet that had been agreed between the First Sea Lord and the US Navy's Chief of Naval Operations.[21] By March 1961 these plans had been postponed, and they were later 'put into cold storage indefinitely'.[22] Other long-established British programmes were also brought to a close. Like Eden before him, Macmillan now required the JIC to prepare a review of all aerial and submarine surveillance tasks, covering both imagery and sigint, so he could assess the value of the intelligence gained from these activities and measure it against the risks.[23] Defence intelligence chiefs were miserable, since the flow of short-range intercepts from these missions had been one of the few precious areas of sigint success. Air Vice Marshal Bufton, head of Air Intelligence, noted: 'The bulk of the intelligence on Soviet scientific research and development on missiles comes from G.C.H.Q. intercepts,' and 'it is "hot" intelligence'.[24]

These developments contained an element of irony. In the early 1950s, Britain and the United States had placed growing emphasis on 'technical means' of espionage, such as sigint-gathering aircraft and overhead photography, because the use of human agents inside Russia had proved increasingly hazardous and, with a few exceptions, rather unproductive. But now, forward surveillance with aircraft and submarines was also proving risky. Safer alternatives certainly existed. As early as 1956 the British had begun cultivating an alternative form of sea-borne surveillance: gathering intelligence on the Soviet fleet from the relative safety of British trawlers operating in northern waters. This was a direct copy of the Soviet sigint trawlers that became a ubiquitous plague by the 1960s. However, the real future of risk-free intelligence-gathering lay with satellites. The Americans were already experimenting with the collection of both sigint and overhead photography from space.[25]

On 22 June 1960, less than two months after the shoot-down of the Gary Powers U-2, the United States launched its first sigint satellite. For many years it was believed that the first operational intelligence-gathering space project was a satellite called 'Corona', which collected imagery. In fact the first intelligence satellite was 'Grab', which stood for 'Galactic Radiation and Background'. It was so secret that no details were released until the late 1990s. Publicly announced as a US Navy satellite designed to monitor the effects of solar radiation on radio communications, in reality it had a more secret second mission, namely gathering elint from Russia. Naval engineers simply took the electronic intelligence antennae that were being used on submarines penetrating Soviet harbours and bolted them onto the outside of the satellite. In the highest traditions of space engineering, the first designs were drawn on the back of a paper placemat when scientists were stranded in a Howard Johnson's restaurant during a snowstorm. Although crude, the Grab satellite was highly effective, and soon torrents of elint from its listening missions high over the Soviet Union were pouring down from space. In the 1960s such satellites remained small, since it was more than a decade before their potential for listening in to communications as well as elint from radars became apparent. However, this was clearly the long-term future of sigint collection, and eventually they would be followed into space by intelligence-gathering giants.[26]

The British and Americans were also enjoying new scientific breakthroughs in the highly secret world of cypher machines. The target of these operations was not the Soviet Union, but rather their West European friends and allies. These countries, whether allied like West Germany or neutral like Sweden, had a curious dual status as both lowly intelligence collaborators and also sigint targets. The management of relations with such allies and neutrals in Europe, some of which eventually became 'third party' members of the UKUSA alliance, was often controversial. As we have seen, immediately after the Second World War, more than half the traffic being analysed by American code-breakers was French.[27] During the late 1950s and early 1960s, one of the big issues for the British and the Americans had been supplying cypher machines to fellow NATO countries. Most of those that had been supplied to European countries after the war were now regarded as insecure.[28] This was because in the 1950s it had been discovered that many cypher machines that produced secure codes nevertheless radiated out a clear signal of the message they were sending over a distance of about a hundred yards – a problem known as 'Tempest'.[29] To deal with this, a new American cypher machine called the KL-7 was rushed into service within NATO, and was also given to other partners, including Rhodesia and South Africa.[30]

Cypher machines are extremely expensive, and the United States bore much of the cost of re-equipping Western Europe's communicators. This was partly to improve security in order to thwart Soviet code-breakers. However, the more secret explanation, which no one wished to admit to, was that NSA and GCHQ wanted to suppress the efforts of European countries to make their own cypher machines.[31] The British and Americans did not want the Continental Europeans to develop their own commercial cypher-machine industry, exporting machines around the world which would then generate messages that would prove difficult for GCHQ or NSA to break. In short, supplying American machines like the KL-7 virtually for free was intended to undercut the market and drive European manufacturers out of business.

Cypher machines remained a hot NATO issue throughout the 1960s. Partly because of their massive resources, the Americans were in the driving seat, and were advancing radical ideas. NSA argued that NATO countries in Europe should be allowed to manufacture British- and American-designed machines under a scheme called 'free licensing'. This meant making these designs available without cost, and ensured that NATO communications would enjoy the greatest degree of commonality and inter-operability. More importantly, the Americans also wished to continue to discourage smaller NATO countries from developing their own cypher-machine industries. Although GCHQ liked the idea, other parts of British government did not. Many in Whitehall felt they had no power to compel British manufacturers of cypher equipment to grant free licences to the Europeans, and would have to pay them expensive compensation. Moreover, London had almost completed negotiations for the Canadians to manufacture the impressive new British Alvis on-line cypher system under licence, and feared that this deal would be undermined.[32]

In June 1962 there was a serious clash between Clive Loehnis, the new Director of GCHQ, and the Ministry of Defence.[33] GCHQ supported the American proposal, explaining that 'SIGINT wanted to avoid the spreading of cryptographic techniques and knowledge,' and that NSA's proposal would remove 'the financial incentive from the development of cryptographic equipment in NATO'. Loehnis's colleague Fred Stannard, who looked after the communications security organisation known as LCSA, heartily agreed.[34] However, commercial interests won the day. To the utter dismay of GCHQ and LCSA, Whitehall offered a stern rejection of the American 'free-licensing' idea. Stannard had the unpleasant duty of telling the Americans that their ideas had been vetoed.[35] He later reported that the news had 'shocked' NSA, and GCHQ's liaison officers in America feared that 'our attitude will in fact impair the relations between NSA and GCHQ and LCSA'.[36]

Loehnis and Stannard did not give up, and now argued that Britain's refusal to cooperate might lead to NSA hardening its approach to Britain, especially in the area of the Mutual Weapons Development Program, a secret route by which the Americans subsidised equipment for both GCHQ and LCSA. NSA also saved Britain costs by assisting with the testing of the security of its new cypher equipment. Loehnis argued that agreeing with NSA on this matter would not only 'prevent damage to our most important and unique SIGINT and COMSEC relations with the United States', but would also save money in the long run.[37] It was certainly true that over the previous decade large amounts of expensive equipment used by GCHQ's sigint programme had been supplied through this scheme, mostly for elint and electronic warfare.[38]

The matter culminated in a remarkable showdown at the Treasury on 10 July 1962. Loehnis and Stannard set out what they insisted was the irreplaceable value of close sigint cooperation between GCHQ and NSA, emphasising that the 'principal feature of the partnership was the full interchange of the "product"'.[39] LCSA's relationship with the communications security division of NSA was, they declared, no less close. With perhaps a little hyperbole, they argued that Britain might 'endanger this partnership' by appearing to act unsympathetically. They warned that:

*

N.S.A. would see United Kingdom reluctance to meet them on free licensing as positively damaging, because they regarded their own proposal as the only way of removing from other N.A.T.O. countries the incentive to do their own research and development in COMSEC. And the continuation of this research and development would, N.S.A. considered, damage the United Kingdom/U.S.A. SIGINT interests.

*

Fundamentals were at stake. Meanwhile, they asserted, the cost of supporting the NSA plan was a relatively small amount of compensation to British companies such as Plessey for the free licensing of its new Alvis machine.[40] In the event GCHQ won the day, and equipment was supplied to NATO nations at a highly subsidised cost.[41]

As an additional backstop, GCHQ and NSA quietly encouraged their NATO allies to introduce legislation that regulated the export of cypher machines in the same way that arms exports were tightly controlled. However, there was an alarming loophole. The restrictions did not apply to neutral countries such as Sweden or Switzerland. Switzerland was one of the world's most advanced manufacturers of a range of technical defence equipment, from optical instruments to radar. It had a long-established record as a manufacturer of excellent cypher machines, the reputation of which was enhanced by public confidence in Swiss neutrality. This 'neutrals problem' was being energetically addressed by GCHQ and NSA. The main issue was a well-known Swiss company called Crypto AG, which was owned by a Swede, Boris Hagelin Senior, one of the world's top experts on cypher machines and a significant innovator in the field of cryptography. Crypto AG had become an increasingly important supplier of cypher equipment after the Second World War, trading on the Swiss reputation for excellent technology and neutrality.

How NSA and GCHQ 'neutralised the neutrals' is an extraordinary tale. The story seems to have begun on 4 September 1956, when the Australian Embassy in Washington 'had a ring from a character who wanted to sell us some cipher machines'.[42] The 'character' was none other than Boris Hagelin Junior, who represented two of his father's companies – Crypto AG in Switzerland and AB Cryptoteknik in Sweden – and ran a sales office in Maryland. He boasted that, together, the two companies had manufactured over 150,000 cypher machines which were in service with over thirty countries.[43]

Hagelin Junior was busy moving around Washington selling cypher machines to the many foreign embassies there. He persisted with his pitch to the Australians, supplying copies of Crypto AG technical literature which the Embassy sent back to Canberra. There it was passed to Vic Rolf at Defence Signals Branch, Australia's sigint agency. In turn, he forwarded it to Fred Stannard and LCSA in London.[44] LCSA was very interested, since the literature revealed that Crypto AG was producing some new and alarmingly advanced machines. LCSA was soon relaying more and more detailed questions about the new machines through its Australian proxy, which now posed plausibly as a buyer. Australian officials in Canberra noted: 'At no stage did we inform our Embassy of the use to which the papers were put.' Later, the Australian code-breakers purchased some samples but did 'not wish to become known to any overseas contact as the ultimate addressee'.[45] Meanwhile, Hagelin remained exceedingly keen to sell its cypher machines and 'random generators' used for making one-time pads.[46]

In August 1957 William Friedman, one of NSA's most experienced code-breakers and a long-standing friend of John Tiltman, was sent on a special mission to Britain. Some have suggested that this was because GCHQ had become suspicious that the Americans had been reading British messages prior to the Suez invasion – something forbidden by the UKUSA agreement – and Friedman was being sent to offer reassurance. But that was not the main purpose of the visit. On 26 August Friedman arrived at GCHQ to be greeted by old friends such as Josh Cooper. For a week he shuttled between GCHQ's new site at Cheltenham and the offices of LCSA in Palmer Street. The main focus of discussion was collaboration against the West Europeans, and a key issue was the increasingly advanced machines being produced by Crypto AG and AB Cryptoteknik. NSA later admitted that the purpose of Friedman's visit was ensuring that it continued to have 'the daily information enabling NSA to read NATO countries' messages'. Friedman's biographer recounts: 'Ciphering machines incorporating ingenious variants and improvements were being produced in Europe by more than one manufacturer and were being bought and adapted by more than one NATO country.' Unsurprisingly, Friedman's subsequent destinations on his European grand tour were Sweden and Switzerland.[47]

Having consulted closely with GCHQ and LCSA, it appears that Friedman came to a private arrangement with a number of companies in 'neutral' Sweden and Switzerland. The exact nature of the negotiations between him and Hagelin remains obscure, but this was a historic meeting, since they were two of the twentieth century's most experienced cypher experts. Certainly by 1975 it appears that NSA was actively involved in subverting the next range of Crypto AG machines. Reportedly, NSA's approach was to introduce a flaw so that the machines secretly broadcast the cypher key, undermining their own encryption. The alleged result was that NSA could read the encoded messages even faster than the intended recipient. This approach is known as a 'trap door', and has also been used more recently in computer encryptions.[48]

The secret of NSA's programme to penetrate much of the traffic carried by 'neutral' cypher machines did not begin to leak out until the 1980s.[49] Publicly, NSA and GCHQ have never admitted the alleged operation against Crypto AG, but by the summer of 1986 many of the details of this sensitive secret had reached the ears of Congressional committees on Capitol Hill, and it seemed only a matter of time before they appeared on the pages of the *New York Times* and the *Washington Post*. General Bill Odom, then the Director of NSA, was furious, and held a personal meeting with Robert Gates, Deputy Director of the CIA, on 6 November 1986. There was only one question on the agenda: 'Who told Cong[ress] about Cry AG?'[50] NSA was also working with the West Germans on this project. In his daily log, Odom referred to a periodic review of the 'Swiss connection' in his meetings with George Wieck, the head of the Bundesnachrichtendienst (BND), the West German intelligence service that handled both sigint and human agents.[51] Cooperation between NSA and the BND was central to the subversion of the neutral machines.[52]

The German newspaper *Der Spiegel* has alleged that later, a secret meeting of the BND had discussed how to change the ownership of Crypto AG, perhaps through a merger. Reportedly, the BND also considered how the Swedish communications company Ericsson might be persuaded, through the medium of its German counterpart Siemens, to terminate its expanding cryptographic business. One former employee of Crypto AG stated that he had to coordinate his developments with shadowy figures 'from Bad Godesberg' – the location of the Central Office for Encryption Affairs of the BND. Employees also recalled the arrival of NSA officials who advised on the use of certain encryption methods.[53] All this is perhaps not as surprising as it appears, since Switzerland and Sweden had been secret de facto allies of NATO since the early Cold War.[54] A recently declassified British document shows that NATO had already come to an unofficial understanding with Switzerland: in peace it would be neutral, but in wartime it would support NATO.[55]

Looming over all these cypher-machine issues like a vast black cloud was the troublesome issue called 'Tempest', the term used for the tendency of all electronic devices to radiate an electro-magnetic field over a short range, usually less than a hundred yards.[56] There has been much debate about when this phenomenon of radiation or 'emanation' was first identified. The NSA official history states that Germans had discovered it during the Second World War, but that its real importance was only recognised by a CIA technician in 1951.[57] Whoever discovered it, during the early 1950s it had become clear that this radiation could allow an enemy to listen in to cypher machines at short range in a way no one had previously envisaged. The British do not seem to have been aware of Tempest until 1952, when it was accidentally discovered that a cypher machine in the Washington Embassy was radiating out the plain text of the messages it was processing. Tempest was a huge problem, because many expensive cypher machines were suddenly found to be vulnerable.[58]

Nevertheless, Tempest also allowed the British to attack the cypher machines of their enemies. In his memoirs the former MI5 officer Peter Wright claims to have been one of the first users of Tempest to eavesdrop on cypher machines in the French and Egyptian Embassies in London. There is no doubt that such operations took place. During the late 1950s and early 1960s Wright joined John Hawkes from SIS in planning these sophisticated activities.[59] Ralph Benjamin, GCHQ's Chief Scientist, remembers Wright as a superb self-taught technician.[60] Wright recounts an operation in 1956 in which British intelligence successfully attacked the Hagelin cypher machines in the Egyptian Embassy in London by picking up emanations from the keyboard using a microphone in an operation code-named 'Engulf'.[61] In the late 1950s, in what appears to have been a coordinated effort with the Americans, British intelligence collected signals generated by French diplomatic cypher machines in London and Washington. These efforts ended in late 1964, when the French finally installed protective copper shielding in their cypher rooms to prevent radiation.[62]

What none of these accounts captures is the exquisite dilemma of offence versus defence. With Tempest, the conflicting demands of offensive sigint and defensive communications security were so complex as to make the head spin. The optimum solution was for GCHQ and NSA to be able to read the traffic of minor allies and neutral countries themselves, but to provide them with enough defensive expertise to make their communications immune to similar code-breaking efforts by the sigint specialists of the KGB. Tempest allowed GCHQ and NSA to launch innovative attacks on all sorts of machines that had not yet been broken, but this was only an unalloyed virtue if the Soviets were lagging behind in its use. This, in turn, raised another awkward question: how much did the Soviets know?

In April 1958 Fred Stannard visited Ottawa to brief the Canadian Cipher Policy Committee on the latest developments. His message was that Tempest was a terrible and complex security problem. While some cypher machines radiated out an electromagnetic field, others gave out an acoustic echo that could travel down a wire for hundreds of feet. Still others caused tell-tale fluctuations in the power supply. Even those machines that did not radiate of their own accord were susceptible to 'interrogation attack'. This meant that the KGB could potentially direct a microwave or laser beam at the cypher room, reflecting back reverberations that might give away the clear text of a message as it was typed on the keyboard. The only saving grace was that the danger was confined to a few hundred yards at most, so the enemy had to get close to the cypher machine they wanted to listen to.[63]

Stannard explained that the most awkward issue presented by Tempest was 'how we may best distribute our responsibilities for advising our allies, particularly in NATO'. Tempest was a nuisance in terms of security, but of course it was beneficial for offensive sigint operations by GCHQ. The British did not want information about Tempest to spread to 'countries or organisations from which signal intelligence is required'. Where the balance of advantage fell depended on the relative importance attached to either sigint or security. Understandably, perhaps, there were some arguments between GCHQ and LCSA over this matter.[64]

By the early 1960s the awkward NATO Tempest question was gradually being resolved. A handbook was provided to the European allies that explained how to install cypher equipment so as to minimise radiation risks from Tempest.[65] However, LCSA emphasised that, within the inner circle constituted by the British, Americans and Canadians, the standard NATO briefing had always to be accompanied by 'advice on certain aspects of the problem which it is undesirable to disseminate to NATO at large'. This circumlocutory language suggests that Britain was offering some of its NATO partners incomplete advice, leaving open certain avenues for exploitation. At the same time, GCHQ hoped fervently that the KGB was not using the same techniques.[66]

At last, after two troublesome decades, Britain's code-breakers and code-makers were finally getting to grips with Tempest. The issue, together with independent cryptography by European NATO allies and neutrals, had presented sensitive and costly problems. However, there had also been enormous achievements, many of which are still shrouded in deep secrecy, which provided continuous access to many streams of diplomatic traffic around the world. The main beneficiaries were K Division at GCHQ, whose task it was to read non-Soviet systems. However, these triumphs also owed much to the work of the unsung heroes of communications security, hiding out in one of Britain's least-known secret service headquarters in Palmer Street in central London. In 1969, their last year of independent operation before they were merged with GCHQ, Fred Stannard's colleagues declared that their secretive influence over cypher machines was the surest route to good intelligence: 'There is no better way to successful Sigint than to influence selected target countries by Comsec advice to use a source of equipment desired by Sigint.' This, they added with quiet satisfaction, 'can sometimes be done'.[67]

Although the problems of Tempest were now being addressed, they were frighteningly expensive to resolve, and in the 1960s money was a major problem for all of Britain's secret services. Indeed, if a single adjective had to be chosen to describe British intelligence during the Cold War, it might well be 'impecunious'. The real world of British secret service at this time was a shabby one, and the persona of the average intelligence officer was less that of Ian Fleming's glamorous James Bond than of Len Deighton's down-at-heel Harry Palmer. In Cheltenham, Berlin, Cyprus or Hong Kong, thousands of intelligence operatives endured dingy offices notable only for their peeling paint and rotting linoleum. Moreover, there was remorseless pressure to economise.

One obvious area for economies was the three sprawling intelligence empires owned by the Royal Navy, the Army and the RAF. As we have seen, each of the armed services had its own intelligence activities. Their largest collection task was sigint, which was mostly picked up by dedicated military units of listeners equipped with headphones sitting in Germany, Cyprus and Hong Kong and working in close collaboration with GCHQ. In December 1960 an inquiry by General Sir Gerald Templer, the 'Tiger of Malaya', argued that the three intelligence service directorates should be merged to form a single Defence Intelligence Staff, and that most of the secret military listeners who did sigint collection should be replaced by civilians and put under the direction of GCHQ. Templer was right, since National Service, which had provided an almost unlimited source of personnel for these military sigint units, was coming to an end.[68]

GCHQ's money problems were made worse by trying to keep up with the Americans. Back in 1955, President Dwight D. Eisenhower had appointed a major inquiry into intelligence, headed by the leading scientist James R. Killian. Like Templer, Killian had concluded that it was now 'exceedingly difficult' to run human agents inside Russia, where the security police were 'brutally effective'. In future the USA would have to depend on science and technology for its intelligence. This would mean spending huge sums of money on spy satellites and code-breaking. American intelligence, he noted, was verging on being a billion-dollar-a-year business. Another intelligence inquiry, the Hoover Commission, came to much the same conclusion. It also proposed an all-out attack on Soviet cyphers using the finest minds and the best computers that money could buy – the equivalent of the Manhattan Project which had produced the first atomic bomb.[69]

By 1962 the cost of British sigint was rising fast, while overall government expenditure was being cut. Something had to give. The issue came to a head in a secretive Whitehall committee called the Permanent Secretaries Committee on the Intelligence Services, or PSIS. Chaired by the Cabinet Secretary, Sir Norman Brook, it allowed the most senior denizens of Whitehall to debate the sharing out of the money allocated to the secret services.[70] In January 1962, PSIS expressed undisguised horror at the rising cost of sigint. While careful to praise GCHQ's achievements, it concluded that it was time for a comprehensive review of the organisation. It was moved in part by the success of Templer's recent inquiry into service intelligence, and hoped fervently for more of the same. Norman Brook called for a wide-ranging investigation into how GCHQ should develop in the face of 'increasing technical difficulties' which were pushing up costs, and whether the expenditure involved was likely to be 'commensurate with the intelligence obtained'. Over the past decade GCHQ had enjoyed two generous allocations of additional funds to boost its work on Soviet high-grade cyphers. These five-year plans for improvement were entitled 'Methods to Improve', or MTI. The first was launched in 1952–53 and the second in 1958–59. Although much knowledge about the Soviet military had been gained from special operations with aircraft and submarines, the golden prize of breaking high-grade cypher traffic and returning to the heady days of 'Ultra' had eluded GCHQ.[71] The review would also look at the future availability of 'overseas sites for interception', since decolonisation was constantly whittling away at GCHQ's precious overseas bases.[72]

GCHQ had been instrumental in the development of some of the best British computers in the 1950s, but was now having to buy from the American company IBM to obtain state-of-the-art machines. These were expensive, but GCHQ knew that without constant investment in better computing it was dead in the water. In 1963–64 it hoped to double its spending on equipment, mostly on new computers, taking its budget from £7.5 million to £11 million. Set against a background of recent Whitehall economies that had imposed a 10 per cent cut on all overseas departments, this was an extravagant request.[73] Moreover, the cost of GCHQ was only half the picture. Some of the costs of British sigint were hidden in the activities of the armed services, and were of a similar size and scale. In fact the total sigint spending was now £20.5 million, and it would soon overtake the cost of the whole of the Foreign Office, with all its embassies and diplomats, of £21.8 million. In other words, the servant would soon be paid more than its master. It was hardly surprising that a serious review had now been triggered.[74]

In mid-May 1962 the Chair of the JIC, Hugh Stephenson, went to the Treasury for an informal brainstorming session with Burke Trend to decide who should chair the review.[75] Trend was a rising star in the Treasury who had a special fascination with the intelligence services, and presided over their budgets. Their eventual choice was Sir Stuart Hampshire, an Oxford philosophy don. Hampshire seemed an improbable figure to review the future of Britain's most technical intelligence agency. With a First in Greats, he may have commanded the respect of civil servants, but he had no background in maths or science. Having been elected a Fellow of All Souls in 1936, he joined the Army in 1940. His otherworldly nature ensured that his superiors were reluctant to let him loose with a compass and a pistol, so he was moved into intelligence. By late 1942 he was in SIS, working alongside Hugh Trevor-Roper and the Radio Security Service. Some of his time was spent at Bletchley Park, and in July 1944 he found himself deliberating over the July Bomb Plot against Hitler with several other young SIS officers.[76] Like Trend, Hampshire had a romantic fascination with intelligence, and he later confessed that he had greatly enjoyed 'the spectacle of duplicity and deceit in secret intelligence during the war'.[77]

GCHQ prepared for the review by producing a report on the 'State of Sigint' and material on 'Interception Deployment in the Sixties and Seventies', and forecasting the costs of research and development.[78] In July it offered a historical summary of its post-war activities running to almost forty pages. The first versions were regarded as evasive by Whitehall, offering 'no assessment of the extent to which their policies had succeeded'. After much coaxing, later drafts identified precisely what had been achieved by the two five-year MTI programmes.[79] Bill Millward, GCHQ's Principal Establishments Officer, offered an account of the core activities against Soviet systems. This was painful for several reasons. It not only put an unsuccessful programme under the spotlight, it also required GCHQ to let the Treasury have 'specially sensitive information'. Millward found this excruciating, and asked that it be seen only by 'the smallest number of people'. The most interesting part of the report detailed GCHQ's expensive failed attack on the main high-grade Soviet diplomatic cyphers. The Treasury was asking whether this should ever have been attempted.[80]

The star performer during the review was Joe Hooper, the Deputy Director of GCHQ. Hooper knew that cooperation with the Americans was Cheltenham's trump card, and went to great lengths to explain how fortunate Britain was to reap the benefits of 'the much more expansive and extravagant effort of the Americans'. He added that senior figures at Cheltenham were genuinely worried about whether they might 'not be making an adequate contribution to the UKUSA partnership'. In the late 1940s sigint had often been a story of British cryptanalytical skill combined with American computer power, but now 'the Americans are becoming less dependent upon us because they are getting better themselves'. The Treasury pressed GCHQ to revisit the UKUSA agreement in order to 'reach a new understanding'. It wanted GCHQ to admit frankly that it could no longer afford to partner NSA's more ambitious programmes, and needed to make a more selective contribution. This made economic sense, but GCHQ regarded such ideas as utterly unthinkable.[81] The Hampshire review also raised the awkward question of 'overlap'. This was ultimately about the degree of mutual trust between GCHQ and NSA. GCHQ had often boasted that there was complete exchange between the British and the Americans, but when pressed hard it admitted that there was duplication of effort – even on the Soviet target. More importantly, the head of K Division, which looked after non-Soviet targets, acknowledged that there was 'considerable and inevitable overlap' in his province, and the British and the Americans were duplicating much of their work on countries in the Middle East, Africa and Asia. 'The reason is we cannot trust each other on sensitive matters,' he admitted. This was because British and American foreign policy diverged in these regions. Inevitably, on intelligence relating to economic matters there was almost no exchange at all. The Treasury demanded 'more of a carve-up and less overlap'.[82]

Hampshire's probe of sigint lasted several months, and included a six-week visit to the sprawling NSA headquarters at Fort Meade that lasted into January 1963.[83] Here, Hampshire was briefed on the super-secret plans of NSA to expand sigint collection using satellites like the highly successful 'Grab' launched in June 1960. He soon concluded that this was one road GCHQ could not travel, since the costs of satellite operations were prohibitive.[84] This also reflected his worries about poor scientific recruitment at GCHQ.[85] His work gave him insights into some of the most secret activities of MI5 and SIS. He met the MI5 officer Peter Wright to discuss GCHQ support for scientific efforts to locate the radios of KGB agents in Britain. Hampshire was broadly supportive of this, but wished to wind up 'Airborne Rafter', the element of the operation conducted with the help of the RAF's 51 Squadron, which was proving very expensive. Wright, a zealous counter-espionage enthusiast, resisted, but eventually agreed with Hampshire that the flights were not cost-effective.[86]

Remarkably, after much debate GCHQ got its money. After 1962, the budgets of most of Britain's overseas departments went down by 10 per cent, but the sigint budget went up by the same amount. This was an astonishing victory delivered by Clive Loehnis and his deputy Joe Hooper. They were greatly helped by the fact that Burke Trend, a fan of secret service, moved from the Treasury to replace Norman Brook as Cabinet Secretary in 1963. Trend and Hampshire had eventually concluded that asking 'value for money' questions about intelligence warning of a future Soviet attack, or indeed about what was now a key element of the Anglo–American relationship, was perhaps wrongheaded. These were core activities that Britain had to continue.[87] The Treasury's biggest worry was airborne sigint, which, as we shall see, remained a perennial problem for decades to come.[88]

Hampshire, having finished his labyrinthine task, left his chair at University College London for Princeton University in the autumn of 1963. Indeed, his recent sojourn with NSA in Maryland had allowed a little time for a preliminary visit to Princeton in neighbouring New Jersey.[89] Doubtless, he thought this would be the end of his involvement in the shadowy world of intelligence. However, this was not the case. A few years later he was visited by Peter Wright, the famed 'Spycatcher' of MI5. Wright had gradually discovered that while many of the more notorious Soviet agents in Britain had been recruited through Cambridge by figures like Anthony Blunt, there was also a more elusive Oxford ring, so he was now looking for further KGB moles. Remarkably, suspicion had fallen upon Hampshire himself.

The irony was intense. Not only had Hampshire been selected to look at the innermost workings of the super-secret Anglo–American code-breaking partnership, he had also presided over decisions on technical support for Wright's own spy-catching activities. Hampshire deals with this rather obliquely in his memoir, recalling, 'Some of my friends who had also worked in secret intelligence during the war were shown to have been secret agents of the Soviet Union.' He then adds: 'I was interrogated about them and their motives.' This is something of an understatement. During his time as an Oxford Fellow, then during his wartime intelligence work, and yet again after the war, Hampshire had continually moved in the circle of 'Stalin's Englishmen'. Moreover, he himself had been directly under suspicion.[90] Amazingly, as an Oxford Fellow in the 1930s he had known both Anthony Blunt and Guy Burgess rather well.[91] Indeed, his friendship with Burgess went back to their time together at the elite Lockers Park prep school.[92] After the war Hampshire had moved to the Foreign Office for three years before returning to academia. There he worked in the private office of Hector McNeil, the Assistant Under-Secretary of State, and shared an office with his old friend Guy Burgess.[93]

The very idea that Hampshire might have been a KGB agent

was unthinkable to the authorities. Accordingly, it was only in 1967 that Wright finally secured permission to interview him at Princeton.[94] To his obvious discomfiture Hampshire was interviewed a second time in 1970, but eventually Sir Dick White, the distinguished head of SIS, concluded that the accusations against him were false. White was almost certainly correct. Although superficially left-wing, Hampshire was fundamentally conservative and a great believer in British institutions. Indeed, his most famous philosophical work, on Spinoza and the nature of free will, implicitly rejected Marxist determinism. Nevertheless, had his past friendships been known in 1962, it is unlikely that he would have been selected to review GCHQ.[95]

Later, when these issues were revealed to the public, Hampshire complained about the 'hypocritical and slimy McCarthyism of the press'. His wartime MI5 colleague Herbert Hart, also the subject of suspicion, hit out at the popular obsession with 'spy pornography'. The two men were representative of a wide circle of people, most of them honest toilers in the vineyards of intelligence, who had worked alongside Anthony Blunt, Guy Burgess and Kim Philby during the war, and now felt distinctly uncomfortable. The end of the Macmillan era and the arrival of Harold Wilson as Prime Minister in 1964 signalled a change of climate. GCHQ was moving from an era of tight-lipped secrecy towards a period of revelations and further spy scandals. Turbulent waters lay ahead.[96]

Harold Wilson – Security Scandals and Spy Revelations

The result is the worst press any P.M. has had in my day . . .
Cecil King, newspaper proprietor, 25 June 1967[1]

For British intelligence, the 1960s was a decade of cultural transformation. Journalists who had been brought up to respect wartime secrecy were discovering that Cold War espionage was a hot subject. It had already burst onto the front pages with the shooting down of Gary Powers' U-2 over Russia in May 1960 and the CIA's ill-fated Bay of Pigs adventure in February 1961, which attempted to unseat Fidel Castro in Cuba. The Profumo affair gripped the British public imagination in the second half of 1963, while the journalist Chapman Pincher broke the news of Britain's secret access to overseas cables in what became known as the 'D-Notice affair' in 1967. The following year was marked by the appearance of Kim Philby's dishonest, but delicious, autobiography, written after his defection to Moscow.

Harold Wilson's first government was beset by security scandals. This was something he had fervently hoped to avoid. In 1963, while still leader of the opposition, Wilson had enjoyed taunting Harold Macmillan over the Profumo scandal, the Vassall spy case which involved a British civil servant passing naval secrets to the Soviets, and Philby's defection. Macmillan resigned a month after Lord Denning released his report on the Profumo affair, proof, if any were needed, that espionage and security were areas of serious political liability. Having seen Macmillan squirm under investigation in the House of Commons, Wilson made a mental note that, once in office, he would toughen up on security in the hope of avoiding the same fate. He also developed an unhealthy fascination with security, and with MI5 in particular.[2] By the summer of 1963 his senior Shadow Ministers had already detected the emerging Wilson hard line on secret matters. Tony Benn noted in his diary:

*

Dick Crossman phoned this morning and we had a talk about security. The Party is making a great fuss about this over the Vassall, Profumo and Philby cases . . . I am afraid it's giving the impression that we want to institute a police state. Dick, who worked for Intelligence during the war, is a fierce security man and said that, as a Minister, he would think it right that his phones should be tapped and all his letters opened. This is quite mad. I am terrified that George Wigg may be made Minister for Security and given power over all our lives.[3]

*

In October 1964 the general election swept Wilson to power and, much as Benn had predicted, George Wigg was given the post of Paymaster General, but with a modified remit, serving as Wilson's intelligence scout and security enforcer. Wigg was a close friend of the Prime Minister, and his particular task was to probe the security arrangements of every department of state in the hope of protecting Wilson from Profumo-like incidents.[4]

Wigg soon turned his attention to GCHQ, which he examined as part of a review of the Foreign Office, although he noted that it was 'autonomous to a considerable extent'. The first thing that struck him was the sheer size and complexity of the organisation. British sigint now employed some 11,500 staff, of whom eight thousand were from GCHQ, while the other 3,500 were service personnel. Indeed, the sigint personnel outnumbered the Diplomatic Service. Almost everyone at Cheltenham was now subject to positive vetting except for a small number of ancillary staff. Despite the fact that GCHQ had a team of twenty-one investigating officers who carried this out, there was a backlog of over a thousand staff, resulting in part from a large transfer of Radio Operators who had recently come over from the services under civilianisation.[5]

Wigg was satisfied that the 'comintsums' and other types of sigint reports that were circulated to decision-makers were well protected because of the tight security procedures laid down by UKUSA. He was also content that overall planning papers produced at GCHQ were fairly secure. However, the specialist branches produced a lot of working material that was not catalogued, and the existence of which was indeed only really known to those who generated it. Tracking this was almost impossible. Wigg was impressed by the new Director, Joe Hooper, who had succeeded Loehnis, but less so by the Security Officer, William Carey-Foster, who was approaching retirement. Although Michael Stewart, the Foreign Secretary, commended his review, Wigg had in fact done a poor job. He had taken the security procedures of the military intercept organisations that supported GCHQ at face value, and did not bother to visit any of the overseas listening stations. It was these far-flung stations, as we shall see, that proved to be the weak links.[6]

Wigg's lack of interest in the service-run intercept stations was doubly surprising, since Berlin had seen its first British sigint defection in 1963. Because of the Profumo affair, the newspapers barely noticed the curious case of a Sergeant Brian Patchett, a sigint specialist who was serving with an obscure signals unit on the outskirts of the British Zone of Berlin. Like one third of the servicemen in the Royal Signals, his trade was interception. Patchett had taken the Sigint Traffic Analysts Course in January 1959, and later completed the Russian Linguist Voice Interceptor Course. He had then been attached to GCHQ at Cheltenham before being sent to a listening unit run by 13 Signals Regiment at the Gatow airbase in Berlin. In both locations he was engaged in shift work, like the civilian Radio Operators who were now being transferred to GCHQ's control.[7] However, Berlin was regarded as a difficult posting, and so remained militarised.

After his defection to the Soviets, Patchett's case was examined by John Drew with a view to extracting lessons from it. Drew had been an MI5 'Double Cross' officer during the war, helping to mastermind the deception activities that cloaked the D-Day landings of 1944. In his opinion, the vetting arrangements for the 'sensitive unit' to which Patchett had been assigned were disastrously weak. Although Patchett was vetted on enlistment, no interviews with his referees were undertaken, and reliance was placed on documents only. His positive vetting status was routinely reviewed in 1963, and he was promoted to the substantive rank of Sergeant on 20 June that year. He defected to the Soviets only two weeks later, on 2 July. For Drew, the whole case turned on one fact: Patchett was known throughout his unit to be a bed-wetter. Drew was astounded that Patchett's commanding officer had discovered this halfway through his training in interception duties in 1960. Despite being referred to a psychiatrist, Patchett was pronounced emotionally fit for duty. He did not defect to the Soviets because of any enthusiasm for Communism. He was simply miserable and depressed in Berlin, and was considered 'a lone wolf with no particular friends'. He had made four applications to be posted elsewhere, all of which were denied. As he explained to a German girlfriend of brief duration, when he decided to run away from the Army he simply found it easier to run east than to run west. There was a clear security failure here, since the service personnel who collected sigint were not vetted to the same level as the staff of GCHQ.[8]

Sigint specialists in Germany pored over the Patchett case, and rightly identified a system under pressure after the end of National Service. A chronic shortage of security personnel had led to a breakdown in vetting. Interceptors were beginning their sigint training before they had even been negatively vetted, i.e. before MI5 had run a simple background check for negative material recorded in their files. They were even beginning operational service in Germany and Cyprus before they had been positively vetted, and were offered little warning about the fact that they might be approached by the KGB or the GRU. It was clear that they needed full briefings with real-life case studies. Issues like Patchett's 'bed-wetting' were always lurking in the background, and officials demanded a selection process that would eliminate people with emotional disorders from duty in sensitive units.[9] However, most of the sensible suggestions were undercut by the extreme shortage of sigint intercept personnel. Sigint managers insisted that the idea of not posting servicemen under the age of twenty-one to places like Berlin was just impossible. They also disliked the idea of some sort of special psychiatric assessment for sigint staff, which they thought would have an adverse effect on recruitment.[10] Only the Army Intelligence Corps introduced psychological testing for all personnel on sensitive postings.[11]

Even as officials debated the Patchett case, further sigint security disasters were in the making. In 1962 Douglas Britten, a thirty-year-old RAF technician, began a six-year spying career for the Soviets. Britten was no ordinary RAF technician. He had joined the Air Force in May 1949, at the age of seventeen, and had spent twenty years as sigint 'special operator' in some of the most important collection stations. After initial training he was sent to Habbaniya in Iraq between 1950 and 1953. He then worked briefly in Egypt, before returning home in 1954. He served with 264 Signals Unit at Ayios Nikolaos in Cyprus between 1956 and 1959, and then again between 1962 and 1966, before being posted to RAF Digby. There was little he did not know about the business of sigint interception. Yet the serious nature of the Britten case was carefully hidden from the public, which was not told about his real duties. The authorities were helped by the fact that he pleaded guilty, ensuring a short trial of which parts were held 'in camera' – away from the public gaze.

Born in Northampton in 1931, Douglas Britten came from a troubled and impoverished background. In 1940 his father joined the RAF and was posted to Bolton for training. There he struck up a relationship with a woman in the house where he was billeted. Britten, aged nine at the time, later recalled violent scenes between his father and his mother, who was a semi-invalid. Eventually she decamped to live with his grandmother. At fourteen, Britten was attending Wellingborough Junior Technical College. However, money was short, so his mother withdrew him from school and he went to work in a series of dull engineering jobs, where he learned little. By the time he was seventeen he had developed an interest in radio, and was attending technical college in the evenings. The Air Force seemed an obvious avenue of escape. After his training he was posted to the RAF station at Hammersley Hayes in Cheadle, which had continued its wartime role as a key sigint collection site, and now focused on the Soviet Air Force.[12]

Britten married a member of WRAF in 1953, and by 1956 they had three daughters. However, there were continual problems with accommodation and money. He recalled that by the late 1950s 'I had begun to get into debt and arguments with my wife became quite common.' He even tried to get farm work on the weekends around RAF Digby in Lincolnshire. Like Patchett before him, Britten was a rather inadequate individual in difficult personal circumstances who was often working in exposed locations. Exactly how the KGB identified him as a likely recruit is not known.[13] However, he was an enthusiastic radio ham, and in late 1962, while visiting the Science Museum in London, he had been approached by a Russian who said he was called 'Yuri'. Yuri claimed he was also a ham radio operator, and addressed Britten by his radio call-sign, 'Golf Three Kilo Foxtrot Lima'. They chatted for a little about radios, and Yuri asked Britten if he could obtain for him the operator's handbook for a Racal 1154 transmitter, as he was from Ukraine and obtaining it there was difficult. This seemed a fairly innocent request, since that radio was fairly out of date, and was commercially available. They agreed to meet about a month later at Southgate tube station.

At that next meeting, the sinister hallmarks of KGB tradecraft were already visible. Britten recalled that Yuri 'walked past me and said to follow him at twenty-metre distances'. In a manner very similar to the William Marshall case more than ten years before, they then 'went all around the houses', the classic procedure whereby a KGB officer tries to 'dry clean' himself and check whether he is under surveillance. After a long time Yuri bent down as if to tie his shoelace. He asked Britten if he had been able to obtain the operator's handbook, and Britten confessed that he hadn't. Yuri nevertheless handed him an envelope containing £10. Britten mentioned that he was shortly to be posted to Cyprus, and Yuri responded by making arrangements for 'a friend' to meet him when he arrived there.

In December 1962, Britten duly arrived in Cyprus. His KGB instructions were to wait outside the Trianon Bar in Famagusta at two in the afternoon on the first Saturday of that month. Again, classic tradecraft was in evidence, with prearranged code words. On the appointed day, just as Yuri had explained, his 'friend' appeared and offered the agreed phrase:

*

'Can you tell me the way to Desdemona's Gardens?'
    Britten replied: 'Go by taxi to the Land Gate in the old city of Famagusta'
    The KGB officer then responded: 'Greetings from Alex.'

*

Britten was asked to show up outside Barclays Bank at 5 o'clock that afternoon. His new KGB controller, who called himself 'Vasiley', turned up in a Ford Taunas with a Russian driver, and they went for a long ride up the Panhandle in eastern Cyprus, before returning to Famagusta. Vasiley took things slowly, asking Britten about his family and his accommodation before giving him an envelope with money and arranging to meet him again two months later, in February 1963.[14]

Britten now had second thoughts. Suddenly 'It really dawned on me exactly what I was getting involved in and the consequences that would follow when and if I was found out.' He resolved to break off all contact with the KGB. However, he found himself getting into debt once more. His marriage was increasingly troubled, and he had started to drink. He resumed contact, and at the next meeting things turned nasty. Vasiley turned up with a woman who he introduced as his wife. The woman, almost certainly another KGB officer, produced a photograph of Britten receiving money from Yuri in London. They said that if he failed to cooperate, 'this photo would be sent to the British intelligence services and I could expect some rough treatment at their hands'. With a sinking feeling he realised that he had been trapped. Everything he had been warned about in security lectures came flooding back. He continued to meet his controllers every four months. All the time 'pressure was being applied'. The KGB had clearly identified him as a weak character, and this was now a coercive relationship.[15]

The KGB demanded that Britten provide details of sigint activities, together with 'telecommunications information' on Britain's signals networks. He was given a Minox camera, a type much favoured by professional spies, and asked to take photos of the inside of his monitoring building, where the operators sat in serried ranks in headphones, but this proved difficult, since he was never alone there. Pressure was put on him to identify other vulnerable individuals. 'I was asked to note and report the bad people in my unit,' he recalled, 'including officers with mistresses.' Vasiley also wanted to know whether 'any of my colleagues indulged in wife-swapping parties or any of the wives prostituted themselves to English or local males'. Such individuals would be ideal victims for future KGB efforts at blackmail. Britten said it would take him a while to discover these things, but Vasiley seemed content, and replied: 'Time is on our side, and we are in no hurry.' Britten was clear in his own mind that he was being used as 'a spotter for potential talent'. Eventually, he recalled, 'I passed my contacts the names of three airmen on my unit who could be recruited by them.' He also supplied general military intelligence, and spent much time driving around the island collecting order of battle information at bases like Dhekelia.[16] The transport he used was a brand-new white Volvo, purchased with the proceeds of his undercover activities – he also sported one of the latest cameras. Quizzed by his RAF colleagues about his newfound affluence, he passed it off as a bequest from a recently deceased relative.[17]

Heavy drinking and adventurous sexual behaviour by signals personnel on Cyprus were not unusual, and presented abiding security problems for the authorities. Working long boring shifts and then returning to unbearably hot billets, operators had little to divert them during their spare time. In the 1960s Major Teddy Thomas spent a long tour as a senior signals officer on Cyprus, and was a regular visitor to most of the communications units on the island, including the sigint units at Episkopi and Ayios Nikolaos. He recalls that a serious security incident occurred early in 1963 involving some WRAC operators: 'It had long been suspected that some of them were practising lesbianism, but that was a matter for their own officers until it came to light that they had involved a young Greek girl in their orgies.' The Greeks on the island were 'jealous of the chastity of their women', and if the affair came to the knowledge of their menfolk, retribution was sure to follow. Thomas considered that the lives of the WRAC operators involved were at risk. Accordingly, they were given an hour to pack their kit and driven straight to Nicosia Airport to board an aircraft for home. Other staff became addicted to alcohol, which was cheap and plentiful on Cyprus. These activities offered opportunities for the KGB, and Teddy Thomas was very much aware of the constant attentions of Soviet intelligence on the island. One of his other duties was ensuring the safe destruction of sensitive cypher equipment once it had worn out. He achieved this by taking it out to sea and dumping it in six hundred fathoms of water.[18]

Douglas Britten recalled that in 1964 Vasiley suddenly announced that the KGB 'wanted to train me properly'. He was given a bag containing four items with designated hiding places. These consisted of two empty Tennent's beer cans with false bottoms, marked 'One' and 'Two', a piece of piping screwed at one end, and a magnetic box container. These were used for passing documents and money. The beer cans were marked 'NAAFI Stores from HM Forces', and were to be left in a telephone box near the Municipal Stadium in Famagusta. The piping was to be discarded casually near a ticket booth at the stadium, while the magnetic box was to be placed beneath a bench on the road from the docks to the Army married quarters at Famagusta. In each case the containers were to be left for thirty minutes. Britten was then to look for a piece of crushed chalk on the road. This was the sign that the device had been collected by the KGB.[19]

During his last year in Cyprus, Britten's relationship with the KGB fluctuated wildly. At times his controllers told him that 'everybody was pleased', and brought him 'greetings from Moscow'. On one occasion they seemed to be offering him sex with a Russian woman he had not met before. At other times they made unpleasant threats. He recalled a meeting on a park bench at which he was warned that if his work did not improve they would 'arrange for me to disappear and something would happen to my family'. On another occasion he was 'pushed against a wall and punched several times in the head and body'. He was told to improve his performance, since he had been given 'an awful lot of money'. The KGB wanted him to opt for a sigint site in Germany as his next posting, but he told them that the choice was not his. Throughout this time his objective was 'to get as much money as I could to buy a house when I got back home'. His posting in Cyprus would finish in October 1966, and from the spring of that year the KGB began to prepare for his return to Britain. There were elaborate procedures for making contact with his new KGB controller. On a particular Saturday in January 1967 he was to go to Brookdale Road in Arnos Grove at 2 o'clock in the afternoon, carrying a copy of *Autocar* magazine. The KGB officer would enquire how to get to Edmonton cemetery, and Britten was to reply, 'You can catch a 219 bus.' The Russian would then reply with the familiar phrase 'Greetings from Alex'.

But back in England, things started to go wrong. The KGB still wanted sigint material, but they also wanted intelligence about the most improbable things. They hoped that Britten could provide information on the experimental TSR2 strike aircraft, and asked for detailed information about police radio frequencies in Leicestershire and Nottinghamshire. They also continued their love affair with elaborate espionage tradecraft. Britten was given a camera disguised as a cigarette case and three film cartridges, for photographing documents. Although he had one-time pads and coding material, he was also assigned a dead-letter box, spy parlance for an innocent-looking place where material could be deposited for collection by the KGB. This was a hollow tree-stump near a signpost for Gypsy Lane in Harlow. Foolishly, Britten resisted the use of dead-letter boxes, and insisted on personal contact with his handler, which was more risky. He recalls that his controller did not like this, but eventually he reluctantly agreed.[20] His controller was called 'Yuri', but was not the same Yuri he had met in London in 1962. He was in fact Alexsandr Ivanovich Borisenko, whose cover was First Secretary at the Soviet Embassy.[21] Yuri would signal his desire for a meeting by sending Britten a copy of *Autocar* magazine via his mother's address. Sometimes his mother was slow forwarding the magazine, and he missed several meetings. He also missed some of his radio signals, to Yuri's annoyance. Britten was warned that the 'arm of the Soviet Secret Service was very long and they had agents all over the UK', and that they would 'only be too pleased' to act against him and his family. He later recalled that he was 'very frightened' by this.[22]

Everything went wrong on 3 February 1968. Britten went to meet his contact, but Yuri was not there. Britten recalled: 'My contact did not turn up at our meeting for the first Saturday of the month and so I went to the Bayswater Road and phoned the Soviet Consulate. Later I went to a café and wrote a letter to my contact, saying I was desperate for money.' He hand-delivered this letter to the Consulate, where he was photographed from a covert MI5 observation post. Furthermore, his telephone call to the Soviet Consulate had almost certainly been intercepted. Thereafter, his angry KGB contact gave him more money and instructions on how to arrange an emergency meeting. This involved placing an innocuous notice in the personal column of the *Daily Telegraph*. But Britten had already compromised himself.[23]

MI5 was working frantically to identify the mysterious visitor to the Soviet Consulate. By August 1968 it had located Britten, and was working with RAF security teams to catch him 'red-handed in the act of handing over classified information to his spy master'. When it failed to achieve this, GCHQ urged that Britten be arrested quickly, having decided that it was no longer reasonable to risk current sigint operations 'in the hope of getting a clear-cut conviction'. MI5 arrested him at 9 o'clock in the morning of Wednesday, 11 September 1968 at RAF Digby. His house, office and car were vigorously searched in the hope that incriminating evidence would be found, as MI5 knew that without it, it would be hard to make the charge of espionage stick.[24] It was not disappointed. A cache of espionage apparatus was recovered, including one-time pads and a timetable of Soviet radio broadcasts with call-sign frequencies. There were directions for meeting with his KGB controller. There was also the camera disguised as a cigarette case.[25]

On 4 November Britten pleaded guilty at the Old Bailey. Ever since he had been recruited he had felt out of his depth. 'I feel a great sense of relief at finally being caught,' he said, adding, 'It is indeed a great relief to be able to talk about these activities.' One of his motivations was clearly money. Although he claimed that over the period of his espionage he received only about £800, both MI5 and the prosecution believed that the true figure was far more. He collaborated superficially with MI5, but they concluded that he was telling less than the whole truth about his activities, and he received a sentence of twenty-one years' imprisonment. Alexsandr Borisenko left London for Moscow six days after Britten's first appearance in court.[26]

The British public had been oblivious to Brian Patchett, and were not very interested in Douglas Britten. The extremely secret nature of Patchett's activities was never revealed, and Britten's decision to plead guilty ensured that his trial was not in the public eye for long. Much more attention was paid to the sensational escape of George Blake from Wormwood Scrubs Prison in October 1966. The authorities thought Blake had been sprung by the KGB; in fact he had been assisted by two peace campaigners and an Irish Republican who thought his record sentence of forty-two years was inhumane. They provided Blake with a rope ladder made from oversized knitting needles, and then one of his friends smuggled him to East Berlin. The cover was a family holiday: Blake was hidden in a VW camper van complete with children.[27]

The British public knew he was an SIS officer, but were still unaware of his highly secret work with sigint. The Blake case certainly reverberated for the Americans. In the White House, President Lyndon B. Johnson's security advisers noted that British security was 'disastrously porous', adding: 'We have had the Fuchs, Burgess, Maclean, Lonsdale, Vassall and Philby parade to remind us.' They argued that had Blake been subjected to a polygraph test when he returned from Korea, the problem might well have been avoided. This was not the last time the Americans would express a wish to see the polygraph adopted in Britain.[28]

On 21 February 1967, to the dismay of GCHQ, sigint finally hit the headlines in Britain as a result of what became known as the 'D-Notice affair'. The *Daily Express* carried a sensational story by Chapman Pincher, its Defence Correspondent, about the government interception of international telegrams and telexes, a process known as 'cable vetting'. It described how all international telegrams and telexes were taken by the carrying companies to government offices for copying, before being sent on their way. Although this traffic included telegrams sent by foreign embassies, the majority of it originated with private companies and ordinary members of the public. GCHQ was the recipient of this material, although it was not directly mentioned in the story, which incorrectly implied that the interested party was MI5.

This affair rapidly became entangled in a heated political debate over the mechanisms by which security-sensitive material was kept out of the British press. This was the 'D-Notice' system, a voluntary arrangement whereby a committee issued the press with warning notices on stories that might damage British national security.[29] Harold Wilson, whose relationship with the press was already experiencing the classic downturn of mid-administration, reacted badly. He later observed that his clumsy handling of the D-Notice affair was 'one of my costliest mistakes of our near six years in office'.[30] The *Daily Express* contended that cable vetting was an instance of 'Big Brother' intrusion into private matters, 'which ranks with telephone tapping and the opening of letters'.[31] Wilson denounced the story in the House of Commons as 'sensationalised and inaccurate', and attacked the *Express* for publishing it in open defiance of the D-Notice system.[32]

Wilson was quite wrong on the facts. In reality, the Permanent Under-Secretary's Department, the section of the Foreign Office that managed intelligence, had got wind of the story on 19 February, two days before it was published, and had quickly decided that it should be suppressed. Colonel Sammy Lohan, the Secretary of the D-Notice Committee, was told to meet Pincher and effect this. The next day, he and Pincher enjoyed a long lunch during which Lohan explained that although he was not keen on the piece being published, it would not actually be in breach of the D-Notice system. In other words, Lohan muffed it. On the night before the article appeared, the Foreign Secretary was contacted in a panic by Denis Greenhill, Chairman of the Joint Intelligence Committee, and told about the impending publication. Greenhill insisted that it would be 'very bad for the national interest', but he was far too late.[33]

Under pressure from Edward Heath, the leader of the opposition, Harold Wilson agreed to set up a committee of Privy Councillors chaired by Lord Radcliffe, one of the Law Lords, to inquire into the matter. Quite rightly, this cleared the *Daily Express* of everything except a minor breach of etiquette. Wilson, however, egged on by George Wigg, denounced the Radcliffe inquiry which he himself had set up. Acting against the advice of his Cabinet Secretary, Burke Trend, he issued his own White Paper, criticising Radcliffe and insisting that the *Daily Express* had deliberately published in defiance of the D-Notice system. His Cabinet colleagues were appalled. 'He is going off his rocker,' remarked Barbara Castle, blaming Wigg for giving poor advice. Many other senior Ministers agreed.[34] The whole affair was made more poignant by the fact that, only months before, Chapman Pincher had been given a major award as 'Journalist of the Decade', presented to him personally by Harold Wilson.[35]

One historian has described Pincher's report in the *Daily Express* as 'trivial'.[36] In fact it was anything but. Pincher had stumbled on a very secret story indeed. It was not only about interception, something which had been hidden from the public for decades, but also about a secret relationship between GCHQ and private companies like Western Union and Cable & Wireless. Although the British government holding in Cable & Wireless was comparatively small, it effectively operated like a nationalised industry. The tradition of handing over all its cable traffic to GCHQ and its antecedents went back to the First World War, and had continued undisturbed for half a century. As early as 1944, when Cable & Wireless was thinking of sending more of its material by wireless, officials were quick to ask how this would impact on 'monitoring'. The use of wireless, they noted, might upset 'the present system in which the company "plays ball" with the authorities concerned'.[37]

The other murky element of the D-Notice affair was the linkage between the secret state and national economic interests. Cable vetting included the interception of a large number of commercial telegrams. One of the main customers for this sort of intelligence was Britain's Director of Economic Intelligence, Michael Kaiser, and his staff, which was located in the Ministry of Defence. Kaiser was described by his superiors as 'a man of enormous personal charm', but also 'a law unto himself'. They went on to outline his duties:

*

A sizeable proportion of the work of his Directorate was devoted to meeting the demands for information from the Confederation of British Industry. A further element went towards producing a publication of such excruciating secrecy that they were rarely if ever read by those many who might best profit from them.[38]

*

This publication was based on intercepts and, as was so often the case with sigint, its very high value militated against its widespread use. Security was especially tight with economic sigint, since this was almost never shared with Britain's UKUSA allies, especially the United States – Britain's military allies were her commercial rivals.

At precisely this moment, Burke Trend was busy revising Britain's central intelligence machinery to take more account of economic and scientific subjects, and indeed commercial rivalry. Clearly this was also meant to translate into stronger economic intelligence targeted to support 'British interest and investments' at a time when Britain's economy was struggling. A second Joint Intelligence Committee was now created to focus on economic, technological and scientific subjects. The Permanent Secretaries Committee on the Intelligence Services was also expanded to include representatives from the Treasury, the Department of Economic Affairs and the Board of Trade.[39] The Bank of England was not represented, but did have regular access to material from GCHQ.[40] Trend's changes to the central machinery also included creating a new part-time post of Cabinet Office Intelligence Coordinator, for which the illustrious Dick White, Chief of SIS, was selected as the first incumbent.[41]

White influenced the merger of Britain's independent comsec unit with GCHQ. It had recently been renamed the Communications-Electronics Security Department after taking over some smaller technical outfits owned by the Post Office.[42]

GCHQ thought a merger would appeal to the sigint planners at NSA. All the other UKUSA countries had combined comsec/ sigint agencies, and it was hoped that a merger would ensure 'continued harmonious Comsec relations' with the allies.[43] Moreover, the controversial matter of 'free licensing' of cypher equipment for NATO countries cast a long shadow, and GCHQ feared that in the future 'a conflict of interest might arise between Comsec and Sigint' over this issue. At all costs it wished to avoid arousing the suspicions of NSA, and a merger would reassure it.[44] Another major factor was the shortage of skilled scientists.[45] Dick White believed that a merger would allow a better exchange of ideas, and would create a scientific research unit with critical mass. By 1973 GCHQ's Chief Scientist was serving as senior scientist for the whole British intelligence community.[46] The merger also strengthened the cover story that everyone at Cheltenham was busy doing defensive communications research.[47] The only opponent was the long-serving head of comsec, Fred Stannard, who departed in dismay and was replaced by Arthur Foden.[48]

Burke Trend and Dick White worked well together, but they were confronted by many challenges. By the late 1960s British intelligence was facing a climate of increasing exposure and revelation, and for some years the press had considered espionage and security to be fair game for stories. Now, with journalists like Chapman Pincher on the prowl and the additional excitement caused by the publication of Kim Philby's memoirs in 1968, the floodgates were opening. Society was becoming less deferential, and newspapers were increasingly reluctant to accept an official definition of what constituted the national interest. Harold Wilson's antagonistic relationship with the press, and his endless talk of conspiracies, made things much worse.[49] Indeed, it was amazing that GCHQ had not been mentioned publicly during the course of the D-Notice affair. NSA was not so lucky: the previous year a series of articles on sigint in the *New York Times* had revealed short-range collection from the

American Embassy in Moscow, as well as satellite interception of the car phones with which Politburo-level Zil limousines were equipped as they sped around Moscow.[50]

Above all, the Vietnam War served as a focus for dissent on both sides of the Atlantic, and crystallised the sense of generational change. Everywhere established authority and conventional attitudes were being challenged. The spring of 1968 was marked by violent anti-war protests on the streets in Washington, London and Paris. In the early summer of that year, Joseph Wenger, one of NSA's most senior code-breakers, confided in a close friend and fellow naval officer that his children did not respect his service to his country, and had complained that he was engaged in a 'shady business'. This had clearly upset him. His friend remarked that Sir Dick White had recently received exactly the same reaction from his own children when his position as Chief of SIS was revealed by the press. White's rejoinder was a good one. He reportedly asked his children, 'Do you consider me to be any less good a husband and father and good citizen?' Upon reflection, his children admitted that they 'guessed not'. Nevertheless, the spirit of the age was presenting new challenges for intelligence officers everywhere.[51]

13

Intelligence for Doomsday

*In March to August 1968 the JIC consistently took the view that
the USSR was unlikely to invade Czechoslovakia.*
Douglas Nicoll, Internal Report on the JIC
and Warning of Aggression[1]

During the early hours of 21 August 1968, Soviet forces invaded
Czechoslovakia. Accompanied by troops from three other Warsaw
Pact countries, their purpose was to crush the 'Prague Spring',
a liberalising tendency within the Eastern Bloc which Moscow
considered dangerous. Czech youths threw petrol bombs at Soviet
tanks as they moved through the streets of Prague. Buses were
set ablaze, and protesters finally massed in Wenceslas Square.
Elsewhere, students actually climbed onto Soviet tanks to argue
with their drivers. However, the Czech Army stayed in their
barracks, and there was no serious fighting. Within a day,
Alexander Dubček, the reformist leader, and his colleagues were
on their way to a KGB compound in the Carpathian Mountains.
Moscow rationalised its move on the basis of the 'Brezhnev
Doctrine', which asserted the right to prevent any member state
from leaving the Warsaw Pact. The Red Army, which had not
hitherto been stationed on Czech soil, arrived in force and
remained as uninvited guests all the way through to 1991.[2]

The best possible sources on Soviet intentions towards
Czechoslovakia during the summer of 1968 were the ultra-secret
short-range sigint stations hidden in the British and American
Embassies in Moscow. These were able to scoop up a variety of
interesting telephone calls, including those made from the cars
of the senior Soviet leadership. Code-named 'Gamma-Guppy',

this material was given a very limited circulation. However, the Soviets were aware of these operations, and were careful about what they said on the phone. In mid-August, Marshal Andrei Grechko, the Chief of Warsaw Pact armed forces, had been flying to various Eastern Bloc capitals to assess opinion on an invasion. On his return, he called Leonid Brezhnev, the Soviet Premier, from Moscow Airport. However, he spoke in a pre-arranged code, and no one in Western intelligence knew if this cryptic conversation meant the invasion was on or off.[3]

For the British, the Soviet invasion was an intelligence disaster of the first order. Dick White, who had just been appointed as Britain's first Cabinet Office Intelligence Coordinator, was horrified by the failure of the JIC to offer any warning that it was imminent. The Defence Secretary Denis Healey and the Chief of the Defence Staff also subjected the recently created Defence Intelligence Staff, with its specific warning role with regard to Soviet military actions, to severe criticism. Dick White set up a small committee to look into the workings of the DIS, and indeed for a while 'its very future seemed fraught with peril'.[4] Conclusions were soon reached. 'Dick White asserted that in 1968 the DIS had been correct in their forecast of the Czech invasion by the Soviets, whereas the FCO [Foreign and Commonwealth Office] and the Friends [SIS] had been wrong.' Sigint had not provided a clear warning, and had been unable to distinguish invasion preparations from routine Warsaw Pact military exercises. By contrast, defence sources had the real information, and so the DIS had come to the right conclusion. However, as White put it, the DIS's 'cutting edge' had not been sharp enough to persuade the JIC.[5]

Although sigint had not offered a definitive warning, Britain had excellent assets on the ground. A team of British military liaison officers known as 'Brixmis' who were stationed in East Germany under a long-standing agreement with the Soviets had been watching the Red Army as it mobilised for a 'major exercise'. The classic question these observers confronted was whether this was an exercise, a bluff, or a real invasion. The fabulous anthropological knowledge that Brixmis had developed over twenty years of watching its subject provided the key warning indicator. It had observed the Red Army going out on exercise countless times, and knew how it behaved. A routine exercise provided an opportunity to leave broken or faulty vehicles in barracks to be worked on by engineers. What marked this out as the 'real thing' was that the Soviets took everything with them. Vehicles were piled high with personal effects, showing that the troops were not expecting to come back for some time. Unserviceable vehicles were also taken. Indeed, there were so many of these that the Soviets ran out of towing chains, and made makeshift ones by plaiting fence chains together. This was a small detail, but to the expert watchers of Brixmis it spoke volumes. The Soviets were definitely up to something.[6]

Why did the JIC get the invasion of Czechoslovakia so badly wrong, despite such excellent indicators? Quite simply because its chairman, a rather lofty diplomat called Denis Greenhill, refused to accept the evidence that was staring him in the face. He insisted that the Soviet mobilisation was only an attempt to apply psychological pressure, and argued that if he was in the Soviets' shoes he would think the wave of international criticism an invasion would provoke too high a price to pay. In other words, he thought like a British decision-maker, not a Russian one – a classic example of a basic analytical mistake called 'mirror-imaging'. The CIA made much the same mistake, and only the West Germans accurately predicted the invasion. After the inquiry, Dick White decided to beef up the Defence Intelligence Staff. His chosen instrument was the redoubtable Admiral Louis Le Bailly, whom he made Director General of Intelligence, or 'DGI', at the Ministry of Defence. The DGI became Deputy Chair of the Joint Intelligence Committee, sitting alongside the senior military intelligence officer, who was already a member of the committee. The DGI was also boosted with his own personal staff. Thereafter, the diplomats and the military fought for control of Britain's central intelligence machinery.[7]

*   *   *

In the late 1960s the West had launched a charm offensive towards the Eastern Bloc called 'détente', which aimed to encourage precisely the liberal tendencies that Brezhnev had now cracked down on. The invasion of Czechoslovakia in August 1968 did not derail Western efforts to pursue détente. However, it did raise awkward questions. NATO forces had presumed a good degree of warning of any Soviet attack on the West, but would they actually receive this warning if a Third World War broke out? The invasion also prompted British commanders in Germany to think harder about intelligence in the first anxious hours of a confrontation between East and West. Although Brixmis provided a fabulous source of both operational and technical intelligence, it was a peacetime mission and was expected to be rounded up before any military action took place. Thereafter, commanders would need a reliable source of intelligence. Their primary need was to track the movement of the main Soviet thrusts, together with reinforcements mustering anything up to three hundred miles to the rear. In a future war, British commanders would hope to disrupt the Warsaw Pact's emerging battle plan and destroy its momentum. The most demanding task would be surveillance well behind the enemy front line.

One might have expected senior British commanders to have turned to sigint and GCHQ. Instead, during the 1960s those in Germany seem to have rejected the wonders of electronic monitoring in favour of the least technical option, human reconnaissance from 'stay-behind patrols'. This was often referred to in the local parlance of hardy special forces soldiers as 'the Mk.1. Eyeball'. From the onset of any future war, intelligence inside the Soviet-occupied areas would have been provided by dedicated stay-behind parties from NATO special forces. Prevailing doctrine suggested that these special forces had several deep-penetration roles in wartime. These included the collection of intelligence by active or passive methods, offensive operations by small parties, cooperation with partisans or guerrillas, and assistance to escapers such as downed pilots. However, in the context of a global war, intelligence was deemed to be the predominant task of SAS-type units. The only sabotage-type activities that were considered important were efforts to destroy enemy nuclear weapons or missile sites.[8] This emphasis on intelligence reflected a growing anxiety that Warsaw Pact forces might move too fast to allow sigint or air reconnaissance to provide effective targeting intelligence for NATO artillery, and eventually tactical nuclear strikes. Everyone knew that NATO commanders would press for early deployment of nuclear weapons, for fear that Warsaw Pact units would deliberately move close to their opponents, making the use of tactical nuclear weapons increasingly difficult.[9]

In the 1960s the British Army on the Rhine developed a secret new force for this important intelligence role. This involved adding a Special Reconnaissance Squadron from the Royal Armoured Corps to strengthen 23 SAS Regiment. During an initial alert, the Special Reconnaissance Squadron was expected to hold the fort until the arrival of 23 SAS, which would be flown in from Britain. These units were on short readiness times: their unofficial motto was 'Wait and Fly – Dig and Die'.[10] After the arrival of 23 SAS the two formations were to operate as a single unit, giving priority to sightings of 'nuclear units, formation HQs, armour, and bridging and ferrying equipment'. Their main task would be to provide the target intelligence for battlefield missile systems and heavy artillery.

These special units were based at Padeborn in central Germany, and were equipped with high-frequency Morse to provide long range and, hopefully, continued communications. The expected onrush of Warsaw Pact tanks meant there was no need for them to practise skills to penetrate the enemy front line. Instead, the drill was to move forward quickly, by any available soft transport, such as three-ton trucks. Special forces would eventually meet the units tasked as the delaying force, and as these elements withdrew, the special forces would stay behind. Preparations for such operations had become quite elaborate by the late 1960s, with pre-identified hides offering good fields of observation over likely routes of advance for the Red Army, and some pre-positioned SAS stocks which had been buried underground. Much of this activity was focused on what commanders referred to as the 'demolition belt'. These were 'killing zones', some way east of the Rhine, where it was hoped that bottlenecks would occur amongst aggressor forces twenty-four hours or so after the Warsaw Pact forces had attacked.[11]

Some special forces units were equipped with Atomic Demolition Munitions (ADMs) which it was hoped would slow the advance of Soviet armour. The US special atomic demolition munitions programme appears to have been code-named 'Green Light', and was active from the mid-1960s to the mid-1980s. In 1960 Sergeant Major Joe Garner of US Army Special Forces was probably the first person to make a parachute jump with a small atomic weapon, which was strapped to his body during a field exercise.[12] Although ADMs posed serious problems of contamination because they would have generated a great deal of fallout, they were nevertheless popular with military planners, since they were considered to be more defensive and less escalatory than other types of tactical nuclear weapons.[13] By 1971, Britain appears to have been moving ahead with its own ADM programme, designated 'Project Clipeus'; however, its full extent is still shrouded in secrecy. Clipeus was a James Bond-type suitcase nuclear weapon, which even now seems to have more in common with spy fiction than reality.[14]

Depending on a few soldiers for the targeting of nuclear artillery and key battlefield missile systems such as 'Corporal' and 'Honest John' during the first few hours of war was an obvious weakness in British plans, and there were increasing concerns about the potential vulnerability of such troops. An extensive programme of research was carried out during 23 SAS's annual autumn training exercise held in Germany, code-named 'Badger's Lair'. Eight SAS teams were deployed on the Soltau training area, while British Army signals teams played the role of the KGB and conducted elaborate tests to investigate their vulnerability to Soviet intercept and direction-finding procedures. RAF units tested concealment procedures by over-flying the SAS hides with thermal-imaging cameras and mono-chrome photography. Vulnerability to searches by dog patrols was also tested. To the dismay of the SAS, of the thirty-nine hides they created, all but two were found within the first six hours. The patrols and dogs proved highly effective, but even more remarkable was the success of electronic warfare sensor vehicles. To the surprise of the research teams, these intercepted not only Morse code but also burst-encrypted traffic, produced by a special radio that stored a message and then sent its entire contents in less than a second, to try to defeat enemy listeners. Direction-finding bearings were achieved at ranges of up to twelve kilometres, and accurate bearings using triangulation between three vehicles at ranges of five kilometres.[15] The ability to track burst transmissions was especially alarming, and prompted a decision to develop better communications equipment for stay-behind parties.[16]

This heavy dependence on SAS-type activities raises profound questions about sigint. After all, it had been a key source of real-time operational intelligence during the Second World War, and as we have seen, had continued to be important in small conflicts such as the Confrontation in Borneo. British commanders in Germany enjoyed their own significant sigint and electronic warfare capability, which was directed by an Intercept Control Centre. In time of war there would have been some additional sigint from airborne collection, albeit these planes' main role would have been to support the British V-bombers. The backbone of this was 225 Signals Squadron, which was tasked to support British forces in Germany. These units had provided an invaluable intelligence contribution in peacetime through their work on the Soviet order of battle. Over the years, operators had learned the radio signatures of individual Soviet units, allowing them to learn a great deal about each distinct formation. However, these tactical sigint units themselves felt that their very success in peacetime had led to a dangerous overestimation of their likely contribution in any future war. They observed:

*

In a war of limited duration in NW Europe, if the standard of security in WP [Warsaw Pact] communication links is good, the timely intelligence and useful steerage that 225 can provide will be very small . . . The problem . . . is not so much one of equipment quantities but rather the difficulty of conducting EW [Electronic Warfare] in a highly mobile tactical environment . . . The wartime limitations of 225 Signal Squadron are not widely known; as a result the squadron's capabilities are overrated.

*

Electronic warfare was one of the few planned intelligence sources for determining the location of enemy headquarters. Yet sigint specialists feared that the Soviets might be routinely 'remoting' the radios associated with their major headquarters, at a distance of perhaps two kilometres, in which case the effectiveness of any direction-finding efforts would be drastically reduced. Their only hope was that under the stress of war, Warsaw Pact communications security might lapse, but this was by no means certain. Indeed, some predicted that for the first twenty-four hours the enemy might advance on predesignated lines and keep near radio silence.[17]

Senior British officers clearly hoped that their tactical sigint organisation would provide some information on enemy deployment patterns as well as intentions in the first few hours of war. They also desired information on the 'location of enemy headquarters and missile launching sites'. However, in reality only the smaller missile-launching sites were likely to be within intercept range, while the more important SCUD missile sites would be outside the typical operating range of tactical sigint, which was forty to fifty kilometres. British commanders were intrigued by the American decision to introduce airborne tactical sigint systems on light aircraft, but noted that these would have to fly far from the battle area in order to survive.[18] In fact, this

American system – known as 'Guardrail' – proved highly effective.[19] The deployment of these small sigint aircraft reflected good previous experiences with the U-2s which had undertaken regular perimeter sigint flights around the Eastern Bloc.[20]

The biggest limitation on Britain's local ground-based sigint capability was range of intercept. Warsaw Pact command and control used VHF radio, and this could only be heard at a maximum distance of forty or fifty kilometres. This reflected both transmitter power and also the need for line-of-sight interception. Accordingly, it was possible to provide adequate comint to divisional commanders, but problems would occur at the level of corps and above, which needed to see further behind the front line. In short, sigint on Warsaw Pact reserve divisions would have arrived too late for the commander of British forces in Germany to react to it. Limitations of range also required sigint collectors to be based as far forward as possible, exposing them to risk and forcing them to move frequently, which was not 'conducive to the best COMINT collection'.[21] General pessimism was reinforced by the knowledge that at the level of divisional headquarters and above, Soviet communications security was excellent. In 1969, the monitoring of large-scale Soviet exercises showed that their ability to 'successfully use communications security measures results in lean intelligence collected by the SIGINT organisation'.[22]

It was only during the mid-1970s that new technology began to provide good alternative sources. Unattended ground sensors, small electronic devices which detected the movement of vehicles, began to become available in Europe. Initially trialled in Vietnam under the 'Igloo White' programme, by the early 1980s these had become a formidable intelligence instrument. Many of the early models – nicknamed 'bump-counters' – were tested during real Warsaw Pact exercises in Eastern Europe, having been put in position by Brixmis personnel.[23] Had war broken out prior to 1970, British commanders in Germany would also have turned to traditional air reconnaissance using aircraft with cameras.[24] However, this source of intelligence would have diminished quickly, because a horrendous aircraft casualty rate of 60 per cent was expected in the first week of any war with Russia.[25] Both captured enemy documents and PoW interrogation were unlikely to be helpful in a fast-moving war.[26]

Did all this planning for a future war matter? After all, deterrence was supposed to ensure that the north German plains would remain the Cold War's frozen front, with little likelihood of real conflict. In fact, by the early 1960s a number of crises had created a climate of growing anxiety. Confrontations over Berlin and Cuba, together with the escalating conflict in Vietnam, made war seem somewhat closer. Alarmingly, American sigint had failed to give much warning about the emerging Cuban Missile Crisis in 1962. The Six-Day War in 1967 and the invasion of Czechoslovakia in 1968 were also unsettling for commanders. More generally, throughout the 1960s there was a growing awareness that NATO's conventional inferiority in numbers, especially in northern Germany, might call for the early use of nuclear weapons to stem the tide of a Warsaw Pact attack. A better intelligence flow was required, not only for warning, but also for decision-making in any nuclear crisis.[27]

Indeed, in 1968, even before the invasion of Czechoslovakia, London and Washington began thinking the unthinkable. Up until recently, sharing anything other than the lowest level of sigint with the European allies had been anathema. However, they now considered upgrading the flow of sigint to the new NATO political headquarters that had just moved to the outskirts of Brussels. Bill Millward, Director of Requirements at GCHQ, had already been out to Brussels for talks with British officials there. However, these plans were plagued by repeated espionage flaps at NATO. In the autumn of 1968 the CIA secured a major counter-espionage coup when it recruited Colonel Ion Iacobescu, the deputy head of the Paris station of the Romanian foreign intelligence service (known as DGIE). Iacobescu revealed that his boss in Paris, Mihai Caraman, was running two high-grade spies inside NATO's Brussels headquarters. One of them was a Turkish staff officer, Colonel Nahit Imre, who had been recruited by DGIE in Ankara, and had been controlled from Paris since his appointment as Deputy Financial Controller of NATO. The other had been recruited by Caraman himself. This was François Roussilhe, who worked as Head of Translation in the NATO registry. The KGB had been so impressed by Caraman's enterprise that it sent one of its own top officers, Vladmir Arhipov, to work alongside him in Paris. Once Caraman's deputy defected to the West, everything began to unravel.[28]

In late 1968 Nahit Imre was publicly revealed to be an agent of the Romanian intelligence service.[29] Once he had been interrogated, his disposal was left to the Turkish authorities. His departure was monitored by the British security team at NATO, who reported that 'when he went on board the Turkish aircraft he was closely followed by two Turkish "gorillas" '. He was tried secretly in Turkey, and executed by firing squad the following year.[30] In London, the Imre case caused real consternation. Ronnie Burroughs of the Foreign Office immediately saw the connection between this case and the recent decision to improve sigint for NATO, and wrote to the senior UK representative on the North Atlantic Council asking 'whether we are right to proceed with our plans to set up an all-NATO GCHQ cell at Evere [near Brussels]'.[31] London eventually decided to press ahead, but was clearly unsettled.[32]

In early 1969, NATO turned to deal with the Roussilhe case. François Roussilhe was a French employee of the international staff who had worked for NATO since 1952, and had gradually risen to be Chief Clerk of the Document Translation Centre. Since 1963 he had provided the Romanian intelligence service with at least five thousand NATO documents, including top-secret material. His motives had apparently been purely materialistic: he had been paid in cash – largely in gold – and up to date had received around a million French francs.[33] The UK Chiefs of Staff took a 'very grave view' of these penetrations, and were determined that they should not be swept under the carpet. There were many voices in London now arguing that Britain was putting its own forces at risk by passing too much information to NATO.[34]

The experienced MI5 representative on NATO's Special Committee, Dick Thistlethwaite, had wanted to run Roussilhe as a deception agent 'to confuse or reduce Soviet assessment' of the information it had received. MI5 went so far as to propose a 'NATO disinformation cell' that would actually turn weak NATO security into an advantage. The British sensed an opportunity to repeat the fabulous achievements of the wartime Double-Cross Committee and the famous D-Day deception. However, this was blocked by the CIA, which disliked the sheer organisational complexities of doing such a thing in Brussels. The British complained that the CIA was timid, and that 'Roussilhe was a lost opportunity'.[35]

The greatest damage caused by these agents was the compromise of operating procedures for nuclear command and control mechanisms. At the same time the British accepted that where more general political policy on nuclear weapons was concerned, there was an avant-garde school of thought which held that 'we should ensure sufficient leakage in order to induce the Soviets to enter the dialogue at this point in our discussions'. Over a hundred copies of Nuclear Planning Group documents were routinely distributed in English and French, and many regarded these as effectively open documents that would soon reach Moscow.[36]

Remarkably, notwithstanding the repeated security breaches in the late 1960s, the GCHQ cell for NATO at Evere went ahead. Without a flow of sigint, NATO's Military Committee was increasingly an obstacle to rapid mobilisation in time of crisis. This was illustrated by a strategic alert in early August 1969, triggered almost entirely by sigint. Monitoring of Soviet units by GCHQ detected an unusual lull in air activity, combined with what seemed to be pre-orders for large-scale troop movements. There had also been a slight rise in signal activity on the Soviet General Staff network. The intelligence suggested 'preparations of a highly unusual character' in Russia and other Eastern Bloc countries. The JIC thought the most likely explanation was an impending Soviet move inside Eastern Europe, against Romania or possibly Yugoslavia. There was even an outside chance of an attack on China.[37] The signals traffic between Moscow and the Strategic Air Command, the Navy and the Strategic Rocket Force remained normal, so all intelligence agencies were convinced that the Soviets were not contemplating hostile action against NATO. Nevertheless, the British Chiefs of Staff found this pattern of Soviet activity 'unusual and disturbing'. They suggested that at the very least there should be some response from NATO, 'so that the Russians would be made aware that we knew of their activities'. They asked General Andrew Goodpaster, the Supreme Allied Commander Europe (SACEUR), who was in charge of all NATO forces in Europe, about the possibility of sending such a signal to the Soviets, ideally by covert means.[38]

On 10 August 1969 Britain instituted a covert mobilisation in collaboration with SACEUR, making war preparations, but only insofar as they would not be publicly visible or cause alarm. Border patrols were increased, and all RAF combat aircraft in Germany were dispersed. Battle-flight practice missions were flown, and all personnel were brought to two hours' notice of readiness. However, efforts to stimulate NATO's Military Committee into action were again frustrated by the difficulties over the release of sigint.[39] This was explained to Denis Healey, the Defence Secretary, by one of his senior officials. The NATO Military Committee had suffered 'paralysis' on this occasion 'because some of its members were not allowed to see the relevant intelligence material', since much of it was sigint and so was CAN/UK/US Eyes Only. He added: 'As early warning will very often be of the COMINT sort we could obviously meet similar difficulties again, and perhaps in more serious circumstances.' By 12 August, further sigint collected from Hong Kong suggested an easing of the immediate situation. However, the issue of NATO sigint had now been identified as an 'unfortunate state of affairs' that simply had to be addressed.[40]

The GCHQ cell at NATO also went ahead because of the recommendations of the Working Group on Sigint set up by NATO's Special Committee. This suggested that the cell might focus only on intelligence that might influence war warning and 'a timely decision to release nuclear weapons'. Sigint for NATO was specifically about intelligence during the critical period between the beginning of a crisis and a request for the release or use of nuclear weapons. In other words, there was never any intention to supply NATO with a broad range of sigint under normal peacetime conditions. Instead, the new arrangements for sigint only sought to regularise the position that had occurred during the Middle East War of 1967, when GCHQ and NSA had provided NATO with most of its intelligence, requiring the laborious production of specially tailored documents that provided detail on the situation, while hiding its source.[41] In 1971, continued anxiety about a possible Soviet invasion of Romania or Yugoslavia prompted the American decision to ask the British to be allowed to run regular SR-71 Blackbird spy-plane missions from RAF Mildenhall, providing the ability to collect imagery and sigint at short notice.[42]

Offsetting some of these anxieties, the late 1960s saw the beginning of arms control agreements and confidence-building measures that were only possible because of intelligence. Improved intelligence from satellites and sigint gave both sides more faith in these agreements. In this way, espionage activities of all kinds seem to have made the international system more stable by the late 1960s. Arguably, the emergence of a regime of reassuring measures, with its emphasis on the avoidance of crisis, also reflected a growing recognition that the command systems on both sides were fundamentally ill-suited to rapid decision-making under pressure. Some British officials had even begun to recognise that, taken together, the intelligence efforts of both sides contributed to a collective calming of nerves. Indeed, during the 1960s the penetration of the NATO registries by Eastern Bloc spies was so complete that the Warsaw Pact had no choice but to conclude that the intentions of Western countries were genuinely defensive and benign.[43] Yet no amount of espionage ever provided complete reassurance. Accordingly, there was little respite for the intelligence agencies, and by the late 1960s ever greater resources were poured into the increasingly high-tech world of sigint and satellites.[44]

Staying Ahead – Sigint Ships
and Spy Planes

. . . no other European NATO countries will have purpose-built aircraft for Sigint collection.
'Nimrod (R)', enclosed in Frank Cooper, Ministry of Defence, to Defence Secretary Denis Healey, 30 July 1968[1]

By the 1960s the British Empire was shrinking fast. Most of Africa was moving rapidly towards independence, and sigint bases in Iraq, Egypt and Ceylon had gone, with much activity being pulled back to Cyprus. Now even Cyprus looked precarious, under pressure from local guerrillas who were campaigning for union with Greece. However, there seemed to be a possible answer to this looming problem: to place one of the large overseas monitoring stations on dedicated sigint ships. This would render it immune to the ploys of post-colonial politicians who wished to twist the tail of the British lion over base rights. It would also permit flexibility, since a floating base could be moved, providing emergency monitoring during the Cold War crises that increasingly erupted in the Third World. These new 'sigint ships' would also help Britain to remain one of the world's leading intelligence powers.

Sigint ships were not new. The aircraft carrier HMS *Albion* and the cruiser HMS *Superb* had been on prolonged sigint cruises in the Baltic as early as 1949; moreover, a number of naval frigates had listening suites installed. Also, as we have seen, several British submarines were modified for intelligence duties and undertook hazardous monitoring operations against Soviet naval bases. There were also listeners on fishery protection vessels and trawlers. However, these were small teams of twos and threes attached to normal ships. Britain had no dedicated sigint ships. By contrast, the Soviets used a flotilla of small spy ships that looked like trawlers. Meanwhile, the American NSA was developing a fleet of Technical Research Ships, consisting of converted supply ships and Second World War Liberty ships (vessels that had been hastily produced for convoy duty); it was these latter developments that had caught Cheltenham's eye.

The first vessel in NSA's Technical Research Ship programme was the USS *Oxford*, a converted Liberty ship which put to sea in 1961. Its flexibility was immediately apparent as it floated from one trouble spot to another, admittedly at an ambulatory pace of just eleven knots. It proved especially successful during the Cuban Missile Crisis. Accordingly, during the 1960s four more ships in the Oxford class were launched: the *Georgetown*, the *Jamestown*, the *Belmont* and the *Liberty*. Three smaller ships joined the listening fleet, based on converted military transports: the *Valdez*, the *Muller* and finally the *Pueblo*, which entered service in 1968. However, the American sigint budgets were tight in the 1960s, and while all these vessels were refurbished, they had nevertheless seen better days.[2]

In 1964, partly as a result of advice from the Hampshire review, GCHQ decided that it would go one better, creating a purpose-built sigint ship, in contrast to the Americans' elderly converted transports.[3] The cover name chosen for this exciting new project was the 'Communications Trials Ship'. The Permanent Secretaries Committee on the Intelligence Services (PSIS) approved the construction of the first ship on 19 July 1965. The ambition was to have a fully fitted-out ship by the summer of 1969, allowing time for trials in the autumn before it entered service in early 1970.[4] There were hopes for two further ships in the same class.[5] In autumn 1965 GCHQ joined the Navy and the Ministry of Transport in sketching out the details.

The sigint ship was to be built to 'extreme naval standard', and capable of worldwide operations, 'including the Persian Gulf'. It needed to be able to cruise at very slow speeds – about five knots – for long periods, and to have a range of eight thousand miles. Substantial size was important, since 'spacing of masts' allowed good direction-finding. The crew was to consist of fourteen officers and fifty-three men. These would be outnumbered by the sigint operators, referred to as the 'Special Trials Party'. This would normally consist of seven officers, fifteen warrant officers and seventy Radio Operators. In an emergency, twenty further operators might be accommodated. The Radio Operators would work in two large receiving bays, and their facilities would include a trials analysis room, a tape-editing room and a 'special facilities' room. There was also to be a strong room for the most secret material.[6] All these 'special features' were to be housed in a main superstructure unit dubbed the 'black box', which would be prefabricated before delivery of the ship.[7]

The GCHQ personnel driving this project were Russell Dudley-Smith from W Division and Michael Herman from S Division, who was effectively the project officer. There was also strong naval representation.[8] Staffing was clearly a big issue. It was agreed that the crew that sailed the ship would be civilian, but the biggest challenge was the 'Special Trials Party'. There were not enough sigint operators available, and no one wanted to pay for them. The Navy asserted that it could only find 'a small proportion' of the sigint staff without cutting back on its shore-based listening sites.[9] Moreover these personnel were now civilians, and there were obvious problems with telling seventy landlubbers that they were suddenly going to sea.

The high point of this remarkable project came in March 1966. GCHQ's plans had grown to envisage a large experimental nuclear-powered sigint vessel. This was intended to be an existing aircraft carrier refitted with a nuclear power plant. It would afford massive space for intercept staff, and would have almost unlimited range for operations. The Atomic Energy Authority was brought in on the planning, and a design study contract was placed with Harland & Wolff of Belfast for 'finalising the proposal in more detail' and estimating costs. Because of the sensitive nature of the project,

the cover story sought to disguise it as a 'floating radio transmitting station on behalf of the Diplomatic Wireless Service'.[10]
This allowed some pre-publicity, and on 5 June 1966 the *Sunday
Express* reported that the ship was designed to allow the Voice of
Britain to be heard 'loud and clear in the world's most troubled
areas'. Journalists were closer to the mark when they argued
that the ship would fill a 'void created by the surrender of British
overseas bases'.[11]

GCHQ's sigint ship project was still going strong in 1967, and
there was a constant stream of new ideas. In their desperate
efforts to find new ways of listening in to the Soviets, American
scientists had come up with a bizarre project called 'Moon-
bounce'. This exploited the possibility of picking up faint echoes
of Soviet communications that were inadvertently reflected back
towards earth from the moon. The special technical equipment
on the sigint ship would be ideal for Moon-bounce, and was to
work in tandem with an American satellite installation at RAF
Oakhanger. The Americans had hoped to build this in Turkey,
but the government in Ankara had been troublesome and the
plan fell through. The British had then rushed forward,
explaining that a site could quickly be made available at
Oakhanger. With the Americans meeting the capital costs, this
was considered 'a good bargain'.[12]

Moon-bounce was a vast programme for the Americans, who
had already begun what was innocuously called the 'Naval Radio
Research Station Program' at Sugar Grove in West Virginia. Six
years of studies had revealed that the moon reflected all kinds
of radio energy from central Siberia with 'minimum distortion'.
This was hailed as facilitating a radically new approach to intelligence-gathering that would provide 'unique daily intercept'
from Soviet radars, communications nets and other electronic
emitting devices. The Sugar Grove facility would work as a
genuine scientific research station for radio astronomy when
the moon was out of view, but as a massive sigint collection
station when it was accessible. However, by the late 1960s satellites were proving to be a better way of collecting these signals,

and were making Moon-bounce redundant.[13] Moreover, back in Britain there were growing arguments over money, with GCHQ and the Navy attempting to offload most of the cost of the sigint ship on each other.[14] Both GCHQ and NSA were encountering serious financial problems, and were having to choose between projects.[15]

The final death knell for Britain's sigint supership was sounded elsewhere. On 8 June 1967, one of NSA's larger sigint ships, the USS *Liberty*, was tracking developments during the Six-Day War between Israel and Egypt in the Sinai Desert. The *Liberty* was busy intercepting both Egyptian and Israeli traffic while anchored twelve miles off the Sinai coast near El Arish. One of its tasks was to try to pick up any evidence of Soviet advisers assisting the Egyptians. Planners were aware that the ship was in a dangerous spot, and ordered the commander to move further away from the coast, but these instructions were not received. During the afternoon the Israelis, who had been keeping the ship under aerial surveillance for several hours, launched a ferocious attack by air and sea. The first was conducted by Mirage jet fighters, and the second by torpedo boats. By the time the torpedo boats attacked, the *Liberty*'s crew had hoisted an enormous flag that measured no less than seven feet by thirteen, declaring her to be an American ship.[16]

Thirty-four of the *Liberty*'s crew died and 170 were wounded. The ship, with eight hundred holes from prolonged rocket and cannon fire, managed to limp away to Malta. In July 1967, the President's Foreign Intelligence Advisory Board, with full access to sigint intercepts of Israeli radio traffic, concluded that although Israeli aircraft had correctly identified the *Liberty* as an American ship, the subsequent attack was the result of incompetence and miscommunication.[17] However, James Bamford, whose sigint history was written with the cooperation of NSA, asserts that the attack was deliberate, and that the *Liberty* was prominently displaying the American flag. He claims that the reason for the attack was that the Israelis feared that the *Liberty* had been eavesdropping on a massacre of Egyptian prisoners of war.

Lieutenant General Marshall Carter, the Director of NSA, also continued to insist that it had been a deliberate attack. The issue of the *Liberty* remains a matter of bitter controversy.[18]

Months later there was a further disaster. In January 1968 the USS *Pueblo*, a smaller NSA vessel, was captured by North Korea while eavesdropping off its coast, leading to an eleven-month stand-off. The crew were poorly trained, and the facilities to destroy secret equipment and documents if threatened were close to non-existent. Accordingly, the haul of cryptological materials secured by the North Koreans and their Soviet advisers was considerable.[19] Some have argued that the real purpose of the capture of the *Pueblo* was acquiring an American KL-47 cypher machine. This would have been invaluable, since the KGB had already received the keys to this cypher from one of its top agents in the United States, John Walker, an American naval communications expert.[20] Sigint ships, which had looked so attractive a few years before, were now considered a liability. The *Liberty* and *Pueblo* disasters had alarmed Cheltenham; however, the main problem was overambitious plans colliding with shrinking budgets. In the autumn of 1968, soon after Dick White was appointed as Cabinet Office Intelligence Coordinator, he was asked to conduct a further inquiry into the alarming issue of the spiralling sigint budget. GCHQ's supership was cancelled. New sigint aircraft were now catching the attention of planners, while what remained for naval sigint was redirected towards the latest submarines.[21]

Hitherto, much of Britain's seaborne sigint effort had consisted of a partnership between GCHQ and the Navy's venerable Super-T submarines. In 1960 the intrepid submarine commander John Coote had taken HMS *Totem* on several listening missions around the Soviet Union's Arctic coast, but he confessed that his vessel was now 'well past . . . her "sell-by" date'.[22] Surprisingly, instead of being scrapped, both the *Totem* and the *Turpin*, two veteran spy subs, were purchased by the Israeli Sea Corps, along with HMS *Truncheon*. In 1965 the ageing submarines were refitted, while a substantial number of Israeli personnel were trained by the British at HMS Dolphin. The *Truncheon* and the *Turpin* then transferred to the main Israeli naval base at Haifa. However, when the *Totem*, now renamed the *Dakar*, Hebrew for 'Swordfish', prepared to set sail on 9 January 1968, those watching on the quayside were alarmed. The Super-Ts were designed to take a crew of sixty, but in order to get all the trainees home, she embarked a total of sixty-nine people. Her new modifications included a special 'wet and dry' air lock alongside the conning tower for the despatch of special forces – which added to her weight.[23] Dockers observing her final preparations on the quayside were also astonished to see many crates of contraband – mostly whisky – also being loaded, followed by dismantled motorcycles. Grossly overloaded, she set sail around midnight.[24]

A week later the *Dakar* arrived safely at Gibraltar, then set out across the Mediterranean. Her last reported position was somewhere east of Crete on 24 January. Nothing more was heard of her. Her wreck was finally discovered in 1999, south-west of Cyprus, at a depth of over nine thousand feet. She was found by the Nauticus Corporation, the same salvage team that located the *Titanic*. Something had caused the submarine to dive below her maximum pressure depth, and she had suffered a catastrophic implosion of her hull. The Israelis salvaged the conning tower, which is now on display at Israel's Naval Museum in Haifa. However, few of those passing this striking memorial are aware of the secret sigint past of the *Dakar* and its sister ships, or of their eventful missions inside the Arctic Circle.

Meanwhile, in Britain, the baton of special submarine operations passed to the new 'O' class submarines, two of which were fitted out for sigint activities. For their commanders, the biggest anxiety was being forced to the surface by Soviet depth-charging or technical failure, and then captured. Alfie Roake, one of Britain's most intrepid spy-sub commanders, recalls that the question they continually asked themselves through the 1970s was how to avoid becoming another *Pueblo*.[25] In December 1968, British naval officers explained the division of labour: 'Some strategic Comint gathering is undertaken for GCHQ, but they carry out the tasking and evaluate the results.' The Navy itself was more interested in elint, and helped to run a cell at Cheltenham which analysed radars that fed into a Comprehensive Comparative Radar Library. Thereafter, ship-borne analysis computers drew on this library of taped intelligence to identify particular Soviet ships.[26] In the late 1960s attention was shifting to an exciting new task: the tracking of the first Soviet submarines capable of carrying ballistic missiles, Moscow's equivalent of Polaris. They first entered service in 1967, and there were normally four parked off the coast of the United States at any one time.

Britain's submarine operations were increasingly carried out in cooperation with her Commonwealth allies, who queued up to buy the new 'O' class submarine, and enjoyed the thrill of replicating her special missions. Australia acquired its first 'O' boats in 1967, and senior British officers and technicians transferred to the Royal Australian Navy with them. The Australian sigint target was the burgeoning Soviet naval power in the Pacific. The 'mystery boats' were always crowded, carrying their standard crew of sixty-two together with up to a dozen civilian sigint specialists. Australia's specialism was the 'underwater look', a perilous manoeuvre that permitted very close reconnaissance of the propellers, propulsion sounds, sonar fit and electronic signature of the enemy ship. Admiral Peter Clarke, who served first in the Royal Navy and then in the Royal Australian Navy, recalls that the ideal position was just outside a harbour, where ships slowed to five knots. The submarine would close on its quarry at depth, and then gradually rise just ahead of the ship. Skilled captains would position their periscope about six feet below the vessel. Special lights and cameras would then scan the underside, while hydrophones and receivers recorded its emissions. A good captain might make two passes. 'But it was a very full-on thing,' adds Clarke. 'You were driving several thousand tons of submarine to within feet of a vessel that you could not see.'[27]

In the 1970s the ships and submarines working for GCHQ were outshone by a new British sigint aircraft called the Nimrod R1. This state-of-the-art spy plane was the prestige intelligence project of the decade, entering service in 1974. Although GCHQ could not afford to join the Americans in the expensive game of satellite collection, a fleet of dedicated sigint aircraft was something no other European country had. Rather like nuclear weapons, it was something that marked Britain out as special.[28] The main advantage of airborne sigint was that it allowed detection of signals at great range, often from within the airspace of a neighbouring friendly country. This in turn meant that a great volume of signals could be collected. Aircraft could also collect in areas where the creation of ground sites was not possible, and could move around rapidly to catch targets of opportunity, typically a major military exercise. The downside was the huge density of signals that were being received by a small number of personnel in one aircraft, who often found themselves overwhelmed by the volume.[29]

Discreet discussions on replacement of the existing Comet sigint aircraft had begun more than a decade earlier, perhaps as early as 1961.[30] A highly secretive group called the Technical Committee of London Signals Intelligence Committee, headed by Ken Perrin, began work on the future direction of elint research in November 1961.[31] Perrin's group had been a key centre for the development of Peter Wright's 'Airborne Rafter' programme that had hunted for KGB spies using a special aircraft. They knew NSA was devoting huge effort to strategic elint, so GCHQ decided to stay away from this area, 'with the exception of special purpose equipment in quiet bands'. GCHQ's plan was to focus upon niche areas, such as tactical collection along the border with the Eastern Bloc.[32] Plessey was awarded a development contract for what was called 'an experimental sideways-looking elint system' in 1962, which was effectively the beginning of the Nimrod R1 programme.[33] This new equipment revealed the ever-increasing complexity of sigint. The existing Comet aircraft depended on teams of human operators wearing headphones who undertook the reception and analysis manually, using narrow-band receivers. However, the growing density and complexity of electronic signals meant that they were simply being overwhelmed. It was 'impossible for the operator to sort out and examine all the active transmissions' in the limited time that an aircraft spent over the search area. This meant that the most interesting material, the unusual signals that might mean new enemy equipment, was being lost. Plessey's new system was designed to do much of the work of the operator, and store what it detected for leisurely analysis after the aircraft had returned from its mission.[34]

The key decisions on the Nimrod were taken in March 1964 by the London Signals Intelligence Committee, which oversaw all of British sigint. It agreed that although the cost of replacing the Comets 'represents a significant proportion of the UK expenditure on Sigint', it was nevertheless essential. It was not just that some signals were otherwise inaccessible, but also that problems over bases meant a continual reduction in ground stations in areas such as Africa, causing GCHQ 'the greatest difficulty'. The committee noted that stations in Iran and Turkey, which were the source of much intelligence on new Soviet radars, 'could be denied to us' at any time, adding 'this had already nearly happened in Turkey'. It then compared the costs of possible aircraft, including the Boeing 707, but the Nimrod R1, which was a specialist variant of the RAF's maritime patrol aircraft, was by far the cheapest.[35]

The Nimrod had strong backing from the Chiefs of Staff.[36] It bolstered the much-prized special Anglo–American intelligence relationship by making a bigger contribution to shared sigint.[37] As Air Vice Marshal Harold Maguire, the Deputy Chief of Defence Staff for Intelligence, explained, there was a limited choice of partners to share burdens with, for although the French ran airborne elint missions, there was no exchange with them. Other NATO partners, such as Norway and Turkey, offered full cooperation, but mostly used ground-based stations, and 'in no case do they receive the full benefits of US resources as we do'. Britain had bilateral elint agreements with other European countries, such as Sweden, offering some of the benefits of airborne elint in exchange for 'basic useful data collected by their ground stations in their own areas'.[38] The Germans had begun to acquire an airborne capability, and were heavily advised by the British, but their aircraft were small.[39] Overall, there was a clear hierarchy. The British were subordinate to the Americans, but enjoyed special status as a sophisticated collector. The Anglo–American partnership in Europe was especially close because of 'common tasking through joint monthly meetings', which allowed the British to focus on searching for new signals or low-level air defence analysis.[40]

Britain was the only NATO country receiving raw American sigint. Accordingly, Maguire explained, it was the only country with the capability to make its 'own assessments in our area of interest and, where necessary, challenge US assessments'. This had been 'critical' when discussions on future NATO weapon-system requirements had occurred. He added: 'We know that our relatively small airborne ELINT programme is appreciated by the Americans as a sharing of the collection task, particularly as their resources are stretched because of worldwide commitments.' Because of the American need to focus on Vietnam in the late 1960s, the RAF was 'covering areas that they leave entirely to us'. Some argued that Washington had come to expect the British to do much of the airborne sigint in Europe, 'and a failure would threaten the massive help they give us in the whole Sigint area'.[41] All this reflected bad relations between NSA and the US Air Force during the Vietnam War, which resulted in a lot of duplication of effort and a drain on American resources.[42]

No one questioned the Nimrod rationale, but hiding the costs almost amounted to a secret operation in its own right.[43] The total cost of £14 million could not be accommodated within the already tight sigint budget. On 26 July 1967, Burke Trend concluded that it was unacceptable for the Nimrods to gobble up all the available funds in that budget; but since they were an essential purchase they were declared to be an integral part of Britain's nuclear strategic weapons programme, as their intelligence supported targeting. Hence the cost of the Nimrods was not only kept out of GCHQ's budget, it was even kept out of the larger and more elusive overall 'Cost of Sigint' spending. Instead it became part of what the RAF called 'our overall contribution to the hidden SIGINT costings'.[44] This meant that all of the RAF's signals activity was swallowed by the more prestigious RAF Strike Command to tie sigint in with nuclear weapons.[45]

As a result, GCHQ began to give more focus to the Nimrods' wartime role.[46] One of their tasks in a future war would be to compensate for the loss of the sigint units in Berlin, which commanders expected to be sabotaged by the KGB on the eve of war and then 'quickly overrun by Soviet forces'.[47] The Nimrods also helped Britain to have a say in nuclear war planning for Europe, which was mostly conducted on an Anglo–American basis.[48] Increasing emphasis on wartime use was reflected in the new ground facilities at RAF Wyton, which included rapid comint transcription facilities and a full analysis-assessment cell. The idea was that 'hot intelligence reports' could be sent quickly to field commanders, while deeper analysis would proceed at a more leisurely pace in GCHQ.[49] In its comint role, planners expected to be able to cram seventeen voice operators and four supervisors inside the Nimrod.[50]

In October 1968, GCHQ's Director of Plans, Ken Perrin, and the RAF sigint managers embarked on a prolonged visit to Germany to grapple with the issue of support for forward commanders. GCHQ was still agonising over the release of sigint to NATO allies 'in the period of extreme tension leading to war'.[51] It also had to decide on the time spent training for wartime tactical sigint, set against what Perrin called 'strategic supplementary tasks', in other words the Nimrods' contribution to GCHQ's work in peacetime.[52]

*　　*　　*

Britain's peacetime sigint targets were increasingly to be found in the Middle East. Egypt and Syria had received growing attention since the Six-Day War in 1967, and activities were coordinated with the Americans, who were also running 'high-level covert flights' against Syria at the rate of six a month.[53] In 1969 the British were flying some sixty sigint flights a year from RAF Sharjah in Oman into Iran and out over the Caspian Sea, which was a superb area for collecting intelligence, since its shores were dotted with defence testing facilities.[54] In 1970 the Shah of Iran personally offered the use of an airfield inside the country as a staging post, and these 'valuable facilities' greatly extended the duration of the RAF sigint operations and what they could achieve.[55]

The American experience in Vietnam influenced Britain's efforts to improve sigint support to commanders in Europe. In April 1972 the RAF's Vice Chief of the Air Staff, Air Marshal Sir Denis Smallwood, met his opposite number, General John C. Meyer, together with their senior officers, for a day of affable discussions, mostly about Vietnam. One of the subjects covered was their 'difference in sigint philosophy'. The British explained that once the Nimrod R1 came on stream, the plan was to feed selected information directly into the NATO intelligence network. In a European war, the Nimrod would fly about fifty miles back from the forward edge of the battle area, out of range of Soviet missiles, providing intelligence direct to operational commanders through a secure link. The RAF wanted to put experienced ground operators into the Nimrods, experts on the Soviet order of battle who would talk direct to operational formations. By contrast, the Americans explained that in Vietnam, the sigint take from their vast EC-135 aircraft was 'fed back to NSA at Fort Meade near Washington and processed by computer sufficiently rapidly for tactical information to be fed back for effective USAF tactical reaction'. The British thought this hopelessly cumbersome – and some Americans were inclined to agree.[56]

Sigint relations between NSA and the American armed services in Vietnam had been a disaster. The American system suffered from the same handicaps witnessed within NATO commands in Germany, with a refusal 'to clear field commanders for the information they so badly needed'. Under Marshall Carter, NSA Director during the late 1960s, a fierce battle developed with the US Joint Chiefs of Staff that 'poisoned the atmosphere', and relations with the military were at 'an all-time low'.[57] John Meyer, who was about to take over at Strategic Air Command, confided that control of sigint in Vietnam was badly split between the communicators, the intelligence people and the operators. The RAF noted privately that NSA was 'an organisation that does not rate highly with General Meyer'. So far no B-52 bombers had been lost, but there was a concern that 'the Russians were learning a lot from the current operations'. By 1972 British sigint personnel were actually in Vietnam observing the performance of a new tactical sigint aircraft called Guardrail 2 which was on a test run by NSA.[58]

In early 1974, Britain's shiny new Nimrod R1s were about to begin their operations on the Soviet periphery. Although their activities were always referred to as 'special', in some ways their missions were routine, at least in the sense that the aircraft often followed a regular pattern. However, on 1 March 1974 these flights were suspended due to the impending British general election. David Omand, an official in the Ministry of Defence with a GCHQ background, explained that for some time past it had been the practice to suspend special intelligence operations at such times, partly to avoid any embarrassing international incidents during the run-up to an election. It was also intended to avoid 'saddling new Ministers who take office after the election (whatever their Party) with the possibility of having to defend activities of which they may not have had an opportunity to hear about and endorse'. As a result, RAF sigint flights from Britain and bases abroad were halted, together with American reconnaissance flights from Britain and special intelligence operations by submarines. Lesser activities such as the overflying of ships of intelligence interest were reduced to 'a low key'. All this underlines the emergence of a sophisticated

British approach to clearing intelligence operations by the early 1970s.[59]

In February 1974, the last operational month before the election, the Americans planned seventeen sigint flights from bases in the UK. Most of them were over the Baltic Sea and West Germany, and were by RC-135 'Looking Glass' aircraft, a vast sigint version of the Boeing 707, flying out of RAF Mildenhall in Suffolk. Because these flights were routine they did not normally require approval by the Prime Minister. Instead they were approved by the Foreign and Commonwealth Office forty-eight hours ahead of take-off.[60] The British were planning similar flights: 'Operation Pat', a series of twelve Comet sorties over the Baltic and the Polish coast, and 'Operation Tibet', seven Comet flights over the same area, all mounted from RAF Wyton. In the Mediterranean, eight Comet sorties were planned under 'Operation Damage', using RAF Akrotiri. Permission was also sought for five flights against targets along the Egyptian and Syrian coast, code-named 'Operation Dolven'. However, in March and April, with the impending election, no activity took place. These flights were the last operations by the venerable Comets, since from May 1974 the RAF began to deploy its newly equipped Nimrod R1s.[61]

Like so much of GCHQ's activity, the whole Nimrod programme was premised on the eternal verities of UKUSA and the Anglo–American special intelligence relationship. It was also carefully calculated to reinforce the distinction in the American mind between Britain as a trusted second party and the Continental Europeans, an altogether lower species of sigint animal. In the late 1960s GCHQ appeared to be building on solid ground. On both sides of the Atlantic most of the senior sigint policy-makers, like Clive Loehnis, Joe Hooper and Joseph Wenger, had served in the Second World War, and had been present during the foundation of the UKUSA alliance. Although Marshall Carter, Director of NSA in the late 1960s, was new to the world of sigint, he was particularly anglophile. When Carter retired in July 1969, Joe Hooper wrote him an effusive letter of farewell, thanking him for his personal contribution to the NSA–GCHQ relationship and praising his 'instinctive feeling for its nature and depth'. However, over the next two decades things would change. In the White House, Westminster and Whitehall a new generation of political leaders and policy-makers was emerging that did not take these things for granted – and there was trouble ahead.[62]

THE 1970s

TURBULENCE AND TERROR

15

Trouble with Henry

Kissinger then said out of the blue . . . that the Special Relationship was collapsing.

Rowley Cromer, British Ambassador to Washington,
24 November 1973[1]

The late 1960s and early 1970s were dominated by the cata-strophic war in Vietnam. Harold Wilson was fêted by the British public for keeping the country out of the quicksand of this prolonged struggle in South-East Asia. What they did not know was that Britain was secretly supporting the conflict by all means short of direct military intervention, and this included 'in country' operations by SIS and special forces. GCHQ made a significant contribution from its sigint sites in Asia, especially Hong Kong, even though North Vietnamese cyphers were noto-riously secure. The gruelling war stretched American intelli-gence resources to breaking point, rendering assistance from GCHQ all the more valuable.

Alongside Vietnam, there was the challenge of an improving relationship between the West and China. The early 1970s also witnessed a dramatic upsurge in Middle East terrorism, with Yasser Arafat and the PLO becoming a major sigint target. In October 1973 the Yom Kippur War suddenly erupted when Egypt and Syria launched a surprise attack on Israel. This was followed in short order by the Turkish invasion of Cyprus. During these dramatic events sigint proved to be the main source of information for world leaders, often constituting two thirds of the intelligence which reached their desks. As a result the sigint bases came to be regarded as so valuable that in some cases their protection steered foreign policy. At remote locations such as the Chagos Islands in the Indian Ocean or Ascension Island in the Atlantic, the future of entire territories was shaped by the need for Anglo–American listening stations. Intelligence had once merely served the 'special relationship', but now secretive intelligence and defence projects lay at its very centre.[2]

Although GCHQ and NSA worked ever more closely in the 1970s, there was also serious political turbulence. In 1969, Richard Nixon arrived in the White House. Nixon was an impressive foreign-policy President, but he was also an archconspirator. Not only did he launch plots and conspiracies, including Watergate, against others, he also saw them all around him. He distrusted his own intelligence services, and indeed most branches of government. One official assessment suggests that 'During Nixon's years in office, the relationship between the President and the CIA reached the lowest point in the Agency's history.'[3] Nixon's obsessive secrecy and paranoia were only exceeded by those of his National Security Adviser, Henry Kissinger, who was as brilliant as he was temperamental. Together they monopolised American foreign policy, kept important secrets from their own intelligence services and tested the patience of their British allies.[4]

James Cable, a senior British diplomat and self-appointed 'Kissinger expert', remarked that in conceding unique influence over foreign affairs to Kissinger, Nixon had 'invested a philosopher with powers greater than those wielded by most of the Princes of this world'. Kissinger had taught strategy at Harvard for many years, and now had his hands on the real levers of power. Seldom has a theorist of international affairs, Cable continued, been given such opportunities to practise what he preached. The problem for the British was that Kissinger's philosophy was deeply realist, and was focused on the manipulative use of power.[5] Worse still, as Cable noted, Kissinger was notorious for his 'fits of petulance', and 'could behave badly on occasion'.[6]

In November 1970 there was a new incumbent in Downing

Street, in the shape of Edward Heath. Britain's new Prime
Minister was not convinced of the value of the special relationship. He tended to question the continual flow of American
requests for new base rights on British territory, and was more
inclined to seek friends in Europe. Over time, personal difficulties between Nixon, Kissinger and Heath led to serious problems in intelligence cooperation. These were only addressed in
March 1974, when Heath departed, following an infamous
winter of trade union unrest in Britain. Richard Nixon resigned
a few months later as a result of Watergate; however, Kissinger
stayed on to serve the new Gerald Ford administration as
Secretary of State until 1977.

Despite the potent mixture of personalities, the Anglo–
American relationship under Nixon and Kissinger began well.
One of Kissinger's many peculiarities was that he often trusted
senior British officials with confidences that he would not
extend to the US State Department. From the outset, the Nixon
presidency was dominated by efforts to resolve the Vietnam
conflict. On 20 July 1970, Kissinger met the outgoing British
Ambassador, John Freeman, to consider a sigint report about
Nikolay Firyubin, the Soviet Deputy Foreign Minister, who
had been overheard discussing the possibility of a major summit
on Vietnam. Kissinger was sceptical, but the sigint report had
clearly intrigued him, since the Soviets were now Hanoi's principal backers. The source was 'intercepts from internal communications' secured during Firyubin's recent visit to Delhi, and
they seemed to show that the Soviets were keen on 'a negotiated end to the war in the not very distant future'. Kissinger
extended further confidences to the British:

*

Firyubin . . . had told the Indians that there had been two
occasions when Washington and Hanoi had been very near
agreement and had failed to achieve it mainly because of
the deep distrust on either side. Kissinger said that this was
in fact true, although the information was only known in
a very restricted circle in the White House. This piece of

information, which had probably not been passed to us over intelligence channels, was of peculiar delicacy.[7]

*

Although Kissinger felt the 'intercept was insufficient evidence to form a judgement on Soviet intention', he was clearly excited. At the same time, his powerful realist instincts pushed him towards the view that greater military pressure on Hanoi over the coming months would make the North Vietnamese more responsive at the negotiating table.[8]

Kissinger's conflicting thoughts about the Firyubin intercept underlined the limitations of Western sigint in the early 1970s. Sigint – and indeed imagery – was delivering fabulous information on Soviet technical and military activity. Supplemented by widespread bugging, it also offered superb insights into diplomatic exchanges at conferences outside Russia, when diplomats were vulnerable to short-range interception. The British had, for example, achieved excellent coverage of Alexei Kosygin, the Soviet Premier, during his recent stay at Claridge's Hotel in London.[9] Sigint was especially valuable against the leadership of North Vietnam, and offered useful insights into negotiations with Hanoi during the late 1960s and early 1970s. Yet the innermost thoughts of the Moscow leadership remained elusive. More than two decades after Black Friday, Soviet high-level diplomatic communications remained largely unreadable. Indiscretions by Soviet diplomats like Nikolay Firyubin on their travels offered only a fleeting glimpse of the thinking of the Politburo.[10]

Some joint Anglo–American intelligence operations were attempting to lift the corner of this veil of secrecy. There had been considerable success in intercepting Soviet government telephone calls, which were carried by microwave relay systems. Much of this material was acquired at short range by technical teams in the British and American Embassies in Moscow. The British operation was code-named 'Tryst', and the American was 'Broadside'. In 1972 the Canadians joined them with their own sigint operation, 'Stephanie'. However, American journalists had blown these embassy-based sigint operations, first in 1966 and then more spectacularly in a long press article in 1971.[11] Afterwards, the Soviets tried to counter such activities by bombarding foreign embassies with microwaves, believing that this disrupted the collection operations. John Nix, who served in the American Embassy in the 1970s, recalls the 'great psychological pressure' that American diplomats lived under in Moscow as the result of KGB activities. The repeated bugging incidents had made people jumpy, but the microwaves made things far worse, because the fact that radiation was being directed at the Embassy 'led to galloping paranoia among everyone'. Nix adds that the health concerns appeared genuine, since the Embassy staff suffered 'a large number of deaths from cancer', and he recalls three occurrences of the wives of Embassy staff giving birth to children with severe defects; these incidents caused a 'climate of near hysteria', which was made worse by the State Department trying to keep the whole matter secret from its employees for as long as it could. Morale amongst Foreign Service officers in Moscow was 'just terrible . . . the worst I've ever seen'.[12]

The arrival of Nixon and Kissinger in the White House marked a revolution in America's practice of foreign affairs. There had also been important changes in Britain, which while not quite so visible at the outset, were also unprecedented. With the advent of Edward Heath as Prime Minister, a new generation of officials, especially within the Foreign Office, had begun to question the relative value of the Anglo–American relationship, set against Britain's new commitments to the European Economic Community which it had finally joined in late 1972.[13] Indeed, the sanctity of the Anglo–American intelligence and defence relationship was being questioned at the very highest levels. Shortly after Heath arrived in office, the Americans had asked for further military bases on British territory. He responded with an uncharacteristically broad question. What, he asked, do 'we get from the Americans in return for the various facilities for which they ask us?' The unhappy recipients of this question were Alec Douglas-Home, the Foreign Secretary, and Lord Carrington, the Defence Secretary. They were uncomfortable for two reasons. First, the question touched on almost every aspect of British intelligence and defence planning. Drawing up an effective summary kept several luckless defence officials busy for two solid weeks. Second, it revealed Heath's temperamental dislike of the special relationship.

Carrington explained that the Anglo–American partnership was perhaps a natural one, given that the two allies' 'geography and size are so different'. Although the scope and scale of Britain's residual empire was continually declining, the small remnants were nonetheless supremely valuable. Carrington continued:

*

Because of the number of our remaining island dependencies, we are able to provide the Americans with facilities which they would get from no one else on a comparable scale. Indeed, the very fact of our possession of these dependencies enables us to make a considerable contribution to an alliance which is important to both of us but in which otherwise our respective contributions might be very ill-balanced.

*

All this allowed Britain to benefit from what he called 'the massive American military technological and intelligence machine'.[14] Carrington argued that the hidden reciprocal benefits to Britain were in three areas: nuclear weapons, research and development, and intelligence. While these things were relatively invisible compared to the requested British real estate, they were nonetheless extremely valuable. Without American intelligence, he argued, 'and particularly that derived from the NSA/GCHQ Agreement', Whitehall would be unable to assess the key military developments inside the Eastern Bloc and China, and indeed would struggle even to produce good intelligence on lesser threats in the Middle East. However, the relationship

was more than just a crude exchange of intelligence for facilities. Carrington argued that Britain was the only other country
thinking on a global basis with whom the Americans could have
'a meaningful exchange on matters of common interest from a
basis of common intelligence'. Meanwhile, defence officials
cautioned Heath that the loss of US intelligence 'would reduce
us to the same position as other European members of NATO'.
Ominously, they also warned that the 'present satisfactory relationship with the USA cannot be taken for granted. It has
suffered setbacks in the past.'[15]

In 1971, London was also keeping secrets from the White
House. A member of the Soviet trade mission in London, the
thirty-four-year-old Oleg Lyalin, had been recruited as an agent
by MI5 in the spring of 1971, and had then defected to Britain.
In reality, Lyalin had been an officer in the sabotage section of
the KGB. While serving in London he had been involved in
developing the most unpleasant operations, including assassinations, that were to be initiated against British government
officials on the eve of any future conflict with the West.[16]
Whitehall was shocked by what he had to tell, and concluded
that this could not be tolerated. Lyalin also revealed the sheer
numbers of KGB officers in London, and the relative freedom
with which they operated. In September 1971, after some debate,
the British government launched 'Operation Foot', in which
close to a hundred Soviet diplomats and officials were declared
persona non grata and expelled.[17] London was aware that the
Americans might resist this action for fear that it would upset
détente, so the British chose not to tell them. Although the
decision to expel the KGB officers was taken in principle in late
May 1971, Nixon and Kissinger were only informed four months
later, after the fact. The excuse offered by London was trans-
parently lame. On 24 September 1971 Kissinger wrote to Nixon:

*

The British Ambassador has just delivered a letter to me
advising of the UK government's action. They will expel
90 Soviet personnel, mostly from various technical missions

(over 550 Soviet personnel are in the UK). The Ambassador asked that I convey to you the Prime Minister's sincere regret. He was unable to advise you in advance as planned. A press leak broke the story and required the government to move immediately this morning.[18]

*

Kissinger sensed that he had been deliberately kept in the dark, and was furious.[19] The following week, Denis Greenhill, the senior official at the Foreign Office, also pondered whether American sigint flights from bases in Britain should be suspended until they had seen Moscow's reaction to the expulsion of so many KGB officers, fearing that the Soviets might retaliate against one of these aircraft.[20]

In Downing Street, discreet resistance to American intelligence activities was gathering strength. During December 1971 Washington asked for permission to carry out more flights with super-secret Blackbird SR-71 Mach 3 reconnaissance aircraft from RAF Mildenhall. Heath took some persuading. However, Douglas-Home and Carrington argued that the targets were of mutual benefit. The most important was monitoring the Arab–Israeli ceasefire agreement reached after the Six-Day War of 1967. The Blackbird SR-71 also offered excellent imagery and sigint capabilities against any crises in Europe – typically, possible Soviet action against the more independently-minded parts of Eastern Europe such as Romania and Yugoslavia. Presciently, Carrington added that a rejection of the American request might strengthen the hand of those in Washington who believed that Britain's entry into the European Economic Community would 'herald some weakening in Anglo–American collaborative arrangements generally'.[21]

Britain's Joint Intelligence Committee was acutely conscious of the tensions between intelligence cooperation with Europe and its long-established close relationship with the Americans. Nevertheless, in April 1972 a delegation from the JIC headed to Paris to meet its French equivalent, the 'Groupe de Synthèse et Prévision'. The French were keen for deep engagement, and clearly did not regard the visit as 'a mere formality'. The British were also enthused, and saw it as an opportunity to 'influence the French further towards the JIC type organisation'.[22] At the same time the British recognised that this raised 'an obvious conflict of interest' between their obligation to routinely share assessments with Washington and the need to 'protect politically sensitive assessments, particularly on France'. Already the JIC was being cautious and keeping most material about France from the eyes of the Americans, but British intelligence officers feared that holding everything back might be noticed, and would 'increase [American] sensitivities on the effect of the UK/USA intelligence alliance of British entry into the EEC'.[23] Washington would have been even less pleased to learn that SIS had raised the possibility of exchanging information on China with the KGB. Senior British officials noted: 'It was not . . . desirable to initiate consultation with intelligence allies on this subject.'[24]

Meanwhile, there were unhappy experiences with major Anglo–American intelligence projects based in Britain. In the late 1960s the British and Americans had agreed to build a large 'Over the Horizon Radar' at Orford Ness on the coast of Suffolk, code-named 'Cobra Mist'. This was an intelligence-gathering system that watched aircraft and missile developments inside the Eastern Bloc, up to two thousand miles away. It also provided a degree of early warning of missile launches. A similar system was already being jointly operated successfully and under conditions of great secrecy in Cyprus. The Americans agreed to provide the capital costs of Cobra Mist, amounting to £13.3 million, while the British provided the land and buildings, at a cost of £1.3 million. The Americans also paid the lion's share of the running costs.[25]

Early trials of Cobra Mist focused on the monitoring of Soviet fighter reactions to RAF sigint flights in the Baltic. However, these tests revealed that the programme was not going well.[26] As early as June 1971, Joe Hooper at GCHQ told Dick White, the Intelligence Co-ordinator, of his private worries. Sir Alan Cottrell, the senior defence scientist, had compiled a damning report, and Hooper thought it contained 'many passages which would be unsuitable for American eyes'.[27] The whole system suffered from enormous amounts of background noise, and the intelligence dividends were thin. Efforts to solve the problems might cost another £20 million, and even then there was no guarantee of success. The whole concept of 'Over the Horizon Radars' might soon be eclipsed by a new generation of satellites that were much better at detecting missile launches.[28] In addition, the limited intelligence that Cobra Mist was giving on Soviet aircraft movements was already available from sigint sources.[29]

Cobra Mist had also caused trouble in unexpected quarters. Keith Joseph, the Secretary of State for Health, was alarmed by the high-power radiation emitted by the radar and its effects on nearby residents. His officials feared that the latest cardiac pacemakers might be neutralised by the radar pulses. Improbably, Joseph argued that the leads which connected directly to the heart muscle 'might pick up sufficient energy from a high frequency high intensity radiation to administer a lethal shock'. While he admitted that it was unlikely that such patients would be 'found wandering along the foreshore at Orford Ness', he nevertheless insisted that some would be 'in grave danger of death'.[30] No sooner had the excitable Joseph been reassured than technicians from the Post Office warned that the nearby town of Aldeburgh might lose all television reception. This rather more plausible prospect seemed to cause officials real anxiety.[31]

On 18 June 1973 the Americans formally announced that they wanted to pull out of Cobra Mist, leaving the British to wind up the operation and lay off hundreds of disgruntled staff.[32] Burke Trend, the Cabinet Secretary, was horrified by the likely drain on Britain's intelligence funds.[33] Louis Le Bailly, the highly capable Director General of Intelligence at the Ministry of Defence, agreed that they were now faced with considerable costs for a white elephant, including restoring the ecology around the Orford Ness site, and 'a considerable public relations problem'.[34] MI5 warned that large numbers of the civilian technicians at Orford Ness were union members, and predicted strikes which might well spread to the missile warning station at Fylingdales in Yorkshire.[35] Michael Herman, a senior GCHQ officer who was serving as Secretary of the JIC, was also concerned by the press discussion of Cobra Mist, because of the public references to 'eavesdropping on Russian communications' which were rare in 1973.[36] In the end the British made the best of a bad job and converted Orford Ness into a Foreign Office transmitter site.[37]

Major failures such as Orford Ness were irritating, but were not unusual in the increasingly high-tech world of intelligence. The more serious problems in the Anglo–American intelligence relationship were political in nature. In March 1973 Britain was still enjoying unique access to Henry Kissinger, and had been working closely with him on arms control. Indeed, Kissinger had prevailed upon the British to produce an early draft of a possible agreement with the Soviets on conventional arms control, or 'Mutual Balanced Force Reductions', while keeping his own State Department firmly out of the loop. For Rowley Cromer, the British Ambassador, this was a clear sign of 'the highly devious nature of Kissinger's intellectual make-up'. At the same time, Cromer was conscious of a change in Kissinger's demeanour. There was now 'an underlying element of strain and perhaps emotion' beneath his outwardly calm exterior, and during their recent meetings Kissinger had verbally attacked almost every country he could think of, whether friend or foe, except the British and the Chinese. He had launched into lengthy tirades about the State Department, the Pentagon, government economists and the Europeans. Cromer found his general scorn for the Europeans 'particularly disturbing', adding, 'I always have an uneasy feeling that we may commit some error which will bring down the Headmaster's censure.' It was, of course, good to enjoy such a close and confidential relationship with

Kissinger, but Cromer warned, 'It is a dangerous and complicated path that we tread.'[38]

Kissinger's underlying nervousness was caused by the emergence of the Watergate scandal, involving Nixon's use of former CIA agents to burgle the Democratic National Committee headquarters in the Watergate building in Washington, and to bug his political opponents there. The story had only just surfaced, but the strain was pronounced by the time Burke Trend and his team travelled to Washington to meet Kissinger again a month later. It was obvious that Watergate was already beginning to undermine the Nixon administration's moral authority. Trend had been taking the lead in these conversations with Kissinger, and he now warned Edward Heath that on the matter of Europe, the Secretary of State was 'a man in a hurry': 'There was a new urgency and impatience in his approach to the problem, which results, I suspect, from his increasing realisation that time is beginning to run against him.' Kissinger said little to Trend about Watergate, other than to observe that he was 'keeping clear of it'. However, everyone could see that he was on edge and his patience was fast running out.[39]

The Headmaster's censure was not long in coming. It arrived unexpectedly during late July 1973 at a meeting in Washington between Kissinger and Trend. Kissinger remonstrated about failures to get a swift European response on his proposals for 'Mutual Balanced Force Reductions'. Trend replied that Kissinger was being unrealistic about the new European institutions, and was 'trying to get the machine to work faster than it was capable of'. He had expected the meeting to be tough, and even Kissinger characterised it as 'a session of recrimination'. The substance of Kissinger's complaint was that Britain had refused to discuss the arms control proposals with Washington before talking to the Europeans. He said rather bitterly that the US had 'never treated Britain as just another country', and warned that this would have 'major consequences for bilateral relations between the US and the UK'. Several times he stressed that Anglo–American relations would be 'severely affected by recent events'.[40] The

Cabinet Office was shocked by this outburst, and kept knowledge of the exchange on the 'strictest need-to-know basis'.[41]

Kissinger was looking for a symbolic area to hit that would send a clear message to London. He chose the intelligence relationship. The next day, intelligence relations between the two countries were halted. NSA went quiet, and officials told Heath that the CIA had 'suspended the supply of certain intelligence materials to us'. NSA and the CIA had been instructed to cease intelligence exchange with GCHQ and SIS. British officials regarded this as 'sinister'.[42] All the American intelligence agencies were surprised, but moved cautiously for fear of incurring the wrath of the White House. Bill Bonsall, who had only just taken over from Joe Hooper as Director of GCHQ, immediately headed off to Washington to see what he could find out. On 16 August Burke Trend was told that the JIC was trying to come up with some recommendations, although the problem was quite unprecedented: 'All the indications are that the JIC are finding it hard to make up their minds.'[43] In fact the JIC discussed Anglo–American intelligence relations at four consecutive meetings during late August and early September as it struggled to address the problem.[44] Kissinger's 'cut-off' had the desired effect, and sent shock waves through the British establishment. This event is so sensitive that even after more than thirty years have passed, the Cabinet Office still refuses to declassify further documents on the subject.[45]

The reactions of the American intelligence agencies to Kissinger's insistence on a cut-off varied. NSA offered a legalistic response, insisting that its relationship with GCHQ was governed by 'a binding international treaty', so it would have to investigate and see what could be done. This was a polite way of telling Kissinger that it intended to ignore him. The CIA also fudged its reply on the matter of human intelligence or reports from agents that were supplied to SIS. Certainly at a station level, some cooperation continued. The area that was hit hardest was imagery, the supply of top-secret photographs from spy planes and satellites. The senior RAF officer tasked with collecting this sensitive imagery, who travelled to Washington once a week on an RAF Comet airliner, turned up and found that 'The bag just was not there.'[46]

Political relations deteriorated further during August and September. Although Edward Heath was urged to write to Nixon on 17 August, it was not until 4 September that officials managed to extract a crawling letter from him.[47] Heath assured the President that there was 'certainly no question of the relationship between your country and our one becoming one of adversaries'. At the same time, he could not resist lecturing Nixon about the complementary nature of Britain's relationships with Europe and the United States.[48] Nixon's response was notably brief and formal.[49] Crispin Tickell, who led a Foreign Office mission to Washington in September 1973, discovered that many staffers on the US National Security Council believed that Britain was now 'more European than the Europeans'. They were complaining loudly that 'The British are pursuing a consistently anti-American policy on a wide variety of subjects.'[50]

Some British officials argued that in 'the intelligence field' the Americans were cutting off their nose to spite their face, since any suspension of cooperation was 'not . . . in their own best interests'.[51] Heath was determined to prove the point, and opportunities for retaliation were not long in arriving. At midday on Saturday, 6 October 1973, a coalition of Arab states inflicted a remarkable surprise attack on Israel that had not been foreseen by any of the world's major intelligence services. The Yom Kippur War ranks alongside Pearl Harbor and Hitler's attack on Russia in 1941 as one of the most extraordinary surprise attacks of all time. Two weeks before, on 25 September, King Hussein of Jordan had flown secretly to Israel to warn the Prime Minister, Golda Meir, of what was coming. However, Israeli intelligence did not believe that Egypt was capable of launching a surprise attack because it lacked air superiority, and so, despite receiving numerous other warnings, they closed their ears. On the morning of 6 October, hours before Egyptian forces pounced,

Meir's Cabinet finally woke up to the fact that the country was about to be attacked. At this point they concluded, probably rightly, that Israel would be better off appearing to the world as an unambiguous victim, rather than trying to pre-empt the invasion.[52]

'In the Yom Kippur War we were all wrong – even Mossad,' recalled Louis Le Bailly, Britain's Director General of Intelligence at the Ministry of Defence. On the Friday morning, two days before the attack, one of the younger colonels in Britain's Defence Intelligence Staff did actually predict the Egyptian moves precisely, but he was overruled by a general who had recently visited the Israeli defences along the Suez Canal, known as the Bar-Lev Line, and insisted they were impregnable 'on the Israeli say-so'. On the Friday afternoon 'a girl from GCHQ' also got it right in a discussion of the Current Intelligence Group on the Middle East, but was similarly shot down by her colleagues. The brilliant Egyptian deception plan, masterminded by the Soviets, had only two flaws. First, the Soviets had evacuated their own families from Damascus to Tripoli by ship on the preceding Thursday evening. Second, on the Friday night the Soviets launched a new satellite over the region. Both of these tell-tale events were missed by Western intelligence.[53] Louis Le Bailly was so convinced that all in the Middle East was quiet that on the Thursday before the Yom Kippur attack he sent his own youngest daughter out to spend the summer working on an Israeli kibbutz.[54]

In terms of collection at least, GCHQ's American partner NSA did rather better. An inquiry led by Congressman Otis Pike later concluded that as early as the last week of September, NSA had been 'picking up clear signals that Egypt and Syria were preparing for a major offensive'. However, this sigint material was voluminous low-grade administrative chatter, and did not attract the interest of rarefied intelligence analysts. Meanwhile, some of the high-grade material that revealed the attack only reached decision-makers in Washington days after the fact. Pike noted ruefully that costly intercepts from NSA's vast sigint machine had detected some of the Egyptian preparations for war, but the intercepts achieved 'scant impact' on high-level reporting, so the most valuable intelligence had never reached the policy-makers.[55]

To the intense anger of Washington, the British adopted a policy of strict neutrality towards the war. This extended even to intelligence, with London implementing tight restrictions on American spy flights from British bases. U-2 spy flights by the CIA from Cyprus were banned, and tough limits were placed on flights from Britain by the larger SR-71 Blackbird reconnaissance aircraft. Not only did the British impose a very cumbersome process for ministerial approval for any American spy flights during the crisis, they also insisted that the resulting 'take' must not on any account be given to Israel. The Germans were equally obstructive. American intelligence officers were furious. According to Richard Helms, who had served as Director of the CIA up to early 1973, British attitudes caused shock at the CIA's Langley headquarters: 'CIA cancelled all contacts . . . when Heath demanded 2 conditions for US landing rights in UK during [the] Middle East Crisis.'[56] In the event, Kissinger baulked at these restrictions, and marathon SR-71 operations were flown from Griffiss Air Force Base in New York State, the nearest unrestricted operational base. It was not for nothing that this secret programme was code-named 'Giant Reach'.[57]

The SR-71 was a futuristic aircraft that flew on the edge of space, but its weakness was that it burned eight thousand gallons of fuel an hour at top speed. During 'Giant Reach' it would need to be refuelled in the air five times from no fewer than sixteen KC-135 tankers, meaning that the chances of something going wrong were greatly increased. Jim Wilson, one of the pilots, recalls one of the early flights from Griffiss Air Force Base. Somewhere south of Crete, 'I lit the afterburners and started acceleration toward the target area.' He then got a red warning light telling him that the engine oil quantity was low. He turned the afterburners off and on before pressing forward, fearing a 'single engine emergency arrival at Ben Gurion airport in Tel Aviv'. Returning from the target, he had only fifteen minutes' worth of fuel left when he met up with the next tanker. On landing, the ground crew had recovered the imagery and the sigint from the aircraft within twenty minutes.[58] Four flights were made from Griffiss before deteriorating weather forced the SR-71 teams to move to Seymour Johnson Air Force Base in North Carolina, which was even further away.[59]

It has been alleged that these missions were helpful to the Israelis, who when handed the material they gathered were able to spot weak points in the Egyptian lines, contributing to their success in the latter stages of the war.[60] Kissinger had also kept up American resupply to the region, and by 16 October the Israelis were pushing confidently into the Sinai.[61] However, by 24 October Kissinger was calling for current intelligence on the exact positions of the two sides, whereupon Bill Colby, the Director of the CIA, admitted: 'I don't have any solid information.' Yet another precarious ultra-long-range SR-71 mission was required. After agonising for some minutes, Kissinger exclaimed, 'Let's fly the thing. We've got to find out what's going on.'[62]

The most controversial event of the Middle East War occurred a day later on Thursday, 25 October. Richard Nixon decided to put American forces on a nuclear alert, or 'Defcon 3', in an effort to send the Soviets a clear signal not to intervene in the conflict. Edward Heath was incensed, since he regarded this move as provocative and unnecessary. What was worse, Heath was the last person to find out. Most senior British officials knew early on the Friday morning, but Heath only found out from news sources in the afternoon. A furious Heath ordered an inquiry by a former Cabinet Secretary, Sir Edward Bridges: 'I wish the highest priority to be given to this with no attempt whatever to hide any defects there may have been in our system at Home or defects in President Nixon's conduct.' Heath insisted that the 'world wide nuclear alert' had done 'immense harm', and complained that 'an American President in the Watergate position [was] apparently willing to go to such lengths at a moment's notice without consultation with his allies', adding that he worried what this meant for the control of American nuclear forces based in Britain.[63] On balance, Percy Cradock and the Assessments Staff agreed with Heath that the US nuclear alert was an overreaction:

*

US Sigint authorities at 0102 hours GMT on 26 October reported that there had been no evidence to suggest the Soviet Union's military forces on a worldwide basis had assumed an increased state of alert. There were no significant anomalies or deviations from normal communications patterns that would indicate that the Russians had placed their forces on a higher degree of readiness. Specifically, there were no Sigint reflections of a change in the posture of strategic rocket forces or increased alert in the Soviet Navy.

*

Although the Assessments Staff tried to hedge, they had to agree with Heath that the Americans had overreacted. Moreover, Kissinger had seemingly misled Rowley Cromer, the British Ambassador, telling him that America was only moving to 'a low level' of military alert.[64] Inexcusably, on the morning of 25 October everyone in Whitehall had been told about the American action except the Prime Minister. News had initially come in by telephone, but was soon confirmed by GCHQ, which had received the information 'in an intelligence context' from NSA. No one thought to tell Edward Heath.[65]

Kissinger railed against the British arms embargo and the restrictions attached to reconnaissance flights from bases in Britain and Cyprus.[66] The new American Secretary of Defense, James Schlesinger, shared his irritation. Schlesinger had been appointed in July 1973, having previously served as a short-lived and intensely unpopular Director of the CIA.[67] He vented his feelings during a heated exchange with Lord Carrington when they met in The Hague on 7 November, making a series of allegations. He insisted that London 'had been in close collusion with the French with the object of frustrating American policy objectives in the Middle East', and accused the British of undermining Egyptian support for a ceasefire resolution put before the United Nations by the Americans. One of Schlesinger's staff at the Department of Defense, almost certainly Harry Bergold, added privately that 'stories about sinister Anglo/French collusion' had been 'fed' to Schlesinger by other mischievous European allies, suggesting that the Dutch were the prime suspects.[68]

Edward Heath was adamant that Britain should also avoid spy flight incidents during the Middle East crisis, and ministers hurriedly reviewed all airborne sigint activities. Routine monitoring flights along the Inner German Border and in the Baltic were considered unproblematic. More worrying was a programme code-named 'Operation Duster' that involved sigint Comets flying out of RAF Akrotiri on Cyprus and along the Egyptian and Syrian coasts, together with Canberras from Luqa on Malta which flew along the Libyan coast. About a dozen missions a month were flown. Even more problematic was 'Operation Hem', a sigint marathon that passed through the region. Flights originated at RAF Wyton and made their way to Luqa before taking the opportunity to loiter along the Libyan coast. They refuelled again at Akrotiri and then headed east once more, listening along the Egyptian coastline, finally arriving at Tehran. They would then operate for a week out of Tehran and Mehrabad in Iran, flying along the borders with Russia and Iraq before heading back to Britain, revisiting Egypt and Libya on the way.[69] Julian Amery, the Foreign Office Minister, emphasised that these flights must continue because of the 'very valuable' intelligence they collected, but over the eastern Mediterranean greatly increased safety distances were maintained, 'keeping the aircraft very close to Cyprus'.[70]

The end of the Heath administration on 4 March 1974 signalled a gradual improvement in relations with the Americans. When Kissinger visited London later that month to talk with Harold

Wilson's second administration, he appeared somewhat chastened. Intelligence was again a symbolic issue. The Middle East War was now over, and Kissinger asked for a resumption of U-2 flights from RAF Akrotiri on Cyprus for monitoring the Arab–Israeli ceasefire. Because the war was over there could now be no question of spy flights favouring the operations of one side or the other, so London was amenable to these operations starting up again. British officials noted that they wished to avoid a repetition of the acrimonious exchanges of October 1973, and were now 'anxious to be as helpful as we can'. Nevertheless, there were worries about the public reputation of the U-2 as a 'spy plane', and the British thought its distinctive shape would soon be noticed. Instead of opting for secrecy, they chose to tell Archbishop Makarios, the President of Cyprus, and President Sadat of Egypt about the flights, and even made a low-key announcement in the press. These U-2 intelligence missions were now to be overt-covert flights.[71]

By April 1974 the damage was being repaired. The CIA had sent another long-distance SR-71 flight over the disengagement area between the Israelis and the Egyptians in the Sinai Desert. This showed that both parties were complying fully with their ceasefire commitments. The CIA told British liaison officers in Washington that in recognition of British helpfulness over restarting the U-2 missions from Cyprus, it was willing to share the results of this flight. It was explained that 'SR-71s would probably not be used in the vicinity of the area of disengagement' once U-2s began operating from Cyprus again. Thereafter, the US National Photographic Intelligence Center would provide the British with 'a duplicate positive copy of the film taken from each U-2 flight' over the Sinai, together with a complete written assessment generated by the CIA for its own purposes.[72]

However, the SR-71 flights over Syria continued, and remained a problem between the British and the Americans as late as July 1974. Admiral Bill Moffit, who worked with the CIA's Office of Special Activities, met British liaison officers in

Washington, and complained that the State Department was still discouraging requests to Britain for SR-71 flights out of RAF Mildenhall, believing it to be an area of continued sensitivity for London.[73] The British explained the distinctions between spy flights during hostilities, which could lead to allegations of partisanship, and monitoring in support of a ceasefire. Moffit wanted permission for SR-71 flights from Mildenhall to monitor the fragile peace in the Middle East. U-2s were fine over the Sinai, but were not favoured for surveillance of the Golan Heights, since they were vulnerable and the Syrians could not be trusted not to fire on them. Although the higher-flying SR-71s were out of range of attack from the ground, the Americans did not want to undertake further marathon missions from the United States, and had recently been flying reconnaissance aircraft from carriers in the Bay of Naples. The British were quick to reassure Moffit that SR-71 flights from Britain could be resumed, adding that 'The last thing we wanted was repetition of the October War misunderstanding.'[74]

In July 1974 there was a further changing of the guard when Richard Nixon finally resigned after struggling with the aftermath of the Watergate break-in for more than a year. Kissinger was staying on, but the British expected that the arrival of the Gerald Ford presidency would 'change the whole environment in which Kissinger at present operates' – a prospect that did not disappoint them.[75] They still wondered what had caused Kissinger to take such a hard line on the Anglo–American relationship, and to impose the remarkable intelligence cut-off during August 1973. Richard Sykes, Rowley Cromer's perceptive deputy at the British Embassy in Washington, asked himself the same question, as many agreed that the Americans' behaviour was not in their own best interests. Sykes thought the answer could be summed up in one word: 'Watergate'. From late April 1973, he argued, this had hung like a black cloud over everything, and if not for that abiding psychological pressure, Nixon and Kissinger would have taken a 'more relaxed view' of events on the inter-

national scene. Watergate had combined with Vietnam and
the Oil Crisis to create a generally depressing political atmosphere in Washington. Sykes continued:

*

I am sometimes asked by English visitors why the
Americans are in such a difficult and touchy frame of mind
today. In reply, I say that they had to go through the equivalent, in our terms, of Suez, the Profumo case and the
devaluation of £, not in a timescale of twelve years as we
did, but in not much more than two. It was, therefore, not
altogether surprising that they were being prickly and difficult.[76]

*

Disaster at Kizildere

Traitors! Pro-American dogs! These English agents were from
NATO forces occupying our country . . . it is our most fundamental
right and debt of honour to kill these agents by shooting them.
Statement by the Turkish People's Liberation Army left
at the village of Kizildere, 30 March 1972[1]

The British intelligence community was not ready for the rise
of terrorism. Although GCHQ's sigint targets were more diver-
sified than those of NSA, it remained terribly anxious to prove
its value to Washington. This meant that Soviet military activity
remained a very high priority for Cheltenham. While GCHQ
and NSA had large-scale collection programmes in the volatile
countries of the Middle East and Africa, especially telephone-
tapping programmes, these too were tuned to watching either
the activities of the Soviets or confrontations between Israel and
its neighbours. In countries such as Iran, Ethiopia and Turkey,
the vast sigint collection programmes of the West were mostly
listening to signals from the Soviet Union. Little attention was
being paid to new religious and social movements within these
countries. It was for this reason that the West was taken by
surprise by the fall of the Shah of Iran in February 1979. Where
there was monitoring of local Middle Eastern traffic, its focus
was often narrowly on oil and arms sales. David Owen, who
was Foreign Secretary at the time of the rise of religious revolutionaries in Iran, laments that one of Britain's mistakes was
to take 'short-term advantage of our Persian linguists to improve
our commercial performance at the expense of in-depth political reporting'. On reflection, he felt that the right kind of monitoring by GCHQ, together with closer cooperation with Mossad,

which knew about the opposition groups in Iran, was what had been required. 'With our electronic sources . . . we could have analysed more and possibly anticipated events.'[2]

Turkey was another country where internal instability and violence impacted on the Western intelligence community because of the vast sigint presence there – over fifteen thousand NATO personnel, most of whom were Americans. In the late 1960s a left-wing movement had opposed growing Western economic and military influence in the country. These groups were broadly based, and counted amongst their numbers many students, academics, bureaucrats and even military officers. Their militancy reflected serious social issues, with soaring inflation and problems in the agricultural sector. In short, there was plenty of combustible material for radical groups to exploit. During the first months of 1970, left-wing activists became more violent, bombing public buildings and machine-gunning police stations.

February 1970 saw the first sign of serious trouble, when a group of eleven students was arrested at Diyarbakir, near the Syrian border. They had been undergoing secret training with the Palestinians near Damascus, and had been liberally supplied with arms and explosives. This training in Syria contributed to the growth of two different militant groups, the Turkish People's Liberation Army (TPLA) and the Turkish People's Liberation Front (TPLF). Both consisted of middle-class intellectuals who regarded themselves as a revolutionary vanguard. Like many revolutionary leaders, they suffered from a 'Che Guevara complex', believing that symbolic acts of violence could trigger a wider social revolution. Che Guevara had come to grief in 1967 during a futile attempt to stir the revolutionary consciousness of Bolivia, and was captured and shot by a police team, advised by the CIA. Turkey's would-be revolutionaries would soon suffer a similar fate. However, in the meantime, the attacks in Turkey focused on the foreign intelligence presence, including sigint collection sites.[3]

NSA and GCHQ should have been more alert. They had

substantial numbers of sigint personnel in Turkey because of the proximity of vast Soviet missile- and aircraft-testing sites around the Caspian Sea. It was the US Air Force that had led the sigint effort here. Back in January 1953, Colonel Arthur Cox from the USAF Security Service had arrived to seek out a site for the first American radio squadron, and selected Karamursel, a small market town forty miles south of Istanbul. The vast compound of seven hundred acres was shared with the US Naval Security Group. Although other monitoring stations were established in Turkey, Karamursel remained the largest, with close to a thousand personnel.[4] It gradually passed under the control of the US Naval Security Group, since its main task was listening to the voice and Morse traffic of the Soviet Navy exercising in the Black Sea. It also hosted NSA's regional communications centre, which relayed sigint from numerous other stations back to NSA headquarters at Fort Meade.[5]

Although Karamursel monitored Soviet space launches, including Yuri Gagarin's historic flight in April 1961, it was not ideally placed to listen to missile tests further east, at places like Kapustin Yar. Accordingly, further sigint sites blossomed along the coast of the Black Sea, at Sinop and Samsun. These specialised in gathering the signals from new Soviet missiles as they were being tested – known as telemetry – and had special intelligence-gathering radars that tracked the missiles in flight.[6] At Samsun, only three hundred miles from the Soviet border, listeners could discover when each missile type was perfected and passed into production. Other stations along Turkey's northern coastline listened in to high-frequency communications.[7]

The intelligence gathered from these stations was a strategic treasure trove: some have suggested that three quarters of the Western intelligence on Soviet strategic weapons systems came from Turkey, together with smaller stations in neighbouring Iran. In the late 1960s, vast sums were invested in a new facility at Pirinclik Air Base, close to the Syrian border at Diyarbakir.

Here the Americans constructed two huge intelligence radar systems, one for detection and the other for tracking. Even more secret were several small intelligence stations on the outskirts of the Turkish capital Ankara. Here the USAF base at Belbasi hosted a seismic intelligence station that captured the vibrations from underground atomic explosions at the Soviet weapon-testing facility at Semipalatinsk. Nearby were other sensitive posts eavesdropping on the diplomatic traffic generated by Ankara, hidden within America's Military Mission headquarters and known as 'TUSLOG'. (This stood for US Logistics Organisation in Turkey, and its inconspicuous name provided the cover for many intelligence activities.) Here the Americans successfully bribed a Turkish code clerk to hand over his own government's cyphers.[8]

In short, Turkey was to the American NSA what Cyprus was to GCHQ, hosting a vast network of aerial farms, dishes and monitoring stations. There was overlap: just as NSA had some small bases on Cyprus, GCHQ had some small stations in Turkey. As early as 1952 the two countries had agreed to 'concert Anglo–American operations in the field' with regard to Turkey. F.M. Smith, the GCHQ officer in charge of the British units in Turkey, worked with local US Army Security Agency units to agree on a suitable division of labour.[9] Britain also carried out many of its sigint and imagery flights from Cyprus over Turkey or Iran, following the border and going out over the Black Sea or the Caspian Sea. In the mid-1960s Britain was carrying out more than a thousand overflights a year across Turkey, many of them for intelligence purposes.[10]

The rising tide of leftist violence and the large foreign intelligence presence inside Turkey was a volatile combination. In the 1960s the sigint facilities were protected by their extreme secrecy. Although large and visible with their domes and dishes, few knew of their real purpose or importance. Instead, the brunt of leftist anger was borne by the CIA, which radicals asserted was exerting a malign influence over the Turkish government, and was behind the growing efforts to repress the left. The

Americans had certainly assisted with the development of MIT, the Turkish intelligence agency, and various groups of special forces. In November 1968 Robert Komer, who had previously served in Vietnam with the CIA, arrived as US Ambassador in Ankara, provoking much comment. In January 1969 his visit to the campus of Ankara's Middle East Technical University, a bastion of radicalism, triggered a major riot.[11]

Increasing numbers of young Turkish officers and government officials joined the radicals, and this translated into an unwelcome interest in the more sensitive installations. On 29 January 1971 a group of about twenty students attacked America's TUSLOG headquarters in Ankara, throwing a bomb and a Molotov cocktail, followed by sporadic small-arms fire. The bomb destroyed a vehicle, and Turkish soldiers returned fire.[12] The next month, an armed group abducted a US Air Force sergeant at Balgat, on the outskirts of Ankara. Although he was freed after seventeen hours, the incident pointed to future trouble.[13] Finally, on 4 March, a group of militants from the TPLA kidnapped four US airmen from a US sigint base in Ankara known as USM-49.[14]

The hostages were returning to their accommodation in an Air Force station wagon manned by a Turkish driver after a monitoring shift. They were following their usual route, a narrow and icy road, when they were forced to stop by a road-block. Several men loitering by the side of the road were suddenly joined by others brandishing sub-machine guns and grenades. The airmen expected to be shot immediately, but instead they were frogmarched away to a waiting car. The whole party then drove off in convoy, led by the captured station wagon. Although they were asked to keep their eyes shut, the Americans were neither bound nor blindfolded. At least one of them reckoned he could probably have made a successful getaway, but he feared the consequences for the remaining captives.[15]

One of the kidnappers then took the station wagon for disposal. Foolishly, he attempted to abandon it near the Soviet

Embassy, which had a strong police presence. He was immediately arrested and successfully interrogated, revealing the names of the leading kidnappers, but not their location. He explained that they had all been trained by the Palestinian group 'Fatah' in Syria during 1970. MIT, the Turkish National Intelligence Agency, concluded that the hostages were being held on the nearby campus of the Middle East Technical University. Accordingly, early on 5 March the campus was cordoned off, and a massive security search began. The campus was vast, and included five miles of underground heating ducts which were examined inch by inch. Armed students barricaded themselves in the dormitories, and there were prolonged exchanges of fire. A student and a soldier were killed, and many were wounded. Weapons were recovered and two thousand students were detained, but there was no sign of the US airmen.[16]

Improbably, the hostages had been taken to a luxury apartment not far from the embassy quarter. For the next five days they were kept cooped up in a closet, interspersed with occasional periods when they were allowed to sit in the hallway for relief. The kidnappers treated their captives respectfully. They provided playing cards, and eventually the airmen developed an improvised chess set. The Americans had offered all their valuables in return for release, but their captors showed no interest. The TPLA began to issue demands, and threatened to put all the four airmen in front of a firing squad unless they were complied with. They included broadcasts of anti-American declamations on Turkish radio, and the payment of $400,000 within thirty-six hours. A little later they contacted the US Embassy, extending the deadline and sending a package containing short letters from the airmen to their families, together with one of their identity cards. There was now extensive press coverage of the crisis, but the real role of the airmen as sigint operators remained a secret.

President Nixon took a hard line. On the day of the abduction he told a White House news conference that he was not asking the Turkish government to negotiate with the kidnappers, and would leave operational decisions to Ankara.[17] Unbeknown to Nixon, the airmen were allowed to listen to the radio, and his comments sent them into a deep depression. They feared their chances were now 'down the drain'. The US Ambassador in Turkey, William J. Hanley, received a cable from Washington on the same day underlining Nixon's tough position and opposing any ransom payment, for fear that it would encourage further kidnappings. Nevertheless, the Turkish government broadcast a version of one of the TPLA's Marxist proclamations, in order to play for time. Meanwhile, MIT masterminded an extraordinary security operation. Thirty thousand troops and police were mobilised in a massive sweep of several sections of Ankara. The security forces combed the poorer areas of the city and revisited parts of the university campus. One member of the Turkish Cabinet declared, 'You don't bargain with bandits.'[18]

Behind the scenes, the US Information Service arranged for Turkish television to interview the pregnant wife of one of the airmen, Jimmie Sexton, and sent photographs of their thirteen-month-old son Anthony to local newspapers. Her direct and emotional appeal had a substantial effect on public opinion. Later, under police questioning, the kidnappers would concede that they had felt the tide of public sentiment turning against them. Once the deadlines expired, the five kidnappers became more nervous. They chose to relieve their anxiety by cleaning their guns in full view of the airmen, and took pleasure in aiming their unloaded weapons at them and pulling the trigger. They clearly loved their abundant weaponry: one of them was so festooned with belts of ammunition and hand grenades that the airmen christened him 'the walking arsenal'. The kidnappers began to discuss taking their captives away to the east and then out of the country. At one point the airmen feared they would be taken to Syria, and then perhaps even on to the Soviet Union.[19]

At about 10 o'clock in the evening of 8 March, by complete chance, local police were called to investigate a domestic quarrel close to the kidnappers' apartment. The kidnappers believed that they had been located, and told the airmen to lie on the floor in the dark. Waiting in the pitch black, they expected a gun battle to erupt at any moment. After a long period of time they realised their kidnappers had fled. Putting on civilian clothes they found in the apartment, they crept out and eventually found a taxi. First they went to the American Embassy, but the huge crowd of press and government officials was so alarming that instead they headed back to their billets, and reported their escape there. It turned out that they had been held only seven hundred yards from the American Embassy. Later, Ambassador Hanley tried to defend the policy of not paying the ransom. The airmen were not impressed, and retorted that when you are being held at gunpoint 'you don't really care about what might happen to somebody else. All you care about is getting out in one piece yourself.'[20]

The broad effect of the kidnap operation was to ratchet up the pressure on all sides. In April 1971 a new government was formed under Nihar Erim, which wasted no time in rounding up hundreds of suspects and declaring martial law in eleven provinces. Many trade unionists and academics who had nothing to do with the TPLA were jailed, and newspapers were shut down.[21] Four of the five kidnappers were caught on their way to the TPLA's headquarters at the mountain stronghold of Malatya in south-eastern Turkey. The only one who remained at large, Sinan Cemgil, was soon planning another attack. The target was the important American intelligence site at Pirinclik Air Base in south-east Turkey, near Diyarbakir. This was a combined radar and elint operation that monitored missiles launched from the ultra-modern Soviet testing grounds at Tyuratam on the Aral Sea.[22] On 28 April, having trained a new cadre of militants, the TPLA force made their way towards the site, but Turkish intelligence had an agent on the inside, and they were intercepted by the security forces. Cemgill and many of his adherents died in the prolonged gun battle that followed.[23]

By early May the security situation seemed superficially to

be under control. One of the kidnappers of the US airmen was dead, and the remaining four were in prison. During the summer three of these prisoners, who were prominent figures in the TPLA, would be sentenced to be hanged. However, it was clear that the terrorists now considered themselves to be at war with the intelligence and security services – not only the Turkish agencies like MIT, but also those of Turkey's allies. Moreover, with good contacts inside the government ministries, they were able to secure sensitive information about which bases had intelligence functions and constituted the most attractive targets. The presence of several key terrorist leaders awaiting the death sentence in Turkish jails was also a likely spur to further action.

Just after midday on 17 May 1971, members of the TPLF kidnapped Ephraim Elrom, the Israeli Consul General in Istanbul, as he returned to his apartment for lunch. He did this every day, never varying his schedule, and his predictable movements made him an easy target. After the kidnapping of the US airmen he had been offered a bodyguard, but had refused. Heavily armed kidnappers took over the flat across the hall from his, holding twelve people prisoner while they waited. Elrom was greeted at gunpoint and resisted, but was pistol-whipped until he was semi-conscious. Bundled into a large leather bag, he was taken away in a stolen car. The terrorists were quick to announce their demands, which amounted simply to the release of all previously captured TPLA members and publicity for their Marxist manifesto. They set a three-day deadline of 5 o'clock on the afternoon of 20 May.

The public were not aware of Ephraim Elrom's true profile. Although fifty-eight years old, he had only entered the Israeli diplomatic corps less than three years previously, after the tragic death of his son in an aircraft accident. Istanbul was his first diplomatic posting, and he had served there for nineteen months. Previously he had been a distinguished security intelligence officer, and Israel's most skilled interrogator. Most importantly, he had been the lead member of the team that had interrogated Adolf Eichmann after his capture by Mossad in Argentina in May 1960. The widespread assumption amongst the foreign diplomatic corps in Ankara was that Elrom had been targeted for anti-Zionist reasons, reflecting his role in bringing Eichmann to justice. However, the British Ambassador in Turkey, Sir Roderick Sarell, knew he had really been selected because of his intelligence liaison role. Elrom's main functions in Turkey seem to have been to exchange intelligence with the Turkish agencies on Turks who had joined Arab terrorist groups such as Fatah, and to help with the training of Turkish counter-terror units. Sarell learned from the Israelis that they had been watching the TPLA, and knew that over a hundred Turks were training in Syria, Jordan and the Lebanon.[24] It was now clear that the extremists were deliberately going after intelligence personnel.[25]

On 17 May the Turkish government warned that if Elrom was not released, many more people would be imprisoned. They were also preparing a law that made sheltering or supporting kidnap groups automatically subject to the death penalty, and threatened to make this retroactive, executing anyone associated with the kidnapping of Elrom. The Israelis backed this tough response. The next day, Turkey's National Security Council met and was given an intelligence briefing by MIT. Afterwards they rounded up four hundred leftists, students and dissidents. Torture was used in the hope of extracting information about the kidnappers. Their hard line reflected a growing conviction on the part of Turkish intelligence that there was strong Syrian or even Soviet support for both the TPLF and the TPLA; some of the activists involved in the kidnapping of the airmen had been part of the original group of eleven students caught on the Syrian border with explosives and guns in 1970.[26]

The TPLF operation to kidnap Elrom was complex. Several apartments had been rented as safe houses, and numerous members of the group were involved indirectly in support teams. On 19 May the kidnappers held a meeting in a nearby safe house with other TPLF leaders, but they were divided about Elrom's fate. On 20 May Elrom's wife issued a public statement asking the kidnappers to release her husband, adding that they had lost their only child, and that she could not bear the further loss of her husband. At this point most Turkish politicians believed that no extremist group would execute a foreign diplomat. The following day, the authorities announced a curfew and began a methodical search of houses in the Istanbul area, a sprawling city of two million people.

By midday, two members of the kidnappers' extensive support team had been caught, and pressure was building. They opted to try to move Elrom using a furniture removal van as cover. Fearing that they had been spotted, they panicked and decided to kill their hostage, flipping a coin to determine who would do the deed before the rest fled to various bolt-holes around Istanbul. Mahir Cayan, to whom the task had fallen, turned a radio up as loud as possible to try to mask the sound of the execution. At exactly 6.30 p.m. he approached Elrom, who was bound to a chair, and fired three shots into his temple. His body was found by a routine search team in the early hours of the following morning, in an apartment block only five hundred yards from the Israeli Consulate.[27]

The government reaction was draconian. Four thousand suspects were arrested, many further leftist newspapers were banned and civil rights were drastically curtailed. All the members of the gang that had taken Elrom were eventually located, and either died resisting arrest or were imprisoned. It transpired that their initial target had been the CIA station in Istanbul, but they had concluded that the security there was too good. With security for military and diplomatic personnel in Turkey's major cities greatly strengthened, many concluded that the spate of kidnappings was now over.

The following autumn the Turkish government announced death sentences for eighteen members of the TPLA and the TPLF. Istanbul's educated elite were shocked, and Western diplomats who moved in middle-class circles reported that many visibly 'shudder at the thought of the barbarities of hanging'. However, in the street, the taxi drivers and cobblers expressed satisfaction; their 'virtually unanimous reaction' was that the 'students must hang'. They added that the terrorists were the 'spoiled children of wealth', and stern action was needed to halt the attacks.[28]

In fact the worst was yet to come. The impending execution of some of their comrades prompted the radical groups to use their ingenuity. On 29 November 1971, five of the most prominent militants escaped from a high-security military prison. They consisted of the three survivors from the killing of Elrom – including Mahir Cayan, who had pulled the trigger – and two members of the group that had kidnapped the sigint airmen. The press reported that they had escaped through a tunnel during an orchestrated riot. In fact the escape was facilitated by military officers sympathetic to the prisoners' anti-imperialist agenda. Some of the guards were later convicted of deliberately not taking roll calls and could not explain how the escapees had been able to drive away calmly in a military vehicle. Meanwhile, the fighters from the terrorist units of the hitherto largely separate TPLF and TPLA had now made common cause in jail.[29]

One of the five escapees was soon killed by the security services, having chosen to hide out in a flat immediately beneath that of one of Istanbul's senior police officers. Another was recaptured in Istanbul. However, in early 1972 the other three were still on the loose.[30] No one doubted that they would seek to obtain the release of their remaining comrades in prison by taking further hostages. Those still incarcerated included Deniz Gezmiş, who had led the kidnapping of the sigint airmen and whose death sentence had been confirmed by the Turkish Court of Appeal on 10 January, and two of the TPLA group that had killed Elrom, who were also sentenced to death. With a total of 353 activists sentenced to long terms in prison and a further eighteen facing the death penalty, the stakes were now high.[31]

Led by Mahir Cayan, the escapees made their way to Ankara,

where they enjoyed a strong network of support. On 24 January the Turkish Interior Minister told parliament that intelligence on further plots had been obtained, and new groups of terrorists were training abroad. As a result, the parliament voted to extend the period of martial law.[32] Although the trials of most of the activists were public, additional military tribunals were proceeding in secret. In March no fewer than fifty-seven officers were removed from the armed forces and were awaiting trial on charges of assisting the TPLA. Their crimes ranged from providing target intelligence and supplying arms, to aiding the five prison escapees in November 1971.[33] Nervous of further escape attempts, some of the convoys taking the accused from jails to the courts were now escorted by tanks.[34]

On 14 March 1972 the American Embassy received a warning from the Turkish intelligence services that because of the impending execution of three of the most prominent terrorists, including Deniz Gezmiş, further kidnap attempts were likely. The Americans regarded the warning as 'particularly significant', and concluded that the danger of kidnapping would remain high for some time to come.[35] A week later, President Cevdet Sunay signed the order for the executions to go ahead in the next few weeks.[36]

Always looking for a high-profile target, the TPLA leader in Istanbul proposed the occupation of a Western embassy, but after some reconnaissance work it was concluded that security was so tight that the scheme was abandoned. Instead, they turned their attention to the more remote intelligence bases. They now chose a GCHQ sigint site at Carsamba, near the Black Sea town of Unye, where new equipment made by Plessey and Marconi was being installed. This was close to a larger American sigint site at Samsun. Surprisingly, despite the kidnapping of the American sigint personnel the previous year, security was poor. The kidnapping operation was led by Mahir Cayan, and had strong local support from left-wing lawyers and teachers who had been sacked as a result of the recent government clampdown, and were happy to assist the militants. They knew that there was no security at the GCHQ accommodation areas, which were in the neighbouring village of Unye.

On 26 March 1972 Cayan and his team, disguised as Turkish officers and carrying Sten guns, were able simply to walk into the accommodation block where eight GCHQ technicians were having dinner. First they forced their captives to open the safe, and stole documents and money. Then they asked, 'Who of you is the toughest?', chose three hostages and tied up the rest, giving themselves a ten-hour start.[37] The abductees were two British nationals, Gordon Banner and Charles Turner, and a Canadian, John Law. All three were sigint technicians whose cover story was that they were staff from Cable & Wireless Ltd doing contract work for the Ministry of Defence. However, recently declassified documents confirm that they were in fact full-time GCHQ staff. Bundled into a truck, they were driven away from the coast over winding roads towards the mountain village of Kizildere, which was a TPLA stronghold. Five more TPLA members were waiting in the house of the local Mayor, which became their base. The Turkish Foreign Ministry later explained that it was worried about the safety of the fifty GCHQ staff working in Turkey at the two other GCHQ sites because it feared that Communist sympathisers within the Turkish Air Force might have tipped off the kidnappers about their routine movements.[38]

The British Foreign Secretary, Alec Douglas-Home, quickly deduced that the main purpose of the kidnapping was to force the release of the three most prominent members of the TPLA and TPLF who were under imminent sentence of death in Istanbul. He asked Roderick Sarell, the British Ambassador in Ankara, to discreetly enquire what was being done about the death sentences. The first thing the Turkish government did was to postpone the executions.[39] On 28 March the Prime Minister, Dr Nihat Erim, wrote to the British Prime Minister, Edward Heath, thanking him for expressing confidence in the Turkish effort and assuring him that the country's 'entire security forces' were attempting the rescue of the three hostages.[40] Although

Douglas-Home had received assurances from Cheltenham, he nevertheless asked Roderick Sarell to double-check that the security precautions to protect the remaining personnel at Unye and the two other Black Sea sites were indeed adequate.[41]

The next day, Douglas-Home made an optimistic statement in the House of Commons. He perpetuated the cover story that the hostages were 'three Ministry of Defence civilian radar operators', working with the Turkish Air Force.[42] However, even as he spoke, the Turkish Prime Minister made a hard-hitting TV address which closed the door on any bargaining with the kidnappers over the impending death sentences. 'It is an empty dream on their part,' he declared, 'to imagine that this kidnapping will yield any result for them.' He was determined to resist 'blackmail', and insisted that the kidnappers would be 'hunted down'. The law, he added, would be enforced 'to the bitter end'.[43] True to his word, a massive search of the area surrounding the half-finished GCHQ facility at Carsamba was launched. Commandos with helicopters were brought in, and by 29 March the hide-out at Kizildere had been located. Operations on the ground were led in person by the Turkish Interior Minister, Ferit Kubat, who was accompanied by a posse of journalists. The next day, at 5.30 in the morning, he began talking directly to the terrorists through an open window in the Mayor's house. When he told them to give up the hostages and surrender, the terrorists insisted on the release of their three comrades awaiting death in Ankara. Later they reduced their demands to their own safe passage to the Syrian border. Kubat insisted that they surrender unconditionally.

These tense personal exchanges continued for some time. Ertugrul Kurku, one of the TPLA gunmen, recalls that at a certain point in the proceedings, the terrorists brought the hostage Charles Turner, who was the leader of the GCHQ party, to the window and allowed him to talk to the Interior Minister. Turner shouted anxiously, 'Don't fire. If you do so they will kill us.' He explained that the kidnappers were desperate, and effectively regarded themselves as a suicide squad, determined to succeed, or else to die in the attempt. The security forces were increasingly frustrated, and shouted back: 'They have no human feelings any more. They will kill you anyway!' Turner repeated that if the security forces opened fire, they would be killed immediately.

Eventually, at about midday a local sympathiser, Sener Sadi, a Marxist lawyer, was brought to the village to try to break the deadlock. He was taken to the operations centre, a farm building not far from the Mayor's house, where he met Kubat and a slightly sinister-looking intelligence chief from MIT, wearing sunglasses and a fur-collared coat. After long discussions, Sadi agreed to advise the kidnappers to surrender. He called to them through a window and through holes they had made in the roof of the Mayor's house, telling them that if they surrendered and did not harm the hostages, nothing would happen to them. This met with expressions of incredulity from the kidnappers. The security forces then shouted that the kidnappers would die in any case.[44] What happened next is disputed, but Ertugrul Kurku, the sole surviving kidnapper, recalls:

*

At 14.20 hours firing started from the houses around us. [Mahir] Cayan, Saffet Alp and I were upstairs. We were taken aback by the firing and jumped down. Mahir [Cayan] shouted 'Ingilizler' [The British] . . . His warm blood was dripping down onto me from upstairs. I saw Mahir Cayan's arm dangling out of the hole upstairs. I ran up. However, because firing continued, I could not pull him down. I touched his body. He had been shot through the head. He was dead. I came down. While I was seeing to Mahir, one or more of our friends had killed the Britishers . . . [45]

*

Accounts differ as to who shot first. The terrorists' supporters insisted that it was the Turkish special forces who began the firing, after which everyone else joined in.[46] The military insist that they only fired once they heard shooting within the house, and presumed that Mayir Cahan was killing the hostages.[47] Either way, the kidnappers and the special forces were now freely exchanging automatic fire. The terrorists threw grenades, and the authorities replied with an RPG-7 rocket launcher and later a mortar. They then tried teargas, but the kidnappers continued to fire as they rushed the building. All three hostages had already been tied up and executed at close range with pistols. After the intense firefight the building was searched, and all but one of the terrorists was also found to be dead.[48]

The surviving terrorist, Ertugrul Kurku, had taken up a position near the door, armed with two sub-machine pistols which he fired together. However, when grenades and rockets started to explode, he retreated into an adjacent barn, and seems to have hidden under a haystack, where he was eventually discovered. Some have alleged that he might have been an informant of the Turkish intelligence service. After the fighting was over, a note was found under a bloodstained pillow near to where the three GCHQ technicians were murdered which suggested that the terrorists were effectively seeking martyrdom. It declared that everyone 'dies sooner or later', and that the 'revolutionary path is difficult' and is 'lighted with blood of every guerrilla that falls'.[49]

Some of the wives, children and friends of the three hostages had gathered at the British Embassy in Ankara, hoping for a successful resolution. The Ambassador now had the sad duty of explaining that things had gone very badly.[50] The Turkish Prime Minister, Nihat Erim, wrote to Edward Heath expressing his shock and grief at the 'senseless murder' of the technicians and asking for his condolences to be passed on to the families. He also offered his assurance that no effort would be spared in tracking down the 'relentless desperadoes' who were responsible for this 'dastardly crime'. Heath responded by praising the energy of the security forces 'despite the tragic outcome'.[51] Roderick Sarell had sent a flash message to Heath's private secretary stating that the kidnappers had blown themselves up, and that the Turkish Army 'to the last refrained from firing'. This was hardly an accurate account of the proceedings.[52] Heath sent messages of sympathy to the wives of Gordon Banner and Charles Turner.[53] In Istanbul the leftists protested against the death of so many of their fighters with a series of bombings around the city on 30 March and again on 5 April.[54]

It was only on 5 April, when Embassy officials received the personal effects of the three GCHQ staff from their apartment at Unye, that they discovered a lengthy ransom note left by the kidnappers. The other five GCHQ technicians, who had been held briefly but not taken, were security-conscious, and had thrown scattered papers, including the ransom note, into a desk and locked it. American officials observed that the existence of the note had been kept a secret, and it had not been shown to the families. They added that 'its late discovery is embarrassing to the British Embassy'. The last section of the overlooked ransom note read:

*

As our Peoples Revolutionary Vanguard we, expressing with action this wish and protest say: if it is wished that in the Turkey of 1972 a single patriots or vanguard warrior's life should be ended by the rope of oligarchy, the Peoples Revolutionary Vanguard, that is us, will liquidate with bullets these British agents also.

If we may put it briefly: For saving the lives of these British agents who work for NATO, the military organ of Anglo–American Imperialism, the chief enemy of the people of the world, our conditions are plain.

The executions will be called off immediately.

*

Richard Fyjis-Walker, the British Counsellor, commented that while the late discovery of the note was embarrassing, had it been found earlier it would not have changed the course of events. More embarrassing was a further discovery made by British intelligence officers who were working with GCHQ to investigate the incident. It turned out that the kidnappers had enjoyed easy access to the GCHQ technicians because they 'had the misfortune to be living above the local cell leader of the

Turkish People's Revolutionary Army'. Whoever had done the security checks on the billets for the GCHQ staff probably had a little explaining to do.[55]

The TPLA were not quite finished with their spate of terror. They attempted three further operations in an effort to secure the release of their jailed colleagues, hijacking a Turkish Airlines flight to Sofia in Bulgaria, then attempting, but failing, to capture two Turkish policemen and to assassinate the Turkish General in charge of martial law in Ankara. Once again the TPLA demonstrated what British officials described as access to 'good local intelligence'.[56] In response, judicial proceedings were accelerated, and the three TPLA leaders who the terrorists had attempted to have freed were hanged on 6 May 1972. Having made a loud proclamation of their belief in Marxist revolution, each was allowed to kick out the chair from under himself. However, being denied the services of a proper gallows, their deaths were prolonged and agonising.[57] On 19 June there was an assassination attempt on another GCHQ technician involved in the same Black Sea project, but he escaped unhurt.[58]

The following year, the widows of the murdered technicians brought a case for compensation against the British government, supported by their trade union.[59] The authorities did not acquit themselves well. One of the issues that appears to have caused official anxiety was the belatedly discovered ransom note. As the court case approached, Georgina Wright, head of the Foreign Office South-East European Department, noted: 'The demand note could cause problems – we did not release information about it at the time as it was found in the flat from which the technicians were kidnapped a week after the murder.'[60] Her colleagues noted that there were other documents that would cause 'serious difficulties' if they were released to the court.[61] There was also a more general wish to conceal GCHQ's involvement in the affair from public view.[62]

In the event, the claims were dealt with by John Somerville, GCHQ's Principal Establishment Officer.[63] Somerville had been out to Turkey in the immediate aftermath of the shooting. He also allowed the solicitors of the widows to speak to two of the technicians who were not taken, once they had been security vetted.[64] With the support of the trade union, Beryl Turner, the widow of Charles Turner, pursued an action alleging government negligence in which her husband was described as 'a civil servant'. She argued that the attack was 'reasonably foreseeable', given that 'certain American personnel employed in a similar capacity to the deceased', as well as the Israeli Consul General, had been kidnapped in the previous twelve months, and that the GCHQ staff were not warned, no secure accommodation was offered and no guards provided. Understandably, what seemed to vex her most was the fact that the landlord who had provided the accommodation for the technicians was a local leader of the TPLA.[65]

GCHQ attempted to argue that, at the time, the violent attacks had seemed to be limited to Ankara and Istanbul. However, this was not the case, since the militants had previously mounted a failed attack on the sigint base at Dakiyir in remote southeast Turkey, making it clear that all such sites were vulnerable. At that point, stronger security measures probably should have been taken. Moreover, although warning circulars reached British staff at diplomatic premises, they were 'not sent to personnel at the operational sites'.[66] In the event, the action never went to trial since GCHQ – wisely perhaps – opted to settle out of court.[67] Compensation of £10,000 was paid to the families, although the GCHQ aspect of the case was not publicly revealed until a debate in the House of Commons ten years later.[68]

For GCHQ, the deaths of Gordon Banner, Charles Turner and John Law were a terrible tragedy. Since the 1950s, the agency had realised that collecting sigint on the Eastern Bloc would mean more short-range collection, more special operations and more risk. Yet the British prided themselves on their professionalism, and had lost no one in their overflights and secret submarine missions, despite some close calls. This reflected a mixture of sound risk-assessment and a measure of good luck.

By contrast, the deaths at Kizildere smacked of incompetence, and were probably avoidable. They followed a period when intelligence personnel were clearly being earmarked as targets by a ruthless group. Indeed, on 1 June 1971, after the capture of the American sigint airmen, the British Ambassador, Roderick Sarell, had expressly warned London of the 'danger of further political kidnappings to be used as a bargaining counter with the authorities'.[69]

It seems unlikely that the Soviets were directly behind the attacks in Turkey. However, Moscow did hope to use the pressure generated by these incidents to reduce the Western intelligence presence in the country. In 1972, NATO and the Warsaw Pact had both withdrawn some troops from central Europe under Kissinger's cherished Mutual Balanced Force Reduction agreement. Turkey was worried that these Soviet forces might be redeployed close to its borders. In 1973, Soviet diplomats aired a possible bilateral Soviet–Turkish security accord. Red Army units would be withdrawn from the border with Turkey, and in return Ankara would close the major US–Turkish airbase at Incirlik and insist on the removal of communications-monitoring sites along the Black Sea coast.[70] The regional stakes were made higher by the rivalry between Greece and Turkey over Cyprus, another critically important listening location. By March 1972 Britain's Joint Intelligence Committee had already warned that trouble was brewing in Cyprus, and that the question was looming larger in Turkey's relations with both Britain and the United States. GCHQ might well have hoped that its troubles in the eastern Mediterranean were now over – but in fact they had only just begun.[71]

Turmoil on Cyprus

At 14.26 hours one of a group of seven Turkish tanks, which had
approached to within a few hundred yards of the NW corner of
the Ayios Nikolaos perimeter, fired three shells into the Sovereign
Base Area . . .

Commander British Forces Near East,
recounting events of 15 August 1974[1]

Cyprus was a powderkeg. Repeatedly conquered by contending
waves of Greeks and Turks down the centuries, it had been
populated by settlers from both communities. In 1878 it was
acquired by the British as a colony, and in 1960 the Cypriot
Republic gained independence from Britain, with its new
President, Archbishop Makarios, presiding over the two communities by means of a complicated constitution which guaranteed an existence for the island that was separate from both
Greece and Turkey. For Britain, and also the United States, a
key goal of the constitutional settlement had been permanent
access to almost a hundred square miles of military bases that
remained British sovereign territory, and the primary purpose
of which was the collection of signals intelligence. However, a
number of prominent Greek Cypriots still hankered after *'enosis'*,
or union with Greece, and since independence Greece and
Turkey had come close to conflict over the island on several
occasions.

Cyprus was of incredible importance to British sigint. Having
lost its stations in Iraq, Egypt and Palestine, the island was
GCHQ's last foothold in the Middle East. For America too, Cyprus
was increasingly important, given the US listening station just
to the north of Nicosia at Yarallakos. Moreover, the Yom Kippur
War of 1973 and the rise of Middle East terrorism ensured that

demand for sigint from the region had rocketed. Therefore, in the mid-1970s something very odd began to happen. Not only did sigint support the making of foreign policy, but foreign policy began to support the collection of sigint. One might argue that during this period the political future of a number of island territories – not just Cyprus, but also Diego Garcia in the Indian Ocean and Ascension Island in the Atlantic – were largely shaped by their value as listening stations. The sigint tail had begun to wag the policy dog. There can be no clearer indication of the importance of GCHQ and NSA in the last quarter of the twentieth century than their powerful influence on the history of Cyprus.

For two decades, Cyprus had not only been a superb source of intelligence on events in the Middle East through comint, it had also provided spectacular intelligence on Soviet strategic weapons and been the West's most important source of war warning. What had long bothered Britain's intelligence experts most was the possibility of surprise attack. If the Soviets opted for full mobilisation, or if they involved the rest of the Warsaw Pact in war preparations, Britain expected to know about it at least a month in advance, since such activities would be hard to disguise. However, if they launched a surprise nuclear attack with missiles and aircraft, the chances of warning about this were poor. The JIC had warned:

*

We could be certain that a decision to attack had been made only if we succeeded in intercepting the decision. We have virtually no chance of doing this and we must, therefore, rely on interpreting the significance of military and other moves and preparations: in the event of a surprise attack we may never obtain such information.

*

In other words, sigint was not expected to offer reliable advance warning. However, British intelligence was working on a top-secret solution to this seemingly impossible problem, codenamed 'Project Sandra'.[2]

Project Sandra was a highly classified facility that was being developed on Cyprus. The equipment involved was partly a form of sigint collection and partly a kind of Over the Horizon Radar.[3] It bounced radio waves off layers in the upper atmosphere and down onto its target well beyond the horizon, as would later be unsuccessfully attempted at Orford Ness. However, in Cyprus, unlike Suffolk, conditions were perfect, giving a range of as much as two thousand miles. This offered the possibility of looking deep inside southern Russia, the heart of the missile- and aircraft-testing area. With many operational rocket sites and bomber bases, this region was also the most likely source of a sneak attack by Russia. The prototype was code-named 'Zinnia', and was initially developed by the Division of Scientific Intelligence with assistance from GCHQ. Begun in its earliest form in 1955, Zinnia was originally intended for the surveillance of aircraft, but by 1959 it had been extended to missiles. Its radar used a constant wave rather than pulsed transmissions to avoid disclosing its purpose.[4] The scientific intelligence branch of the CIA became a development partner, and in late 1960 new versions of Zinnia were tested at Cape Canaveral, detecting the full range of American rocketry, including Atlas, Jupiter, Thor, Titan and even an early version of the Polaris missile. Twenty missiles were fired in all, and Zinnia performed brilliantly.[5]

The final decision to initiate Project Sandra, taken on 1 November 1961, was a difficult one, since Britain enjoyed other secret sources of intelligence on Soviet missiles.[6] The previous year, SIS had achieved one of the greatest agent recruitments of the Cold War. This was Colonel Oleg Penkovsky, a Soviet Army missile expert who was providing superb intelligence on Moscow's strategic forces. Burke Trend, the Cabinet Secretary, explained the complex relationship between Project Sandra and the material provided by Penkovsky: 'Sited in Cyprus . . . it would afford a check on intelligence obtained from another source and in the event of the failure of the latter, would become much more important. But in addition it would provide significant intelligence which the other source could not.'[7] Trend understood that the situation of any agent inside the Eastern Bloc was perilous, and indeed his observations turned out to be all too prescient. Penkovsky was caught meeting a go-between of SIS in the autumn of 1962. Arrested by the KGB and put on trial, he was shot the following year, even before the construction of Sandra was completed.[8] Work now accelerated, with Sandra's transmitter located in the west of Cyprus at RAF Akrotiri, while the receiver was located in the east, at the RAF sigint base at Pergamos.[9]

Project Sandra provided early warning to all of NATO, and had a top-secret link to the American Sixth Fleet in the Mediterranean. Its success was the inspiration for further stations in Pakistan and Taiwan in the 1960s, as well as the failed experiment at Orford Ness in the early 1970s.[10] Sandra's high performance had much to do with the peculiarly beneficial location of Cyprus for the reception of signals, and for this reason the island simply bristled with aerials.[11] However, by 1970 the nature of the intelligence stations on Cyprus was changing. Alongside the veteran Project Sandra, the Americans had been permitted to construct their own special installation, code-named 'Cobra Shoe', to improve early warning to the US Sixth Fleet.[12] Cobra Shoe was a more powerful and up-to-date version of Sandra. The Americans also built a new missile-early-warning system alongside it.[13] This was the most advanced intelligence site covering Russia, and was 'run by the RAF for the USAF', although that fact was hidden from the Cypriot government.[14] Indeed, the island's authorities were highly allergic to any US intelligence presence, so American technicians visiting the twin sites had to keep a very low profile.[15]

All through the early 1970s there were signs of inter-communal trouble on Cyprus. On 8 March 1970 the President, Archbishop Makarios, escaped an assassination attempt by a whisker. A few days later, Polycarpos Georkadijis, the long-serving Minister of the Interior, was killed in a similar attack. Georkadijis's death was perhaps not surprising, since he was, according to local American diplomats, 'the arch-conspirator' of Cyprus, a 'survivor of many plots and gun battles' and 'the repository of many dark secrets'. The attempt to kill Archbishop Makarios was more shocking, since he was widely accepted as the political, emotional and indeed religious leader of all Greek Cypriots. These dramatic events brought into question many of the fundamental assumptions about the island's politics. In the short term, the position of Makarios had strengthened, but the future was uncertain. British and American officials thought it not unlikely that Greek officers dreaming of union with Greece might have been behind the attack, and concluded that the renegades might well try again.[16]

On the morning of 15 July 1974, the Greek junta in Athens launched a surprise coup attempt against the government of Makarios, who was opposed to *enosis*. The junta's chosen instrument was some officers they had loaned to the Greek Cypriot National Guard, which served as a focus for the radical pro-*enosis* faction. Under orders from Athens, they stormed the presidential palace in an attempt to kill Makarios. Despite the fact that the CIA was close to the junta, American intelligence received no warning. Athens claimed, implausibly, that its hand had been forced by impetuous local officers, but its CIA patrons did not believe this for a moment.[17] The British rescued Makarios by helicopter, and whisked him away to safety on Malta. Fighting now developed across the whole island, threatening the status quo between the two communities. All sides recognised that this reckless move was likely to trigger a Turkish military intervention. The British Foreign Secretary, James Callaghan, hoped to persuade Henry Kissinger that it was worth putting pressure on the Greek junta to end their ill-considered adventure, but Washington was treading carefully for fear that Athens would retaliate by withdrawing base rights for the American Sixth Fleet.[18]

On Cyprus, British commanders were initially faced with the task of trying to return some 3,500 local civilian base workers from RAF Akrotiri to their homes in the capital of Limassol. Officers thought they had negotiated safe passage for them, but as they made their way along the road towards Limassol, there was renewed fighting. By late afternoon the convoy had become stranded, and was unable to turn around. A large band of Greek irregulars had drawn up alongside it, 'armed with anything from muzzle-loaders to World War II Japanese field guns'. Heavy fighting was developing only a few hundred yards away, and the convoy eventually retreated back to Akrotiri. In Limassol, some British married quarters were commandeered by the various factions as machine-gun positions. 'One wife who suffered such an intrusion recovered several hundred expended cartridge cases from her living room carpet next morning.'[19]

The initial coup against Makarios took British intelligence by surprise: the Foreign Secretary at the time, James Callaghan, recalled that he had no idea what was about to unfold.[20] However, coverage of the subsequent crisis was good, partly from inter-ception of high-level Turkish military communications.[21] On 17 July the JIC provided a clear forecast of the Turkish response, which was a large-scale invasion. More than two days before the Turks landed, it warned: 'We believe that the Turks are now militarily ready to intervene if the Turkish Cypriot community is physically threatened or if Enosis is declared, but will try for the moment, through diplomatic efforts, to bring about a solu-tion by other means.' Diplomatic efforts failed, and the Turkish invasion was triggered.[22] In fact, Turkish emissaries had arrived at Downing Street on the evening of 17 July, hoping to persuade the British 'to declare war with them' and intervene jointly. Bernard Donoughue, Prime Minister Harold Wilson's Senior Policy Adviser, noted in his diary that when the British refused the Turkish delegation left, saying 'they would do it themselves anyway'. His impression was that 'they would not take long'. Sigint from GCHQ relating to the crisis was quickly forwarded to Washington, but the Americans were not in a position to make good use of the material. At the end of the month Richard Nixon would resign his presidency as a result of the Watergate scandal. Indeed, the fact that Turkey knew the White House was in turmoil contributed to its decision to invade.[23]

On the morning of 19 July, British sigint reported that the Turkish 39th Division, which had long been earmarked for possible intervention in Cyprus, was getting ready to move. At 2.50 that afternoon the JIC issued what the British commander on Cyprus, Sir John Aiken, called a 'remarkably accurate assessment' of Turkish objectives in Cyprus and capabilities.[24] Thirty minutes later came reports of a large force sailing from southern Turkey.[25] The progress of this armada was tracked by Nimrod sorties over the night of 19–20 July. After an 'extremely tense night', the Nimrod detected the main force of thirty-four vessels off the north coast of Cyprus, and at 4.30 a.m. it reported that the Turkish fleet was turning towards the coast. Meanwhile, ground stations captured sigint from Turkish strike aircraft lifting off from Antalya and Incirlik. These planes were on an attack course. 'The Nimrod was speedily withdrawn and actually cleared the area only a minute or so before the first wave of Turkish aircraft arrived.'[26] This sigint was being shared in real time with Washington. On the evening of 19 July – early in the morning of 20 July on Cyprus – US Secretary of Defense James Schlesinger phoned Kissinger and reported: 'Turks took several F-100s off about 3 hours ago from one of their bases in Turkey – they were loaded up . . . My own guess is they have a notion that before you land on a beach you are supposed to drop bombs on it.' By daylight a major Turkish offensive was in progress, with a large parachute drop north of Nicosia.[27] Kissinger had done all he could to prevent the crisis, but now lamented that 'The animals are out of their cages.'[28]

Heavy fighting developed over the next ten days, and at the end of July, with things hotting up, Aiken, the British commander in chief, decided to cease British reconnaissance flights over Cyprus for fear of an incident.[29] Britain's SIS remained active because of its large station on Cyprus, and was at pains to keep the senior CIA officers at the American Embassy in London supplied with up-to-date reports. The CIA's own sources on Cyprus were rather thin, so on 31 July Bill Colby, who had just taken over as Director of the CIA, wrote personally to the British to express his thanks for the detailed reporting.[30] During August the Turks consolidated their hold on the city of Famagusta, at the eastern end of the island. The biggest problem for the British was the threat to the GCHQ's large sigint base at Ayios Nikolaos, not far away on the edge of the eastern Sovereign Base Area of Dhekelia. As the Turks advanced, thousands of Greek refugees fled for the protection of the British base. Aiken recalled that they came on foot, in smart cars, on tractors and mule-drawn carts. Local commanders found it 'a daunting experience to see so many people with dazed and fearful expressions peering through the windows'.[31]

On 14 August, as Turkish ground forces continued to advance towards the sigint base, the Foreign Office made urgent representations to the Turkish Ambassador in London, stressing the 'specially sensitive problem of the British units at Ayios Nikolaos'. The Turks reaffirmed their respect for the British bases. However, assurances in London were one thing, and action on the ground was another. Dawn on 15 August heralded a major upsurge in violence, with mortar and heavy-machine-gun fire and large artillery explosions all around the old city. 'The atmosphere was very tense,' since no one knew if the Turks would stop at the boundary of the British bases, or encircle them. The perimeter of Ayios Nikolaos was being defended by the 3rd Battalion Royal Regiment of Fusiliers. At about 1.30 p.m. they spotted thirty-five Turkish armoured vehicles three miles north of the base. Some headed south, and 'At 14.26 hours one of a group of seven Turkish tanks, which had approached to within a few hundred yards of the NW corner of the Ayios Nikolaos perimeter, fired three shells into the base area, narrowly missing a Ferret Scout car of the 16/5 L[ancers] and a white van belonging to Thames TV.' The television crew all scrambled aboard an exceedingly crowded Ferret scout car, which then 'hastily withdrew'.[32]

The day was saved by heroic action on the ground. At 4 p.m., Colonel Hugh Johnstone, Commander of 9 Signals Regiment, the main sigint operators at Ayios Nikolaos, accompanied by Colonel Ian Cartwright, the commanding officer of the Fusiliers, walked out from the base towards the Turkish forces. An hour later they encountered three squadrons of tanks and some armoured personnel carriers, which appeared to have stopped for a 'brew-up'. A happy accommodation was reached after the British officers explained the demarcation of the boundary. Magically, the local Turkish commander then appeared and gave assurances that there would be no further trouble. As dusk approached, just as the situation appeared to be calming down, a lone Turkish tank appeared menacingly at a checkpoint at the entrance to the base. It transpired that its crew 'were totally lost, they had no radio, they had run out of main armament ammunition, their 0.5 machine gun had jammed and they had run out of fuel'. Petrol was 'hurriedly produced' and the tank was sent lumbering back towards Famagusta.[33]

By the end of August things were looking up, and a ceasefire was in place. Turkey had halted its forces, having occupied the eastern third of the island, and although 'the difficulties ahead were very great', Aiken noted that the long, slow diplomatic haul towards peace had started. Ironically, the security of the Sovereign Base Areas was 'firmer than it has been for some time', and apart from the ongoing refugee problems the situation was quiet. In London, intelligence chiefs had worried about Turkish attitudes towards Britain's secret listening units. But the local information was reassuring, and Aiken explained that contrary to what he had been told, 'the longer-term security of the signal unit and Ayios Nikolaos would seem to be better guaranteed by the close presence of the Turkish Army than it had been under the Makarios administration. The Turks understood – and approved! – its function in the NATO context.'[34] In fact, during the crisis Britain had passed almost no intelligence to NATO, given that 'both contestants are members'. Sigint personnel now resumed their normal duties, although NSA decided to abandon Yarallakos and join the British inside the safer Sovereign Base Areas.[35]

*   *   *

Surprisingly, the main threat to the sigint sites now came from London. During July 1974, officials had agonised over what to do about Cyprus in the long term. Two problems had now converged. First, the sprawling nature of the sigint sites on Cyprus, which needed vast aerial farms, made them hard to defend. Second, the increasing troop requirements generated by the growing troubles in Northern Ireland meant that strategic reserves earmarked to reinforce Cyprus in a crisis were being depleted. In short, there was no longer a 'fire brigade' to come to the rescue in a future crisis.[36] This coincided with a major defence review, begun by Harold Wilson, reflecting the dire state of the British economy. The Cabinet decided that British forces, including the sigint units, should be withdrawn completely from Cyprus as soon as possible. Wilson's objective was that this should be carried out by 31 March 1976, saving £60 million. Senior officials, including the Cabinet Secretary Sir John Hunt, warned that Washington 'will press us hard not to withdraw from Cyprus', but hoped that it could be dressed up as 'an integral part of the settlement of the Cyprus problem'. However, they also observed that: 'The American Intelligence Community is a powerful lobby in Washington. So our eventual decisions on Cyprus may affect not only the continuance of the present valuable Anglo–American intelligence relationship but also the general American reaction to our overall Defence Review proposals.'[37]

Wilson pressed on with his decision to leave Cyprus, and Hunt travelled to Washington to break the bad news as gently as possible. On 12 November 1974 he met privately with Henry Kissinger, James Schlesinger and William Colby. The meeting did not go well. Kissinger's reaction was especially explosive, involving a remarkable stream of expletives.[38] Indeed, the Americans objected so strongly that the British decision was put on hold.[39] Kissinger, worried about the loss of the intelligence bases and thinking withdrawal would have a destabilising effect on the region, was determined that the British 'continue to occupy this square on the world chessboard'. London eventually capitulated, 'given the global importance of working closely with the Americans'.[40] Two weeks later, Foreign Secretary Jim Callaghan formally assured Kissinger that 'We shall not in the present circumstances proceed with our preferred policy of withdrawing from the Sovereign Base Area altogether.'[41]

But everything was not as it appeared. Cabinet Ministers believed that Hunt had been sent to Washington to tell the Americans about the demise of the Cyprus bases. In reality, GCHQ and the Cabinet Secretary seem to have been involved in an audacious game of poker with the Americans. The idea was to persuade them to pay for the presence on Cyprus. On the very day that Hunt endured the invective of Kissinger, Schlesinger and Colby in Washington, Derek Tonkin from the Permanent Under-Secretary's Department was explaining the underlying strategy 'in the strictest confidence' to planners from the BBC monitoring service. The BBC was about to discuss its own radio monitoring station on Cyprus with its American associates who performed the same task for the CIA. Tonkin made it clear that despite the Cabinet decision to withdraw, nothing should be taken for granted. 'It might be,' he explained, 'that the Americans would offer to pay for some of the facilities in Cyprus.' Indeed, he was rather optimistic and hoped the Americans would be willing to provide 'substantial financial assistance'. He lamented that the British financial position was so bad that the country 'had long passed the time when we might have felt embarrassed' about asking the Americans for money. Meanwhile, the BBC was advised to plan on the basis of a continued British presence on Cyprus.[42]

America's willingness to pay towards the costs of bases on Cyprus was connected to the steep deterioration of its relations with Turkey during the invasion. Ankara had expected Washington to put pressure on Athens to stop the coup attempt against Makarios. Kissinger had not done this, and instead, once the Turkish invasion began, the United States suspended military assistance to Turkey. The Turks, already nurturing resentment over American efforts to deter a Turkish invasion of Cyprus ten years earlier, retaliated by closing down the vast complex of American bases that sprawled across their country. At a stroke, the United States lost the use of numerous intelligence-gathering facilities which had cost tens of millions of dollars to create and had been staffed by literally thousands of operatives. This was an earthquake in the sigint world, and the net result was that NSA became more dependent on Cyprus.[43] Kissinger regarded the loss of the Turkish bases as nothing short of 'a disaster'.[44] NSA's relations with Turkey had been difficult for some time. During the 1960s the deal had been that NSA would help Turkey to expand its own sigint capability in return for access to 'certain intelligence sites'. However, by the early 1970s the cost of sigint assistance to Turkey was rising 'astronomically'. The Americans had tried to revise the agreement, but this had been indignantly rejected by Ankara.[45]

In February 1975 Sir John Aiken was told that British forces on Cyprus were not going home after all. However, the island was now reshaped into an intelligence-only base. This meant the sigint, communications and radar facilities would stay, together with airfields to provide a foothold for British and American intelligence-gathering aircraft. Beyond this, the only other forces remaining were those required to defend them. In practice this meant about a thousand personnel, including two hundred civilians from GCHQ.[46] The search for economies was a strain for GCHQ, with quite a few duties being done by staff on short visits, and there was a struggle to find volunteers.[47] Little of the cost of staying on Cyprus appears to have been drawn from the intelligence budget.[48] The British were now keen to assist the Americans in using all the facilities in Cyprus. In April 1975 America requested spy flights to investigate Soviet arms shipments to Syria via the ports of Latakia and Tartus. These needed to be launched frequently and at short notice, yet there was 'no suitable US programme that would provide the intelligence'. Predictably, British intelligence officers were delighted to offer a Cyprus-based operation, and explained that:

*

When faced with attempting to provide some return for the enormous amounts of intelligence material provided by the US, the UK is always at a disadvantage by having so few opportunities to gain information, especially air photography. To redress the imbalance, any opportunity that presents itself should be exploited to the full. The reconnaissance of the ports of Latakia and Tartus is such an opportunity, especially as it has resulted from a direct request for assistance.[49]

*

This coincided with the expansion of the American U-2 detachment on Cyprus. The additional personnel and ground equipment arrived by American transport aircraft which were requested to arrive and depart after dark, to avoid local curiosity.[50]

The American Defense Secretary, James Schlesinger, remained anxious about British defence cuts. In early September 1975, during a NATO Nuclear Planning Group meeting at Monterey in California, Schlesinger had taken Roy Mason, the British Defence Secretary, aside and told him that he would deplore further reductions in British defence expenditure. Indeed, he threatened that if this happened the United States would have to 'reconsider its bilateral arrangements' in areas such as communications intelligence, and also on assistance in respect of nuclear weapons, including improvements to Britain's Polaris missiles. He emphasised that he was conveying the attitude of the US government as a whole.[51] When Schlesinger visited London on 24 September he was given renewed assurances that Britain had halted any plans for withdrawal from Cyprus which had 'impactions for US defence facilities there'. He also took the opportunity to emphasise the 'crucial importance' of American base expansion on the British island of Diego Garcia in the Indian Ocean.[52]

London and Washington continued to think about sigint on Cyprus, pondering how to meet their shared intelligence-gathering needs in the most economical way.[53] In February 1977 Dr David Owen, who had taken over as Foreign Secretary under the Callaghan government, spoke with Clark Clifford, American Special Emissary to the eastern Mediterranean, who was taking the lead on Cyprus. Clifford had recently been on a tour of the region, and conferred with Owen in London on his way home. On intelligence, Owen wanted to put on the record Britain's 'deep gratitude for the privileged treatment they had received from the US in this field'. He then explained that while Britain had kept the Cyprus bases because of their immense value to 'the joint intelligence effort' of the two countries, the presence there was expensive, and so remained 'a natural target for cuts'. He added, 'We had intended in 1974 to withdraw from the SBAs, but had decided not to do so in response to an American request to remain.' However, Britain's finances were in a parlous state, and the question needed to be looked at again. In short, the British needed further subsidies. Clifford admitted that, while the intelligence from Cyprus was 'not unique', with America's Turkish bases out of action it was 'very useful at present'. He asked exactly how much the Cyprus bases were costing, and after a little thought offered the prospect of 'some economic arrangement'. Owen was visibly cheered.[54]

Britain and the United States were now a rather odd couple. During the early 1970s their alliance relationship had suffered a number of vexations. The Americans had been disconcerted by Britain's irritating shift towards Europe, while Washington had alarmed London with its tendency to act unilaterally, especially in the Middle East. Yet for that very reason the British were determined to try to preserve the intelligence connection. Derek Tonkin, who looked after intelligence coordination at the Foreign Office, put this rather well, explaining that because of these political tensions 'The intelligence exchange with the Americans is perhaps the last bastion of the "special relationship".' Moreover, he added, for the British the intelligence relationship was now as much about watching Washington as about watching the rest of the world.[55]

Despite their growing political differences, in the late 1970s Britain and America shared many practical problems in the realm of sigint. Both NSA and GCHQ suffered deep cuts in their budgets. On 13 July 1976, Joe Hooper, the Cabinet Office Intelligence Coordinator, briefed the British Chiefs of Staff on the impact of the cuts. Intelligence spending was scheduled to fall by 10 per cent over a period of four years, and Hooper warned that any further reduction would mean both losses of intelligence on targets of the highest priority and 'serious risk to US/UK relations both in intelligence and other fields'. The Chiefs of Staff, led by Michael Carver, responded that Britain 'above all should preserve its special intelligence relationship with the US'.[56] However, not everything was gloomy. Hooper argued that Britain should take every opportunity to gather intelligence from Cyprus, capitalising on the Americans' loss of their facilities in Turkey and the continuing volatility of the Middle East.[57]

The dramatic events in Turkey and Cyprus illustrated another serious problem shared by Britain and the USA, namely the shrinking pattern of bases in the Third World. Whether they were owned by the British or the Americans, overseas bases were a perennial source of conflict with nationalist politicians. Back in May 1964 the US National Security Council had reviewed the problem of 'politically unstable or unreliable countries' in which the Americans had intelligence facilities. The list was long, and included Cyprus, Greece, Turkey, Ethiopia, Libya, Kenya, Morocco, India and Pakistan.[58] However, in the Indian Ocean the British seemed to have come up with a novel plan to sidestep these problems by seeking to create an Anglo–American base in a country without any indigenous people. Britain persuaded Mauritius and the Seychelles to detach a string of small islands in order to create a new sovereign area to be called the British Indian Ocean Territories, or 'BIOT'. The fly in the ointment was that in reality there was a small indigenous population, so the plan called for their enforced removal to Mauritius. What had seemed like a good idea quickly turned into a source of grave embarrassment.[59]

The main focus was the tiny island of Diego Garcia. The Pentagon had made its first request for a possible communication station there in August 1963.[60] An agreement was reached at the end of December 1966 and a station was built in late 1970. The original intention was that Britain would meet the cost of resettling the island's inhabitants and 'buying the agreement of Mauritius and the Seychelles', while the Americans would pay for the installations. However, as time went on it became clear that the 'sweetener' demanded by Mauritius and the Seychelles to give up the islands was larger than expected – in the region of £10 million. Ministers decided that Washington should contribute to this, and American defence officials reluctantly agreed, on condition that this neocolonial activity could be hidden. The arrangement was carried out secretly, by deducting the American contribution from money that Britain owed for buying Polaris missiles.[61] By the following year a full financial agreement had been drawn up, stating that the United States would 'forgo the R&D surcharge to the extent of $14 million'.[62] American defence officials knew that Congress would not approve of America subsidising the 'separation of the Chagos archipelago' to create a new British colony. Indeed, British Treasury officials seemed to enjoy the discomfort of their allies and noted, 'There is plenty of reason for embarrassment.'[63] If anyone asked whether there had been any American financial contribution they were to say that 'no payment had been made by the US Government'.[64] In April 1967, Richard Sykes of the Foreign Office noted that 'in view of the extreme delicacy of this subject' the circulation of papers was being kept to the absolute minimum. Nevertheless, the Americans were increasingly nervous about telling what was 'frankly an outright lie'.[65]

Almost as soon as the communications facility had been built on Diego Garcia, the Americans were requesting further expansion. This was linked to an earlier imperial sigint episode in East Africa. During the Second World War the British had given America permission to build a sigint station at Kagnew in

Ethiopia. By March 1951 there were over 1,312 staff there, providing what NSA's Director, General Ralph Canine, described as 'unique and profitable intercept coverage'.[66] Some of the work at Kagnew was focused on the Soviets, but the base also collected manual Morse from much of Africa and the Middle East. This was especially valuable during the Congo crisis of 1960, when the different factions fought for control over the province of Katanga, and the US Ambassador to the United Nations later sent a letter of commendation to the commander of the Kagnew station for his excellent support to the UN mission, provided through intercepts. Most of the automatic high-speed Morse intercepted was commercial, and some of it related to Middle East oil deals. At its most active period Kagnew's vast antennae farms sprawled over some 3,400 acres, and its five thousand personnel had all the facilities of a small town, including tennis courts and swimming pools. However, by 1969 this ideal spot for sigint collection was threatened by growing fighting between the Ethiopian military, which was supported by the Americans, and the rebel Eritrean Liberation Front, backed by Syria and the Soviet Union.[67] By 1972 there were only nine hundred personnel, and by 1974 Kagnew was simply a relay station for nuclear submarine communications, with a staff of little over a hundred. Two kidnapping episodes in 1975 helped accelerate its final closure in 1977.[68]

In June 1973 American officials in London explained to the British that they had been forced 'to reduce certain activities conducted by the US Army at Kagnew Station, Asmara', and the most practical way of compensating for this would be the enlargement of the station on Diego Garcia. This would restore 'coverage in Gulf of Oman, Arabian Sea and Western Indian Ocean, where Kagnew phase-out would have caused temporary degradation' to signals intelligence operations.[69] The British were taken aback at this 'very considerable' expansion of the facilities.[70] The cost of Diego Garcia now doubled. Part of the increased expenditure was for a sigint system designed to track Soviet submarines. The American trump card was ongoing support for

Britain's own nuclear strategic submarines: Kissinger and Schlesinger did not hesitate to link Diego Garcia to ongoing discussions about the successor to the Polaris system that formed the core of the British nuclear deterrent. Kissinger specifically referred to a recent message from Heath to Nixon enquiring about this matter, adding that 'A favourable reply on Diego Garcia would be very welcome and useful in the context of your message.'[71] In fact the British Ambassador to Washington, Rowley Cromer, had already signalled to the Americans that the expansion of Diego Garcia would be conditional on 'US willingness to assist Britain to carry through its Super Antelope program aimed at modernising and upgrading its Polaris submarine force'. Who articulated this deal first is unclear, but both sides saw it as a quid pro quo.[72]

The deal almost came unstuck because of the confrontation about intelligence and bases between Heath and Kissinger in late 1973. The hot question was whether the Americans would be given what they called 'unrestricted access' to the base at Diego Garcia in a crisis.[73] Having seen Heath restrict access to bases in both Cyprus and Britain during the Yom Kippur War of October 1973, Washington was not about to make the same mistake again. But Heath wanted precisely these sorts of restrictions on Diego Garcia. On 10 January 1974 Sir John Hunt warned Heath, 'This will not be easy.'[74] Three weeks later it was a hapless Hunt who was sent on a special mission to the White House to find an agreed formula. On 30 January he and Kissinger met at the White House with their officials. Kissinger, who clearly had the confrontations with Heath over intelligence flights in October 1973 fresh in his mind, explained that they might well be 'confronted with the same sort of differences between our two Governments as there had been at the time of the Middle East War'. If Heath refused access in some future crisis, the Diego Garcia facilities on which America would have spent many millions would be 'useless'. Britain 'had to be realistic'.[75]

With Hunt due to fly back to London within hours, he met

Kissinger privately to try to resolve the deadlock. Their solution was a remarkable one. Publicly, the position would be a 'joint decision' on the use of the bases in a crisis, seemingly retaining the British veto. However, behind the scenes there would be a highly secret exchange of letters between Heath and Nixon that effectively changed this to mere consultation. Sure enough, on 5 February Heath wrote a carefully crafted letter assuring Nixon of this 'on a very personal basis'. 'These understandings are agreeable to me,' replied Nixon.[76] The British Embassy assured London that the exchange was being handled 'very restrictively indeed in the White House'.[77]

The difficulties that would dog Diego Garcia for years had only just begun. In September 1975 Harold Wilson was told by his officials that there were continuing problems with the indigenous population. 'Our real difficulty,' they admitted, 'arises from the failure of the Mauritius Government to use the money we gave them to resettle those evacuated from Diego Garcia.' Mauritius had been paid over £12 million, but this money had seemingly disappeared. Officials said that they were doing what they could to persuade the Mauritian government to meet their responsibilities, but they had been 'dragging their feet'.[78] Meanwhile, Diego Garcia became a byword for misrule, and a point of transatlantic friction. In 1981 the State Department complained that the local Royal Navy contingent that was supposed to keep order on the island was 'unable to cope with spreading lawlessness'. It noted, 'the drug problem is out of hand', and that recently 'rampaging construction workers and sailors reportedly have smashed up the British Club'.[79]

In their different ways, events in Turkey, Cyprus and Diego Garcia are important examples of how the ruthless requirement for signals intelligence bases has impacted on the wider fabric of the international system. On Diego Garcia the effect was especially stark, translating into a Canute-like resistance to the end of empire and the cruel deportation of an island population. This was surely one of the more dismal episodes in recent British history. Many of the deportees were second- or third-generation islanders, for whom Diego Garcia was their rightful home. Ahead lay years of legal battles as the indigenous islanders attempted – unsuccessfully – to end their forced resettlement and achieve the right to return.[80] When the original secret deal over Diego Garcia was done, Sir Paul Gore Booth, the Permanent Under-Secretary at the Foreign Office, had expressed the British attitude frankly: 'We must surely be very tough about this. The object of the exercise is to get some rocks which will remain *ours*. There will be no indigenous people except the seagulls...'[81]

Unmasking GCHQ: The ABC Trial

We've been to MI5, MI6, Scotland Yard, Parliament and many more. Now we're going where much of the dirty work goes on –
CHELTENHAM!
ABC trial campaign newsletter, 27 May 1978[1]

During the late 1960s and early 1970s, signals intelligence was changing fast. The big players were discovering a whole new world of super-secret interception which provided a different sort of signals intelligence. This new source was telephone calls. As we have already seen, tapping telephones was hardly new, and had boomed in the 1950s in response to problems with reading high-grade codes. However, telephone calls were now increasingly being routed away from old-fashioned cables, which were hard to intercept, especially within secure states like the Soviet Union, and being carried by the more modern means of radio links, using microwave towers and satellites. This was a vastly more efficient system of communication, especially for long-distance or international calls. One of the side-effects was that conversations now spilled freely into the ether, making the possibilities for interception almost limitless. The best thing about this new source was that the material was often not encrypted so it provided a veritable fountain of intelligence virtually for free. A sigint revolution was just around the corner.

The downside of these new developments was that they produced inconceivable volumes of material. Computers were no longer needed just for breaking codes, but also for combing through the intelligence, storing it and distributing it to customers. The volume of sigint that was being collected was too large for any human to read. Moreover, the vast complexes of domes and satellite dishes that now accompanied the supposedly super-secret intelligence activities of NSA and GCHQ meant that they were more and more visible. Sooner rather than later, an enterprising investigative journalist was bound to point to these surreal installations and shout the dreaded words 'Signals intelligence.' It is amazing that in the mid-1970s GCHQ was still managing to pass itself off as a glorified communications relay station, hiding its real activities from public view. Anonymity would not last much longer.

What we now recognise as the first glimmerings of a global telecommunications revolution seemed to be in the interests of the world's major sigint agencies. A fascinating example of this was an operation carried out jointly by the British and Americans in 1969. NSA was gathering a great deal of intelligence from telephone calls between Fidel Castro's Cuba and the many Cuban exiles living in Florida. Using sigint ships, it was also possible to intercept some calls from Havana to other parts of Cuba. This was of some importance, since an elaborate game of cat and mouse was being played between the CIA and the Cuban intelligence service among the exile communities of Florida. Most of the calls were carried on a radio network called a tropospheric scatter system, owned by the Radio Corporation of Cuba, which also carried teletype traffic. The Radio Corporation of Cuba was a subsidiary of the American telecommunications giant ITT which had been gleefully nationalised by Castro when he came to power in 1959, along with all other American businesses on the island. The radio installation in Cuba was in need of a substantial upgrade, requiring new condensers and transistors, leading the Americans to fear that the link would cease to function, and the telephone calls would be sent by a different route, perhaps by cable, which was much harder to intercept.

Because America maintained a strict economic blockade of Cuba, it needed to subvert its own embargo in order for the necessary material to reach the island – besides which, if it came direct from America, the uncharacteristic generosity would alert the Cubans to the interception. The Americans turned to Britain, which had no embargo on Cuba, explaining that 'The intelligence community regards the maintenance of the link as being of considerable importance.'[2] The British, for their part, welcomed the opportunity of placing the Americans in their debt by participating in a covert operation.[3] The materials were duly shipped to Britain, and then re-exported. NSA ensured that the suppliers were indemnified against legal action for breaking the embargo, while ITT used its subsidiary in Britain, Standard Telegraph & Cable Ltd, as a cover to make the delivery.

One of GCHQ's largest ventures into the world of vacuuming up telephone calls was launched in Cornwall in 1967. At Goonhilly Downs on the Lizard peninsula there was a satellite receiving station for one of the world's first commercial communications satellites, Intelsat. Intelsat was a booming commercial venture that carried a growing proportion of the world's private communications, and was partly responsible for the explosion of international telephone calls. The system grew from 240 channels when it opened in 1964 to thirty thousand in 1983.[4] Displaying a certain amount of barefaced cheek, GCHQ built a duplicate receiving station about sixty miles down the road, near the village of Morwenstow, on the site of a former RAF wartime airfield. Here it could scoop up the same telephone traffic by simply collecting the 'spillage' as commercial satellites beamed messages down to earth. This station, with its distinctive domes and satellite dishes littered along the Cornish clifftops, was initially called CSO Morwenstow, and later changed its name to GCHQ Bude. Morwenstow was a classic Anglo–American intelligence venture. NSA paid for most of the infrastructure and the technology, while GCHQ contributed the land and paid for the staff and running costs. The massive flow of intelligence it received was shared and processed jointly.[5]

In 1969 GCHQ was working hard to develop revolutionary new systems for analysing and distributing the huge volume of intelligence intercepts, with computers being used to search for keywords that indicated subjects of interest. On 3 March Joe Hooper, the Director of GCHQ, explained to Dick White, the Cabinet Office Intelligence Coordinator, that the sigint collected at Bude would shortly be fed into a computer database that would be used by Britain and the USA to select product. The main challenge was restricting access to information at the right level to people with the right clearances. This, Hooper explained, involved 'a complicated system of "gating" in the computer programmes'. This was the first British venture with secure multi-level access computer systems for delivering intelligence.[6]

GCHQ was at the cutting edge of what would eventually be a transformative technology for all kinds of researchers. In the past, anyone who wanted to look at large volumes of newspapers would have to trawl laboriously through them physically. The time and effort involved meant that they could focus on only a few chosen titles. Today, accessing the world's press is effortless and can be done at the click of a mouse, because it is available electronically. The downside, again, is 'too much information'. Nobody can read all the world's press, so modern researchers use word-search facilities like Google Alert. In exactly the same way, NSA and GCHQ could not listen in to the entire world's satellite telephone calls, telexes and faxes. So they fed all the material into computers and built a top-secret equivalent of Google Alert, constructing computers that combed the traffic for keywords and predesignated phrases. This system was called 'Dictionary'.[7]

Each new form of interception presents fresh legal challenges. GCHQ's collection operation at Bude took three forms. At its most expansive it involved baseband trawling, which meant moving through large volumes of traffic from each country that was being monitored to find out whether material of interest was passing through particular channels. Next, there was a system that allowed the interception of all the traffic from a particular telephone dialling code, in other words perhaps one section of a city. Thirdly, there was the monitoring of specific telephone numbers. Initially, the GCHQ staff were uncertain about the legality of some of the broadband trawling, which included some British channels. For reasons that are not entirely clear, managers eventually persuaded them that it was not a legal issue. Allegedly, specific British numbers were targeted, and these were known as 'P-Numbers'. GCHQ was already beginning to encounter what we now recognise as one of the key characteristics of globalisation – the mixing up of what is inside and outside the nation state. Previously there had been a clear dividing line between domestic and international communications, which made for useful legal distinctions in the realm of interception. During the 1970s these distinctions were beginning to break down.[8]

Even telephone messages that were not carried by satellite were vulnerable, because they were increasingly being beamed between microwave radio towers. The beams travelled in a straight line, eventually spilling out into space because of the curvature of the earth. This led to yet another collection revolution, since the Americans discovered that much of this telephone traffic was vulnerable to interception by a new generation of sigint satellites. By the 1970s these were scooping enormous amounts of communications from space. One of the first major dividends was an improved ability to listen in to Moscow. NSA began to listen in to telephone calls in the Soviet capital, and also to the radio messages of taxi drivers and the Zil limousines used by the Politburo. The drivers gossiped constantly about their passengers, revealing fascinating insights into life amongst Russia's elite. Alas, this was revealed publicly in the *Washington Post* in September 1971 by the renegade American journalist Jack Anderson.[9]

The ability to listen in to telephone calls carried by radio waves meant a radical shift in GCHQ's business all around the world. In August 1974, British officials noted with delight that Syrian communications security was unsophisticated, and that 'In some quarters the open telephone is treated as if it were secure.'[10] GCHQ also had to assist friends and allies to protect them against the new sigint techniques: in Oman, for example, speech security equipment was installed.[11] The Joint Intelligence Committee also began to rethink Britain's intelligence targets in Europe because of this telephone sigint bonanza, which it coyly referred to as 'advances in intelligence-gathering by technical means'.[12] By 1973, new subjects had joined Russia as 'Priority One'. These included the 'Stability of the UK', which required intelligence to look inwards. Specific new targets included the IRA and extremist organisations within Britain. The other new priority, which had been growing fast since the 1960s, was Western Europe. Intelligence on West Germany was now far more valuable than intelligence on East Germany. Britain needed to know what Bonn thought about Britain's diplomatic recognition of East Germany, Britain's entry into the Common Market and major arms deals such as the new NATO Tornado Multi-Role Combat Aircraft that would eventually equip the air forces of Britain, West Germany and Italy. Britain's senior policy-makers also wanted better support for the sort of guerrilla wars that had flared in Cyprus, Aden and Oman during the 1960s and 1970s.[13]

NSA was already experimenting with sophisticated satellites that would revolutionise sigint activity by focusing on signals that were above the high-frequency range.[14] On 19 July 1970 America launched its first operational Ryolite satellites, which stayed broadly in the same place above the earth, requiring ground stations in specific locations to receive the voluminous sigint that they beamed down.[15] These stations were constructed at Pine Gap in Australia and at Menwith Hill near Harrogate in Yorkshire. Menwith Hill had been a field collection station for the US Army Security Agency since the 1950s, but was later taken over and run directly by NSA. By the 1970s it had been vastly expanded, and had become the largest American overseas intelligence base in the world. Its dozens of space-age domes, each of which hid a satellite dish, looked somewhat incongruous amongst the grazing cattle of the Yorkshire countryside. Now, its main purpose was to download torrents of sigint collected by the new generations of American sigint satellites. About 15 per cent of this 'overhead' material was diverted to Cheltenham, where a new super-secret section of GCHQ's Soviet Section (J Division) – code-named J-Operations or 'J-Ops' – was set up to handle this new influx of sigint.[16]

Much of the popular anxiety about the vast American ground station at Menwith Hill, nominally disguised as an RAF station, has focused on its connection to the nearby Hunters Stones Post Office Tower, which forms part of the British microwave telephone network. For years, campaigners protesting against the American base insisted that this allowed NSA to eavesdrop on British domestic communications. This was fervently denied by Albert Braeuninger, the base commander in the early 1980s, who insisted that NSA was merely a customer of British Telecom. This statement was correct, but it actually hid a different secret. Much of the product from the Ryolite satellites was being routed over this microwave network to GCHQ's secretive J-Ops section, where it was processed locally on behalf of NSA. This indicated an important change in status for GCHQ in the late 1970s and 1980s, since it increasingly became part of the processing system for what NSA collected.[17]

NSA's new satellites were actually a major problem for the Americans by the late 1970s. The 'take' from these sources was enormous and still growing, yet funding for NSA was being reduced as a result of post-Vietnam defence budget cuts. NSA's own historian, Robert Johnson, notes: 'Scarce resources meant reliance on outside help. As the budget got slimmer, NSA turned increasingly to the help that foreigners could provide. This trend accelerated in the 1970s to a greater degree than at any time in post-World War II cryptological history.' The collaboration between GCHQ and NSA was 'almost total', and at 'each bend in the road, NSA made the conscious decision to remain engaged'. Indeed, these developments, which also involved other friendly countries, were so important that NSA appointed a 'Third Party Manager' to look after the increasingly complex relationship with allies.[18]

*   *   *

The sigint satellite revolution was an unsettling experience for GCHQ. Although the British were 'in' on developments such as Bude and Menwith Hill, they were not 'of' them, since they had no satellites of their own. The golden age of high-frequency ground-based interception by manual operators sitting in nissen huts was drawing to a close. Major overseas sigint sites, such as Cyprus, were still vital, especially for missile surveillance. However, broadly speaking, the satellite revolution, together with the possibilities of remote collection, was gradually downgrading the value of GCHQ's exotic real estate. Meanwhile, the advent of satellites created a new super-club of sigint powers, of which there were only two members, America and Russia. It was a club that GCHQ ached to join.

In one area, GCHQ was joining the satellite club. This was the field of communications satellites for forwarding sigint from collection stations to GCHQ, and for communicating with NSA. In the early 1950s, communications between GCHQ and NSA were poor, due to insufficient cables and inadequate clear radio frequencies.[19] In 1956, the transatlantic channels between the two agencies were suffering outages of over four hours a day.[20] The main worry was enemy disruption in any future conflict. A secret study had concluded that the Soviets were likely to try a range of sabotage tactics in war, among the easiest of which was trawling up cables and cutting them. Transatlantic cables were at 'trawl depth' for long stretches, and the Soviets were expected to deploy specially modified nuclear submarines for the task. Other options were available, including the use of KGB agents to place 'clandestine, low-powered jammers' close to the relay stations.[21] By the 1970s Britain would be overcoming some of these problems with its own military communications satellite, called 'Skynet'. Skynet also provided secure encrypted speech facilities to the military wherever a Skynet terminal existed. The first Skynet satellite was expected in 1969, followed by a progressive build-up of further satellites and ground terminals. In obscure locations such as Bahrain, GCHQ was the largest

Skynet user. On Cyprus it required no fewer than eight channels, and was responsible for more than 80 per cent of the traffic coming back to Britain. Much of this was data on Soviet missiles from Project Sandra and Project Cobra Shoe.[22]

Skynet was a major scientific achievement, and represented Britain's first significant step into space. The launch of the satellite was regarded as a cause for national celebration. In November 1969 the RAF was invited onto the BBC children's programme *Blue Peter* to display a mock-up of the satellite which was admired by the presenters Valerie Singleton, John Noakes and Peter Purves. The programme also described Britain's new satellite control centre at RAF Oakhanger. However, no public mention was made on *Blue Peter*, or indeed anywhere, of Skynet's biggest single customer, namely GCHQ.[23]

The capacity provided by Skynet was enormous, yet the planners noted that it was 'adequate for all users of data except GCHQ'. The unimaginably huge amount of intelligence it was sharing with its main partners meant that GCHQ still required its own dedicated cables to NSA, the Canadian CBNRC and the Australian DSD.[24] By February 1972, the Cabinet Office was beginning to look at the next generation of Skynet satellites and its alternatives, at a cost of about £50 million. Again, the biggest customer was GCHQ.[25] All of its allies, especially the CIA, were now 'satellite-conscious'.[26] GCHQ pressed for closer integration with the United States, arguing for an off-the-shelf American Type-777 satellite, which was hardened to withstand some of the effects of a nuclear explosion. However, government Ministers were desperate to maintain a British national space programme, so they chose Skynet III.[27]

Preserving UK national reserves of knowledge and expertise was something that GCHQ touched on in many ways. For example, it had long helped to steer policy on the teaching of languages like Chinese in British universities.[28] More importantly, it had a role in the development of British computing. Code-breaking had driven important breakthroughs in computing both during and after the Second World War, led by luminary figures such as Alan Turing. The most famous example is 'Colossus', which was used to attack 'Tunny', the encyphered teleprinter used by the German High Command. Ten examples of Colossus II were in operation by the end of the war. Other early computers called 'Robinson' and 'Aquarius' were no less innovative. Both Robinson and Colossus were designed and built at the Post Office Research Station at Dollis Hill by the celebrated Tommy Flowers, now recognised as one of the most enterprising scientists Britain produced during the war. At the end of the war a number of engineers moved from Dollis Hill and the British Tabulating Machine Company at Letchworth to join GCHQ at nearby Eastcote.[29]

Colossus marched on into the early Cold War period. The last two Colossus II machines were assembled at Eastcote rather than Bletchley, and code-named 'Blue' and 'Red'. These were rebuilt between 1948 and 1951, before being taken to Cheltenham in 1953 and employed until 1961. Also using the Colossus circuits were four new Robinson machines that were installed at Eastcote. These were eventually overtaken by 'Colorob', a new specialist machine developed with help from the defence electronics firm Ferranti and Manchester University. The most important GCHQ computer development was 'Oedipus', the first machine to exploit high-speed storage. Begun in 1951, Oedipus could store ten thousand fifteen-character phrases on its drum memory, an achievement far ahead of its time.[30] The significance of Oedipus was that it was a powerful rapid-character-comparison machine with a capability greatly exceeding that of any general stored programme machine available commercially in the 1950s and 1960s. Much of this elaborate technology was devoted to unsuccessful attacks on high-grade Soviet diplomatic cyphers.[31]

However, GCHQ's impact on computer development was not as great as that of NSA. Although NSA pursued a 'policy of anonymity', it was nevertheless later able to claim a string of very considerable computer firsts. Typically, the 'Atlas 1', delivered to NSA in December 1950, was the first parallel electronic computer with a drum memory. Its successor, 'Atlas 2', delivered in December 1953, was the first core memory computer. In March 1958 NSA received the first computer that relied wholly on transistors, called 'Solo', which became the model for many of Philco's later commercial designs. In February 1962 it took delivery of 'Harvest', the first large computer with a completely automated tape library. Harvest strongly influenced the design of the IBM System 360, a breakthrough machine which was a familiar sight in GCHQ's vast computer hall by the late 1960s.[32] The later IBM-700 series was soon the mainstay of core operations at NSA and GCHQ. By 1968 Marshall Carter, NSA's Director, could boast that he had over a hundred computers occupying almost five acres of floor space.[33]

In 1977 GCHQ took delivery of the first of its advanced American-built Cray super-computers. A super-computer breaks a problem down into many tasks that can all be done at the same time. By using different parts of its brain in parallel it can undertake vast calculations unbelievably quickly. The main applications are code-breaking, designing nuclear weapons and weather forecasting. At this time the world of super-computers was led by Seymour Cray, and the first production model rolled out of his company's factory at Chippewa Falls, Minnesota in the spring of 1976. This was delivered to NSA, while the second went to NSA's mathematical think tank at Princeton University.[34] Remarkably, a Cray machine for Cheltenham was already under construction, and was shipped across the Atlantic the following year. In the autumn of 1976 the impending arrival of the Cray drove some of the construction work at GCHQ's Benhall site, including a new building for the computer staff – known as X Division – together with a new Special Compartmentalised Intelligence Facility with reinforced strongrooms to hold their documents.[35] The new Cray machine was so powerful that it required elaborate cooling, and much of the redevelopment at Cheltenham was in order to provide special ventilation and a supply of 'chilled water direct to computers'.[36] All this reflected a strategic decision by NSA to place more emphasis on supercomputing, a decision which was followed by GCHQ.[37] They were soon rewarded, for in 1976 the West recovered the long-lost ability to read some high-level Soviet communications, including telegrams between Moscow and the Soviet Embassy in Washington.[38]

GCHQ was also making an important transition from using computers just for cryptanalysis to using them for everything, including sending sigint to customers. This was the beginning of a revolutionary breakthrough. As early as August 1967, Foreign Office planners remarked, 'We hope to get proposals shortly from G.C.H.Q. in Cheltenham which would provide methods of random access by desk officers to the computer itself.' GCHQ hoped that this would provide something like near real-time distribution of its precious sigint product to users in Whitehall. In the 1970s the old 'blue jacket' files full of sigint intercepts started to disappear, and online access for policy-makers slowly began to take over.[39] Computers were also being used widely inside GCHQ. In 1967, Ken Sly, who had commanded the sigint unit at Hong Kong, took over from Nicodemus Doniach as head of a GCHQ branch called the Joint Technical Language Service, a group of thirty highly qualified linguists who not only undertook translations, but also compiled material ranging from dictionaries of Soviet military terms to handbooks of Arab names. When Sly took over they were working from a vast wall of index cards thirty yards long. He began a determined programme of computerisation, so this vast body of knowledge gradually became available to everyone in GCHQ.[40]

This change was of the first importance. GCHQ could see that computers were the shape of the future, and wanted to use them to improve every stage of the intelligence process. However, the gap between ambition and reality was huge. In 1973 GCHQ was still at the basic stage of trying to get lists of its previous files onto computer, moving away from card indexes. The ambition was to get enough information about the files into the system to allow for keyword searching. However, there was a mountain of files, and Gerry Bontoft, who presided over records, needed more staff and was battling a freeze on recruitment.[41] GCHQ also kept personnel files for longer than most other departments in case they were needed for security enquiries.[42] As a result, it was now bulging with records. Its Registry held a massive twenty-three thousand shelf feet of records generated by GCHQ's twenty different divisions, and was adding four thousand files every year.[43] The Registry predicted that it would hit a quarter of a million files by the year 2000. Matters were made worse by the determination of each division to keep its own over-stuffed registry. Managers wanted to destroy older sigint records received from US and Commonwealth allies, but the divisions resisted, pointing out that the United States in particular could not be relied upon to keep complete sets of its own reports.[44]

GCHQ did at least have good American-made IBM computers, whereas other areas of government were continually under pressure to take underperforming machines from the ailing British computer industry. The agency could always play the trump card of Anglo–American compatibility. By the mid-1960s, IBM was in a position that British officials described as an 'oligopoly', enjoying three quarters of the world's computer market and spending £30 million a year on research and development. It recovered these costs easily through production runs of thousands of machines. GCHQ bought IBM computers not only because of NSA compatibility, but because its machines were cutting edge.[45] Nevertheless, GCHQ still had an impact on the British computing industry during the 1970s. This came largely in the form of one person, Teddy Poulden, who was lent by GCHQ to the Cabinet Office as an adviser. Poulden was, in many ways, an unlikely figure for this role. He was a general sigint manager rather than a computer specialist. He had begun his career helping to run the vast British naval sigint station on Ceylon during the war, and his first post-war job had been to head the new Australian sigint organisation. However, he then spent a couple of years as the liaison officer at NSA at a time of increasing automation, and had learned to love computers. He became Coordinator of Technical Services at GCHQ, working closely with the computer section known as X Division.

Dick White, the go-ahead new Intelligence Coordinator in the Cabinet Office, was another avid computer enthusiast. In February 1969 he was chatting to Joe Hooper, the Director of GCHQ, about how computers were transforming the world of intelligence. Hooper happened to mention a new American system called 'COINS' (Community On-line Intelligence System) that was intended to provide a shared database across the whole US intelligence community. White was excited by this idea, and asked him for a detailed appraisal. Hooper rather relished giving White the doleful story. Begun in 1965 as a presidential initiative by Lyndon Johnson, after four years and vast expense it was still not working. The idea was to allow all the different American intelligence agencies to access each other's computerised files, together with 'read-only' access for the Pentagon and the State Department. However, there were major difficulties with different file formats and terminology. The committee set up to address this had got nowhere, and was caught up in bitter bureaucratic wrangling.[46]

White was not deterred. By early 1970 he had persuaded the Joint Intelligence Committee to get busy in the area of new technology. Brian Stewart, Secretary of the JIC, created a joint team on Automatic Data Processing which also comprised MI5, SIS, the Defence Intelligence Staff and the Foreign Office. Teddy Poulden from GCHQ was given the job of chairing it.[47] GCHQ and NSA had just completed a shared computer project to standardise the spelling of geographical locations in Russian.[48] What GCHQ really thirsted for was progress on machine translation that would do some of the jobs currently undertaken by linguists, but so far this had failed on grounds of high costs and complexity.[49] The Defence Intelligence Staff had looked at storing more of its material on computer, but had been horrified by the sheer labour required to keep such databases current. Despite these disappointments, they all recognised that NSA's growing use of computers for data storage meant this was the future. 'Most Sigint end-product already contained simple machine symbols' as a result of its journey through the communications system, and NSA already maintained 'an almost complete file of Sigint end-product for retrieval' on computer. In June 1971 Poulden was rightly predicting that these changes would spread through the entire Western intelligence community over the next ten years.[50] By 1974, Dick White's successors as Intelligence Coordinator would be looking to computers in a desperate effort to cut staff numbers in the face of swingeing cuts to the intelligence and defence budgets.[51]

In the early 1970s the public knew almost nothing about the breathtaking achievements of high-tech espionage. Overhead, satellites were collecting millions of telephone calls which were then being word-searched by computers of mind-boggling complexity. Yet the British people were still not even aware of the wartime achievements of Bletchley Park. Ultra and its conquest of the German Enigma machine were still shrouded in government secrecy. Indeed, the official histories of the Second World War had been artfully constructed to hide code-breaking and deception from public view. But in 1974 all was suddenly revealed in a memoir called *The Ultra Secret* by Frederick Winterbotham, who had looked after the distribution of Ultra to operational commanders in the field. Those who had worked at Bletchley Park had taken their vows of secrecy very seriously, and in some cases for thirty years had not told even their husbands or wives what they had worked on during the war. Now they could speak about what they had done.[52]

Kim Philby was a major reason why the government eventually chose not to oppose the publication of Winterbotham's tell-all memoir. Burke Trend, the Cabinet Secretary, hoped that the revelations it contained would help restore the reputation of British intelligence, which had taken a battering in recent years as a result of the vast publicity given to the defection of the KGB moles who had burrowed deep inside the intelligence services. Philby's deliberately misleading memoir, published in 1968, was especially damaging, and had prompted the government to produce its own official history of intelligence, and even to release some wartime sigint records from Bletchley Park for use by historians.[53] Managing the public image of the intelligence community was entirely new territory for the authorities, who now faced the nightmare task of screening top-secret files before they reached the Public Record Office at Kew. The archives from the Second World War were enormous, and weeding them to extract the specific bits of intelligence material that were still deemed too sensitive for release was a Herculean task. However, officials were spurred on by news that the Soviets were taking a close interest in what was released. In July 1970 the Security Department of the Foreign Office warned that the Soviets had sent a researcher from Moscow to look through the newly released records at Kew, 'not merely from a historical point of view but also with an eye on current British government procedures'. Officials observed that 'Time spent in cleansing the record of intelligence . . . is not spent in vain.'[54]

What the KGB had already managed to find out about current GCHQ activities had formed part of the deliberations over the release of wartime sigint records from Bletchley Park. 'The Russians in particular know of our sigint successes,' noted one official, adding that the worst leaks had occurred because of 'three defectors from NSA who were fully informed on Anglo/US sigint in the '50s and early '60s'. Primarily, this was a reference to the defection in 1960 of the American code-breakers William Martin and Bernon Mitchell, who had talked enthusiastically at a press conference in Moscow about the way in which the West had collected and broken the diplomatic traffic of countries like Egypt and Indonesia. The third NSA defector was Jack Dunlap, who revealed a great deal about code-breaking to the Soviets in 1963. The British officials failed to mention their own security problems with figures such as Douglas Britten.[55]

Whitehall and Washington were now badly out of step. Timorous figures from GCHQ had spent the early 1970s worrying over the protection of wartime secrets. Suddenly, in 1974, to the horror of British officials, the Americans began to expose current secrets. In Washington the secret state was in full retreat as the American psyche suffered the triple blows of Watergate, Vietnam and the Oil Crisis. One of the manifestations of this new self-questioning political climate was court decisions which upheld the rights of dissident intelligence officers to write their memoirs. A CIA officer called Victor Marchetti had teamed up with a diplomat to write one of the first revelatory accounts of the CIA. The US government had demanded over two hundred deletions, but the courts later reduced this to twenty-two. Britain was alarmed. One of the joint operations revealed in the Marchetti book was the shared nature of Britain's massive sigint and radar complex on Cyprus. In April 1974 Harold Wilson had just begun his second administration, and his new Cabinet Secretary, John Hunt, warned him of a 'potential danger' to the continued operation of Sandra and Cobra Shoe, with their ability to look deep into Soviet airspace, since the Cypriots did not know about American participation in these projects.[56]

The following year, the British intelligence community was shocked to the core by Congressional inquiries into intelligence under Senator Frank Church. The revelations included discussion of planned assassinations by the CIA. Richard Helms, who had been Director of the CIA until 1973, confided his feelings to his friend the former Hut Six code-breaker Bill Bundy. Helms felt he had 'maintained discipline' during his own tenure, but now 'the dam had broken' and secrets of all kinds were spilling out.[57] British intelligence applied continuous pressure on the Americans to avoid revelations about their joint operations. In early April 1976 George Bush, the fourth new CIA Director in as many years, came to visit Harold Wilson. One of his purposes was to reassure the British that the Americans had curbed the Church Committee hearings, with their 'vociferous demand for general disclosure of intelligence procedures'. British officials hoped that at last the pendulum had begun to swing back in favour of secrecy. John Hunt asked Wilson to take the opportunity during their discussions to reassure Bush about the high value Britain continued to place on the Anglo–American intelligence relationship. Hunt added that this relationship was on the up, because the Americans were under financial pressure and had lost listening stations in South-East Asia and in Turkey, making them more dependent on British help.[58]

Harold Wilson, now moving towards the end of his second term as Prime Minister, was both fascinated and terrified by intelligence matters. Unlike his officials, he seemed to rather enjoy the revelations of the Church inquiry. Indeed, only a month before George Bush arrived at Downing Street, Wilson had been visited by Frank Church, and spent longer chatting with him than he did with Bush. Church explained the workings of his Congressional inquiry at length, and Wilson responded that he 'had always been assured that the CIA were not engaged in covert operations in this country', adding that he thought this was '98 per cent true'. Church said that he had been given the same assurance, and 'agreed with his qualification'. Wilson then began to reveal some of his own espionage obsessions, especially his fears about South African intelligence agents in Britain who were active in the cause of apartheid, explaining that he thought both the CIA and the notorious South African secret service (BOSS) were behind the recent recruitment of British mercenaries for service in the Angolan civil war. Wilson also pressed Church on the possibility of the CIA having paid bribes to British companies. Church departed, assuring Wilson that he would send him his findings on CIA activities in Chile.[59] Even more remarkable than the Church inquiry into the nefarious doings of the CIA was a parallel Congressional inquiry into NSA during 1975 which had uncovered 'Project Minaret', the illegal monitoring of domestic radicals. Although this inquiry had been secret, the material reached the front page of the *New York Times* in January 1976.[60] By February, former NSA director Lew Allen was embroiled in legal action.[61]

This vast outpouring of secrets and scandals soon reverberated in Britain. The most obvious target for British journalists was the activities of the CIA station in London. On 1 July 1976, three days before the bicentennial anniversary of American Independence, Maurice Oldfield, the Chief of SIS, spoke on the subject of Anglo–American intelligence relations. The occasion was the departure of the retiring head of the CIA station in London, Cord Meyer. Oldfield chose to praise Meyer's extreme forbearance under 'continuous and continuing press bombardment'. The Americans only had themselves to blame, since almost incredible stories were spilling onto the front pages of their newspapers. All enterprising British journalists had to do was read the latest spy revelations in the New York Times and the Washington Post, then think about what the British connections to these stories might be. Many of the latest exposures concerned NSA's high-tech world of sigint, satellites and computers, and the press in London was soon asking questions about a mysterious British organisation called 'GCHQ'.[62]

GCHQ was unmasked in the summer of 1976 when the British investigative journalist Duncan Campbell wrote a pathbreaking article in Time Out magazine entitled 'The Eavesdroppers' with an American colleague called Mark Hosenball, giving great detail about both GCHQ and NSA activities.[63] In Campbell's own words, this was 'the importation from the United States of post-Watergate investigative journalism', something that was adopted by radical and left journalists in Britain 'at considerable speed'.[64] Campbell had interviewed a dissident former member of NSA who was visiting London, and then carried out his own research on GCHQ, piecing the story together from overlooked fragments of published material. The article was the first public exposure of what the agency actually did, and revealed significant details about the latest high-tech methods of interception. Cheltenham was horrified, and Mark Hosenball was quickly deported by the government as a threat to national security.

Shortly after the 'Eavesdroppers' story appeared, Campbell and another radical journalist, Crispin Aubrey, were contacted by John Berry, a soldier who had served for many years with 9 Signals at the Ayios Nikolaos sigint base and who had read the article. Berry recounted his own experiences, which included listening in on armoured formations during the Yom Kippur War. He had once 'heard a cry to Allah by an Egyptian soldier as his tank was hit by an Israeli shell'. Alerted by the 'Eavesdroppers' story, MI5 had been watching Campbell closely, and after meeting at Berry's flat in February 1977, Aubrey, Berry and Campbell were arrested and prosecuted under the Official Secrets Act. This soon became known as the 'ABC trial', after the initials of the three defendants' surnames.[65]

The ABC trial was all about suppressing sigint secrets, and quickly became a *cause célèbre*. The prosecution fielded various sigint experts as witnesses, but tried to keep their identities secret, introducing them only as 'Colonel A', 'Colonel B' and so forth. A furore erupted when 'Colonel B' was revealed in the House of Commons to be none other than the redoubtable Colonel Hugh Johnstone, who had marched out to face down the Turkish tanks on the perimeter of the Ayios Nikolaos facility on Cyprus in July 1974.[66] At the trial, the defence counsel discovered that not only had the prosecution secretly applied to the judge to vet the jury, but that the jury contained three members who had signed the Official Secrets Act – indeed, the foreman was boasting to fellow jurors of his exploits in the SAS. When this was revealed on a television programme hosted by Russell Harty, the judge felt the process had been compromised and discharged the jury. A retrial had to be initiated, and proceedings were still ongoing in the summer of 1978.[67]

A vigorous 'ABC Defence Committee' was operating from the *Time Out* offices in Southampton Street in London in support of the accused. The government took great interest in the ABC Defence Committee, and a vast amount of very recently declassified material in government files suggests that the authorities had people infiltrating the campaign. Government officials had only recently been debating whether to unveil the wartime Ultra secret, and now – to their disbelief – GCHQ's current activities from locations such as Cyprus were in the public eye. The trial only raised the public profile of GCHQ further. On 10 March

1978 the ABC Defence Committee's provocative newsletter announced a demonstration planned for 25 March which would begin at GCHQ's Benhall site and end up at the main site at GCHQ Oakley. It urged:

*

Now we have an excellent opportunity to get across – not least to the people of Cheltenham – what SIGINT is really doing, the fact that it's illegal and the role of GCHQ as the hub of the system . . . We've been to MI5, MI6, Scotland Yard, parliament and many more. Now we're going where much of the dirty work goes on – CHELTENHAM![68]

*

GCHQ had noted that Duncan Campbell had been investigating the American sigint site at Chicksands in Bedfordshire, that focused on the Soviet Air Force, and was clearly anxious about how the Americans would react to this.[69]

When the ABC trial recommenced in the summer of 1978, the government was severely embarrassed. It turned out that most of the information that it deemed secret, including the duties of Colonel Hugh Johnstone at Ayios Nikolaos, was freely available to the public in the journal of the Royal Signals Regiment, *The Wire*. In August the defence took advantage of its increasingly strong position and offered a plea bargain.[70] David Owen, the Foreign Secretary, had initially supported the prosecution, but now badly wanted the case dropped, urging that 'Almost any accommodation is to be preferred.'[71] As a result, Aubrey, Berry and Campbell were convicted of minor breaches of the Official Secrets Act, but most of the charges were dropped. Anthony Duff, the new Coordinator of Intelligence, considered that the overall impact of the case was 'to make it more difficult to continue to refuse to acknowledge that we undertake SIGINT in peacetime or that GCHQ is involved'.[72] The Foreign Office legal adviser had been inspired by the case to look into whether the interception of communications between diplomatic missions in London and their home capitals was legal. He concluded that 'It now seems clear that it is at least a dubious practice.'[73]

The ABC trial was a landmark event. GCHQ had now been publicly 'outed' as Britain's signals intelligence centre – even though government officials steadfastly refused to acknowledge the fact. Moreover, it inspired radical campaign groups to begin 'watching the watchers'. They now probed constantly for new examples of secret activity that they could discuss in the radical press. The group that officials found most alarming was the State Research Association, which had been fostered by the National Council for Civil Liberties and was funded by the Rowntree Foundation. Its purpose was to publish material on recent developments in internal security and espionage, and its membership overlapped with the ABC Defence Committee. Its secretary was Tony Bunyan, and horrified defence officials noted that all the members 'can be broadly described as unaffiliated revolutionaries'.[74] Michael Hanley, the Director General of MI5, identified Duncan Campbell as the person of greatest interest.[75]

The ABC trial showed that sigint, with its vast satellite dishes and computers, was now just too big to hide. In 1978, as the trial drew to a close, the Cabinet Secretary, John Hunt, advised Prime Minister James Callaghan that there had been numerous press references to 'the intelligence role of GCHQ, to its Director, to some of its stations, to its relationship with NSA and to the fact that it succeeded the Government Code and Cypher School'.[76] The government has repeatedly claimed that GCHQ's identity as an intelligence organisation was only revealed in the 1980s. In reality, it was already widely known by 1976. What finally pulled the lid off Cheltenham was a revelatory book called *The Puzzle Palace* by the investigative journalist James Bamford. Published on 23 September 1982, it detailed the super-secret relationship between NSA and GCHQ by using the same methodical open source research employed by Duncan Campbell. This relationship was still very secret, and in NSA's own words, 'GCHQ was not amused.' Yet much of what Bamford revealed about sigint lay in unclassified newsletters and obscure libraries; he had only pointed to what was in plain sight. NSA concedes that Bamford's research was 'meticulous', and that he 'wrote the book' on how to research a reclusive organisation from open sources.[77] Together, Duncan Campbell and James Bamford confirmed a fundamental truth: that there are no secrets, only lazy researchers.[78] Nevertheless, these new investigative writers were regarded as a serious threat, and one of NSA's Directors later asserted that *The Puzzle Palace* was used by the Soviet Union and China to target Western sigint operations.[79]

Remarkably, in 1982, even as Bamford's book came out, GCHQ was still trying to keep a lid on certain technical aspects of Ultra. Although the importance of Ultra in assisting Allied wartime strategy had now been revealed, little had been said about the dark arts of code-breaking that had been practised in Bletchley Park's Hut Six. Just as GCHQ had feared, once the general Ultra secret was out, veterans, historians and journalists rushed forward to write about code-breaking in more and more detail.[80] Gordon Welchman, who had been head of Hut Six, was one of these would-be authors. In 1941 he had drafted the famous plea sent to Churchill asking for more resources for Bletchley Park, to which Churchill had famously responded 'Action This Day'.[81] Once he had heard about Frederick Winterbotham's book *The Ultra Secret*, Welchman was burning to tell his own story, 'regardless of the Official Secrets Act'.[82] He went to GCHQ for a chat with two senior figures, George Goodall and Douglas Nicoll. Although they were 'very friendly', they said they had no choice but to keep to the 'party line', and told Welchman that he must not give away the 'methodological secrets' of code-breaking.[83]

Welchman went ahead regardless. When he finally 'sprung' his book on GCHQ in 1982, it was horrified. Entitled *The Hut Six Story*, it first appeared in the United States in order to evade censorship. Welchman continued to publish on code-breaking history, and in 1985 he wrote an article in a new journal founded by the historians Christopher Andrew and Michael Handel which would soon become the premier outlet for the new field of intelligence history. Welchman followed proper procedure and submitted his article to the D-Notice Committee, which requested no deletions. However, a few days later he received a stiff letter from the new Director of GCHQ that spoke of the 'great shock' his book had caused at GCHQ, and claimed his writings had done 'direct damage to security' and had 'let us down'. The tone was rude at best, and caused indignation amongst veteran code-breakers.[84] The Welchman affair touched Bletchley Park veterans on both sides of the Atlantic: in 1985 his American friend Bill Bundy was asked to give a talk about Bletchley Park to a veterans' group of 'former cryptographic types', but NSA called him to say that 'in no circumstances' should he talk about any Hut Six techniques.[85]

Silly arguments about wartime secrets were soon swept away by the infamous *Spycatcher* affair. In 1985 Peter Wright, an MI5 officer who had worked closely with GCHQ's Ken Perrin on short-range sigint, published his sensational but unreliable memoirs, subtitled *The Candid Autobiography of a Senior Intelligence Officer*. The book revealed the level of paranoia about Soviet moles inside Western governments during the 1960s and 1970s, and the scale of MI5's efforts to catch them. Like Welchman, in order to get around the Official Secrets Act Wright chose to publish overseas – in Australia, where he then lived. Sir Robert Armstrong, the Cabinet Secretary, made a farcical attempt in the Australian courts to defend Prime Minister Margaret Thatcher's policy of blanket secrecy. Even now, *Spycatcher* remains the only memoir by a British intelligence officer that deals in any detail with post-war sigint. GCHQ informed NSA that it was 'upset' about Wright's book, and now considered that many aspects of sigint were 'at risk'.[86] Indeed, the publication of *Spycatcher* prompted GCHQ to ask Margaret Thatcher for a tougher Official Secrets Act, 'making it a crime to leak' and giving it the power to reduce the pensions of those found guilty of leaking.[87]

Many found this decade of revelations bewildering. In early 1974, wartime Ultra was still a secret. By 1986, the shelves of bookshops were groaning under the weight of spy books. Intelligence history – both popular and academic – had arrived with a vengeance. Bletchley Park veterans such as Gordon Welchman, Bill Bundy and Stuart Milner-Barry were all avid readers of this new material. Milner-Barry felt obliged to read *Spycatcher*, partly because it accused so many of his former associates of being Soviet spies. Having read the book, he then purchased John Costello's *Mask of Treachery* (1988), a biography of Anthony Blunt, which he judged 'interminable'. Milner-Barry thought Costello was 'paranoiac about homosexuals who abound on every page', but he read on because there was a whole chapter devoted to John Cairncross, the 'Fifth Man', who had been in Hut Three. Oddly, Milner-Barry noted that 'Neither I nor anybody I have asked in Hut 3 can remember Cairncross at all.' He complained to his friend Bill Bundy: 'I seem to have been reading nothing but moles for weeks and I am heartily sick of them all.'[88]

Britain's new Prime Minister, Margaret Thatcher, was also fed up with moles. On 17 November 1979, only months after her election, she was embarrassed and angered by the unmasking of Sir Anthony Blunt, Surveyor of the Queen's Pictures, as the 'Fourth Man'. She was also incandescent with rage at the publication of *Spycatcher*. As with her predecessors Harold Macmillan and Harold Wilson, the House of Commons greatly enjoyed baiting her about these security failures. Thatcher was so exasperated by the continual spy revelations that she ordered a clampdown, even forbidding the publication of any further volumes in the government's own official intelligence history series, initiated by Burke Trend and Dick White. The final volumes, including one by the world-famous military historian Michael Howard, were suppressed for almost a decade by the same groups of secret servants that had commissioned them in the first place.[89] Meanwhile, Westminster and Whitehall were now plunged into a legendary period of controversy and confrontation – the Thatcher era.[90]

THE 1980s

INTO THE
THATCHER ERA

Geoffrey Prime – The GCHQ Mole

. . . because of the nature of GCHQ's work and their need for staff with esoteric specialisms they attracted many odd and eccentric characters. Prime did not stand out as he might have done elsewhere.

UK Security Commission, Report on Geoffrey Prime,
May 1983[1]

The Thatcher era was partly defined by mole-mania. In the autumn of 1979 Margaret Thatcher made an announcement in the House of Commons identifying Sir Anthony Blunt as the 'Fourth Man', one of a ring of Cambridge spies that had included Kim Philby, Guy Burgess and Donald Maclean. Her hand had been forced because several newspapers had hinted strongly at Blunt's KGB identity. Because of Blunt's close associations with the royal family – he was Surveyor of the Queen's Pictures – this was as much a social as a security scandal. It also confirmed the public perception of the Establishment as bungling toffs who were not to be trusted with security matters. Although the authorities had known about the Blunt case for more than a decade, his public exposure unleashed a worldwide media quest to uncover further traitors. A blizzard of unlikely names filled the pages of the newspapers, including three former senior members of MI5: Sir Roger Hollis, Graham Mitchell and Guy Liddell.[2]

Margaret Thatcher found these matters intensely vexing. She was also extremely agitated about what she called 'hostile forces' attempting to foment industrial unrest. These included a broad swathe of Trotskyites and militants, some of whom were in touch with foreign governments, who wished to use industrial action for political purposes. Strikes at British Leyland, Britain's last large-scale car manufacturer, which were intended to disrupt a government recovery plan, had been organised with the co-operation of the Communist Party of Great Britain, which was in turn taking money from the Soviet Union. Although the miners' strike of 1982 had genuinely domestic origins, the Soviet Communist Party nevertheless funded it to the tune of more than half a million pounds, albeit against the advice of the KGB. Such active intervention in British internal affairs generated a certain amount of paranoia in British government. This extended to the Campaign for Nuclear Disarmament, which was also watched closely by MI5 for evidence of foreign influence. Several leading figures in CND were subjected to surveillance, including the future Cabinet Minister Harriet Harman. The Ministry of Defence was so worried about CND that it set up a special unit, DS.19, to counteract its activities, and wild rumours abounded that some of the protesters outside American bases were really Soviet special forces or 'Spetnaz' in disguise. In fact, during the 1980s the most dangerous KGB mole was in none of these places – instead he was at GCHQ.[3]

Security within GCHQ had always been a nightmare. Elsewhere in government, a person who was regarded as a possible security risk could be gradually transferred to a less sensitive area. This option did not exist within GCHQ, since everywhere was sensitive. Security problems overlapped with trade union worries. Even in the mid-1950s, some GCHQ managers were anxious about Communist influence in the Electrical Trades Union, which was prominent at Cheltenham.[4] There was also the sheer scale of positive vetting required in such a large organisation: as we have seen, despite an increase in the numbers of investigating officers, a backlog had built up. Most of all there was the problem of document security. All of GCHQ's basic 'working material' was highly secret, yet it was so super-abundant that it could not be catalogued. In other words it would be easy for a spy to smuggle out papers that his or her branch was working on.[5] In the 1970s the Security Commission had called for the certified destruction of top-secret documents that were no longer required. However, this concept was completely unworkable within GCHQ, since there was just too much such material. One of GCHQ's key customers, the Warsaw Pact order of battle cell within the Defence Intelligence Staff, handled 'about 10,000 CODEWORD signals' each week. It was impossible to record all of these signals, still less to certify their destruction.[6]

There had been countless security reviews during the 1960s and 1970s, yet all had missed the most important chink in GCHQ's armour: the armed services personnel who worked for the sigint arms of the military. Somehow, because they wore a uniform, these individuals were thought to be more reliable than civilian staff. Yet they were harder to vet because of their itinerant backgrounds, undertook the most repetitive and demoralising work, and were often posted to inhospitable locations. At these far-flung military outstations morale was often low, and operators were vulnerable to KGB recruiters. Berlin and Cyprus were subject to frequent KGB predation, and it is unlikely that all the Soviet recruitment successes have yet come to light. Brian Patchett and Douglas Britten were examples of this, and there were others yet to be uncovered.[7]

Growing up in Staffordshire, Geoffrey Prime suffered a difficult childhood. His mother and father had an unhappy relationship, and Prime had problems making friends at school. He was sexually assaulted by an adult relative, which probably left lasting effects upon him. After securing good 'O' levels, mostly in languages, Prime left St Joseph's Catholic College, Stoke-on-Trent, and began dull work at a factory as a junior wages clerk. Two years later, in 1956, National Service in the RAF offered him a happy escape from this existence. He nurtured ambitions to train as flight crew, hoping perhaps to serve as a Radio Operator, but due to colour blindness he was relegated to duties as a storesman. Eventually his talent for languages was spotted, and he was sent to RAF Crail in Scotland to begin the Russian Language course. The fact that he was required to sign up for regular service was of no consequence to him, since he hoped to gain professional qualifications. Excelling at Russian, he was soon an acting sergeant. He was then sent to London University on an advanced Russian course, but he did not fit in well and failed the course after three months. His rank and privileges were taken from him, and he returned to a mundane life in the stores.[8]

Still only twenty-one, Prime secured a posting to Kenya, and was promoted back to corporal. He filled his spare time by learning Swahili, becoming fluent and speaking with the native labour force at his airbase. He was shocked by the poverty and what he saw as the colonial exploitation of Kenya. He also disliked the racist attitudes of the long-term European settlers, and on one occasion reported an officer for treating a Kenyan badly. It was at this point in his life that Prime began to take an interest in Communist radio broadcasts and to read the magazine *Soviet Weekly*. By the time he returned to Britain in April 1962 he was more mature, and confident enough to apply for training in languages again. He spent a year at the Joint Technical Services Language School at Tangmere in Surrey, and in May 1964 was posted to the large sigint unit at RAF Gatow in Berlin, although he was not vetted until May 1966. He carried out his function as a wireless operator on the monitoring of Russian voice transmissions well enough to resume the rank of sergeant in May 1968.[9]

West Berlin was in effect a rather small, inhospitable island surrounded by East Germany. Most Allied troops arrived by sealed train, and this was how Prime came to the notice of the Soviets. As his train moved slowly through a checkpoint, he threw a message offering his services as a spy at the feet of a nearby Soviet sentry. The KGB followed it up, and eventually placed a mysterious magnetic cylinder under the handle of the door of Prime's car. Hidden inside were instructions telling him to travel on the underground train to Friedrichstrasse station in East Berlin. After several meetings he persuaded the KGB that he was sincere in his desire to work for them. Prime insisted that he was ideologically motivated, but the KGB pressed money upon him, a standard gambit designed to entrap a new agent. Knowing that Prime's enlistment was about to run out after twelve years in the RAF, the Soviets encouraged him to apply for a post with GCHQ at Cheltenham. To his surprise he was successful, and returned to Britain.[10]

The KGB now began work in earnest. Prime was invited to make a secret visit back to Germany, and was instructed to change planes in Amsterdam to cover his tracks. On arrival in East Berlin he was installed in a flat at Karlshorst, the main KGB centre, where he was given a full training in spycraft. All the time he was watched, and each night he was locked in. The KGB also made clumsy attempts to explore his sexual preferences, and presumed he was gay. Prime was angered by this, protesting continually that he was offering to assist the KGB for ideological reasons. Although this was true, the money he was offered seems to have become more important to him over time.[11] His KGB case officers went by the cover names 'Igor' and 'Valya', and instructed him in the exotic paraphernalia of espionage, including invisible inks, one-time pads and microdots. He was supplied with a Minox camera which he later used to photograph sensitive documents, and was also given £400 which he hid, along with the equipment, in a briefcase with a concealed compartment. His handlers told him that all further meetings had to be in either Finland or Austria, and Prime chose Austria.[12] The last thing they did was tell him his code name, which was 'Rowlands'.

The meetings abroad were an odd aspect of KGB tradecraft. As we have seen, other KGB agents such as Douglas Britten had local KGB officers assigned to them as handlers wherever they went. Prime's different arrangements reflect the circumstances of his recruitment. His initial message, thrown from a troop train, had been taken by a Soviet soldier to his security officer. From there it had naturally reached the Third Directorate of the KGB, which looked after military security within Soviet Army units. Running agents in the West was not its main responsibility, but having found Prime by accident, it was not about to let him go.[13] Just like Western intelligence, the KGB was riven by interdepartmental jealousies. Ideally, Prime should have been run by a KGB officer based in Britain, which would have offered him the support and companionship that is critical to the successful development of a spy. However, these activities were controlled by the First Directorate of the KGB, which undertook espionage. Arguably, had Prime been handled by the First Directorate he might well have lasted longer and done much more damage.[14]

Once back in England, Prime began his employment with GCHQ. By night he received radio messages, and was told about a dead-letter drop location at Esher in Surrey. There he found a note of congratulations and another payment of £400. Energised, he now went to work with his Minox, copying GCHQ documents at home and initially sending them on to his control in East Berlin in the form of microdots. He communicated with his handlers through a short-wave radio, encyphering his messages using one-time pads. More dead-letter boxes were developed in the Abbey Wood area of south-east London and at Banstead railway station in Surrey. His meetings with controllers were rare and almost always abroad, reflecting Prime's rather awkward Third Directorate ownership. He seems to have rendezvoused with them in Vienna in 1969, Ireland in 1970, Rome in 1970 and Cyprus in 1972. He preferred these personal meetings, since the dead-letter boxes could not accommodate the large number of films his espionage was producing.[15] Nevertheless, he made some use of dead-letter boxes in Britain. MI5's Stella Rimington recalls that he used classic tradecraft, including an empty Coca-Cola can, to convey messages, as well as chalk marks on telegraph poles and trees.[16]

Although Prime now worked for GCHQ, he was not based in Cheltenham. Instead, he was part of a translator pool called the London Processing Group (LPG), a curious leftover from the MI6 Y Section which had run the Berlin tunnel operation in the 1950s. A large and varied group of translators had been assembled at the LPG offices in Carlton Gardens. Some of them were Baltic émigrés, chosen both for their excellent Russian and their hatred of the Soviet Union; some were former Indian Army officers; some were new graduates. When the Berlin tunnel was uncovered in 1956 there was still an enormous backlog of intelligence material, but by 1958 it was judged to be out of date. SIS handed its translator team on to GCHQ, where it processed the increasing flow of material from telephone intercepts and aggressive bugging by all the secret agencies. Realising that the arrival of dozens of Baltic émigrés in the Cotswolds would raise awkward questions, GCHQ decided to keep this unit separate. An office was found at St Dunstan's Hill in the City of London, where it formed an 'isolated cell'.[17]

Starting work there on 9 September 1968, Prime initially spent several months in the Control Unit, where all the various transcripts were checked for quality before being forwarded to Cheltenham. This gave him a wonderful overview of everything being produced at LPG.[18] He was part of a new wave of staff. The wartime Baltic émigrés were ageing, and could not be replenished. Their replacements were ex-services sigint people like himself, and university Russian graduates. This prompted a culture change at LPG. The work was often tiring, tedious and difficult, but the émigrés had been content to carry it out 'in a void', knowing nothing of its context or importance. This was not true of the younger British intake, who were bored and dissatisfied, leading to a high resignation rate. In order to motivate them they were informed about the importance and context of their work, encouraged to ask questions about the whole intelligence framework, and deliberately told more than they needed to know. Prime thrived in this new atmosphere.[19]

In 1975 he returned to Vienna for one of his periodic meetings with his handlers. He had important news. Most of the Baltic staff had now retired, so LPG was in the process of being moved to Cheltenham.[20] The KGB officers were very pleased, smelling the possibility of wider espionage within GCHQ. Their delight was expressed in a gift of £800 before Prime's departure. On 22 March 1976 he arrived at Cheltenham and joined J30, part of J Division 'Special Sigint', which handled Soviet traffic. J30 was in a security-compartmentalised spur in B Block. Like many divisions it had its own vault, and Prime was one of the three senior officers in his section with access to it. It was easy for him to remove documents at will, take them home and photograph them, returning them the next day. He was also able to photocopy documents during his lunch break, since the amount of paper being used in the copiers was never checked.

On 30 June 1976, only three months after arriving at Cheltenham, Prime was promoted to Higher Linguist Specialist, and became the leader of a small group of transcribers in J25, a different part of J Division.[21] In November he was transferred to another unit that was more focused on the intelligence analysis of transcribed material. He also became Personal Security Supervisor for his section. Prime was moving onwards and upwards.[22] One of his duties in his newly elevated post was delivering occasional lectures. As a nervous and intensely introverted man he loathed this part of his job, and would become agitated about the prospect some days in advance. On 22 September 1977 he failed to show up for a lecture, and resigned shortly afterwards.[23] GCHQ's Security Division believed that his decision to leave was partly caused by having to manage office staff, which he was bad at, and the lectures, 'which terrified him'. However, it also reflected changes in his personal life.[24]

Back in August 1969, while still working for LPG in London, Prime had met a woman called Helena Organ through a marriage bureau, and they eventually married. The union was not successful, perhaps due to Prime's introverted nature and peculiar sexual proclivities, which included an interest in young girls. Helena Prime found a large sum of money in their home in April 1973, and it is now thought that Prime confessed to her in outline that he was helping the Soviets, and that this was how he had accrued the money. She panicked, and not knowing where to turn, confided in a close friend, a Mrs Barsby. Remarkably, Mrs Barsby was one of Prime's referees for his security clearance, and in time a routine positive vetting check became due. However, the security officer who visited Mrs Barsby was so abrupt, and asked her questions of such a personal nature, that she took an instant dislike to him. As a result she did not reveal anything about Helena Prime's suspicions. Geoffrey and Helena Prime agreed to a divorce the following year.

When Prime moved to Cheltenham in 1976 he found lodgings at Laburnum Cottage in Pittville Crescent Lane, owned by a thirty-three-year-old divorcee, Rhona Ratcliffe. They got on well, and on 18 June 1977 they married. Apart from a wife, Prime also gained three young children. By all accounts he was respected by the children, took an interest in their lives and provided for them well. The changes in his personal life seemed to feed into his decision to resign from GCHQ in September of that year, and after a disastrous attempt at selling quality wines he became a taxi driver. Prime was now at something of a crossroads in his life. He later told his interrogators that at this point he twice resolved to defect to the Soviets, but did not go through with it. He no longer listened to the KGB messages, and ceased to operate as an agent. Because he was run at a distance by the Third Directorate, there was no local KGB case officer to try to dissuade him from this decision. Ken Sly, his manager at Cheltenham, was puzzled by his resignation, recalling, 'He certainly wasn't pushed out by the Head of his Branch and there seemed to be no reason why he should leave a very lucrative post at GCHQ.'[25]

In April 1980, nearly three years after he had left GCHQ, Prime was contacted again by the KGB. He travelled to see them in Vienna, and spent three pleasant days with his handlers on a river cruise to Hungary and back. The Soviets hoped to persuade him to rejoin GCHQ. In fact, some believe that he was still working for GCHQ on a casual basis, since it used taxi drivers to take certain kinds of sigint product to RAF Brize Norton airbase for despatch to the United States, and preferred ex-GCHQ employees with live security clearances to transport especially sensitive material.[26] Although Prime refused to rejoin

GCHQ, he had been canny. Prior to his resignation he had had the foresight to take copies of five hundred secret documents, which he was then able to hand over in segments. On 16 May 1980 he delivered fifteen reels of film to the KGB in Vienna, for which he was paid £600. More than a year later, on 16 November 1981, he travelled to East Berlin, where his stock of espionage equipment was replenished. He still refused to rejoin GCHQ, but now handed over his last haul of stored material. This was top-grade stuff, signified by the fact that he now received £4,000 from the delighted Soviets. The head of GCHQ's Security Division would later conclude that while all of Prime's espionage was 'very grave', the 'most damaging of all' was the material he handed over in Berlin in 1981.[27]

Britain's security authorities have always maintained that 'The damage inflicted by Prime was of a very high order.'[28] NSA has concurred, concluding that 'Prime's case was of major importance for cryptology.'[29] What exactly had he handed over to his KGB masters? When he moved from London to GCHQ Cheltenham he had become a Higher Linguist in J Division, and was given a 'Byeman' clearance to work on material from the new American sigint satellites. The key satellites were code-named 'Ryolite' and 'Canyon', and had first been launched in 1969. They had been designed primarily to pick up Soviet missile launches and collect telemetry from missiles, which the Soviets were not bothering to encrypt. Surprisingly, they also proved capable of collecting huge amounts of communications in the VHF and UHF wavebands that were spilling into space, and microwave telephone traffic. Space was an undiscovered sigint goldmine. By the mid-1970s there were more than a dozen of these satellites in orbit, producing a fantastic amount of intelligence on Russia, China, Vietnam and the Middle East, much of it from telephone calls. Because the 'take' was so enormous, NSA had been forced to ask its UKUSA allies to help process it. It was for this reason that Prime was pressed into service on 'Canyon' intercepts.[30]

Prime's material dovetailed nicely with intelligence provided by John Walker, a US Navy Warrant Officer working on top-secret communications who had been recruited by the KGB at about the same time as him. It was also supplemented by material that the KGB was receiving from yet another spy, called Ed Boyce, who was working for TRW Inc., the American company that made some of the most secret spy satellites, and who told the Soviets about the latest 'Argus' and 'Pyramider' satellites. Argus formed part of a project that had the capability to listen in on the microwave links used in Russia's phone network. Together, Prime, Walker and Boyce inflicted horrific damage upon Western sigint and comsec operations. In the late 1970s, after thirty years of effort, the Americans had begun to make some headway with high-grade Soviet diplomatic traffic, and this was one of the many secrets that was given away.[31] Indeed, Prime, Walker and Boyce were so productive that they spurred a major reorganisation within the KGB. Hitherto all sigint and comsec had been handled by the KGB's Eighth Directorate. In 1969 a new Sixteenth Directorate was established to deal with the increased flow of sigint, leaving the Eighth Directorate to focus exclusively on the defensive challenge posed by Western sigint, about which it now knew a great deal.[32]

Prime's most damaging revelation concerned the vast, top-secret and highly expensive Anglo–American effort to track Soviet strategic submarines. The official line was that ballistic-missile-carrying submarines were undetectable, since this reinforced the stability of deterrence for both sides in the Cold War. Secretly, however, the West was enjoying significant success in tracking these submarines. By the early 1970s this involved three technologies. The first was SOSUS, a line of undersea microphones that listened for the engines of Soviet submarines. A joint UK/US project team had identified RAF Brawdy on the coast of Wales as the ideal site for an additional SOSUS centre. Britain had provided the land and the capital costs, while the United States contributed the personnel and the equipment for the intelligence analysis.[33] The second element was airborne maritime patrol aircraft with sonar. The third and most hidden element, code-named 'Project Sambo', was efforts to track the low-frequency radio transmissions of submarines when they rose closer to the surface to communicate with their head-quarters in Moscow or with supply ships. This was an integrated UKUSA effort, with NSA running twenty-one listening stations and the allies running a further eight.[34] Prime revealed this super-secret programme.

Prime was not caught as a result of his spying, but because of his criminal paedophile activities. He had a long history of making obscene phone calls, and during 1981 he became more dangerous, and began to indulge his desire to perform sexual acts in front of young girls, carrying out attacks on two occa-sions and escaping undiscovered. However, later in the year he attacked a third girl, a fourteen-year-old gymnast, in her own home. When the girl screamed, Prime was frightened and ran off. He fled the scene in his car, which he had parked in a lane near a farm. One of the nearby farm workers knew a lot about cars, and was able to give a detailed description of the vehicle to the police, stating with certainty that it was an 'S' reg brown two-tone Mark IV Ford Cortina. Although there were 426 'S' reg Cortinas in the immediate surrounding area, only a dozen were coloured 'Roman Bronze'.

The next day Geoffrey Prime opened the front door of his home to two detectives from Hereford CID. Detective Sergeant Wilkes and Detective Constable Miriam Rhodes asked him about the two-tone 'S' reg Cortina parked in the drive outside. Wilkes noticed that Prime bore an uncanny resemblance to the iden-tikit photo of the suspect, and was wearing the same style of checked shirt. Prime must have realised that he was a promin-ent suspect, and became very agitated when Wilkes asked him for his fingerprints. Although he was not yet arrested, Prime knew it was only a matter of time. That evening, he took his wife Rhona out to Cleeve Hill, a local beauty spot, and after a heavy silence blurted out, 'It's me they want.' He then told her the truth about his sexual activities. Only that evening, over a glass of brandy, did he finally confess that he had also been a

KGB spy for over a decade. In fact Rhona already suspected the espionage, and initially decided to stand by her husband. The next day Prime was arrested, and his car and house were searched. Apart from 2,287 record cards, bearing notes about and photographs of young girls, which were bagged and taken away as evidence, a black leather briefcase was also seized. This was later opened by Prime, in the presence of police officers, to reveal the secret compartment filled with KGB equipment, including a camera and one-time pads. For now, the police remained quite unaware of his espionage activities.[35]

Rhona Prime was now having doubts. On 23 May 1982 she contacted the police and informed them about Prime's work for the KGB.[36] The trigger for this was her discovery of a mass of espionage equipment in the house, including many envelopes addressed to places in East Germany, two one-time pads with columns of five-figure numbers, and some manuals on microdot production. She also gave the police a wallet with a schedule of radio frequencies. Later a team of specialists combed Laburnum Cottage with minute thoroughness:

*

For two days they searched, leaving nothing to chance: wall cavities explored with cameras controlled by flexible cables; insulating material removed from the loft; chimney, drains and sewers examined; fitted furniture dismantled; soft furnishings X-rayed; carpets and floorboards lifted . . . The house gradually surrendered its secrets.

*

The police eventually uncovered a tape recorder and another list of radio frequencies and schedules, together with documents from GCHQ. On 25 June, Detective Inspector David Cole interviewed Prime and switched on the tape recorder. Coded messages in German filled the room – the unmistakable sound of espionage. Prime offered the reply that it was merely his hobby, listening to the radio and twiddling the tuning knob. However, the game was clearly up, and at 4.30 p.m. the next day he made a complete confession.[37] On Wednesday, 10 November 1982,

Geoffrey Arthur Prime, then aged forty-four, pleaded guilty to seven counts of espionage and three further sexual offences at the Old Bailey. For spying, he received a sentence of thirty-five years, plus a further three years for the sexual offences. The total of thirty-eight years meant that he would be eighty-two on his release in 2020 if he served the full term. He was paroled after serving half his sentence, and was released to a secret address in 2001.[38]

The Gloucestershire police who investigated Prime had worked tirelessly on the case. They travelled the length and breadth of the country, combing RAF personnel archives and persuading travel agents to hunt through mountains of past receipts for evidence of Prime's visits to meet his KGB controllers. Yet, to their surprise, the senior management of GCHQ were less than helpful. When Detective Inspector Cole, who led the case, visited GCHQ to confirm that items found in Prime's possession had been unlawfully taken from its premises, he and a colleague received a 'less than welcoming' reception. He asked senior figures for formal evidential statements, but was met with a 'point-blank refusal' on the grounds that the material was 'far too sensitive to be discussed'. Cole recalled that in twenty-five years of police investigations he had 'rarely encountered such a distasteful reaction'. GCHQ gave him the impression that he was 'a thorough bloody nuisance' and that it believed these matters to be 'way above his head'. Cole also detected the grade-consciousness and even class-consciousness that marked GCHQ at this time. The policemen were blanked by the code-breakers and sent on their way. As they left by Oakley's main gate, they realised that GCHQ would have preferred to see the whole embarrassing matter buried, and had not even wanted Prime prosecuted.[39]

Geoffrey Prime was caught by accident, not by GCHQ's standard security defences, and this posed some awkward questions for the authorities.[40] General Sir Hugh Beach led the subsequent inquiry by the Security Commission. Both the Commission and GCHQ concluded that the security procedures had worked as well as they could. Some things could be tightened up, but nothing that was in place at the time would have stopped Prime for certain. Even random searches at the gates of GCHQ could have been evaded by a concealed camera in a bag. In any case, the most damaging information Prime had passed on concerned what streams of intelligence GCHQ had access to, and he could easily have committed this to memory, even though agent runners love to have documents to send their controllers. What the Security Commission was looking for were new kinds of procedures that would greatly improve security.[41] Basic issues, such as access to photocopiers, were tightened up, not only at GCHQ but right across the UKUSA system, including at CSE in Ottawa, but ideally it wanted a new security system.[42]

In February 1983 Beach took his Commission on a visit to Washington, which they found to be 'most valuable'. All the Americans and 'particularly the NSA and CIA made no secret of their belief that their personnel security procedures are more effective than our own'.[43] What impressed them most was the routine use of the polygraph. They noted that in 1962 a secret and unpublished section of the Radcliffe Inquiry into security procedures in the Civil Service had recommended its use. The Security Commission thought it significant that during his inter-rogation Prime had conceded that if he had faced a polygraph test prior to joining GCHQ in 1968, he would not have applied to the organisation. Their strongest recommendation was a pilot scheme for the introduction of the polygraph at Cheltenham. They accepted that it would take time to build up expertise in its use, and that the political obstacles to its introduction would be 'formidable'.[44] Benson Buffham, a former Deputy Director of NSA who had recently served as the American Liaison Officer to GCHQ, or 'SUSLO', visited London to confer on security, and made it very clear that the Americans were keen to see the polygraph arrive at GCHQ.[45] The Security Commission also recommended that vetting teams should be granted access to medical records in order to check for problems such as depres-sion. However, this was shot down immediately by the BMA's

Civil Service Medical Officers Group as 'neither necessary nor justified'.[46]

The Prime case left some loose ends. The Security Commission accepted that Prime might not have been the Soviets' only source within GCHQ, and in May 1983, more than a year after Prime's arrest, a team from MI5 was probing the possibility of sub-agents. The Security Commission noted that the press had claimed that Prime had been blackmailing some of his colleagues, but it had no evidence either to substantiate this or to safely discount it.[47] The biggest question that has lingered over Prime is whether he assisted the KGB in recruiting others by simply identifying unhappy or vulnerable colleagues. Arguably, one of the most valuable things that a spy in Prime's position could offer the Soviets was not access to information, but tips on which colleagues had problems with drink or debt, or had patterns of sexual behaviour that might leave them open to blackmail. This was precisely the sort of information that the KGB had sought from Douglas Britten on Cyprus a decade before.

In the wake of the Prime case there was extensive press speculation seeking to link a contemporaneous spate of suicides with possible KGB recruitment at Cheltenham and the ongoing inquiries by the security services. Interest was initially sparked by the death of George Franks, a Radio Operator who worked at the GCHQ's Empress building near Earl's Court, which monitored diplomatic and commercial traffic out of London. Franks died of a heart attack after drinking a large quantity of whisky, but had reportedly also tried to hang himself. However, colleagues insisted that his death was most likely to be due to stress. Drink had always been an issue amongst the Radio Operators, not least because many spent time at remote service bases such as Cyprus where the consumption of duty-free alcohol was considerable. The long shifts were also stressful, and down the years quite a few were treated at the Cooney Hill psychiatric hospital in Gloucester.

A further spate of three deaths looked more suspicious. The

first was Captain Timothy Fetherstone-Haugh, a twenty-nine-year-old officer who worked at the sigint station at Gatow in Berlin. In February 1982 he was found at the wheel of his car inside a garage filled with exhaust fumes. The second was Jack Wolfenden, a senior radio officer at GCHQ who died when his glider crashed into a Cotswold hillside in July 1982. Wolfenden's girlfriend, Judith Pither, told the inquest that he had 'acted oddly after returning from a trip abroad'. The third was Ernst Brockway, a GCHQ radio officer who was found dead at his home in October 1982. However, in reality many of the suicides that aroused the interest of the press were by people who worked at other scientific establishments, and the number of GCHQ staff who committed suicide in this period was not statistically significant. Moreover, given that Prime was handled by the Third Directorate of the KGB, it would have been hard for them to employ the information he supplied to recruit more agents.[48]

Nevertheless, further KGB recruitment efforts against British sigint were already under way. While the Security Commission was flying off to America to look at polygraph machines, and the British newspapers were worrying about people mysteriously crashing their gliders, Soviet intelligence officers had simply returned to their tried and trusted source: vulnerable young men employed on sigint duties in the armed services who were based far from home. In 1984 eight servicemen serving with 9 Signals Regiment at the Ayios Nikolaos sigint base on Cyprus were charged with espionage for the KGB under Section One of the Official Secrets Act. This 'Army unit' was in fact a mixed outfit of soldiers, airmen and civilians working for GCHQ. All those arrested had confessed, however they later retracted their confessions, citing the grim circumstances of their interrogation. On this basis all eight were acquitted. The prosecution had alleged that a vast amount of highly classified information had been passed to the Soviets when one of the accused was blackmailed by an Arab called 'John' after becoming involved in homosexual acts. The government claimed that a KGB officer code-named 'Alex' had then worked with 'John' and one of the defendants to exert pressure on the other defendants. Much of the material was reportedly handed over at the Chiquito nightclub at Larnaca on Cyprus, and several exotic cabaret singers were flown to London to give evidence. However, the prosecution failed due to the incompetent and coercive interrogations.[49]

The Security Commission was rolled out yet again. This time it could not miss the elementary clues. In October 1986 it reported that it had discovered that there were security difficulties with the employment of young and fairly immature people on top-secret activities in obscure locations. Officers had taken little interest in their off-duty activities, and document security at 9 Signals Regiment at Ayios Nikolaos had been poor.[50] The Commission reported this as if it was a revelation, but in fact it had been obvious since the Patchett and Britten cases in the 1960s. There were further parallels in the British clerical and support staff who the Soviets had managed to recruit at Britain's Moscow Embassy, most of whom have not yet been publicly named.[51]

Meanwhile, GCHQ rejoiced at the uncovering of American spies like Edward Howard in the CIA and Ronald Pelton in NSA. They joined a growing throng of KGB spies inside the United States, including John Walker and his family, that helpfully put the Geoffrey Prime case in the shade. Ronald Pelton was especially damaging. He had pursued a career path almost identical to that of Prime, learning Russian while serving in a front-line Air Force sigint unit doing voice intercept at Peshawar in Pakistan in the mid-1960s. He then transferred to NSA, and worked there until 1980. In 1984 he ran into financial difficulty, and decided to travel to Austria, where he sold his knowledge of NSA activities to the KGB. One important programme he compromised was 'Ivy Bells', a joint NSA–US Navy operation which tapped Soviet undersea communication cables using submarines. Pelton confessed under interrogation in 1986, and was given three consecutive life sentences.[52] In 1985 William Odom, Director of NSA, worried that there might be other agents. He was also concerned that some of the defending lawyers were 'radical', and would deliberately try to use the trials to expose more sigint secrets, especially NSA's very successful programmes of covert comint collection from embassies in the Middle East.[53]

In the 1980s the American intelligence community uncovered many KGB spies within its ranks, and was entering a period of mole-mania, not dissimilar to the one previously endured by the British. The American equivalent of Kim Philby, a senior CIA officer named Aldrich Ames, was yet to be unmasked. By contrast, the British were at last winning the spy war against the Soviets. SIS had recruited a senior KGB officer, Oleg Gordievsky, a prolific source who bravely stayed in place and provided vital intelligence during the last decade of the Cold War. It is widely thought that his information led to the 'Cyprus Eight' prosecution in 1984.[54] More importantly, by 1985 GCHQ had managed to decode some of the messages of the agents working for the East German intelligence service in Britain, which led to charges being made against them. For the first time, after anxious deliberation, GCHQ presented intercepts as evidence during closed court sessions.[55]

MI5 continued to debrief Geoffrey Prime regularly, long after he reached Wormwood Scrubs Prison. 'They come up once or twice a week,' said Prime, 'and ask an awful lot of questions.' Prime was the first KGB agent to be held in a British prison for some years. Dave Wait, one of his fellow inmates at Wormwood Scrubs, explains that the authorities still remembered the spectacular escape of George Blake, who in 1966 had leapt to freedom from a window in D Wing of the same prison. As a result, Prime was accompanied everywhere by two warders, and had his own specially designed, escape-proof exercise area: 'Two sides are brick walls, the other two are honeycombed concrete and thick unbreakable glass, a box twenty feet high for Prime to walk around on his own.' At this time Wait, who was serving a life sentence for murder, was passing his time serving as the prison librarian. He recalls Prime's first visit to the library. Prime asked how many books he was allowed to borrow at one time, and Wait replied with a grin that officially he could have six, but he would stretch the allowance a bit, as long as he didn't 'run off with them' to Russia. Prime chose six books including a volume of advanced mathematics, Plato's *The Republic* and Chapman Pincher's recent book about the KGB penetration of the West, *Their Trade is Treachery*.[56]

A Surprise Attack – The Falklands War

. . . a series of intercepted signals . . . left little doubt that an invasion was planned for the morning of Friday 2 April.

John Nott, Secretary of State for Defence[1]

GCHQ's intelligence about the Soviet invasion of Afghanistan in the last days of 1979 was excellent, but other recent surprise attacks and military interventions had taken the British completely unawares.[2] Over the previous decade or so there had been quite a few. In 1968, as we have seen, the Joint Intelligence Committee had spectacularly failed to predict the Russian invasion of Czechoslovakia and the subsequent crushing of the Prague Spring. Over the next ten years there had been other nasty surprises, including the Arab–Israeli War of 1973 and the Chinese attack on Vietnam in 1979. The invasion of Afghanistan in late 1979 and early 1980 was quickly followed by Soviet intervention in Poland.

The overall performance of British intelligence in spotting these surprise attacks and military crises was at best mediocre. Brooks Richards, the Cabinet Intelligence Coordinator, decided to probe what has been called 'the dog that didn't bark'.[3] In other words, he wanted to know why the record of Britain's JIC was poor when it came to warning of military aggression.[4] The person he chose to investigate was Douglas Nicoll, a veteran of Bletchley Park's Hut Six.[5] Working alongside Gordon Welchman and Stuart Milner-Barry, he had spent the Second World War puzzling over the intricate code-breaking problems of Enigma. After the war he was one of a minority who had stayed on at GCHQ, and by the early 1970s he had been in charge of Z Division, which passed finished intelligence to the customers in Whitehall. Now, after half a lifetime of work at GCHQ, he had been given a rather different puzzle.[6]

By late 1981 Nicoll had finished what had become a massive study of surprise attack. His findings were important. He concluded that although 'provision of warning of aggression' was a core duty of the JIC, it was actually ill-suited to the task, since it was really a body that had been set up to produce strategic estimates. In short, the problems it thought about were large and complex, and the time cycles were long. By contrast, warning was really all about tactical intelligence, since aggression was often long in the planning but short in the execution. Moreover, Nicoll argued that Britain's intelligence analysts tended to suffer from two psychological neuroses. First, they found it difficult to believe that an aggressor would ever find the use of force politically acceptable. They tended to think about what the British would do if they were in the shoes of their enemies. In fact, the political regimes they were looking at were often unstable, and therefore much more inclined to commit acts of violent aggression. Nicoll also identified something that he called 'perseveration'. This was the tendency of intelligence analysts to come up with a view about a problem early on, and then to refuse to change it. Given that intelligence officers were often asked to look at the same problem repeatedly, this was a serious failing.[7]

On 2 April 1982, only three months after the Nicoll report on surprise attack had been completed, Argentina invaded the Falkland Islands. British intelligence manifestly failed to spot this coming, and within months Nicoll had been recalled to mount a second inquiry that focused on the Falklands intelligence failure. Although he had been tough on Britain's intelligence analysts about their performance over the past decade, he was kinder to them about the Falklands. He concluded that the invasion had been very hard to detect in advance. The

Argentineans had caught the British by surprise because they launched their operation earlier than they had themselves intended, and with almost no preparation. The Argentinean military planners had expected six months of build-up, but Buenos Aires had suddenly ordered a snap invasion in the space of just six days. There were simply no preparations to see. As Lord Carrington, Britain's forlorn Foreign Secretary, later put it: 'It's all very well when you can see soldiers moving about on the ground, but you can't see someone's intentions.'[8] Nevertheless, senior intelligence officers conceded that despite increased diplomatic rumblings over the Falklands, the islands had remained a 'low intelligence priority'.[9]

The Argentinean junta that took power in a coup in 1976 was, in the words of Lord Carrington, a 'brutal' one.[10] Its more unpleasant activities included a loathsome 'Dirty War' in which leftists, intellectuals, trade unionists and human rights campaigners 'disappeared'. The notorious Naval Mechanics School in Buenos Aires became the main torture centre, and many junior officers were forced to participate in the liquidation of forty thousand of their fellow citizens. Argentinean naval intelligence played a leading role in the secret execution of intellectuals and union leaders, and this in turn underlined the strength of the naval faction in the new junta. Invading the Falklands would be a predominantly naval operation, and almost immediately after the coup there were worrying signs. In November 1976 the aggressive Commander in Chief of the Argentine Navy, Admiral Jorge Anaya, arranged for the symbolic occupation of the tiny uninhabited British island of Southern Thule. More remarkably, on 22 September 1977 Anaya ordered the capture of four Soviet trawlers that were fishing in Falklands waters as an assertion of Argentina's sovereignty. The incident was messy, with an exchange of fire and the death of one Russian sailor. This should have signalled that Buenos Aires was now run by violent men. Argentinean death squads operated not only at home but abroad. Elena Holmberg, the Argentine Cultural Attaché in Paris, compiled a dossier on the way in which Argentine naval intelligence officers were extending their terror operations to Europe to kill dissident Argentines there. Sadly, she was recalled to Buenos Aires and herself secretly killed in January 1979.[11]

The main impediment to the junta's Falklands ambitions had been the arrival of the highly principled Jimmy Carter in the White House in 1977. The junta had been thinking about repeating the Southern Thule episode by capturing South Georgia, a dependency of the Falklands and a larger island than Thule, which London would not be able to ignore. This, the Argentineans believed, would allow them to negotiate from a position of strength on the issue of the Falklands, which they had long regarded as Argentinean territory. However, Carter placed a moratorium on American arms exports to Argentina because of its horrific human rights violations. By contrast, the Europeans behaved like unprincipled bagmen. The British rushed to sell the Argentineans some of their latest frigates, but were outpaced by the Germans. The French sold them Super Etendard jets and the latest Exocet sea-skimming missiles. The Italians, Spanish and Belgians followed in their wake. All these countries overlooked the disappearance of their own nationals in Argentina as part of the 'Dirty War': in the case of Germany, no fewer than forty-eight of their citizens had vanished without trace. Britain secured a contract for the training of Argentinean special forces, and even supplied a hundred specially silenced Sterling sub-machine guns. In April 1982 these elite Argentinean troops were in the first wave of invaders, and infamously displayed captured British Royal Marines in front of Government House at Port Stanley, the islands' capital.[12]

Incredibly, when the Argentinean junta seized the tiny unin-habited island of Southern Thule in 1976, the Foreign Office covered this up, and it was only admitted to Parliament a year later. Ted Rowlands, a junior Foreign Office Minister, was sent to Argentina to undertake another round of appeasement. Rowlands made pathetic pleas to Buenos Aires not to mention the embarrassing Southern Thule incident publicly, resulting in open mockery from the Argentineans. By 1977 the JIC had looked at the occupation of Southern Thule and concluded, rightly, that the Falklands were now a *cause célèbre* for the junta, and that a further escapade might be on the cards. The Foreign Secretary, David Owen, decided that frigates and a nuclear submarine should be sent to the South Atlantic as a show of resolve, and the Prime Minister, James Callaghan, backed him. It is widely thought that SIS was asked by Callaghan to gently leak the presence of this secret task force to the Argentineans to increase its deterrent value.[13]

Given that warning of an attack on the islands would always be difficult to secure, visible deterrence was critical. The most important element of the British military presence in the South Atlantic was a curious-looking ship called HMS *Endurance*, variously described as an ice-patrol ship or a survey vessel. Painted an indeterminate shade of reddish-orange, she was known affectionately by her crew as 'The Plum'. Armed with only a 20mm cannon and a helicopter, she moved around between South Georgia, the Falklands and Argentina, transporting small contingents of Royal Marines and conducting scientific survey work. However, her most important role was a covert one, as her Captain, Nick Barker, later explained:

*

It could be argued that the main armament of the ship was the listening suite. This was a small box parked on top of the hangar which contained a comprehensive set of monitoring equipment. It could also receive frequencies in most bands at sea or on station. Our communications technicians were Spanish linguists which meant they were well informed whenever we went alongside in South America ... The *Endurance* was, in effect, a listening station. The two senior ratings most concerned were known as 'The Spies' by the ship's company.[14]

*

As Barker recounts, it did not take the Argentineans long to realise that the curious boxes on the roof of the hangar contained something slightly more exciting than brooms for sweeping down the decks. Sir Anthony Williams, Britain's Ambassador to Buenos Aires later explained that *Endurance* was not only listening to Argentina, but was gathering signals intelligence from throughout South America.[15] Much of Cheltenham's best material on Argentina came from the *Endurance*. However, the Thule incident had also prompted GCHQ to revive its small station on Ascension Island off the west coast of Africa, which had only been closed down the year before. The cover for this activity was the small settlement called Two Boats, which nominally belonged to Cable & Wireless Ltd.[16]

In 1980 an unsuspecting Foreign Office Minister, Nicholas Ridley, was lured by pro-Argentinean British diplomats into trying to transfer the islands' sovereignty by stealth. The idea was that the Falklands would quietly be given to the Argentineans, but then leased back from them by Britain for a number of years. Ridley tried valiantly to sell the idea of 'leaseback' to the islanders, but they were not impressed, and wished to remain British subjects. In December 1980 he expounded the plan to the House of Commons, and walked into a well-prepared ambush by the Falklands lobby. He was subjected to a wilting attack from all sides, denouncing what they called the Foreign Office's 'shameful schemes'.[17] Nonetheless, curious conspiracies were still going on in Whitehall a year later. When Admiral Fieldhouse, the new Commander in Chief of the Fleet, took over in 1981, he recalls repeatedly asking about contingency plans for the defence of the Falklands. The Foreign Office told him there was no need, as 'they were negotiating and could handle it'.[18] More alarmingly, HMS *Endurance* was scheduled to be withdrawn in late 1981 because of defence cuts. Argentina had detected that the civil servants of Whitehall were not anxious to defend the Falklands, but it was equally clear that a negotiated solution would never get past the House of Commons. For the Argentineans, the only logical answer was now invasion. The person who was most aware of the developing crisis was the man on the spot, Sir Anthony Williams, Britain's Ambassador in Buenos Aires. He had been anxious about the Falklands for some time, and in the autumn of 1981 had sent 'a very much more acute warning' to the Foreign Office. However, London was not persuaded: 'They were by no means convinced that my information was necessarily better than what they were getting through . . . the interception of Argentina's diplomatic cypher traffic by Government Communications Headquarters.'[19]

In fact, Argentinean orders to prepare for the invasion of the Falklands were given secretly by word of mouth. On the sunny morning of Tuesday, 15 December 1981, Admiral Anaya flew into Puerto Belgrano, which served as the main centre of operations for the Argentine Navy. His presence there was seemingly ceremonial: he had arrived to oversee the installation of the new Chief of Naval Operations, Vice Admiral Juan Lombardo. Bands played, sailors paraded and were inspected, everything passed off faultlessly. However, a surprise awaited Lombardo. A few hours after the parade, Anaya asked to speak to him alone. To his amazement he was ordered to prepare for the invasion of the Falklands. Absolute secrecy, Anaya emphasised, was paramount.[20] In mid-January 1982 the Army and the Air Force were told, and by early March the outline planning for invasion was ready. The target date was mid-September, following the abatement of the foul South Atlantic winter weather, between April and August. The 2nd Marine Infantry Battalion, which was to lead the invasion, began quietly exercising on the coast of Patagonia, using a beach that resembled that of Port Stanley. Only a handful of their officers knew the real purpose of the exercises, and radio silence ensured that it was not picked up by GCHQ.[21]

Bizarrely, the British now triggered an earlier than scheduled invasion of the Falklands, and so, in a way, inflicted surprise upon themselves. During March 1982 a minor incident occurred on South Georgia, which was also claimed by Argentina. A group of Argentine scrap-metal workers had been contracted to remove some old machinery from an abandoned whale factory on the island. During their visit they raised an Argentinean flag, and refused to seek a landing permit. The British Foreign Secretary, Lord Carrington, repeatedly insisted on their removal, and despatched HMS *Endurance*, with a party of twenty Royal Marines, from the Falklands. This was reported to Buenos Aires, which sent a similar-sized ship, the *Bahia Paraios*, with a small party of troops. By the end of March two armed parties, Lilliputian in size, were on South Georgia, twenty miles apart. Crucially, this minor confrontation accelerated the invasion of the Falklands. The junta now ordered immediate action. Argentinean military officers had almost no time to prepare the invasion, and British intelligence had few preparations to observe.[22]

The Argentinean junta saw South Georgia as a crisis. The removal of the scrap men by force would be an unbearable slight to their prestige, yet they would not be ready for military action against the British for months. All crises consist of both danger and opportunity. In the end, Buenos Aires decided to seize the opportunity, and used the confrontation over South Georgia as a pretext to launch a snap invasion of the Falklands. On 23 March the planning group was asked how quickly they could produce a detailed scheme for invasion. Their answer was early April, but they were told to be ready to sail on 28 March. Air Vice Commodore Carlos Bloomer-Reeve, who was to become Secretary General of the new Argentinean administration on what they called the 'Islas Malvinas', was only told of his role on 27 March.[23] The extreme short notice helped to defeat sigint. One of GCHQ's key indicators of a possible invasion was that intelligence analysts had identified a number of Argentine military units as likely participants, and their signals were tracked as warning features. Among these indicator units were elite army formations along the border with Chile.[24] While they remained there, so orthodoxy maintained, an invasion could not be under way. Rather like the Israelis in 1973, who had a model of what forces the Egyptians would need to assemble if they planned an invasion, GCHQ also had a fixed concept. Instead, the initial operations were carried out almost entirely by the Argentinean Navy and Marines. Meanwhile the crack army units remained on the Chilean border.[25]

At sea, both the Argentineans and the Chileans were engaged in large-scale exercises, resulting in a cacophony of signals from dozens of ships, all seemingly 'on operations'.[26] In fact sigint contributed to British confusion. Reports received around 24 March indicated that two Argentine warships had been sent to intercept HMS *Endurance*, then making its way to South Georgia with Marines. It was this sigint material that triggered a discussion of the situation on South Georgia in Whitehall on Thursday, 25 March. The Defence Secretary, John Nott, who had been away in Washington, saw the same material over the weekend, and went to see the First Sea Lord, Henry Leach, about it early on the following Monday morning. GCHQ had picked up a signal from Admiral Anaya in Buenos Aires ordering two Argentinean frigates, *Drummond* and *Granville*, to sail south to reinforce the *Bahia Paraios* and its small party of Marines on South Georgia. In fact Admiral Lombardo objected to this move, insisting that he needed the frigates for the main operation against the Falklands, so they were recalled. However, such is the power of sigint in painting the picture for commanders that most British accounts, including Nott's own precise memoir, still insist that these ships went to South Georgia. Oddly, a deployment that never actually occurred now began the slide towards war.[27]

Over the weekend of 27–28 March, the British Ambassador in Buenos Aires was told by the Argentines that South Georgia was now a 'closed issue', and would not be discussed further. This ominous sign was accompanied by general instructions to Argentinean embassies around the world to cancel all leave. All this was collected by GCHQ. The JIC still believed in a model of gradually escalating tension, and did not think the crisis over South Georgia would have immediate implications for the Falklands. However, GCHQ maintained its long-established practice of selecting choice items of raw intelligence for Downing Street, known as the Blue Book. This was a favourite with

Margaret Thatcher, who loved intelligence, despite the fact that her staff referred to these reports rather sneeringly as 'Comic Cuts'.[28] When she and Carrington saw the raw sigint on South Georgia, their gut instincts were much better than those of the intelligence analysts. Conversing over the phone on the evening of 28 March, and again on an aircraft that took them to a summit in Brussels on Monday, 29 March, they decided to send three nuclear submarines south immediately. At this point the focus of British anxiety still seems to have been South Georgia. However, to Carrington's credit, these submarines were sailing south within perhaps three days of the moment at which the junta had decided to invade.[29]

In the two weeks between the arrival of the scrap-metal workers and the invasion of the Falklands, much of the intelligence material pouring in was low-grade naval sigint collected by *Endurance*. Because of John Nott's attempts to trim the British fleet in 1981, *Endurance* had been earmarked for retirement. Therefore her warnings of increasing Argentine bellicosity, based on the interception of low-level operational traffic, were dismissed by some as an effort to save the ship from being withdrawn from service.[30] Working under the JIC were several Current Intelligence Groups covering different regions. The Group covering Latin America, headed by Brigadier Adam Gurdon, thought the material was not very definitive. Something was going on, but the vast volume of low-grade naval traffic was confusing. Key elements of the Argentine Army were still on the border with Chile. Moreover, the momentum seemed less than in 1977, when the JIC had sounded the alarm but no attack had taken place. So for the time being they watched and waited.[31] What Douglas Nicoll had called 'perseveration' was also in evidence. The intelligence analysts rehearsed the familiar line on the Falklands that invasion would not occur suddenly, but would follow a gradual increase in diplomatic pressure by Buenos Aires. Moreover, the gathering tempo of the Cold War, with fighting in Afghanistan and then trouble in Poland, took their attention elsewhere. Over a two-year period between November 1977 and November 1979, the JIC had reviewed the situation in the Falklands eight times. However, over the next two and a half years, between November 1979 and March 1982, it revisited the threat to the islands only three times.[32]

On Wednesday, 31 March 1982, sigint finally picked up unambiguous signs of a Falklands invasion at two days' notice. GCHQ intercepted a message to the Argentine submarine *Santa Fe*, which was landing a special forces reconnaissance team on the beach at Mullett Creek on the Falklands. There was only one possible interpretation that could be placed on this – invasion was very close. This unpleasant news was flashed to the Cabinet Office.[33] During that morning there had also been a very rapid rise in the volume of signals traffic. Suddenly, it was hard to escape the conclusion that an invasion fleet was mustering off the Falklands. By the same afternoon a crash assessment had reached John Nott's desk, but he was busy in the House of Commons.[34] At 6 o'clock in the evening, Nott still had 'no conception' that a major crisis was about to unfold. However, aware that there were problems, he had asked a team from the Defence Intelligence Staff to come to his room in the House of Commons to give him a briefing:

*

They then produced a series of intercepted signals and other intelligence which left little doubt that an invasion was planned for the morning of Friday 2 April. We knew four things: that an Argentine submarine had been deployed to the area around Port Stanley . . . That the Argentine fleet, which had been on exercises, had broken up into smaller units and seemed to be reassembling for an invasion, that an army commander had been embarked separately on a merchant ship and seemed likely to be the commander of an amphibious force; and finally that the fleet had been ordered to destroy all its documents.[35]

*

Sigint might not have given early warning of Argentinean intentions, but now the invasion was under way, it rendered everything horribly transparent. This triggered action. Nott asked to

see the Prime Minister immediately in her room in the
Commons. An informal meeting of Ministers and Permanent
Under-Secretaries gathered to discuss initial reactions. Margaret
Thatcher recalls that the sigint from GCHQ was extremely
compelling, and there was 'no ground to question the intelligence'.[36] She sent Ronald Reagan a message, 'asking whether
he was aware of the Signals intelligence that we had just
received'. David Omand, Nott's private secretary, was sent to
see if the material from GCHQ had yet been forwarded to NSA.
'At this early stage it had not.'[37]

Just before the meeting broke up, Henry Leach, the First Sea
Lord, arrived outside the Prime Minister's room asking to see
Nott. They invited him in to join the proceedings. He entered
in full uniform, making an immediate impression on the Prime
Minister, who recalls it as a moment of 'comedy' in an otherwise dark episode.[38] Thatcher asked him for his views. With
'supreme self-confidence and assertiveness' he explained that
much of the British fleet just happened to be exercising off
Gibraltar. It would be possible to send a large task force within
a week. He predicted that the Argentines would flee at the sight
of the White Ensign. Could he have permission? Thatcher
acceded immediately and with visible relief.[39] She already knew
that her government was in very serious trouble, and the
showing of her Ministers in the ensuing emergency debates did
nothing to dispel the general air of incompetence.[40] John Major,
a backbencher at the time, recalls that an angry House of
Commons was close to 'mob rule' and was febrile with 'rumours
that the Foreign Office had received the plans of the invasion
days earlier'.[41] Many have concluded that if the risky decision
to send the Task Force had not been taken, the Thatcher government would not have survived.[42]

On Thursday, 1 April, further sigint arrived from GCHQ. The
Argentine forces had been ordered to rendezvous off the
Falklands at 6 o'clock the next morning, confirming the inva-
sion date of 2 April suggested in earlier intercepts.[43] How was
GCHQ reading the Argentinean communications with such ease?

The answer was quite simple. Some of Argentina's high-grade military and diplomatic communications systems made use of expensive but thoroughly compromised European cypher machines, while some Argentinean military field units employed American-manufactured systems which were also vulnerable; oddly, their medium-grade traffic sometimes took longer to break.[44] NSA also had the capability to read Argentine traffic, but was not giving it any priority due to its focus on Russia and China. In late April, Admiral Bobby Ray Inman, who was just completing his tour as Deputy Director of the Central Intelligence Agency (and who had been Director of NSA under Carter), explained the situation. US technical intelligence in Germany was now so good that a Russian surprise attack there was all but impossible. But, Inman insisted, Washington did not have 'foreknowledge of the Argentine government's intention to invade the Falklands Islands'. It just did not have enough staff to follow global trends, so in remoter areas it often did 'very poorly'.[45] In Britain, a number of senior ex-Ministers, including Denis Healey, who had taken a close interest in intelligence over the years, suspected that the Americans had known about the Argentinean invasion in advance. Antony Duff, who had replaced Richard Brooks as the new Cabinet Office Intelligence Coordinator, was busy giving private assurances to these individuals that this was not the case.[46]

GCHQ was now expecting a sigint bonanza. With Argentinean military operations rolling along, Cheltenham hoped that their readable communications, together with avid collection by friends and allies, would render their opponent an open book. They had not reckoned on Ted Rowlands, Labour MP for Clwyd, who had led the embarrassing negotiation mission to Argentina in 1977 as junior Foreign Office Minister. During his period in office he had been privy to sigint decrypts of Argentinean traffic. The word 'privy' is used advisedly, since he was now a Privy Councillor, a role to which special discretion is attached. However, in the heat of the Falklands debate in April 1982, he chose to blurt out all he knew about sigint. Anxious to extract maximum political advantage, he insisted that the invasion could not have been a surprise. 'I shall make disclosure,' he said rather pompously. 'As well as trying to read the mind of the enemy, we have been reading its telegrams for many years.'[47]

The gasps of horror in the House of Commons were audible. The groans of agony were even louder at Cheltenham. No Member of Parliament had committed such a public sigint gaffe since Stanley Baldwin had infamously baited the Russians by reading out their own cypher traffic in the House of Commons in 1927. Margaret Thatcher later said that the Rowlands blunder had been 'totally and utterly devastating in the amount which it gave away to those against whom intelligence was directed', adding, 'The moment you say too much the sources dry up.'[48] What was the cost of the Rowlands security gaffe? Some have argued that it was so great that some major reverses of the Falklands War, such as the attack on the Sir Galahad at Bluff Cove, might have been averted had Rowlands kept his mouth shut.[49] The reality seems to be that while the Argentineans may have improved their cypher security, their material became harder to break, rather than unbreakable. They improved their procedures, changed their codes more frequently and in some cases double encyphered, but to little avail, since their actual machines were compromised. Commander Robert Denton Green, who was the Intelligence Officer at Fleet Headquarters in Northwood, offers the best assessment:

*

But amid all this difficulty, GCHQ managed to break the Argentine codes. They were not terribly sophisticated, but we got a lot of very high quality political and battle-planning intelligence. It took us between twelve and twenty-four hours to decipher and translate the messages, so we were always trying to extrapolate forward to see what they meant for us now.

*

Denton Green concludes that although the material was some-times ambiguous, GCHQ intercepts gave it a reasonable picture of what was going on inside the minds of the main Argentine commanders. By contrast, the GCHQ material on the political side was 'a little bit confusing', but this reflected the genuine turbulence within the ruling circles in Buenos Aires at the time. Some of the delay was caused by the challenge of sifting through the vast volume of messages that were intercepted and deciding what was useful.[50] The Argentinean Air Force's traffic was the hardest to read, since it had recently invested in new encrypted communications made by a subsidiary of the British defence company Racal, based in South Africa.[51] One of the most irritating aspects of the Rowlands affair for GCHQ was that other countries in the Southern Hemisphere took the hint and set about improving their own cypher facilities.[52]

As the Task Force headed south, intelligence activities by other interested parties presented awkward questions. What should be done about the ever-present Soviet spy trawlers, 'bristling with radio antennae', that followed the Task Force?[53] Overhead, they were watched by vast Russian TU-20D 'Bear' elint reconnaissance aircraft, with a range of eleven thousand miles, while GCHQ soon reported that the Russians had launched extra satellites to watch the spectacle.[54] Remarkably, throughout the conflict the Norwegian signals intelligence base located at Fauske in the far north regularly intercepted the Soviet satellite intelligence data. This was then sent direct to the British, who used it to find the Argentinean fleet. One British intelligence officer recalls: 'When the war broke out, we ourselves almost didn't have any intelligence information from this area. It was here we got help from the Norwegians, who gave us a stream of information about the Argentine warships' positions. The information came to us all the time and straight to our war headquarters at Northwood. The information was continuously updated and told us exactly where the Argentine ships were.' Meanwhile, the Soviets passed nothing on to Argentina.[55]

In early April, Britain's intelligence analysts were playing catch-up. One of the areas in which sigint offers huge benefits is its ability to build up a picture of the enemy's order of battle, including the size of each unit, its position and the extent to which it is mobile. Partly because of the difficulties with high-grade Russian sigint during the Cold War, GCHQ and the sigint elements of the three services had devoted vast effort to mapping every subsection of Warsaw Pact forces. However, this sort of activity is time-consuming and labour-intensive. Armies of listeners are required to shadow the real armies on the ground. No such effort had been devoted to the armed forces of Argentina, and their order of battle was a mystery. Thus, on 4 April 1982, when Major General Julian Thompson, the Royal Marines commander, looked to his Brigade Intelligence Officer, Vivian Rowe, for a briefing about the three thousand Argentine troops, the main source of intelligence was reference books in Plymouth Public Library.[56] Things did not look much better in the Defence Intelligence Staff in London, which had little material on the Argentinean order of battle. Eventually it found a British naval officer who followed the Argentinean forces as a hobby.[57] Later, the CIA and Chile handed over their own order of battle materials on Argentina, which were complete.[58]

Meanwhile, Cheltenham had set up an operations room, presided over by Rod Little of K Division, the section of GCHQ that specialised in non-Russian comint, in one of the unprepossessing single-storey spurs on the main site at Oakley. In a room nearby, elint was presided over by the head of J Division, Michael Herman, who had vast experience of airborne signals collection.[59] One of the biggest problems was forward distribution of the product. At the Fleet Headquarters at Northwood, Commander Robert Denton Green had secure communications giving him an excellent feed of material from both GCHQ and NSA. However, the abiding Cold War mindset had resulted in little attention being given to the ability to push sigint forward to operational commanders, especially during expeditionary operations in far-flung locations. The main connection between GCHQ and Commander Sandy Woodward's flagship in the South Atlantic, the aircraft carrier HMS *Hermes*, was a secure encrypted telephone link using Skynet, which allowed the operations room at Cheltenham to talk directly to the intelligence officers on the ship. However, distribution to lower levels was more difficult. As Denton Green observed, the Falklands War was 'very strange', and many arrangements had to be improvised.[60]

A set of bizarre circumstances soon made communications yet more difficult. In common with many British government agencies in the 1980s, GCHQ was now required to outsource its building maintenance rather than relying on a local workforce. Some weeks into the Falklands War, a gang of contractors appeared outside the Falklands operations room in Cheltenham and announced that they had come to resurface the roof. In times gone by they would have been sent away with a flea in their ear, but this would now involve hefty cancellation charges. So, with the nerve centre of sigint operations operating below, the labourers began work on the roof of the single-storey office building, ripping off the old felt, spreading fresh sealant and recovering. Vats of boiling tar surrounded the hapless sigint teams. As late spring turned to early summer the temperature rose, but the windows could not be opened. The tar men were not cleared for comint, or indeed any kind of 'int'. For a week, conversations with HMS *Hermes* were hilarious. The intelligence officer on Woodward's staff would say, 'Hang on, I can't hear you. Some Harriers are just taking off!' Cheltenham would reply, 'Well, we can't hear you either, there's too much banging on the roof!'[61]

During late April, even as the Task Force headed south, General Alexander Haig, Reagan's Secretary of State, had been engaged in a slightly comic reprise of Kissinger's famous 1970s 'Shuttle Diplomacy'. Presenting himself to Margaret Thatcher as an honest broker, he had been subjected to a severe tongue-lashing by the Prime Minister, in which she made ready comparisons between the military dictators in Buenos Aires and Adolf Hitler. Despite her obvious vexations at American attempts to play the honest broker, Thatcher entered into the diplomatic exchanges in good faith. Rather to her relief, on 19 April the

Argentinean government rejected Haig's latest peace plan. Ronald Reagan now reluctantly terminated Haig's mission, declaring American support for Britain. Britain announced a two-hundred-mile Exclusion Zone around the Falklands. On 1 May the RAF launched the first long-range Vulcan bomber raid on Stanley airport. On the same day, Sea Harriers attacked Goose Green and three Argentinean aircraft were brought down. The talking was over and the shooting war had begun.

On 2 May, the most controversial action of the war occurred when the Argentine cruiser *General Belgrano* was sunk by the British nuclear attack submarine HMS *Conqueror*. The *Belgrano* was a large cruiser accompanied by destroyers, and the British were anxious about losing track of her as she headed towards the Exclusion Zone. Her main threat was her powerful radar, which could detect the British fleet at long range, while the fire-power actually lay with the Exocet-carrying destroyers that accompanied her. The *Belgrano* group constituted a serious danger to the Task Force, and was therefore being shadowed by the *Conqueror* under Commander Christopher Wreford-Brown, who had arrived on the submarine only a few weeks previously. The Admiralty requested a change to the rules of engagement to allow an attack on the cruiser while she was outside the Exclusion Zone, and the War Cabinet gave its approval at 10 o'clock in the morning. This had not been given lightly. Willie Whitelaw, the Deputy Prime Minister, asked what many regarded as the key question. If the *Conqueror* was asked merely to shadow the *Belgrano* group for the time being, could she be certain to maintain contact? The answer was an emphatic 'no'. In fact, the *Conqueror* had previously been shadowing the Argentine aircraft carrier *25 Mayo*, but had lost contact during bad weather.[62]

Even while this fraught discussion was going on, the *Belgrano* group changed course and, gently zig-zagging, began heading away from the Falklands. At 1.30 in the afternoon the *Conqueror* rose and accessed the satellite, which gave her the changed rules of engagement and permission to attack. Choosing old-fashioned Mark 8 torpedoes of a Second World War vintage,

Wreford-Brown had to manoeuvre to within less than two miles of the *Belgrano*. This took until 6.30 p.m. At the last moment he thought he had misjudged the approach. Peering through the periscope, he muttered, 'Damn. Too close.' But after a few seconds' hesitation he fired three torpedoes. Less than a minute later, the first torpedo hit the *Belgrano* just ahead of the front gun turret. A massive flash lit up the sky, and the explosion nearly blew the entire bow of the ship off. The *Belgrano* was already doomed when the second torpedo slammed home. The third also found its mark, but failed to explode. The *Belgrano* was sunk thirty miles outside the Exclusion Zone, and 386 Argentine sailors perished. By the following day, all Argentinean naval vessels had been recalled to within a few miles of the coast.[63]

Sigint bears strongly on the *Belgrano* story. During the conflict, and for some years afterward, Margaret Thatcher was severely criticised for permitting the attack outside the Exclusion Zone. It now seems that the key signals intelligence concerning this controversial action reached British commanders and politicians in London after the fact. Events turned largely upon a sequence of Argentine Navy signals that were intercepted and read by GCHQ. On 1 May 1982 the Argentine Navy was told to locate the British Task Force around the Falklands and launch a 'massive attack' as soon as possible. The *Belgrano* was ordered south and into the Exclusion Zone. This alarming signal was intercepted by GCHQ, and strongly informed the government's deliberations. Shortly afterwards, the War Cabinet met at the Prime Minister's country residence, Chequers, and authorised an attack on the *Belgrano*. Sigint showed that, although at this moment she still lay outside the Exclusion Zone, her orders were clear, and she constituted a serious threat. Later, further intercepted signals revealed that the Argentinean military chiefs had ordered the *Belgrano* to reverse course and resume her previous position, probably because she had been spotted by British aircraft. However, as we have seen, Argentinean traffic took some time to process, and the new intercepts were not distributed on the British side until the following day, and so had no impact on the day's events.[64] Accusations were later made that Thatcher pursued this action in order to 'torpedo' an American-backed Peruvian peace plan. It is now clear that the *Belgrano* was sunk for operational rather than political reasons.[65]

The Argentineans were not slow to respond. They deployed their French-built Super Etendard jets equipped with an air-launched version of the massive anti-ship missile, the Exocet. Almost everything that British intelligence thought it knew about Argentine use of this system was wrong. The naval operations staff in Whitehall had been assured that the Argentinean Exocets were not ready to be deployed.[66] Although Britain knew the Argentines only had five missiles, they believed there was only one launch aircraft, when in fact there were five. The Task Force had been told the range of the aircraft was only 425 miles, but this did not take into account the possibility of mid-air refuelling. Thus, on 4 May, when the British detected an Argentine Neptune surveillance aircraft, they did not realise that it was helping to guide the attacking aircraft, and dismissed it as a search aircraft looking for survivors from the *Belgrano*. Only when two Etendards approached the Task Force, and rose slightly to acquire their targets with their radar, was the alert sounded. HMS *Glasgow* and HMS *Coventry* had mere seconds to respond, but escaped by firing large clouds of aluminium chaff, which deflected the missiles. However, twenty miles away, for reasons that are still obscure, HMS *Sheffield* had her radar turned off, and did not hear the warnings from her sister ships. Seconds later she was hit in the forward engine compartment by an Exocet.[67] The missile failed to explode, but the ship was still destroyed by its force and its remaining propellant. Twenty members of the crew died. Everyone had known that the lack of air cover was the Achilles heel of the Task Force, and indeed, for this very reason some in the Cabinet had privately thought that its despatch was 'ludicrous'.[68]

It was public knowledge that Argentina had only a limited number of Exocets, and several remarkable operations were now launched to reduce their effectiveness. First of all, warning was needed of when the Exocet-armed Super Etendard jet fighters took off. This meant deploying special forces inside Argentina. Robert Denton Green recalls: 'The idea was to get a guy onto the runway to tell us whenever aircraft took off. It worked, to a certain extent, but was very hit and miss.'[69] Second, the French were persuaded to hand over the technical details and elint profiles of the missiles. Most importantly, SIS launched an operation to prevent more missiles being bought on the open market. Roberto Calvi, an Italian banker who aided a global Argentinean effort to procure more Exocets, ended up dead under Blackfriars Bridge in June 1982.[70] Calvi was also the banker to the Papacy in Rome, and had Mafia connections. We now know a little more about this murky subject. David Fischer, an American diplomat, claims to have met the man who killed Calvi sitting on a toilet in a restaurant in Rome clutching an AK-47. This improbable figure was an ex-Mafia hitman who had been developed as an American agent during the hunt for a kidnapped commander of American forces in Italy, General James Dozier. By 1982 he was clearly a confirmed CIA asset, suggesting that the Americans were perhaps assisting SIS on the ground in their anti-Exocet campaign.[71]

Meanwhile, in the South Atlantic, there was a concerted effort to degrade any Argentine intelligence systems. Typically, there were suspicions about an Argentine trawler called the *Narwal* which was shadowing the Task Force and which appeared to be a sigint spy trawler. Eventually Admiral Woodward ordered Captain Jeremy Black, the commander of the carrier HMS *Invincible*, to go and capture her. After careful reconnaissance she was attacked with cannon fire by two Harriers in the hope of disabling her. When she failed to stop, a thousand-pound bomb was dropped, which failed to detonate. After more cannon fire the trawler was stopped, and slowly began to sink. Helicopters were despatched with an SBS boarding party. Although the *Narwal* had indeed been gathering intelligence, she was not a sophisticated 'elint trawler' of the Russian type. She had once been a normal fishing vessel, and had been commandeered by Lieutenant Commander Gonzales Llanos of the Argentinean Navy at pistol point. The twenty-four fishermen on board, one of whom had been killed in the Harrier attack, were a rather miserable press-ganged crew. Llanos was about to throw his intelligence materials overboard, but was warned sternly by the SBS party that if he did so, he would follow them into the ocean. Captain Black was relieved to hear that an Argentinean intelligence officer had been captured on board, complete with all his files, codes and equipment, making the operation what Woodward called 'a fair cop'.[72]

Three weeks earlier in the conflict, the British had a much narrower squeak with an Argentinean military Boeing 707 reconnaissance plane. Decked out in Argentinean Air Force regalia, it was presumed to be the equivalent of a Nimrod sigint aircraft. On 21 April it was buzzed by a Harrier, but could not be shot down because the fleet was not yet in the Exclusion Zone. Nicknamed 'the Burglar', this aircraft was a daily visitor, and a cause of some anxiety. Woodward was given permission via the Skynet secure phone to shoot it down if he was close and had positive identification. Three days later, after more unwelcome visits the British achieved a good lock-on with the radar of their Sea Dart missile system. Woodward recalls that the aircraft approached at 350 knots, and within two minutes would be within the permitted range for shootdown – 'At which point he is ours.' But with twenty seconds to spare Woodward yelled 'Weapons tight!', withdrawing permission to fire. It was not 'the Burglar' but a Brazilian airliner running from Durban to Rio de Janeiro. On 3 July 1988 the American cruiser USS *Vincennes* infamously shot down an Iranian airliner bound for Dubai over the Gulf, mistaking it for an attacking fighter aircraft and killing all 290 people on board. The British had been only inches from a similar disaster.[73]

Special operations to prepare a path for British amphibious landings on the islands began on 20 May. The initial landings were destined for San Carlos Water, a calm inlet on East Falkland. However, the narrow entrance to the inlet was commanded by a steep bluff called Fanning Head that offered a superb vantage of the surrounding area. Sigint had intercepted orders for an Argentine heavy weapons company with 105mm guns and mortars to move into the area. The exact location was uncertain, because the sigint operatives were still puzzling over the way in which the Argentines transmitted their map references. Later in the campaign, sigint was brought together with captured maps marked up in pen, obtained from prisoners of war, that resolved the mystery.[74] On the night of 20 May an operation was launched using the SBS to find and neutralise the heavy weapons unit. They would be accompanied by a Royal Marine naval gunfire controller, Captain Hugh McManners, who would direct shellfire from HMS *Antrim* onto the edge of the enemy positions. When they judged that the Argentineans had had enough, another officer, Captain Rod Bell, who spoke excellent Spanish, would call on them to surrender using a loudspeaker.[75]

This rather elaborate plan was concocted in the wake of the recent surrender of Argentine forces on South Georgia, and reflected the fact that British commanders now believed that much of the garrison would probably give up without a fight, if offered the option. The plan was to insert the SBS party from *Antrim* by night, using two helicopters. However, the operation was complicated by the fact that the sigint pointed to three possible enemy locations that were quite widely dispersed. To deal with this, a preliminary reconnaissance flight was undertaken by a modified Wessex helicopter with a newly installed thermal image camera – so new in fact that the crew were still reading the manual. The helicopter was a rather improbable-looking beast, earning it the nickname 'Humphrey'. During this mission all the occupants, who included the SBS commander and McManners, were nervous because a Sea King helicopter had just been lost at sea with eighteen members of the SAS. However, the new equipment worked perfectly, 'vacuuming up' thermal images, first picking up the bungalows of the settlement at the far end of the San Carlos inlet and eventually revealing the Argentine heavy weapons company as a cluster of 'bright green glow worms'. They returned to brief the whole patrol, which departed an hour later in two helicopters so heavily laden that they struggled to get airborne.

The excessive weight was caused by the fact that every second member of the thirty-man SBS fighting patrol carried a belt-feed General Purpose Machine Gun, in the hope that this massive firepower, together with tracer ammunition, would allow them to pretend to be a much bigger force than they really were. By the time the patrol approached Fanning Head, the Argentine heavy weapons company were already firing their artillery out to sea. McManners immediately called in a heavy barrage from *Antrim* which consisted of twenty salvoes set as airbursts, exploding fifty feet above the ground. The massive explosions turned night into day, and the Argentine guns quickly fell silent. McManners then called in sporadic rounds to keep the position busy while his patrol advanced. But Captain Bell's loudspeaker failed, and efforts to persuade the remaining enemy to surrender were only partly effective. With dawn fast approaching, an inter-mittent firefight developed, vast clouds of tracer bullets skim-ming towards the enemy. Fanning Head was soon secure, and the SBS patrol made its way down to the beach to watch the main landing force heading up San Carlos Water towards its landing points. Overhead, Argentine aircraft had already begun to attack the landing ships and their escorts, extracting a high cost. Mirage jets from the Argentine Air Force streaked by the SBS patrol, only fifty feet above the water.[76]

It was now the morning of 21 May, and the troubled land-ings at San Carlos Water began in earnest. Brigadier Julian Thompson had arranged for a diversionary attack to be put in by D Squadron of the SAS at Darwin and Goose Green, where there were large concentrations of Argentine troops. These parties were able to call in gunfire from HMS *Ardent* and HMS *Glamorgan* to make their attack look serious: 'Signals intercept traffic afterwards revealed that the Argentineans believed they were under attack from the main force, which was our inten-tion.'[77] Sigint continued to be fed in a steady stream to Admiral

Woodward on *Hermes*, and informed the air and naval war. However, once Brigadier Thompson and his 3 Commando Brigade HQ were ashore at San Carlos, it was harder to get sigint to the land forces. Remarkably, because of its highly classified nature, some information was withheld from Thompson's intelligence staff, so initially they had difficulty figuring out Argentinean strengths and positions. The withheld information was mostly sigint, and the authorities were adamant that it could not be released.[78]

Thompson ended up generating much of his own local sigint. Fortunately his intelligence staff had picked up a local radio link transmitting messages from enemy troops on the Falklands to their families in Argentina. Not only were these messages in clear, they also carried the name, rank, unit and location of the sender. This amazing security lapse by the Argentineans gave Thompson much of the information he needed on the enemy positions. Good intelligence came from local interception by tactical sigint from the Royal Marines' own Y Troop sigint unit, or from patrolling by the SAS and SBS. Nevertheless, the failure to push national sigint from GCHQ to the front line seems to have led to problems. Notably, 450 British paratroopers led by Colonel H. Jones captured Goose Green, at considerable cost, defeating a force four times their size. The Defence Intelligence Staff in London seem to have received a full picture of the enemy forces at Goose Green, but it does not appear that local British commanders were ever fully aware of the size or nature of the force they were confronting.[79]

Brigadier Thompson himself recalls how poorly he was served by national intelligence, and the rather fragmented information that was available to him once his troops were on the ground:

*

We had very little intelligence, and what we had was often wrong. For example, the Argentinean commander Menendez was labelled a hard-hitting tough guy, but actually was a conciliatory sort of chap, probably selected to be governor, who in my view was not a good choice to fight a battle. The intelligence picture did improve, mainly from radio intelligence monitoring. Although we built up an accurate picture of which units were where on the islands, we didn't know what equipment they had.[80]

*

Rather as the British Army of the Rhine had planned in Germany in the 1960s and 1970s, the intelligence gap was filled not from national assets, but by the local commander's own Y Troop and by special forces, who were often moving within yards of the Argentine positions.

Useful intelligence also came from the islanders. The most remarkable was perhaps Reg Silvey, the keeper of the lighthouse at Cape Pembroke. When Argentine patrols required him to hand over his radio transmitter, he only handed over his second set. Having dismantled his radio mast, he then used the steel core of his washing line and his remaining transmitter to send information on Argentine troop movements to the British. He also listened in on transmissions by the Argentine forces, which they mistakenly considered immune to interception because they were low-power and short-range. Moreover, he created confusion by recording Argentine radio traffic and then rebroadcasting it later on the same frequency. Perhaps the most valuable information he provided was the fact that there were no islanders on the Stanley Airport peninsula, clearing the way for sustained shelling and several marathon bombing raids by RAF Vulcans, code-named 'Black Buck'.[81] General Mario Menendez, the Argentine military governor, confirms that some islanders were caught communicating with the British fleet, and although the Argentinean forces would have been within their rights to shoot them, their treatment was restrained.[82] Carlos Bloomer-Reeve, the Argentine Secretary General, also recalls that the senior officers were 'trying to arrest a lot of people' in their search for 'an illegal radio station'.[83]

The Argentineans were clearly doing their own tactical sigint. General Menendez claims: 'We intercepted all communications by radio from the British troops,' but what this actually amounted to, and how it was used, is not clear.[84] In the latter stages of the campaign Brigadier Thompson was treated to a brief but dramatic insight into the hazards of enemy radio direction-finding. The headquarters of his 3 Commando Brigade had been set up on the reverse slopes of Mount Kent as the Royal Marines prepared to attack Mount Tumbledown, and he recalls that the Argentineans located them using radio direction-finding. Nearby helicopters also helped to give away their position. His headquarters were soon attacked by two A4 Skyhawks which dropped seven thousand-pound bombs in two passes, and then attacked with cannon fire. It was a miracle no one was killed. The tent in which Thompson was about to give attack orders to his commanders was pepper-potted with shrapnel, and the chairs they were about to sit on had their aluminium legs sliced off.[85]

On 15 June, British troops marched into Port Stanley and the Argentinean forces surrendered. A month later the last prisoner was exchanged and released. On 12 October there was a victory parade through London. Three days later, Lieutenant General Sir James Glover, Britain's most senior Army intelligence officer, visited Washington and gave a detailed briefing on intelligence and the Falklands War to his opposite number General William Odom, head of US Army intelligence. In the Falklands campaign, Glover said, sigint had provided 90 per cent of intelligence. Comint had performed exceedingly well, and had proved 'invaluable'. Elint had proved more of a 'mixed blessing'. The most important lesson – soon forgotten, of course – was that local army sigint units often found they were collecting strategic sigint that related to high policy, while strategic sigint collectors using national resources found they were often collecting tactical sigint of more use to those in the front line. The systems were not well designed to move this material in a sophisticated way to the right customers. There had been time delays when targets changed, and problems with getting sigint to the fighting units as the pattern of battles changed hour by hour.[86] Nevertheless, sigint had been hugely important, and at the end of the campaign

Brian Tovey, the Director of GCHQ, sent a message to all the staff at Cheltenham which read: 'High level praise. Never has so much praise been accorded. There can be no doubt that this praise has been well deserved. It has been earned by hard and dedicated work by you as individuals.'[87]

Sigint shone partly because of the weakness of other sources. Imagery was often unavailable due to cloud cover. The Army had no drones, and aircraft were only covering sporadic tactical targets. SIS was 'slow to develop' in the region, but its work with the Defence Intelligence Staff against Exocet shipments had been invaluable. PoW interrogations and the islanders themselves had been helpful. Intelligence weaknesses for forward operations required much use of special forces, which had made a 'critical contribution'. The need for intelligence prior to the landings had really stretched the special forces. The other missing element, again a perennial problem in British military operations, was good, reliable, secure communications. The British had become aware from their own sigint of their vulnerability to Argentinean sigint. What the Army now wanted was a jump forward to 'burst communications' that would defeat enemy listening. Deception was fairly successful, but tended to consist of small-scale activities and lacked an overall strategic theme.[88] The poor performance of the Nimrods, on which Britain had blown such a large slice of its sigint budget, is still a mystery. Lt Colonel David Chaundler, who served in the Defence Intelligence Staff until halfway through the campaign, asserted, 'The Nimrods were achieving very little,' despite the enormous effort that was being put into refuelling them.[89] At least eight maritime reconnaissance Nimrods operated from Ascension Island, and one R1 sigint aircraft seems to have flown from the Chilean base at Punta Arenas.[90]

In a crisis you find out who your friends are. In 1982 the Americans were very helpful, but Britain's European allies rallied to her cause even quicker.[91] The Defence Secretary, John Nott, remarked: 'In so many ways [President] Mitterrand and the

French were our greatest allies.' This included considerable assistance with signals intelligence. Recent revelations suggest that sigint from French Guyana, and also from the Dutch site at Eemnes, was important in assisting the British effort.[92] Margaret Thatcher also pronounced Mitterrand to be an 'absolutely staunch' ally.[93] Not only did the French refuse to hand over the Exocets that the Argentineans had already paid for, they offered the British details of the electronic signatures of the missiles. The Spanish also proved to be firm friends, shutting down a covert operation by an Argentine underwater demolition team to attack British ships at Gibraltar. Surprisingly, Israel supplied weapons and training to the neo-fascist Argentinean regime during the conflict. This continued after the war, when the Israelis refitted three Argentinean Air Force 707s of the 'Burglar' variety with new sigint equipment so they became the equivalent of Britain's Nimrod R1 listening aircraft.[94]

The Falklands War was profoundly important for the development of British sigint, and triggered GCHQ's ill-fated experiment with an independent sigint satellite system in the mid-1980s. During the Falklands War, American defence and intelligence agencies had certainly been very helpful. NSA had allowed the retargeting of one of its powerful sigint satellites for a few hours each day, and handed the 'take' over to GCHQ. After some argument, imagery satellites had also been diverted at considerable financial cost, since their operational lives were shortened. However, this episode also illuminated a dangerous dependency on American satellite technology for future military operations. By 1983 Cheltenham had begun to ask, what would happen if one day the Americans decided not to be quite so accommodating? Flushed with success from a good sigint performance in the Falklands campaign, GCHQ's Director, Brian Tovey, now stepped forward with a proposal. The result was plans for GCHQ's own sigint satellite, code-named 'Zircon' – by far the most secret British defence project of the 1980s.[95]

Thatcher and the GCHQ
Trade Union Ban

*. . . it was carefully prepared in secret and it came as a bolt from
the blue – bang!*
Mike Grindley, Chinese linguist, GCHQ[1]

The acrimonious GCHQ trade union dispute that occurred in
early 1984 has to be seen in the context of a wider struggle.
For more than a decade both Labour and Conservative governments had been challenged by union power, especially in the
area of economic policy. Margaret Thatcher was determined to
end this, and during its first term in office her government
passed a range of trade union legislation, restricting activities
such as strikes and picketing. Although the unions had vowed
to resist this, the moderate leader of the TUC, Len Murray, told
his colleagues that if the Conservatives were elected for a second
term in 1983, they would have to accept it. The Conservatives
were re-elected, but confrontation continued. By the autumn
of 1983 there was a high-profile printing dispute at Warrington
and an ongoing miners' strike led by Arthur Scargill. It was
against this volatile background that the Thatcher government
decided to ban unions at GCHQ, in a surprise decision announced
in January 1984.

The ban caused a furore throughout the union movement,
and even the most moderate trade unionists were appalled. The
personal position of Len Murray was undermined. He worked
with the Cabinet Secretary, Sir Robert Armstrong, to put together
a compromise in the spring of 1984 which he hoped would be
acceptable to the Cabinet, but it was rejected on the personal

whim of the Prime Minister. Jim Prior, the Northern Ireland Secretary, recalls that at that moment, 'Len Murray was lost.' It is hard to escape the conclusion that both Margaret Thatcher and the major unions used GCHQ as a pawn in a wider ideological battle. Neither the managers nor the trade unionists at GCHQ were directly responsible for what followed.[2]

The issue of trade unions at Cheltenham is synonymous with the Thatcher era. After its eruption in early 1984, it constituted a running sore until it was resolved in 1997. Yet it is rarely realised that union issues were not new to the secret world, or indeed to GCHQ. Paradoxically, GCHQ had always had trade unions because it was even more secret than its sister services, MI5 and SIS, which did not. This was because many GCHQ workers were hidden inside other units – such as the Diplomatic Wireless Staff (DWS) – that might reasonably expect union representation. Moreover, unlike MI5 or SIS, Cheltenham was effectively a vast factory that produced intelligence on an industrial scale. The majority of employees at GCHQ and its outstations were working a shift system. In all factories, even secret ones, there is a clear hierarchy, and good labour relations are of the first importance. Yet the managers at GCHQ could be remote figures who were rather conscious of their grades. As a result, union issues had raged beneath the surface of British sigint since the 1950s.

Disruption of GCHQ's activities through union action was not the only source of anxiety. Officials believed there were also security issues. Although they conceded that no union official had ever been detected acting as a spy, nevertheless they worried that a significant proportion of officials in some key unions were Communists. Spy cases during the 1950s and 1960s had shown beyond any doubt that Communist Party membership often meant espionage, and Foreign Office officials feared 'a direct, unfettered and undetectable line of liaison between staff having knowledge of secret affairs and Communists'. Some senior officials had pondered the alternative of a staff association, in other words a tame internal union not affiliated to the TUC, for staff in specialist establishments like GCHQ and Hanslope Park.³ Managers at both the DWS and GCHQ had liked the idea, but Ministers baulked at the political difficulties – it would mean withdrawing normal union membership from many existing staff, and conflict was anticipated. Without concrete evidence of union-related espionage it was decided to continue with the present situation.⁴ In fact, the main problem was labour relations, not espionage. GCHQ had faced constant issues with Radio Operators because of changing communications technology. New equipment and work of increased complexity meant new grades and many different levels of pay.

On 11 November 1955, John Winnifrith, a Treasury official who looked after security matters, had reported, 'Trouble is brewing in GCHQ.' This was because of a complex dispute involving competing unions which wished to represent the Slip-Readers who worked alongside the Radio Operators, turning the electronic signals captured as sound into processible messages. The Civil Service Union was battling it out with the smaller Government and Overseas Cable and Wireless Operators Association, but Winnifrith explained to his superiors that 'the politics go far further than that'. He had been told 'in confidence' that what was really behind this dispute was the fact that 'management at GCHQ had deliberately brought this smaller association in to spike the guns of CSU', as they did not want the Slip-Readers to join an already over-mighty union.⁵ This deliberate policy of 'divide and rule' on the part of Eric Jones, GCHQ's Director in the early 1950s, was probably a mistake.

In April 1962 the Radcliffe Inquiry into Security in the Civil Service had resurrected security fears about trade unions. MI5 now estimated that one third of full-time officials in the major Civil Service unions were either Communists or Communist sympathisers. The Electrical Trades Union had Communist full-time officials. At a number of secret establishments, primarily the Atomic Weapons Establishment at Aldermaston, MI5 was looking closely at specific trade union officials. However, this was slippery territory, since MI5 did not want GCHQ or Aldermaston to take precautionary action that would jeopardise its sources. Their greatest worry was that trade unionists, whose legitimate role was to hear staff grievances, would be able to 'talent spot' for the KGB, identifying disgruntled individuals who might be willing to act as 'hostile intelligence agents'. Once again, management pressed for staff associations that had no links to mainstream unions. However, when Privy Councillors consulted the TUC they were warned that such a move would 'meet with the strongest possible Trade Union opposition'. Fearing political confrontation, the government backed away.[6]

Michael Herman, who was head of the prestigious J Division, dealing with Russian problems, observes that by and large there was not much union militancy at GCHQ. However, the Radio Operators had some genuinely awkward problems, including 'age bulges' resulting from the recruitment of a lot of wartime staff which blighted promotion prospects. Working conditions in some of the outstations like Cyprus and Hong Kong were also poor.[7] In early September 1969, all this boiled over in a five-day strike. This was notionally a work-to-rule after the rejection of a recent pay claim. Some 2,200 Radio Operators were affected, and product from Cyprus and Hong Kong slowed to a trickle. Much of the operators' work involved searching for radio traffic. During the dispute they found very little, but once it was over, production mysteriously bounced back to normal. Joe Hooper, the Director, intervened personally to persuade the Treasury to reconsider the rejected pay claim. John Somerville, his Principal Establishment Officer, later admitted that industrial action now became a 'sword of Damocles', because the 1969 work-to-rule had 'an immediate and drastic effect on the work of GCHQ'.[8] In the long term, the agency responded by moving away from manual collection by people who sat in huts with headphones on, towards more of the sort of automated systems already used by the Americans.[9]

In February 1973 the Civil and Public Servants Association

had called a one-day strike as part of a general dispute over government public-sector pay policy. Principal Establishment Officers from across the Foreign Office met to review the likely damage to operations. John Somerville explained that at GCHQ the situation was complex, since there were 7,500 staff distributed amongst forty different classes or grades. Half belonged to the Civil and Public Servants Association, and the majority favoured action. The Civil Service Union had also lodged a new pay claim that was likely to lead to trouble. Somerville's main worry was the impact this might have on sensitive activities: 'The principal area involved would be the computer centre which might have to be shut down.' This was because the computers that undertook the core cryptanalysis ran around the clock, and depended on shift work. All this, he added, would have 'unfortunate effects on certain aspects of bi-lateral cooperation' by which he meant GCHQ's collaboration with NSA.[10]

The next serious dispute with the Radio Operators did not arrive until 1979. The strikes of that year, which rumbled on until 1981, were partly caused by an acceleration of the Cold War, driven by the Russian invasion of Afghanistan. Normally, fresh monitoring equipment for the Radio Operators at locations such as Cyprus and Hong Kong underwent a long period of development and operational testing. However, from 1979 a series of crises drove the emergency deployment of new sigint equipment, with little discussion about procedure. This time it was the local managers, or Station Radio Officers, who were upset. The Station Radio Officer was the local manager of resources, and his key role was tactical targeting. If an international event occurred that was of interest, he had responsibility to shift the station's effort from routine targets to new targets of opportunity. Such redirection was required frequently during the multiple international crises that occurred between late 1979 and early 1980.

Peter Little, who had been head of K Division, the part of GCHQ dealing with non-Soviet traffic, in the early 1980s, later identified the four international events which coincided with this long-running dispute: the invasion of Afghanistan in 1979, the hostage crisis in Iran, the invasion of Poland by Russia in 1980–81, and the main annual Soviet military exercise in September 1981. K Division was heavily involved in these issues.[11] GCHQ's allies had helped out by covering for the lost interception as a result of the dispute, but the disruption was embarrassing. Typically, additional coverage during the Polish crisis had been provided by Sweden's sigint service, the FRA.[12] There were other reasons for poor GCHQ performance during the Polish crisis, including the breakdown of equipment. However, unhappiness with coverage of this event fed into the ongoing Douglas Nicoll review.[13] Michael Herman recalls his 'feeling of sadness and shame . . . when a Cold War 24-hour surveillance unit for which I was responsible closed down for a night watch as part of a departmental pay dispute'. Again, the allies, including NSA, had to 'take the strain'.[14]

The Anglo–American relationship loomed large here, since the strikes impacted directly and painfully on GCHQ's growing role as a processor of the 'take' from NSA's new satellites. As we have seen, in the 1970s NSA was picking up vastly more product because of its new Ryolite satellites, but had less human processing power because of budget cuts. GCHQ, the Canadian and Australian sigint services had helped out by offering to analyse some of the material. Much of GCHQ was now a processing unit for the streams of sigint that NSA was beaming down to Menwith Hill in Yorkshire, and it feared anything that would disrupt this. In other words, GCHQ and NSA were now wired together in a way that they had not quite been before. Meanwhile, with union relations in Britain generally looking difficult, GCHQ anticipated more strikes across the whole Civil Service than in the past. Accordingly, Cheltenham's managers now returned to the idea of a staff association to replace unions that had been floated in the 1950s and 1960s.

Brian Tovey, a bullish figure who had taken over as Director of GCHQ in 1979, recalls that the strikes of that year were 'the turning point' for him. He was always puzzled by the presence of the unions at GCHQ, unlike NSA, which he characterised as a 'cast-iron organisation' with a military complexion. GCHQ's industrial action was now impacting on the two agencies' shared projects. Tovey would have to tell NSA: 'We've had to drop this because of industrial unrest. Could you pick it up for us?' The Americans found this bizarre. Something else had begun to bother Tovey. Traditionally, union strike action had tended to focus on departments that delivered mainstream public services, such as the National Insurance Office or the Department of Health and Social Security, since this disruption attracted publicity. However, during the late 1970s the union leaders in London had 'twigged' that disruption at GCHQ bothered the government.[15]

By 1981, general industrial strife was accelerating, and in Tovey's words the unions had made it 'brutally clear' that they regarded GCHQ as a 'damn good place to hit'. As a result, he noticed 'a reluctance to enter into work-sharing' on the part of the Americans. When GCHQ offered further joint projects, NSA tended to think: 'Oh Lord, we don't know if we can rely on the British.' Accordingly, in early 1981, when Tovey quietly informed his NSA opposite number, Bobby Ray Inman, of his plans to get the unions banned, Inman replied, 'That's marvellous.'[16] Indeed, the perception of a threat to the Anglo–American intelligence relationship was now widely shared across government. Jim Prior, who was Secretary of State for Northern Ireland at the time, recalled that union action at GCHQ in 1981 'had very much upset the Americans'.[17]

The next strike, on 9 March 1981, was part of a general day of action by the Civil Service Union. About a quarter of GCHQ staff walked out. Even at the time, local CSU officials at Cheltenham worried that this was a bad idea. Mike Vernon, a member of the CSU's committee that looked after Radio Operators, was conscious of GCHQ's declining position as a producer in the wider world of sigint agencies. GCHQ was looking old and tired alongside younger agencies such as the West German BND. Everyone knew that NSA was thinking about a closer relationship with the BND, and was investing heavily in its station at Bad Aibling in Germany. America had also repaired its relationship with Turkey, reducing the value of Cyprus. Vernon thought that jobs at some of GCHQ's outstations were in jeopardy.[18] Mike Bradshaw, another union official, admits that the CSU's tactics between 1979 and 1981 included trying to embarrass GCHQ in front of its American partners. If the intention was to provoke a reaction, it worked.[19]

Exactly why Margaret Thatcher chose to confront the unions over GCHQ in January 1984, rather than in 1981, remains a mystery. Brian Tovey had discussed the union matter at length with his board of directors in 1980, and had drawn up a secret plan for de-unionisation, code-named 'Status'.[20] He formally asked the government for a union ban following the CSU's 9 March 1981 day of action, but as in the 1950s and 1960s, government Ministers recoiled in horror. The main opponent was the Foreign Secretary Lord Carrington, who objected on principle, viewing trade union membership as a basic human right. Even within the Permanent Secretaries' Committee on the Intelligence Services (PSIS), Sir Douglas Vass at the Treasury and Frank Cooper at the Ministry of Defence argued that it would cause too much trouble.[21] Francis Pym, Carrington's successor as Foreign Secretary in 1982, would also have nothing to do with the idea of a union ban at GCHQ.[22]

Margaret Thatcher later misrepresented this. Hiding ministerial dissent, she insisted that the reason no action was taken in 1981 was because it would have drawn undue attention to GCHQ's intelligence-gathering activities, which were not yet publicly avowed. By contrast, she claimed after the Geoffrey Prime affair of 1982 that the truth about GCHQ's duties was in the open.[23] This is simply not a plausible explanation. The real nature of GCHQ had been revealed to the Russians by countless defectors, including the NSA operatives Martin and Mitchell in 1960, and to the British public by Duncan Campbell and the infamous ABC trial in 1978.[24] So what suddenly changed Margaret Thatcher's mind in 1984? Part of the reason was politics. Lord

Carrington, one of the staunchest objectors to a union ban, had resigned over the Falklands. Now in her second administration, with a large post-Falklands majority, she was more confident. However, another issue lurked underneath: the much-feared polygraph. As we have seen, in July 1983, having reviewed the Prime case and visited NSA, the Security Commission had recommended the introduction of the polygraph at GCHQ. The unions feared that the polygraph was inaccurate, and that many innocent individuals would fail the test. Staunch union resistance was guaranteed, so the removal of the unions seemed to be a prerequisite for the introduction of this unpopular security measure.[25]

The dark shadow of the polygraph also explains why government did not pursue obvious options such as a 'continuity of service' agreement – effectively a non-strike agreement – with the unions. Brian Tovey told the Employment Select Committee of the House of Commons that this would have left him perfectly satisfied. However, it would not have solved the underlying problem of union resistance to the polygraph. This left managers with no choice but to go down the more radical road of replacing the unions with a staff federation. The polygraph also shut off the other sensible option of closing union membership to new joiners. Given that union membership at Cheltenham was only about half the staff, this would have reduced it significantly over a decade, with the unions gradually withering on the vine. However, the polygraph issue required them to be removed abruptly.[26]

NSA did not give GCHQ any sort of directive on the issue. Brian Tovey has stated that the Americans never explicitly requested the removal of trade unions at GCHQ, and that it was his own initiative. However, they had directly and repeatedly requested the introduction of the polygraph, and former Deputy Director of NSA Benson Buffham had come to London to reinforce this. The team NSA sent to Britain to assess the damage caused by Geoffrey Prime concluded that while the systems for handling sigint product securely were standardised throughout the UKUSA alliance system, the protocols for personnel security were lamentably weak. The sense of urgency was increased by the fact that some believed that Prime had assisted the KGB with the recruitment of further moles. The pressure for the polygraph influenced the way in which the trade union ban was implemented.[27]

The unions were clearly petrified by the polygraph. In May 1983 the Cabinet Secretary, Sir Robert Armstrong, assured them that 'no loyal servant has anything to fear' from the polygraph, and promised further talks before it was introduced. However, the unions believed it would be introduced quickly, and perhaps operated by Americans.[28] In July 1983 Armstrong explained that there was 'a risk that the USA would question UKUSA exchange if the UK did not at least, run a pilot scheme to see if the polygraph was feasible'. He assured the unions that the machines would not be operated by Americans, but by MI5 personnel who were even now undertaking a fourteen-week training course in the USA.[29] The unions now saw the intro-duction of the polygraph as a foregone conclusion. At Cheltenham, both security (R Division) and personnel (E Division) were thought to be keen, since it was known that Russian agents were briefed to avoid exposure to the polygraph if at all possible.[30] By November 1983 the unions suspected that E3, part of the personnel division, already had machines hidden on the premises at GCHQ, although there were fervent denials.[31] The following month, senior staff at GCHQ volunteered to act as guinea pigs, and a pilot machine was allocated to Personnel Security Branch (R12).[32] Margaret Thatcher was personally committed to the polygraph, arguing that 'people employed in work which makes them privy to that nation's highest secrets would . . . accept the logic' and realise that it was aimed at strengthening their organisation against 'hostile penetration'.[33]

The trade unions had good reason to resist the polygraph. The Royal Commission on Criminal Justice Procedure had recently examined the device, and concluded that while the claimed 86 per cent success rate sounded good, what it meant in practice was that there existed a high chance of honest people being branded a security risk. Moreover, any agents who slipped past the polygraph – which required only a modicum of training – would have their reliability falsely confirmed.[34] No fewer than four NSA staff who defected to the Russians had taken and passed the polygraph test.[35] Researchers at the University of Pennsylvania medical school had found that an effective way of fooling the machine was to take 400mg of a widely available drug called Meprobamate.[36] The worry was not so much the testing of new entrants to GCHQ, but that many loyal staff with years of service might fail the test and have their clearances removed. In October 1983 the Society of Civil and Public Servants produced a campaign booklet with a chapter entitled 'How to Beat the Polygraph'.[37]

In December 1983 a secret Cabinet subcommittee was created to implement a GCHQ trade union ban. The members of this committee were Margaret Thatcher, the Defence Secretary Michael Heseltine, the Foreign Secretary Geoffrey Howe, the Employment Secretary Tom King and Deputy Prime Minister Willie Whitelaw. Howe recalled that this committee gave 'a good deal of thought, or so we believed, to sugaring the pill', and finally decided to offer GCHQ employees financial compensation for the loss of their union rights. In gloomy tones he noted that somehow 'it fell to me' to present this to the House of Commons in a 'surprise' statement on 25 January 1984. In fact the whole thing was prepared with such obsessive secrecy that Howe now recalls it with 'astonishment'. Only two other major figures were told in advance. TUC General Secretary Len Murray and Shadow Foreign Secretary Denis Healey, both Privy Councillors, were called to Howe's office in the Commons to be informed a few hours before the announcement. Healey, one of the most intelligent people ever to hold ministerial office, immediately recognised the scale of the impending blunder, and was 'beside himself' with delight at the political hay he would be able to make. 'From the moment when I made my statement to the House,' recalls Howe, 'a huge storm of denunciation broke about my head.'[38]

At GCHQ the implementation was also handled with pantomime secrecy. Brian Tovey, one of the foremost advocates of the ban, had now departed, and it fell to his successor, Peter Marychurch, to implement it. A general letter to all staff from John Adye, the Principal Establishment Officer, was photocopied in the United States and flown in. Its distribution, timed for the afternoon of Howe's Commons statement, was handled by E Division, located in A Block at GCHQ's Oakley site. The timing was complex, since there were many overseas stations, and the managers were called to Britain for a briefing.[39] John Adye's letter explained to staff that the option of belonging to mainstream trade unions was being withdrawn. They now had the option of giving up their right to union membership – even if they did not actually belong to a union – and receiving £1,000 in compensation. This was known as 'Option A'. Alternatively, they could ask for redeployment elsewhere in the Civil Service, which was known as 'Option B'. Those who refused to take either course risked being fired. The unions would be replaced by a new in-house staff federation. At 3 p.m., while the letter was being distributed to staff, John Adye met union leaders to give them a briefing.[40]

The union representatives were in shock. They urged members not to sign away their rights, and then convened at Cheltenham's Pittville Pump Room late in the afternoon to decide what to do. The strategy the unions chose to pursue was fairly reactive. Although they had the overwhelming support of most MPs, including many Conservatives, and the press, they had been stunned by the surprise announcement. Most believed that the government would accept a compromise. On 1 February Len Murray led a fourteen-strong TUC delegation to Downing Street, where they met Margaret Thatcher, Geoffrey Howe, Tom King, Willie Whitelaw and Robert Armstrong. The unions accepted that the anxiety about disruption to intelligence was not absurd, but took issue with the way the issue had been handled. They offered a 'no disruption agreement'. King, Whitelaw and Howe also urged a compromise, Howe suggesting that staff could remain union members if they agreed not to engage in strike activity.[41]

The fly in the ointment was Bernard Ingham, Margaret Thatcher's Press Secretary. Howe captures Ingham's role perfectly when he says that his strength lay in 'his ability to articulate the Prime Minister's prejudices more crisply even than she could herself'. Ingham told Thatcher that the press would see a compromise as a sign of weakness – in effect a 'U-turn'. Lord Gowrie, Minister for the Civil Service, and Thatcher's Principal Private Secretary, Sir Robin Butler, were also against compromise.[42] Accordingly, on 28 February there was a second meeting, and the compromise was rejected. The unions then played into Thatcher's hands by calling a one-day strike. The TUC had given a lot of ground, and Robert Armstrong, the Cabinet Secretary, had expected the compromise to be accepted. Indeed, he had signalled as much to the unions, and was now embarrassed. The Foreign Office later argued that the deal offered did not provide 'sufficient guarantees'. In truth, it was rejected on a prime ministerial whim.[43]

John Somerville, who served as GCHQ's Principal Establishment Officer throughout the 1970s, observed: 'When the union put their teeth on the table in February 1984, I cannot understand why the Prime Minister did not pick them up.'[44] Brian Tovey also told the Employment Select Committee that the no-strike deal offered by Len Murray during the talks at Downing Street would have been much preferable to a ban on union membership.[45] However, the Prime Minister was now very much in the driving seat. Indeed, in setting up the new Government Communications Staff Federation, which was designed to replace the unions, Peter Marychurch was very careful to refer back to London to identify the precise terms under which this body would be acceptable to the government.[46] They included making its activities subject to veto by both the Director of GCHQ and the Foreign Secretary.[47]

On 27 February 1984 an acrimonious House of Commons debated the GCHQ ban. The nub of the issue was disruption, and several trade unions had handed Margaret Thatcher price-less ammunition. Militants had boasted about creating difficulty at GCHQ, and appeared to gloat at the idea of interrupting intel-ligence work at such a sensitive security location. Thatcher quoted directly from two union documents, including a CSU campaign report of 1981 which spoke approvingly of applying pressure in 'sensitive areas'.[48] It also claimed that the day of action in March 1981 had caused 'serious disruption and incon-venience', and that 'international relationships with other governments had been under great strain' – an obvious refer-ence to NSA.[49] Other unions had claimed that '48-hour walk-outs have severely hit secret monitoring stations', and that the government was 'clearly worried and will be subject to huge pressure from NATO allies'. These union statements were uncomfortable facts that could not be denied.[50]

Nevertheless, Denis Healey had a field day deriding Geoffrey Howe, and denounced the new Government Communications Staff Federation as a 'yellow-dog union'. The exact degree of union disruption was disputed on all sides of the Commons. Sir John Nott, who had been Defence Secretary during the recent Falklands War, asserted, 'Up to now they have not in any way affected operational capability in any area.' Both proponents and opponents of the ban tended to fixate on the headline issue of the number of working days lost. The government claimed that ten thousand were lost due to the disputes of 1979–81, and stressed the fact that they occurred during a number of international crises. Opponents argued this was only a tiny frac-tion of the working days in a year. Neither side recognised that the real issue was the impact on specific sensitive programmes like J-Ops, which was far harder to measure.[51] However, the later claim made by William Waldegrave, a Minister of State at the Foreign Office, on the BBC Radio 4 *Today* programme that 'GCHQ was constantly out of action' was certainly a wild exag-geration.[52]

If the whole workforce at GCHQ had refused to sign away their rights, or had asked to be transferred, the ban would have failed. But the unions were on a losing wicket from the start. Firstly, GCHQ was only about half unionised. So for those who were not members, the offer of a £1,000 payment (equivalent to £3,500 at current prices) for giving up something they did not value was most attractive. Out of eight thousand staff, 7,700 eventually signed 'Option A' and happily collected their payment. Only 150 opted for a transfer, and about the same number refused to sign. Resistance to de-unionisation had melted away like the morning mist. Down the road in Cheltenham town centre, the effects were dramatic, since the payments immediately pumped almost £5 million into the local economy.[53] Cheltenham retailers loved it, and a vast spending spree followed. Thomas Cook reported mammoth holiday bookings. One family booked a trip to Dallas, saying gleefully: 'We are going courtesy of Mrs Thatcher.' The manager of Cheltenham's largest department store reported brisk sales of washing machines, videos and televisions, and some retailers arranged 'emergency deliveries' of luxury goods.[54]

The more stalwart union members realised that they required a long-term strategy. The most important decision they took was to establish a GCHQ Free Trade Union led by Mike Grindley, a Chinese linguist. Created on 1 March 1984, it consisted of members of the six existing trade unions at Cheltenham and representatives from the UK outstations. It met in the GCHQ canteen on a Monday evening, and launched a regular campaign publication entitled *Warning Signal*. It adopted a three-pronged approach: firstly, mobilising strong support within the wider union movement; secondly, seeking a judicial review of government policy; and thirdly, securing firm promises from the opposition that full union rights would be restored under a future Labour government.

During May 1984 attention switched to the courts. The unions had successfully obtained permission for a judicial review. The judge, Mr Justice Glidwell, focused on the cavalier nature of Margaret Thatcher's initial decision to ban the unions, a simple verbal instruction to Sir Robert Armstrong on 22 December 1983, issued without discussion or process. Glidwell decided that the oral instruction had no standing, and moreover, that the GCHQ workers were entitled to consultation before such a dramatic change in their work practices took place. By contrast, the government case rested heavily on reference to the 1982 Civil Service Order in Council, an instrument which harked back to Royal Prerogative. This, the government argued, gave it the power to do pretty much whatever it liked without consulting Parliament. Glidwell was unimpressed, observing dryly that this was 'an unusual way to legislate'. On 16 July he overturned the ban, reading out a judgement of no fewer than sixty-four pages which, as he put it, 'raised matters of considerable constitutional importance'.[55] The government had anticipated Glidwell's judgement, since the previous day Geoffrey Howe had flown to GCHQ by helicopter for an emergency conference with Peter Marychurch.[56]

In the wake of this, John Adye, the Principal Establishment Officer, warned staff that, pending a hearing on appeal, the position of GCHQ management would not change.[57] Nevertheless, a hundred GCHQ employees now merrily skipped back and rejoined their unions, despite having spent their £1,000 'Thatcher payment' in the department stores of Cheltenham. Their euphoria did not last long. Glidwell's judgement was overturned in the Court of Appeal, where the government case focused determinedly on national security. The case then went to the House of Lords, where the five Law Lords, including Lord Scarman, all accepted that national security was paramount, something of a tradition amongst senior British judges. The Law Lords complained about the government's use of outdated statutes, and muttered about 'the clanking of the medieval chains of the ghosts of the past'.[58] Nevertheless, they found in favour of the government in one of the most important legal judgements of the late twentieth century.[59]

GCHQ now proceeded at leisure. It waited until 1986 before taking any action against the remaining union members, moving first against the 'rejoiners' who had scampered back to their unions. One of the problems for officials was Geoffrey Howe's rash undertaking that there would be only one round of disciplinary proceedings, a promise that was soon broken. As the various employees fell into a range of categories, this was always likely to be a messy and prolonged business.[60] For GCHQ, the small numbers of those who had refused to leave their union or had rejoined it was not the issue. The main problem was the impact on relations with the sizeable minority of employees who had signed away their rights only reluctantly, typically because of family commitments. GCHQ managers had expected trouble from the Radio Operators, but not from the more cerebral employees. In fact many of the mathematicians and computer experts reasoned that it was illogical for the West to be trumpeting the rights of free trade unions like Solidarity in Poland, yet to be clamping down on unions at home. Some mathematicians and cryptographers who worked in H Division chose to leave. This unit was GCHQ's most valued human resource, and the damage was serious.[61]

Alexander Hamilton, a leading cryptanalyst, decided to take early retirement. Hamilton was so eminent that his name had been given to several systems for decryption. George Toumlin, also in H Division, held out and expected to be sacked, but reached retirement age before this occurred.[62] H Division's anger at the management coalesced with other factors including poor pay and limited equipment budgets. George Brauntoltz, who worked at a senior level in H Division and had been with GCHQ for thirty years, was particularly outspoken. He argued that while the strikes had caused embarrassment, they had done little serious damage, which had in fact been inflicted by government pay policies which discriminated against scientists and engineers, making it hard to get the cutting-edge staff that codebreaking needed. There had also been continual cuts in capital expenditure at GCHQ, making it difficult to 'get the tools to do the job'.[63]

The point of exodus was frequently the Golden Valley Hotel on the edge of Cheltenham, which had long been used by ATV for the external shots for the daytime soap opera *Crossroads*.

Inside, large electronics companies including GEC-Marconi, Racal and Plessey – some of GCHQ's main suppliers – were busy offering GCHQ staff employment at 30 per cent above their existing salaries. Having taken a pleasing £1,000 from the government, many then chose to move on to well-paid employment in the private sector. GCHQ lost half of its Higher Executive Officer computer experts between 1984 and 1985. In 1983 it had lost none.[64] 'The sharks are now round GCHQ,' claimed Denis Healey, adding with some amusement that Brian Tovey, the architect of the ban, was now also a consultant for Plessey.[65]

The GCHQ trade unions had high hopes of the European Court. However, on 20 January 1987 the European Commission of Human Rights ruled their case inadmissible on the grounds that GCHQ resembled the armed forces, since its duties were intimately connected to national security. This was hardly surprising, given that the European Convention gives explicit exemptions on national security grounds. The government's action was described as 'drastic' but 'in no way arbitrary'. With all legal remedies now exhausted, the focus of the GCHQ trade unions' campaign was now the repeated promises from the Labour Party to restore union rights in full.[66] In 1983 the Labour leader, Michael Foot, had pledged himself to 'restore in full all rights of the trade unionists at GCHQ'. In 1984 and again in 1987 his successor Neil Kinnock gave the same undertaking. The Labour Manifesto for the July 1987 general election included the promise, but Margaret Thatcher was returned to power for a third time, albeit with a reduced majority.[67] The last trade unionist at GCHQ, Gareth Morris, was sacked on 2 March 1989.[68]

Ironically, the government's drive to bring in the polygraph, arguably the main reason for the abrupt nature of the ban in January 1984, failed. In 1985 the House of Commons Select Committee on Employment took a close look at the polygraph with experts from the British Psychological Society. They were scathing, and dismissed the machine as useless. Whitehall now chose to run a field test on members of MI5, hoping to prove its effectiveness. Although the tests were secret, the results were leaked to the *Sunday Times* by mutinous officials. Two hundred members of MI5 were tested. No less than 37 per cent failed, and in theory would now have to be removed from their posts as security risks.[69] The government did not want to admit to the Americans that things were not going well. On 3 March 1986, Bill Odom, Director of NSA, made a note to himself to 'Ask Peter Marychurch about poly of his people,' but he does not seem to have had a clear answer from his British counterpart.[70] By the end of the year, NSA realised that GCHQ was dragging its feet, and was reported to be 'angered and dismayed'.[71]

It was not until 8 December 1988 that Margaret Thatcher quietly announced that, after considering a new report by the Medical Research Council, and a further report by the Security Commission, the so-called 'second phase of trials would not now go ahead'.[72] This was a quiet admission of defeat. Everyone knew that the polygraph was unscientific and inaccurate. Its main value was that it deterred those with a guilty conscience. NSA had observed that the greatest benefits it provided were the things people confessed to before or immediately after taking a polygraph test because of the state of anxiety it created. Infamously, President Nixon once discussed the polygraph with his inner circle and offered remarks in much the same vain: 'I don't know anything about polygraphs, and I don't know how accurate they are, but I know they scare the hell out of people.'[73]

Was the government correct to seek to remove union rights at Cheltenham? On balance, the answer is probably yes. It is not widely understood that union issues had been a persistent problem over several decades, and the presence of the unions at GCHQ was anomalous compared to MI5 and SIS. In the late 1970s, as the highly secret J-Ops section of GCHQ became a processing component for NSA's massive satellite 'hoovering' operations, the possibility of disruption in sensitive areas, such as round-the-clock computer processing, caused a collective neuralgic twinge on the part of intelligence chiefs. By that time GCHQ was not only being affected by local grading disputes, but also by national disputes in which the agency was seen as a useful 'sore spot' to annoy government. Something had to be done.

However, Thatcher's approach was incompetent. It put GCHQ in the spotlight, a place it was not supposed to be, and also damaged morale. Summarily removing trade union rights from those who already had them raised profound issues of principle. Michael Herman, the former head of J Division, offers a characteristically acute observation, noting that the sight of senior civil servants 'marching in Cheltenham with the National Union of Mineworkers in the annual rally of protest sums up the effects'.[74] There were several better options available. The First Division Association wisely recommended a continuity of service agreement. Alternatively, if government had been determined to move to a staff association, it could have taken a decision simply to allow no new union members. This, together with an offer of £1,000 to voluntarily relinquish rights to union membership, would have driven numbers down quickly. Hounding the few remaining unionists was unwise and vindictive.

For GCHQ, the worst effect was upon staff commitment. The nature of its work made it peculiarly dependent on corporate spirit and collegiality. Nancy Duffton, a GCHQ worker, told the House of Commons, 'Morale is very low since the union ban . . . The important thing, as far as the work is concerned, is that the sort of dedication that people used to have to the job is beginning to dwindle.'[75] GCHQ workers told the *Economist* that morale was at 'an all-time low', and because of this the agency was working at only 80 per cent of its normal volume. In some of the outstations like Hong Kong, many of the Radio Operators just put their feet up and drew their pay. Most were agreed that the main fault lay with Margaret Thatcher. Whether right or wrong in principle, the government handled GCHQ with astonishing heavy-handedness and inflexibility.[76] The arguments would drag on until 1997, when the trade union ban was reversed by the incoming Labour government of Tony Blair. Meanwhile, the secret activities of GCHQ received enormous publicity.[77] Geoffrey Howe, in a remarkably honest assessment, conceded that: 'Almost every aspect of the work and location of GCHQ was rehearsed again and again in the press. Our most secret service had become almost the most public.'[78]

NSA and the Zircon Project

Thatcher said 'we will strain every sinew' to have Zircon.
Peter Marychurch, Director of GCHQ, 1 May 1987[1]

On 24 January 1985 the American space shuttle *Discovery* was launched from Cape Canaveral. So far there had been fifteen shuttle launches, but this particular flight was unique. It was the first shuttle to be deployed on an intelligence mission, and it carried a highly secret new sigint satellite code-named 'Orion'. Weighing almost six thousand pounds, the satellite was guided from the cargo bay by two military astronauts before being powered into its final orbit by rocket boosters. Once there, it unfurled two massive parabolic antennae that looked like huge umbrellas, each stretching out more than a hundred yards. One of these collected signals, including low-power radio transmissions that no sigint satellite had hitherto been able to hear. The other beamed the 'take' back to earth. The United States had been operating sigint satellites for more than twenty years, but this was by far the most powerful and impressive example, confirming the status of the USA as the world's premier intelligence collector.[2]

Sigint satellites, rather like fibre-optic cables and then personal computers, were part of an unstoppable world communications revolution.[3] These technical breakthroughs had profound implications for sigint, and on both sides of the Atlantic intelligence chiefs recognised that this was changing the UKUSA alliance relationship. As a result of the growth of satellite collection,

GCHQ was working more closely with NSA than ever before, notably by processing about 15 per cent of the 'overhead' material in its highly secret J-Ops section. Yet, paradoxically, GCHQ was also being left behind, and the underlying feeling was one of growing 'unspecialness'. Indeed, with the possibility of machine translation beckoning, there was even a danger that the Americans might eventually view GCHQ as expendable. Therefore, in the 1980s both GCHQ and NSA were reconsidering their intelligence alliances, not only with each other, but also with the long-established 'second party' members of the original UKUSA agreements such as New Zealand, and even with the 'third party' sigint services in Western Europe, such as Sweden's FRA and Germany's BND.

Any venture into space meant tough political as well as technical choices. In the mid-1960s Harold Wilson's Cabinet had opted for the British-made Skynet military communication satellite, instead of GCHQ's preferred option of an American-made model. Whether to buy cheap and reliable from the Americans, or to invest in expensive British national capacity (and jobs), or indeed even to join with the Europeans, was a perennial issue. The same dilemma of dependence or independence presented itself in other high-tech areas such as nuclear weapons and computing, as had recently been illustrated most starkly by a further British venture into space code-named 'Chevaline'. This was a programme to upgrade Britain's Polaris nuclear missiles by improving the final stage of the rocket – in effect a small space-ship – that carried the warhead on the last part of its journey towards its target. Chevaline was the direct precursor of Britain's remarkable adventure with a sigint satellite called 'Zircon' in the 1980s.

Britain's main nuclear deterrent consisted of American-made Polaris missiles carried on submarines. No sooner had Britain taken delivery of Polaris than it started to look outdated. The Russians and Americans had begun to experiment with elaborate anti-ballistic-missile systems to defend their cities, threatening a new spiral in the arms race. Unless Britain's Polaris missiles were either replaced or upgraded, they would most likely be defeated by Moscow's anti-missile defences, rendering Britain's independent nuclear deterrent implausible. The ability to hit Moscow was considered to be the key criterion for an effective British deterrent.[4] Throughout the early 1970s British defence chiefs pressed for the purchase of a new American missile called 'Poseidon', with multiple warheads powerful enough to overwhelm Soviet defences. One of the reasons they wanted to buy American was because they had always recognised that 'Without US intelligence support any nuclear deterrent system would lose credibility in a few years.'[5] In other words, access to American sigint was vital for targeting British nuclear weapons.

However, Britain's political leaders had recognised that there would be a diplomatic furore if Britain bought Poseidon. The country had just entered the Common Market, and the French would certainly not appreciate such a public reaffirmation of the 'special relationship' at this crucial moment. Accordingly, in late 1973 the Edward Heath government rejected the Poseidon option and chose a British programme to update and improve the ageing Polaris missiles, code-named 'Chevaline'. At the time, officials believed that this code name was French for a nimble mountain goat. In fact, when the Chevaline saga unravelled some years later in the House of Commons, it turned out that its true meaning was either someone who sells rotten horse flesh, or an ugly woman. There was considerable humour at the government's expense.[6]

Britain's defence scientists were delighted by the Chevaline decision, which effectively gave them their own mini-space programme and a substantial secret budget for advanced science. Some defence intelligence experts were less impressed. Louis Le Bailly, Director General of Intelligence at the Ministry of Defence, was working closely with the CIA, and enjoyed the best insights into the Russian anti-ballistic-missile systems which Chevaline was supposed to defeat. He was not optimistic about its chances: 'I personally laboured with my advisers for the best part of six months to transpose this deeply technical data into layman's language so that my colleagues on the JIC could understand its impact, which I believed to be profound.' However, at the last moment senior scientists persuaded the Cabinet Secretary to have intelligence reports criticising the Chevaline decision withdrawn from circulation. The chairman of the Joint Intelligence Committee was reportedly 'almost prostrate with hysteria'.[7] In protest, on 17 July 1974 Le Bailly handed in his resignation to the Cabinet Office Intelligence Coordinator. Chevaline was quite simply the hottest defence issue of the decade.[8]

It was also very secret. In March 1974, when a Labour government took over from Edward Heath, Harold Wilson was anxious to hide the project from his own backbenchers, who were not at all sympathetic to nuclear weapons. Indeed, Wilson even hid it from some of his Cabinet Ministers. Therefore, despite the huge sums involved, the existence of Chevaline was not revealed to the House of Commons Public Accounts Committee, or indeed reported to Parliament in any way.

Meanwhile, the super-secret programme was not going well. For years Chevaline, which was effectively a mini-space capsule that provided a new front end for Britain's Polaris missiles, was test fired but failed to work properly. The cost escalated from an initial £175 million to £600 million, and then £800 million. In 1982, when the highly secret programme was finally exposed, there was an almighty row, not least because both front benches had been involved in an elaborate deception of Parliament. Officials had to confess that they had conspired to spend close to a billion pounds in complete secrecy on a failed project. This was a major public scandal, since Parliament was supposed to control major expenditure. Shortly afterward, a special 'Never Again' agreement was drawn up, with officials promising faithfully not to hide large defence projects from Parliament.[9]

The 'Never Again' agreement did not last long. The cause of its demise was GCHQ's desire to venture into space. By late 1983,

Britain's alliance relationships were being re-examined in the light of the recent Falklands War. Once Alexander Haig's effort to find a peaceful compromise had ended in late April 1982, American military assistance had flowed towards the British in vast quantities. The rapid provision of the latest American Sidewinder air-to-air missiles for the Royal Navy's Harrier jets alone had done much to decide the war in Britain's favour. Casper Weinberger, the American Secretary of Defense, had gone so far as to say that if Britain lost an aircraft carrier, he would happily provide a replacement. The same applied broadly to intelligence assistance, and during the war some of the corridors in the CIA headquarters at Langley in Virginia were actually decked out in Union Jack bunting. Yet in Cheltenham, GCHQ's evaluation of the 'special relationship' was somewhat mixed. Imagery satellites were not especially helpful because of the almost complete cloud cover over the Falklands during the South Atlantic winter. For sigint coverage, GCHQ had pleaded for the use of an NSA listening satellite that was then focused on Central America, supporting the Contra struggle against El Salvador and Nicaragua, which was of high importance to the Reagan administration. In order to cover the Falklands the satellite had to be moved, and NSA was willing to do this for only a few hours a day. Persuading it to do even this much had taken a good deal of argument on the part of GCHQ's Director, Brian Tovey.[10]

GCHQ now had to face some unpalatable facts. It had been left behind in space, which was clearly the future of sigint. Given that sigint provided more than 80 per cent of Britain's intelligence, and took a similar proportion of the budget, this was a serious matter, conjuring up the possibility that during some future crisis the United States might be unwilling or unable to divert its resources to help Britain, either because they differed on an issue politically, or because NSA was preoccupied elsewhere. All the senior staff at Cheltenham recalled Kissinger's sinister attempts to 'cut off' the intelligence flow to Britain in August 1973, and even now a similar spat was looming between the United States and New Zealand. Thus, in his last year as GCHQ Director the energetic Brian Tovey proposed that Britain should launch its own sigint spy satellite, code-named 'Zircon'. He reasoned that GCHQ was judged to have performed well during the Falklands War, so this was the right moment to press Margaret Thatcher for a substantial reward. Zircon was bound to be very expensive. Like the Nimrod R1 in the 1970s, it could not be accommodated within the routine 'Cost of Sigint' budget. Some have estimated that the satellite and its associated ground installations might have cost £500 million over five years, and thereafter it would need replacing.[11]

Many believe that Zircon had originally been conceived by Brian Tovey 'to keep the special relationship sweet' and to take his organisation into space.[12] However, others have read it as a deep questioning of the 'special relationship'. As Bill Odom, Director of NSA after 1985, put it, 'You do not invest all that money in a satellite system if you believe that the Americans will continue to give it to you for free. That would be plain stupid.'[13] Some believed that GCHQ's satellite venture was part of a radical new strategy. Tovey was sympathetically disposed towards some of the European 'third parties', such as Germany and Holland, and had provided them with more material than was generally realised. In particular, he enjoyed a good rela-tionship with the charismatic Alexandre de Marenches, head of the French secret intelligence service, SDECE.[14] It is not inconceivable that Zircon was about GCHQ becoming the biggest fish in a European pool. A sigint satellite like Zircon, working in cooperation with the French satellite imagery programme, would have made Europe a serious intelligence collector. At the very least, Zircon guaranteed Britain an alternative option at a time when the European 'third parties' were becoming more powerful and influential.[15] Indeed, the Europeans had recently set up their own mini-UKUSA alliance called 'The Ring of Five', consisting of the sigint agencies of Germany, the Netherlands, France, Belgium and Denmark – although this did not prevent them from intercepting and reading each other's communications traffic.[16]

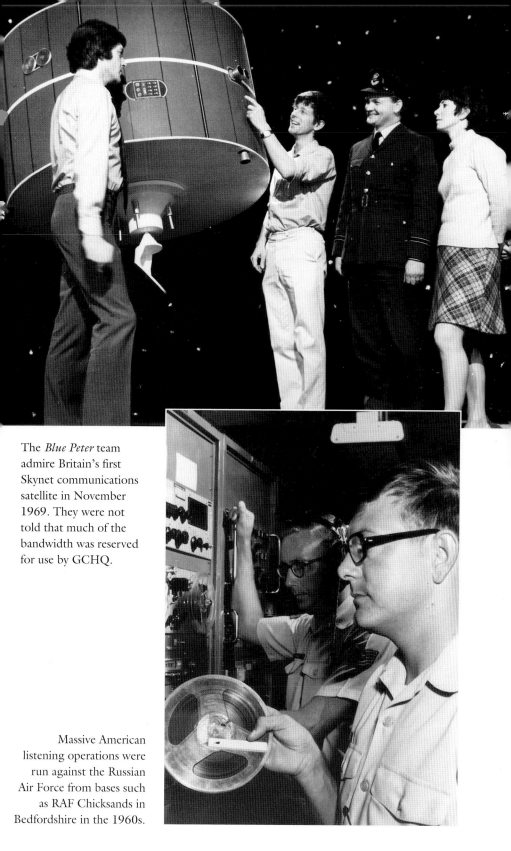

The *Blue Peter* team admire Britain's first Skynet communications satellite in November 1969. They were not told that much of the bandwidth was reserved for use by GCHQ.

Massive American listening operations were run against the Russian Air Force from bases such as RAF Chicksands in Bedfordshire in the 1960s.

Benhall, one of the two GCHQ
sites at Cheltenham in the 1970s.

USS *Oxford*, one of America's spy ships and a sister to
the *Liberty*. GCHQ had plans to emulate NSA's secret
navy with its own nuclear-powered vessel in the 1960s.

US President Richard Nixon and CIA Director Richard Helms. Helms recalls that Nixon and Kissinger tried to cut off the intelligence flow to Britain in 1973 after they lost patience with British Prime Minister Edward Heath.

Heath retaliated by placing restrictions on American SR-71 Blackbird spy-plane flights from RAF Mildenhall during the Yom Kippur War of October 1973.

The bloody aftermath of the shoot-out at Kizildere, where three GCHQ staff were held hostage in March 1972. The photograph shows the bodies of some of the kidnappers.

The ruins of the Mayor's house at Kizildere immediately after the end of the siege.

HMS *Endurance*, a key sigint platform in the South Atlantic during the Falklands War.

HMS *Conqueror* displays the traditional skull and crossbones after sinking the Argentine cruiser *General Belgrano*. The episode largely turned on sigint.

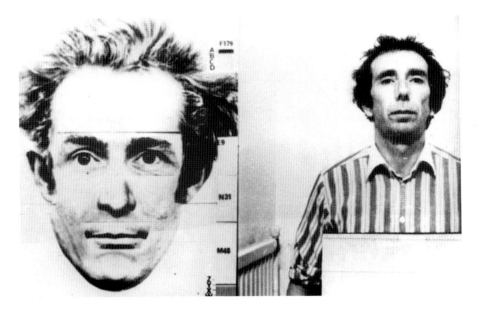

Geoffrey Prime and his indentikit photo. Special measures were taken at Wormwood Scrubs prison to prevent the KGB from 'springing' him.

Benson Buffham (centre), who served as SUSLO in Britain in the late 1970s, touring a sigint site in Korea. He was sent to Britain by NSA in 1982 to probe the Prime case.

GCHQ protesters march through
Cheltenham in 1984 after a surprise
announcement banned trade unions.

An 'Odette' intercept unit deploys
during the Gulf War in 1991.

John Scarlett, Chair of the Joint Intelligence Committee, and Sir David Omand, who in 1996 set GCHQ on its 'Change Journey', leave the High Court in London on 26 August 2003 after giving evidence at the Hutton Inquiry into the death of Dr David Kelly.

'The Doughnut', GCHQ's new building at Cheltenham which was opened in 2003.

The idea of GCHQ teaming up with the Europeans was not a bad one. European sigint services such as those of the Norwegians, the Germans and the Dutch were highly professional, and had made many important contributions to Western intelligence down the years, not least during the Falklands War. They often displayed brilliant lateral thinking. When Soviet naval ships entered Dutch harbours in the 1980s, their hosts would often complain that the Soviet radar was interfering with local television broadcasts and insist on a snap technical inspection. The crafty Dutch used this opportunity to plant a small tracking device high up on the Soviet ships that was no more than the size of a brick. This tracking device was so successful that it became a standard technique across the Western secret services. Typically, a small group of British SBS personnel worked with SIS and GCHQ on similar tasks in the 1990s.[17]

GCHQ's relationship with its American partner was about people as well as projects. General Bill Odom arrived as the new Director of NSA in March 1985. Odom was a tough-talking Army officer with an extremely abrupt manner. He saw himself as a new broom, complaining that his predecessor 'would not favour radical change' and that the staff at NSA were 'too laid-back'.[18] He also looked afresh at the Anglo–American sigint relationship, and was deeply unimpressed, observing that 'The name of the British game is to show up with one card and expect to call all the shots.'[19] Ingenious old-fashioned British cryptanalysis was being overtaken by the raw power of America's Cray supercomputers, and this had been underlined by some remarkable NSA breakthroughs with Soviet high-grade diplomatic traffic in the late 1970s.[20] Odom noted that, 'What the British brought in World War II, they do not bring any more . . . Today, this business requires huge investment, and Britain doesn't have that.' Britain's decision to buy Zircon signalled GCHQ's renewed commitment to spend big money on sigint.[21]

Bill Odom's first year as Director at NSA was a traumatic one. Washington soon dubbed 1985 'the Year of the Spy', since it brought the exposure of Ronald Pelton, a damaging mole who worked in 'A5', NSA's sensitive Soviet section. With a photo-graphic memory, Pelton proved even more disastrous to Western code-breaking than Geoffrey Prime. At almost the same time the Walker family, a whole group of spies working within US naval intelligence and communications, was uncovered. Edward Lee Howard, a CIA officer, was also revealed to be working for the Russians. To cap it all, in November 1985 it was discovered that Jonathan Pollard, a Mossad spy inside the Pentagon, had been handing over very sensitive material to the Israelis. The Americans had not yet uncovered the two best covert sources employed by the Soviets, namely a CIA officer called Aldrich Ames and an FBI officer, Robert Hanssen.[22] These frightening cases of KGB espionage had a direct impact on the British, since they made Bill Odom all the keener to see the polygraph deployed by GCHQ at Cheltenham.[23]

Alongside KGB espionage, the other big issue of the time was relations between the Western sigint allies. In 1985 the United States cut off the intelligence flow to New Zealand, one of the 'second party' members of UKUSA. Similarly to the 'cut-off' that Kissinger had imposed on Britain in 1973, this was trig-gered by wider defence issues, rather than sigint specifically. New Zealand was sensitive about nuclear weapons, given that the south-west Pacific had been used for many years by both the Americans and the French as an atomic test zone. In 1985 David Lange's Labour government introduced a general ban on ships carrying nuclear weapons entering New Zealand's harbours. This effectively excluded many American naval vessels which routinely carried nuclear depth charges. Washington was keen to deter other countries from following a similar course – perhaps creating a Pacific nuclear-free zone – and earmarked New Zealand for exemplary punishment. Intelligence was the chosen instrument.[24]

A remarkable confrontation now occurred. Paul Cleveland, the American Ambassador in Wellington, informed Lange that henceforth his country would not be receiving NSA's precious sigint jewels. Lange responded tartly that they were not jewels by any means, and the intelligence cut-off was probably a good thing, since he would now 'have more time to do the cross-word'.[25] Cleveland, flabbergasted by Lange's sangfroid, got to work on some of his Cabinet colleagues. He asked David Caygill, the Finance Minister, whether he realised quite how important the intelligence issue was. Caygill recalls, 'I asked him what he meant,' and Cleveland responded that it was all about 'trust', explaining that the UKUSA intelligence alliance depended on mutual confidence, and now that had completely evaporated. 'We have not spied on each other,' continued Cleveland. 'If you go ahead with your policies we will not be able to trust you.' Caygill later explained to Lange that what the American Ambassador had meant was that 'The US would no longer feel any inhibition in conducting intelligence-gathering operations against us.'[26] The new Director at GCHQ, Peter Marychurch, was particularly upset by this rift, having just spent a couple of years attached to New Zealand's sigint agency, the Government Communications Security Bureau (GCSB).

Hitherto, relations between New Zealand's GCSB and its bigger partners, GCHQ and NSA, had been close. Highly sensitive material, recently released only by accident, affords us a rare glimpse of their joint activities. When Helen Bain, the political editor of the New Zealand newspaper the *Sunday Star-Times*, asked for permission to look at Lange's papers from when he had been Prime Minister, which had just arrived in the archives in Wellington, she was supposed to be given individual files, but by mistake an entire unsorted box was handed over. This contained a highly classified annual report from the mid-1980s that revealed the relationship of GCSB with its allies.[27] Working closely with NSA and GCHQ, the New Zealanders were actually devoting much of their time to spying on allies, friends and neutrals. In 1985 New Zealand was reading diplomatic telegrams and telephone satellite communications from France, Japan and the Philippines, as well as a host of South Pacific island states. It was also intercepting the communications of some United

Nations organisations in the Pacific, together with those of non-governmental organisations such as Greenpeace.[28]

In many cases NSA or GCHQ provided 'raw traffic' that was of interest to the New Zealanders, or which matched their translation skills. A great deal of attention had been given to Japanese communications by the three partners. New Zealand's GCSB had produced 238 intelligence reports on Japanese diplomatic cables, using 'raw traffic from GCHQ/NSA sources'. However, it lamented that the recent implementation of a new high-grade Japanese cypher machine had seriously reduced its output. Diplomatic traffic from Fiji, Vietnam and Laos was being intercepted, as was South African military traffic and Argentinean naval traffic. The GCSB relied heavily on the collection capabilities of its British and American allies to provide French communications that were out of range of its own monitoring stations. American overhead satellites, including the new 'Orion', were crucial in this respect. After the Greenpeace ship *Rainbow Warrior* was attacked and sunk in Auckland harbour by the French secret intelligence service in July 1985, killing one of its crew, GCSB set in train a special collection effort in the region. NSA and GCHQ were asked to monitor targets in France, including certain Paris telephone lines. In short, all three allies worked closely together on a very wide range of targets, so, despite Lange's apparent insouciance, New Zealand had in fact lost valuable material as a result of being banished in 1985.[29] Both GCHQ and the Australian sigint agency, DSD, did their best to subvert the American ban by supplying the New Zealanders with sigint of their own.[30]

As had been the case with the Kissinger 'cut-off' in August 1973, NSA also worked gently to subvert the ban, and over time came to ignore it. In return, New Zealand agreed to host more elaborate satellite receiving stations on behalf of NSA. Nevertheless, in the short term this confrontation had profound effects on all the venerable Commonwealth countries which had helped to found the UKUSA sigint alliance and were known as the 'second parties'. Odom now pondered some big ques-

tions, writing in his notebook: 'If 2nd party status disappears –
What then?' He complained that Britain, Canada and Australia
had made a fuss and tended to 'over do [the] banishing of NZ',
but he also understood that they wished to be supportive of
their Commonwealth ally.[31] The situation also created fiendishly
complex problems, because UKUSA sigint had become so closely
wired together in the 1980s. Peter Hunt, Director of Canada's
sigint agency, the CSE, asked Odom's advice about what to do
with 'integrees', staff on loan from New Zealand's GCSB who
were embedded in the headquarters of his own organisation in
Ottawa.[32]

This turbulence in Western sigint relations only seemed to
confirm the wisdom of GCHQ's decision to develop Zircon,
offering Britain some measure of independence in the realm of
sigint. Although NSA did not like the Pentagon decision to cut
New Zealand off, in the 1980s there was general American disil-
lusionment with all the UKUSA 'second parties' – especially
with Canada. In the summer of 1985 Peter Hunt confessed that
he had been having great difficulty persuading Canadian policy-
makers of the value of CSE's sigint product, although this situation was now improving. Despite the fact that CSE had been
helping NSA and GCHQ with increased covert collection from
Canadian Embassies, when Odom met officials from the US
Embassy in Ottawa to discuss intelligence cooperation they all
agreed 'how poor the Canadian effort is!'[33] By contrast, NSA
was increasingly impressed by the West European 'third parties',
like the West Germans, who were achieving very good results
against the diplomatic traffic of Eastern Europe countries like
Czechoslovakia, using ground stations.[34]

In 1985 Odom decided to make improved NSA relations with
the West Germans a high priority. Hitherto NSA had hesitated,
since the German foreign intelligence service, the BND, was
known to be penetrated by Eastern Bloc spies. But after the
Geoffrey Prime affair in Britain and the damaging Pelton, Walker
and Howard cases in the United States, the German security

problems seemed less unique. 'Sure, we knew they were leaky,' recalls Odom, 'but we felt we had a way of compartmentalising sigint carefully to deal with this.' What mattered to him was that the Germans were investing more and more money in sigint, and were becoming a bigger player in Europe. They had already demonstrated their technical proficiency in some excellent electronic warfare projects conducted jointly with Israel. In the pragmatic world of sigint alliances, diversifying partners made perfect sense. However, GCHQ 'went up the wall' when they heard about it, Odom recalled with a wry grin, 'since it undermined their specialness'.[35]

One of the top priorities for any Director of GCHQ is to ensure smooth dealings with NSA. Relations between intelligence chiefs are often rather personal. For example, 'Pat' Carter, who had been Director of NSA in the late 1970s, was exceedingly anglophile, and established a happy bond with his opposite number at GCHQ, Joe Hooper. By contrast, Bill Odom took an initial dislike to Peter Marychurch, who he referred to as 'the Sheep'. Indeed, Odom hated all the qualities that had prompted Whitehall to choose Marychurch. Following the tenure of his gung-ho predecessor Brian Tovey, GCHQ wanted a more stable and avuncular figure. Marychurch was not a great intellectual, but he was an effective administrator and a good diplomat. After he had spent a period of time as GCHQ's representative in New Zealand, some were surprised to see him recalled to become Director. He had spent less time in London than many of his contemporaries, and so seemed rather disconnected from the big defence debates of the day. By contrast, Bill Odom prided himself on his intellectual toughness and his ability to talk global strategy, having been the right-hand man to Zbigniew Brzezinski, President Jimmy Carter's National Security Adviser.[36]

One of the reasons Odom liked the West Germans was that they agreed with him that NATO armed forces in Europe had long been starved of sigint. Under existing rules, only when war actually broke out would high-grade sigint from UKUSA be released to the West Europeans and also pushed forward to commanders on the front line. The lack of current sigint support for front-line units was not only causing problems in Germany. One of the commanders of the main US sigint station in South Korea confided to Odom that there too, 'The requirements of the field commander were their lowest priority,' and that 'NSA fought every attempt to collect and disseminate "tactical" intelligence' to military formations. Bill Odom was a soldier at heart, and he wanted current sigint to reach those who would be in the front line if a major war ever broke out.[37]

In the early summer of 1985 Odom set out on a European tour to press this personal agenda. He took with him Peter Aldridge, Director of the National Reconnaissance Office, the agency which provided America's spy satellites. On 7 June they met Peter Marychurch in Cheltenham, and discussed progress on Britain's Zircon sigint satellite. Marychurch was forced to admit that GCHQ was hitting problems, partly of cost and partly of competency. This was likely to delay the project, and also pushed the British towards the use of more US contractors, for which he needed to ask their permission.[38] One of the ironies of so-called 'British' space defence projects was that while they were supposed to increase national independence, they often needed backdoor American technical support to get them off the ground.[39] There were other irritants in the relationship. NSA's largest base overseas, Menwith Hill, set as it was on a remote spot on the Yorkshire moors, was proving to be an especially unpopular posting with NSA personnel, and Bill Odom noted that there were too few volunteers and too many draftees.[40] The substantial cost of NSA sigint bases in Britain was a further factor that pushed him towards Continental Europe, since the price of operating from West Germany was lower.[41]

Britain's Zircon satellite was also rattling Odom's cage. A few days after his meetings with Marychurch he chewed over the whole matter of Anglo–American cooperation in a discussion with Dick Kern, NSA's liaison officer in Britain. Odom expressed the view that the relationship with GCHQ 'had grown too big', and 'needed to be managed better'. They agreed that the Zircon programme was an unwanted intrusion into the realm of space, which they did not want to share with any of their allies, and this was viewed as a problem. Ultimately, NSA wanted to monopolise the Western flow of sigint from space, giving America the 'potential to turn off the flow in future'. Odom and Kern both felt that they needed to reconsider certain areas of cooperation with GCHQ, including the 'integration of personnel'. All this was to be offset by improving relations with third parties like the Germans.[42]

A week later, Bill Odom headed to Bergen in Norway for a 'European Principals Meeting', an annual gathering of all the sigint chiefs in Western Europe, hosted this year by the Norwegian Chief of Intelligence, Rear Admiral Jan Ingebrigtsen. Significantly, the members of this elite club only stretched as far south as France, since NSA equated the reliability of sigint partners in Europe with their distance from the Mediterranean. The Greeks ranked bottom in this hierarchy, since their communications were known to be horrifically insecure. Odom was like a social anthropologist, and enjoyed recording the 'traditional national suspicions and jealousies' displayed by the cast of characters at the meeting in his daily log. He liked his Norwegian host, who he found 'pleasant, dignified, and pro-American'. He also warmed to the Germans, who had come forward with a 'most constructive proposal' which most of the group was ready to accept. However, the British, he noted, 'can't accept happily their own loss of pre-eminence in this business'.[43] Odom was especially fond of the German chief, Eberhard Blum, remarking that they 'had a good talk, some good laughs, and a few reminiscences'. Blum, he noted, was inclined to defend NSA, even when other West German officials complained of the Americans' 'Big Brother' approach, arguing that in fact they had always dealt fairly and generously with their smaller sigint partners. However, Blum was coming up for retirement, and Odom recorded sadly that while his German colleagues shared his views, they were rather more hesitant when it came to 'putting down the British'.[44]

The 'most constructive proposal' that the BND had brought forward was a scheme code-named 'Sigdasys', which aimed to improve the flow of operational sigint to NATO's front-line commanders in Europe.[45] Peter Marychurch was dead against it, since the British had long been hesitant about sharing sigint with military units in peacetime.[46] Ironically, Sigdasys was just what the British Army's electronic warfare operators on the front line had been requesting for years. This was because their own short-range 'Y' units were having a tough time listening in on the Soviets, since Warsaw Pact radio security had continually improved, making eavesdropping difficult. 'Traditionally,' they noted, 'the signal intercept service has been the primary source of tactical intelligence,' but now its value was fading as Soviet divisional headquarters refined their communications security.[47] By the 1980s, tactical listening was reduced to direction-finding work against front-line formations.[48]

GCHQ's trenchant opposition to the German proposals at Bergen brought out Bill Odom's intense dislike of Peter Marychurch. On 11 June Odom went home, and penned his thoughts on the various European sigint chiefs, including the Director of GCHQ:

*

Peter Marychurch, my UK counterpart, is the least attractive of the lot. A tense, nervous, slightly insecure civil servant, he has as his main task to stay fully entangled with the US system, to try and act as our equivalent in Europe, to stand between us and the other Europeans if possible. He and his immediate subordinates hold, in my view, a vastly inflated view of their own competence and talents.[49]

*

Predictably, the abrasive Odom had got his way at Bergen, and noted with ill-disguised delight that this would 'embarrass the GCHQ coalition'. Conflict, he wrote, 'abounds in our bilateral ties' with GCHQ at every point, including resources, security

and UKUSA third party rules. Re-evaluating the Anglo–
American sigint relationship was now a higher priority. For the
Americans, the key question was whether geographic access to
Britain and its overseas bases was worth the cost. In his own
mind Odom had already answered the question, adding that
the USA was not getting very much in return for 'this excessively entangled bilateral connection'.[50] A notoriously impatient
man, he now observed: 'Socially, I no longer find the British
amusing, merely a pain in the ass.'[51]

Odom was a soldier with very considerable military experience, and he wanted to see sigint used to support fighting. He
was absolutely correct about the need to push sigint further
forward, a lesson underlined by Britain's own experience in the
Falklands and again in the Gulf in 1991, where operational
commanders were indifferently served. Odom had been instrumental in the development of the US Army's Intelligence Support
Activity, an innovative special forces unit that combined SAS-
type operations with short-range sigint. This unit, which made
use of listening equipment in helicopters, had been used successfully in Italy during the mid-1980s as part of efforts to find the
NATO commander General James Dozier, who had been
kidnapped by leftist terrorists.[52] Odom was always keen to see
sigint actually used in the field. Typically, in June 1985 he pushed
hard to use it tactically against the New People's Army, a Marxist
guerrilla group in the Philippines.[53]

However, Odom was impulsive, and had only come to the
world of sigint recently. By contrast, the affable Peter
Marychurch had spent decades at GCHQ, and knew more about
the complex world of secret listening. It was soon clear that
Marychurch also knew much more about the hazards of working
with the West Germans. Only a month after the Bergen meeting,
Odom's close friend Eberhard Blum retired as President of the
BND, to be succeeded by Heribert Hellenbroich, the long-serving
and respected head of Germany's domestic security service, the
BfV. At forty-eight years old, Hellenbroich seemed set to follow
an upward path, not dissimilar to that of Britain's famed

spymaster Dick White, who had successfully headed MI5 and then SIS. Alas, this was not to be. On 27 August 1985 the BfV was hit by an extraordinary spy scandal when one of Hellenbroich's immediate subordinates, who was also a close friend, defected to East Germany. This triggered a general panic, with some of the West's most valuable agents in East Germany hurriedly defecting in the other direction, for fear that their identities had been compromised and their lives were in danger. The West German Chancellor Helmut Kohl ordered an inquiry, which discovered that Hellenbroich had kept his friend in his post despite his notoriously heavy drinking and personal problems. Hellenbroich was summarily dismissed, becoming the shortest-serving BND chief in the agency's history.[54]

The West German defection had direct repercussions for both MI5 and GCHQ. For some time MI5 had been mounting covert surveillance on an unremarkable rented house at 249 Waye Avenue in Cranford, near Heathrow Airport on the western edge of London. This was inhabited by Reinhard and Sonja Schulze, a quiet German couple in their mid-thirties who worked respectively as a kitchen designer and a translator. In fact they were agents of the East German foreign intelligence agency, the HVA. Unusually, they were 'illegals' – in other words they lived under deep cover, rather than pretending to be Eastern Bloc diplomats. At the same time as the BfV security flap in West Germany, the Metropolitan Police Special Branch raided the house and the Schulzes were arrested. Specialists then spent several weeks ripping up floorboards and dismantling every item in the house. They were not disappointed. In the garden shed they found wallets with one-time pads for encyphering and decyphering messages, together with a radio receiver. There was also an escape kit with money and false passports. The authorities had moved quickly because they feared that the Schulzes might flee, joining the flurry of anxious double agents moving between East and West.[55] GCHQ had been reading many of the messages that the agents received in high-frequency Morse. This breakthrough was a great achievement for Cheltenham, a mini-version of Venona.

In contrast to Venona, which was never used in court, GCHQ intercepts of the HVA communications were cited as prosecution evidence when the Schulzes came to trial in June 1987, ensuring that they each received ten years in prison.[56]

Surprisingly, Odom was not deterred by these serious security problems within the West German intelligence services, and continued to press ahead with his German plan. There were bureaucratic obstacles, since the BND was engaged in a fierce turf battle over tactical sigint with the West German Army which closely resembled the tussles between NSA and America's own armed forces.[57] Nevertheless, by the summer of 1986 NSA, the BND and indeed GCHQ were building the new Sigdasys system proposed by the Germans, which gave a better supply of sigint to NATO operational commanders and allowed partners to pool their military sigint on the Soviets. This was paid for on a three-way split between the British, the Americans and the Germans, with the French joining soon after.[58] In September 1987 Peter Marychurch suggested the Swedish FRA join as a 'sleeping partner', since Sigdasys was saving costs for everyone by eliminating overlap.[59] The Americans continued to be impressed by the BND's aggressive and expanding global sigint programme, for example its cooperation with the code-breaking agency in Taiwan.[60]

Sadly, Odom's desire to give more sigint to NATO's front-line divisions was twenty years too late. By 1986 the new Russian Premier, Mikhail Gorbachev, was beginning to transform world affairs. In the Pentagon and the Ministry of Defence, Gorbachev was welcomed with cautious optimism. Observers were not only watching him but also the 'exceptionally able' Russian Ambassador in Washington, Anatoly Dobrynin, who was a natural diplomat.[61] Meanwhile, the Middle East and Africa were becoming more important to NSA, which was anxiously watching the conflict in Angola between the Marxist regime and rebel forces of Joseph Savimbi, who received support from both South Africa and the CIA. NSA was pondering how to expand its coverage of sub-Saharan Africa, and at a meeting with his senior staff on 16 July 1986 Odom expressed high hopes of an ambitious new GCHQ covert collection operation that was being mounted from the British Embassy in Luanda, the Angolan capital. He also pondered using more sigint ships, and asking the BND to do some work in southern Africa. South Africa's communications security was improving, with burst transmission and frequency-hopping, forcing GCHQ and NSA to concentrate on clear voice traffic.[62]

Terrorism was now an extremely high-profile concern, with Libya the main focus because it was directly aiding terrorist groups in the West, including the IRA. Indeed, a low-level war with Libya was gradually developing. During the early 1980s the eccentric Libyan leader, Colonel Muammar Gaddafi, had become increasingly paranoid about dissidents and exiles who opposed his regime. After hanging two students outside the gates of Tripoli University, he had ordered his secret service to attack what he called 'stray dogs' abroad, resulting in a series of bombings and shootings against opposition groups based in Britain. With the help of MI5, three Libyan assassins were caught and sentenced to life imprisonment. Some of these attacks had been organised from within the Libyan Embassy at 5 St James's Square in London, now renamed the 'Libyan People's Bureau'. GCHQ was decoding Libyan communications freely, and during the early 1980s it had intercepted several of Gaddafi's alarming messages demanding violent action.[63]

However, on the morning of Tuesday, 17 April 1984 the British authorities were taken unawares by a new wave of violence. Seventy-five demonstrators were protesting outside the Libyan People's Bureau over the recent execution of further students in Tripoli who had been critical of Gaddafi, and the police were trying to keep them separate from an angry group of pro-Gaddafi loyalists. At 10.18 a.m. a prolonged burst of automatic fire from two Sterling sub-machine guns came from the windows of the Libyan People's Bureau, resulting in the death of twenty-five-year-old WPC Yvonne Fletcher. Eleven demonstrators were also injured. A former MI5 officer, Annie Machon, has claimed that GCHQ had advance warning of the incident. Cheltenham was still successfully reading communications between Gaddafi's office in Tripoli and the People's Bureau, and one message, intercepted on the day before the shooting, asked loyal Libyans 'to open fire on the dissidents'. Machon would write:

*

As a prior warning of a possible attack, it was very useful intelligence or would have been, if it had been handed on in a timely fashion. But it wasn't as the nine-to-five bureaucrats at GCHQ had gone home for the night. As a result the report did not go to the police or MI5 that day. In the meantime WPC Yvonne Fletcher was fatally shot from the window of the LPB [Libyan People's Bureau].[64]

*

The recent authorised history of MI5 largely confirms this highly controversial claim. What GCHQ had actually intercepted the previous day was a telex sent by staff within the Libyan People's Bureau to Tripoli, discussing possible means of dealing with the planned demonstrations by exiles and dissidents. One option that they suggested was: 'To fire on them from within the Bureau.' In fact this intelligence was not passed to MI5 or the Metropolitan Police Special Branch until the day after the shooting.[65] The initial incident was followed by a ten-day siege of the embassy, after which Britain broke off diplomatic relations with Libya. In common with a number of other terrorist incidents in the 1980s and 1990s, GCHQ was criticised and there were internal arguments about how intelligence was circulated. All this underlined the new challenge of dealing with terrorism, which required responses in 'real time', something that a Cold War security apparatus was not remotely accustomed to. In the wake of the shooting at the Libyan People's Bureau, there was a deliberate attempt to develop resources that could work on a twenty-four-hour basis and achieve the rapid response times required by counter-terrorism.[66]

In March 1986 there was a major naval confrontation between

the Americans and President Gaddafi's forces in the Gulf of Sidra, off the coast of Libya, where the extent of territorial waters was disputed. After US fighters attacked Libyan missile batteries and patrol boats, Gaddafi demanded that his secret services retaliate, and on 4 April Libya organised the terrorist bombing of La Belle discothèque in West Berlin, killing two American servicemen. NSA had intercepted the message from the head of the Libyan secret service ordering terrorist attacks throughout Europe, and newspapers had already revealed that Libyan communications were being read, so President Ronald Reagan decided there was nothing to be lost by using sigint publicly and in some detail to underline the fact that Gaddafi was the culprit. Three days later, Bill Odom was told by Reagan's CIA chief, Bill Casey, that the President 'wants to go public with SIGINT on Libyan activity in Berlin – [CIA Deputy Director] R[obert] Gates will work out "text" '. However, both GCHQ and NSA were horrified that NSA's reading of Libyan diplomatic traffic was going to be made public.[67] Predictably, the Libyans responded by immediately changing all their codes and cyphers, and they also purchased expensive new cypher machines from Crypto AG in Switzerland.[68]

Reagan's public use of sigint to blame Gaddafi for the Berlin discothèque bombing was intended to justify a US air strike on Tripoli. Eighteen USAF F-111 bombers took off from RAF Upper Heyford, but were denied overflight rights by France, Italy and Spain, and so were compelled to take a circuitous route to their targets. One of these targets was President Gaddafi's own compound. He escaped death by minutes because the Prime Minister of Malta warned the Libyans by telephone of the approaching military aircraft. However, Gaddafi's fifteen-month-old adopted daughter was killed and two of his sons were injured.[69] In 1987 the CIA, SIS and the French secret intelligence service assembled a vast mercenary army that pummelled Gaddafi's forces during the ongoing border war between Libya and Chad. The conflict between Libya and the West flared again in December 1988 with the bombing of Pan Am Flight 103 over

Lockerbie in Scotland, although responsibility for this attack remains a matter of dispute.[70]

Although Bill Odom had not warmed to Peter Marychurch, GCHQ's Director was an energetic administrator and had notched up some impressive achievements in the late 1980s.[71] He was trying to modernise GCHQ, moving away from old-style sigint operations which used rows of people sitting in nissen huts with headphones on. Radio Operators who did the front-line listening now had computer consoles which allowed them to feed the most interesting intelligence directly into a central computer, and were using better recording equipment called 'Keepnet' and a new system that allowed them to compare different signals, called 'Livebait'. Like most GCHQ computers, the local computers – invariably Honeywells – were of American manufacture, so as to be in step with NSA. The terminals used by each operator could hold about a million words, meaning that the product could be word-searched and then distributed electronically, something GCHQ had hankered after for two decades.[72]

Marychurch's biggest headache was the perennial issue of budgets, which slowed the recruitment of higher-grade technical staff.[73] Money problems had also impacted on Zircon, perhaps Britain's most sensitive defence project during the mid-1980s. Bill Odom was not disappointed when Andrew Saunders, Britain's liaison officer within NSA at Fort Meade, confided to him as early as February 1986 that in his personal opinion, as a result of defence cuts, 'Zircon probably will go.'[74] By April 1986 Marychurch had persuaded America's National Reconnaissance Office to give him further assistance with Zircon. However, it now had an unnerving 'on–off' status, and understandably the British Treasury was scheming to kill off this highly secret project.[75]

Zircon did not remain secret for much longer. In early 1987, to the horror of Whitehall civil servants, the project was exposed by Duncan Campbell, the journalist who almost a decade before had been at the centre of the 'ABC trial'. For the past ten years his investigative journalism, mostly for the New Statesman magazine, had tracked the British secret state, and he was regarded as a significant problem by the authorities. In November 1985 he had been commissioned by BBC Scotland to make a series of programmes called Secret Society, and had decided to use this to reveal Zircon. However, it was only in the summer of 1986 that he uncovered the biggest secret. Speaking to Robert Sheldon, the Chair of the House of Commons Public Accounts Committee, he discovered that Parliament knew absolutely nothing about the project. The fact that this very large spending item had been hidden from Parliament – a reprise of the previous defence spending scandal over Chevaline – now became the core issue. Meanwhile, GCHQ had got wind of the planned documentary, and on 5 December 1986 there was a hurried meeting between Peter Marychurch and the BBC. In early January 1987 Alasdair Milne, the Director General of the BBC, announced that he had banned the programme on grounds of national security.[76]

On 21 January the High Court granted an injunction against Duncan Campbell. This restrained him from either showing the documentary or revealing any details of its contents. The next day the New Statesman published an article asserting that the real issue was nothing less than the sovereignty of Parliament itself, and that a deception had been perpetrated on the Public Accounts Committee. Campbell tried to have the film shown to MPs in the House of Commons, but was prevented by the intransigent Speaker of the House, Bernard Weatherill.[77] Then, over the weekend of 24–25 January the Special Branch raided the offices of the BBC and the New Statesman, together with the homes of Duncan Campbell and several other journalists who had worked with him. There was high drama as television cameras filmed a search team breaking down the front door to Campbell's London flat.[78] The New Statesman's solicitor was soon contacting everyone mentioned in the programme, including the GCHQ trade unions at Cheltenham, warning them that they might also be raided by the local constabulary.[79]

Nigel Lawson, then Chancellor of the Exchequer, claims that he had actually killed off Zircon in the autumn of 1986, some months before the Campbell story broke. 'Well before all this blew up,' he recounts, 'I had succeeded in getting the ZIRCON project cancelled on grounds of cost.' For this reason, he declares rather triumphantly, the satellite 'did not in any sense leave the ground'.[80] In fact, this is by no means the whole story. Whitehall opposition to Zircon was certainly mounting during late 1986, and key defence advisers had lost faith in it.[81] However, Bill Odom's personal daily log, only recently released, makes it very clear that in the spring of 1987 Britain's political leaders were still completely committed to some form of space-based sigint, and that a variant of the project – still called 'Zircon' – was going forward. Indeed, what is remarkable is the strength of Margaret Thatcher's continued personal commitment. In May 1987 Peter Marychurch visited NSA and personally told Bill Odom: 'Thatcher says "we will strain every sinew" to get Zircon.'[82]

What did Marychurch mean by this? By late 1986 the costs of Zircon were threatening to spiral out of control. Therefore, by the summer of 1987 he was exploring the possibility of purchasing a single American-built satellite 'off the shelf'. However, a single satellite would not give Britain global coverage: the comprehensive collection of sigint would require no fewer than three satellites. By 1988 a more sensible solution had emerged. Britain opted to pay £500 million as a direct subscriber to the American satellite system. Then Foreign Secretary Geoffrey Howe recalls: 'Beggars can't be choosers. If you can't afford a wholly independent operation then you have to put in a share.' Each of the three latest American sigint satellites cost £500 million, and Britain effectively bought a one third time-share, giving it a guaranteed supply of 'overhead' sigint. This not only delivered global coverage, but also a much bigger advantage: quite simply the system worked well, unlike Britain's ill-fated space adventures.[83] Satellite experts suggest that 'Zircon', such as it now was, arrived in space on 4 September 1990. A Titan

34D rocket from Cape Canaveral put it in position under the cover of a Skynet 4C launch, and the satellite was positioned over Asia.

In some ways Zircon symbolised the increasingly awkward sigint partnerships of the 1980s, a curious mixture of collaboration and animosity. Together with the Geoffrey Prime affair, the Falklands War and the trade union issue, it underlined the deep transatlantic tensions that now existed in the world of code-breaking. Nevertheless, the new 'time-share' relationship went down well in Washington. Brian Tovey's seemingly upstart bid for GCHQ independence in space had been bought off, and NSA breathed a sigh of relief that another power, albeit a close ally, had not acquired its own space sigint capability. Meanwhile, despite Bill Odom's bluster about Britain's failure to play in the big league of sigint powers, NSA's own budgets were stretched to breaking point in the late 1980s. With the Cold War drawing to a close, many were predicting savage cuts in intelligence budgets, so GCHQ's monetary contributions to the secret satellite programme were doubly welcome. Accordingly, the somewhat battered GCHQ–NSA relationship marched on, out of the Cold War and into a new era of 'hot peace'.[84]

AFTER 1989

GCHQ GOES GLOBAL

23

From Cold War to Hot Peace –
The Gulf War and Bosnia

We had the place 'swept' regularly, but it made no difference.
That building . . . was built around bugs.

Captain Milos Stankovic on the UN
Headquarters in Sarajevo[1]

Intelligence organisations everywhere failed to predict the end
of the Cold War. GCHQ and NSA certainly did not foresee it,
nor did Britain's Joint Intelligence Committee.[2] The changes that
swept across the Warsaw Pact countries in 1989 also took
Communist leaders by surprise, despite the intense surveillance
conducted within their own societies. The exact moment at
which the Eastern Bloc collapsed was hard to pinpoint, because
ultimately it amounted to a failure of self-belief. Once the
Communist leadership was unwilling to shoot its own people,
the game was up. The closest anyone from Britain had come to
a prediction of the end of the Cold War was in the writings of
the journalist Timothy Garton Ash, reporting on the free trade
union 'Solidarity' in Poland in the early 1980s. Having witnessed
the mass defiance of the Soviets by trade unionists in the Polish
shipyards, he had forecast that Moscow's empire might well
crumble in short order – and he was quite right.[3]

Bizarrely, the end of the Cold War was not accompanied by
an onrush of new threats, but by the surprise appearance of an
old threat. On 2 August 1990, Iraq launched a surprise attack
against its neighbour Kuwait. This was arguably an event that
GCHQ had been awaiting for three decades. Iraq had long
professed claims to areas of Kuwaiti territory; meanwhile Britain
had sought to deter an Iraqi attack because of its friendship

with the Kuwaiti royal family. Back in January 1965, shortly after Joe Hooper took over from Clive Loehnis as Director of GCHQ, one of his first tasks was to discuss the future of a small GCHQ team in Kuwait whose brief was to constantly sweep the airwaves for signs of an Iraqi attack. 'While the team was a reasonable insurance factor in providing timely warning of an external attack,' he explained to the JIC, 'it could do little or nothing to give Sigint warning of internal unrest or a coup.' Hooper was pressed for resources, and wondered whether the team's task could be carried out by the bigger sigint stations on Cyprus. However, GCHQ did not want to suffer the 'loss of tactical Sigint information on the Basra brigade', the key unit of the Iraqi Army. This could only be collected at short range, so it decided the team should stay in place.[4] Sigint against Iraq did not operate in isolation. There was also regular photographic intelligence from a Canberra photo reconnaissance aircraft flying along the edge of the Iraqi frontier to detect an Iraqi military build-up. In an emergency, typically a warning from SIS or GCHQ, British diplomats in the Persian Gulf could order high-level photographic flights over the Basra area of southern Iraq, penetrating up to fifty-five miles inside the border, to confirm or disprove indications of a coming attack.[5]

No less than twenty-five years later, the alert system worked. On 27 July 1990, five days before Iraq's attack on Kuwait, the JIC gave a clear warning that aggression was likely.[6] Although no one spotted the precise timing, warning signals continued to grow.[7] On 29 July, Iraq's Soviet-built long-range radar units, code-named 'Tall King', became very active, having been silent for some months. There was now a considerable programme of satellite monitoring of Iraq, mostly through imagery, which was expected to provide twenty-four hours' notice of an attack. However, despite warnings of troops massing on the Kuwait border, the prevailing thinking in the White House and Downing Street was that this was a bluff. What had made anticipating Iraq's intentions harder was the sophisticated training that the United States had itself offered to the country in the mid-1980s during the war between Iraq and Iran. This included lessons on secure communications, encouraging the extensive use of land-lines with fibre-optic cables, together with many reserve communication channels. Nevertheless, the intelligence community had warned of a likely invasion, but political leaders simply discounted it. As with the Falklands, they had difficulty with the concept that there were old-fashioned military dictators around who still liked going to war.[8] Reassurances from Egypt's President Hosni Mubarak that, despite the military build-up, nothing would happen also misled the West.[9]

Operation 'Desert Storm', designed to retake Kuwait, was unleashed on 17 January 1991 with a wave of air attacks. Oddly, this conflict resembled the vast tank battles that NATO had prepared to fight with the Soviets in central Europe during the Cold War. The United States supplied by far the largest component of troops, and Britain the next. Ranged alongside them were contributions from France, Australia and many Middle Eastern states, including Egypt and Saudi Arabia. Once the Gulf War began in earnest, British and American sigint experts became involved in complex discussions about how much of the Iraqi signals infrastructure should be left intact to permit continued monitoring, perhaps with the intention of locating Saddam Hussein. They also had to think about their own deception operations, which were distributing false orders to Iraqi battalions. British forces conducted a classic operational deception, superintended by a unit code-named 'Rhino Force'. On several field exercises by Britain's First Armoured Division, messages were transmitted on low power to avoid interception by Iraqi signals intelligence units. During the actual ground attack, on 23 January, recordings of these earlier transmissions were played back at full power. They were then heard clearly by the Iraqis. By that time most of the British forces had moved about 125 miles to the west to link up with the main US Seventh Army Corps in their attack, yet the Iraqis thought they were heading in the opposite direction. The British tuned in to what remained of the Iraqi command network, and further signals intelligence showed that the Iraqis had bought this deception in its entirety. Meanwhile, a secret radio station based in Saudi Arabia pretended to be 'Radio Kuwait', and broadcast the false news that Kuwait City had already fallen to the allies, causing several Iraqi units to flee for fear of being cut off.[10]

Operation 'Desert Storm' illustrated the close relationship between special forces and sigint. The main task assigned to British special forces was hunting down Iraqi Scud missile launchers. The SBS was given responsibility for eastern Iraq, while the SAS was allocated the west. In addition to the Scuds, the SBS was given a further important target: a major terminal for the fibre-optic cables that provided the backbone of Iraq's remarkably modern and secure communications network. This nexus was located about thirty miles from Baghdad, alongside an oil pipeline. A team of thirty-six men, with four hundred pounds of explosive, was taken to the site by two Chinook helicopters during the night of 22 January.[11] Their task was to disable a section of the communications network which lay a few feet beneath the sand.

The flight time was at least two hours each way, leaving only a limited period of darkness in which to complete the mission. Most of the party formed a defensive circle with machine guns and grenade launchers, while the remainder began searching for their target. After much scurrying about with ground scanners and cable locators a number of holes were dug, but infuriatingly no cable was found. Dawn was fast approaching, and the helicopter crews were becoming more and more anxious. Eventually the commander chose the hole that seemed most likely to be close to the cable, filled it with all their explosives and set a charge, hoping they were near enough. On their return to base they were told that they had indeed severed the cable. The main task of the mission was to force the Iraq regime 'up onto the air', in other words to make it use wireless communications that could then be intercepted, and there was indeed an increase in high-frequency radio traffic. However, not all the fibre-optic networks were destroyed, and thereafter the cables proved largely invulnerable to bombing.[12]

Forcing the Iraqis to rely more on high-frequency radio offered GCHQ several advantages. It is widely alleged that radio equipment sold to Baghdad prior to the Gulf War was subtly adapted so that the British could monitor its transmissions more easily. This is not to suggest that the British manufacturers, Racal, were aware that their equipment had been altered in this way. Racal, which had long experience of making such equipment, were the main suppliers of rack radios to GCHQ for its own monitoring operations. Several senior staff from GCHQ had become directors of Racal. The alleged decision to modify the radios was taken perhaps as early as 1985, when Iraq spent £42 million on state-of-the-art Racal Jaguar V radios, equipped with frequency-hopping to allow them to counter Iranian monitoring and jamming on the battlefield. Remarkably, Racal was building a radio factory in Iraq when the Gulf War broke out in 1991. In any case, exchanges between Iraqi commanders could be read by both GCHQ and NSA.[13]

Iraqi communications discipline was very good, and sigint failed to find the location of a single Scud missile during the Gulf War.[14] The conflict revealed once more the familiar weaknesses that existed in British intelligence support for major expeditionary operations – something witnessed in the Falklands ten years before. At each level, British Army formations depended mostly on their own intelligence assets, and there was little inter-service cooperation. Information flowed from GCHQ and from the imagery centre at RAF Brampton in Cambridgeshire, but mostly because officers at Divisional HQ in the Gulf had 'mates' at the desk level in Cheltenham who they could telephone directly. The tactical exploitation of national intelligence assets was poor. However, this time the lessons were learned, and by 1996 Britain had created a Permanent Joint Headquarters at Northwood with an intelligence division specifically tasked with solving many of these problems.[15]

In contrast to the situation in previous conflicts, by 1991 GCHQ was no longer invisible to the British public. During the approach of the Gulf War a prankster had taken advantage of this and posted hundreds of letters using forged GCHQ notepaper, ordering people to report to Lichfield barracks in Staffordshire to commence two weeks of crash training prior to being flown out to the Gulf by an RAF Hercules transport plane. The recipients, apparently chosen at random and mostly with no previous military service, endured not a little anxiety.[16] Senior managers at GCHQ were forced to issue warnings telling the public to ignore the hoax letters.

One of the big discoveries of the Gulf War of 1991 was the scale of Iraq's stocks of chemical weapons. The task of monitoring their destruction after the end of hostilities was allocated to a mission of UN inspectors called the United Nations Special Commission, or UNSCOM. They picked their way through innumerable military sites and palaces, some of them with as many as five hundred separate buildings, looking for weapons declared illegal under UN rulings. Soon a number of these observers, who in many cases were British, Australian or American military personnel on loan, were conducting short-range sigint using scanners, and delivering the material to their national intelligence agencies and also to the Israelis. This so-called Special Collection Element within UNSCOM was suggested by Scott Ritter, a former US Marine officer who had been working with UNSCOM since 1995. It often recorded Iraqi warnings to weapons facilities that the inspectors were on their way, but given that the material took weeks to process, this was of little help to the inspectors on the ground. Arguments soon developed. Israel's sigint agency, called Unit 8200, was helpful and provided the inspectors with complete transcripts, but the Americans only returned small amounts of redacted material to UNSCOM.[17]

NSA and GCHQ would use UNSCOM as short-range collectors up until 1996, but predictably they were paranoid about sharing any decrypted product which carried the ominous caveat 'Special Compartmented Intelligence – Top Secret/Final Curtain'. As a result, relations between the inspectors and NSA were increasingly frosty. When Scott Ritter came to Britain in the hope of developing closer relations between his Special Collection Element and GCHQ, his contact at GCHQ apologised and said that they could not assist him. He explained: 'Even if we could handle the material, the special relationship between the UK and the Americans prevents us from sharing the take with an outside agency, such as UNSCOM, without the express permission of the Americans,' and added apologetically, 'This permission isn't being given.' Later, another British official explained the full picture to him. The GCHQ station on Cyprus had identified strange burst transmissions coming from the UN headquarters in Iraq. GCHQ concluded that there was a separate CIA communications intercept operation inside the building, put in place by its local agents. This was an automated 'black box' operation that collected local Iraqi signals and then compressed them to be sent as a short 'burst' signal to American U-2 aircraft which flew over Baghdad about once a day. In short, GCHQ had concluded that America no longer had any need of UNSCOM to collect sigint inside Iraq.[18]

One of the important features of intelligence in the 1990s was the improving relations between the UKUSA countries and Israel. A few years earlier, Bill Odom, the Director of NSA, had denounced the head of Israel's intelligence agency Mossad, Nahum Admoni, as 'a nasty slippery man' who had refused to cooperate with NSA and GCHQ on sigint programmes against the Soviets. Admoni retired in 1989, and was replaced by Shabtai Shavit, who was regarded as much more amenable.[19] NSA, GCHQ and the Israelis now worked much more closely on Iraq, yet at the same time they were at loggerheads elsewhere, most obviously in the former Yugoslavia, which by the summer of 1991 was collapsing into a series of bitter civil wars. Many Western intelligence services suddenly found themselves seriously at odds with each other in this complex conflict, with its bewildering factions. The United States worked closely with Germany's BND to assist the Croats and Bosnian Muslims in an effort to create a level playing field. Meanwhile, it regarded the British as too friendly with the Bosnian Serb headquarters at Pale, where SIS undoubtedly enjoyed good sources of intelligence. Along with the secret services of Greece and the Ukraine, Mossad was openly pro-Serbian, and was concerned by the CIA's close cooperation with Turkey and Iran in a covert operation to fly in arms and jihadist fighters from the Middle East to bolster the Muslim cause, in clear contravention of the United Nations arms embargo. The former Yugoslavia also offered some fascinating lessons in the tortuous politics of allied signals intelligence.[20]

Bosnia was a place where relations between GCHQ and NSA were tense. Intelligence sharing between the two allies on the Balkans was limited, and NSA was very reluctant to provide its British partner with any intelligence on the Muslim factions that were favoured by Washington. Meanwhile, General Sir Michael Rose, a former head of the SAS and now the British Commander in Chief of the United Nations Protection Force, found that his biggest problem was the insecure and elderly communications equipment that the British Army had endured for years. The need for better radios had been one of the obvious lessons from the Falklands, but Britain's defence bureaucrats had bungled hopelessly. Rose realised that his UN headquarters in Sarajevo were effectively under surveillance by the Americans. He himself was regarded as a 'legitimate target' for sigint collection by the USA, since he was officially serving as a UN military chief, rather than as a British commander.[21]

NSA worked closely with the German BND to offer sigint support to the various Muslim elements, not least to Croatia, which had suffered badly at the hands of the Serbs in the fighting of 1991 and 1992. They focused on boosting the work of Admiral Davor Domazet, chief of Croatia's military intelligence during the struggle against secessionist Serbian guerrillas in the east of the country. This was especially visible during 1993, when Croatian forces pushed forward into the Medak Pocket, and again in August 1995, when they conducted a lightning offensive known as 'Operation Storm'. This was supported by unmanned intelligence-gathering drones which allowed

Croatian artillery to locate the positions of rebel Serbs on the ground. Reportedly, the drones were operated by the CIA from a base at Zadar on the Adriatic coast. More importantly, NSA supplied Croatian signals intelligence units with improved satellite dishes for electronic surveillance of telephone traffic.[22]

Sigint was a major factor in the Croatian success. The Croatian equivalent of NSA, the National Central Electronic Reconnaissance Agency (NSEI), was the most significant and secretive part of the country's intelligence system. In 1995 it was able to listen in on panicked phone calls to Slobodan Milošević, the Serbian leader in Belgrade, pleading for help as Serb forces were pushed back during 'Operation Storm'. It was also able to follow Milošević in his efforts to put pressure on neighbouring Montenegro. NSEI successfully monitored other key participants across all regions of the former Yugoslavia. These included the British, who found themselves subject to aggressive sigint collection by multiple elements. However, while NSEI was good on sigint, it was bad on its own communications security. Accordingly, when the Croatians shared the sigint they had collected on the British amongst themselves, this was in turn picked up by additional parties and shared again.[23]

Milos Stankovic, a British major from the Parachute Regiment who was serving on General Rose's United Nations staff at Sarajevo, explains this strange situation in a section of his memoirs appropriately entitled 'The Mad Hatter's Tea Party'. It was accepted by the long-serving British officers accompanying Rose that their offices were under technical surveillance by the Americans, and probably the Croatians and Bosnian Muslims too. However, the Bosnian Serb leaders in Pale, such as Radovan Karadžić and Ratko Mladić, also seemed to have advance warning of any British initiative. Stankovic patiently explained the situation to a new initiate on the British team:

*

. . . the Serbs were bugging the buggers . . . if you'll excuse the pun. Everyone was bugging each other. No secrets in the Balkans. The only people not playing this game was the UN. It's simple: Rose is discussing [NATO Commander in Chief, US General John] Galvin's programme in his office the previous day, the Yanks or the Bosnians bug that conversation, and then the Serbs listen in to what the Bosnians are saying to each other. Before you know it that little tidbit had landed on Mladić's desk . . .

*

NSA actually had a covert listening station in the American Embassy in Sarajevo which was 'busy hoovering up every single little electronic bleep and fart'. The NSA team had arrived in Yugoslavia under military cover as US Army officers, but 'could not carry it off very well'.[24] By November 1994, numerous incidents of uncanny preknowledge on the part of the Bosnian Muslims offered multiple confirmation of technical surveillance. General Michael Rose was conscious of this, and sometimes used it for deception purposes. However, it made attempts to negotiate difficult, since the Bosnian Muslims always had the upper hand over the Serbs because of their better technical coverage.[25] To cap it all, Britain could hear itself being listened to. Its own sigint operations were being conducted on the ground, using 'Odette' and 'Vampire' intercept units.[26] Sigint was also collected by two Royal Navy frigates based in the Adriatic, and RAF Nimrod R1s flying out of NATO bases in Italy.[27]

By early 1995 Rose had been succeeded as UN Commander in Bosnia by another senior British officer, General Rupert Smith. One day shortly after his arrival, Smith made a number of urgent calls to London on a supposedly secure scrambler phone, and then hurried from his headquarters to the nearby American Embassy for a meeting. While he spoke with senior Americans on the top floor, his military aide wandered around the lower floors of the Embassy. To his amazement, despite the fact that Smith was on the top floor, the aide could hear his commander's voice coming from a room at the end of a corridor. This proved to house an interception centre, where staff were busy listening to one of the telephone conversations Smith had held with

London only an hour before. As a result of this confirmation that a joint CIA–NSA listening operation was being directed towards the UN headquarters, Smith was more careful with his communications thereafter, often using the encrypted radios of the Special Air Service, which he believed to be more secure.[28]

Perhaps the most historic change for GCHQ in the early 1990s was the loss of its listening station in Hong Kong, which, but for a brief interruption during the Second World War, had been there since the early days of GC&CS. This was triggered by the impending transfer of Hong Kong to Chinese rule. Washington viewed Hong Kong as an irreplaceable watchtower on China. For years British diplomats had complained that Britain was collecting more intelligence about China than it could possibly need, and had asked why this target was so important. The underlying rationale was exchange with the Americans. Hong Kong was the single most valuable British collection station to NSA, providing offset in an otherwise unbalanced Anglo–American intelligence relationship.[29]

Notwithstanding the fact that NSA knew the British would have to leave in 1997, it had poured huge investment into British sigint at Hong Kong. In 1982 the GCHQ station at Little Sai Wan, which had depended on listeners with headphones, had been closed down and replaced by a new operation at Chum Hom Kok, on the south side of the island, which monitored satellite activity.[30] This new station was initially given the code name 'Demos-1'.[31] The problem with the location was accommodating the massive dishes – there were eventually five – on what was a narrow shelf of rock overlooking the South China Sea.[32] Chinese agents took a close interest in the station, so there were tight procedures whereby a 'cleared expatriate' supervised the moving of classified waste to a vast 'Refudoc' incinerator in the main building. The burn bags full of top-secret sigint material were huge, standing three feet high and weighing about thirty pounds.[33]

Despite the problems of its precarious site, Demos-1 had

continued to grow during the 1980s. A further programme code-named 'Demos-4' provided yet more enormous dishes to capture civil traffic from China's growing network of communications satellites, and also telemetry from missile tests. Perched on top of a cliff, this was an astonishing feat of civil construction, five years in the making. Elaborate earthworks and retaining walls were required to prevent the whole facility slipping into the sea. Roy Chiverton, one of the senior staff in GCHQ's F Division, was exasperated by the complexity of the project: 'The situation changes so frequently . . . I keep tearing up drafts.' He added, 'I am not deterred – but my wastepaper basket gets fuller.'[34] The vast dish antennae, constructed to the latest NSA design, were supplied by Lockheed from its Sunnyvale facility in California.[35] Much of the equipment was very delicate, and it was suscep-tible to damage in transit, prompting officials to refer scathingly to what they called 'crushed dish syndrome'.[36] Nevertheless, when the Chum Hom Kok station was finished, John Adye, who became Director of GCHQ in 1989, wrote to the site engineers praising their efforts. Building had continued in bad monsoon weather, and he added that he had seen 'some horrific photo-graphs of a mechanical excavator poised on the edge of a very steep slope'. He conveyed GCHQ's sincere thanks to all who had contributed to a project on which 'a great deal depended'.[37]

The investment was repaid with excellent intercepts of Chinese military traffic that revealed, for instance, Beijing's thinking around the time of the Tiananmen Square massacre in June 1989.[38] Yet even while this new station was being completed, the British were reminding NSA that their time on Hong Kong was running out. Odom had suggested that Britain should try to keep control of the Commander British Forces HQ building in Hong Kong even after handover, because it was by far the best medium-wave sigint collection site in the territory. However, despite concerted pressure from the Americans, the British were 'unenthusiastic' about this idea.[39] NSA and GCHQ had already begun to ponder future alternative sites. Odom noted in his ever-present daily logbook: 'Hong Kong – where to move our gear?'[40]

At midnight on 1 July 1997 the colony of Hong Kong was finally returned to China, signalling the end of Britain's ninety-nine-year lease on the New Territories. All the intercept equipment had already been moved to Geraldton, a DSD site in Western Australia. It was hoped that the loss of interception from Hong Kong would be partly offset by a sophisticated monitoring operation against the new Chinese Embassy in Canberra. The West had devoted enormous attention to state-of-the-art surveillance of this new diplomatic complex, and the resulting intelligence 'take' was so great that there were often thirty transcribers in the Australian capital processing it, a miniature version of the team recruited to translate the Berlin tunnel material in the 1950s. Secret collection from the Chinese Embassy included not only sound, but even video footage. This opened a priceless window on Chinese communications, which had always been very hard to break. However, just like the Berlin tunnel, the duration of this operation was short, and to the fury of GCHQ and its allies the operation was blown by the Australian press in 1995.[41]

Hong Kong also illustrates the shift towards using sigint against organised crime after the end of the Cold War. During the last days of the colony the Royal Navy was part of an Anti-Smuggling Task Force that was struggling to keep up with the extremely fast boats used by local criminals who were stealing luxury cars on the streets of Hong Kong and shipping them to mainland China. Once in China, the smugglers were paid for the cars in heroin, which they then brought back for sale in the colony. Boarding the vessels of the smugglers, which could achieve seventy miles per hour, was dangerous, and the crews were often armed with automatic weapons, so the Task Force decided to try sigint. Using two well-trained sigint operators with the latest frequency scanners, it was able to tune in to the smugglers' radios and locate the point of exchange. The Task Force swooped on the quiet dock where the smugglers were offloading forty-five pounds of heroin in return for a BMW 7 series that had been stolen off the streets of Hong Kong only that day.[42]

GCHQ GOES GLOBAL

After the handover of Hong Kong, China remained an important intelligence target. Some Western sigint agencies exploited the growing volume of container shipping that thronged Chinese ports and proceeded along China's major waterways for perhaps a thousand miles inland by installing remote collection equipment deep in the bowels of the vessels of friendly container companies, timed to begin recording once the ship came close to China. The more sophisticated versions beamed their 'take' up to overhead satellites for rapid exploitation.[43]

In Europe, too, the iconic watchtowers were tumbling. One very public manifestation of the end of the Cold War was the closure of the vast Teufelsberg station overlooking Berlin, after thirty years of operation.[44] Yet at GCHQ there was no rapid shift of resources away from Russia, merely a gentle drift of numbers towards K Division, which handled non-Russian sigint.[45] This was understandable, since for the first time in decades Russia was now a promising intelligence target. In the early 1990s the market was being flooded with would-be KGB defectors hoping for a comfortable resettlement package in the West. Amid this embarrassment of riches, it was sometimes hard to know which ageing KGB men should be taken onto SIS's dwindling payroll. Britain's ability to absorb defectors, rehabilitate them and offer them a pension, as had been done with Oleg Gordievsky in the 1980s, was very limited. Nevertheless, one defector was judged of sufficiently high value to make such an investment worthwhile. This was Colonel Alexander Simakov, a missile specialist who had worked in mission control for every ballistic missile test the Russians had conducted between 1984 and 1990. In 1991 he had introduced himself to a British Army sergeant running in the Moscow marathon, and through this chance contact had been put in touch with SIS. Simakov was the human end of all the missile telemetry that GCHQ and NSA had been assiduously collecting from locations such as Turkey and Cyprus for almost half a century. 'The guy's a goldmine,' remarked the SIS rocket specialists. 'We've got to get him residency here.'

Simakov defected in 1992, and was soon providing a full rundown on Russia's new strategic command bunker. The opportunity to marry up sigint with human agent material was electrifying: SIS officers enthused, 'We've hit the jackpot.'[46]

With the end of the Cold War, the world was positively crawling with redundant intelligence officers of every hue, offering their services for a fee. In Russia, many former KGB officers drifted off into private security work or organised crime – the two spheres often overlapped to an alarming degree. Other parts of the world saw intelligence officers setting up private military companies that were active in Africa, and would become prominent in the Middle East after the 2003 invasion of Iraq. In Britain too, the long years of the Cold War, together with an extended struggle against organisations like the IRA, meant that many had been trained in the dark arts of telephone interception and bugging. Their services were now available for hire. By the early 1990s this was having an impact on public life in Britain, largely through the growing use of freelance interception and other forms of privatised intelligence-gathering by tabloid journalists. One of the targets of this new privatised sigint activity was the royal family.

In the first weeks of 1990, Cyril Reenan, a retired bank manager, parked outside Didcot railway station not far from his house in Abingdon, a quiet town in Oxfordshire. In his spare time Reenan was an amateur eavesdropper who used a radio scanner to listen in to all types of radio transmissions, including mobile phones, for his private amusement. At his home he had arranged an old 1960s-style reel-to-reel tape recorder next to his scanner to capture anything interesting that he overheard. He believed he had captured an extremely intimate conversation between Diana, Princess of Wales, and James Gilbey, a childhood friend who owned a Lotus car dealership and was heir to the Gilbey's Gin fortune. He was now about to hand the tape over to the *Sun* newspaper.

The tape was not published by the *Sun* until August 1992. Gilbey initially insisted the story was false, but the paper took the remarkable step of setting up a dedicated phone-line which allowed callers to hear the whole tape at a cost of 36 pence per minute. In fact this was not the whole tape, since even the *Sun* had blushed at certain sections of the recording, and had edited some passages out. Diana offered a lengthy description of her treatment at the hands of the royal family, and detailed what she considered to be the Queen's condescension and pity towards her. Gilbey referred to the Princess alternately as 'Darling' or 'Squidgy'. The latter name, used fifty-three times during the conversation, was soon adopted by the press, which routinely referred to the affair as 'Squidgygate'.[47]

Through the early 1990s, interest in the tapes was sustained by the so-called 'War of the Waleses' during which the Prince and Princess of Wales battled for public sympathy. This included the leaking of material to trusted journalists, and finally entire television programmes. Each week the tabloids offered new revelations, including accounts of the Princess's depression and failed suicide attempts. Increasing attention was given to Charles's long-standing relationship with Camilla Parker-Bowles, which many journalists had known about, but which now entered the public domain. The growing public interest prompted the *Sunday Times* to ask a company of surveillance specialists called Audiotel International to analyse the Diana tape obtained by the *Sun*. They quickly realised that this was not a conversation that could have been recorded on a simple radio scanner in the manner recounted by Cyril Reenan.

First of all there were what Audiotel called 'data bursts', or 'pips', which were indicators used for charging a call. This seemingly innocuous fact was important, since these 'pips' are not broadcast over the radio system that carries mobile telephone calls, but are filtered out at the local exchange. This, and the fact that two other amateur scanners had also recorded the conversation, suggested strongly that the tape had been recorded by professionals and then rebroadcast, whereupon it was picked up by Reenan. Within a few days the *Sunday Times* asked a second set of audio experts retained by Sony International to examine the tape. They agreed that this was not a conversation captured by a scanner, partly because scanners usually capture only one half of a conversation clearly. More importantly, there was a 'hum' in the background, which they noted was the usual effect of trying to record a telephone conversation via a direct physical tap on a landline.

Given that Gilbey was speaking from a mobile telephone, this pointed strongly to the possibility that a professional telephone tap had been secretly attached to Diana's landline inside Sandringham. The experts believed that the doctoring of the tape constituted a crude attempt to make a tap on a landline sound as if it was an intercepted mobile telephone call. A little later there was further confirmation when Cellnet, the company that supported Gilbey's mobile phone, revealed that the sensational press stories had triggered an internal investigation, as the company feared that its security had been breached. It too concluded that this was a professional tap on a landline. Tellingly, all the amateur listeners who intercepted the call on their scanners, heard it several days after the real call was actually made.

This information was dynamite, since many believed it pointed to the involvement of the intelligence and security services. However, the Home Secretary, Kenneth Clarke, denounced the idea as 'extremely silly', since tapping was rigidly controlled, and insisted that he was 'absolutely certain' that this had nothing to do with MI5, SIS or GCHQ. Instead, he blamed the newspapers, which he suspected of freelance interception. The annual report of the Interception Commissioner, Lord Bingham of Cornhill, also implicitly cleared the agencies. However, the Chairman of the Broadcasting Standards Authority, Lord Rees-Mogg, expressed a different view. He wondered whether the tapes were the result of a legitimate monitoring operation that was part of the protection of the royal family, adding that once the sensational recording had been made, it was almost inevitable that it would be leaked. At first glance this seemed an absurd suggestion, but few members of the public were aware of the security services' intense anxiety about the threat from the IRA.

Elaborate measures had been taken to protect prominent people, including senior officials, after the assassination of the Conservative MP Ian Gow by the IRA in July 1990, including the setting up of a new central unit focused on personal security. Fantastically complex monitoring equipment and alarms had been installed in the homes of VIPs by a veritable army of technicians, some of whom were from the police and security services and some of whom were contract workers. The same was true of the royal palaces, and this surge of technical protection had provided endless opportunities for freelance activity.[48]

The Queen was particularly disturbed by the 'Squidgygate' affair, because she immediately recognised what it meant for the security of all royal communications. Accordingly, in January 1993 she requested that the authorities carry out an internal investigation to find the culprits. At this point there was a flurry of meetings and correspondence involving the heads of both GCHQ and MI5. However, Kenneth Clarke was highly reluctant to initiate an inquiry, for fear of what might be uncovered, and was anxious that its findings would themselves leak, triggering another round of scurrilous stories.[49] The person most affected by the 'Squidgygate' affair was Diana herself, who became increasingly obsessed with the threat of audio surveillance. This extended beyond the telephone, and there was constant fear of bugs all over her apartments. In 1993 she arranged for a team of communications security experts recommended to her by the Duchess of York to sweep her rooms at Kensington Palace for bugs. They arrived disguised as carpet-fitters and searched for hidden microphones, but were denied access to the main telephone exchange.[50] By this point, tapes of conversations between Prince Charles and Camilla Parker-Bowles had also surfaced, and the Cabinet Secretary Robin Butler suggested having all the royal premises checked for evidence of interference with landlines.[51]

Since her tragic death on 31 August 1997, Princess Diana's fears of more widespread monitoring have partly been confirmed. A news agency submitted a Freedom of Information

Act request to NSA for all its documents on Diana. Although NSA took the standard approach of sigint agencies, refusing to declassify so much as a page, it did admit that the US government had a dossier of over 1,056 pages on the Princess. This included thirty-nine NSA documents, some of which were transcripts of telephone calls. Most of these would have been collected as the result of her work overseas for various charities, including against landmines in Africa, which would have resulted in her being flagged up in channels which NSA routinely monitors. The American journalist Gerald Posner was later allowed to hear extracts from NSA recordings of an intercepted phone call made by Diana to a friend in the Brazilian Embassy in Washington.[52]

More than a decade later, the matter was still a live public issue. In January 2008 Diana's former bodyguard, ex-policeman Ken Wharfe, told the formal inquiry into her death that he believed the tapes had been deliberately broadcast by GCHQ in the sure knowledge that radio hams would pick them up. However, he conceded that he had absolutely no evidence of GCHQ involvement. Later, John Adye, Director of GCHQ between 1989 and 1996, testified that there had been no monitoring of Diana by GCHQ, and certainly no warrant. He added that audit trails at GCHQ were sufficiently good to identify unauthorised monitoring. Adye was of the opinion that the recording of the telephone conversations was possibly a criminal activity – in other words, freelance bugging by an illegal agent. However, this raises the awkward issue of how such individuals gained physical access to some of the most sensitive areas of the royal palaces. The most likely explanation remains a rogue individual working in a security capacity who enjoyed legitimate access to Sandringham.[53]

By the early 1990s there was a general shift towards the tighter regulation of intelligence. A key driving force here was the European Convention on Human Rights. The Swedish security service had recently been criticised by the European Court, because the agency had no legal existence and little oversight. This triggered a headlong rush towards regulation right across Europe. More importantly, it generated cultural change. During the Cold War the agencies had thought of themselves as 'secret services' which could get away with their operations because nobody saw them. A symptom of this was GCHQ's improbable attempt to pretend that its vast installations and worldwide activities did not exist. Now, however, they were obliged to conceive of themselves as intelligence services with a legal identity. They had less to fear from exposure, since all they had to do was show that their activities were proportionate. Civil rights campaigners found this a continual source of disappointment. Having presumed that more regulation would mean more restrictions on the secret state, they soon discovered that this was permissive legislation. Being 'legit' often meant that the agencies could carry out even more operations.[54]

As a result, GCHQ was given a firm place on the statute books through the Intelligence Services Act of 1994, which stated clearly what the organisation did and greatly strengthened its legal authority. A new oversight body also appeared called the Intelligence and Security Committee, composed of parliamentarians. Although this looked like a Parliamentary Select Committee, it was in fact responsible to the Prime Minister, and lacked many of the powers normally associated with select committees. It reported to Downing Street and its powers were relatively weak. Meanwhile, the real Parliamentary Select Committees with a legitimate interest in intelligence, such as Defence and Foreign Affairs, were finding that government now tended to resist their efforts to probe secret matters. Instead, they were told that intelligence was now the province of the Intelligence and Security Committee. Some have argued that John Major's experiment with openness was really about reaffirming secrecy.[55]

Surprisingly, when the Lord Chancellor, Lord Mackay of Clashfern, introduced the Intelligence Services Act in the House of Lords in December 1993, he actually felt that he had to make a case for the continued existence of the British intelligence and security services. He argued that superpower rivalry during the Cold War had offered 'its own grim version of stability', and that while the collapse of Communism had reduced one cataclysmic threat, it had also brought many new dangers. He spoke of a 'rising tide of nationalism and fanaticism, untried alliances, untested groupings, new rivalries and new ambitions'. Rather philosophically, he added: 'Greed, envy and corruption . . . are as prevalent as ever.' Few were inclined to argue. In the ensuing debate, former Cabinet Secretaries and former Prime Ministers held forth, reflecting decades of experience as both managers and customers of the British intelligence community. Jim Callaghan argued that the intelligence services had grown large and powerful during the Cold War, and 'cost a great deal of money'. He urged that the most urgent task facing the new Intelligence and Security Committee was to review the future of GCHQ, which he described as 'a full blown bureaucracy', and added that the new oversight bodies should 'investigate whether all the functions that GCHQ carries out today are still necessary'. He was not the only one asking this question. With the Cold War over, some were now daring to ask what the future purpose of GCHQ might be.[56]

The New Age of Ubiquitous Computing

Mobile cell phones increased from sixteen million to 741 million
... Internet users went from about four million to 361 million.
General Michael Hayden, Director of NSA,
commenting on the 1990s[1]

In the autumn of 1994, elite counter-drugs forces were searching a compound in an affluent neighbourhood of the Colombian city of Cali, home to some of the world's major cocaine cartels. This time, instead of finding drugs, they uncovered a large computer centre, with six technicians slaving over an IBM AS400 mainframe around the clock. The presumption was that this had something to do with major underworld financial transactions, so the computer was dismantled and taken to the United States for analysis. In fact, the drug cartel had loaded all the office and home telephone numbers of US diplomats and counter-narcotics agents based in Colombia. They had then added the entire regional telephone log containing the call history of the last two years, purchased illegally from the commercial telephone company in Cali. This was being systematically analysed, using 'data-mining' software of the kind now commonly used by intelligence agencies, to identify all the people who had been calling the counter-narcotics officers on a regular basis. The drug barons were engaged in sophisticated sigint to uncover informants in their ranks. Chillingly, a dozen had already been assassinated, and this was the machine that had uncovered them.[2]

At about the same time, a team from GCHQ were assisting with an investigation into blackouts of the national power grid that had struck Auckland in New Zealand. They proved to be the result of electronic attacks on the country's electricity distribution network, launched over the internet. Australia's signals intelligence agency, the DSD, confirmed that intermittent blackouts across Queensland were the result of attacks from the same source. The culprits were a group of hackers called the 'Anti-Christ Doom Squad' who were able to move effortlessly across the computer systems of many countries using 'spoofed' user names and stolen passwords to hide who they were. Once they gained access to the computers controlling New Zealand's power supply, they focused on the distribution systems, picking a point where all five main power lines converged before coming into Auckland. By changing the temperature within the sensitive cables they quickly put them out of action. Remarkably, the whole attack was run from a laptop in a drug café in the back streets of Amsterdam. The offenders had then snaked a pathway through host computers in a dozen different countries, and GCHQ thought it was unlikely that it could ever bring a prosecution against them.[3]

In 1995 GCHQ also found itself investigating cyber attacks on banks in the City of London. Working with the Department of Trade and Industry and the Bank of England, it began to probe crimes which the banks were extremely anxious to hide. Outwardly, they claimed to be secure, but in fact they had paid out millions of pounds to blackmailers who had gained entry to their systems and threatened to wipe their computer databases. GCHQ was hampered by limited cooperation from the banks, which were reluctant to admit the extent to which they had been damaged, for fear of undermining the confidence of investors. Nevertheless, GCHQ was able to identify forty-six attacks that had taken place over a period of two years, including attacks on three British banks and one American investment house. One of the questions GCHQ was asking was how the blackmailers had gained access to 'hacking' technologies that had been developed by military scientists.[4]

Taken together, these computer attacks represented an

alarming revolution. The identity of GCHQ had supposedly been 'modernised' through the Intelligence Services Act of the previous year. But the language of this legislation was archaic, employing time-worn phrases such as 'wireless telegraphy'. Moreover, the intelligence agencies were struggling to embrace the new age of personal computing and the internet.[5] Of course, GCHQ and NSA had been intimately involved in the development of cutting-edge computing, but the sigint agencies tended to think big. The great prize had always been access to high-grade Soviet cyphers, and for this they needed massive super-computers. The code-breakers had been much less interested in the development of personal computing and the internet. In the 1980s, email had been an eccentric form of communication used mostly by bearded scientists in universities who wanted to chat about quarks and quasars. However, by the 1990s email was rapidly becoming ubiquitous, and global commerce was increasingly dependent on a 'wired world' provided by the internet. This in turn led to growing anxiety about the safety of 'critical national infrastructure', the ever-growing electronic networks which underpinned not only banking, but also the maintenance of many essential public services.

For GCHQ this was a paradigm shift. Alongside its traditional code-breaking role, Cheltenham was increasingly under pressure to defend the whole underlying electronic system upon which banking, commerce and indeed all the public services that supported national life now depended. GCHQ did not like this, since it resurrected the familiar dilemma of 'offence versus defence' in the realm of code-breaking, but in a much more unmanageable form. The dependence of banks and businesses upon ubiquitous networked computers led to a growing demand for widely available computer security and confidential messaging. Yet the very thing that GCHQ and NSA had been battling against for years was the possibility of widely available cyphers and secure communications, since this would undermine the whole business of sigint. Indeed, government was now asking them to advise large swathes of the private sector on the hitherto dark secrets of how to maintain computer security. Even as they did so, they were privately agonising over how to stop the spread of the very same technology.

In the past, NSA and GCHQ had dealt with the demand for encryption from banks and businesses by forcing IBM, the computer industry leader, to weaken its Data Encryption Standard or 'DES', a cypher which protected communications between computers. The idea was that DES should be strong enough to prevent rival commercial companies or hackers from breaking it, but weak enough to allow NSA and GCHQ to read it if they needed to.[6] In June 1985 British, French, German and American code-breakers had come together for a secret quadripartite meeting in London about this problem, chaired by GCHQ. They agreed that the Japanese computer industry would be a problem 'for the foreseeable future', since it was not party to this collective agreement. GCHQ arranged a division of labour, with each sigint agency tracking the work of particular companies: the British would watch Nokia in Finland, the French were to track the French arms company Thompson-CSF, and the Americans followed Japanese activities. They all agreed that they needed a long-term programme to 'destabilise' DES and any successors. As they suspected, by the 1990s DES was looking weak, and demands for stronger encryption by banks and businesses were emerging everywhere.[7]

In fact, the nemesis of the code-breaking agencies was not large corporations, but a group of maverick scientists. They explicitly set themselves the task of recovering truly private communication for the ordinary citizen after decades of government surveillance. For them the Holy Grail was something they called 'Public Key Cryptography'. The growing popularity of desktop computers in the 1990s, and their growing processor power, had opened up the possibility of ordinary people creating their own codes of mind-boggling complexity. The problem that confronted these mavericks was key distribution. It was no good being able to send a message secretly halfway around the world if the recipient could not read it. To do this the recipient needed the key to unlock the code, and without the paraphernalia of a government courier system, distributing the key safely and without interception was a problem. However, the mavericks now made a breakthrough. The most common analogy used to explain it is a series of padlocks. The sender, who we will call 'Alice', secures her message to her friend 'Bob' with a cypher that works like a padlock to which Bob does not have the key. When Bob receives it, instead of trying to open it, he adds a second padlock that depends on a cypher of his own devising, and sends it back to Alice. Alice then removes only her original padlock and sends it back to Bob, by which time it is only secured by Bob's padlock. Bob can now open the box and read the message. They have communicated securely, yet there has been no key distribution.[8]

This was a revolutionary breakthrough. The arrival of Public Key Cryptography triggered a veritable war between civil libertarians and the code-breaking agencies. For the mavericks, the possibility of email secrecy and anonymous web activity offered the prize of a return to the golden age of privacy for the citizen. For the sigint agencies, the military and the police this conjured up a world in which criminals, drug dealers and terrorists would be able to avoid the interception of their communications and encrypt what was on their computers. The double irony was that the global telecommunications revolution that had helped to bring all this about was also placing the sigint agencies under growing pressure from their own governments to assist with secure e-commerce. Some time after his retirement, Sir Brian Tovey, a former Director of GCHQ, explained the dilemma:

*

The question is: how in the world does one reconcile these two? How does one on the one hand assure industry that its communications are confidential and reliable, and how on the other hand is Government under these very carefully defined circumstances to continue to derive important information, be it about drug running, terrorism et cetera, from the interception of communications . . . ?

*

Either way, the tide of technology and economic activity, one might even say the tide of globalisation, was moving in favour of ever greater security and against the sigint agencies. Taken together with the huge increase in the use of fibre-optic cables to carry telecom traffic, which was hard to tap into, this spelt disaster for GCHQ.[9]

Just like fibre-optics, Public Key Cryptography appears to have been discovered first by the British. Arguably the most important development in secure communications for several centuries, it was partly invented by James Ellis at GCHQ in the 1970s. However, Ellis's achievement was so far ahead of its time that neither GCHQ nor NSA could initially see any application for it, since the internet did not then exist. Sean Wyllie, one of GCHQ's top mathematicians, had raised the issue of Ellis's invention during a visit to Washington and asked if it had any uses, but it did not seem significant at the time.[10] There was some talk of using it to distribute the 'go-codes' for nuclear weapons, but that was it. In the 1980s Whitfield Diffie and Martin Hellman, two American computer scientists, discovered Public Key Cryptography quite independently at a time when the development of desktop computers and the internet rendered it a breakthrough development. They immediately recognised its importance, and took it much further, developing ideas such as digital signatures.[11] The US government responded by threatening to prosecute them. Martin Hellman recalls: 'Some of my friends who had worked in the intelligence community even told me that my life could be in danger.'[12]

In 1993 these matters were brought to a head by a software engineer living in Boulder, Colorado, called Phil Zimmermann. He developed a code-making programme for desktop personal computers called 'PGP', which stood for 'Pretty Good Privacy', and then gave it away on the internet for free. Zimmermann had developed a quick and easy-to-use version of Public Key Cryptography that retained much of its strength, but greatly simplified its use. Now even the most non-technical computer user enjoyed access to strong cyphers and secure email communications. The American government was horrified, declaring that Zimmermann had effectively 'exported munitions', and actually began a public prosecution, hoping to put him in jail. After three years, the case – which became a *cause célèbre* – collapsed. Zimmermann asserted triumphantly: 'This technology belongs to everybody.'[13]

GCHQ had debated the possibility of announcing its own early discovery of Public Key Cryptography as early as 1984. However, even while it pondered this, the controversy over Peter Wright's *Spycatcher* memoirs erupted, inflaming Margaret Thatcher's notorious obsession with secrecy. GCHQ's senior management, who were also embattled over the trade union issue, took fright and decided to keep quiet. It was more than a decade before GCHQ summoned up the courage to make a public avowal of its remarkable achievements. Cabinet Office approval for a public announcement was finally granted in late December 1997. Tragically, James Ellis, a true hero of sigint who certainly ranks alongside the greats such as Alan Turing, had died just a month earlier, on 25 November 1997. He never received proper recognition within his lifetime.[14]

Throughout the 1990s, both NSA and GCHQ doggedly fought Public Key Cryptography. The Clinton administration came up with the idea of the so-called 'Clipper Chip', a small device in every computer that could be directly accessed by government to bypass any encryption used by the owner. However, it was soon shown that this device was easily disabled. Later, NSA suggested that American computer manufacturers should be permitted to export computers with strong encryption if a spare set of decoding keys was accessible to the government through a trusted third party. The proposals, known as 'Key Recovery' or 'Key Escrow', were bitterly criticised by privacy advocates. In fact, this scheme was soon rendered unworkable by the export of strong computer encryption from other countries like Switzerland, France, Germany and Belgium. This was a rerun of the European cypher machine problem encountered in the 1960s. The difficulties only increased when mobile phones appeared that also boasted strong encryption, which were quickly purchased by the Chinese government. In the 1990s the communications revolution continually favoured the code-makers, and pushed the code-breakers firmly into second place.[15]

Keeping up with the internet revolution was proving expensive for the code-breakers. Yet just as GCHQ was faced with these major challenges, its budget was severely cut. In the summer of 1993 the British government began to call for defence cuts following the end of the Cold War. The Soviet Union had visibly disintegrated, and the huge arsenals maintained by the West for half a century no longer seemed necessary. When intelligence chiefs tried to justify their budgets, there was no shortage of security problems in the world, but most looked quite small in scale. They included narcotics, money laundering, people trafficking, terrorism, nuclear proliferation and the illegal light weapons trade. There was now more emphasis on economic intelligence. GCHQ was also giving more attention to 'economic well-being'. Robin Robison, who worked in the Cabinet Office, declared in 1992 that he had seen 'sack loads' of economic material making its way from GCHQ to the JIC.[16] However, this did not keep the economisers at bay. In late 1993 Sir Michael Quinlan, former Permanent Under-Secretary at the Ministry of Defence, was asked to carry out a 'Review of Intelligence Requirements and Resources'. This was completed in early 1994, and suggested only some gentle retailoring.[17] Quinlan was a great friend of the intelligence services, yet even the modest cut of 3 per cent that he imposed on GCHQ was painful. Cold War icons were wound up, including the long-serving 13 Signals Regiment which had listened to the Soviets along the Inner German Border for four decades.[18]

GCHQ now became entangled with the fate of a single individual. This was a rising star in the Conservative Party called Jonathan Aitken. Having previously been a Minister for Defence, in 1994 he was appointed Chief Secretary to the Treasury, perhaps the most coveted post amongst younger Ministers and carrying Cabinet rank. Britain was in the middle of another expenditure crisis, and Aitken's main task was to look for savings. One of the effects of the end of the Cold War had been to allow the Treasury to strip away a little of the mystery of secret services funding. For decades this had been grouped together as the 'Secret Vote' and decided upon by the Prime Minister. In 1994 the Treasury managed to make some inroads here, requiring each agency chief to face bilateral discussions with the Chief Secretary like ordinary mortals. As a result, much more of Britain's carefully hidden intelligence spending became visible. At this point formal British intelligence spending was about £1.1 billion per year, of which GCHQ claimed the lion's share as ever, at £850 million. MI5 and SIS received the crumbs from under the table, at £125 million each.[19]

MI5 and SIS performed faultlessly in their meetings with Aitken. David Spedding, the new chief of SIS, was a Middle East expert and was at home in the post-Cold War environment. He explained how his networks of agents were a long-term business, and could not be rebuilt quickly in a crisis if they were cut back. Stella Rimington, Director General of MI5, together with her deputy, Stephen Lander, made a convincing case for protection of its budget focused on the IRA. They argued that while the Republicans were engaged in talks, they were also secretly re-arming, so MI5 too escaped lightly. Aitken confessed that he was 'actually convinced by some of the arguments against cuts put forward by the spooks'.

By contrast, John Adye, leading the GCHQ team, performed badly. Initially GCHQ produced 'bewildering countermeasures' by moving into the stratosphere of 'technical incomprehensibility'. As Aitken studied the agency more closely, burning the ministerial midnight oil, he became convinced that there was something wrong. GCHQ, he concluded, was 'suffering from out-of-date methods of management and out-of date methods for assessing priorities'. There was undoubtedly great technical wizardry. GCHQ was monitoring communications between Russian tank commanders in Chechnya – but what, asked

Aitken, was the real value of this to British national interests?[20]

Aitken sensed weakness. He pressed for a deep probe of GCHQ led jointly by Foreign Secretary Douglas Hurd and himself for the Treasury. The real work was to be led by an outsider – Roger Hurn, the successful chairman of Smiths Industries, which made technical instruments.[21] Hurn's review team was formidable. It included Alice Perkins (a.k.a. Mrs Jack Straw), one of the most effective Treasury officials, and David Omand, 'a fearlessly outspoken Deputy Secretary at the MoD'.[22] The schedule was tight. Commissioned on 12 December 1994, the team reported back to Ministers on 25 March 1995.[23] GCHQ suffered a body blow. Hurn took almost £200 million per annum off Cheltenham's budget in one bite, somewhere close to a quarter of its spending. This left managers in deep shock. No British intelligence agency had suffered such deep retrenchment since the end of the Second World War.[24] These cuts heralded 'massive and dramatic change', and staff understandably had 'fears for the future'. The vast Cold War 'silos' were broken up, resulting in the death of the mighty J Division, which handled sigint on Russia, and K Division, which handled the rest of the world. Even greater changes lay in store for the communications security wing. Hurn suggested that this should go over to charging its Whitehall customers on a cost-recovery basis.[25]

If this was not enough, on 23 November 1995 it was announced that the GCHQ Director, John Adye, would be replaced by someone from outside the agency. This was David Omand, a senior official who had been part of the Hurn Review team. Many at GCHQ greeted this news with 'consternation and disappointment', since it seemed to signal that internal candidates were not good enough. Some pondered aloud whether Omand was yet another 'axe man' sent to further downsize GCHQ.[26] In fact it was inaccurate to say that Omand was an 'outsider', since he had joined GCHQ straight from Corpus Christi College, Cambridge, in the 1970s. However, an obvious high-flyer, he had soon moved on to the Ministry of Defence.

Omand's reputation for tough management and intellectual rigour caused visible panic at GCHQ.[27] Wild rumours abounded that the target figure for further job losses was at least three thousand, leaving a staff of perhaps just over two thousand at GCHQ by the end of the century.[28] In reality, Omand was GCHQ's saviour, rapidly reordering it for the post-Cold War world and putting in place imaginative new plans that central government would fund. Meanwhile, the planned cuts were far more modest than the doom-mongers had suggested. GCHQ stood at 5,900 staff in April 1995, and managers envisaged a move to 5,300 over two years.[29]

Omand performed open-heart surgery on GCHQ. He realised that both rapidly shifting targets and the increasing pace of technological evolution would mean abandoning the old structures. The central concept was now something called 'Sinews', or 'Sigint NEW Systems', which gained massive momentum by 2000. The aim of Sinews was to provide maximum flexibility of operations while avoiding wasteful overlap. In practice it resulted in the creation of fourteen domains, each with a defined area of work. The key to success was a small team of programme managers who could move people rapidly from task to task, and a lot of time was now spent balancing competing intelligence requirements. The whole purpose was to come to grips with the messy post-Cold War environment, with its myriad targets and changing priorities. One of the most important drivers of Sinews was a recognition that the culture of GCHQ had to change from a highly secretive 'need to know' towards 'need to share'.[30]

When David Omand took over on 1 July 1996, the most striking aspect of GCHQ was its physical dilapidation. His own office was a drab 1950s affair in C Block on the Oakley site. Even as GCHQ's management sought to anticipate the challenges of the twenty-first century, their own windows looked out on a heritage theme park covered with 1940s prefabs. The contrast was made all the sharper by the fact that SIS had just moved into distinctive new London offices at Vauxhall Cross, by the side of the Thames, designed by the architect Terry Farrell,

that could easily have been the work of the visionary television producer Gerry Anderson, creator of the 1960s puppet
series *Thunderbirds*. More importantly, one of the obstacles to
improving GCHQ was the fact that it was spread across innumerable small buildings on two sites, at Oakley and Benhall.[31]
Accordingly, in September 1996 Omand began to consider a
Private Finance Initiative to provide new accommodation. He
also improved the agency's profile with a new high-level GCHQ
post in Whitehall and new London facilities in Albany Court,
across the road from its existing offices in Palmer Street.[32]

The future shape of GCHQ was round – or to be more precise,
doughnut-shaped. Under Omand's new plan, by 2003 all of
GCHQ's activities were to be brought together on the Benhall
site, in a vast new circular building with an open centre. The
optimistic idea of post-Cold War peace was still in the air, and
it was thought that while the building would take all of GCHQ's
staff, by the time it was completed lower numbers might even
allow them to rent out some of the space.[33] GCHQ would actually lease rather than buy its new quarters. When construction
began in the late 1990s it was the largest building ever initiated by the British government, and indeed the largest construction project then in progress in Europe. The plan included an
underground road to service the main building, and massive
basement computer halls. Above ground, it required sixteen
miles of carpet and provided more than a million square feet
of office space. There was great excitement about 'the Doughnut',
but also some trepidation. The new MI5 and SIS headquarters
had each cost more than three times their original estimated
price, largely due to computer problems, and by 1999 the
projected figures for the GCHQ building were already being
looked on with some scepticism.[34]

In Britain, the advent of a new Labour government in 1997
brought further change. At the start of the 1990s a young Tony
Blair – then Shadow Employment Secretary – told an enthusiastic GCHQ trade union rally that the first act of a Labour
government would be to restore union rights to Cheltenham.[35]

The union issue had not been dormant. By the 1990s the GCHQ Trade Union Campaign was a small but hardened machine, working remorselessly to stay in touch with Blair, continually thanking him for speaking about GCHQ, congratulating him on the attainment of each Shadow Cabinet post and keeping him up to date with the campaign. Blair always responded warmly and enthusiastically.[36] Gordon Brown was also energetic and sincere in his offers of assistance.[37] Other key members of Blair's team, including Peter Mandelson and Tessa Jowell, had continually praised what they called a brave and admirable activity. Now Labour was back in power, the unions were coming back to Cheltenham, with cloth caps, brass bands and banners flying, all somewhat out of step with David Omand's new mood of modernisation.[38]

In the two years before the election, Tony Blair regularly repeated his pledge to restore full trade union rights at Cheltenham. During the period June to September 1995 he repeated the undertaking on no fewer than four separate occasions.[39] Yet trust between the GCHQ trade unions and the Labour Ministers who had backed them unstintingly for thirteen years was surprisingly fragile. Although publicly thanking the new Foreign Secretary Robin Cook, they suspected him of capitulating on the matter of a no-strike deal, and were sufficiently anxious to write to him asking him to deny rumours to this effect. Despite plaintive reassurances from Tony Blair, the last remaining GCHQ trade unionists expected to be sold down the river. In fact, Cook went for a voluntary agreement, exactly as the GCHQ Trade Union Campaign desired.[40] The complex process of negotiating the 'collective agreement' began with the Director of GCHQ, Kevin Tebbit, making it clear that he wanted 'no outside inducement to disruption'. The only sticking point was that the unions wanted an agreement on non-disruption by arbitration, while the managers desired a solid legal agreement.[41]

IRA terrorism stood out as the seemingly perennial sigint target in the early 1990s. Down the years, perhaps GCHQ's biggest contribution in Northern Ireland was in the electronic war against the radio-controlled bombs used by terrorists. Once the IRA moved away from old-fashioned command wires towards radio-controlled bombs, researchers at GCHQ came up with special equipment that inundated the Province with random radio signals on the bomb command frequencies. This caused a number of bombs to detonate while they were being constructed and tested. It was only after a number of volunteers had been killed or injured by their own bombs exploding in their secret workshops that the IRA realised what was happening. A scientific war developed, with the IRA creating a new type of bomb that was triggered by two separate coded signals. GCHQ eventually discovered this, and took further countermeasures, resulting in more IRA deaths. To counter this, the IRA tried to move to using other kinds of trigger, including adapting radar guns used by the police in speed traps.[42]

The main source of technical collection on the IRA was local telephone tapping, most of which was undertaken by the Royal Ulster Constabulary Special Branch, together with bugging with microphones facilitated by the Army and MI5. The scale of bugging was so great that in the 1980s extra Army personnel had to be borrowed from units such as the Royal Electrical and Mechanical Engineers to do the work. Telephone interception was an especially skilled business because of the sensitivity of the IRA to surveillance. The core analysis was provided by about thirty women working for the RUC in a building nicknamed 'the hen house', where real-time listening continued twenty-four hours a day. The analysts required the most acute skills, since it was often the inflection in a voice, the particular way in which someone said, 'Are you coming out for a drink then?', or even a period of silence, that suggested imminent activity. GCHQ had responsibility for longer-distance communications, including telephone lines between Northern Ireland, the British mainland and the Republic of Ireland. The IRA was known to run its own ingenious sigint operations, dismantling old television sets to obtain UHF/VHF receivers to allow them to listen in on the high-frequency radios used by the Army and the RUC.[43]

Intelligence was no less vital during the mid-1990s, when the British government had entered into tentative dialogue with the Republicans. Key participants included Sinn Féin's Martin McGuinness and senior British government figures including Mo Mowlam, the Northern Ireland Secretary, and Jonathan Powell, Tony Blair's Chief of Staff. Blair's immediate circle soon noticed that the Sinn Féin President Gerry Adams was sensitive to surveillance, and 'went without a mobile . . . because he knew he could be tracked on it'.[44] Like not a few government Ministers, Mo Mowlam struggled to deal with the intricacies of using intercepts. She was regularly provided with transcripts of IRA conversations derived from surveillance, yet she would discuss sensitive political subjects, such as her battle to stop the Prime Minister sacking her, with Martin McGuinness in circumstances in which she was also likely to be captured by British technical collection. More alarmingly, she sometimes introduced details into her conversations with Adams and McGuinness that she could only have been privy to from technical collection. This led the Republicans to uncover listening devices in one of their key safe houses. In May 1998 the security agencies accused Mowlam of revealing a listening operation that had been mounted against Gerry Kelly, a leading Sinn Féin official living in Belfast. A wooden rafter in his house had been hollowed out and packed full of listening equipment, which had been providing good intelligence for three years.[45] Needless to say, the intelligence and security services did not consider Mo Mowlam their all-time-favourite Northern Ireland Secretary.

The most striking physical feature of GCHQ's participation in the intelligence war against the IRA was a 150-foot-high concrete tower built in 1989 within a secure compound at Capenhurst in Cheshire owned by British Nuclear Fuels Ltd. It was on a direct line between the British Telecom Medium Wave Tower at Holyhead in Anglesey and another tower at Sutton Common near Macclesfield, a microwave link which carried most of the telephone calls between mainland Britain and Ireland. The tower contained seven floors of secret monitoring equipment and three floors of aerials. Its staff were rumoured to be drawn from the Royal Radar Establishment at Malvern. The tower was closed in 1998 when the Irish government protested strongly and insisted on telephone calls being sent by a different route. Over a decade the Capenhurst tower had allowed GCHQ to intercept a vast volume of telephone traffic for analysis. A similar station on Croslieve Mountain in South Armagh is thought to have taken traffic between Belfast and Dublin. This was a classic example of the bonanza of clear voice material that could be provided by microwave telephone interception. Unsurprisingly, during the Peace Process in the 1990s the IRA was most anxious to see the physical architecture of surveillance in Northern Ireland removed, including the watchtowers that bristled with aerials and antennae.[46]

On 15 August 1998, twenty-nine people died at the town of Omagh in County Tyrone in the most deadly bomb attack ever carried out in Ireland. This was the work of a small break-away faction called the 'Real IRA'. Recently, dramatic claims have been made suggesting that the Omagh bombing could have been disrupted by the security forces had intelligence from GCHQ been properly utilised. BBC investigative journalists said that GCHQ intercepted mobile phone calls from members of the Real IRA in the car carrying the bomb towards the target, and that these should have indicated that a major attack was being launched. There is no doubt that the RUC had asked for the mobiles in question to be given a very high priority for monitoring. Ray White, a former Assistant Chief Constable in the RUC, recalls that Special Branch had requested 'live' monitoring of particular mobile phone numbers in the hope of stopping such attacks.

In September 2008 the BBC's *Panorama* claimed that just ninety minutes before the attack, GCHQ captured a call to a suspect phone which contained the phrase: 'We're crossing the line,' meaning the car carrying the bombers was passing from Eire into

Northern Ireland. Forty minutes before the explosion, the words 'The bricks are in the wall' were heard on the same phone, a code understood to mean the bomb was in place. White claims that when Special Branch later asked why the information came so late, GCHQ said: 'We missed it.'[47] Understandably, the assertions that GCHQ had intercepted mobile phone calls prior to the detonation caused a public furore. Eventually the Intelligence Commissioner, Sir Peter Gibson, was called on to investigate.

GCHQ is such a sensitive topic that Gibson's report was never made public. Instead, a short summary was produced that was hedged around by the excruciating secrecy that still accompanies sigint. Nevertheless, to the discerning eye much was revealed. Gibson effectively conceded that the mobile phones of the Real IRA were indeed being monitored live by GCHQ – which underlines that these people were a very high priority. But there were two problems. First, the Real IRA knew this, and used obscure code words. It is unlikely that the conversations GCHQ captured prior to the bombing indicated clearly that an attack was under way. Second, GCHQ had insisted on convoluted procedures that restricted sigint very tightly to a few people in Northern Ireland. Some GCHQ staff had been lent out to RUC's intelligence headquarters in Belfast; however, Gibson himself concedes that:

*

Once intercept material reached RUC HQ and Special Branch South, any further publication and release of that material, even to another part, or other members, of Special Branch, was subject to strict conditions imposed by GCHQ . . . If those persons within the RUC HQ and Special Branch South who received intelligence from GCHQ wanted to disseminate it within the RUC or even within Special Branch a set procedure had to be followed . . . and a form of words cleared with GCHQ.

*

This was hardly a procedure designed to permit immediate action. Moreover, Gibson also shows that GCHQ had prioritised the flow of sigint to RUC headquarters in Belfast and the border areas. Omagh was in a quiet area west of Belfast, and had been given a lower priority.[48] Whatever the shortcomings of the system, it remains unlikely that the security forces could have responded in the limited time-frame available. Even with the most attentive real-time listening, for GCHQ to have analysed the conversations, contacted the right units in Northern Ireland, and for them in turn to have put several roadblocks in place, in a little more than an hour, is improbable. Quite simply, in real life, response times are not that fast.[49]

Much more convincing are the complaints about the way in which the dead hand of sigint security rules impeded the subsequent police investigation. GCHQ shared intelligence with the RUC Special Branch, which it saw as another intelligence service, but not with the CID officers pursuing the criminal investigations. Gibson concedes that this led to 'a tension between Special Branch and CID'.[50] GCHQ's voice recordings might well have assisted in the CID's subsequent efforts to identify and arrest the perpetrators. Instead they spent months trawling through call logs, in effect doing their own more primitive sigint, and as a result the trail went cold.[51]

The Omagh bombing underlined that 'need to share' was a major problem right across the British intelligence community. The sort of targets that were of rising importance in the late 1990s, including Middle Eastern terrorists, Colombian drug cartels and warlords in the former Yugoslavia, required closer and faster cooperation with MI5 and SIS. A well-worn system of liaison already existed. GCHQ had a small unit called 'Z Division', whose job it was to pass material to the other secret services and to agree on the use to which it could be put. However, the formal regulations surrounding the use of sigint, called 'IRSIG', largely drawn up by NSA, were proving cumbersome and made 'Action On' very difficult. ('Action On' was the phrase used to indicate permission to share sigint with colleagues with a view to taking positive action.) GCHQ's instinct was always to hide its source. Now, a younger generation of MI5

and SIS officers was tending to bypass these obstacles, prefer-
ring to meet up informally with GCHQ personnel in the pleasant
Cotswolds pubs around Cheltenham. This was a grassroots revolt,
and during the late 1990s top managers in the British intelligence community had to accept the new trend. Organic connections were developing fast between the three secret agencies
under the pressure of fast-moving day-to-day operations.[52]

In the summer of 1998, after only six months in office, Kevin
Tebbit handed over to Francis Richards, who would be GCHQ's
fourth Director in as many years. Like his immediate predecessors, Richards was an outsider, but he was not entirely unac-
quainted with the secret world. He had served in the Army,
including on Cyprus, and had then joined the diplomatic service.
His father, Brooks Richards, had served in SOE during the war,
and had been Cabinet Office Coordinator of Intelligence in the
late 1970s. For Richards, and for Britain's other intelligence
chiefs, one of the pleasing aspects of the Blair administration
was that the Prime Minister took intelligence seriously, partly
because of his abiding enthusiasm for military intervention.
However, in the late 1990s the emerging security issue was the
rising tide of global organised crime. In early December 1999,
Richards joined the Chief of SIS and the Director General of
MI5 in an extended meeting at Downing Street on the 'crime
emergency' facing Britain, including the threat from the Russian
Mafia. GCHQ was asked to work more closely with the National
Criminal Intelligence Service and to help set up a new unit
called the Government Telecommunications Advisory Centre,
which addressed the growing use of email and encrypted
computers by organised crime.[53]

By the late 1990s the main threats that preoccupied government arose from shadowy non-state organisations rather than
foreign countries. They included terrorism, organised crime and
warlordism, together with a proliferation of private networks interested in nuclear, chemical and biological weapons. The common
element among these new threats was that many of them operated clandestinely. The British response was to give more emphasis

to intelligence-led activity. Indeed, as Britain's borders became more porous, and with the growing volumes of international trade, there was little else that could be done. The expansion of the European Union seemed to suggest practically an open frontier for Britain that extended as far as the Urals.[54] In June 2000 the shocking discovery of fifty-eight Chinese illegal immigrants who had perished in a container lorry at Dover highlighted how serious these matters were. The government was now reversing the cuts it had imposed on the intelligence agencies, because they seemed a plausible antidote to these intractable problems.[55]

GCHQ's contributions in this realm were valuable. This was illustrated by the capture of the exceedingly dangerous criminal Kenneth Noye. In 1996 Noye was the prime suspect in the notorious murder of Stephen Cameron in a road-rage incident on the M25 motorway. The perpetrator fled the motorway junction where the attack took place in a black Range Rover. Noye was also linked to a string of high-profile crimes, including the disposal of the assets from the Brinks Mat bullion robbery at Heathrow airport in 1983. After the murder, Noye slipped abroad: the police would visit no fewer than thirteen countries, including Russia and northern Cyprus, in their quest for him. Huge efforts were made to keep the search secret, since some police officers and one senior politician were thought to be in Noye's pay. All the police had to go on were reports that he was in Spain and his current mobile phone number. In 1998 GCHQ used cell-site tracking of his mobile phone to identify his movements, and this allowed him to be located in Spain, despite numerous false identities. Stephen Cameron's girlfriend, Danielle Cable, who had witnessed the M25 murder, was flown out to Spain to assist in his identification. One evening Noye was eating dinner in an expensive restaurant when four undercover detectives in T-shirts and shorts surprised him and handcuffed him. Britain's most wanted criminal had been caught. Jack Straw, the Home Secretary, signed Public Interest Immunity certificates on 8 February 2000 to ensure that details of GCHQ's role in finding Noye were not revealed in court.[56]

The police were so anxious about the safety of their witnesses that they were protected in a police station in north London with three separate air locks. Each witness was guarded by an armed policeman who had been specially vetted to ensure that he had no links to south London, where Noye operated. This caution was justified. Danielle Cable courageously gave evidence at Noye's trial in 2000, and was later given a new identity. Alan Decabral, an eye-witness to the murder who also gave evidence, refused a new identity and was shot dead in his car in Ashford in Kent on 5 October 2001.[57] To the dismay of GCHQ, its role in the effort against Noye was being discussed in the news-papers even before the case came to trial. This triggered a further operation, this time against journalists and their sources. Code-named 'Operation Nigeria', it caught journalists from tabloid newspapers on tape during a surveillance operation that showed they were procuring intelligence from a private detective agency which, in turn, obtained its information from corrupt police officers. Over the summer of 1999 the detective agency in ques-tion, known as Southern Investigations, was secretly bugged by the Metropolitan Police's anti-corruption squad, CIB3, and one leading figure was recorded discussing how he had sold a story to a reporter about GCHQ's role in tracking down Noye. It was also found that Southern Investigations had an informant in the Diplomatic Protection Squad at Buckingham Palace.[58]

No one could possibly argue that the identification and arrest of Kenneth Noye was anything other than an immense public good. Yet, because crime recognises no borders, this sort of work meant that GCHQ was being inexorably drawn into the contro-versial realm of domestic surveillance as well as having to engage with the contentious politics of internet privacy. During 1996 GCHQ and NSA had joined forces to put forward a solution to the problem of publicly available encryption, called 'Key Escrow'. However, this idea had proved unworkable, and in any case the new Blair government was unsympathetic to it. On 26 May 1999 Stephen Byers, Secretary of State at the Department of Trade and Industry, revealed the latest thinking on 'Encryption and Law

Enforcement'. Speaking at the Cabinet Office, he confirmed that 'Key Escrow' was finished, and now emphasised cooperating closely with the computer industry rather than fighting it. The government accepted that no single magic technique was likely to sustain interception in the face of rising use of encryption by criminals.[59] Instead, it placed its hopes on new legislation called the Regulation of Investigatory Powers Act 2000, under which criminals would face serious penalties for refusing to offer up the keys to encrypted material.[60]

In addition, there would be a new dedicated computer unit called the Government Technical Assistance Centre (GTAC), intended to break the codes that criminals used to encrypt their emails and computer hard drives. While this was nominally a Home Office unit, in reality code-breaking and code-making always meant GCHQ, and officials joked privately that 'GTAC' actually stood for 'GCHQ Technical Assistance Centre'. Sure enough, in July 2000 GCHQ was asked to lend one of its top experts, Brian Paterson, to the Home Office to establish the unit.[61] Even Paterson called GTAC a 'euphemistic title' for what was in effect a code-cracking unit at the Home Office. He explained that modern criminals tended to use the internet in three different ways. First, as a simple extension of ordinary crimes, such as fraud, theft and smuggling. Second, there were crimes which had only developed because of the existence of the internet, such as hacking and virus attacks.[62] Third, there was the use of the internet by criminals as a means of communications or storage. When it came to the third problem, Paterson explained that domestic interception presented multiple difficulties. It required warrants literally signed by the Home Secretary, 'even if it means getting him out of bed'. Moreover, in the era of the internet, interception was being made 'very much more difficult by new technology'.[63] Surprisingly, GTAC was developed, staffed, and then little used. Always partly run by GCHQ, it was quietly transferred to Cheltenham in April 2006.[64]

The number of criminals encrypting their emails and computer files proved to be fairly small. In fact, for a decade both NSA and

GCHQ had been barking up the wrong tree in terms of their obsession with the dangers of Public Key Encryption. This was a small problem, compared to the sheer explosion of open communications, especially those based around the internet. In October 2002 General Michael Hayden, Director of NSA, explained to Congress that in the 1990s the number of mobile phones in the world had increased from sixteen million to 741 million. At the same time, internet users went from about four million to 361 million. Half as many landlines were laid between 1994 and 2000 as in the whole previous history of the world. International telephone traffic went from thirty-eight billion minutes a year to over a hundred billion.[65] Both NSA and GCHQ were simply overwhelmed by a tidal wave of data, despite the fact that almost none of it was in code. One insider recounted that NSA had created a special facility with three years' worth of storage capacity for intercepted internet traffic. 'They filled it in eleven months.'[66]

By 2000, some intelligence chiefs had even begun to question the value of sigint in this era of superabundant communication. GCHQ and NSA could collect all of this new traffic, but they could not begin to listen to it or process it – so intelligence chiefs were at a loss to know what to do with it. One disillusioned code-breaker observed that it was like trying to pour a glass of water with a firehose. The costs of collecting all this material were huge, and the benefits were uncertain. In the United States, the price of satellite collection was threatening to overwhelm the whole intelligence budget, while in Britain the cost of transferring GCHQ's massive computers to the new building had begun to rise alarmingly. More importantly, the new sigint, which focused on emails and mobile phone calls, only worked if you knew precisely who you wanted to listen to, since trying to listen to everyone in a globalising world was impossible. Was this the right kind of intelligence-gathering for the twenty-first century? Even as security agencies pondered this question, frightening events were lurking just around the corner that would give it a sharper edge.[67]

The 9/11 Attacks and the Iraq War

Tomorrow is zero hour . . .
Intercepted phone message, 10 September 2001[1]

Shortly before 3 o'clock on the afternoon of 11 September 2001, Tony Blair was speaking before the Trades Union Congress in Brighton. His speech was hastily improvised, and was far removed from the subject he had expected to speak about. In the previous hour he had been informed of dramatic events unfolding in New York, where it was still morning. Two passenger aircraft laden with fuel had just hit the twin towers of the World Trade Center, which were soon billowing infernos. It was already clear that this was a deliberate attack, and Blair told his audience: 'This mass terrorism is the new evil in our world today.' At 2.59 p.m. British time, almost as Blair left the podium, the South Tower collapsed. The unprecedented scale of destruction was just beginning to dawn on the Prime Minister's immediate circle.

Special Branch officers were worried about an attack on Blair's car, perhaps by helicopter, so he was taken back to London by train. Later that afternoon he spoke to his intelligence chiefs, who were almost certain that the Islamic terrorist organisation al Qaeda was responsible. John Scarlett, Chair of the Joint Intelligence Committee, offered the view that it was the only group with the capability to mount such an attack. Blair was an avid reader of intelligence, but al Qaeda was not familiar to him. At 5.30 he chaired a formal meeting of 'Cobra', the Cabinet emergency planning committee, in its special bunker under

Whitehall, which focused on the imminent threat to Britain. Privately, his main anxiety was that the Americans might over-react, retaliating immediately and massively.[2] The next day, the heads of the three British intelligence and security services flew to Washington to express solidarity and to underline their deter-mination to do everything to assist. It was a gesture that was greatly appreciated by the Americans.[3]

In London, the Stock Exchange had been evacuated on the day of the attack, along with Canary Wharf. The skies over London, Paris and other European capitals had been closed to civilian air traffic. Cabinet Ministers felt safe enough meeting in 'Cobra', deep below ground, but eventually normal routines had to resume. The Labour Party conference in Brighton was only a few weeks away, and security for the Cabinet there was now a massive headache. The Ministry of Defence wanted to park a warship armed with surface-to-air missiles just off the seafront in case 'unauthorised planes looked as if they were going to attack the conference centre or the hotel'. David Blunkett, the Home Secretary, thought this was a little exces-sive. It was then suggested that missiles should be mounted on the roof of the conference centre, or in lorries nearby. In the end, the security forces settled for crash barriers to prevent vehicle-borne bombs.[4]

In America, an intelligence post-mortem had already begun. On 10 September NSA had intercepted two messages from Afghanistan. One of them said 'The match is about to begin,' and the other 'Tomorrow is zero hour.' The messages were in Arabic, and were not translated until the day after the attacks. Much was made of these messages in the weeks and months that followed, but their significance is now debatable. Even had they been translated immediately, they were not actionable. Although they appear to allude to an impending attack, they do not specify where, when or how. 'On Sept. 12 when they looked at these intercepts, no one knew who these people were,' noted one official.[5]

Al Qaeda had been NSA's number-one target since 7 August

1998, when it had bombed the American Embassies in Kenya and Tanzania.[6] By contrast, GCHQ had begun to take a pronounced interest in the organisation only relatively recently. The Director of GCHQ, Francis Richards, confirmed that the al Qaeda leader Osama bin Laden had only been 'a major preoccupation' for Cheltenham since 2000.[7] Nevertheless, GCHQ had picked up some of the growing 'chatter' during the summer of 2001, including messages to Middle Eastern journalists based in London. There was much talk about impending attacks, and Western embassies were already on high alert. On 6 August the crescendo of imprecise warnings had resulted in a section of President Bush's Daily Brief headed 'Bin Laden Determined to Strike in the US', which underlined the al Qaeda leader's determination to retaliate for previous Cruise-missile strikes against his training compounds in Afghanistan. It also reminded Bush that al Qaeda had bombed the World Trade Center in 1993. But no intercept gave any direct indication of the time or place of the planned attacks. Senior members of the Bush Cabinet were sceptical about the idea that al Qaeda was responsible for the attacks on the twin towers and the Pentagon, and Secretary of Defense Donald Rumsfeld went so far as to say the intercepted messages were possibly a hoax or a deception.[8]

After 9/11, the sigint agencies found themselves in crisis. For much of the 1990s the absence of a single high-profile threat had led to cuts in their budgets, just at the time when NSA and GCHQ were struggling to keep up with rapid changes in communications technology. Indeed, one of the problems later identified by the 9/11 Commission set up to inquire into the attacks was that the intelligence agencies had taken on very few new staff in the 1990s. In the wake of 9/11 they moved from famine to feast, and after further terrorist attacks such as that in Bali in October 2002, money was no object. Everywhere there were calls for more intelligence, and for wider international cooperation between intelligence and security services. Even the United Nations, an institution that was traditionally allergic to intelligence agencies, passed Security Council Resolution 1373, which placed a legal duty on all states to 'find ways of intensifying and accelerating the exchange of operational information, especially regarding actions or movements of terrorist persons or networks'.[9]

Immediately after 9/11, GCHQ doubled the size of its counter-terrorism team. However, the attacks underlined the weakness of the sigint agencies. Over the past decade, not only had they lost the battle over Public Key Encryption, but they were collecting more data than they could remotely process. NSA and GCHQ possessed phenomenal computing power, but it was being outstripped by the scale of the global communications revolution. Moreover, while only a small number of people were using publicly available encryption, many more were being careful about their communications. Interception was no longer secret, and monitoring was widely reported in the press. Groups like al Qaeda had become aware that they were vulnerable to eaves-dropping. Warlords, terrorists and criminals were starting to engage in opaque conversations, placing an even greater strain on the analysts, since intercepted messages were increasingly filled with the verbal equivalent of nods and winks which required a highly trained ear to deduce their meaning. Some of the nods and winks were in Pashtu, Farsi and other obscure languages. NSA and GCHQ were having to run fast to stand still.[10]

Language had been a major challenge for the sigint agencies for a decade. In the early 1990s the war in Bosnia had required GCHQ to make a significant investment of effort in the Balkans. By the late 1990s this was paying dividends, and policy-makers complimented Cheltenham on the 'flexible and in-depth service' it provided during Britain's involvement in Kosovo.[11] In 1999, when NATO air forces launched a massive air offensive against the Serbs, almost all the bombing targets were pinpointed by sigint provided by GCHQ and NSA.[12] The former Yugoslavia had remained a subject of constant interest to British policy-makers for an entire decade, but it was now common for target coun-tries to change rapidly, and GCHQ conceded that it was expe-riencing difficulties in recruiting personnel who were familiar with rarer languages. Although there were people in Britain with the required skills, many did not meet the residency requirement necessary to pass security vetting.[13]

The 9/11 Commission that investigated the attacks on the World Trade Center and the Pentagon examined how much al Qaeda knew about the fact that it was being listened to by the sigint agencies. It specifically pointed to a *Washington Times* article in 1998 which, it claimed, resulted in bin Laden deciding to cease making calls from a portable satellite phone. Others have argued that the bombarding of his encampment with Cruise missiles only a few days before the article appeared might also have sent the message that he needed to be a little more careful with his communications. What is certain is that NSA had charts on its walls that showed how mobile-phone chatter and email volumes amongst terrorists dropped off markedly after each reference to interception in the international press. In fact, NSA had only itself to blame, since it had enjoyed showing off to visiting politicians at its Fort Meade headquarters by playing tapes of bin Laden talking to his mother on his satellite phone.[14] The agency has since made an active effort to educate media correspondents on this issue.[15]

Because of the extreme caution terrorists now employed when using communications, GCHQ and NSA were sometimes reduced to 'traffic analysis', examining patterns of calls in order to deduce the groups they sketched out. Sigint rarely revealed plans or plots, but it could identify terrorist networks. Increasingly sophisticated software, often using neural network computers, was able to dredge useful data from something as simple as a list of numbers that had been called from a particular phone – often known as a call log. GCHQ also began to notice a regular phenomenon. In the week before 9/11, and also before the Bali bombing and the suicide attacks in Riyadh in early 2003, there was a surge in 'electronic chatter', followed by a period of silence before each attack. Some groups were clearly aware that GCHQ's computers were programmed to sniff email traffic for key words. For example, emails from the kidnappers of the American journalist Daniel Pearl, who was murdered by his captors in early 2002, contained deliberately misspelled words, such as 'Amreeka', 'Terrarism' and 'Pakstan', designed to avoid alerting the authorities.[16] Nevertheless, good communications security discipline is difficult, and one slip by the terrorists could give away a key player.[17]

Terrorists and drug dealers alike had also learned to change their mobile phones and sim cards frequently, as often as once every three days. The sigint agencies responded by using recorded 'voice prints', which allowed them to search volumes of traffic for people who 'sounded like' the suspects. The British were apparently the first to provide an authentic recording of bin Laden's voice, which was then used in this way.[18] The technique also revealed the location of Ramzi Binalshibh, a senior al Qaeda operative who was caught in Pakistan in September 2002. It appears that a sample of his voice, taken from an al-Jazeera television interview, was used to conduct a computer search against vast volumes of telephone traffic collected by satellite. Exactly a year after the 9/11 attacks, on the morning of Wednesday, 11 September 2002, the Pakistani intelligence service, ISI, surrounded a four-storey block of flats in Karachi. Their initial assault surprised five men who had returned to bed in one of the apartments after early-morning prayers. While they were being taken out at gunpoint, sympathisers in the adjacent apartment threw a grenade at the intelligence officers. A gun battle developed, and those inside hurled more grenades at the authorities.[19] Terrified neighbours called the local police, who were unaware of the super-secret activities of the ISI. In the ensuing confusion twenty policemen were injured, many by friendly fire.[20] Ramzi Binalshibh was among those captured.

In the spring of 2003 an intercepted email led to the arrest of Khalid Sheikh Mohammed, who was very close to bin Laden, and had been a key figure in the planning of the 9/11 attacks.[21] He was arrested at a house in Rawalpindi in a joint operation by ISI and the CIA's paramilitary force, the Special Activities

Division,[22] and taken to one of the CIA's secret prisons in northern Poland, where the US government has confirmed that he was repeatedly subjected to 'simulated drowning', or 'waterboarding'. Some of the information extracted from him related to Britain. Dame Eliza Manningham-Buller, the Director General of MI5, has commented:

*

When he was in detention in 2003, place unknown, he provided [the pseudonyms of] six individuals . . . who were involved in AQ activities in or against the UK. The Americans gave us this information . . . These included high-profile terrorists – an illustration of the huge amount of significant information that came from one man in detention in an unknown place.[23]

*

Interception had led to the capture of key suspects and informants. Thereafter, however, their handling left much to be desired. Cruelty and incompetence stood in for what should have been a sophisticated and patient in-depth interrogation. For example, Khalid Sheikh Mohammed was mostly questioned by a CIA officer who had never previously conducted an interrogation, and who did not speak Arabic.[24]

During 2002, both the British public and the security agencies remained convinced that Islamic terrorism was something that happened abroad.[25] However, in February 2003 the mood darkened following a warning of an imminent attack on Heathrow provided by GCHQ. At 6 o'clock on the morning of Tuesday, 11 February, Tony Blair authorised the deployment of 1,500 armed police and troops at the airport, together with light tanks from the Household Cavalry. A Nimrod MR2 reconnaissance aircraft patrolled the skies overhead to provide an immediate communications link-up for the forces. GCHQ had picked up information of an imminent 'spectacular' by extremists in London, involving a plan to smuggle Russian-made shoulder-launched Sam-7 surface-to-air missiles into the country, with the intention of bringing down an airliner. Almost immediately this was conflated by some journalists with government efforts to prepare public opinion for war with Iraq. John Reid, the Defence Secretary, reacted angrily to these suggestions, and insisted that the Heathrow plot was real: 'This is not a game. This is about a threat of the nature that massacred thousands of people in New York.'[26]

By 2003, counter-terrorism represented GCHQ's single largest allocation of effort. Moreover, the agency decided to increase its counter-terrorism activity by half as much again in 2004–05. Inevitably, this meant cuts elsewhere. It was decided to decrease collection in most geographical areas, and even to reduce the attention given to the proliferation of nuclear weapons. The only area that remained untouched was serious crime. Languages remained a problem at every level of sigint, whether at Cheltenham or on the front line, where, typically, exotic-language skills were required for the crews of Nimrod R1s flying sigint missions over Afghanistan. GCHQ established a specialist office in which staff (particularly linguists) who could not be granted high-level clearance could still do useful translation work. However, the Nimrod crews were often 50 per cent short of the ideal complement of linguists.[27]

Even while GCHQ was in the middle of a high-tempo counter-terrorist campaign, it was confronted with the distracting issue of Iraq. Political leaders in London and Washington were keen to highlight the country's reluctance to comply with UN resolutions requiring it to disarm. They now wanted to use secret intelligence for public education. For years Britain had insisted that intelligence from MI5, SIS and GCHQ was deadly secret. Suddenly, the Cabinet Office now decided that intelligence material should be disseminated to the general public in two dossiers. The first, produced on 24 September 2002, claimed to reveal the Iraqi President Saddam Hussein's continued nuclear, chemical and biological weapons activity. The second, released on 3 February 2003, dealt with Saddam's security agencies and the persecution of his people. The idea of war with Iraq was highly controversial, since the country appeared to have little connection with 9/11 or the current concerns about al Qaeda, and the unprecedented step of placing intelligence in the public domain to support the case for war raised a political storm. Journalists accused the Prime Minister's Press Secretary, Alastair Campbell, of undue influence in the intelligence process, and Campbell reacted angrily. Downing Street and the BBC then engaged in a prolonged sparring match throughout early 2003. For GCHQ, the dossier issues were relatively peripheral, since most of the intelligence Britain had gathered on Iraq's weapons came from human agents or defectors held by allied countries.[28]

However, if GCHQ thought it was comfortably out of the firing line on Iraq, it was wrong. At this point Blair had persuaded George Bush, rather against the President's judgement, to seek a second resolution in the UN Security Council, in the hope of strengthening the case for war. On Sunday, 2 March, the *Observer* revealed a highly sensitive memo from NSA to GCHQ asking for an accelerated eavesdropping campaign against the non-permanent members of the Security Council, such as Chile and Mexico. This was intended to permit greater diplomatic pressure to be applied to these smaller countries, whose votes were critical in the American effort to build support for military action against Iraq. The publication of this message caused an international furore. Sent by Frank Koza, a mid-level manager at NSA, it not only revealed the monitoring of allies and neutral nations, but also seemed to suggest the gerrymandering of votes in the hallowed councils of the United Nations. Unusually, the *Observer* printed it in full on its front page:

*

To: [Recipients withheld]
From: FRANK KOZA, Def Chief of Staff (Regional Targets)
CIV/NSA
Sent on Jan 31 2003 0:16
Subject: Reflections of Iraq Debate/Votes at UN-RT Actions +
          Potential for Related Contributions
Importance: HIGH
Top Secret//COMINT//X1

All,

As you've likely heard by now, the Agency is mounting a surge particularly directed at the UN Security Council (UNSC) members (minus US and GBR of course) for insights as to how the membership is reacting to the on-going debate RE: Iraq, plans to vote on any related resolutions, what related policies/negotiating positions they may be considering, alliances/dependencies, etc – the whole gamut of information that could give US policymakers an edge in obtaining results favorable to US goals or to head off surprises. In RT [Radio Traffic], that means a QRC [Quick Reaction Capability] surge effort to revive/create efforts against UNSC members Angola, Cameroon, Chile, Bulgaria and Guinea, as well as extra focus on Pakistan UN matters.

We've also asked ALL RT topi's [Radio Traffic – Targets of Primary Interest teams] to emphasize and make sure they pay attention to existing non-UNSC member UN-related and domestic comms for anything useful related to the UNSC deliberations/debates/votes. We have a lot of special UN-related diplomatic coverage (various UN delegations) from countries not sitting on the UNSC right now that could contribute related perspectives/insights/whatever. We recognize that we can't afford to ignore this possible source.

We'd appreciate your support in getting the word to your analysts who might have similar, more in-direct access to valuable information from accesses in your product lines. I suspect that you'll be hearing more along these lines in formal channels – especially as this effort will probably peak (at least for this specific focus) in the middle of next week, following the SecState's presentation to the UNSC.

Thanks for your help.[29]

*

The countries identified for increased targeting were members of a group called the 'Middle Six' on the Security Council, which was looking for a compromise solution. Their votes were being eagerly sought by both pro-war and anti-war factions. Pakistan and Bulgaria were thought to favour the United States, although it was by no means certain, while the rest were undecided. Nine votes were needed in the fifteen-member Security Council to approve a second resolution authorising military action against Iraq. Blair needed this resolution badly, but it was thought to be a close-run thing.[30]

The international atmosphere was febrile. Sigint was being publicly discussed everywhere. Intelligence experts were not surprised by the leaked Koza message, observing that listening in on the United Nations was routine. Indeed, in 1945 the United States had pressed for the UN headquarters to be in New York precisely in order to make eavesdropping easier.[31] However, the memo did a great deal of diplomatic damage to the British and American positions.[32] During early March Tony Blair was becoming increasingly frantic about securing a majority vote in the Security Council, since he felt his position as Prime Minister might depend on it.[33] In Chile, the public had long been sensitive to reports of 'dirty tricks' by intelligence agencies because of the alleged CIA coup that installed the dictator General Augusto Pinochet in 1973.[34] President Ricardo Lagos telephoned Blair on Sunday, 2 March, within hours of the *Observer* story appearing, and then twice again on the following Wednesday. The country's Foreign Minister, Soledad Alvear, fired a series of awkward questions about GCHQ at his opposite number in Britain, Jack Straw.[35]

The Mexican government was no less angry, and there were heated telephone calls to Downing Street. Months later the Mexicans were still pursuing the matter with Straw. The Mexican Foreign Minister wrote to him in December 2003, pressing him again on whether GCHQ was still spying on its friends in the United Nations. Aguilar Zinser, who had been Mexican Ambassador to the United Nations at the time, later explained

that in the week before what was expected to be a second resolution, the diplomats from the 'Group of Six' were in fact
working on their own secret plans for a compromise solution
which they hoped would avert war. 'Only the people in the
room knew what the document said,' recalls Zinser. He added
that the surprising thing was the very rapid nature of the
American response to the proposal. The meeting putting it
together took place in the evening, and Zinser received a call
from US diplomats early the next morning. He told them the
group was looking for a compromise. The Americans' response
was: 'Do not attempt it.' In the end it was the French who
pulled the plug on the possibility of a second UN resolution.
On 10 March President Jacques Chirac announced that France
would use its veto in the Security Council to block any such
move, resulting in public acrimony between Paris and
Washington. Few realised that war was now only ten days
away.[36]

Although the French and German governments were strongly
opposed to war with Iraq, their own intelligence services insisted
that the country had an active weapons of mass destruction
(WMD) programme. The fact that the respected German BND
loudly asserted this, even though Chancellor Gerhard Schröder
was opposed to war, convinced many independent observers
that there must be some hard evidence of Iraqi WMD. The
French DGSE was also telling President Chirac that Iraq had
WMD. However, the sagacious Chirac made his own assessments, and believed that the Western intelligence services were
deluded. In January 2003 he visited Hans Blix, the head of the
UN Monitoring, Inspection and Verification Commission, who
had been searching Iraq for evidence of WMD for many years.
Blix recalls that by then his team 'had begun to have some
doubts', although, by and large, even he still thought Iraq was
hiding some weapons. By contrast, Chirac was highly suspicious, and 'was among the first who doubted the intelligence
reports'. He understood how the Western intelligence agencies
worked, continually bringing their specialists together and devel-

oping a collective outlook that is often called 'groupthink'. Chirac put it rather well, asserting that the intelligence agencies had tended to 'intoxicate each other'.[37]

The leaked message to GCHQ reverberated for a long time. One of the challenges that had faced the *Observer*, before publishing it, had been verifying it as genuine. The world's top experts on sigint were certain that it was the real thing. James Bamford noted that words such as 'surge' and 'product lines' were NSA 'lingo', while Matthew Aid revealed that the purported author, Frank Koza, was indeed a senior operational manager at NSA.[38] They did not have to wait long for confirmation. A few days after the story was published, Katharine Gun, a twenty-eight-year-old Mandarin linguist at GCHQ, walked into the Cheltenham headquarters and told her supervisor, 'The leaker is me.' This was a surprise for GCHQ managers, who had never had a serious 'whistleblower'. SIS had struggled to silence its own whistleblower, Richard Tomlinson, in the 1990s, even arranging a dream job for him with a Formula One racing team in the hope of keeping him quiet. MI5 had pursued another whistleblower, the eccentric David Shayler, through the courts, and had tried to prevent its own former Director General, Stella Rimington, from publishing her memoirs. However, Cheltenham somehow never quite thought it would happen to them.[39]

Katharine Gun's decision to expose the NSA message was taken on the spur of the moment. On Friday, 31 January 2003 she had gone to work at GCHQ as usual. At about 10 o'clock she opened her emails. 'I could not believe what was on the screen,' she said. 'My thoughts were racing, really bizarre thoughts for me. I had never intended to do anything like that . . . ' In other words, she had not been looking for material to leak, but now she felt she was privy to the 'most secret workings of top government'. Moreover, it struck her that this document – if leaked – might well be used to impede military action against Iraq. Gun's critics have since denounced her for naïvety, asserting that someone working for GCHQ should have understood that sigint agencies monitor everyone, including friends and neutrals, even the United

Nations. Her response to this was that the memo exposed a lie. London and Washington claimed to be working for a diplomatic solution, but in fact they seemed to be trying to avoid one.[40] They also seemed to be trying to manipulate the key vote in the Security Council by 'bullying' the smaller members. She recalls being horrified and angry.[41]

The Monday morning after the story broke, GCHQ began an immediate leak inquiry, interviewing over a hundred staff who had seen the email. Gun had not expected the *Observer* to reproduce the entire text on the front page, and had been 'absolutely terrified' when she saw it. Although she denied her action during her security interview, a few days later her nerve crumbled and she confessed to her line manager. She was taken to GCHQ's Security Division, then interviewed by Special Branch from London. She never returned to GCHQ.[42] The case, which ran for over a year, was headline news. To her supporters she was the 'the spy who tried to stop a war'. Others were less complimentary. David Blunkett, the Home Secretary, insisted that the NSA memo had been 'doctored' before publication, and believed that Gun was motivated by the fact that her husband, a Kurdish asylum-seeker, was being removed from the country.[43]

No less significant than the leaked email from NSA was another message that had been sent to all staff in GCHQ the previous week. The issue of possible war against Iraq was causing growing anxiety among staff at Cheltenham, and a senior official had tried to address their concerns, assuring them that they would not be asked to participate in anything unlawful, and that British troops would not go into action unless the Attorney General, Lord Goldsmith, had advised the Prime Minister that it was legal. This was to prove important nine months later, since Katharine Gun's acquittal of charges under the Official Secrets Act turned precisely upon the Attorney General's legal opinion on military action. Because of the GCHQ email underlining the importance of lawfulness, Gun's defence team asked to see the full text of Goldsmith's opinion on the legality of the Iraq War. At this point the government's lawyers crumbled.

Despite the fact that Gun had admitted her actions, the Crown Prosecution Service dropped the case 'for lack of evidence' within twenty-four hours. The government did not wish to reveal Goldsmith's full legal opinion under any circumstances, since it was equivocal. This in turn underlined the fact that journalists had been barking up the wrong tree with their obsession over the Iraq dossiers, their testy arguments with Alastair Campbell and the supposed fact that Saddam would be capable of deploying his WMD at forty-five minutes' notice. The Katharine Gun case showed, rather belatedly, that some of the bigger issues relating to the approach of war had been missed by the press.[44]

GCHQ monitoring of the United Nations remained stubbornly in the headlines. In February 2004, Clare Short, who had resigned her Cabinet post as Minister for Overseas Development, offered her own testimony about listening in on the UN, declaring on prime-time television that she had routinely seen sigint on Secretary General Kofi Annan's conversations that had taken place in his private office at the UN headquarters in New York during the period before the war. Just as with Mo Mowlam in Northern Ireland in the 1990s, the whole matter of interception had a rather surreal quality. Short said: 'I have seen transcripts of Kofi Annan's conversations. In fact, I have had conversations with Kofi in the run-up to war thinking, "Oh dear, there will be a transcript of this, and people will see what he and I are saying." '[45] This was embarrassing, since it not only showed that GCHQ had been intercepting Annan's phone calls and emails, but also that a clandestine listening device had been surreptitiously planted in his office.[46]

As war drew closer, Clare Short took an unusual step. 'I had decided that I ought to inform Kofi that transcripts of his conversations as well as draft papers were circulated by British intelligence.' This monitoring had seemed harmless when Britain was working closely with the Secretary General, but now she considered that it had become 'insidious'. When the Katharine Gun case erupted, Short spoke on BBC Radio 4's *Today* programme and revealed that 'We were also spying on Kofi Annan's office.' Following this interview, she recalls, 'All hell broke loose,' and she received a warning from Tony Blair.[47] However, she was not deterred. On 29 February 2004 she was a guest on the Jonathan Dimbleby programme on ITV. Here she displayed a letter from the Cabinet Secretary, Andrew Turnbull, rebuking her for discussing signals intelligence in public and threatening her with unspecified 'further action' if she did not stop talking about GCHQ.[48]

GCHQ's most important potential military contribution to the war against Iraq was in its first few hours. Reportedly, late on 19 March 2003, Cheltenham discovered that Saddam Hussein was meeting senior commanders at a house called Dora Farms in the prosperous Mansour district on the southern outskirts of Baghdad. A number of special forces personnel from Britain and the United States were already operating inside Baghdad, as were two members of Germany's BND. They were asked to confirm the information. At about 6 o'clock on the morning of 20 March, Baghdad time, the opening of hostilities saw two American F-117 bombers hammer the area, dropping four two-thousand-pound bunker-busting bombs, leaving a crater sixty feet deep.[49] Two weeks later, the British asserted that they had intelligence from GCHQ that Saddam left the area minutes before the bombing, but had been injured. However, the CIA remained 'cautiously optimistic they got him'. Reporters later discovered that the bombs had missed their target, and had instead flattened three neighbouring buildings. Reportedly, the strike was triggered by the Iraqi leadership's use for communications among themselves of an old system made by the British company Racal which had been monitored.[50]

Accompanying Britain's land forces were two mobile sigint units, in the form of the Army's 14 Signals Regiment and the Royal Marines' Y Troop. Most of the staff of Y Troop flew out to Kuwait in the last week of January 2003. Usefully, some of them had recently been on an eight-week Arabic course. They were located at a Kuwaiti training camp, allowing some of their detachments to be deployed to Mutlar Ridge, overlooking the Iraqi frontier, which allowed them to test equipment and to liaise with the US Marines' 1st Radio Battalion, which was also a field sigint unit. After about a month, Y Troop spread out along the border in small detachments to listen to the enemy and await instructions to advance. Their main equipment was three Odette sigint systems, mounted on Land Rovers with their distinctive twenty-foot aerials. However, there were technical problems, so most of Y Troop was sent forward with smaller man packs as radio reconnaissance teams, working alongside 40 Commando. This was front-line work, and they were soon amongst the tanks of the Queen's Dragoon Guards, listening in on enemy positions at very close range as British armour advanced towards the southern town of Basra.[51]

Eventually the technical problems with the Odette aerials were fixed by 14 Signals Regiment, the Army's main electronic warfare unit, allowing Y Troop to go back to longer-range intercept work. At this point a small Iraqi patrol found them, and managed to launch some RPG rockets at their encampment before being seen off with a barrage of automatic fire. There were no casualties, but it was a sharp reminder of the hazards of forward interception. Thereafter, the number of targets they were tracking became progressively smaller as Iraqi soldiers deserted their positions. A notable discovery was the location of their counterparts, the Iraqi 124 Electronic Warfare Regiment. It was noted with satisfaction that this became '124 Crater Regiment' after the application of well-directed artillery fire.[52]

As the British First Armoured Division advanced towards Basra, sigint provided timely warnings of ambushes that had been set up by Saddam's Fedayeen guerrillas. It also obtained good information on the movements of key Iraqi leaders inside Basra itself.[53] Sigint performed well in Iraq because many of the old problems of intelligence support to the front-line soldier had been solved. For the first time in perhaps fifty years, sigint flowed freely from national assets down to operational units, a stunning breakthrough when set against the history of patchy

GCHQ support for previous major campaigns. Instead, the problem was sharing between allies. The Americans were well-equipped with pilotless drones that collected both imagery and sigint, of which the British felt the lack. As the initial invasion turned into a gruelling insurgency there was also a shortage of personnel who were experienced in running human agents. Some British sigint was being fed into American databases which then proved to be 'for American eyes only', causing frustration at the front line. There was no sharing of sigint with minor allies. In fairness to British and American intelligence agencies, while they had performed poorly on the issue of Iraqi WMD, they had accurately predicted the difficulties of a hostile occupation and the prolonged insurgency.[54]

As the Iraq War commenced, GCHQ's Director, Sir Francis Richards, was preparing to depart to become Governor of Gibraltar. After a succession of three 'outsiders' as Director, GCHQ was being handed back to one of its own, the fifty-five-year-old Dr David Pepper. Joining GCHQ in 1972 after completing a D.Phil. in physics at Oxford University, he had risen to be Director of Administration by 1995, and served as 'aide de camp' during the Roger Hurn review.[55] Pepper not only had a new role, he also had a brand-new office, located behind the gleaming glass doors of 'the Doughnut', GCHQ's impressive new headquarters at Benhall. The first wave of staff was preparing to move in during August 2003, and senior officials assured reporters that even the builders had gone through security checks: 'We didn't want a repeat of the American Embassy in Moscow, which was riddled with bugs.' The building was secure, but unfortunately it was not big enough. Planned during the 1990s contraction of intelligence, it was now too small to hold all of the GCHQ staff, which with the surge against terrorism was now approaching 5,300. About five hundred of these could not be permanently accommodated, so some buildings were retained on the old Oakley site, and 'hot desking' was the order of the day.[56]

'The Doughnut' had proved to be surprisingly troublesome. In late 1999 there had been dire warnings about a massive overspend on its computer equipment, and as a result the Cabinet Secretary, Richard Wilson, had asked Lieutenant General Sir Edmund Burton to review every aspect of GCHQ's business management.[57] Burton had some good ideas, but he could not fix the IT overspend which had triggered the review. When GCHQ planned its new building in the late 1990s, its technicians were still mentally living in the late 1980s. As David Pepper later explained, at that time its computers tended to be stand-alone systems, often quite large, but not interconnected. This reflected the fact that GCHQ's main adversaries were also 'large, monolithic, essentially static targets' like Russia. By the mid-1990s the organisation was faced with much more volatile targets, requiring flexible approaches, and this accelerated GCHQ's move towards computer networking. Yet the planners still envisaged a simple box-move into the new building, which meant switching everything off. Nobody stood back and said, 'Just a minute. It's not going to work like that, because of the degree of networking.'[58]

GCHQ's original guess at the cost of moving its computers had been £41 million over two years. It was now a breathtaking £450 million.[59] Parliament was incensed, and MPs were doubly angry because this kind of mistake had happened many times before. The computer costs of the new MI5 and SIS buildings had also rocketed. There were other precedents. The most obvious was a secret defence programme called 'Project Pindar', a top-level command bunker hidden under the southern end of the Ministry of Defence main building.[60] This vast complex also included facilities for 'Cobra', the Cabinet emergency committee room.[61] Although partly a civil project, the costs were buried within the Ministry of Defence budget.[62] The agreed cost eventually quadrupled, and much of this had to do with the computers and communications equipment. There had been a similar experience with a disastrous Defence Intelligence Staff computer scheme called 'Trawlerman', which had to be abandoned. In 1996, MI5's computerised system code-named 'Grant' had also failed miserably, and was scrapped at a total cost of over £20 million.[63] Indeed, there were so many precedents that MPs could not begin to understand why officials had not learned from this string of disasters.[64]

GCHQ's mammoth overspend caused real friction within the intelligence community, since MI5 and SIS feared that their budgets would be squeezed to make up the cost.[65] In the event, David Pepper was saved by circumstances, since the increased tempo of counter-terrorist activity made the case for uninterrupted operations unanswerable. Nevertheless, in the autumn of 2003 Parliament discovered that GCHQ had wasted further millions on new systems that had been bought to intercept terrorist communications. A costly prototype of a system that GCHQ hoped would increase its ability to listen in to terrorist traffic had only 'partly delivered'.[66] This was coded Whitehall language for 'The computer system has failed and has been scrapped.' MPs complained that 'Security cannot be used as a smokescreen for incompetence.'[67] Notwithstanding this, it has to be conceded that operational continuity at GCHQ had proved valuable in the recent past. On 24 January 2000 a catastrophic failure of NSA's powerful computers halted the processing of American intelligence at Fort Meade in Maryland for more than three days. GCHQ took up some of the strain, and American customers were served directly from Cheltenham.[68]

By the summer of 2003, no one was taking much notice of GCHQ's financial misdemeanours. Instead, the hot intelligence issue was the 'missing' Iraqi WMD, which had been the main justification for going to war. Four months after the invasion, no WMD had been found. The decision to invade Iraq had been politically divisive, and the patience of the British public had run out. There followed an unprecedented 'season of inquiry' into the secret services, with no fewer than four British investigations into intelligence aspects of Iraqi WMD between July 2003 and July 2004. The issues were looked at by the

Parliamentary Select Committee on Foreign Affairs, and then by the Intelligence and Security Committee. A third inquiry, chaired by Lord Hutton, looked into the death of Dr David Kelly, a government scientist who had been a key defence intelligence expert, and who was closely cross-examined during the first inquiry. None of this assuaged the intense public anger, so finally, in early 2004, Lord Butler, who had been Cabinet Secretary under John Major, was called in to conduct a much wider investigation into British intelligence and WMD over the previous decade.

The controversy persuaded veteran Cheltenham staff to break their customary silence. In a letter to *The Times* in February 2004, Douglas Nicoll, the senior GCHQ officer who had previously reviewed the JIC's performance on attack warning, denounced Tony Blair's recent explanations before Parliament about how the JIC had interacted with other parts of the intelligence machine over Iraq as having 'the highest degree of improbability', and asserted that 'politicos' from No.10 had become involved in the intelligence process. Nicoll considered that this was 'unprecedented', and that there was much for Lord Butler to investigate.[69]

Everyone was asking the same question. Was the Iraqi WMD fiasco a product of intelligence failure by the agencies, or of deception by politicians and spin doctors? Inevitably, the answer is 'both'. Having badly underestimated Iraqi WMD stocks prior to the First Gulf War in 1991, intelligence officers did not want to be caught out a second time, and so opted for 'worst-case analysis'. In other words, they over-corrected. Moreover, the allies cooperated so closely on WMD estimates that, far from challenging each other's findings, they succumbed to a form of 'groupthink'. Only the Dutch and Canadian intelligence communities expressed serious doubts. Butler revealed that a lot of British intelligence had come from a handful of human agents run by SIS who were not properly 'validated', and whose material was mediocre at best.[70] The awkward evidence still continues to accumulate. Tyler Drumheller, the CIA Europe

Division Chief, who worked closely with Britain's SIS, has revealed that Naji Sabri, Iraq's Foreign Minister, did a deal to reveal the country's military secrets. Drumheller recounts that once policy-makers learned what Sabri had to say – that Iraq had no active WMD programme – 'They stopped being interested in the intelligence.'[71]

There was also blatant political dishonesty. The British government had made three assertions in its WMD dossier. First, that there was plausible intelligence to suggest that the Iraqis might have hidden some old biological or chemical stocks from 1991. This was true, but these weapons were unlikely to be usable, and were at best of historical interest. Second, that there was evidence that Iraq continued to seek nuclear components on the world market, and nurtured future ambitions. This was also true, but no one thought for a moment that the country had got far with reconstituting its nuclear programme. Everything turned on the third claim, that Iraq was engaged in continued production of WMD. This assertion was made forcibly by the Prime Minister in his personal foreword to the Iraqi WMD dossier in September 2002. There was no credible evidence for this.[72] Later, Blair assured the House of Commons that the intelligence was 'extensive, detailed, authoritative'. This statement was also deeply misleading.[73] Equally, Butler noticed that there was no change in the intelligence reports on Iraqi WMD during the period between 2002 and 2003, when the British government shifted dramatically from a policy of containing Iraq to one of confrontation.[74] Alastair Campbell summed this up best in his diary, noting that the hardest question was: 'Why now? What was it that we knew now that we didn't before that made us believe that we had to do it now?'[75]

In one respect, Lord Butler's report was odd. As we have seen, GCHQ produces the majority of Britain's intelligence. Astonishingly, in the 216 pages of the report 'GCHQ' appears only once, and that is in the list of abbreviations. It seems that Cheltenham was referred to in the text of an earlier draft, but in the published version all discussion of it has mysteriously disappeared. In fact Peter Freeman, a veteran GCHQ officer who served as the link between Cheltenham and the inquiry team, persuaded Butler to remove all direct references to GCHQ from the report.[76] The Butler inquiry is also an example of the masterly drawing of remits. Although it was not permitted to look at the link between intelligence and policy-making over Iraq, which is what everyone wanted to know about, curiously, it was allowed to make meandering historical digressions into intelligence on other WMD episodes as far back as 1990. These included work against the AQ Khan proliferation network in Pakistan and the winding up of President Gaddafi's nuclear programme in Libya. The case studies were selective: Butler went far enough back to find some successes, but not far enough to find other failures.[77]

Butler's inquiry into British intelligence, and parallel inquiries in the United States, underlined the strange new climate the intelligence agencies were working in. Although not exactly transparent, they were under the spotlight of investigation as never before. Trust in them had been badly corroded, and many thought it would take a decade to repair the damage. International teams of journalists, aided by dissident officials, were ripping the lid off each sensitive story in short order. Moreover, the British public was now highly suspicious about the increasing levels of surveillance at home and abroad. Yet simultaneously, the upsurge in international terrorism had led governments to call for a massive increase in secret intelligence activity of every kind. Understandably, no politicians wanted another 9/11 to happen on their watch. The balance between liberty and security was already a hot issue, and during 2005 it would become even hotter.[78]

From Bletchley Park to a
Brave New World?

*These new proposals suggest an intention to capture anything and
everything . . .*

UK internet service providers commenting on
government plans, August 2009[1]

At 8.50 on the morning of Thursday, 7 July 2005, four suicide
bombers attacked London. Following the classic al Qaeda
approach of multiple strikes, they bombed three tube trains
within the space of a minute, and an hour later attacked a bus
in Tavistock Square. Fifty-two people died and over seven
hundred were injured in what proved to be the most deadly
attack on the capital since the Second World War. Tony Blair
was away at the G-8 Summit at Gleneagles in Scotland, as
indeed were numerous specialist police units from London, sent
there to guard the visiting world leaders from marauding anti-
globalisation protesters. In the immediate wake of the attacks,
George Bush and Italy's Prime Minister Silvio Berlusconi argued
over whether the G-8 leaders should come to London to show
solidarity. In the end, Blair left his international guests in
Scotland and flew back to London to join his Cabinet colleagues
in the increasingly familiar surroundings of 'Cobra', deep
beneath Whitehall. Two weeks later, another wave of bombers
attempted a second attack, but failed due to technical problems
with their explosive devices. What most shocked the British
population was that these were suicide attacks by their own
nationals.[2] Dr David Pepper, Director of GCHQ, observed that
'What happened in July [2005] was a demonstration that there
were conspiracies going on about which we essentially knew

nothing.' The British government now had to rethink its surveillance strategy.[3]

GCHQ was now fighting on three fronts. It was taking a leading role in the so-called 'War on Terror' while supporting British forces in two major conflicts, in Iraq and Afghanistan. In the context of the prolonged insurgencies that had developed in both countries, the new idea was the 'Total Information Battlespace' that sought to connect strategic intelligence-gathering from satellites, and every other kind of source, with soldiers on the ground. The old idea that GCHQ would mostly support the 'high-ups' in Whitehall while the troops fended for themselves with their own tactical sigint collection or 'Y units' in ageing Land Rovers had been completely abandoned. The challenge was to bring together sigint from many sources, and indeed from many intelligence services, since both campaigns involved numerous national contingents from places as diverse as Spain, Denmark and Ukraine. Sigint connectivity with the Americans was still a difficult issue. British, Australian and Canadian special forces, which were never shy when it came to speaking their minds, asserted that this problem had cost allied lives in the early part of the campaign in Afghanistan. Almost no sigint was shared with the Iraqi or Afghan forces, despite the efforts to rebuild them.

One of the most effective allied sigint operations was run by a Dutch intelligence chief who belonged to NATO's International Security Assistance Force (ISAF) around Kabul. General Joop van der Reijn spent the months before his departure to Afghanistan joining up the intelligence practices of the Dutch and German forces. Once he had arrived, one of his most valuable innovations was improvised local sigint. He took over a building and filled it with low-cost 'off the shelf' radio intercept equipment that was commercially available. Two dozen former Afghan policemen were selected to become translators and eventually sigint monitors. Any problems with the rudimentary equipment were more than offset by the ability of this unit to comprehend the innumerable dialects and opaque inferences in the Taliban conversations they intercepted. This unit took a little time to set up 'given the Afghan way of doing business', but eventually it became an invaluable part of the Joint Security Coordination Centre, which was ISAF's intelligence hub.[4]

On the ground, much of the British sigint work in Afghanistan and Iraq was conducted by Light Electronic Warfare Teams, or LEWTs, from Britain's last remaining dedicated field sigint unit, 14 Signals Regiment.[5] Although it deployed the same vehicle-mounted equipment that had been effective in Yugoslavia, namely the Odette sigint system and the Vampire direction-finding system, much of the important work was done on foot at dangerously close range. The main instrument of the sigint war in Afghanistan was 'Scarus', a portable interception kit operated by four-man teams which looked rather like a back-pack radio with oversized aerials. This was introduced in the summer of 2003, and by 2004 a dozen units were operational. The range of Scarus is only ten miles, and this meant forward monitoring operations. Scarus was often supplemented by commercially purchased hand-held scanners of the sort used by aircraft enthusiasts to listen in to air traffic control towers. Again this was improvised sigint, since these could be used most effectively by Afghan guides accompanying infantry patrols.[6]

British sigint operators often worked with their NATO colleagues. In 2006 they teamed up with Danish electronic warfare operators in Afghanistan's Helmand province under the Sigint/EW Operations Centre in Regional Command (South). Their work earned them praise as 'battle-winners', providing real-time force protection and situational awareness. Many of the senior army commanders were experiencing the enormous potential of sigint for the first time. Intense operational pressure led to experimentation. The most remarkable achievement was linking up sigint aircraft circling overhead to the four-man LEWTs embedded with Parachute Regiment companies, and also serving the platoon-sized long-range patrols.

However, the cost was high. LEWT troops lost four men in

action in the period up to January 2008.[7] Among those killed
was Lance Corporal Jabron Hashmi, the first British Muslim
soldier to be killed on active duty in Afghanistan. He died along
with another sigint specialist, Corporal Peter Thorpe, when they
were hit by a rocket-propelled grenade during a firefight near
Sangin. Born in Pakistan, less than an hour from the border
with Afghanistan, Hashmi had come to Britain with his family
when he was aged twelve. He had joined the Army and undergone specialist training at the Defence Intelligence and Security
Centre at Chicksands before being posted to the Army's main
sigint unit. The local Parachute Regiment commanders spoke
of the vital protection his specialist work had provided to their
patrols.[8] GCHQ also sent significant numbers of people out to
Iraq and Afghanistan: managers were surprised by the willingness of staff from Cheltenham to volunteer for these very
arduous postings.[9]

The Royal Marines were prominent in the Afghanistan
campaign, and had their own dedicated tactical sigint unit, in
the form of Y Squadron from 3 Commando Brigade. Again the
emphasis was on a front-line approach, with mobile Radio
Reconnaissance Teams accompanying patrols. In May 2007 the
Royal Marines located and eventually killed the Taliban's most
important chief, Mullah Dadullah, in an operation that was
driven by sigint. He had been tracked across Helmand province
by intercepting the calls he made to his brother on a satellite
phone.[10] By January 2009, commanders boasted of six thousand significant intercepts and in the region of seven hundred
enemy call signs identified. The most significant contribution
was advance warnings of enemy ambushes in Helmand which
saved many lives. Once patrols understood what Y Squadron's
capabilities were, they wanted to take a Radio Reconnaissance
Team with them every time they went out on patrol. Fusing
sigint from tactical, operational and even strategic platforms was
the new style of intelligence operations. The main vehicle for
this was the recently formed in-theatre Sigint Electronic Warfare
Operation Centre. Experiences in Afghanistan after 2002 led to

a new overall sigint approach for NATO, tried out first in Operation 'Trail Hammer' in 2006. The objective was to share sigint seamlessly between GCHQ, the Nimrods of 51 Squadron, ships with dedicated sigint collection suites like HMS *Cornwall*, and forward sigint collectors. A high priority is extending this sort of support to units like the SAS.[11]

Circling overhead in Afghanistan were Nimrod R1 reconnaissance aircraft. Although the R1 sigint variants of these planes operate regularly over Afghanistan, the majority of Nimrods used there were maritime reconnaissance aircraft, originally designed to search for submarines. Given that Afghanistan is without benefit of a coastline, or even large stretches of water, this may seem peculiar. Their presence was required because until 2010, Britain lacked effective unmanned reconnaissance aircraft, or 'drones', of the sort operated by the Americans, since the type of drone initially purchased by the British, called 'Phoenix', was much inferior, and would not fly in hot weather or at the altitudes required for operations in Afghanistan.[12] Indeed, when deployed in Iraq in 2003, one drone had been lost for every six missions flown. As a result, the ageing fleet of Nimrod maritime reconnaissance aircraft, six of which had some real-time video surveillance capability, was stretched to the limit serving as temporary drones and sigint collectors. One of these planes suffered a calamitous explosion in September 2006, with the loss of sixteen lives. In-flight refuelling of Nimrods was halted for a period, and then they were all grounded, leaving troops dangerously exposed.[13]

Belatedly, the British purchased larger and more effective foreign-made drones. The most important model was the Watchkeeper 450, which had an impressive ability to listen in to Taliban communications. This was an Israeli-made device that had been used extensively to conduct missile attacks over Lebanon in 2006, and later over Gaza. For the British, the Watchkeeper provided much-needed video coverage and also greatly improved sigint, since at altitude, interception range is much better. Currently, the elderly Odette intercept system is being replaced with 'Soothsayer', which offers greater inter-operability with the Americans and a much higher level of automation. Significant investment in front-line sigint equipment to serve the troops is, at last, being made.

While circling over Afghanistan, the RAF's Nimrod R1s noticed something rather interesting. From 2005, it was increasingly common for these surveillance planes monitoring Taliban radio communications to come across militants speaking with Bradford or Birmingham accents. A case in point was Rashid Rauf, a Birmingham man sought by British police in connection with an August 2006 plot to bomb transatlantic airliners. He is believed to have escaped from a Pakistan prison in 2007, and was killed just inside Pakistan in a CIA missile attack on a militant stronghold in 2008. Intelligence officers observed privately: 'He's not the only British Muslim to die out here.' Predictably, this raised fears that experienced fighters might have returned home from Afghanistan to plot attacks in Britain, and it was not long before RAF aircraft with similar listening equipment began circling over British cities searching for returned Afghan fighters. Their brief was to seek out suspects using 'voice prints' of fighters with British accents that had been collected by the Nimrods from Taliban battlefield communications.[14]

The surveillance effort between the war in Afghanistan and the 'war' at home was now seamlessly connected. The RAF had purchased three Britten-Norman Islander aircraft which were equipped with sigint suites and used as airborne listening stations. Based at RAF Northolt in west London, they are used for covert surveillance by MI5, which provides the monitoring staff in the aircraft. In early 2007 they were used to support the West Midlands Police when tracking suspects connected to a plot to kidnap and behead a British Muslim soldier. These aircraft can fly at fairly high altitude, and have been seen loitering over the East End of London for long periods. They are also known to operate out of Leeds-Bradford Airport. Many have presumed that they were deployed as part of a post-9/11 surveillance effort, but newspapers have published photographs of an MI5 officer standing next to one of them as long ago as 1999.[15] Although run jointly by the RAF and MI5, like other 'Home Office' interception projects, this is partly a GCHQ activity, using technicians on temporary loan to the Home Office. It recalls Peter Wright's 'Airborne Rafter' programme in the late 1950s, again run jointly by MI5 and GCHQ, which searched for KGB spies by tracking their radios.[16] The residents in Muslim areas of Birmingham, Bradford, Leeds and London are not necessarily aware of the sigint flights, but they are highly sensitised to surveillance. 'You are always looking over your shoulder here,' remarked one local – even council workmen digging a hole in the road 'means MI5, GCHQ, and the installation of monitoring devices'.[17]

These British monitoring aircraft use a technology that was developed during the drug wars in Colombia in the early 1990s, when the sigint agencies were involved in a technical war against well-resourced cocaine cartels. Once Pablo Escobar, the head of the Medellin drugs cartel, had been killed in December 1993, other drug lords became more anxious about the vulnerability of their cell phones. Their response was to frequently change their phones to confuse the eavesdroppers. Remarkably, they could even make use of scanners to steal the identities of the phones of passers-by, which were then cloned. The answer was a new aerial technology which depended on small spy planes. Cessnas and other light aircraft were fitted with directional antennae and wide-band recorders to take all the traffic from across the major bands on the entire spectrum used by cell phones. A single aircraft could take much of the mobile phone traffic of an entire city by circling at a high altitude and sucking up the microwave signals that connect the cell sites to the phone networks. The plane then pushed the product to a ground station where a massive computer examined the audio content of each conversation using voice-recognition software. This technique has not been effective everywhere, since some regions do not have much in the way of cell phone systems. However, in the skies over Britain this is now an important element in the armoury of the intelligence agencies.[18]

Comparing voices recorded over Britain with voices recorded over Afghanistan underlined the fact that the boundary between foreign wars and domestic terrorism was now perilously thin. In 2006 GCHQ launched two new programmes subsumed under the broader 'SIGMod initiative', or sigint modernisation programme. The exact nature of this remains classified, but it clearly focuses on the way in which GCHQ collects, analyses, presents and disseminates intelligence about terrorism. The anxiety that Britain's oversight body, the Intelligence and Security Committee, has expressed about the need 'to ensure that new interception techniques are regulated by a proper legal framework' is another indication that the boundary between domestic and foreign communications is rapidly collapsing.[19] SIGMod has resulted in a twentyfold increase in GCHQ's ability to access, process and store material from internet-based communications, and 'vast sums of money' were spent on these two projects. Meanwhile, GCHQ decided to deploy yet more analysts to work alongside MI5 and other partners engaged in counter-terrorism.[20]

What was GCHQ's own reading of its growing place in what had proved to be an American-led 'War on Terror'? Detecting the broader political sensibilities of an entire secret service is not easy. However, by early 2006 there was a steady rise in staff asking difficult questions about legality, set against the background of high-profile issues such as CIA secret prisons in Europe that were spilling onto the front pages of Britain's newspapers. Inquiries by the Council of Europe and the European Parliament into this matter prompted the Intelligence and Security Committee to look at British involvement in what were often called 'extraordinary renditions', in other words the secret apprehension and transfer of terrorist suspects without warrant. The heads of MI5, SIS and GCHQ were all asked for their views. When questioned, Sir David Pepper, GCHQ's Director, seemed especially anxious to distance his organisation from the affair. On 29 November 2006 he explained that GCHQ had 'never knowingly provided support to a US rendition operation and we would not authorise the use of intelligence for that purpose . . . and we have never been asked to do so'. He added that GCHQ's only knowledge of the rendition programme 'has essentially flowed from what SIS have learnt and told the other Agencies'. On rendition, he insisted, GCHQ had no independent source of information, and had merely 'followed SIS's growing understanding of what the U.S. was doing'. Pepper then outlined the standard guidance given to GCHQ's analysts for situations in which they fear that unlawful behaviour might result from supplying intelligence to a foreign partner. This included possible upward referral, 'ultimately to Ministerial level'. One gets a strong sense that not all aspects of the 'War on Terror' have sat comfortably with GCHQ's management board.[21]

The stormiest current issues for GCHQ have little to do with the United States. Instead they have everything to do with the troubled business of domestic interception. While the British government tends to present GCHQ as a foreign intelligence service like SIS, mainly concerned with the interception of foreign communications, as we have seen, the distinction between foreign and domestic is eroding fast. The claim that all domestic interception is now authorised by individual warrants requires an increasingly ingenious interpretation of the law, and there is considerable evidence of wholesale collection of communications. Indeed, several new developments mean that GCHQ has little choice but to head down the road towards wholesale collection, since many international groups such as terrorists and criminal gangs overlap seamlessly, with dispersed elements within British society.[22]

The issue of what is a domestic communication and what is foreign has been further muddied by Britain's membership of the European Union. In recent years Britain has been attempting to persuade Europe to take on some of the odious burden of legislating for electronic surveillance of its own population. British Ministers wanted Europe to pass legislation that would require mobile phone companies and internet service providers to retain vast amounts of records relating to personal emails, details of web pages accessed and telephone calls for ten years, and for these to be made accessible to the police and intelligence services on request. The proposals were denounced by privacy campaigners as among the most wide-ranging extensions of government security surveillance over private individuals.[23] Their main opponent was the internet industry itself, which resisted them vehemently, again stressing issues of privacy. In reality, its anxieties reflected pressure from business customers, since the authorities have a track record of being cavalier with personal data. They also reflect concerns about the high cost of storing data including the names and addresses of customers, the source and destination of their emails, websites visited and phone numbers called. All of this would be freely available to the authorities, since only access to the actual content of emails and telephone calls would require a warrant. GCHQ continually pressed for this, and in 2006 it finally passed into European law.[24]

GCHQ has also constituted a powerful but hidden voice in the debate over the proposed use of telephone intercepts in court. The British police and customs would like to see this legalised, but Cheltenham is adamantly opposed, arguing that it would sensitise GCHQ targets to the fact that they were vulnerable to surveillance. This is an element of the age-old tension between secret knowledge and the active use of secret knowledge, which has bedevilled sigint since its inception. Since 2001, several Home Secretaries have pressed for a review of the law, and have questioned why intercepted telephone conversations can only serve in court as 'intelligence', with their existence concealed from the defence. In 2004, Cabinet Ministers were presented with an inter-agency study entitled 'Review of Intercept as Evidence', the fifth occasion in ten years on which this matter had been debated. In 2005, limited use of intercepts as evidence appeared about to be approved when GCHQ intervened at the last minute, citing new technical developments and, remarkably, exercising a veto.[25] There are strange anomalies in the law as it stands. A conversation collected by a radio microphone bug is admissible in court, but telephone intercepts are not. Moreover, telephone intercepts collected in other countries are admissible in British courts: when a former Merseyside narcotics squad chief was convicted over his corrupt relationship with a drugs baron, the prosecution depended on wiretap evidence from Holland.[26] Rather sniffily, GCHQ explained that intercept evidence from other European countries can be used freely because Britain 'is the only country which has . . . a strategic intercept and SIGINT capacity that is worth protecting'.[27]

GCHQ's bizarre policy on phone-tap evidence is highlighted by American attempts to extradite the radical Muslim cleric Abu Hamza al-Masri (known to the British tabloid press as 'Hooky') on terrorist charges. Cheltenham had allegedly intercepted telephone discussions between Abu Hamza and a group that had kidnapped Western tourists in Yemen. Secret recordings of these conversations were made in December 1998 by experts from GCHQ who listened in on a specially purchased satellite phone. The transcripts were passed to MI5 and Special Branch in early 1999. This material cannot be used in British courts. However, almost identical material collected by NSA is likely to be central to any case against Abu Hamza mounted by the Americans. The British authorities are reportedly highly embarrassed that they have been shown to have evidence suggestive of persons involved in kidnapping and murder, yet did not take stronger action.[28] In March 2009 the use of telephone intercept evidence was revisited for the sixth time in a decade, and it is now technically permitted, but is subject to so many conditions – including a GCHQ veto – that experts believe that in practice it will never be used in court. Iain Lobban, the current Director of GCHQ, has continued to assert that its use would represent 'a very, very serious blow back to our capability'.[29]

Each time the use of intercept evidence in court has been suggested, it has been supported by the Prime Minister and the

Home Secretary. The current Director of Public Prosecutions, Keir Starmer, and his predecessor, Ken Macdonald, are also in favour, and recently blamed 'the spying agencies' for the lack of progress. The ability of GCHQ to block the proposal is testimony to its considerable secret power within Whitehall and Westminster. Quite apart from the issue of secrecy, GCHQ does not wish to be drawn into the time-consuming business of preparing evidence for court proceedings. However, intercepts would resolve many difficult cases, including some of those relating to people currently held under what is effectively house arrest by means of controversial Control Orders. Many believe that the intercepts that supported these Control Orders would also have facilitated effective prosecutions.[30]

In 2008 the Home Secretary Jacqui Smith unveiled a new domestic intercept plan of truly breathtaking proportions when she announced the remarkable Intercept Modernisation Programme, or 'IMP'. Costing an estimated £12 billion pounds, this project dwarfed even the massive Cheltenham 'Doughnut', and amounted to a surveillance concept so vast that it was beyond the bounds of the imagination. Given that intelligence-related IT projects have routinely run over budget by several times their agreed cost, it is hardly surprising that the Treasury squeaked with fear at the very mention of such an idea. The oddest feature of the IMP was that, despite the fact that Europe had finally agreed to compel internet service providers to retain all of their customers' communications data within their own companies, the plan was to build a vast government-run silo to duplicate exactly the same function, recording and storing the details of every telephone call, email, text message and instance of web access by every person in Britain. The scheme was initially associated with the innocuously titled Communications Data Bill scheduled for 2009. Its stated purpose was bland – to 'allow communications data capabilities for the prevention and detection of crime and protection of national security to keep up with changing technology'. However, Lord Carlile of Berriew QC, Britain's independent reviewer of antiterrorist legislation, immediately expressed anxiety about the new government-run database: 'As a raw idea it is awful.' He added that it would lead to the authorities undertaking searches 'willy-nilly' and without review. Richard Thomas, the Information Commissioner, also denounced the IMP plans as 'a step too far', and entirely contrary to the British way of life.[31]

In late 2008, growing public hostility to IMP prompted the government to withdraw the Bill at the last minute. Instead, it has resolved to advance the plan by stealth. Remarkably, and without any legislation, a pilot scheme at an estimated cost of £2 billion is already under way, with sample 'probes' established at the facilities of one major fixed line telecom operator and one major mobile phone provider. The Home Office Minister, Lord West, has emphasised the important place of the private sector in this scheme. One alleged beneficiary is the security company Detica, which was bought in 2008 by BAE Systems Ltd. Located in Guildford, it manufactures the strange black boxes – which enjoy the unlikely title of 'deep packet sniffers' – that enable intelligence services to siphon off material from the internet. Unlike the current black boxes that vacuum up content, the IMP would be a vast database of 'who contacted who' and 'who looked at what'. By analysing a person's social network as defined by their telephone calls, texts and emails, and then overlaying their internet use or combining it with their credit-card activity, an enormously detailed picture can be constructed of every individual and those they associate with.[32]

The British government has always insisted that IMP is merely about maintaining an existing and traditional capability to carry out interception in a world of rapidly changing technology. However, the reality looks rather different. In April 2009 the government advertised for senior staff to direct an ambitious programme called 'Mastering the Internet'. With a title that might well have been borrowed from an episode of *Doctor Who*, this initiative could have been deliberately calculated to provoke anxiety on the part of privacy campaigners. Indeed, there was so much controversy in the press that, unusually, in May 2009

GCHQ had to issue an express denial. It stated: 'GCHQ is not developing technology to enable the monitoring of all internet use and phone calls in Britain, or to target everyone in the UK.' GCHQ's argument is that the nature of telephone calls is changing, and they are increasingly passed over the internet. Without this new programme it will lose the intercept capability it has always had. However, this glosses over the fact that because it is difficult to separate out telephone calls from other kinds of internet traffic, and equally difficult to separate out records of who called who from actual call content, this modernisation unavoidably means a vast increase in collection.[33]

In August 2009, GCHQ's denial that it had ambitions for massive surveillance met a direct challenge when Britain's own telecommunications firms and internet service providers, including British Telecom and Virgin, condemned the IMP plan as an unwarranted intrusion into people's privacy. The very companies that the British government was depending upon to help it to implement the scheme asserted strongly that government officials were not being straight with the public about the vast scale of monitoring they were planning. Their statement told the government that:

*

We view the description of the government's proposals as 'maintaining' the capability as disingenuous: the volume of data the government now proposes [we] should collect and retain will be unprecedented, as is the overall level of intrusion into the privacy of citizenry . . . This is a purely political description that serves to win consent by hiding the extent of the proposed extension of powers for the state.

*

The companies also boggled at the mammoth scale of the private information they were being asked to retain on the telephone and internet use of British citizens: they complained that they did not even know of any equipment that would enable them to acquire and retain such a wide range of data.[34]

What does government want with all this detail? Even more

puzzling is the fact that it is prepared to spend vast amounts of money to store this data itself, when it has already compelled the telecom companies and internet service providers to hold the same information. The answer is 'data-mining', the use of computers to comb through unimaginable amounts of information looking for patterns and statistical relationships. This practice now constitutes the most insidious threat to personal liberty. What makes surveillance different in the age of ubiquitous computing and the mobile phone is that our data is never thrown away. Machines routinely store millions of details about our everyday lives, and at some point in the future it will be possible to bring these all together and search them. Devices which were introduced to make life more convenient are also generating a detailed electronic narrative of our lives. In 2009 the British public sent sixty billion text messages, a fantastically detailed record of our personal interactions. At 'Googleplex', the corporate headquarters of Google, located at Mountain View in California, the company retains a record of every Google search a person has made on the internet for two years. In other words, in its memory banks Google effectively contains 'virtual individuals' that consist of a cross section of each user's interests, tastes and thoughts. A decade ago, such data was discarded by many companies, but with the cost of warehousing it halving every two years, many now choose to retain it.[35]

NSA is already close to completing its own mammoth data silo. Located in a remote desert area of Utah, this facility is 'above top secret' and boasts a million square feet of space. Here, America's largest intelligence agency stores the electronic detritus of the everyday lives of the nation's citizens. Billons of phone calls, text messages, emails, web searches, passenger lists and parking tickets will be warehoused here forever. Supercomputers will use elaborate programmes to trawl for suspicious relationships and patterns within this data.[36] Where NSA goes today, GCHQ will go tomorrow. Sure enough, industry insiders have alleged that a similar centre is now being created inside 'the Doughnut' at Cheltenham, where a vast room of super-computers will hold an immense pool of personal information and protected data. Because it is not actual call or email content, no warrants are required for the authorities to gain access to this material, allowing limitless trawling of everyone.[37] This is a whole new world of intelligence. Indeed, it is not really intelligence as we have traditionally understood it. In one sense it is a kind of sigint, given that much of it is derived from telephone calls, emails, texts and internet activity sent by means of a signal. However, very little of it is in code, so it is merely private or 'protected information' rather than 'top secret'. Moreover, much of this information is from passenger transport lists and credit-card transactions, so it is initially collected by corporations, not government. What governments now wish to do is take this data over and use it to produce a wholly new kind of intelligence.

Data-mining, which allows governments to search for individuals or groups of people with particular types of behaviour, and to profile them as suspicious, is as powerful as it is dangerous. It is powerful because it allows the sifting of titanic amounts of private information, and it is dangerous because it often throws up 'false positives'. In other words, some people will look suspicious because a number of chance activities have coalesced to generate something which a computer thinks is a problem.[38] At present, data-mining is limited because government can only access so much information. But the appetite is clearly there. Under the Regulation of Investigatory Powers Act (RIPA) 2000, the British authorities can ask internet service providers or mobile phone companies to hand over details of the phone, email and internet habits of specific individuals without seeking a warrant. A staggering 504,073 such requests were made in 2008. Although this is too many, it is still 'retail surveillance', because it relates to individual persons. Data-mining is the next step, and to do this the authorities need constant access to everyone's data.

IMP has been presented as a Home Office project, but just like GTAC, it will be impossible to implement without the participation of GCHQ. Predictably, GCHQ is now recruiting more experts in data-mining. Recent job advertisements for Cheltenham state: 'At GCHQ, we are leaders in the emerging field of data stream mining,' and that 'the next few years are guaranteed to be an exciting time' because of several new technologies which are 'set to dramatically change the way large volumes of information are analysed'. Areas in which GCHQ is currently looking for skilled personnel include 'development and interrogation of large databases', 'data-warehousing' and 'machine learning'. The latter is defined as 'classification, prediction, clustering, pattern finding'.[39]

The growth of this powerful technical surveillance has alarmed senior lawyers and judges. On 20 October 2008, Sir Ken Macdonald QC, the Director of Public Prosecutions, delivered a public lecture shortly before his retirement. Entitled 'Coming Out of the Shadows', its subject was nothing less than technology and the future of freedom. He explained that the same technology that has given us the impression that everything in the world is at our fingertips, and has made our lives immeasurably richer, has simultaneously given the state enormous powers. Because mobile phones and computers are ubiquitous, the government now has access to information about each one of us, and the ability to collect and store it at will 'every second of the day, in everything we do'. He added that while this technology is important in the struggle against serious crime, the public also needs to understand that we are rapidly approaching a cliff-edge. He warned that

*

... decisions taken in the next few months and years about how the State may use these powers, and to what extent, are likely to be irreversible. They will be with us forever. And they in turn will be built upon. So we should take very great care to imagine the world we are creating before we build it. We might end up living with something we can't bear.[40]

*

Such ominous warnings from the Director of Public Prosecutions are rare, and should give us real pause for thought.

GCHQ has travelled a long and winding road. That road stretches from the wooden huts of Bletchley Park, past the domes and dishes of the Cold War, and on towards what some suggest will be the omniscient state of a Brave New World. As we look to the future, the docile and passive society described by Aldous Huxley in his *Brave New World* is perhaps a more appropriate analogy than the starkly totalitarian predictions offered by George Orwell's *Nineteen Eighty-Four*. Bizarrely, many British citizens are quite content in this new climate of hyper-surveillance, since it is their own lifestyle choices that have helped to create it. GCHQ and its partners at NSA did not invent our current 'wired world' – or even wish for it, for as we have seen, the new torrents of data have been a source of endless trouble for the overstretched secret agencies. As Ken Macdonald rightly points out, the real drivers of our wired world have been private companies looking for growth, and private individuals in search of luxury and convenience at the click of a mouse. The sigint agencies have merely been handed the impossible task of making an interconnected society perfectly secure and risk-free, against the background of a globalised world that presents many unpredictable threats, and now has few boundaries or borders to protect us.

Who, then, is to blame for the rapid intensification of electronic surveillance? Instinctively, many might reply Osama bin Laden, or perhaps Pablo Escobar. Others might respond that governments have used these villains as a convenient excuse to extend state control. At first glance, the massive growth of security activity, which includes not only eavesdropping but also biometric monitoring, face recognition, universal fingerprinting and the gathering of DNA, looks like a direct response to new kinds of miscreants. However, the sad reality is that the Brave New World that looms ahead of us is ultimately a reflection of ourselves. It is driven by technologies such as text messaging and customer loyalty cards that we are free to accept or reject as we choose. The public debate on surveillance is often cast in terms of a trade-off between security and privacy. The truth is that luxury and convenience have been pre-eminent themes in the last decade, and we have given them a much higher priority than either security or privacy. We have all embraced the world of surveillance with remarkable eagerness, surfing the internet in a global search for a better bargain, better friends, even a better partner.

GCHQ's vast new circular headquarters is sometimes represented as a 'ring of power', exercising unparalleled levels of surveillance over citizens at home and abroad, collecting every email, every telephone call and every instance of internet access. It has even been asserted that GCHQ is engaged in nothing short of 'algorithmic warfare' as part of a battle for control of global communications. By contrast, the occupants of Cheltenham's 'Doughnut' claim that in reality they are increasingly weak, having been left behind by the unstoppable electronic revolution with its unimaginable volumes of communications that they cannot hope to listen to, still less analyse or make sense of. In fact, the frightening truth is that no one is in control. No person, no intelligence agency and no government is steering the accelerating electronic processes that may eventually enslave us. Most of the devices that cause us to leave a continual digital trail of everything we think or do were not devised by the state, but are merely symptoms of modernity.[41] GCHQ is simply a vast mirror, and it reflects the spirit of the age.

Appendix 1

Directors of Government Communications
Headquarters

Sir Alastair Denniston	1921–1944
Sir Edward Travis	1944–1952
Sir Eric Jones	1952–1960
Sir Clive ('Joe') Loehnis	1960–1964
Sir Leonard ('Joe') Hooper	1965–1973
Arthur ('Bill') Bonsall	1973–1978
Sir Brian Tovey	1978–1983
Sir Peter Marychurch	1983–1989
Sir John Anthony Adye	1989–1996
Sir David Omand	1996–1998
Kevin Tebbit	1998
Sir Francis Richards	1998–2003
Dr David Pepper	2003–2008
Iain Lobban	2008–

Directors of Communications-Electronics Security
Group and its predecessors

Director of the Cypher Policy Committee
Sir Stewart Menzies   1942–1944

Director of the Cypher Policy Board
Sir Stewart Menzies   1944–1952
Secretary to the Cypher Policy Board
Captain Edmund Wilson RN   1944–1947
Captain T.R.W. Burton-Miller RN 1947–1952

Directors of London Communications Security Agency
General William Penney   1953–1957
Captain R.F.T. ('Fred') Stannard RN 1957–1963

Director of London Communications-Electronics Security Agency
Captain R.F.T. ('Fred') Stannard RN 1964–1965

Director of the Communications-Electronics Security Department
Captain R.F.T. ('Fred') Stannard RN 1965–1969

Directors of Communications-Electronics Security Group 1969–
Air Vice Marshal Arthur Foden   1969–1975
Brian Tovey   1975–1978
Dr John Johnson   1978–1980
Major Gen Alistair Anderson   1980–1985
Paul Foster   1985–1989
Air Vice Marshal John Porter   1989–1991
Andrew Saunders   1991–1998
Richard Walton   1999–2002
Huw Rees   2002–2005
Dr John Widdowson   2005–

Appendix 2

GCHQ Timeline

1 Nov. 1919	GC&CS formed from a merger of the Army's MI1b and the Navy's Room 40
1921	Alastair Denniston becomes Director of GG&CS
Aug. 1939	GC&CS moves to Bletchley Park to avoid wartime bombing
1942	Holden agreement on Anglo–American naval sigint
1943	BRUSA agreement on Anglo–American military sigint
1944	Revised Holden agreement on Anglo–American naval sigint
1944	Edward Travis becomes Director of GC&CS
Feb. 1944	Cypher Policy Board created due to penetration of Allied cyphers
15 Sept. 1945	US Army code-breakers redesignated Army Security Agency (ASA)
22 Feb. 1946	Commonwealth sigint cooperation conference in London begins
5 Mar. 1946	Revised BRUSA agreement on Anglo–American sigint cooperation
May 1946	Revised BRUSA technical appendices on Anglo–American sigint cooperation

Jul. 1948   UK–USA Communications Intelligence
               Agreement
1 Aug. 1948   Captain Edmund Wilson and his team are
               shown over Oakley and Benhall sites
29 Oct. 1948   'Black Friday' – a major change occurs in
               Russian cypher procedures
1 Nov. 1948   The term 'London Signals Intelligence Centre'
               is abolished in favour of GCHQ
20 May 1949   US Armed Forces Security Agency created, a
               weak forerunner of NSA
Aug. 1949   Loss of the USS *Cochino*
1949   Vienna tunnel operations begin
10 Mar. 1950   US Communications Intelligence Board created
Mar. 1952   Eric Jones becomes Director of GCHQ, taking
               over from Edward Travis
Jul. 1952   Move from Eastcote to Cheltenham begins
24 Oct. 1952   President Truman signs order to create NSA,
               following failure to warn of Korean War
1953   LCSA created with Major General William
               Penney as Director
12 Mar. 1953   Loss of an RAF Lincoln over the Inner German
               Border
Feb. 1954   Move from Eastcote to Cheltenham completed
2 Sept. 1954   Work on the Berlin tunnel begins
21 Apr. 1956   Eastern Bloc troops break into the Berlin
               tunnel
1956   NSA moves to new headquarters at Fort
               Meade
1957   RAF Hambuhren handed over to German
               communications units
1957   Move from HMS Anderson sigint site to Perkar
               on Ceylon
1957   Government White Paper suggests coming end
               of National Service
1957   Karamursel NSA station built in Turkey to the
               south of Istanbul

11 Oct. 1957   Jodrell Bank, the first radiotelescope, is
               completed and is also used for sigint
1 Nov. 1957   Captain Robert Stannard RN becomes Director
               of LCSA, taking over from William Penney
21 Aug. 1958   The RAF's sigint unit, 192 Squadron, is renum-
               bered as 51 Squadron
2 Sept. 1958   US Sigint C-130A Hercules shot down over
               Armenia with loss of seventeen crew
1958   Berlin tunnel translators move from SIS to
               GCHQ as London Processing Group
1958   Comet sigint aircraft enter service with 51
               Squadron
1959   1 Special Wireless Regiment renamed 13
               Signals Regiment
May 1959   RAF Habbaniya in Iraq closed and sigint
               personnel moved to Cyprus
3 Jun. 1959   One of 51 Squadron's new Comets destroyed
               by fire
1 Sept. 1959   2 Wireless Regiment at Ayios Nikolaos
               renamed 9 Signals Regiment
12 Nov. 1959   The first dedicated US sigint-gathering ship,
               USS *Oxford*, is authorised
1 May 1960   Shooting down of Gary Powers' U-2 spy
               plane
1960   Clive Loehnis becomes Director of GCHQ,
               taking over from Eric Jones
Sept. 1960   Joe Hooper introduces joint sigint equipment
               purchase with services
Dec. 1960   Templer Report on integration of service inter-
               ception
1961   George Blake arrested and early compromise of
               Berlin tunnel realised
1961   Collection begins from Teufelsberg in Berlin
               operating out of ASA vans
Nov. 1961   Project Sandra receives Treasury approval
1962   Perkar sigint site on Ceylon closed

Jul. 1962	Sir Stuart Hampshire's review of GCHQ
Dec. 1962	Hampshire visits NSA for three weeks
Mar. 1963	LCSA becomes London Communications–Electronics Security Agency
May 1963	Hampshire review of GCHQ completed
Jun. 1963	Permission for a communications facility on Diego Garcia requested
1963	MC 74/1 – NATO Cryptographic Policy agreed
1963	Project Sandra begins operations on Cyprus
1 Jan. 1964	Little Sai Wan station in Hong Kong passes from RAF control to GCHQ
Sept. 1964	Cypher clerks at the British Embassy in Moscow repel KGB 'firemen'
1965	Joe Hooper becomes Director of GCHQ, taking over from Clive Loehnis
1965	LCSA takes over SCDU and JSRU and is renamed CESD
Nov. 1965	Diego Garcia agreement completed and 2,300 inhabitants removed
1966	Pine Gap station opened in Australia
Oct. 1966	Decision taken to replace sigint Comets with Nimrod R1s
1967	Scharfoldendorf station near the Inner German Border closed
7 Jun. 1967	USS *Liberty* AGTR ship attacked off Israel
1967	Chapman Pincher and the 'D-Notice affair' exposes cable vetting
1967	Teufelsberg sigint site in Berlin begins operations
Dec. 1967	First voyage of the USS *Pueblo*
Jan. 1968	Geoffrey Prime offers his services to the KGB
23 Jan. 1968	USS *Pueblo* ALGER-2 ship captured by North Korea
24 Jan. 1968	HMS *Totem*, now renamed *Dakar*, sinks off Cyprus
20 Aug. 1968	Russian invasion of Czechoslovakia takes GCHQ and NSA by surprise

Late 1968	Dick White review of DIS and JIC in the wake of Czech invasion
Late 1968	Dick White inquiry into rising sigint costs
9 Sept. 1968	Geoffrey Prime begins work at GCHQ's London Processing Group
1969	GCHQ's nuclear-powered sigint ship project abandoned
Jun. 1969	Decision to merge CESD with GCHQ and change its name to CESG
1969	Arthur Foden becomes Director of CESG, taking over from Robert Stannard
30 Mar. 1972	Kizildere incident: eight GCHQ staff taken hostage and three killed by TPLA terrorists
Apr. 1972	JIC (A) delegation meets Groupe de Synthèse et Prévision in Paris
1972	Skynet III decision
6 Mar. 1973	Ryolite satellite launched to verify the SALT 1 arms control treaty
18 Jun. 1973	Closure of Cobra Mist facility at Orford Ness announced
Aug. 1973	Arthur Bonsall becomes Director of GCHQ, taking over from Joe Hooper
Aug. 1973	Nixon–Kissinger 'cut-off' of intelligence cooperation attempted
1973	Transfer of London Processing Group to Cheltenham begun
1973	James Ellis discovers the asymmetric algorithm, later the foundation of RSA
3 May 1974	First operational flight by a Nimrod R1
1974	Cyprus invasion by Turkey
1974	US sigint bases in Turkey shut down
Feb. 1975	Government Secure Speech Network cancelled
Jul. 1975	Ivy Bells undersea cable-tapping operation begins using USS *Halibut*
Aug. 1975	Work on Diego Garcia expansion begins
1975	GCHQ Mauritius station closed

1975	NSA takes delivery of its first Cray computer
Sept. 1975	Brian Tovey becomes Director of CESG, taking over from Arthur Foden
22 Mar. 1976	Geoffrey Prime moved from London to Cheltenham
1976	'ABC trial' of Aubrey, Berry and Campbell begins
1976	Geoffrey Prime promoted to Section Head in J Division
1977	Transfer of London Processing Group to Cheltenham completed
1977	14 Signals Regiment (Electronic Warfare) formed
1977	GCHQ's Wincombe station closed
1977	GCHQ's Flowerdown station closed
28 Sept. 1977	Geoffrey Prime resigns from GCHQ
1978	GCHQ's Gilnahirk station in Northern Ireland closed
1978	Special Collection Service, a joint NSA–CIA black-bag unit created
1978	GCHQ station at Two Boats on Ascension Island reactivated
1978	John Johnson becomes Director of CESG, taking over from Brian Tovey
1978	Brian Tovey becomes Director of GCHQ, taking over from Arthur Bonsall
Jan. 1979	Iranian revolution – NSA and GCHQ listening posts in Iran are lost
23 Feb. 1979	One-day strike triggers Brian Tovey's thinking on union removal at GCHQ
1980	Alastair Anderson becomes Director of CESG, taking over from John Johnson
1980	Ivy Bells submarine tapping operation blown by Ronald Pelton, KGB agent in NSA
9 Mar. 1981	One-day strike at GCHQ, then disruptive action to April
16 Nov. 1981	Geoffrey Prime makes his last contact with the KGB in East Berlin

1982	Gordon Welchman threatened with OSA over *Hut Six Story*
1982	GCHQ's Little Sai Wan closed down and moved to Chum Hom Kok
26 Jun. 1982	Geoffrey Prime confesses
15 Jul. 1982	Prime remanded in custody on OSA charges
23 Sept. 1982	James Bamford's *Puzzle Palace* published
10 Nov. 1982	Geoffrey Prime pleads guilty
1983	STU-III secure speech unit introduced by NSA
Sept. 1983	Peter Marychurch becomes Director of GCHQ, taking over from Brian Tovey
1 Dec. 1983	Pilot polygraph machine arrives at R12 at Cheltenham
Dec. 1983	Decision on de-unionisation taken by ad hoc Cabinet committee
25 Jan. 1984	GCHQ staff receive GN 100/84 letter on unions
17 Apr. 1984	WPC Yvonne Fletcher shot outside the Libyan People's Bureau in London
1984	GCHQ's Brora station in Sutherland closed
1985	Paul Foster becomes Director of CESG, taking over from Alastair Anderson
1985	Interception of Communications Act
1 Aug. 1985	KGB officer Vitaly Yurchenko defects and reveals NSA spy Ronald Pelton
5 Jun. 1986	Pelton convicted of espionage for the KGB
6 Jun. 1986	Jonathan Pollard pleads guilty to espionage for Mossad
1986	Joint Speech Research Unit at GCHQ amalgamated with Speech Research Group at RSRE to form Speech Research Unit
20 Jan. 1987	European Commission for Human Rights declares GCHQ trade union case inadmissible
31 Jul. 1988	Hawklaw station in Fife closed
1989	Hilltop station at Teufelberg in Berlin closed
1989	John Porter becomes Director of CESG, taking over from Paul Foster

1989	John Adye becomes Director of GCHQ, taking over from Peter Marychurch
Mar. 1991	Andrew Saunders becomes Director of CESG, taking over from John Porter
Late 1993	Sir Michael Quinlan asked to look at government spending on intelligence
22 Dec. 1993	T of R for Quinlan's 'Review of Intelligence Requirements and Resources' agreed
Jun. 1994	'Review of Intelligence Requirements and Resources' completed
1994	GCHQ's Earl's Court station at Empress Building closed
Oct. 1994	Operations at GCHQ's Chum Hom Kok station end
2 Nov. 1994	Intelligence Services Act
12 Dec. 1994	Roger Hurn Special Study of GCHQ commissioned
Jan. 1995	Chum Hom Kok closed down and operations move to Geraldton in Australia
Jan. 1995	Operations at Cheadle end and station closed in June
25 Mar. 1995	Roger Hurn Special Study completed
Mar. 1995	13 Signals Regiment in Germany disbanded, some move to JSSU at RAF Digby
16 May 1995	XW666, one of the three sigint Nimrod R1s, ditches in the Moray Firth
1995	RAF 51 Squadron moves from RAF Wyton to RAF Waddington
16 Oct. 1995	New high-level post created to represent GCHQ in London
6 Nov. 1995	J, K and V Divisions abolished. M, Q, U and W Divisions created
10 Nov. 1995	GCHQ's Central Training School at Taunton closes
23 Nov. 1995	Impending appointment of David Omand announced

Jan. 1996	Sideslip/Caid/Cental and Yardage introduced for Radio Operators/RDs
1 Jul. 1996	David Omand becomes Director of GCHQ, taking over from John Adye
1996	RAF Pergamos closes
1 Jan. 1997	Corporate Communications Unit created
16 Jan. 1997	GCHQ relaxes regulation on the employment of gays and lesbians
1 Apr. 1997	CESG moves to cost recovery and completes restructuring
28 Apr. 1997	XV249, the Nimrod R1 replacement for XW666, becomes operational
15 May 1997	Robin Cook announces the end of the GCHQ trade union ban
Oct. 1997	NSA station at Edzell in Scotland which focused on Soviet naval traffic is closed
Jan. 1998	Kevin Tebbit becomes Director of GCHQ, taking over from David Omand
Jun. 1998	Lead 21 management training scheme begins
Jul. 1998	Francis Richards becomes Director of GCHQ, taking over from Kevin Tebbit
4 Jan. 1999	Richard Walton becomes Director of CESG, taking over from Andrew Saunders
1999	GCHQ station at Culmhead in Somerset closed, functions transferred to Scarborough
1999	Speech Research Unit privatised
Sept.1999	Cabinet Secretary asks Lieutenant General Sir Edmund Burton to review GCHQ
Jan. 2000	GCHQ assists NSA during its major computer failure
2000	Burton review completed, focusing on cost overruns on new accommodation
Jul. 2000	Brian Paterson from GCHQ develops Government Technical Assistance Centre (GTAC)
13 Mar. 2001	Geoffrey Prime released from Rochester Prison on parole

12 Sept. 2001 Directors of MI5, MI6 and GCHQ fly to Washington

2002 Huw Rees becomes Director of CESG, taking over from Richard Walton

2 Jun. 2002 JTAC begins operations in the MI5 headquarters at Thames House

3 Mar. 2003 *Observer* publishes NSA document on the monitoring of UN delegations

20 Mar. 2003 Iraq War begins with targeted strike against Saddam Hussein

Apr. 2003 Dr David Pepper becomes Director of GCHQ, taking over from Francis Richards

16 Jul. 2003 National Audit Office publishes report on new accommodation IT cost

Jul. 2003 Scarus manpack sigint equipment arrives in Afghanistan

17 Sept. 2003 Staff begin to move into 'the Doughnut'

14 Nov. 2003 Katharine Gun charged under Official Secrets Act on UN revelations

Feb. 2004 Katharine Gun acquitted

May 2004 Move to new accommodation completed

Sept. 2005 John Widdowson becomes Director of CESG, taking over from Huw Rees

Oct. 2005 Heilbronn Institute for Mathematical Research set up at University of Bristol

Apr. 2006 NTAC (formerly GTAC) transferred from Home Office to GCHQ

30 Jul. 2008 Iain Lobban becomes Director of GCHQ, taking over from Dr David Pepper

Aug. 2008 Intercept Modernisation Programme announced

10 Mar. 2010 Cyber Security Operations Centre opens

Appendix 3 – GCHQ Organisation in 1946

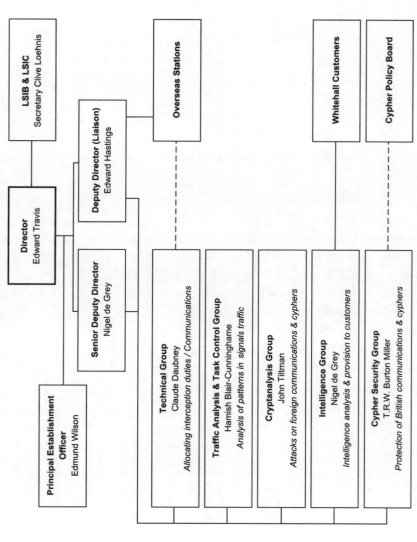

LSIB & LSIC
Secretary Clive Loehnis

Director
Edward Travis

Principal Establishment Officer
Edmund Wilson

Senior Deputy Director
Nigel de Grey

Deputy Director (Liaison)
Edward Hastings

Overseas Stations

Whitehall Customers

Cypher Policy Board

Technical Group
Claude Daubney
Allocating interception duties / Communications

Traffic Analysis & Task Control Group
Hamish Blair-Cunninghame
Analysis of patterns in signals traffic

Cryptanalysis Group
John Tiltman
Attacks on foreign communications & cyphers

Intelligence Group
Nigel de Grey
Intelligence analysis & provision to customers

Cypher Security Group
T.R.W. Burton Miller
Protection of British communications & cyphers

Appendix 4 – GCHQ Organisation in 1970

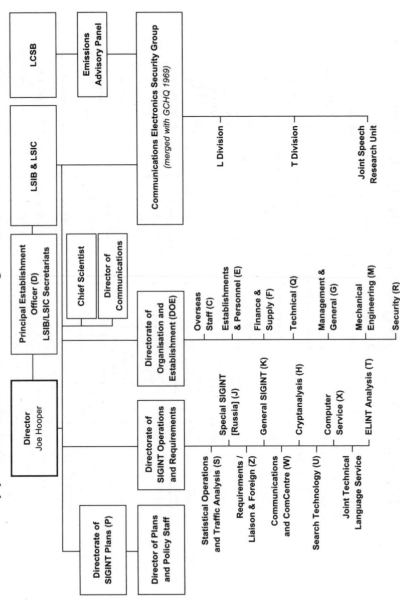

Appendix 5 – GCHQ Organisation in 1998

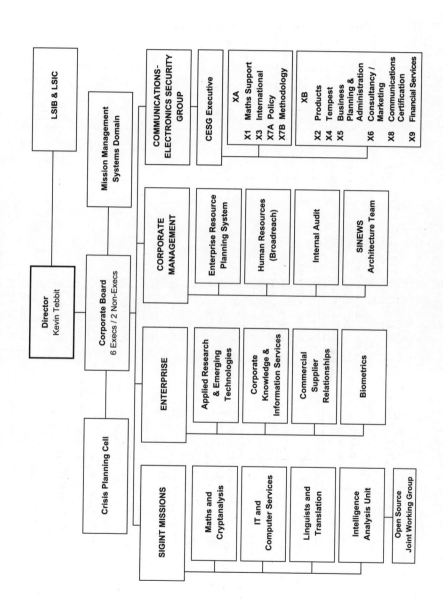

Acknowledgements

On 9 December 1993 the Lord Chancellor, Lord Mackay of Clashfern, introduced the Intelligence Services Act in the House of Lords. He declared that the declassifying of hitherto highly secret documents on intelligence was part of the new accountability of the British intelligence services. Lord Mackay also emphasised that government had 'released a number of previously withheld government records' as an important component of the new commitment to openness – and planned to release more: 'Things have moved on. The climate has changed. Greater openness has gained momentum.' Initially, I greeted these words with profound scepticism. However, by the late 1990s it was clear that the authorities had been as good as their word. Remarkable historical materials were making their way to the National Archives at Kew, where they could be viewed by ordinary mortals. A number of Whitehall departments, most notably the Treasury under Gordon Brown, were very generous in releasing material on GCHQ. Overwhelmingly, the present study is based on this newly declassified material. Without this commendable shift towards openness and the generous new release of hitherto highly secret documents on GCHQ by many departments of state, this book would not have been possible.

Because the work stretches back over more than a decade, I happily find myself in the debt of a wide array of individuals and institutions, and it is a pleasure to have the opportunity to offer my thanks here. For legal reasons I have chosen not to interview former British officials; however, I have occasionally spoken to 'friends and allies', and indeed 'rivals', overseas. The study has been compiled from open sources, and no classified material has been utilised. In a sense it is no more, and no less, than a summation of the documents about GCHQ that the various authorities have chosen to place in the public domain. Errors, of course, remain entirely my own, and given that I am writing about a secret agency from unsecret sources, there are likely to be more than a few. Those who wish to write to me with comments or corrections are most welcome, and I can be reached at r.j.aldrich@warwick.ac.uk or at the Department of Politics and International Studies, University of Warwick, Coventry CV4 7AL.

Many academic friends and colleagues have guided me to documents or commented on early findings. I would particularly like to thank David Alvarez, Peter Catterall, Philip Davies, Stephen Dorril, David Easter, David Edgerton, Geoffrey Elliott, Ralph Erskine, Rob Evans, John Ferris, M.R.D. Foot, Stevyn Gibson, Roy Giles, Michael Goodman, Chris Grey, David Hamer, Michael Handel, Michael Herman, Peter Jackson, Rhodri Jeffreys-Jones, Matthew Jones, Sheila Kerr, Paul Lashmar, Julian Lewis, W. Scott Lucas, Paul Maddrell, Sir David Omand, Martin Rudner, Len Scott, Mark Seaman, Michael Smith, David Stafford, Andy Sturdy, Stephen Twigge, Wesley K. Wark, Donald Cameron Watt and John W. Young. I am also fortunate to enjoy the company of a number of very talented research students and research fellows whose input has been invaluable.

On a project such as this, the assistance of departmental record officers and official historians is especially important. I would like to thank the many individuals who have declassified material for me, allowed me sight of documents, or simply explained the meaning of documents to me. I would like to thank Christopher Simpson at the Attorney General's Office; Alan Glennie, Brian Hogan and Shumailla Moinuddin at the Cabinet Office; Gill Bennett, Lynsey Hughes, Janet James, Penny Prior,

Duncan Stewart, Stuart Taylor and Stephen Twigge at the Foreign and Commonwealth Office; Iain Goode, Simon Marsh and Steve Roper at the Ministry of Defence; Rosemary Banner, Ashley Britten, Darren Creamer, Francis Houston, Kate Jenkins and Sean Molloy at the Treasury; Patrick Driscoll at Treasury Solicitors. Ray Nolan at the Ministry of Defence needs to be singled out for a special mention, having tirelessly reviewed no fewer than 166 files for me. Tessa Stirling, the head of the Historians and Openness Unit at the Cabinet Office, has been notably generous with her time, allowing me to inspect additional material on site at the Cabinet Office.

I have enjoyed kind assistance with my many queries from the GCHQ historians at Cheltenham, including the current incumbent and his immediate predecessor, whom I shall refer to here only as the mysterious 'M'. For much of the duration of this project the GCHQ historian was the late Peter Freeman, who was always encouraging, and I regret he did not see its completion. Chris Wilson in the GCHQ press office has been helpful with more recent queries. The archivists of SIS and MI5 have also assisted at various points. David Hatch, the historian at NSA's Center for Cryptologic History, has also been kind in answering questions.

Armies of archivists and librarians – tireless in their efforts – have extended their kindness, and cannot all be named here. In Washington, I would like to mention Nicholas Scheetz at the Special Collections Center, the Lauinger Library at Georgetown University; and Lia Apodocia and Jeffrey M. Flannery at the Library of Congress together with Dane Hartgrove, Will Mahoney, Kathy McCastro, Ed Reese and the legendary late John E. Taylor at NARA. Above all it is the staff of the National Archives (Public Record Office), overworked and often confronted with an irascible researcher, but unfailingly courteous and helpful, who have facilitated this book. The University of Warwick has provided a friendly environment during the years over which this study was completed, and also hosts the wonderful Modern Records Centre, under the direction of Helen Ford, with its collection of GCHQ trade union materials. The Warwick Institute of Advanced

Study provided a constant stream of visiting fellows and research colloquia with their fresh inspirations. I would like to thank the Director, Margot Finn, and her colleagues for all their kindness.

Early research was begun under the auspices of a British Academy Large Grant in 2003 which funded lengthy trips to the United States, Australia and Canada. Lee, Al and Della offered a happy home in Rock Creek Park while I was working in Washington. University House at ANU was a wonderful home in Canberra, and the Canadian Association for the Study of Intelligence and Security has made each visit to Ottawa a joy. The American dimension was also made possible by an earlier American Studies Fellowship supported by the American Council of Learned Societies, the British American Studies Association and the Fulbright Programme. Most importantly, a year of study leave supported by the University of Warwick allowed the book's completion.

There are a few individuals to whom I owe a particularly heavy debt of gratitude. My literary agent, Andrew Lownie, deserves special thanks for his faith in this project and for his unique sense of timing. Richard Johnson, Martin Redfern and his colleagues at HarperCollins have been especially supportive and forbearing during a process that has taken longer than we had hoped. Robert Lacey, David Havilland and Barry Holmes have run an expert eye over advanced drafts. Matthew Aid, Christopher Andrew, Peter Hennessy and Cees Wiebes have offered crucial assistance and constant inspiration. Above all, I owe an enormous debt to my family for their encouragement over the years. My brother James cast his critical eye over the final draft. My children, Nicholas and Harriet, deserve special thanks for their wonderful musical distractions and theatrical diversions during the book's progress. As ever my wife Libby offered boundless love, support and sound advice on a project that seemed to have no end.

Richard J. Aldrich
March 2010

Notes

Abbreviations

ACAS(I)	Assistant Chief of the Air Staff (Intelligence)	COS	Chiefs of Staff
ACSI	Assistant Chief of Staff Intelligence [American]	CPB	Cypher Policy Board, succeeded by LCSA
AFSA	Armed Forces Security Agency [American]	CSC	Cabinet Security Committee
		CTSD	Communications Technical Services Department
AWM	Australian War Memorial	CWIHP	Cold War International History Project
BAFB	Bollings Air Force Base, Washington DC	DA	GCHQ Director of Administration – 1990s successor to PEO
BDEE	British Documents on End of Empire		
BGS Int	Brigadier General Staff Intelligence, the senior Army intelligence officer	DCI	Director of Central Intelligence, the head of the CIA
BJSM	British Joint Services Mission, Washington	DDEL	Dwight D. Eisenhower Library, Abilene, Kansas
BL	British Library	DDRS	Declassified Document Reference System
BLPES	British Library of Political and Economic Science	D/GCHQ	Director of GCHQ
BNS	Briefing Notes Subseries (NSC)	DMI	Director of Military Intelligence
BOD	Bodleian Library	DNI	Director of Naval Intelligence
BRO	Brotherton Library	D of I	USAF Director of Intelligence
BUL	Birmingham University Library	DPS	GCHQ Difficult Post Supplement – where discomfort and hazard is involved
CAFH	Center for Air Force History, Bollings Air Force Base		
CAS	Chief of the Air Staff	DSI	Director of Scientific Intelligence
CCC	Churchill College, Cambridge		
C/GSPS	Controller, Government Signals Planning Staff	DSSS	Defence Secure Speech System – satellite-based 1970s
CIG	Central Intelligence Group, regional function subset of the JIC	DSTI	Director of Scientific and Technical Intelligence (MoD)
		FAOHP	Foreign Affairs Oral History Programme
CIGS	Chief of the Imperial General Staff	FECOM	Far Eastern Command [American]
CNA	Canadian National Archives		
CNO	Chief of Naval Operations [American]	FOIA	Document obtained by Freedom of Information Act
CNS	Chief of the Naval Staff		

FRUS	*Foreign Relations of the United States*	NPM	Nixon Presidential Materials at College Park, now moved to the Nixon Library
GCHQ-UR	GCHQ union records at WMRC	NSG	Naval Security Group [American]
GCSF	Government Communications Staff Federation, which replaced unions in 1984	NY	New York
		OAB, WNY	Operational Archives Branch, Washington Navy Yard
GSPS	Government Signals Planning Staff	OR	Office of Intelligence and Research in the State Department
HL	Hartley Library, University of Southampton		
HoC	House of Commons	OSANSA	Office of the Special Assistant for National Security Affairs
HQSBAA	HQ Sovereign Base Area Administration, Episkopi, Cyprus	OTHR	Over the horizon radar or ionospheric reflection radar
HSTL	Harry S. Truman Library, Independence, Missouri	PFIAB	President's Foreign Intelligence Advisory Board [American]
IC	Cabinet Office Intelligence Coordinator	POF	President's Official File
		PS/SAS	Presidential Subseries, Special Assistant Series, DDEL
IJICI	*International Journal of Intelligence and Counter Intelligence*	PSF	President's Secretaries Files
I∂NS	*Intelligence and National Security*	PUSD	Permanent Under-Secretary's Department
INSCOM	Intelligence and Security Command [American]	RG	Record Group of the US National Archives and Canadian National Archives
IOLR	India Office Library and Records, Blackfriars, London, now held at the British Library	RNSM	Royal Naval Submarine Museum, Gosport
IWM	Imperial War Museum	RSI (CWP)	Review of Service Intelligence (Civilianisation Working Party)
J.	Journal		
JCS	Joint Chiefs of Staff [American]	RSM	Royal Signals Museum, Blandford Forum
JFKL	John F. Kennedy Library, Boston	SAC	US Air Force Strategic Air Command
JIB	Joint Intelligence Bureau	SACMED	Supreme Allied Commander Mediterranean
JTLS	Joint Technical Language Service	SAM	Surface to Air Missile
LBJL	Lyndon Baines Johnson Library, Austin, Texas	SCARL	Signals Command Air Radio Laboratory, RAF Watton
LC	Library of Congress	SD	State Department [American]
LHCMA	Liddell Hart Centre for Military Archives, King's College London	SPDR	Strategic Plans Division Records
		TC/LSIC	Technical Committee of London Signals Intelligence Committee
LL	Lauinger Library, Georgetown University		
LSIB	London Signals Intelligence Board	USCIB	US Communications Intelligence Board
LSIC	London Signals Intelligence Committee	USMHI	US Military History Institute, Carlisle Barracks
MI8	Military Intelligence section dealing with signals intelligence	USNOA	US Navy Operational Archive, Navy Yard, Washington DC
MoS	Ministry of Supply files	WHO	White House Office
NAA	National Archives of Australia	WMRC	Warwick Modern Records Centre
NARA	National Archives and Record Administration, Washington DC	W/T	Wireless Telegraphy
NMLH	National Museum of Labour History, Manchester		

Introduction: GCHQ – The Last Secret?

1 HC Deb 55, 107, 27.02.84, pp.37–8.

2 There are no books devoted to GCHQ's post-war history, although in 1986 Nigel West provided an excellent overview of British code-breaking in the twentieth century in his book *GCHQ*.

3 MacEachin, *The Final Months of War with Japan*; www.cia.gov/library/publications/index.html.

4 Andrew, 'Intelligence and International Relations', pp.321–3.

5 Important writings about GCHQ are submerged within wider accounts. See in particular: Aid, *Secret Sentry*; Bamford, *The Puzzle Palace*; Richelson and Ball, *Ties that Bind*; Campbell, *Unsinkable Aircraft Carrier*; Smith, *The Ultra–Magic Deals* and Wiebes, *Intelligence and the War in Bosnia*. Important episodes have also been recounted by Stafford in *Beneath Berlin* and Urban, *UK Eyes Alpha*. Seminal articles include Andrew, 'The Growth of the Australian Intelligence Community' and 'The Making of the Anglo–American SIGINT Alliance', together with Easter, 'GCHQ' and Rudner, 'Betwixt and Between'.

6 HC Deb, 11.10.04, Col 51W.

7 Nicholas Henderson interview, British Diplomatic Oral History project, CCC.

8 Entries for 1.04.74, 5.02.76 and 18.02.76, Donoughue, *Downing Street Diaries*, pp.85, 656, 670.

9 Young, *The Labour Governments, 1964–70*, p.15.

10 S.I. Khrushchev, 'My Father Nikita's Downfall', 14.11.88, *Time*.

11 RFE Background Report, 'Vukmanovic Describes His Last Meeting with Khrushchev: How Rankovic "Bugged" Tito's Bedroom', by Slovan Stankovic, 25.01.71, 79–4–239, Open Society Archives.

12 Heath, *The Course of My Life*, p.493.

13 Entry for 5.11.01, Campbell, *The Blair Years*, p.577.

14 Lewis, *Changing Direction*, pp.178–241.

15 Bruce Schneier, 'NSA and Bush's Illegal Eavesdropping', 20.12.05, http://www.schneier.com/blog/archives/2005/12/nsa_and_bushs_i.html.

THE 1940s: BLETCHLEY PARK AND BEYOND

Chapter 1: Schooldays

1 Kipling, 'Wireless', p.238.

2 Ibid., pp.238–9.

3 Vincent, *Culture of Secrecy*, pp.26–31; Smith, *Spying Game*, pp.43–5.

4 Smith, *Spying Game*, pp.257–8.

5 Andrew, *Secret Service*, pp.108–13.

6 Ibid., pp.259–60; Denniston, *Thirty Secret Years*, p.54.

7 Vincent, *Culture of Secrecy*, p.207.

8 Calvocoressi, *Top Secret Ultra*, p.9.

9 Smith, *Spying Game*, p.261.

10 Ball and Horner, *Breaking the Code*, p.179; Andrew, *Secret Service*, pp.331–3.

11 Paterson, *Voices*, p.30.

12 Erskine and Freeman, 'Brigadier John Tiltman', pp.294–6.

13 Best, *British Intelligence and the Japanese Challenge*, pp.56–7.

14 Calvocoressi, *Top Secret Ultra*, p.5.

15 Paterson, *Voices*, p.31.

16 Ratcliff, *Delusions of Intelligence*, p.11.

17 Sebag-Montefiore, *The Battle for the Code*, p.10.

18 Smith, *Station X*, p.5.

19 Calvocoressi, *Top Secret Ultra*, p.13.

20 Winterbotham, *The Ultra Secret*, p.12.

21 Diary entries, 04.11.39 and 05.11.39, Cadogan diary, ACAD 1/8, 1939, Cadogan papers, CCC.

22 Bennett, *Morton*, pp.210–12.

23 Ibid. p.248.

24 Diary entry, 14.03.41, Cadogan diary, ACAD 1/10 1941, Cadogan papers, CCC.

25 Bennett, *Morton*, p.267. These matters were delegated to Peter Loxley, his private secretary.

26 Calvocoressi, *Top Secret Ultra*, pp.13, 19.

27 Bennett, *Morton*, p.252.

28 Davies, *MI6 and the Machinery of Spying*, pp.188–9.

29 Grey and Sturdy, 'A Chaos that Worked', pp.47–50.

30 Denniston, *Thirty Secret Years*, pp.68–75.

31 Lewin, *Ultra*, pp.30–61.

32 Entry for 11.01.41, ACAD 1/10, 1941, Cadogan papers, CCC.

33 Smith, *Station X*, p.78.

34 Davies, 'GC&CS and Institution-Building in Sigint', pp.397–9.

35 Denniston, *Thirty Secret Years*, pp.73–5.

36 The idea came from Gordon Welchman; see Milner-Barry, 'Action This Day', pp.272–6.

37 Smith, *Spying Game*, pp.283–4.

38 Grey and Sturdy, 'Reorganisation', pp.311–13.

39 Davies, 'GC&CS and Institution-Building in Sigint', pp.397–9.

40 Loehnis to Beesly, 10.08.80, MLBE, CCC.

41 The pre-eminent account is Gannon, *Colossus*.

42 Clark, *The Man Who Broke Purple*, pp.119–21.

Chapter 2: Friends and Allies

1 Chapter VIII, 'The Russian Liaison', HW 3/101.
2 Hinsley, *British Intelligence*, Vol.II, pp.618–19.
3 DMI memo, 'Expansion of "Y" Service in India', 29.10.41, L/WS/1/897, IOLR.
4 Ball and Horner, *Breaking the Code*, p.183.
5 Aldrich, *War Against Japan*, pp.164–5.
6 Loehnis to Denniston (D/GCandCS), 06.10.39, HW 14/1; Memo by MGM, 'Russian Navy – Y Investigation', 01.10.39, ibid.
7 GC&CS History, 'Russian Naval', HW 3/151.
8 GC&CS memo, 14.01.40, HW 14/3.
9 Erskine and Freeman, 'Brigadier John Tiltman', p.299.
10 GC&CS History, 'Russian Naval', HW 3/151.
11 Ibid.
12 Hinsley, *British Intelligence*, Vol.I, pp.438–40.
13 Gorodetsky, *Grand Delusion*, pp.281–3.
14 Chapter VIII, 'The Russian Liaison', HW 3/101.
15 Scott-Farnie memo, 'Y Liaison Visit to Russia', 03.10.41, HW 34/23.
16 Chapter VIII, 'The Russian Liaison', HW 3/101.
17 Cooper (RAF Section GCC) to Blandy (DDSY), 03.10.41, HW 34/23.
18 Chapter VIII, 'The Russian Liaison', HW 3/101.
19 Ibid.
20 Winterbotham (GC&CS) to DD(S), n.d., 10.06.42?, HW40/5. See also Grant (GC&CS) to Travis (GC&CS), 9.06.42, ibid.
21 Grant (GC&CS), 'Report on German Cryptography on the Russian Front', ibid.
22 De Grey (GC&CS) to Hatton Hall (GC&CS), 16.06.42, ibid.
23 Crankshaw (Moscow) to Chairman Y Committee, 29.10.42, HW 14/56.
24 Chapter VIII, 'The Russian Liaison', HW 3/101.
25 LSIB decision discussed in Rushbrooke (DNI) min., 04.03.44, ADM 1/28903.
26 Andrew and Gordievsky, *KGB*, pp.247–9; Tom Bower, Obituary: John Cairncross, *Independent*, 10.10.95.
27 Ibid. One of the MI5 officers searching the flat of Guy Burgess was Anthony Blunt.
28 Denniston memo, 'Third Mtg of Liaison Officers on 21 October', 27.10.42, HW 14/56.
29 Smith, *Spying Game*, pp.291–2
30 Erskine, 'Anglo–US Cryptological Co-operation'; conversation with John Croft.
31 Budiansky, 'Bletchley Park', p.213.
32 Kahn, *The Reader of Gentlemen's Mail*, p.212.
33 Johnson, *American Cryptology*, Vol.1, p.14.
34 Erskine, 'When a Purple Machine Went Missing', pp.185–6.
35 Budiansky, 'Bletchley Park', p.220
36 Smith, *The Emperor's Codes*, pp.75–7.
37 Alvarez, 'GC&CS and American Diplomatic Cryptanalysis', pp.163–5.
38 Entry for 04.06.41, Leutze (ed.) *London Observer*. See also JIC (41) 15th mtg (1) and Annex I and II, 06.06.41, CAB 81/88.
39 Smith, *Ultra-Magic Deals*, pp.84–5.
40 Andrew, *President's Eyes Only*, p.108.
41 WO to C. in C. Far East, 22.08.41, WO 208/2049A.
42 Brown, 'Intelligence and the Decision to Collect It', pp.449–68; Croft, 'Reminiscences', pp.133–44. Private information.
43 Entry for 04.06.41, Leutze (ed.), *The London Observer*.
44 Budiansky, 'Bletchley Park', p.217.
45 Croft, 'Wartime at Berkeley Street', pp.133–44.
46 Aldrich, *Intelligence and the War Against Japan*, pp.82–3; Bowen, Socony Vaccum Oil, NY, to Barry, Socony Vacuum Oil, London, incepted tel., 12.04.44, U3271/3271/70, FO 371/40776.
47 Erskine, 'Churchill and the Start of the Ultra–Magic Deals', p.59.
48 CPB (45) 4th mtg Agenda, Item 2, Statement by Secretary, 'Suggested approach to the USA for Complete Exchange of Information of Cypher Machine Development between UK and USA Governments', 09.02.45, CAB 21/2522.
49 CPB (45), 4th mtg, 21.02.45, ibid.
50 Johnson, *American Cryptology*, Vol.1, p.14.
51 Budiansky, 'Bletchley Park', pp.226–7.
52 Erskine, 'The Holden Agreement', pp.187–97.
53 Budiansky, 'Bletchley Park', p.233.
54 Denniston to Tiltman, 'Notes on Diplomatic Liaison with USA', 08.03.42, HW 14/46.
55 Alvarez, 'Most Helpful', in Smith and Erskine (eds), *Action this Day*, pp.161–4.
56 Ibid. pp.168–70.
57 Cadogan (FO) to Menzies ('C'), 03.07.44, HW37/4. See also Bissell to Menzies ('C'), 20.05.44, ibid.

58 Budiansky, 'Bletchley Park', p.234.
59 Stevens to Tiltman, 31.07.42, HW 14/47.
60 Aid, 'The Russian Target', pp.7–8.
61 Aldrich, *Hidden Hand*, p.67.
62 Johnson, *American Cryptology*, Vol.1, p.15; Aid, 'The Russian Target', p.8

Chapter 3: Every War Must Have an End
1 De Grey to Menzies (C), 14.09.44, HW 14/111.
2 Travis (GCHQ) to Wenger (NSS), 05.01.46, Box 101, CNSG records, RG 38, NARA.
3 Parrish, *The Ultra Americans*, pp.279–86.
4 Ibid.
5 Ibid.; Smith, *Spying Game*, pp.292–3.
6 Whitaker and Kruh, 'From Bletchley Park to the Berchtesgaden', pp.129–30.
7 Director's Order no.61, 'TICOM Captured Document Committee', 15.06.45, HW 64/68. See also Aid, 'The Russian Target', p.17.
8 Johnson, *American Cryptology*, Vol.1, p.3.
9 West, *Venona*, p.33.
10 Col Kurt Gottschling, 'The Radio Intercept Service of the German Air Force', Vol.2, KL13.107-191, 8-115-21 (E)K10262, CAFH.
11 Jenkins, *Life*, p.57. Conversation with Roy Jenkins at the Bletchley Park conference, Christ Church College, Oxford, 2002.
12 Chairman, LSIB to Chair ME Signals Intelligence Committee, 31.05.44, HW 41/391.
13 Penney min. to SAC, 22.09.45, WO203/-5051; Russell, *Sheridan's Story*; Donini, 'The Cryptographic Services of the Royal (British) and Italian Navies', pp.97–127.
14 AFHQ to MI8 London, 10.07.45, 'SID Cryptographic Documents', WO 208/5073. Also AFHQ to MI8 London, 'Diplomatic Interception in Northern Italy', 16.05.45, and Annex, 'SIM Success on British and US Diplo', ibid.
15 Churchill (PM) to Eden (SoS FO), 25.11.44, U7917/180/70, FO 371/40720; Brown, 'Interplay of Information'; Schlesinger, 'Cryptanalysis for Peacetime'; private information.
16 Clark Kerr to Eden (SoS FO), 12.11.43, N6739/22/38, FO 371/36926; Thomas, 'France in British Signals Intelligence', pp.64–6.
17 Good examples of intercepted high-level French traffic from their ambassadors in London, Washington and Moscow back to Paris for September 1945, together with Greek and Portuguese traffic, are at HW39/16.

18 Johnson, *American Cryptology*, Vol.1, p.10.
19 Aid, 'The Russian Target', p.13.
20 Alvarez, 'Behind Venona', p.184.
21 Travis (GCHQ) to Wenger, 13.08.45, HW 14/133. See also 'Future of the French Section', mtg 04.08.45, ibid.
22 McKane (MI8) to DDY, 'Italian Sigint Service', 15.05.46, WO 208/5073.
23 McKane (MI8) to Director LSIC (for Head of TA Group), 31.05.46, enclosing 'Further notes on Italian Cover', WO 208/5073; McKane to K.H. Sachse (LSIC), 'Italian Intercept Organisation', 04.06.46, ibid.
24 Ball and Horner, *Breaking the Code*, p.110.
25 Cypher Security Committee, mins. of the 78th mtg, 12.04.44, FO 850/133.
26 Ratcliff, *Delusions of Intelligence*, pp.49–51
27 Chitty to Codrington (FO), 'Scrutiny of Government Cypher Traffic in London', 13.10.43, CAB 21/2522.
28 Ibid.
29 Bridges (Cab Sec) to Cadogan (PUS FO), 17.03.44, enclosing 'Security of British and Allied Communications. Formation Cypher Policy Board', 17.03.44, FO 850/133.
30 Burton-Miller (GCHQ), 10 Chesterfield St, W1 to Hawkins (Stockholm), 04.12.50, letter in the author's possession.
31 Bridges (Cab Sec) to Menzies ('C'), 'Future Cypher Machine Development', 14.09.44, CAB 21/2522. See also CPB (44) 3rd mtg, 05.10.44, ibid.
32 Menzies ('C') to Bridges (CAB), 02.06.44, C/6658, enclosing 'Preliminary Notes on Rockex II', 23.05.44, CAB 21/2522.
33 Pidgeon, *The Secret Wireless War*, pp.17–19.
34 Burrows (Cairo) to Dinlop (FO), YD125/G, FO 850/46A.
35 Davies, *MI6 and the Machinery of Spying*, pp.188–9.
36 Bertrand, *Enigma*, p.256.
37 Harris, 'Foreword' in Paterson, *Voices*, p.6.
38 Hinsley, 'The influence of Ultra in the Second World War' in Hinsley and Stripp (eds), *Code-Breakers*, pp.11–12.
39 Parrish, *The Ultra Americans*, pp.285–6
40 Bennett, *Behind the Battle*, pp.xvi–xviii.
41 Calvocoressi, *Top Secret Ultra*, p.4. See also Kahn, 'Code-Breaking in World Wars I and II', p.638.
42 Paterson, *Voices*, p.46.
43 The term GCHQ had been inaugurated as a cover name perhaps as early as late 1939, because of the growing volume of deliveries to the Bletchley site (see the correspondence in HW 14/3). I am indebted to the GCHQ historian for this point.

44 Calvocoressi, *Top Secret Ultra*, pp.11–13.
45 Ibid., p.15.
46 Millward, 'Life in and out of Hut 3', in Hinsley and Stripp (eds), *Code-Breakers*, p.27.
47 See for example Clayton, *The Enemy is Listening*.
48 Grey and Sturdy, 'The 1942 Reorganization', pp.311–33.
49 Bennett, *Morton*, p.267.
50 Welchman, *The Hut Six Story*, pp.179–80.
51 Welchman, Hinsley and Crankshaw to Travis, 'A Note on the Future of G.C. and C.S.', 17.09.44, HW 3/169.
52 Ibid. On Slim's complaints see Aldrich, *Intelligence and the War Against Japan*, pp.316–17.
53 Part 1, 'The General Problem of Intelligence and Security in Peace' (personal for Director), Preliminary Draft, 09.44, HW 3/169.
54 Clarke, 'Post War Organisation', pp.118–22
55 Tiltman (GC&CS), 'Note by the Chairman; Brigadier Tiltman on Mr Welchman's Statement', 04.10.44, HW 3/30.
56 Bentinck, 'The Intelligence Machine', 10.01.45, CAB 163/6.
57 Information kindly supplied by the GCHQ historian.
58 Travis (D/GCHQ), 'Post-War Sigint Organsation',14.09.45, HW 64/68.
59 Winnifrith memo, 'GC&CS – Post War Reorganisation', 13.10.45, FO 366/1518.
60 Travis (D/GCHQ) to Crombie (T), 19.12.45, FO 366/1518.
61 Wilson had already realised that retention and promotion would be a problem. Keeping people in jobs where they were best suited for the period of the war was one thing, but developing the careers of such specialists over decades was another. Wilson (GCHQ) to Crombie (T), 'Rejoinder to Treasury Counter-Proposals', 13.11.45, FO 366/1518.
62 Bodsworth (GCHQ) to Wenger (NSS), 09.06.46, Box 104, CNSG records, RG 38, NARA.
63 Special Order by Sir Edward Travis, Director, GC&CS, 07.05.45, HW 3/29.
64 Keith (Anderson) to Travis (D/GCHQ), 22.10.45, HW14/136.
65 Director's Order 89, 'Eastcote', 24.01.46, HW 14/164.
66 There would be ninety-three technical staff, 180 in TA, 475 in Cryptographic, eighty-three in intelligence, 150 in cypher security, plus thirty-six administrative staff. Director's Order, 'Move of GC&CS', 31.10.45, ibid.
67 See for example Treasury to Wilson (GCHQ), 24.06.46, T 220/1356, TNA, which give Wilson's address as 'Station X'.
68 Smith, *Station X*, p.177.
69 Newman (Manchester University) to DDA (GCHQ), 12.11.45, HW 64/59.
70 Bromley (FO), 'Distribution of BJ's in the Foreign Office', 26.09.45, HW 64/80; Crawshaw to Travis, reports on distribution, 3–13.10.45, ibid.
71 Ibid.

Chapter 4: The KGB and the Venona Project

1 Haynes and Klehr, *Venona*, pp.51–2.
2 'Venona' is the last and best-known code name for this programme, but it appears to have no meaning, and no one knows why it was chosen
3 Andrew, *Defence of the Realm*, p.369
4 Albright and Kunstel, *Bombshell*, pp.209–10; Andrew, *Defence of the Realm*, pp.367–8.
5 Andrew, 'The Venona Secret', pp.209–13.
6 Unpublished memoir, ch.12, 'Soviet Spies and the Atomic Bomb', George Strauss papers, STRS 1/2 CCC.
7 West, *Venona*, p.15.
8 Aid, *Secret Sentry*, p.5.
9 Benson and Warner, *Introductory History of Venona*, pp.2–4.
10 Aid, *Secret Sentry*, pp.2–3.
11 West, *Venona*, p.11; Aid, 'The Russian Target', p.3
12 Ibid., pp.4–5.
13 Benson and Warner, *Introductory History of Venona*, xxi.
14 Albright and Kunstel, *Bombshell*, pp.205–7.
15 Haynes and Klehr, *Venona*, p.31.
16 Ball and Horner, *Breaking the Code*, p.196.
17 Lamphere claimed that there had been some helpful 'black bag jobs', ibid., p.208.
18 Meredith Gardner, undated report on the compartmentalisation of Venona, HW15/58.
19 Ibid.
20 Ibid.
21 Aid, *Secret Sentry*, p.15; Smith, *Spying Game*, pp.296–7. On Coleridge, see also 'Summary of War Diary' G4A, April 1946, 06.05.46, Box 160, CNSG records, RG 38, NARA. I am indebted to Ralph Erskine for this document.
22 Ball and Horner, *Breaking the Code*, pp.197–8.
23 Ibid.; West, *Venona*, p.27.

24 Wenger (NSS) to Loehnis (GCHQ), 11.08.47, Box 103, CNSG records, RG 38, NARA.
25 About 1,800 were in London, and the rest were at intercept stations. Wilson (GCHQ) to Pitbaldo (T), DAW/199, 25.02.48, enclosing 'GCHQ "B" Class Officers', T 220/1410; Wilson (GCHQ) to Peck (T), 23.11.48, ibid.
26 DD/SP to CSS, 'USSR (Comintern) W/T Transmissions', 03.06.43, HW 34/23. See also Steward memo, 'MU Case No.19 (X/285)', 20.05.43, ibid.
27 Wenger (NSS) to Bodsworth (GCHQ), 03.07.46, Box 101, CNSG records, RG 38, NARA. In June 1946 Bodsworth replaced Pritchard, who had left to work in the City.
28 West, Venona, p.29.
29 Weinstein and Vassiliev, The Haunted Wood, p.262.
30 Andrew and Gordievsky, KGB, pp.308–9.
31 The National Cryptological School, On Watch: Profiles from the National Security Agency's Past 40 years, Chapter Three – 'Treachery and Triumph: Black Friday', pp.19–22 (FOIA).
32 This material from RG 38 is excellently summarised in Alvarez, 'Behind Venona', p.180.
33 Andrew, 'The Venona Secret', p.219.
34 Borovik, Philby Files, pp.259–62.
35 Haynes and Klehr, Venona, pp.51–2.
36 Modin, My Five Cambridge Friends, p.185.
37 Borovik, Philby Files, pp.259–62.
38 Ibid.
39 Andrew, Defence of the Realm, p.379; Ball and Horner, Breaking the Code, p.202.
40 Andrew, Defence of the Realm, p.374.
41 'Development of the "G" – "Homer" ["Gomer"] Case', 11.11.51, HW 15/58.
42 Haynes and Klehr, Venona, p.55
43 Entry for 08.07.47, Montgomery Diary, 180/34, IWM.
44 Aldrich, Hidden Hand, p.110.
45 Ibid., pp.110–11; Manne, Petrov, pp.180–1.
46 Cain, 'Venona in Australia', pp.242–7; presentation by Oleg Tsarev, Oxford Conference, September 1999.
47 Ball and Horner, Breaking the Code, p.177.
48 Andrew, 'Australian Intelligence Community', pp.127–9; McKnight, Australia's Spies, pp.10–11. MI5 Report, 'Security in the Dominions', Appendix to JIC (48) 127 (Final) Guard, 17.12.48, L/WS/1/1074, IOLR.
49 McKnight, Australia's Spies, pp.19–22.
50 Andrew, 'The Venona Secret', p.217;

McKnight, Australia's Spies, pp.30–1, 49–50.
51 Cain, 'Venona in Australia', p.247.
52 Hennessy, Secret State, pp.90–1.
53 West, Venona, p.xiv.

Chapter 5: UKUSA – Creating the Global Sigint Alliance

1 Entry, 21.11.45, Cunningham diary, MSS 52578, BL.
2 Wark, 'Cryptographic Innocence', p.659.
3 Richard Mottram, the Permanent Secretary, Intelligence, Security and Resilience, has declared, 'There is no "UK/USA Treaty 1948".' Mottram to Professor Peter Hennessy, Queen Mary College London, 23.08.06. I am most indebted to Peter Hennessy for sight of this letter. However, most disconcertingly, Burton-Miller refers to 'the UK–USA Comint Treaty of 1948' in Burton-Miller (GCHQ) to Anderson (CAB), R/1712/207/4, 11.07.61, CAB 163/12. There was clearly some sort of further agreement concluded in 1948.
4 Thorne, Allies of a Kind.
5 Richelson, US Intelligence Community, p.269.
6 Paige to Espe (Op.23-Y), 'American Codes Held by Stella Polaris', 08.05.46, Box 64, Entry 171A, RG226. See also Smith, Spying Game, pp.294–5.
7 Ibid., p.16.
8 Entry 21.11.45, Cunningham diary, MSS 52578, BL; Wark, 'Cryptographic Innocence', pp.558–9; Andrew, President's Eyes Only, p.161.
9 He was accompanied by Harry Hinsley, Clive Loehnis and Rear Admiral Rushbrooke, the Director of Naval Intelligence.
10 Andrew, 'The Making of the Anglo–American Sigint Alliance', pp.103–6; Ball and Horner, Breaking the Code, p.165.
11 DNI to ACNS, 20.09.45, ADM 223/397.
12 GBNIET (Sydney) to DNI, 10.11.45, ADM 223/385.
13 DNI to NZ Navy Board, 27.11.45, ADM 223/397.
14 C in C EIS to DNI, 13.01.46, ibid.
15 Ball and Horner, Breaking the Code, p.166.
16 Shedden to Travis (GCHQ), 06.07.46 (Cream), ADM 223/385, TNA; Ball and Horner, Breaking the Code, p.162.
17 Poulden also headed up Australian comsec, presided over by Cypher Security Committee. See Freneton memo, 'Cypher Security', 06.02.48, item 1, CRS A1209, NAA.
18 There are widely different accounts of

Thompson's start date. John Rendle, a GCHQ officer, seems to have been Acting Director in 1951, and then D.M. Moriarty by the spring of 1952. Thompson took over shortly after. See Moriarty (Acting Director DSB) to Fleming (DFA), 'Purchase of High Frequency Direction Finders for the Technical Section, DSB', 15.04.52, CRS A816 48/302/110, NAA.

19 Ball and Horner, *Breaking the Code*, pp.167–8; Andrew, 'Australian Intelligence Community', pp.223–5; Blaxland, *Signals Swift and Sure*, p.47.

20 Aid, *Secret Sentry*, p.13.

21 Wark, 'Cryptographic Innocence', pp.639–65; Sawatsky, *For Services Rendered*, p.29. I am much indebted to the guidance of Matthew Aid on these matters.

22 Jensen, *Cautious Beginnings*, pp.134–5.

23 Andrew, 'Australian Intelligence Community', pp.223–5.

24 Johnson, *American Cryptology*, Vol.1, p.17; Aid, 'The Russian Target', p.11.

25 BPC/F/1, 'Comint Relations with Third Parties Affecting BRUSA Relationships', Appendix P, 14.02.52, Top Secret Eider, NSA FOIA.

26 Wenger (NSS) to Jones (GCHQ), 4.06.46, Box 101, CNSG records, RG 38, NARA.

27 Director's Order 94, 'Eastcote', 16.02.46, HW 14/164.

28 Ball and Horner, *Breaking the Code*, p.184.

29 Johnson, *American Cryptology*, Vol.1, p.160.

30 A-2 to Naval Communications Annex, 'Request for British Comintsum Publications', 19.03.48, 21450, Box 41, USAF D of I records, RG 341, NARA.

31 Cabell to Air Police Division, 28.04.48, 21200, Box 40, ibid.

32 JIC (48) 15th mtg Confidential Annex, 'Circulation of JIC Reports to the Central Intelligence Agency', 20.02.48, CAB 159/3.

33 Aid, *Secret Sentry*, p.10

34 USCIB 18th mtg, 08.01.47, FOIA.

35 Brigadier General USAF, Acting Director of Intelligence, Walter R. Agee, to US Coordinator of Joint Operations, 07.06.48, 'Proposed U.S.-Canadian Agreement', USAF D of I records, File 2-1200/2-1299, Box 40, RG 341, NARA.

36 Johnson, *American Cryptology*, Vol.1, p.18

37 Ibid., p.19.

38 Ratcliff, *Delusions of Intelligence*, pp.167–8.

39 Hayes (Chief) ASA, 'US and British Collaboration on Combined Cipher Machine Development', 01.04.47, File 381, Box 5, Army Int. TS-Decimal File,

1945–52, Entry 47A, RG 319, NARA.

40 Matthew Aid, 'US Humint and Comint in the Korean War: From the Approach of War to the Chinese Intervention', pp.15–50.

41 Riste, *Norwegian Intelligence Service*, pp.95–7; Tamnes, *Cold War in the High North*, pp.76–7.

42 UKHC Ceylon to Defence Dept, 21.04.50, DO 35/2418.

43 Aid, *Secret Sentry*, pp.25–7; Johnson, *American Cryptology*, Vol.1, p.39.

44 JCS 2010/19, 'Expanded Requirement of the Armed Forces Security Agency (AFSA) in View of Current World Situation', 24.07.50, Box 105, Entry 335, RG 341, NARA.

45 Young (USAF) to Coordinator USCIB, 'Site Requirement', 15.07.52, 224100-, Box 66, ibid.

46 Johnson, *American Cryptology*, Vol.1, p.74.

47 NSA, *On Watch: Profiles from the National Security Agency's Past 40 Years*, p.17, declassified by NSA under FOIA.

48 Samford (D of I USAF) to Twining, 06.08.52, 224400, Box 66, USAF D of I records, RG 341, NARA.

49 Memo for Sec. of Defense, 'Formal Implementation of NSCID No.9 Revised', 20.11.52, 311.5, Box 343, Entry 199, RG 330, NARA.

50 Aid, 'The Russian Target', p.9.

51 Bradley (JCS), 'Proposed Cryptologic Establishment Outside the Washington Area', 27.11.51, File 380.01, Box 7, Army Int. TS Decimal File, 1945–52, Entry 47A, RG 319, NARA.

52 JCS 2010/60, 'National Security Agency Construction Project', 03.11.52, Box 105, Entry 335 RG 341, NARA.

53 Freeman, *How GCHQ Came to Cheltenham*, pp.1–12.

54 Jones, *Reflections on Intelligence*, pp.14–15.

55 Lewin, *Ultra Goes to War*, pp.129–33; Jones, *Reflections on Intelligence*, p.15.

56 'Protest Greets Howe at GCHQ', *Gloucestershire Echo*, 15.07.84.

57 Freeman, *How GCHQ Came to Cheltenham*, pp.11–33. For similar reasons of 'fit' into buildings, the Americans had carried out a de facto separation of their comsec element at the same time. Johnson, *American Cryptology*, Vol.1, p.27.

58 Freeman, *How GCHQ Came to Cheltenham*, pp.15–33. Private information.

59 Sturdy and Grey, 'A Chaos that Worked', pp.47–68.

THE 1950s: FIGHTING THE ELECTRONIC WAR

Chapter 6: 'Elint' and the Soviet Nuclear Target

1 JIC (47) 65 (0), 'Summary of Principal External Factors Affecting Commonwealth Security', 29.10.47, L/WS/1/986, IOLR.
2 Holloway, *Stalin and the Bomb*, pp.215–19.
3 The best account of this is offered in Goodman, *Spying on the Nuclear Bear*, pp.36–56.
4 Ibid.
5 JIC (48) (0) (second revised draft), 'Sigint intelligence requirements', 11.05.48, L/WS/1196, IOLR.
6 Ibid.
7 Stripp, *Code-Breaker in the Far East*, pp.50–60; Jones, *Reflections*, pp.14–16.
8 Aid, 'The Russian Target', p.13
9 Confidential Annex, 'Sigint Intelligence Requirements – 1948', 02.48, CAB 159/3.
10 SEAC Noise Investigation Bureau report for May 1945, WO 203/4089.
11 R.V. Jones, *Most Secret War*, p.92.
12 Bonsall, 'Bletchley Park and the RAF Y Service'.
13 Johnson, *American Cryptology*, Vol.1, p.10.
14 Hughes to Hodges (Asst CoAS A-2), 26.02.45, File 1945, Box 77, Vandenberg Papers, LC; *Condensed Analysis of the Ninth Air Force in the European Theatre of Operations*, 1984, 120, CAFH.
15 Captain Wenger, US Navy Coordinator of Joint Operations, to Colonel R.P. Klocko, USAF, CJO 0001922, 12.03.48, memo: 'British Proposal for Liaison on "Noise Investigation" ', USAF D of I records, File 2-1100/2-1199, Box 40, RG 341, NARA.
16 As a quid pro quo Jones was made scientific adviser to GCHQ with a deputy based permanently at Cheltenham. This eventually blossomed into the post of GCHQ Chief Scientist, the first incumbent being the talented Gerald Touch, a lifelong friend of Jones. Jones, *Reflections on Intelligence*, pp.15–17.
17 McMurtie (JSM), to Moore (Pentagon), 20.11.48, File 2-8300–2-8399, USAF D of I records, RG 341, NARA.
18 Aid, *Secret Sentry*, pp.56–7.
19 Memo for D of I and CNI, 17.11.48, Microfilm Reel 1031, CAFH.
20 Addison (AOC 60 Grp) to Porter (DDS B/1), 25.03.46, AIR 40/2591.
21 It had previously been located at Medmenham.
22 Mtg to discuss a paper on Tactical Sigint, 23.07.47, AIR 40/2591, TNA
23 Peter Long, *In Support of So Many*.
24 Air Technical Intelligence Study, 'Soviet Electronic Countermeasures', 10.06.51, 20034, Box 149, USAF D of I records, RG 341, NARA; Air Technical Intelligence Study, 'Soviet Air Communications', 12.07.51, 20032, ibid.
25 Sontag and Drew, *Blind Man's Buff*, pp.12–23.
26 Oscar Martinez, 'The Account of the Sinking of the USS *Cochino*', 08.49, http://www.sid.hill.com/ntins/bbs-034a.htm
27 Lederer, *The Last Cruise*, pp.78–9.
28 Sontag and Drew, *Blind Man's Buff*, pp.7–24.
29 Packard, *Century*, pp.195–7; Tamnes, *High North*, p.77; Burrows, *By Any Means Necessary*, pp.108–9.
30 Bradley memos, 'Special Electronic Airborne Search Operations', 05.05.50 and 22.07.50, and Truman minute 19.05.50, HST microfilm, Pt.2, Reel 3, HUL.
31 Tamnes, *High North*, p.79; Riste, *Norwegian Intelligence*, pp.62–3.
32 Tamnes, *High North*, pp.122–3.
33 Porter (DS) to RWE Watton, 27.02.46, enclosing DD of Sigs (B), 'Tactical Signals Intelligence in Peace and War', 22.02.46, AIR 40/2591.
34 Addison (AOC 60 Grp) to Porter (DDS B/1), 25.03.46, ibid.
35 JIC (51) 96th mtg,(5), 'Inter Service Scheme for the Training of Russian Linguists for War', 14.09.51, CAB 159/10.
36 William Trites and Forrest G. Hogg took up equivalent roles in the UK. See Tamnes, *High North*, pp.116–17; D of I USAF to US Air Attaché London, 'Liaison with GCHQ', 26.10.52, 235700, Box 68, D of I records, RG 341, NARA.
37 JIC 611/1, 'Intelligence Estimate of Technical Characteristics and Tactical Employment of Soviet Electronic Devices', 18.06.52, JCS 1951-3 350.09 USSR (12-19-49) Sec.1 RG 218, NARA.
38 AFOIN-T to D of I USAF, 16.04.52, 223200, Box 64, USAF D of I records, RG 341, NARA.
39 Ibid.
40 Cook (USAF) to Lang (BJSM), 02.06.52, 2-23600, Box 65, ibid.
41 Eubank (COS) to Rowlands (MoS), 31.01.52, DEFE 11/350; Eubank to DRPC, 31.01.52, ibid.
42 COS (52) 152nd mtg (1) Confidential Annex, 04.11.52, ibid.

43 Wenger (NSS) to Travis (GCHQ), 05.03.46, Box 101, CNSG records, RG 38, NARA.
44 Millward, 'Life in and out of Hut 3', in Hinsley and Stripp (eds), *Code-Breakers*, p.26.
45 Jones (GCHQ) to Wenger (NSS), 09.05.46, Box 101, CNSG records, RG 38, NARA.
46 COS (52) 152nd mtg (1) Confidential Annex, 04.11.52, DEFE 11/350.
47 DSI/JTIC (52) 17th mtg, 23.09.52, DEFE 10/497.
48 DSI/JTIC (52) 14th mtg, 22.07.52, ibid.
49 These were WZ966, WZ967 and WZ968, together with a standard bomber version as a trainer, WW346.
50 'Boeing B-29/F-13A/RVB-29A/RB-29A Washington/RB-50'
http://www.spyflight.co.uk/rb29.htm
51 DSI/JTIC (52) 13th mtg, 06.07.52, DEFE 10/497.
52 DSI/JTIC (53) 5th mtg, 17.03.53, ibid.
53 DSI/JTIC (52) 22nd mtg, 16.12.52, ibid.
54 Hooper (GCHQ) to Treasury, 10.04.61, DEFE 25/11. See also Peter Long, 'In Support of So Many'.
55 Brief on Fifth Report to the President by PBCFIA (Recommendation Concerning Fusion of Comint-Elint Activities), 11.03.60, File: 1960 Mtgs. with President Vol. 1 (5), Box 4, Presidential Subseries, Special Assistant Series, OSANA, WHO, Dwight D. Eisenhower Library, Abilene, Kansas.
56 DCEM 1017, 'Control of Radio Countermeasures', 14.02.55, JCS 1954–6, 311 (3-2-7-42) Sec.11, RG 218.
57 The first one after Korea was held in May 1954. JCEC 894/5, 'US/UK Electronic Warfare Discussions', 19.09.55, JCS 1954–6, 337 (9-6-51) Sec.1, RG 218, NARA.
58 McCabe (ASA), 'Electronic Counter-measures Responsibilities', 10.10.52, File 010, Box 1, Army Int. TS Decimal File, 1945–52, Entry 47A, RG 319, NARA.
59 DSI/JTIC (53) 16th mtg, 10.11.53, DEFE 10/497.
60 DSI/JTIC (54) 3rd mtg, 02.02.54, ibid.
61 DSI/JTIC (54) 1st mtg, 05.01.54, ibid.
62 Alexander (SoS Def) to PM, 'Radio Intelligence Flights', 01.10.52, AIR 40/2552.
63 Ibid.

Chapter 7: The Voyages of HMS *Turpin*

1 Tony Beasley, personal recollections (LHCMA).
2 They remained effective until the advent of frequency-hopping radars, which forced the jammers to dilute their power.

3 Lashmar, *Spy-Flights*, pp.60–75.
4 Lord De Lisle and Dudley (SoS Air) to Churchill, 19.03.53, AIR 19/675.
5 Undated map showing course of both Lincoln and MiGs at AIR 55/291.
6 Statement of a witness: Wilma Muller, 13.03.53, AIR55/291. All the witness statements are on this file.
7 FCO to Wahnerheide, No.252, 15.04.53, W1226/83, FO 371/104052.
8 Parliamentary question by George Odey, MP for Beverley, HC Deb, 15.04.53.
9 Roberts (FO) min. to Strang (FO), 21.04.53, CW1226/113(1), FO 371/104054.
10 Hancock (FO) min. 18.06.53, W1226/160, FO 371/104056.
11 The full crew was: S/L Harold J. Fitz, F/Lt Stephen V. Wyles, F/Sgt Peter J. Dunnell, Sgt Ronald F. Stevens, Sgt George B. Long, Sgt William R. Mason, Sgt Kenneth J. Jones. 'Lincoln Bomber Crew', April 1953, AIR 19/675.
12 Private information.
13 James to Pendred (Flying Training Command), 5.05.53, AIR 19/675.
14 Warner min. 28.04.53, W1226/105, FO 371/104054.
15 However, guns no longer had to be 'cocked'. See D.L.D. min. to Eden (PM), 23.09.55, PREM 11/856; Eden (PM) min. 24.09.55, ibid.
16 Burrows, *By Any Means Necessary*, p.5.
17 Makins (Washington) to FO, No.2253, 15.10.53, W1226/220, FO 371/104059. See also Burrows, *By Any Means Necessary*, pp.35–40, where he insists that some of the crew were taken prisoner and not released.
18 HQ 2nd TAF to Air Min., 13.03.53, AIR 19/675; Sec. of State to Churchill, 23.09.53, ibid.
19 Kirkpatrick (Wahnerheide) to (FO), No.405, 16.04.53, W1226/94, FO 371/104052.
20 Ward to AVM Jones (2ATAF), 23.07.53, CW1226/184, FO 371/104058.
21 Kirkpatrick (Wahnerheide) to (FO), No.405, 16.04.53, W1226/94, FO 371/104052.
22 Peter Long, *In Support of So Many*.
23 DSI/JTIC (50) 13th mtg, 26.09.50, DEFE 10/496.
24 DSI/JTIC (54) 15th mtg, 17.08.54, DEFE 10/497.
25 DSI/JTIC (54) 16th mtg, 07.09.54, ibid.
26 Lashmar, *Spy-Flights*, pp.124–5.
27 Comments by E.M. Jones (GCHQ) at Confidential Annex to JIC (55) 99th mtg, 15.11.55, CAB 159/50.

28 Tony Beasley, personal recollections (LHCMA).
29 'Material for a Biography' enclosed in Roake to McGeogh (former FO S/M), 24.04.04, Roake papers, RNSM.
30 Tony Beasley, personal recollections (LHCMA).
31 Lennox-Conyngham (DSD) to DNI, 'Communications Security in Operation Defiant', Top Secret – Froth, 16.12.54, ADM 1/26923.
32 All from Tony Beasley's personal account, with his kind permission.
33 James, *Anthony Eden*, pp.436–7; Goodman, 'Tentacles of Failure', pp.768–73.
34 Eden to Bridges, M.104.56, 9.05.56, AP20/32/78, Avon Papers, Birmingham University Library (BUL).
35 See Goodman, 'The Tentacles of Failure', pp.774–82.
36 Eden (PM) to Antony Head (Min. Def.), 22.12.56, AP20/21/228, Avon Papers, BUL.
37 Aldrich, *Hidden Hand*, p.526.
38 'Sinbad' Sinclair (MI6) to Penney (LCSA), 01.07.56, 1/17, Penney papers, LHCMA.
39 There had also been tussles between JIC and LSIB over the coordination of sigint. See comments of Clive Loehnis at JIC (58) 8th mtg (7), 23.01.58, CAB 159/29; also JIC (58) 55th mtg (6) 14.08.58, CAB 159/30.
40 Elkins (BJSM) to Mountbatten, 16.10.56, ADM 205/110.
41 Elkins (BJSM) to Mountbatten, 31.11.56, ibid. See also Coote, *Submariner*, pp.206–7.
42 Entries for 4, 11 and 12.09.57, Diary of M.J. Hurley, 'Early T-Boat Patrols in the Cold War', RNSM.
43 Entries for 19, 25 and 28.09.57, ibid.
44 Entries for 15, 17, and 19.03.58, ibid.
45 Entries for 28.03.58, 29.03.58 and 1.04.58, ibid.
46 In 1962, the JIC set out special rules for submarines 'designed to apply to operations close to the Soviet coast'. See Butler (SoS) to Carrington (Adm), 'Operation Bargold', 19.06.63, DEFE 13/255.
47 Entries for 4 and 5.04.58, Diary of M.J. Hurley, 'Early T-Boat Patrols in the Cold War', RNSM.
48 Entries for 16, 21 and 27.04.58, ibid.
49 Roake to McGeogh (former FO S/M), 24.04.04, Roake papers, RNSM.
50 Alfie Roake, 'Cold War Warrior', pp.2–4, unpublished MSS, A1999/163, RNSM
51 Roake to McGeogh (former FO S/M), 24.04.04, Roake papers, RNSM.

Chapter 8: Sigint in the Sun – GCHQ's Overseas Empire

1 Porritt, 'Tim Hardy', pp.7–8.
2 Canine (NSA), memo for Sec. of Defense, 'Communication Intelligence Overseas Base Requirements', 10.04.53, 311.5, Box 21, Entry 199, RG 330, NARA.
3 C(51)59, 'Malaya', 21.12.51, Stockwell (ed.) *BDEE, Malaya*, B/3, Part II, p.345.
4 Presentation given by Wg. Cmdr. B. Paton of 51 Sqdn at 'Cold War Intelligence Gathering', Hendon, 18.04.00. I am grateful to Anthony Short for information about radios.
5 Cloake, *Templer*, pp.224–6.
6 Interview with Sir Andrew Gilchrist, 1992; Gilchrist, *Cod Wars*, pp.11–27.
7 Aid, 'The Russian Target', p.22
8 Aldrich, *Intelligence and the War Against Japan*, pp.288–9.
9 Aldrich and Hopkins, *Intelligence*, p.233.
10 JCS to CINCFE Tokyo, JCS 86211, 20.03.51, FECOM Records, RG 4, Box 43, DMM. I am indebted to Matthew Aid for a copy of this document.
11 Young (USAF) to Coordinator USCIB, 'Site Requirement', 15.07.52, 224100, Box 66, D of I records, RG 341, NARA.
12 JCS to CINCFE Tokyo, JCS 86211, 20.03.51, FECOM Records, RG 9, Box 43, DMM. I am indebted to Matthew Aid for a copy of this document.
13 Counter-draft, 'Formosa-US Government on Radio Communications Units', 08.03.55, Box 55, Records of the Office of Chinese Affairs, Lot 56 D625, RG 59, NARA.
14 Prime Minister's Meeting on the Future of Hong Kong and the Colonial Territories in the South-West Pacific, Brief for the Minister of Defence (Hong Kong), DEFE 13/309.
15 'Schematic Analysis of Utility of Functions Performed by UK Military Forces in Various Overseas Locations', annex to 'US Preferred Positions on British Overseas Deployments', 1967, SD to US Embassy London, 21.08.63, Box 1, Lot Files, UK – Office of Northern European Affairs, RG 59, NARA.
16 Redman (VCIGS), Note by COS Representative on the Mason Committee, 'Operation Debenture', 22.06.54, AIR 40/2552.
17 Note for Secretary, 'Defence Signals Branch Tasks', 07.48, item 36, CRS A5964, NAA. The targets have been redacted but remain (just) legible.

18 Whitely (367 SU) to SIO RAF Hong Kong, 'RAAF Linguist Training', 30.07.56, item 106e, CRS A1838, NAA.

19 VCAS memo, 'Manning of Special Signals Units', 01.57, AIR 20/10100. Vietnamese was taught at an Air Force language school at Point Cook in Victoria.

20 Sly, *Horse Grows Horns*, pp.166–7.

21 Ibid., pp.162–4.

22 Ken Sly replaced Nicodemus 'Naky' Doniach as head of JTLS in 1966.

23 Bramall (CBFHK) to Carver (CDS), 'Force Levels in Hong Kong', 03.07.74, FCO 46/1172.

24 Hunt, Russell and Scott, *Mandarin Blue*, pp.121–2.

25 http://www.rafmtd.co.uk/vintage/vintage.html.

26 Potts (DD/AEI) minutes, 'Chinese Interest in Nuclear Weapons', 15 and 17.06.60, IAE410/8G, FO 371/149546.

27 Eden to Selwyn Lloyd, 30.04.56, M.86/56, AP 20/21/84, Avon Papers, BUL.

28 Eden to Selwyn Lloyd, 04.05.56, M.95/56, AP20/21/94, ibid.

29 Lashmar and Oliver, *Britain's Secret Propaganda War*, p.69.

30 Zuluetta to Millard, 25.05.56, PREM 11/1450; Eden min., 26.05.56, ibid.

31 MoD to GHQ Middle East Land Forces, DEF 4572, 19.09.56, AIR 20/9228.

32 MoD to GHQ Middle East Land Forces, DEF 4386, 17.08.56, ibid.

33 Packard, *Century*, pp.432–3.

34 Johnson, *American Cryptology*, Vol.1, pp.236, 239.

35 Aldrich, *Hidden Hand*, p.486.

36 Ranelagh, *The Agency*, pp.301–3.

37 This was known as the Paramount Committee.

38 Pedlow and Welzenbach, *The CIA and the U-2*, pp.115–17.

39 DDE Diary, 28.10.56, DDEL. On American reactions see especially Andrew, *President's Eyes Only*, pp.230–2.

40 Dulles to Phleger, 11.05.64, Folder 31, Box 53, Allen Dulles papers, Princeton University.

41 Hahn, *United States, Great Britain and Egypt*, pp.224–30; Dorril, *MI6*, pp.642–3.

42 Johnson, *American Cryptology*, Vol.1, p.235.

43 Selwyn Lloyd to Director of GCHQ, E.M. Jones (D/GCHQ), 20.09.56, AIR20/10621 (I am indebted to W. Scott Lucas for drawing this document to my attention); GHQ ME to MoD, 17.08.56, AIR20/9228.

44 Presentation given by Wg Cmdr B. Paton, 51 Squadron, on 'Cold War Intelligence Gathering', RAF Hendon, 18.04.00.

45 Horne, *Macmillan 1957–1986*, p.96.

46 Wright, *Spycatcher*, pp.109–11.

47 P. Hennessy, 'What the Queen Knew', *Independent on Sunday*, 21.12.94.

48 VCAS memo, 'Manning of Special Signals Units', 01.57, AIR 20/10100.

49 Hailsham to Eden, 17.10.56, DEFE13/230; Draft Brief, 01.12.56, ibid; D(57) 3, 'Defence Facilities in Ceylon', 21.01.57, ibid. See also 'W/T Stations and Perkar', T 225/1486.

50 UKHC Ceylon to Defence Dept, 21.04.50, DO 35/2418.

51 Mtg at the Admiralty, 26.10.51, DO35/2418; L62/370A, 'Ceylon, Anderson WT Station', 6.07.54, ADM 1/25489, TNA; Milt Branch to C in C EI, 23.03.55, ADM 1/24680.

52 'Note on Retention of Those Service Facilities in Ceylon which are Vital to the Defence of the Commonwealth', T225/485.

53 Hailsham to Eden, 17.10.56, DEFE 13/230; Draft Brief, 01.12.56, ibid; D(57) 3, 'Defence Facilities in Ceylon', 21.01.57, ibid. See also 'W/T Stations and Perkar', T225/1486.

54 Horne, *Macmillan 1957–1986*, pp.96–7. See also Macmillan diary, 17.07.58, BOD.

55 Youle (ADC(D)), 'Report on the Disposal of Equipment and Stores and on Various Accounting and Contracts Aspects Arising From the RAF Withdrawal from Iraq, April–May 1959', 26.06.59, AIR 20/10769.

56 Ibid.

57 Philpott to VCAS, 'RAF Requirements in Cyprus', 27.04.59, AIR 20/10328.

58 Stanford (AIR) to Herbecq (T), 15.05.57, T 225/753.

59 Easter, 'GCHQ', p.684.

60 Cyprus Committee, 'The Boundaries of the Sovereign Base Areas in Cyprus', memo by Minister of Defence, 07.05.59, AIR 20/10328.

61 Carruthers (HQSBAA) to Heskett (MoD), 23.11.70, AIR 20/10260.

62 COS.715/27/5/60, Sec. COS to Wright (MoD), 'Sovereign Base Areas', 27.05.60, AIR20/10932.

63 COS (61) 447, 'Cyprus – Future Policy', 23.11.61, AIR 20/11067.

64 Thorneycroft (Min Def) to Douglas-Home (PM), 'Retention of our Facilities in Cyprus', 3.01.64, DEFE 1/396. Also COS 6/64 'Cyprus', 03.01.63, ibid.

65 See the brilliant account in Jones, *Britain and the Yemen Civil War*, pp.35, 116–17.

66 COS 1447/11/7/9 enclosure, Cheyne to

Bayne (Sec. COS), 08.07.69, DEFE 32/18.

67 ANZAM JIC Report No3/1964, 'The Military and Subversive Threat from Indonesia', 01.07.64, AWM 121125/G/1.

68 Blaxland, *Signals Swift and Sure*, pp.97–8.

69 Porritt, 'Tim Hardy', pp.7–8.

70 COS 1447/11/7/9 enclosure, Cheyne to Bayne (Sec. COS), 08.07.69, DEFE 32/18. Hence most of the SAS memoir accounts do not mention tactical sigint.

71 Walker, 'Borneo', pp.7–15.

72 Here 9 Signals Regiment became 9 ANZUK Signals Regiment, with Australia's 121 Signals Squadron doing most of the sigint work until it was withdrawn by the Whitlam government in the 1970s.

73 Blaxland, *Signals Swift and Sure*, pp.94–5.

74 JIC Aust Report No.4/1968, 'Australian Intelligence Priorities', 29.05.68, AWM 121 25/B/1.

75 JIC (FE) 17/65 (Final), 'An Assessment for Planning Purposes of the Likely Duration of the Confrontation', 04.03.65, AIR23/8646.

76 COS 219/65, 'Possible Military Responses to Continued Confrontation', 30.12.65, ibid.

77 Van der Bijl, *Confrontation*, p.139.

78 COS 1447/11/7/9 enclosure, Cheyne to Bayne (Sec. COS), 08.07.69, DEFE 32/18.

79 Easter, *British Policy Towards Indonesia*, pp.23, 28, 108, 125, 207, 223. Easter's book is excellent on the matter of sigint.

80 McNaughton memo, 'McNamara–Healey Conversation in London', 30.05.65, File: Klein Memos, Box 5, NSF – Name Files, LBJL.

81 Van der Bijl, *Confrontation*, p.80.

82 Blaxland, *Signals Swift and Sure*, pp.94–5.

83 The SAS remained in Brunei into the 1970s, largely in the context of counter-coup activity. The SAS 'Special Task Squadron' trained the Special Branch unit designated to be the Sultan's bodyguard. They also trained an additional unit known as the 'snatch squad', whose role was to rescue the Sultan in the event of a coup. Only the leader of the unit was told of its covert role; even the Sultan was not informed for fear he would talk. See HQ Special Air Service Group memo, 'SAS Assistance for RBMR', 08.05.72, FCO 24/1390.

Chapter 9: Blake, Bugs and the Berlin Tunnel

1 Macmillan diary, 21.02.59–3.03.59, BOD. I am most indebted to Peter Catterall for drawing my attention to this passage.

2 Clandestine Services History, 'The Berlin Tunnel Operation', 25.08.67, CIA microfilm, Europe, Reel 2, LL.

3 BSCB 17th mtg, 'Appendix E, 'Scramble Facilities for CCG (BE)', 07.10.46, FO 371/54986, TNA; BSCB 12th mtg, Appendix F, 'Directory Enquiries', 10.05.46, FO 371/54984.

4 Assistant Deputy Commissioner ACABRIT to FO, Sec.4134, 'Signal Security', 23.02.48, CG1114/G, FO 371/70897.

5 CC(M) (49) 16, 04.08.49, DEFE 41/78; JIC (52) 73, 'German Security', 21.11.52, CAB 158/74.

6 Davies, *SIS and the Machinery of Spying*, pp.215–16.

7 Ibid.

8 Stafford, *Spies Beneath Berlin*, 2nd edn, pp.131–2.

9 Davies, *SIS and the Machinery of Spying*, pp.215–16.

10 Blake, *No Other Choice*, pp.180–1.

11 Clandestine Services History, 'The Berlin Tunnel Operation', 25.08.67, CIA microfilm, Europe, Reel 2, LL.

12 Stafford, *Spies Beneath Berlin*, 2nd edn, pp.141–2.

13 CIA internal histories reproduced in Steury, *Front Line*, pp.328–405; Clandestine Services History, 'The Berlin Tunnel Operation', 25.08.67, CIA microfilm, Europe, Reel 2, LL.

14 Richelson and Ball, *Ties that Bind*, pp.260–1. Stafford is sceptical on this point. *Spies Beneath Berlin*, 2nd edn, pp.39–42.

15 Aid, *Secret Sentry*, pp.46–7.

16 Johnson, *American Cryptology*, Vol.1, pp.92–3. Information from Matthew Aid.

17 Johnson, *American Cryptology*, Vol.2, pp.341–2.

18 Blake, *No Other Choice*, p.181.

19 By 5 May 1956 there had been over two thousand visitors. Political Branch (Berlin) to Chancery, 08.05.56, WG 1373/5, FO 371/124647.

20 Peck (Berlin) to Hope (Bonn), 04.05.56, WG 1373/4, ibid.

21 Blake, *No Other Choice*, p.216; Andrew, *Defence of the Realm*, p.488.

22 BBC2, *Cold War: Espionage* (Ted Turner Productions), broadcast 18.04.99.

23 CIA internal histories in Steury, *Front Line*, pp.328–405; Wallace and Melton, *Spycraft*, pp.138–9.

24 Leary, 'George Blake and the Berlin Tunnel'.

25 White to Dulles, 29.09.61, Folder 30, Box 57, Allen Dulles papers, Princeton University.

26 Strong (JIB) to Minister of Defence, Harold Watkinson, 29.08.60, DEFE 13/9. Also private information.
27 Riste, *Norwegian Intelligence Service*, p.11.
28 Aldrich, *Espionage, Security and Intelligence*, pp.147–9. See also Radford (JCS) memorandum, 'Clandestine Listening Devices', 06.04.56, file: Presidential papers 1956 (8), Box 3, Presidential subseries, Special Assistant Series, OSANA, WHO, DDEL.
29 Kennan, *Memoirs, 1950–1963*, p.157.
30 Colville to Morrison, 09.10.52, DEFE 13/16; MoD memo, 'Russian Eavesdropping', enclosed in Morrison (MoD) to Colville, 13.10.52, ibid.
31 Eden to Churchill, 25.10.52, PREM 11/760; Alexander to Churchill, 'Russian Eavesdropping', 15.07.54, ibid.
32 Blake, *No Other Choice*, pp.162–3.
33 Ibid., pp.163–4.
34 Montgomery Hyde, *George Blake*, pp.43–5.
35 Macmillan diary, 21.02.59–3.03.59, BOD. I am most indebted to Peter Catterall for drawing my attention to this passage.
36 SM–276–56, 'Clandestine Listening Devices', 6.04.56, JCS records 1954–6, 371.2 (1-31-56) Sec.1 RB, RG 218, NARA.
37 Kahn, 'Soviet Comint', p.17.
38 Bryant, *Dog Days at the White House*, p.27.
39 State Dept to Moscow, No.3499, 19.03.64, File: Hidden Microphones, Box 9, NSF – Intelligence File, LBJL.
40 Conversation with members of the Borehamwood Local History Society.
41 His assistant at Chester Road was Major C.R. Crooker of SIS. Notes of a mtg at 4 Chester Rd, Borehamwood, 30.11.56, T220/1444. Also Pidgeon, *Secret Wireless War*, pp.177–9
42 Skidmore (T) to Rigby (T), 10.06.58, T 220/1220. This file has since been lost by the Treasury, and I am indebted to Philip Davies for sight of his copies made at an earlier date.
43 Bridges (T) to Strang (FO), 18.08.52, ibid
44 Scott (FCO) to Pumphrey (T), 22.10.56, T 220/1220. Re-equipment costs in 1956 were £41,000.
45 COS (57) 49th mtg 'Research on Eavesdropping', Confidential Annex, 25.06.57, AIR 20/10100.
46 Skidmore (T) to Rigby (T), 10.06.58, T 220/1220.
47 Pumphrey (FO) to Skidmore (T), 03.01.57, T 220/1446.
48 Pumphrey (FO) to Skidmore (T), 11.01.57, ibid.

49 Skidmore, note on visit to Hanslope on 18.01.57, ibid.

Chapter 10: Embassy Wars

1 Jones (T) to Edminston (T), 'Sensitivity Check File', 16.12.86, T 220/1220. This file, detailing the 'bug shop', has since been lost by the Treasury, and I am most indebted to Philip Davies for sight of his copies made at an earlier date.
2 B.5. Report re: movements of P.S. Kuznetsov, 29.04.52, KV 2/1636.
3 The William Marshall case is discussed in Chapman Pincher, *Traitors*, pp.86–7.
4 Note of a meeting between MI5, MI6 and Gambier-Parry, head of DWS, 30.04.52, KV 2/1636.
5 Titchner (Moscow) to Carey-Foster (FO), 09.05.52, KV 2/1636.
6 Ibid.
7 MI5 report by Storrier, 'W.M. Marshall', 20.05.52, KV 2/1667.
8 MI5 report by Storrier, 'W.M. Marshall', 19.05.52, ibid.
9 MI5, note of a meeting with Director of B Division, 10.05.52, ibid.
10 MI5 note of a meeting with Maltby (DWS) by Simkin, 11.06.52, ibid.
11 MI5 note of a meeting with Churchill and Cherwell by Dick White (MI5), 16.06.52, ibid.
12 MI5 memo, 'The Case of William Marshall', 19.06.52, ibid.
13 Simkin (MI5) min to B2A, 27.06.52, KV 2/1638.
14 MI5, note of a meeting at Leconfield House, 20.06.52, ibid. See also White (MI5) to Sillitoe (DG/MI5), 23.06.52, ibid.
15 Eden (SoS FO) to Churchill (PM), PM/52/64, 'W.M. Marshall', 26.06.52, ibid.
16 MI5 report on visit to Hanslope Park, 08.05.52, Appendix, 'List of DWS Personnel in Moscow from December 1950 to December 1951', KV 2/1636. Ker had an MI5 personal file, no.702,720.
17 MI5 memo, 15.06.52, KV 2/1641.
18 Burbidge (MI5) to Carey-Foster (FO), 'William Marshall', 05.07.52, KV 2/1639.
19 B2A, note for the file, interview with Hibberson, 22.07.52, ibid. The implication was probably that he did not think Marshall was homosexual.
20 West, *A Matter of Trust*, pp.47–8.
21 Titchner (Moscow) to Carey-Foster (FO), 9.05.52, KV 2/1636. Smythe PF.751,565 and Howarth PF.759,863.
22 Aldrich, *Hidden Hand*, pp.403–4.
23 Slessor to Sec of State, enclosing 'TASS

Agency Monitoring Station', 13.07.51, AIR 75/92.

24 JIC (51) 83rd mtg.(3), 'TASS Agency Radio Monitoring Station', CAB 159/10

25 Ross (PUSD) min. 23.08.51, NS1921/15, FO 371/94949.

26 Yerofereev to Morrison (SoS FO), 15.08.51, ibid.; Holder min. 26.09.51, ibid.

27 SRT (58) 2(Final) (Revised) Appendix D, 'The Threat to Radio Transmissions from the UK from Soviet and Satellite Forward Signals Intelligence Operations', 23.07.58, DEFE 21/70.

28 'I was one of only two senior people in GCHQ who in 1953 was solidly in favour of setting up LCSA separately from this place! The other of course was Eric [Jones].' Hooper (GCHQ) to Penney (LCSA), 1/29, Penney papers, LHCMA

29 Cypher Policy Board was gradually replaced by a London Communications Security Board, whose title echoed that of the main sigint controlerate, the London Signals Intelligence Board. Report of the CESD Working Party, Annex A, 'Historical Background', 13.05.69, DEFE 32/18.

30 When DWS was wound up in 1972, officials lamented, 'The buccaneering days are over; the Captains Morgan, Blood and Sharkey are now either dead or wearing a sober uniform.' Oakeshott, 04.09.72, Oakeshott Report, CAB 185/12.

31 JIC (53) 92nd mtg. (2), 26.08.53, CAB 159/14

32 MI5 report on visit to Hanslope Park, 8.05.52, KV 2/1636.

33 Statement by Victor Sheymov before the Joint Economic Committee United States Congress, Wednesday, 20.05.98, 'The Low Energy Radio Frequency Weapons Threat to Critical Infrastructure', http://www.fas.org/irp/congress/1998_hr/sheymov.htm

34 Interview, Sir Roderic Braithwaite, p.8, CCC. See also Benjamin, Five Lives in One, pp.149–51. A similar event occurred at the US Embassy in Moscow in 1977.

35 Interview with Victor Sheymov by George Lardner, 04.04.90, File 6, Box 226, Lardner papers, LC.

36 Cradock, Experiences of China, pp.63–7.

37 Peking to FCO, 31.08.67, FCO 21/29.

38 Information kindly provided by the SIS archivist.

39 Cypher Systems Working Party, 3rd mtg, 12.06.68, FCO 19/18.

40 Campbell (Paris) to Denson (FCO), 'Communications with Peking', 01.09.67, FCO 21/29.

41 Jones (SD), 'Inspector Plitt's Report of the Taiwan Situation', 29.06.57, 794a.00/6-2957.1.G, File.116.11, Decimal File 1955–9, RG 59, NARA.

42 Marshall Carter (Acting Director CIA) to Mcgeorge Bundy, 'Audio-Surveillance and Countermeasures Problems Within the United States Intelligence Community', 23.09.64, FOIA, File: NSAM 317, Box 5, NSF, LBJL.

43 Cheasley, 'Century House, 1000 Westminster Bridge Road, SE1, Occupational Services for G.C.B.', March 1966, WORK12/670.

44 'Report of a Visit to East Berlin to Review Security Arrangements', 4990/12, FCO 33/2393.

45 Reeve, Cocktails, Crises and Cockroaches, p.209.

46 By 1973 the Diplomatic Technical Maintenance Staff had become the Communications Technical Services Department.

47 Edkins (CTSD) to Miller (Berlin), 07.06.73, WRE 25/1, FCO 33/2092.

48 Edkins (CTSD), 'East Berlin Embassy – Programme of Works', EBE/NWB/20/73, 07.05.73, ibid.

49 'Report of a Visit to East Berlin to Review Security Arrangements', 4990/12, FCO 33/2393. See also Benjamin, Five Lives in One, pp.153–4.

50 Reeve, Cocktails, Crises and Cockroaches, pp.212–13. The same issues arose over expanded Soviet diplomatic premises in West Berlin. The British requested that the Soviets be allocated premises with 'the characteristics and layout which offer opportunity for technical attack'. Ian Cameron (BSSO (G)) to Jackson (BMG) and copied to John Jones (MI5), 22.07.71, FCO 33/1546.

THE 1960s: SPACE, SPY SHIPS AND SCANDALS

Chapter 11: Harold Macmillan – Shootdowns, Cyphers and Spending

1 Macmillan (PM) to Home (Foreign Secretary), M271/60, 01.08.60, DEFE 13/15.

2 Burrows, By Any Means Necessary, pp.243–4.

3 Pocock, U-2 Spyplane, p.187.

4 Taubman, Secret Empire, pp.305–9.

5 Aid, Secret Sentry, pp.53–5; Horne, Macmillan 1957–1986, pp.224–6.

6 Beschloss, Mayday, pp.356–7.

7 Ambrose, Eisenhower the President, Vol.2, p.584; Burrows, By Any Means Necessary, pp.250–5.

8 Reilly (Moscow) to (FO), Nos. 954 and 957, 11.07.60, 213/4/G, FO 371/173538.

9 Reilly (Moscow) to (FO), 14.06.60, NS1381/82, FO 371/152002.

10 Horne, *Macmillan 1957–1986*, p.225

11 Reilly (Moscow) to (FO), 12.07.60, 213/4/G, FO 371/173538. The subsequent JIC paper was JIC (60) 43 (Final), 'Soviet Threats Against Reconnaissance Flight Bases Following the U-2 Incident', and is summarised in DEFE 13/342.

12 Reilly (Moscow) to FO, 19.07.60, 13/44, FO 371/173540.

13 'Soviet Reply Note on RB-47 Incident', Moscow Home Service, 18.05 GMT, 15.07.60, SU/387.A1/1, SWB. See also Johnson, *American Cryptology*, Vol.1, p.148.

14 Macmillan to Eisenhower, 12.07.60, Z13/23/G, FO 371/173539.

15 'Memorandum on Buzzing of Soviet Ships', Tass in English, 17.47 GMT, 16.07.60, SU/387.A1/1, SWB.

16 Johnson, *American Cryptology*, Vol.1, p.141.

17 Michel (FO) to Wilkison (H/PUSD) 21.07.60 and Wilkinson to Michel, 22.07.60, 13/44, FO371/173540.

18 Andrew, *Defence of the Realm*, pp.484, 493.

19 Macmillan (PM) to Home (Foreign Secretary), M271/60, 01.08.60, DEFE 13/15.

20 Mtg held in the PM's Rooms at the House of Commons, JIC 1850/60, 'Radio Proving Flights', Daunt, 10.11.60, ibid.

21 Minutes, 'Surveillance Meeting', 26.04.60, 16/W/160, ADM 1/27680.

22 Minute by head of Military Branch II, 10.03.61, ibid.

23 Memorandum from PS to V.C.A.S. to PS to S. of S., 'Aircraft Approach Restrictions – Operation TIARA/GARNET', 10.60, AIR 20/12222. The JIC paper prepared for Macmillan was JIC (60) 62 (Revised), 01.09.60.

24 Bufton (ACAS(I)) memo, 'Comments on JIB's memorandum', 08.60, enclosing Hunt (Cab) to Bufton, JIC/1482/60, 09.09.60, AIR 8/1953.

25 On continuing British submarine intelligence operations in the 1960s see Riste, *Norwegian Intelligence Service*, p.228.

26 Speech by Keith Hall, Director NRO, Naval Research Laboratory 75th Anniversary Event,http://www.globalsecurity.org/space/library/news/1998/grab–698.htm

27 Smith (IG), 'Procurement of Foreign Cryptographic Material', 14.04.49, File 310.13, Box 9, Army Int. TS-Decimal File, 1945–52, Entry 47A, RG 319, NARA

28 Ralph Erskine, 'The Admiralty and Cipher Machines'; CPB (52), 1st mtg, Appendix E, CPB/52/1, 'NATO Cryptomaterial: Plan for Production, Distribution, Accounting and Security Control', note by the Secretary, 25.09.52, HW 9/28.

29 FCO to British Defence Liaison Staff (NZ), 19.06.69, FCO19/90, discussed in Matt Russell, BID/60 (Singlet) http://www.jproc.ca/crypto/bid60.html.

30 Johnson, *American Cryptology*, Vol.1, pp.212–18.

31 SM-2721-52, Memo of the Reps. of the British COS, 'Report of the UK/US Communications Security Conference 1952', JCS 1951–3, CCS311 (1-10-42) Sec.15, RG 218, NARA.

32 Alvis was indeed a good system, and was eventually operated in many countries, including Canada and Australia. It was still in use in Canberra in the 1980s.

33 The paper was LCSB (62) 6, 22.05.62.

34 'Provision of On-Line Cryptographic Equipment for NATO', note of a meeting in Mr Trend's Room at the Treasury, 07.06.62, 73/155/01, T 225/2074.

35 Captain Robert F.T. Stannard, CBE, DSO, RN, took over from Major General Sir William Ronald C. Penney, KBE, CB, DSO, MC, as D/LCSA on 01.11.57. I am indebted to Peter Freeman for this information.

36 Summarised in Stephenson (FO) to Trend (Treasury) 29.06.62, T 225/2074.

37 Ibid.

38 UK-46-MWD-N-59 and UK-47-N-59, discussed in Reeve (MoD) to Mitchell (T), 28.08.61, enclosing 'MWDP Agreements Signed Since the MWDP Meeting 22.12.50', T 225/1758.

39 As we shall see in the next chapter, this assertion was far from true.

40 'Provision of On-Line Cryptographic Equipment for NATO', note of mtg 10.07.62, T 225/2074.

41 Stannard (LCESA) to Stephenson (FO), BM55/0504, 29.01.63, T 225/2074.

42 The official who took the call was not impressed, and noted: 'He got nowhere as far as I was concerned.' Hartley (Washington) to Walshe (DEA), 04.09.56, item.2, CRS A1838, NAA

43 Hagelin to Australian Embassy (Washington), 10.56, item 65, ibid. See also Crypto AG (Switzerland), 'Analysis of the CX-52 Machine from the Point of View of Cryptographic Security', 02.54, item.59, ibid.

44 'I am . . . in correspondence with LCSA on the subject.' Rolf (DSB) to Walshe (DEA), 14.12.56, 48/253/630, item 13, ibid.

45 JPW min. Communications Branch, N1223/19.07.58, item.78, ibid., NAA. See also Rolf (DSB) to Walshe (DEA), 'Hagelin Brochures', 02.12.57, item.70, ibid.

46 Hagelin to Hartley (Washington), 27.09.58, item.91, ibid.

47 Clark, *The Man Who Broke Purple*, pp.185–9.

48 Campbell, *Interception Capabilities*, p.vii.

49 The first mention of this subject horrified NSA when it appeared in Bamford, *Puzzle Palace*, pp.321–3.

50 'Gates', Odom (NSA) daily log, 06.11.86, File 8, Box 25, Odom papers, LC. Their suspicions allegedly focused on John McMahon, a senior CIA officer who had been Deputy Director and the predecessor to Gates until 28.03.86.

51 'Wieck', Odom (NSA) daily log, 23.01.86, File 7, Box 25, Odom papers, LC.

52 Wayne Madsen, 'Crypto AG: The NSA's Trojan Whore?', *Covert Action Quarterly*, No.63 (Winter 1998), pp.36–7.

53 'No Such Agency, Part 4: Rigging the Game,' *Baltimore Sun*, 04.12.95; 'NSA's Crypto Sting', *Baltimore Sun*, 10.12.95. The fullest account is given in the biography of Hans Bühler: Strehle, *Verschlüsselt* [Encrypted]: *Der Fall Hans Bühler*.

54 For references to Swedish sigint cooperation see for example Wright, *Spycatcher*, pp.113, 186.

55 See the detailed coverage of Montgomery's conversations during his visits to Yugoslavia and Switzerland in PREM11/1224.

56 LCSB/23/68 (Conclusions), 'The State of Communications-Electronic Security and Measures to Improve it, 1968', CAB164/312. See also Gardiner (CESD) to Cottrell (Cabinet Office), 13.11.68, ibid.

57 Johnson, *American Cryptology*, Vol.1, p.221.

58 CPB (52), 1st mtg, Item 8, 'Current Technical Problems', 06.10.52, HW 9/28.

59 Mins of TC/LSIC, 25.05.61, T 225/2496. Ken Perrin was in the chair.

60 Benjamin, *Five Lives in One*, pp.145–6. However, Michael Hanley, the Director General of MI5, specifically warned Benjamin not to trust Wright's judgement on the issue of moles.

61 Wright, *Spycatcher*, pp.84, 108–14.

62 Ibid., pp.110–13, 240–1.

63 'What is Being Done About Radiation', Stannard (D/LCSA), address to 38th mtg of the [Canadian] Cipher Policy Committee, Apr. 1958, File TS 1325-3 'Communications Security – Crypto Systems', Canadian Department of National Defence, Box 31, RG 24, CNA.

64 Ibid.

65 The handbook was designated AMSP522.

66 LCSC (59) 10 (Final), 'Radiation: Review of Measures Taken or in Hand', 19.06.59, File TS 1325-3 'Communications Security – Crypto Systems', Canadian Department of National Defence, Box 31, RG 24, CNA.

67 Burrough to Ryland, 03.06.69, attached 'Report of the CESD Working Party', DEFE 32/18, cited in Easter, 'GCHQ and British External Policy in the 1960s', p.692.

68 Drew (MoD) min. 'The Templer Report', 03.02.61, ibid.

69 Johnson, *American Cryptology*, Vol.1, pp.227–9.

70 PSIS was created during the 1950s, and eventually had numerous sub-committees.

71 Min. to Collier (T), 'GCHQ', reporting a conversation with Clive Loehnis, 11.04.62, T 213/844.

72 Ibid.

73 Collier (T) to Millward (GCHQ), 18.05.62, T 213/844.

74 GCHQ spending had gone from £4,894,000 in 1953–54 to £7,903,000 in 1962–63, while the total sigint spend had gone from £10,239,000 to £20,520,000 in the same period. Wyatt note, 'Increase in Sigint expenditure in the last decade compared with changes in other Government expenditure', 10.10.62, ibid.

75 Wyatt (T) to Trend (T), 'The Sigint Review, 1962', 05.62, ibid.

76 Winter, 'British Intelligence and the July Bomb Plot', pp.468–94.

77 Hampshire, *Innocence and Experience*, p.11.

78 Loehnis (D/GCHQ) to Stephenson (JIC), D/0948/1/14, 24.06.64, T 213/884.

79 Collier (T) to Trend (T), 'The Sigint Review', 13.07.62, ibid.

80 This paper no longer exists in the Treasury file, having been pulled back by GCHQ even as the review ended, but discussion of its contents is extant.

81 Wyatt (T) to Collier (T), 'The Sigint Review', 17.08.62, T 213/884.

82 Ibid.

83 Collier (T), note of meeting between Hampshire and Trend, 30.10.62, ibid.

84 Wright, *Spycatcher*, pp.246–7. Wright misdates the Hampshire review to 1964, and mistakenly attributes the initiative to the incoming Labour government of

Harold Wilson. However, in other respects his detailed account is remarkably accurate.

85 Collier (T) to Trend (T), 'Hampshire', 26.10.62, T 213/884.

86 Wright, *Spycatcher*, pp.246-7.

87 Thimont (T), to Collier (T), 24.11.64, T199/1089. This subcommittee included the Treasury Third Secretary who looked after expenditure in support of overseas policy.

88 Wyatt (T), 'Review of Sigint: Note for the Record', 14.09.62, T 213/884.

89 Private information.

90 Hampshire, *Innocence and Experience*, p.10.

91 Collini, 'A Life of H.L.A. Hart', pp.108-14.

92 Rees, *Looking for Mr Nobody*, p.85.

93 Lacey, *Hart*, pp.92-3.

94 Wright, *Spycatcher*, pp.246-7.

95 Hampshire, *Innocence and Experience*, p.11; 'Hampshire', *Telegraph*, 15.06.04.

96 Lacey, *Hart*, p.339.

Chapter 12: Harold Wilson – Security Scandals and Spy Revelations

1 King, *The Cecil King Diary*, p.128

2 Jenkins, *A Life at the Centre*, p.383.

3 Entry for 03.07.63, Benn, *Out of the Wilderness*. p.37.

4 Young, 'George Wigg', pp.198-9; Andrew, *Defence of the Realm*, pp.522-5

5 'The Organisation for Security in the Diplomatic Service and Government Communications Headquarters', Aug. 1966, PREM13/1203, fully reproduced in Young, 'George Wigg', pp.203-8.

6 Ibid.

7 Godber (SoS for War) to Thorneycroft (SoS Defence), 16.07.63, DEFE 13/17.

8 Drew (MoD) to Secretary, 'Sergeant Patchett', 03.12.63, ibid.

9 SIC (Germany) (64) 4 (Final), D/6800/1402/28, 06.07.64, discussed at 'Ad Hoc Committee on Personnel Security in Sigint Units in Germany', 17.03.65, AIR 2/17290.

10 LSIB, minutes of a limited mtg on 29.04.65, D/7246/1402/28/LSIB, 11.05.65, ibid.

11 *Report of the Security Commission May 1983*, Cmnd.8876, p.38.

12 Regina vs. Douglas Ronald Britten, Central Criminal Court, No. 7602/B/68, Old Bailey, 04.11.68, pp.12-13, BA 19/45.

13 The recruitment seems to have been KGB rather than GRU. See Andrew and Mitrokhin, *The Sword and the Shield*, p.414.

14 Britten never learned the real identity of 'Vasiley', who had previously served as a

KGB officer in Greece, a posting he had much preferred.

15 Regina vs. Douglas Ronald Britten, Central Criminal Court, No. 7602/B/68, Old Bailey, 04.11.68, pp.4-5, BA 19/45.

16 Ibid., p.6

17 Private information.

18 Thomas, *Signal Success*, pp.368-9.

19 Regina vs. Douglas Ronald Britten, Central Criminal Court, No. 7602/B/68, Old Bailey, 04.11.68, pp.4-5, BA 19/45, p.6

20 Ibid., p.23.

21 West, *A Matter of Trust*, p.161.

22 Regina vs. Douglas Ronald Britten, Central Criminal Court, No. 7602/B/68, Old Bailey, 04.11.68, pp.4-5, BA 19/45, p.6

23 Ibid., pp.10, 23.

24 Bunnett (MoD) to Armstrong (TS), PUS/68/1601/54/3, 10.09.68, BA 19/45.

25 Regina vs. Douglas Ronald Britten, Central Criminal Court, No. 7602/B/68, Old Bailey, 04.11.68, BA 19/45.

26 Pincher, *Too Secret*, p.463; West, *MI5*, pp.161-2

27 Blake, *No Other Choice*, pp.222-57

28 Jessup to Rostow, 'Reflections on the Blake Case', 01.11.66, File: Memo for Rostow, Box 2, National Security File/Intelligence File, LBJL.

29 Ziegler, *Wilson*, pp.267-8.

30 Wilson, *The Labour Government*, p.478.

31 Pimlott, *Wilson*, p.444

32 Ziegler, *Wilson*, pp.267-8.

33 Creevy, 'A Critical Review', p.213.

34 Ziegler, *Wilson*, pp.267-8.

35 Creevy, 'A Critical Review', p.213.

36 Pimlott, *Wilson*, p.444.

37 Jones (FO) min., 06.11.44, FO 850/137.

38 Le Bailly (DGI), 'The Development of the Defence Intelligence Staff: Staff II, 1970-1973', Folder 6, Box 7, Le Bailly papers, CCC.

39 Trend (Cab Sec) to Armstrong (CSD), 05.03.68, enclosing 'Reorganisation of Interdepartmental Intelligence Committee Structure', BA25/41.

40 Littler to Pitchforth, 'Intelligence', 17.08.67, ibid.

41 Young, *The Labour Governments, 1964-70*, p.16.

42 In 1965 its predecessor, the London Communications-Electronics Security Agency, had taken over the Joint Speech Research Unit and also the Services Cypher Development Unit.

43 Albeit the working party noted that American comsec and sigint still did not get on well.

44 'Report of the CESD Working Party', 13.05.69, DEFE 32/18.
45 Gardiner (CESD) to Cottrell (MoD), 13.11.68, CAB 164/312.
46 Benjamin, *Five Lives in One*, pp.143–5.
47 'Report of the CESD Working Party', 13.05.69, DEFE 32/18.
48 Burroughs (FCO) to Ryland (GPO), 'Future of CESD', 3.06.69, ibid.
49 Creevy, 'A Critical Review', p.212.
50 Young, *The Labour Governments, 1964–70*, pp.14–15; Johnson, *American Cryptology*, Vol.2, pp.458–9
51 Taylor (USN) to Wenger (NSA), 28.06.68, Box 104, CNSG records, RG 38, NARA.

Chapter 13: Intelligence for Doomsday
1 Reproduced in Goodman, 'The Dog that Didn't Bark', pp.529–51
2 Friedman, *The Fifty-Year War*, p.351.
3 Aid, *Secret Sentry*, p.144.
4 Le Bailly, 'The Development of the Defence Intelligence Staff: Staff II, 1970–1973', Folder 6, Box 7, Le Bailly papers, CCC.
5 Le Bailly to Butler (Cab Sec), 09.12.93, Folder 5, Box 21, ibid. See also Butler (Cab Sec) to Le Bailly, 14.12.93, ibid.
6 Cradock, *Know Your Enemy*, pp.249–56; also private information. The Americans had realised that the invasion was on by midday on 19 August. Johnson, *American Cryptology*, Vol.2, pp.458–9.
7 Le Bailly to 'Charlie', 01.07.82, Folder 3, Box 7, Le Bailly papers, CCC. See also Aid, *Secret Sentry*, pp.142–6; Cradock, *Know Your Enemy*, pp.241–58.
8 DMO memo, 'Future Requirement for SAS Type Operations', 14.07.58, WO 32/19472. See also memo by Lt Col. Pat Hart, 'The Special Air Service', 1958, McLeod papers, 2/5, LHCMA.
9 257 Signals Squadron provided the communications links from Northag HQ to UK and German missile batteries.
10 Private information.
11 'Operational Directive to 23 SAS and Special Reconnaissance Squadron RAC', Annex to B 2014/10 G (Ops and Plans) 11.09.62, WO 32/19472.
12 Garner, *Codename Copperhead*, pp.19–25.
13 NATO Special Committee – Nuclear Planning Working Group: Role of Tactical Nuclear Weapons (paper by the UK), 12.04.66, CAB 163/38.
14 AWRE Report 012/73, 'Clipeus Reference Documents and the UK ADM Policy 1953–1971', ES4/1372.

15 DOAE M7404, 'Exercise Badger's Lair: The Detectability of Stay-Behind Parties', 06.74, DEFE 48/279.
16 LCSC (61) 17 (Final), ' "Short Burst" Radio Communications Systems', 31.12.61, CAB 21/4601.
17 DOAE M7424, 'An Assessment of the Value to 1(BR) Corps of ESM Provided by 225 Signal Squadron', 01.75, DEFE 48/294.
18 Ibid.
19 What Northag lacked was a local equivalent of the American Guardrail system. Stacy, *US Army Border Operations in Germany, 1945–1983*, p.243.
20 Pocock, *The U-2 Spyplane*, p.81. I am indebted to Chris Pocock for his comments on U-2 sigint systems.
21 DOAE Study No 229, 'The Communications Electronic Support Measures Provided by 225 Signal Squadron to 1 (BR) Corps in War', 10.75, DEFE 48/806.
22 DOAE Project 147, 'The NATO Intelligence System', 06.69, DEFE 48/496.
23 'Experiments on the Use of Information Gained from Remote Sensors on the Battlefield', 1976, DEFE 48/318; Nicholls, 'Unattended Ground Sensors', pp.6–11. Also private information.
24 2ATAF was comprised of squadrons from the Belgian, Netherlands, German and Royal Air Forces.
25 DOAE Project 147, 'The NATO Intelligence System', 06.69, DEFE 48/496.
26 JSP 120 (5), *Manual of Service Intelligence Volume 5: North Atlantic Treaty Organization Standardization Agreements (Stanags) Intelligence*, 11.73, DEFE 73/12.
27 Johnson, *American Cryptology*, Vol.2, p.332.
28 Deletant, *Ceausescu and the Securitate*, p.55.
29 Burrough (UK FCO) to Stewart (Secretary UK JIC (A)), 'NATO Security – Nahit Imre', 28.01.69, FCO 41/441. See also DPS 1006/22/1/69, 'Assessment of Military Damage Done to the UK as a Result of the Imre Affair', 01.69, ibid.
30 Bushell (UK NATO Deleg) to Ashe (FCO), 'NATO – Spy Case', 27.09.68, FO 1116/39.
31 Burrough (UK FCO) to Burrows (UK Rep NAC), EJC 10/579/4, 18.02.69, ibid.
32 Pemberton-Pigott (UK NATO Deleg.) to Burrough (FCO), 07.03.69, ibid.
33 Pemberton-Piggot (UK NATO Deleg.) to Holmer (FCO), 06.08.69, ibid.
34 Frank Cooper (UK MoD) to Bernard Burrows (UK Rep NAC), DSS (P)/7779, 'The Roussilhe Case', 21.11.69, FO1116/40.

35 COS 1102/4/2/70, 'Security breach in NATO', 04.02.70, DEFE 32/19.
36 Ibid. On warning indicators see Hennessy, *Secret State*, pp.9–12.
37 Acting Chief of Defence Staff to Healey (MoD), 'Widespread Lull in Soviet Air Activity', 08.08.69, DEFE13/901. See also Taylor to Healey (MoD), 08.08.69, ibid.
38 COS (I) 7/8/69, Item 1, 'Soviet Military Activity in August 1969', 07.08.69, discussing JIC(A) 69 (SA) 52, 06.08.69, DEFE 32/18.
39 Acting Chief of Defence Staff to Healey (MoD), 'Widespread Lull in Soviet Air Activity', 12.08.69, DEFE 13/901.
40 Taylor (MoD) to Healey, 'Soviet Military Activity' 12.08.69, ibid.
41 Parsons (FCO) to Bushell (UK NATO Deleg), 31.05.67, FCO 41/146.
42 Douglas-Home (SoS FCO) to Heath (PM), 'Proposed Occasional Basing of US SR-71 Photographic Reconnaissance Aircraft in Britain', 16.12.71, DEFE 13/898.
43 Mastny, *A Cardboard Castle*, pp.404, 522.
44 On the impact of intelligence see Herman, 'The Cold War: Did Intelligence Make a Difference?', pp.159–63.

Chapter 14: Staying Ahead – Sigint Ships and Spy Planes

1 Hastie-Smith, 'Nimrod (R)' enclosed in Frank Cooper (DUS (P)) to Healey (Def Sec), 30.07.68, DEFE 68/76.
2 Johnson, *American Cryptology*, Vol.2, pp.315–17, 395.
3 Figg (FCO), 'US/UK Cooperation in Moon Relay Communications', 23.02.67, FCO 46/218.
4 CTS/P(66)1, 'Communications Trials Ship Watch Committee: State of the Project and Future Programme', 25.01.66, MT 40/207.
5 Mins. of 6th Mtg of Working Group B, 06.02.67, DEFE 61/8.
6 'Communications Trials Ship: Sketch Staff Requirements', 1965, MT 40/207.
7 'Government Communications Trials Ship', mins. of a mtg at MoD, 30.06.65, ibid. A prototype of the ship's special trials communications system was built by Racal Special Systems Division at Slough and trialled on 11.12.68. Grantham (DG Weapons Naval) to GCHQ, 29.11.68, DEFE 61/8.
8 'Communications Trials Ship', Notes of a mtg 30.11.65, MT 40/207.
9 CTS/P(66)2, 'Communications Trials Ship Watch Committee: Allocation of Responsibility Between Departments', 25.01.66, ibid.

10 Kay (AEA) to Murray Smith (BT), 'Application of Nuclear Power', 15.03.66, ibid.
11 P. Vane, 'Britain Plans Atom Ship as Radio Voice in Ocean', *Sunday Express*, 05.06.66. See also Communications Trials Ship Watch Committee: Working Group "E" – Finance', mins of mtg 6.07.66, MT 40/207
12 Figg (FCO), 'US/UK Cooperation in Moon Relay Communications', 23.02.67, FCO 46/218; min., 27.02.67, ibid.
13 1957 Elint, 'Naval Radio Research Program', Box 104, CNSG records, RG 38, NARA
14 Mountfield (T), memo, 'Divisional Responsibility: G.C.H.Q, C.E.S.D and D.W.S', 01.04.66, T 199/1089.
15 Carter (NSA) to Sec Def, 'Reductions of Overseas Cryptological Manpower', 10.02.68, File: National Security Agency, Box 43, NSF-Agency File, LBJL.
16 Johnson, *American Cryptology*, Vol.2, p.437.
17 PFIAB, 'The Israeli Attack on the USS *Liberty*', 18.07.67, File: ME Crisis Misc. Material 2, Box 115, NSF-Country File, LBJL.
18 Bamford, *Body of Secrets*, pp.187–239. However, see Johnson, *American Cryptology*, Vol.2, pp.436–7, which argues that this was the result of miscommunication.
19 Lerner, *The Pueblo Incident*, pp.33, 79.
20 Cherkashin, *Spy Handler*, pp.182–3.
21 The files on the Dick White inquiry into sigint costs are at CAB 163/79 and CAB 163/284, but they remain closed.
22 Coote, *Submariner*, pp.194–5.
23 Ibid.
24 'Material for a Biography' enclosed in Roake to McGeogh (former FO S/M), 24.04.04, Roake papers, RNSM. Also private information.
25 Alfie Roake, 'Cold War Warrior', p.5, unpublished MSS, A1999/163, RNSM.
26 Mins of an Electronic Warfare Committee Working Party No.4 mtg, 23.12.68, AIR 2/18910.
27 Barker, 'The Mystery Boats', pp.16–18.
28 France was the only other European country with an independent nuclear deterrent.
29 Hughes (GCHQ) to MoA, 'S band SAM radars', S/0875/1000/49, 24.09.63, AVIA 13/1341.
30 Smith (GCHQ) to Kimbrey (RAF), 'Draft Air Staff Targets Nos.CR/3614 and 3615', S/0038/947/1, 16.01.61, ibid.
31 Richardson (Sec TC/LSIC) to Hunt (RAE),

'Airborne Elint R & D', S/4507/265/3, 14.11.61, ibid.

32 Richardson (Sec TC/LSIC) memo, 'Review of Airborne Elint', and ETAP 1//61, C/30/61, 31.10.61, ibid.

33 T.A. Lewis (GCHQ) to Todd (RAE), 'Sideways Looking System', M/1332/9000/11C, 10.05.63, ibid.

34 Air Staff Requirement No 817, 'Sideways Looking Airborne Search Reviewing System', 05.08.64, ibid.

35 LSIC/10/64, 'Airborne Sigint Collection', 12.03.64, AIR 40/2820.

36 JCG/S/24, Operational Requirements Committee, 19.07.67, AIR 20/11747.

37 LSIB/12/66 (Final) 20.10.66, discussed in WD 86/87 'Air Staff Requirement No.389 (HS801(R))', 07.12.67, DEFE 68/76.

38 Within NATO Britain had full cooperation on elint with Norway, Denmark, Germany and Turkey. There was limited cooperation with Italy on naval tactical elint. Holland did naval elint but there was 'no cooperation', and with France there was also 'no exchange'. DCDS (I) Maguire memo, 'Elint Collection in NATO', and annex, 27.11.67, AIR 20/11747.

39 Britain's cooperation with the BND Technical Sub-Committee is discussed in SZ/CSA/116/4 A.G. Touch, 1961, Zuckerman papers, University of East Anglia Library.

40 DCDS (I) Maguire memo, 'Elint Collection in NATO', 27.11.67, AIR 20/11747. See also DASB Brief for mtg with CDS, 22.11.67, ibid.

41 Ibid.

42 Johnson, American Cryptology, Vol.2, p.359.

43 LSIB/1/67, 16.02.67, discussed in WD 86/87 'Air Staff Requirement No. 389 (HS801(R))', 07.12.67, DEFE 68/76.

44 Aiken (AC(I)) memo, 'Replacement Aircraft – No 51 Squadron', 01.08.67, AIR20/12072. A working party on airborne sigint was running under Dr Cottrell, the Chief Scientist at the MoD.

45 In the subsequent flurry of relabelling the Signals Command Air Radio Laboratory (SCARL) changed to Signals Air Radio Laboratory (SARL) in 1969.

46 Humphreys (DS9) to PUS (E), 'Nimrod (R)', 01.08.68, DEFE 68/76.

47 Brief No. 7 – 'ACAS(Pol) for Discussions with VCOS USAF: Differences in Sigint Philosophy', 04.72, AIR 2/12574.

48 Cooper (DUS (P)) to PS to S of S, 'Nimrod (R)', 30.07.68, DEFE 68/76.

49 Dixon (DD Ops), 'MoD Air Electronic Warfare Committee Working Party No.4: Final Report', 11.03.69, AIR 2/18910.

50 Hellawell (DD Sigs 3), 'HS801 (R) – Special Operator Voice for Comint Role 51 Squadron', 11.03.69, ibid.

51 Perrin (GCHQ) to Dixon (RAF), 'MOD (AIR) Electronic Warfare Committee Working Party No.4', P/0230/8102/13, 15.04.69, ibid.

52 Perrin (GCHQ) to Dixon (DD Ops Recce), 'Tasking of Airborne Sigint', P/4359/8102/13, 21.03.69, ibid.

53 VCAS, 'Radio Proving Flights Against UAR and Syria', 14.03.69, DEFE 13/894.

54 Burnett (VCAS) to Healey (Sec Def), 'Radio Proving Flights – July 1967', 17.06.67, AIR 20/12133.

55 VCAS to Def Sec, 'Mounting of RAF Radio Proving Flights from an Iranian Airfield', 6.05.69, DEFE 13/894.

56 Brief No. 7 – 'ACAS (Pol) for Discussions with VCOS USAF: Differences in Sigint Philosophy', 04.72, AIR 2/12574.

57 Johnson, American Cryptology, Vol.2, pp.359–60.

58 Record of Vice-Chief to Vice-Chief Discussions in Washington, 18.04.72, AIR 2/12574. The first B-52 lost to enemy fire was brought down by a SAM on 22.11.72. Over the next three years fourteen more would be lost.

59 Omand (MoD) to SoS Defence, 'Intelligence Gathering Operations – Ministerial Authority', 6.02.74, DEFE 13/985.

60 VCAS, 'US Radio Proving Flights – February 1974', 21.01.74. ibid.

61 Ibid.

62 Hooper (GCHQ) to Carter (NSA), 22.07.69, reproduced in Bamford, Puzzle Palace, p.337.

THE 1970s: TURBULENCE AND TERROR

Chapter 15: Trouble with Henry

1 Cromer to FCO, personal for SoS, 24.11.73, FCO 82/288.

2 Dumbrell, A Special Relationship, pp.125–46.

3 Gustafson, Hostile Intent, p.17.

4 Andrew, President's Eyes Only, pp.351–3.

5 Cable (FCO), 'Dr Kissinger's Ideas', 31.07.73, PREM 15/1983.

6 Cable (FCO), 'Dear Henry', 12.07.73, ibid.

7 Millard (FCO) to Greenhill (PUS), 20.07.70, 'Top Secret – Personal-Guard-Umbra', FCO 73/162.

8 Ibid.

9 Young, *The Labour Governments, 1964–70*, p.15.
10 Johnson, *American Cryptology*, Vol.2, pp.315–17
11 Aid, *Secret Sentry*, pp.152–3.
12 John Nix, pp.15–16, Foreign Affairs Oral History Collection (5), LL.
13 Forster, 'No Entry', pp.139–46.
14 Douglas-Home (FCO) to Heath (PM), 18.09.70, enclosing 'Provision of Facilities for the United States Administration', DEFE 24/603. The officials complained that 'the task . . . has been a big one'. Gibson (MoD) to Tesh (FCO), 16.09.70, ibid.
15 Ibid. A retired NSA director has confirmed to the author that the ability to compare world views was no less valuable a British contribution than raw intelligence.
16 Andrew and Gordievsky, *KGB*, pp.435–6.
17 Record of mtg in the Permanent Under-Secretary's Office, 25.05.71, in Bennett and Hamilton (eds), *DBPO, III, Vol.1, Britain and the Soviet Union, 1968–72*, No.66, pp.339–43.
18 Kissinger to Nixon, 24.09.71, and attached memo 'Defection in the UK by a Soviet KGB Official', Subject File: Defectors and Refugees, Jun 1971–Apr 1973, Box 318, National Security Files, NPM, NARA.
19 Walden, *Lucky George*, pp.144–8.
20 Greenhill (PUS FCO) to Douglas-Home (SoS FCO), 30.09.71, DEFE 13/898.
21 Douglas-Home (SoS FCO) to Heath (PM), 'Proposed Occasional Basing of US SR-71 Photographic Reconnaissance Aircraft in Britain', 16.12.71, ibid.
22 JIC (A) (72) 23rd mtg (4) Confidential Annex, 'Intelligence Exchanges with the French', 22.06.72, CAB 185/10.
23 JIC (A) (72) 17th mtg (4) Confidential Annex, 'Release of Assessments on France to the United States', 04.05.72, ibid.
24 SIS paper INT 9 (70) 1 'Soviet Approaches for Intelligence in China', attachment to No.4601/70, CAB190/9; JIC Working Party on Soviet Approaches for Intelligence on China, 1st mtg, 02.12.70, ibid.
25 Eventually the capital costs rose to £35 million.
26 D.DSTI/31/2/4/4, 'Cobra Mist: Status and Future UK Policy', 21.11.72, AIR 2/18797.
27 Hooper (D/GCHQ) to White (IC), D/2709/1402/42, 24.06.71, DEFE 31/155.
28 DUS (Air) to PS/SoS MoD, 'Cobra Mist, Orfordness', 19.06.73, ibid.
29 Le Bailly to PUS MoD, 'Cobra Mist', and attachment, 11.06.73, ibid.

30 Joseph (SoS DHSS) to Carrington (Min Def), 05.02.71, HO 255/1108.
31 Min. Post and Telecommunications, note on mtg 26.03.71, ibid.
32 Carrington (Def Sec) to Heath (PM), MO 10/7, 'Cobra Mist, Orfordness', 21.06.73, DEFE 31/155.
33 Trend (CAB) to Dunnett (PUS MoD), 'Cobra Mist OTHR', 12.06.73, ibid.
34 Le Bailly to PUS MoD, 'Cobra Mist', and attachment, 11.06.73, ibid.
35 HD of S9 (Air) to DUS (Air), 'RAF Orfordness', 28.06.73, ibid.
36 Nicoll (GCHQ) to Herman (Sec JIC), 'Cobra Mist', Z/1096/80002/15, 18.07.73, ibid.
37 Rothery (FCO Hanslope) to Rogers (PSA), 'Future Use of the Crowborough Site', 06.06.83, CM 37/21.
38 Cromer (Washington) to Brimelow (FCO), 07.03.73, FCO 73/135.
39 Trend (Cab Sec) to Heath (PM), 24.04.73, PREM 15/1362.
40 Record of mtg at the White House, 30.07.73, FCO 82/311.
41 Webster (CAB) to Cradock (FCO), 29.08.73, CAB 164/1235.
42 Trend memo, 'United States/Europe Relations', 17.08.73, ibid. Also private information.
43 Robertson (CAB) to Trend (Cab Sec), 16.08.73, CAB 164/1235.
44 JIC (73) 31st mtg (4), 16.08.73; JIC (73) 32nd mtg (7), 28.08.73, JIC (73) 33rd mtg (3), 30.08.73, JIC (73) 34th mtg (2), 06.09.73, CAB 185/13.
45 Cabinet Office to the author, 21.05.07.
46 Information from former American officials, 06.04.09.
47 Trend (?) memo, 'United States/Europe Relations', 17.08.73, CAB 164/1235.
48 Heath to Nixon, 04.09.73, ibid.
49 Nixon to Heath, 09.09.73, PREM 15/1981.
50 Tickell (Washington) to Wiggin (FCO), 'Talks on MBFR – The Problem', 12.10.73, FCO 41/1242.
51 Sykes (Washington) to Brimelow (FCO), 13.08.73, DEFE 13/981.
52 Bergman and Meltzer, *Yom Kippur War, Real Time*, pp.123–7.
53 Le Bailly to '?', 01.01.83, Folder 3, Box 7, Le Bailly papers, CCC.
54 Le Bailly to 'Charlie', 01.07.82, Folder 3, Box 7, Le Bailly papers, CCC.
55 Andrew, *President's Eyes Only*, pp.391–2.
56 Notes of an interview by Henry Brandon with Richard Helms, File 8 'Helms', Box 57, Henry Brandon papers, LC.
57 NRO memo for Dr McLucas, 'November

Forecast of NRP Satellite and Aircraft Overflight Activities', 19.10.73, National Security Archive. See also JCS Memo for the Members of Special Committee, 'Proposed SR–71 Deployment', 08.10.73, ibid.

58 Account by Colonel Jim Wilson, 'OL-Griffiss AFB, Rome, New York, 1973 Yom Kippur War', http://www.wvi.com/~sr71 webmater/griffiss.html.

59 See also Brugioni, 'The Effects of Aerial and Satellite Imagery'.

60 Van der Art, *Aerial Espionage*, p.67

61 Siniver, *Nixon, Kissinger and US Foreign Policy Making*, pp.201–3.

62 William Colby/Kissinger, 9.40 a.m., 24.10.73, Kissinger Telecons, NPM, NARA

63 Heath (PM) to Bridges (T), 28.10.73, PREM 15/1382.

64 Note by the Assessments Staff, 'The US Alert of 25 October', 29.10.73, ibid.

65 Smith (CAB) to Bridges (T), 'The American Alert of 25 October 1973', ibid; Hunt (Cab Sec) to Heath (PM), 'Crisis Management', 19.12.73, ibid.

66 Overton (FCO), 'US/UK Relations', 12.11.73, FCO 82/306.

67 Simons (Washington Embassy) to Herman (JIC), JIC 2/3, 'New Director of Central Intelligence (DCI)', 12.01.73, DEFE 13/891.

68 Mumford (MoD) to Carrington (Def Sec), 07.11.73, ibid. See also record of a mtg between Carrington and Schlesinger in The Hague, 07.11.73, ibid. Harry Bergold was Deputy Assistant Secretary for European and NATO Affairs at the Department of Defense.

69 Carrington (SoS MoD) to Douglas-Home (SoS FO), MO15/2/1 and annex, 26.10.73, ibid.

70 Amery (FCO) to Carrington (SoS MoD), 01.11.73, DEFE 13/900.

71 'Visit of US Secretary of State: US Request for Reconnaissance Flight Facilities in Cyprus', 28.03.74, FCO82/441.

72 Simons (Washington) to Arthur (FCO), JIC 2/12, 'Information about Israeli/Egyptian Disengagement from US Reconnaissance Flights', 24.04.74, FCO 93/401.

73 NRO memo for Dr McLucas, 'Denied Area Aircraft Reconnaissance', 25.10.73, National Security Archive.

74 BDS Washington to MoD, 23.07.74, DEFE 25/345.

75 Killick to PUS, 16.01.74, FCO 82/443.

76 Sykes (Washington) to Brimelow (FCO), 13.08.73, FCO 82/311. Richard Sykes was

later Ambassador to the Netherlands, and was shot and killed there by the IRA on 22 March 1979. It is widely thought that he was mistaken for the Chief of SIS, who had visited The Hague the previous day.

Chapter 16: Disaster at Kizildere

1 Ankara to SoS, No.2593, 'Kidnapping of NATO Tech Reps', 07.04.72, Subject Numeric Box 2638, RG 59 NARA.

2 Owen, *Time to Declare*, pp.391–2.

3 There were also suggestions of assistance from Kuwait. Amman to SoS, No.1060, 'Turkish Terrorist–Faydeen Relations', 13.03.71, Subject Numeric Box 2229, RG 59 NARA.

4 Richelson, *American Espionage*, p.84; Bamford, *Puzzle Palace*, p.159

5 Bamford, *Body of Secrets*, p.43.

6 Richelson, *Century*, pp.258–60

7 Richelson, *American Espionage*, pp.85–9; Bamford, *Puzzle Palace*, p.159

8 Richelson, *Wizards of Langley*, p.36.

9 Mitchell (BJSM), 'Ground Noise Listening Operations – Turkey', 12.05.52, AFS/1700/6/Int, 12.05.52, File 381, Box 5, Army Int. TS Decimal File, 1945–52, Entry 47A, RG 319, NARA

10 Allen (Ankara) to Rennie (FO), 13.04.64, C119/2, FO 371/174762.

11 'Envoy Komer's Car Burned in Turkey', *Washington Post*, 07.01.69.

12 Ankara to SoS, No.669, 'TUSLOG Bombed', 29.01.71, Subject Numeric Box 2229, RG 59 NARA.

13 This was James Finley. Baumann, *Diplomatic Kidnapping*, p.89.

14 Bamford, *Puzzle Palace*, p.159

15 The four airmen were S/Sgt Jimmie Sexton and three Airmen 1st Class: James M. Gholson, Larry Heavner and Richard Caraszi. 'No More Tribute for Terrorism', *Time*, 22.03.71.

16 Ankara to SoS, No.933, 'Kidnapped Airmen: Situation Mid-Morning 5 March', 5.03.71, Subject Numeric Box 2229, RG 59 NARA.

17 Kissinger to Nixon, 'Kidnappings in Turkey', 06.03.71, *FRUS*, 1969–76, Vol.XXIX, pp.1082–3

18 Krahenbuhl, 'Political Kidnappings in Turkey', pp.45–7

19 Ibid., pp.39–40

20 Ibid., p.48

21 The terrorists were Deniz Gezmiş, Yusuf Aslan, Huesyin Inan, Sinan Cemgil and Mete Ertekin. Baumann, *Diplomatic Kidnappings*, pp.89–91

22 Bamford, *Puzzle Palace*, p.160.

23 Krahenbuhl, 'Political Kidnappings in Turkey', p.6

24 Sarell (Ankara) to FCO, 08.06.71, FCO 9/1468. Also private information.

25 'A Tempting Target', *Time*, 31.05.71.

26 Krahenbuhl, 'Political Kidnappings in Turkey', p.4

27 Baumann, *Diplomatic Kidnappings*, p.173

28 Ankara to SoS, No.721, 'Istanbul Reaction to Deniz Gezmiş Gang Death Sentences', 13.10.71, Subject Numeric Box 2639, RG 59 NARA

29 Ankara to SoS, No.167, 'Erim Announces Military Involvement in Cayan Escape', 01.05.72, Subject Numeric Box 2638, RG59 NARA.

30 Short (Ankara) to FCO, 'Turkey: Internal Security', 22.02.72, FCO 9/1604.

31 Sam Cohen, 'Appeal by Three Rejected', *Guardian*, 11.01.72. See also Short (Ankara) to FCO, 'Turkey: Trials of Extremists', 07.12.71, FCO 9/1604.

32 Short (Ankara) to FCO, 'Turkey: Martial Law', 25.01.72, FCO 9/1604.

33 Sam Cohen, 'Turkey Purges Army "Rebels" ', *Guardian*, 13.03.72.

34 Sam Cohen, 'Death Penalty for Two', *Guardian*, 28.12.71.

35 Ankara to SoS, No.282, 'Important Development in Internal Security Situation', 14.03.72, Subject Numeric Box 2638, RG 59 NARA

36 Ankara to SoS, No.607, 'President Signs Three Death Sentences', 24.03.72, Subject Numeric Box 2637, RG 59 NARA

37 Ankara to SoS, No.379, 'Developments on Kidnapping of NATO Tech Reps', 28.03.72, Subject Numeric Box 2638, RG 59 NARA; 'Britons Who Escaped Tell of Their Ordeal', *The Times*, 01.04.72.

38 Ankara to SoS, No.476, 'Kidnapping of Three British Tech Reps', 27.03.72, ibid.

39 Douglas-Home to Sarell, tel. no.31, 27.03.72, PREM 15/1256.

40 Erim to Heath, PM's Personal Message T125/72, 28.03.72, ibid.

41 Douglas-Home to Sarell, tel. no.31, 27.03.72, ibid.

42 Statement by SoS FO in House of Commons, 28.03.72, ibid.

43 Ankara to SoS, No.876, 'Kidnapping of Three Tech Reps: PM's Statement', 29.03.72, Subject Numeric Box 2638, RG 59 NARA

44 Everett (PUSD) minute, 'Kizildere Trial', 07.06.73, FCO 9/1849. Also Sam Cohen,

'Guerrillas Killed British Experts', *Guardian*, 01.05.73.

45 Brown (Ankara) to FCO, 'Kizildere Trial', 05.06.73, FCO 9/1849.

46 Leeland (Ankara) to FCO, 'Kizildere Trial', 31.08.73, enclosing extract from *Gunaydin*, 23.08.73, ibid.

47 Brown (Ankara) to FCO, 'Kizildere Trial', 05.06.73, ibid.

48 Ankara to SoS, No.2593, 'Kidnapping of NATO Tech Reps', 07.04.72, Subject Numeric Box 2638, RG 59 NARA. See also Sarell (Ankara) to FCO, tel. no.412, 30.03.72, PREM 15/1256.

49 Ibid. The commandos later recovered four machine guns, twenty-seven pistols, 2,358 rounds of ammunition, thirty-six grenades and two radio sets. SWB report, ME/3962/C/1, 13.04.72.

50 Obituary, Sir Roderick Sarell, *Telegraph*, 22.11.01.

51 Erim to Heath, PM's Personal Message T126/72, in immediate Ankara tel. no.471, 31.03.72, PREM 15/1256; Heath to Erim, PM's Personal Message T128/72, in immediate Ankara telegram No. 473, 31.03.72, ibid. Also Wright (FCO) to Downing St, 31.03.72, ibid.

52 Sarell (Ankara) to Heath (PM), 30.03.72, ibid.

53 Heath to Mrs G. Banner and Mrs C. Taylor, 30.03.72, ibid.

54 Kennedy (Ankara) to FCO, 10.04.72, FCO 9/1604; Ankara to SoS, No.914, 'Student Protest Shoot-Out at Kizildere', 04.04.72, Subject Numeric Box 2638, RG 59 NARA; Ankara to SoS, No.507, 'Incidents at Istanbul University', 06.04.72, ibid.

55 Ankara to SoS, No.2593, 'Ransom Note Finally Found', 11.04.72, Subject Numeric Box 2638, RG 59 NARA.

56 Fyjis-Walker (Ankara) to FCO, 08.05.72, FCO 9/1605.

57 Krahenbuhl, 'The Turkish Communists', pp.405–13.

58 Short (Ankara) to FCO, 07.07.72, FCO 9/1605.

59 Golden and Youatt (Solicitors) to Graham (FCO), 'The Late John Stuart Law', 07.07.72, DEFE 13/1332.

60 Wright minute, 01.07.72, on Brown (Ankara) to FCO, 'Kizildere Trial', 22.05.73, FCO 9/1849.

61 FCO to Brown (Ankara), 02.02.73, ibid.

62 GCHQ is mentioned directly in Prendergast min. 'J.S. Law Deceased', 27.06.72, ibid.

63 On John Somerville as PEO see Benjamin, *Five Lives in One*, pp.150–1.

64 Wolfe (FCO) to Leeming (CSD) 'Charles Turner Deceased and Gordon Banner Deceased', 27.02.73, FCO 9/1849.

65 In the High Court of Justice, Queen's Bench Division, Writ issued between Beryl Elizabeth Turner and the Attorney General, 1973, ibid.

66 Fyjis-Walker (Ankara) to FCO, tel. no.216, 08.02.73, ibid.

67 Everett (PUSD) minute, 'Kizildere Trial' 07.06.73, ibid.

68 HC Deb 55, 107, 27.02.84, col.93.

69 Sarell (Ankara) to FCO, 'Turkey: Internal Situation and Martial Law', 01.06.71, FCO 9/1468.

70 McCauliffe (US Mission NATO) to US Sec of S, 19.01.73, NATO 353, Subject Numeric Box 1812 DEF15 Tur-US, RG 59, NARA.

71 Fearn minute, 'JIC Paper: Outlook for Turkey', 16.03.72, WSTI/I, FCO 9/1604.

Chapter 17: Turmoil on Cyprus

1 Annex TT, 'The Turkish Advance on Famagusta – As Seen from Ayios Nikolaos, 15 Aug. 1974', BNFE/1500/24, 'Report by Commander British Forces Near East on the Cyprus Emergency, 15 Jul.–16 Aug. 1974', TT 1–4, 15.04.75, AIR 8/2628.

2 JIC (56) 21 (Final), 'Likelihood of Global War and Warning of Attack', 01.04.56, CAB 34/1315.

3 The Treasury pondered whether it was an Air Ministry project or else 'in the GCHQ nexus'. They plumped for the former. Wilding (T) memo, 'Sandra and Zinnia', 24.10.60, T 225/2198.

4 Benjamin (RAE), 'Zinnia: An Ionospheric Reflection Radar', 02.62, AVIA 6/17569.

5 DSI memo No 65, 'Zinnia: Trials in the United States (Project Bart)', 04.60, DEFE 44/1140.

6 'Sandra: Minutes of a Mtg in the Treasury', 01.1161, T 225/2198.

7 Trend (T) to Wood (Air), 'Sandra', 25.01.60, ibid.

8 Scott, *Macmillan, Kennedy and the Cuban Missile Crisis*, p.177.

9 Maguire (DGI) memo, 'Sir Alan Cottrell's Enquiry into OTHR Systems', 18.04.71, DEFE 23/100.

10 Richelson, *Wizards of Langley*, pp.36–7.

11 COS (61) 19, 'Review of Strengths of the Cyprus Garrison', 19.01.61, DO 181/11.

12 Douglas-Home (FCO) to Heath (PM), 18.09.70, enclosing 'Provision of Facilities for the United States Administration', DEFE 24/603.

13 Maguire (DGI) memo, 'Sir Alan Cottrell's Enquiry into OTHR Systems', 18.04.71, DEFE 23/100.

14 The cost was £350,000 per annum. Le Bailly to PUS MoD, 'Cobra Mist', and attachment 11.06.73, DEFE 31/155.

15 SD to London, 'Even-Steven: Adam–Sisco Exchange', 19.11.70, Subject Numeric Box 2656, RG 59, NARA.

16 (Popper) US Embassy Nicosia to Dept of State, 17.04.70, File: Pol 27 Cyp, Subject Numeric Box 2226, RG 59, NARA.

17 *FRUS*, Vol. XXX, Doc. No. 88.

18 Callaghan, *Time and Chance*, pp.337–41.

19 BNFE/1500/24, 'Report by Commander British Forces Near East on the Cyprus Emergency, 15 Jul.–16 Aug. 1974', pp.4–6, 15.04.75, AIR 8/2628.

20 Callaghan, *Time and Chance*, pp.335–6.

21 See for example discussion of decisions by the Turkish General Staff in 'Cyprus Emergency, Akrotiri', Annex A, HQ Near East Air Force, 25.11.74, AIR 23/8715.

22 Extract of JIC assessment prepared by the Cabinet Office, Wed. 17.07.74, fo.31, DEFE 13/966.

23 Entry for 17.07.74, Donoughue, *Downing Street Diary*, p.166.

24 BNFE/1500/24, 'Report by Commander British Forces Near East on the Cyprus Emergency, 15 Jul.–16 Aug. 1974', pp.18–19, 15.05.75, AIR 8/2628.

25 JIC(A) 74 (SA)70, 19.07.74, in Annex Q, BNFE/1500/24, ibid.

26 BNFE/1500/24, 'Report by Commander British Forces Near East on the Cyprus Emergency, 15 Jul.–16 Aug. 1974', pp.18–19, 15.05.75, AIR 8/2628. Also private information.

27 James Schlesinger/Kissinger, 9.10 p.m., 19.07.74, Kissinger Telecons, NPM, NARA.

28 Tom Braden/Kissinger, 11.50 a.m., 21.07.74, ibid.

29 Mumford (PS to SoS MoD) to CDS, 'RAF Reconnaissance Flights Over Cyprus', 29.07.74, AIR 8/2628.

30 The main focus of cooperation was Cord Meyer, the Head of Station in London, and his analytical chief Sid Bearman. See Colby (DCI) to Le Bailly (DGI), 31.07.74, Folder 5, Box 21, Le Bailly papers, CCC.

31 BNFE/1500/24, 'Report by Commander British Forces Near East on the Cyprus Emergency, 15 Jul.–16 Aug. 1974', pp.89–90, 15.05.75, AIR 8/2628.

32 Annex TT, 'The Turkish Advance on Famagusta – As Seen from Ayios Nikolaos,

15 Aug. 1974', BNFE/1500/24, 'Report by Commander British Forces Near East on the Cyprus Emergency, 15 Jul.–16 Aug. 1974', TT 1–4, 15.05.75, ibid.

33 Ibid.

34 Biles (CGS staff), 'Notes of an Informal Meeting Between A/CDS (CGS) and CBFNE', 27.08.74, DEFE 24/578.

35 Le Bailly (DGI) to CDS, 'Promulgation of Intelligence in the Cyprus Situation to UKMILREP', 24.07.74, DEFE 25/345.

36 Hockaday (MoD) to Arthur (FCO), 'Cyprus', 29.07.74, ibid.

37 OPD (74) 35, 'Defence Review: International Consultations', note by the Secretaries, 18.10.74, CAB 148/145. I am indebted to Matthew Jones for this reference.

38 Tonkin (PUSD), 'Coverage of Middle East Broadcasting Stations', 12.11.74, AIR 20/12691. Private information.

39 D/DS11/3/4, 'Cyprus: Foreign and Commonwealth Secretary's Talk with Mr Clark Clifford', 25.02.77, AIR 8/2747. The Cabinet decision was CC(74) 41st conclusions.

40 Weston (FCO) to Lane (Ankara), 'British Interests in the Eastern Mediterranean', 11.04.75, FCO 46/1248.

41 D/DS11/3/4, 'Cyprus: Foreign and Commonwealth Secretary's Talk with Mr Clark Clifford', 25.02.77, AIR 8/2747. The Cabinet decision was CC(74) 41st conclusions.

42 Tonkin (PUSD), 'Coverage of Middle East Broadcasting Stations', 12.11.74, AIR 20/12691.

43 JIC (75) 12th mtg, 13.03.75, discussing JIC (75) 9, 'The Implications for Turkish Foreign Policy of the Suspension of United States Military Assistance', CAB 185/17.

44 Robert Kleiman/Kissinger, 7.10 p.m., 25.07.75, Kissinger Telecons, NPM, NARA.

45 Dillon (NEA SD), 'Troublesome Times Ahead in Relations with Turkey', 10.07.73, Subject Numeric Box 2639, RG 59 NARA. See also the discussion of NSA's Woods Study in Johnson, *American Cryptology*, Vol.2, p.391.

46 Bagnall (Sec to COS) to CBFNE, 'Cyprus Future Force Levels', COS 1055/733A, 27.02.75, DEFE 25/340.

47 DP6/75 (Final), 'Cyprus – Future Force Level', 03.07.75, DEFE 11/874.

48 About £60 million. PSIS (75) 1st mtg (3), discussed in ibid.

49 Adams (JARIB) to DS8, 'US Navy Request for Reconnaissance of Eastern Mediter-

ranean Ports', 08.04.75, AIR 2/18991.

50 Leslie (DS8), 'American U2 Operations in Cyprus', 07.04.75, AIR 20/12652.

51 McDonnell (DS1 MoD) 'Dr Schlesinger's Visit', 22.09.75, T 225/4177. See also Mason to PM, MO 25/2/50/1, 19.06.75, ibid.

52 Hall (MoD) to PPS, 'Dr Schlesinger's Visit on 24 September', 09.75, ibid.

53 D/DS11/3/4, 'Cyprus: Foreign and Commonwealth Secretary's Talk with Mr Clark Clifford', 25.02.77, AIR 8/2747. The Cabinet decision was CC(74) 41st conclusions.

54 Mtg between Owen (SoS FO) and Clifford, London, 28.02.77, AIR 8/2747.

55 Aldrich, 'The UK–US Intelligence Alliance in 1975'.

56 UK intelligence spending was £147.1 million in 1976–77, and was now scheduled to fall by £12.8 million at current prices by 1980–81. COS (76) 12th mtg (2), Confidential Annex, 'The Intelligence Coordinator's Annual Review of Intelligence 1976', 13.07.76, DEFE 32/23.

57 COS (76) 3rd mtg (1), 03.02.76, 'Defence Intelligence Staff Annual Report 1975', DEFE 32/23. See also Johnson, *American Cryptology*, Vol.3, p.160.

58 McGeorge Bundy, NSAM 301, 'Intelligence Installations', 19.05.64, File: NSAM 301, Box 4, National Security File – NSAMs, LBJL.

59 The island that was initially of interest was Aldabra, the most westerly in the BIOT group. However, Aldabra was home to the world's largest population of giant tortoises, estimated at some 100,000. Protests prompted the officials to turn their attention to the neighbouring atoll of Diego Garcia. See Morland (MoD) memo, 'Aldabra', 22.04.66, T 225/3052.

60 SD to US Embassy London, 21.08.63, Lot Files, UK (1962–74) – Office of Northern European Affairs, Box 5, RG 59, NARA.

61 Downey (T) memo, 'Indian Ocean', 02.07.65, T 225/3474.

62 'British Indian Ocean Territory, Amended Draft; Financial Agreement', enclosure B in Bruce to State Dept, No.6275, 02.07.66, File UK Cables Vol.VIII, Box 209, NSF – Country Files, LBJL.

63 Draft note from SoS Def to Foreign Secretary, June 1966, T 225/3052.

64 FCO to Washington, No.4030, 25.04.67, ibid.

65 Sykes (FCO) to Campbell (MoD), 'British Indian Ocean Territories: Financial Arrangements', 26.04.67, ibid.

66 Bolling (ASA), 'Negotiations with Ethiopia Concerning Retention of D/A Facilities in Eritrea', 20.03.51, File 350.09, Box 1, Army Int. TS Decimal File, 1945–52, Entry 47A, RG 319, NARA

67 Campbell (Consul Asmara) to Alsop, 02.05.69, File 4, Box 79, Alsop papers, HGARC.

68 G. Cook, 'Kagnew Station – Tract C', http://www.kagnewstation.com/stories/4 9.html

69 Dept of State to US London Embassy, tel.118250, 18.06.73, *FRUS, 1969–76*, Vol.E-8, *South East Asia, 1973–76*, Doc. 57.

70 DS5 to SoS MoD, 'Expansion of Diego Garcia Communications Facility', 27.06.73, DEFE 17/726.

71 Douglas-Home (SoS FCO) to Heath (PM), PM/74/4, 'Diego Garcia: US Proposals for Expanded Facilities', 10.01.74, PREM15/2233. See also Douglas-Home (SoS FCO) to Freedman (Washington), 16.01.74, DEFE 17/726.

72 Weiss (PM/SD) to SoS, 'DOD Plans for Upgrading Diego Garcia Facility', 01.74, Box 6, Lot Files, UK (1964–72) – Office of Northern European Affairs, RG 59, NARA. I am indebted to Matthew Jones for guidance on this point.

73 Buell (SD), 'Diego Garcia- Current Status', 28.01.74, Box 1, Lot Files, UK (1964–72) – Office of Northern European Affairs, RG 59, NARA.

74 Hunt (Cab Sec) to Heath (PM), A06004, 'Diego Garcia', 10.01.74.

75 Mtg between Hunt (Cab Sec) and Kissinger, 30.01.74, PREM 15/2233.

76 Nixon to Heath (PM), T60/74, 20.02.74, ibid.

77 Sykes (Washington) to Bridges (Downing St), 20.02.74, ibid.

78 Whitmore (MoD) to Bryard (Cab), 'Mr Schlesinger's Visit: Briefs for the Prime Minister', 23.09.75, T 225/4177.

79 US Embassy London to Department of State, No.2597, 17.02.81, DDRS.

80 Hyam, *Britain's Declining Empire*, p.391.

81 Pilger, *Freedom Next Time*, p.38.

Chapter 18: Unmasking GCHQ: The ABC Trial

1 ABC Newsletter 10.03.78, 'Cheltenham 27 May – "B" There!', DEFE 13/1303.

2 Freeman (Washington) to FCO, 30.10.69, FCO 7/1235.

3 Ibid. See also Aid, *Secret Sentry*, pp.61–3.

4 In 2008 Goonhilly was scheduled to close, with operations moving to the Madley Communications Centre in Herefordshire.

5 Lanning and Norton-Taylor, *Conflict of Loyalties*, p.33

6 Hooper (D/GCHQ) to White (CAB), D/7873/1802/13, 03.03.69, CAB 163/119.

7 Lanning and Norton-Taylor, *Conflict of Loyalties*, p.64.

8 Ibid., p.69.

9 Andrew, *President's Eyes Only*, pp.358–9.

10 SPM (74) 19, 'State of Security in Syria', 16.08.74, CAB 134/3843.

11 SPM (74) 22, 'State of Security in Oman', 22.10.74, ibid.

12 INT 15 (73) 1, JIC (A), 'Intelligence Priorities: Particular Issues', CAB 190/44.

13 'Annex A: Intelligence Requirements Order of Priorities List 1', Note to VCDS, 'Defence Intelligence Priorities in the 1970s', May 1970, DEFE 27/1.

14 Johnson, *American Cryptology*, Vol.2, p.397.

15 Andronov, 'American Geosynchronous Sigint Satellites', pp.37–43.

16 Information from William Odom, April 2008.

17 D. Campbell, 'Phone Tappers and the State', *New Statesman*, 1981, pp.54–5.

18 The position was initially filled by Robert Drake. Johnson, *American Cryptology*, Vol.3, pp.156–7, 162.

19 Corput (Director, Communications Electronics) to Canine (D/NSA), 'Unsatisfactory Communications Between National Security Agency, Washington and GCHQ', 20.07.53, JCS 1954–6, 337 (9-6-51), RG 218, NARA.

20 CNO to Dir, Communication Electronics, 'Transatlantic Channels Allocated to National Security Agency', 30.03.56, JCS 1954–6, CCS 334 DCE (10-5-55) Sec.1, ibid.

21 S.I. 1/9, 'Threat of Soviet Interdiction of Allied Communications', 20.07.59, DEFE 26/6.

22 DCN/3/12, Annex A, 'Defence Communications Network: Communications Staff Requirement, 1970–71', 03.05.68, FCO 19/10.

23 John Adcock, Director, *Blue Peter*, to David Lloyd, British Space Centre RAF Oakhanger, 18.11.69, AIR 29/3905.

24 This channel – known as TGP5 – was shared with the Joint Intelligence Committee. Webber (Office of the Canadian Chief of Defence Staff) to DSB, 'Transatlantic Communications Consolidation', 26.04.68, FCO19/43. See also Burrough (C/GSPS) to Bates (FCO),

21.08.69, 'Telegraph Cable Channels to Australia', FCO 19/50.

25 'Satellite Communications Post-SKYNET II', mtg at Cabinet Office, 16.02.71, FCO 19/183. GCHQ was represented at the Skynet discussions by John Burrough, who was Director of Plans, and accompanied by two senior GCHQ colleagues, Katherine Fox and John Adye, the latter becoming Director in 1989. This was Burrough's last post; by 1976 he would be chairman of Racal. See Burrough (GCHQ) to Le Bailly (DGI), 05.06.72, Folder 3, Box 21, Le Bailly papers, CCC.

26 Snelling (FCO), 'Satellite Communications', 23.03.72, FCO 19/183.

27 DSB 10/72 (Draft), 'Replenishment of Skynet Phase II Satellites in 1976/77', 07.06.72, ibid.

28 In the 1960s Cheltenham had helped to steer national policy on language-teaching. Indeed, Arthur Cooper, GCHQ's senior sinologist (and brother to the well-known Bletchley Park veteran Josh Cooper), had been loaned to the Department of Education and Science as Research Adviser on the Development of Modern Languages. He had also assisted the University Funding Council as a special adviser during its national review of the teaching of Chinese. See Young (Nuffield) to Hooper (D/GCHQ), 07.02.67, FCO 79/20; ML (67) 1st mtg, Appendix, 'Inter-Universities Chinese Language School', 28.02.67, ED 181/110.

29 Lavington, 'In the Footsteps of Colossus', pp.44–7.

30 This was developed at Eastcote by Tony Riddington of GCHQ and Harry Carpenter from Elliott Brothers Ltd, based at Borehamwood. Ferranti also assisted with this work.

31 There were also comsec machines at Eastcote called 'Donald Duck' and 'High Speed Checker'. Ibid.

32 SRH003, Samuel S. Snyder, 'Influence of US Cryptological Organizations on the Digital Computer Industry', 1977, File 5750/363, Box 142, CNSG records, RG 38, NARA.

33 Johnson, American Cryptology, Vol.1, p.204; Johnson, American Cryptology, Vol.2, p.368.

34 Bamford, Puzzle Palace, pp.137–8.

35 Brundle to Veale, 15.06.77, enclosing 'Oakley and Benhall – Long Term Planning Study', F/4752/6000/22, CM 23/133.

36 Burnett, Tait and Partners, 'GCHQ Phase II, Benhall Site, Cheltenham', 09.09.76, ibid.

37 This was partly the work of the 1976 Perry Commission. See Johnson, American Cryptology, Vol.3, pp.217–18.

38 Aid, Secret Sentry, pp.164–5.

39 GCHQ was already processing the calculations for Foreign Office pay. Heath (FCO) min. to Hillyard (FCO), 11.08.67, 'The Use of Computers in the Diplomatic Service', FCO 19/5.

40 Sly, Horse Grows Horns, pp.210–11

41 Bontoft (GCHQ) to McDonald (PRO), G/9374/1315/1, 'Records Review and Indexing', 13.11.73, PRO 69/219.

42 Bontoft (GCHQ) to McDonald (PRO), G/9542/1315/1, 'Personal Files', 03.12.74, ibid.

43 About 6,500 feet was 'end product' which was of long-term value. Another 14,500 feet was essentially historical material that was used infrequently. There were also six hundred feet of personal files and 1,400 feet of registered files relating to policy. McDonald (PRO), memo, 'Visit to GCHQ', 29.10.73, ibid.

44 Anslow (PRO), 'Note on Visit to GCHQ, 15–16 June 1971', ibid.

45 Laver (T) to Lees (T), 4.01.65, T 224/1127. See also Couzens (T) to Henley (DEA) memo, 'The Government and the British Computer Industry', 04.01.65, ibid.

46 Hooper (D/GCHQ) to White (CAB), D/7873/1802/13, 3.03.69, CAB 163/119.

47 Poulden (GCHQ) to Stewart (Sec. JIC), D/8987/1402/37, 'JIC (A) Sub-Committee on Automatic Data Processing', 29.09.69, ibid. Poulden was in the chair, the GCHQ rep was H. Long, and the secretary, also provided by GCHQ, was J.R. Cheadle.

48 JIC (A) (ADP) (71) 1st mtg, 15.02.71, CAB 182/81.

49 JIC (A) (ADP) (70) 2nd mtg, 03.08.70, CAB 182/75.

50 JIC (A) (ADP) (71) 2nd mtg, 14.06.71, CAB 182/81.

51 COS (73) 13th mtg (4), 'The Intelligence Coordinator's Annual Review of Intelligence 1975 and his Report on Reductions in Intelligence Expenditure', 15.05.75, DEFE 32/22.

52 Aldrich, 'Policing the Past'.

53 Trend (Cab Sec) to Heath (PM), 09.10.70, enclosing JIC (A) memo, 'Release of SIGINT Records', DEFE 23/107.

54 Romeril (FCO) to Williams (PRO), 'Soviet Interest in British Documents Released Under 30-Year Rule', 30.07.70, DEFE 31/7.

55 DCDS(I) to Def Sec, DCDS (I)/10, 'Release of Sigint Records', 15.05.69, DEFE 13/615.

56 Hunt (Cab Sec) to Wilson (PM), 'Marchetti and Marks and Winterbotham', 08.04.74, PREM 16/670.

57 Helms to Bundy, 28.11.76, File: Richard Helms, Box 2, 2nd Series, William Bundy papers, Princeton University Library.

58 Hunt (Cab Sec) memo, 'Visit of Mr George Bush', 24.03.76, PREM 16/1151. Wilson to Bush (DCI), 5.04.76 and Bush (DCI) to Wilson, 07.04.76, ibid.

59 Note for the Record, 16.02.76, PREM 16/1150.

60 Johnson, American Cryptology, Vol.3, pp.65, 97–9.

61 Banner (NSA) to Phillips, 06.02.76, D6/31/76, Box 144, File 9, Phillips papers, LC.

62 Oldfield (C/SIS) speech, 'Cord Meyer, Farewell 1 July 1976', Box 2, File 6, Meyer papers, LC.

63 D. Campbell and M. Hosenball, 'The Eavesdroppers', Time Out, 21.05.76.

64 Campbell, 'Official Secrecy and British Libertarianism', p.77.

65 Robertson, The Justice Game, p.110; N. Wilkinson, Secrecy and the Media, p.366.

66 McEwan memo, 'The Aubrey Berry Campbell Defence Committee', 30.03.78, DEFE 13/1303.

67 Robertson, The Justice Game, pp.107–9, 127–9.

68 ABC Newsletter, 10.03.78, 'Cheltenham 27 May – "B" There!', DEFE 13/1303.

69 DIS (CS), '(2) The American Connection', 14.07.77, DEFE 47/34.

70 2nd PUS memo, 'The ABC Case', 02.08.78, DEFE 13/1303.

71 Brind (MoD) memo, 'The ABC Case', 07.08.78, ibid. See also Owen, Time to Declare, pp.344–5.

72 Duff to PUS, 'ABC Case', 09.11.78, ibid.

73 Hockaday to D of HQ Sy, 27.06.78, DEFE 47/34.

74 Young (DD Sy), 'State Research Association', 06.04.78, ibid.

75 Hanley (DG MI5) to Allen (CSD), 30.06.77, ibid.

76 Hunt (Cab Sec) to Callaghan (PM), 22.05.78, DEFE 13/1304.

77 Johnson, American Cryptology, Vol.4, p.427.

78 Constance, 'How Jim Bamford Probed the NSA', pp.71–4.

79 'Pelton', Odom (NSA) daily log, 12.11.86, File 8, Box 25, Odom papers, LC.

80 Not everyone was thrilled. Hugh Alexander, who had spent the 1950s working for LCSA, was utterly furious that Ultra had been revealed.

81 Milner-Barry, 'Action This Day', pp.272–6.

82 Welchman to Milner-Barry, 30.04.89, File: Bletchley Material, Box 1, 2nd Series, William Bundy papers, Princeton University Library.

83 Milner-Barry to Hooper (Cab), 27.02.75, MNBY 1, CCC.

84 Reproduced in Andrew, 'Gordon Welchman', pp.277–9.

85 Bundy to Milner-Barry, 30.10.85, File: Milner-Barry, Box 1, 2nd Series, William Bundy papers, Princeton University Library.

86 'Peter Wright MSS', Odom (NSA) daily log, 29.05.87, File 1, Box 26, Odom papers, LC.

87 He also came up with the idea of a Staff Counsellor to 'deal with problems of conscience'. See 'Peter Marychurch', Odom (NSA) daily log, 09.09.87, File 2, Box 26, Odom papers, LC.

88 Milner-Barry to Bundy, 30.04.89, File: Milner-Barry, Box 1, 2nd Series, William Bundy papers, Princeton University Library.

89 Howard, 'Reflections', p.241. Margaret Thatcher's memoirs, The Downing Street Years, do not mention either Peter Wright or the GCHQ trade unions affair.

90 Wesley Wark, 'In Never Never Land?', pp.196–203.

THE 1980s: INTO THE THATCHER ERA

Chapter 19: Geoffrey Prime – The GCHQ Mole

1 Report of the Security Commission May 1983, Cmnd 8876, p.19.

2 Andrew, Defence of the Realm, pp.706–7.

3 Ibid., pp.670–81; Heseltine, Life in the Jungle, p.247.

4 Aldrich, Hidden Hand, p.546; CIA, Special Report – Office of Current Intelligence, 'The British Communist Party', OCI No. 275638, File UK General, 1963, Box 171, NSF Files, JFKL.

5 Paymaster General George Wigg, to Prime Minister Harold Wilson, enclosing 'The Organisation of Security in the Diplomatic Service and Government Communications Headquarters', 17.08.66, PREM 13/1203.

6 SPM (74) 4, 'Double Certification of Destruction of Secret and Top Secret Documents – Exemptions', 11.01.74, CAB 134/3843.

7 Cole, *Geoffrey Prime*, pp.54–76.
8 Ibid, pp.39–40.
9 *Report of the Security Commission May 1983*, Cmnd 8876, p.2.
10 Cole, *Geoffrey Prime*, pp.114–17.
11 Ibid., pp.117–19
12 *Report of the Security Commission May 1983*, Cmnd 8876, pp.13–14.
13 Andrew, *Defence of the Realm*, p.578.
14 Anton and Pemrobuch, *Radioespionage*, pp.238–41. Also private information.
15 Cole, *Geoffrey Prime*, pp.135–6.
16 Statement of Stella Rimington (MI5), 09.11.92, 'Police Witness Statements', p.62, Regina vs. Michael John Smith, http://cryptome.or/smith-witness-statement.doc
17 *Report of the Security Commission May 1983*, Cmnd 8876, pp.7–8.
18 Ibid., p.7.
19 Ibid, pp.8–9.
20 LPG was moved in phases between 1974 and 1977.
21 Lumley (GCHQ), Head of Security Division (R), 'The Prime Case: Security Commission', RLO 170, 10.06.83, MSS.384/3/57, GCHQ-UR, WMRC.
22 *Report of the Security Commission May 1983*, Cmnd 8876, p.9.
23 Ibid., pp.9–10.
24 Lumley (GCHQ), Head of Security Division (R), 'The Prime Case: Security Commission', RLO 170, 10.06.83, MSS.384/3/57, GCHQ-UR, WMRC.
25 Sly, *Horse Grows Horns*, p.213.
26 Lanning and Norton-Taylor, *Conflict of Loyalties*, p.49.
27 Lumley (GCHQ), Head of Security Division (R), 'The Prime Case: Security Commission', RLO 170, 10.06.83, MSS.384/3/57, GCHQ-UR, WMRC.
28 *Report of the Security Commission May 1983*, Cmnd 8876, p.2.
29 Johnson, *American Cryptology*, Vol.4, p.407.
30 Richelson, *The Wizards of Langley*, pp.157, 203–5
31 Andrew and Gordievsky, *KGB*, pp.438–43; Aid, *Secret Sentry*, pp.164, 183–7; Johnson, *American Cryptology*, Vol.4, p.407.
32 Andrew and Gordievsky, *More Instructions from the Centre*, pp.100–1.
33 Head of Naval Home Division memo, 'Project Neat', 10.11.70, AIR 20/12879.
34 Lanning and Norton-Taylor, *Conflict of Loyalties*, p.51; Aid, *Secret Sentry*, p.129.
35 Prime, *Time of Trial*, pp.21–5.
36 Ibid., pp.72–3.
37 Cole, *Geoffrey Prime*, pp.62–3, 136–9.

38 He left Rochester Prison on 13 March 2001, after serving half his thirty-eight-year sentence.
39 Cole, *Geoffrey Prime*, pp.156–7
40 *Report of the Security Commission May 1983*, Cmnd 8876, pp.20–1.
41 Lumley (GCHQ), Head of Security Division (R), 'The Prime Case: Security Commission', RLO 170, 10.06.83, MSS 384/3/57, GCHQ-UR, WMRC.
42 Conversation with Steve Woolner (CSE), Odom (NSA) daily log, 08.08.85, File 5, Box 25, Odom papers, LC
43 *Report of the Security Commission May 1983*, Cmnd 8876, p.4.
44 Ibid., p.34.
45 Wynn (GCHQ), 'Improved Physical Security at Oakley', F/6007/9/1, 24.02.87, MSS.384/3/35, GCHQ-UR, WMRC.
46 Woods (BMA) to Duffton (SCPS GCHQ Main Branch), RVW/JNL/FB, 15.12.83, MSS.84/3/19, GCHQ-UR, WMRC.
47 *Report of the Security Commission May 1983*, Cmnd 8876, p.3.
48 John Coats and Ian Batley, 'Stress of Eavesdropping', *Sunday Times*, 15.04.84. See also 'Secret of GCHQ Suicide', *Daily Mail*, 07.04.84.
49 Thomas, *Espionage and Secrecy*, pp.141–2, 194–8.
50 *Report of the Security Commission, October 1986*, Cmnd 9923, pp.27–9.
51 The American problems are discussed in P. Earley, 'Spy Fiasco', *Washington Post*, 07.02.88.
52 Bearden and Risen, *The Main Enemy*, pp.324–6.
53 'Walker Case', Odom (NSA) daily log, 21.10.85, File 6 Box 25, Odom papers, LC.
54 Lanning and Norton-Taylor, *Conflict of Loyalties*, p.53.
55 'Items for Peter Marychurch', Odom (NSA) daily log, 15.09.85, File 6 Box 25, Odom papers, LC.
56 Smith, *Inside Time*, pp.87–9.

Chapter 20: A Surprise Attack – The Falklands War

1 Nott, *Here Today*, p.252.
2 Cooley, *Unholy Wars*, pp.17–18, 78. Even on Afghanistan, despite nine months of military preparations, the JIC had insisted that there would be no invasion, and only changed its mind in mid-December 1979.
3 One wonders whether this was triggered by knowledge of similar research that had been undertaken for the US government by Richard Betts.

4 Goodman, 'The Dog that Didn't Bark', pp.38–42.

5 Milner-Barry to Hooper (Cab), 27.02.75, MNBY 1, CCC.

6 Nicoll (GCHQ) to Stewart (Sec JIC), 'Central Monitoring Point for Requirements', Z/1187/8005/10, 3.06.71, CAB190/19.

7 Goodman, 'The Dog that Didn't Bark', pp.38–42.

8 Price, 'Interview: Lord Carrington', pp.2–4.

9 Lt General Sir James Glover (BGS Int), 'Falkland Islands Campaign', briefing to Odom (NSA) daily log, 15.10.82, File 1, Box 21, Odom papers, LC.

10 Carrington, Reflections on Things Past, p.358.

11 Bicheno, Razor's Edge, pp.64–7.

12 Ibid., p.69. As Bicheno rightly pointed out, it was the Europeans, not the Americans, who bolstered the junta in this period.

13 Hastings and Jenkins, The Battle for the Falklands, pp.36–59

14 Barker, Beyond Endurance, pp.30–1.

15 Bilton and Kosminksy, Speaking Out, p.33, fn.2.

16 Lanning and Norton-Taylor, A Conflict of Loyalties, pp.12–13.

17 Hastings and Jenkins, The Battle for the Falklands, pp.58–9

18 Commander Robert Denton Green in McManners, Forgotten Voices, p.15.

19 Bilton and Kosminsky (eds), Speaking Out, p.32.

20 Middlebrook, The Fight for the 'Malvinas', p.1.

21 Ibid., pp.2–5.

22 Ibid., pp.6–12.

23 Air Vice Commodore Carlos Bloomer-Reeve in McManners, Forgotten Voices, p.23.

24 Keegan, Intelligence in War, p.305.

25 Middlebrook, The Fight for the 'Malvinas', pp.14–15.

26 Keegan, Intelligence in War, p.299

27 See, for example, Nott, Here Today, p.252; Hastings and Jenkins, The Battle for the Falklands, p.77.

28 C. Powell, 'Reading Behind the Lines', Spectator, 02.03.02.

29 Hastings and Jenkins, The Battle for the Falklands, pp.77–8.

30 Ibid., p.69

31 Ibid., pp.75–6.

32 Franks, Falkland Islands Review, para.306.

33 West, The Secret War for the Falklands, p.44.

34 Hastings and Jenkins, The Battle for the Falklands, pp.83–4.

35 Nott, Here Today, p.257.

36 Thatcher, The Downing Street Years, p.178.

37 Nott, Here Today, p.257.

38 Thatcher, The Downing Street Years, p.179.

39 Nott, Here Today, p.258

40 Alan Clark records in his diary that John Nott's performance before the House as Defence Secretary was 'a disaster', adding that he 'faltered and fluttered and fumbled'. Entry for 3.04.82, Clark, Diaries: Into Politics, pp.312–13.

41 Major, The Autobiography, pp.76–7.

42 Entry for 05.04.82, Clark, Diaries: Into Politics, p.314.

43 Ibid., p.261.

44 Private information.

45 Wallace Turner, 'Adm. Inman Says US has Intelligence Gaps', International Herald Tribune, 29.04.82.

46 Duff (IC) to Le Bailly, 12.05.82, Folder 3, Box 9, Le Bailly papers, CCC. Admiral Bobby Ray Inman, Deputy Director of the CIA, also insisted the Americans did not know in advance. Wallace Turner, 'Adm. Inman Says US has Intelligence Gaps', International Herald Tribune, 29.04.82.

47 Freedman and Gamba-Stonehouse, Signals of War, pp.131–2. See also Bicheno, Razor's Edge, pp.121–2.

48 Richard Norton-Taylor, 'The Chance Remark Reopens Row Over GCHQ', Guardian, 08.05.84.

49 Bicheno has pondered whether Rowlands contributed to operational reverses. We are unlikely to know the truth of the matter for many years. Razor's Edge, pp.121–2.

50 Commander Robert Denton Green in McManners, Forgotten Voices, p.58.

51 West, The Secret War for the Falklands, p.67.

52 Freedman and Gamba-Stonehouse, Signals of War, p.131.

53 McManners, Falklands Commando, p.83.

54 Nott, Here Today, p.272. Private information.

55 http://www.nrk.no/programmer/tv/brennpunkt/1861285.html. Article about the Fauske II station (in Norwegian).

56 Hastings and Jenkins, The Battle for the Falklands, p.111.

57 Freedman, Falklands: Official History, Vol.II, p.70.

58 West, The Secret War for the Falklands, p.48.

59 Information from the late Peter Freeman, GCHQ Historian.

60 Commander Robert Denton Green, Intelligence Officer to Commander in Chief, Fleet HQ, Northwood, in

McManners, *Forgotten Voices*, p.14. On DSSS via Skynet see Woodward, *One Hundred Days*, p.143.

61 Private information.

62 Whitelaw, *Memoirs*, p.207.

63 Woodward, *One Hundred Days*, pp.213–21

64 Freedman, *Falklands: Official History*, Vol.II, pp.285, 290.

65 Heseltine's account of the forlorn efforts of a motley band of ministers, senior officials and intelligence chiefs to formulate an agreed account of the *Belgrano* decision not long after is more than fascinating to any contemporary historian. *Life in the Jungle*, p.281.

66 Rear Admiral Anthony John Whetstone, in McManners, *Forgotten Voices*, p.170.

67 Keegan, *Intelligence in War*, pp.306–7.

68 Major, *The Autobiography*, pp.76–7.

69 Commander Robert Denton Green in McManners, *Forgotten Voices*, p.325.

70 West, *The Secret War for the Falklands*, pp.180–94.

71 David Fischer, pp.151–2, Foreign Affairs Oral History Program (4), LL.

72 Captain Jeremy Black in McManners, *Forgotten Voices*, pp.184–5; Woodward, *One Hundred Days*, pp.267–9; Falconer, *First into Action*, p.369.

73 Woodward, *One Hundred Days*, pp.143–5.

74 Van der Bijl. *Nine Battles to Stanley*, p.160.

75 McManners, *Falklands Commando*, p.97.

76 Ibid., pp.99–108.

77 Captain Christopher Brown in McManners, *Forgotten Voices*, pp.197–8; see also p.194.

78 Van der Bijl, *Nine Battles to Stanley*, p.115.

79 Ibid., pp.115–16; Hastings and Jenkins, *The Battle for the Falklands*, pp.287–8.

80 Brigadier Julian Thompson in McManners, *Forgotten Voices*, p.57.

81 Perrett, *Weapons of the Falklands Conflict*, pp.135–6.

82 General Mario Menendez in McManners, *Forgotten Voices*, p.84.

83 Air Vice Commodore Carlos Bloomer-Reeve in ibid., p.79.

84 General Mario Menendez in ibid., p.23.

85 Brigadier Julian Thompson in ibid., p.397.

86 Lt General Sir James Glover (BGS Int), 'Falkland Islands Campaign', briefing to Odom (NSA) daily log, 15.10.82, File 1, Box 21, Odom papers, LC. Also conversations with the late William Odom.

87 HC Deb 55, 107, 27.02.84, pp.37–8.

88 Lt General Sir James Glover (BGS Int), 'Falkland Islands Campaign', briefing to

Odom (NSA) daily log, 15.10.82, File 1, Box 21, Odom papers, LC. Also conversations with the late William Odom.

89 Lt Colonel David Chaundler in McManners, *Forgotten Voices*, pp.295–6.

90 Lake, 'Nimrod R1', p.31.

91 See also Edwards, 'Europe and the Falklands Crisis', pp.295–313.

92 Freedman, *Falklands: Official History*, Vol.II, pp.720–1.

93 Thatcher, *The Downing Street Years*, p.227.

94 Wiebes, 'Dutch Sigint During the Cold War, 1945–94', p.275.

95 The most detailed account is given in Urban, *UK Eyes Alpha*, pp.57–69.

Chapter 21: Thatcher and the GCHQ Trade Union Ban

1 Transcript of interview with Mike Grindley, formerly a Chinese Scientific and Technical Linguist, 14.02.94, GCHQ-UR, MSS.384/3/50 WMRC.

2 Prior, *Balance of Power*, pp.255–6.

3 'Comments on Clough's Letter of 6th October', n.d., FO366/2998.

4 'Communist Trade Union Officials and Secret Departments', n.d., 10.52?, ibid.

5 Winnifrith min., 11.11.55, T215/391.

6 'Communist Officials in Civil Service Trade Unions', 02.08.61, T 216/914.

7 Herman, *Intelligence Services*, pp.184–5.

8 Somerville (GCHQ) to Attfield (CSD), E/3005/23/D/9403, 07.03.72, T 322/50.

9 Lanning and Norton-Taylor, *Conflict of Loyalties*, pp.18–23. See also Herman, 'Sir Leonard Hooper'.

10 APC (73) 3rd mtg, 'Record of the Administrative Planning Committee', 3.02.73, FCO 79/286. See also Somerville (GCHQ) to Youde (FCO), D/6442/1106/6, 8.02.73, ibid.

11 Lanning and Norton-Taylor, *Conflict of Loyalties*, p.18.

12 R.H. Greenfield, 'What Happens at GCHQ', *Sunday Telegraph*, 5.02.84.

13 HC Deb 55, 107, 27.02.84, col.94.

14 Herman, *Intelligence Services*, p.189.

15 Tovey, interview in 'Secret War', *Sunday Times*, 05.02.84. Richard Evans, 'Ban on Unions Essential, Former GCHQ Chief Says', *The Times*, 06.02.84.

16 Ibid.

17 Prior, *Balance of Power*, p.256.

18 Mike Vernon to CSU, 14.04.82, cited in Lanning and Norton-Taylor, *Conflict of Loyalties*, pp.34–6.

19 Lanning and Norton-Taylor, *Conflict of Loyalties*, p.36.

20 Tovey, interview in 'Secret War', *Sunday Times*, 05.02.84.

21 'Adieu Adye', *Warning Signal*, No.145, July 1996, p.1.

22 Transcript of interview with Mike Grindley, 14.02.94, GCHQ-UR, MSS.384/3/50 WMRC.

23 Lanning and Norton-Taylor, *Conflict of Loyalties*, p.87.

24 Denis Healey put this argument eloquently in the House of Commons, HC Deb 55, 107, 27.02.84, pp.37–8.

25 Ibid.

26 Lanning and Norton-Taylor, *Conflict of Loyalties*, p.4.

27 Ibid., p.38.

28 Armstrong (Cab Sec) to Jones (CPSU), 'Security Commission Report', AO83/1412, 18.05.83, GCHQ-UR, MSS.384/3/57 WMRC.

29 SCPS memo, 'Secret Commission Report (SCR) – Developments', 19.07.83, ibid.

30 Nicholls (GCHQ) to Verrion (DWC TUs), E/9435GA/1007/32, 15.06.83, GCHQ-UR, MSS.384/3/57 WMRC.

31 Meeting of CCSU coordinating committee, 17.11.83, ibid.

32 Hall (GCHQ) to Bryant (DWC TUs), 'R12 Complement', E/7525GA/3022/3/6, ibid.

33 Thatcher (PM) to Oonagh McDonald MP, 17.04.84, GCHQ-UR, MSS.384/3/58 WMRC.

34 Dufton (CCSU) to Irving (MP Cheltenham), 24.10.83, GCHQ-UR, MSS.384/3/57 WMRC.

35 Bamford, *Puzzle Palace*, pp.118–54.

36 'Meprobamate Reduces Accuracy of Psychological Testing of Deception', *Science*, 03.04.81.

37 CPS, *The Case Against the Polygraph* (London: October 1983).

38 Howe, *Conflict of Loyalty*, pp.341–3.

39 Lanning and Norton-Taylor, *Conflict of Loyalties*, p.12.

40 Marychurch (D/GCHQ) to all members of staff, D/8489DQ1501/29A, 25.01.84, GCHQ-UR, MSS.384/3/17, WMRC.

41 Lanning and Norton-Taylor, *Conflict of Loyalties*, pp.87–8.

42 Howe, *Conflict of Loyalty*, p.345.

43 Link (PUSD) to Goddard (GDTC), 17.11.86, MSS.384/3/26, GCHQ-UR, WMRC.

44 Lanning and Norton-Taylor, *Conflict of Loyalties*, p.103.

45 HC Deb 55, 107, 27.02.84, pp.43–4.

46 Armstrong (Cab Sec) to Marychurch (D/GCHQ), 07.02.84, MSS.384/3/30, GCHQ-UR, WMRC.

47 Marychurch (D/GCHQ) to Moore (Chair SRSC), 'The Government Communications Staff Federation', D/1151DQ/1101/21, 20.12.84, MSS.384/3/37, GCHQ-UR, WMRC.

48 Ivor Owen, 'Union Documents Used to Justify GCHQ Ban', *Financial Times*, 01.02.84.

49 Lanning and Norton-Taylor, *Conflict of Loyalties*, pp.28–33.

50 HC Deb 55, 107, 27.02.84, pp.77–8.

51 Lanning and Norton-Taylor, *Conflict of Loyalties*, pp.3, 28.

52 Lanning (NUCPS) to Hart, Oct 1988, 'Union Official Challenges to Government Facts Over GCHQ' MSS.384/3/20, GCHQ-UR, WMRC.

53 'GCHQ Banana Skins Become a Bonanza', *Telegraph*, 29.03.84.

54 P. Dobbie, 'GCHQ Goes on Spending Spree', *Sunday Telegraph*, 01.04.84. The author spoke to a local car dealer who lamented that there would never again be a year like 1984.

55 Lanning and Norton-Taylor, *Conflict of Loyalties*, pp.126–8.

56 'Protest Greets Howe at GCHQ', *Gloucestershire Echo*, 15.07.84.

57 Adye (GCHQ) to all staff, 'Judicial Review', D/9936DQ/1101/23, 19.07.84, MSS.384/3/44, GCHQ-UR, WMRC.

58 Will Bennett, 'Security "Outweighs" Earlier Ruling on Ban', *The Times*, 07.08.84.

59 Lustgarten and Leigh, *In From the Cold*, pp.329–33.

60 Kemp (T), to Hawken (Customs and Excise), 'GCHQ'. Enclosing 'GCHQ – Disciplinary Action Against Optant A Rejoiners', 25.06.86, FD 7/1944.

61 Benjamin, *Five Lives in One*, pp.149–51.

62 Lanning and Norton-Taylor, *Conflict of Loyalties*, pp.175–6.

63 G.H. Brauntoltz, text of speech to IPCS at Harrogate, 15.03.84, GCHQ-UR, MSS.384/3/17, WMRC.

64 Lanning and Norton-Taylor, *Conflict of Loyalties*, p.137.

65 HC Deb 55, 107, 27.02.84, pp.39–40; M. Weaver, 'Electronic Firms go Head-Hunting for GCHQ Staff', *Telegraph*, 13.02.84

66 Lanning and Norton-Taylor, *Conflict of Loyalties*, p.151

67 Appendix: 'Examples of Labour Party Leadership Pledges on GCHQ', Grindley (Chair GCHQ TUs) to Brett (IPMS), 02.04.96, MSS.384/3/20, GCHQ-UR, WMRC.

68 Lanning and Norton-Taylor, *Conflict of Loyalties*, p.174.
69 Ibid., pp.141–2.
70 'Navy Spec. Program', Odom (NSA) daily log, 03.03.86, File 7, Box 25, Odom papers, LC.
71 Norman Kirkham, 'New Lie Detector Row Looms Over Secret Whitehall Centre', *Sunday Telegraph*, 21.12.86.
72 'Polygraph Victory', *Warning Signal*, 12.12.88, p.4
73 Conversation between President Nixon, John D. Erlichman and H.R. Haldeman in the Oval Office between 12.36 p.m. and 1.00 p.m., 24.07.71, Conv. No 545–3 (rev.9/98), NPM, NARA.
74 Herman, *Intelligence Services*, pp.180–1.
75 Evidence to the Employment Select Committee of the House of Commons, 20.06.84, p.122. para. 302.
76 'The Refuseniks of Cheltenham', *Economist*, 10.03.84, p.26.
77 Drewry and Butcher, *The Civil Service Today*, pp.124–7.
78 Howe, *Conflict of Loyalty*, p.356.

Chapter 22: NSA and the Zircon Project
1 'Marychurch', Odom (NSA) daily log, 01.05.87, File 1, Box 26, Odom papers, LC.
2 Richelson, *The Wizards of Langley*, pp.234–5.
3 The arrival of fibre-optic cables deserves a chapter in itself, and resulted from work at the giant Post Office Research Department that had relocated from Dollis Hill to a new space-age site at Martelsham Heath in Suffolk. T (75) 13, 'Research and Development in Support of Government Communications', 07.08.75, CAB 134/3967.
4 Baylis, 'British Nuclear Doctrine', pp.53–65.
5 COS (71) 41st mtg (1), 'Strategic Nuclear Deterrent Force', 30.11.71, DEFE 32/21.
6 Freedman, *British Nuclear Weapons*, p.48.
7 Le Bailly, 'The Development of the Defence Intelligence Staff: Staff II, 1970–1973', Folder 6, Box 7, Le Bailly papers, CCC.
8 Hooper (IC) to Le Bailly (DGI), 18.07.74, Folder 5, Box 21, Le Bailly papers, CCC.
9 Baylis, 'British Nuclear Doctrine', pp.56–65.
10 Urban, *UK Eyes Alpha*, pp.59–61; Freedman and Gamba-Stonehouse, *Signals of War*, pp.181–2.
11 Urban, *UK Eyes Alpha*, pp.56–63. Urban's

superb account of Zircon remains unsurpassed.
12 Richelson, 'US Intelligence', p.344.
13 Interview with William Odom, 18.04.08.
14 Cooley, *Unholy Wars*, pp.17–18, 78.
15 Interview with Bill Odom, 18.04.08.
16 The Dutch were reading both German and Belgian diplomatic traffic at this time. Private information.
17 Tomlinson, *The Big Breach*, p.77.
18 Odom (NSA) daily log, 10.05.85, File 5, Box 25, Odom papers, LC.
19 Urban, *UK Eyes Alpha*, p.60.
20 This was known as 'success with the A5 problem', after the part of NSA that worked on Soviet diplomatic traffic. Aid, *Secret Sentry*, p.165.
21 Urban, *UK Eyes Alpha*, p.60
22 Cherkashin, *Spy Handler*, pp.224–5.
23 Odom daily log, 08.1181, File 3, Box 20, Odom papers, LC.
24 Cranston, 'US Signals Intelligence to New Zealand Blocked', p.243: Tow, 'The ANZUS Alliance', pp.61–6; Johnson, *American Cryptology*, Vol.4, p.304.
25 Helen Bain, 'Lange's Secret Papers Reveal USA's Bully Tactics', *Sunday Star-Times*, 15.01.06.
26 'Lange Papers Reveal US Spy Threats', *New Zealand Herald*, 15.01.06. See also 'US–New Zealand Nuclear Feud Detailed', *International Herald Tribune*, 15.01.06.
27 The document seems to have been 'Government Communications Security Bureau 1985/86 Annual Report', which was headed 'Top Secret Umbra Handle via Comint Channels Only'.
28 Helen Bain, 'Lange's Secrets', *Sunday Star-Times*, 15.01.06.
29 Ibid.
30 Barker, 'The Mystery Boats', pp.16–18
31 'New Zealand – Tucker', Odom (NSA) daily log, 06.11.86, File 7, Box 25, Odom papers, LC.
32 'Peter Hunt', Odom (NSA) daily log, 18.11.87, File 2, Box 26, Odom papers, LC.
33 Conversation with Peter Hunt (D/CSE), Odom (NSA) daily log, 08.08.85, File 5, Box 25, Odom papers, LC. On embassy collection see Frost, *Spyworld*, pp.154–78.
34 Odom (NSA) daily log, 01.08.85, File 5, Box 25, Odom papers, LC
35 Interview with William Odom, 2008.
36 Ibid.
37 Gorman to Odom (ACSI), 26.04.85, File 7, Box 17, Odom papers, LC.
38 'GCHQ/ZIRKON mtg London', Odom

(NSA) daily log, 07.05.85, File 5, Box 5, Odom papers, LC.

39 Record of a mtg with Weinberger, Odom (NSA) daily log, 31.05.85, ibid.

40 'Jarry Masz – Menwith Hill Station', Odom (NSA) daily log, 15.09.85, File 6, Box 25, Odom papers, LC.

41 Odom (NSA) daily log, 11.06.85, File 5, Box 25, Odom papers, LC

42 'GCHQ: Post mortem w/Dick Kern', Odom (NSA) daily log, 07.06.85, File 5, Box 25, Odom papers, LC. Kern served as SUSLO from Dec. 1983 to Jul. 1986.

43 'Notes and Observations on London and Bergen Mtgs', Odom (NSA) daily log, 11.06.85, File 5, Box 25, Odom papers, LC

44 Ibid.

45 The best account of Sigdasys is in Wiebes, 'Dutch Sigint 1945–94', in Aid and Wiebes, *Secrets of Signals Intelligence*, pp.276–8.

46 Mistakenly, Odom blamed Foreign Office influence on GCHQ for Marychurch's views.

47 ACIC, A/101/5, Annex A, 'The Role of Electronic Warfare, 1980–1990', WO 32/21273.

48 RARDE Technical Report 9/79, 'Evaluation of the Warsaw Pact Threat to I (BR) Corps Communications Post 1985', DEFE 15/2582.

49 'Notes and Observations on London and Bergen Mtgs', Odom (NSA) daily log, 11.06.85, File 5, Box 25, Odom papers, LC.

50 Ibid.

51 He added: 'Marychurch and Johnson must take me for an ordinary American with no education to speak of. They don't have a good grasp either of current strategic affairs or history. They are semi-educated newspaper readers, not intel[ligence] analysts worthy of national-level posts.' Ibid.

52 Smith, *Killer Elite*, pp.41–5.

53 Odom (NSA) daily log, 20.06.85, File 5, Box 25, Odom papers, LC.

54 M. Johnson et al., 'West Germany: Spies, Spies and More Spies', *Time*, 09.09.85. Private information.

55 *The Times*, 20.06.87.

56 Odom (NSA) daily log, Box 25, Odom papers, LC

57 Odom (NSA) daily log, 10.07.85, File 5, Box 25, Odom papers, LC

58 'Wiek – Issues', Odom (NSA) daily log, 09.09.86, File 8, Box 25, Odom papers, LC.

59 'Peter Marychurch', Odom (NSA) daily log, 09.09.87, File 2, Box 26, Odom papers, LC.

60 'Wieck', Odom (NSA) daily log, 23.01.86, File 8, Box 25, Odom papers, LC.

61 Le Bailly to Whitmore (PUS MoD), 13.06.86, Folder 1, Box 10, Le Bailly papers, CCC.

62 'G-94 Sub-Saharan Africa', Odom (NSA) daily log, 16.07.86, File 7, Box 25, Odom papers, LC.

63 Andrew, *Defence of the Realm*, p.689.

64 Machon, *Spies, Lies and Whistleblowers*, pp.300–1.

65 Andrew, *Defence of the Realm*, p.701.

66 Ibid. See also I. Black, 'Machine Gun Burst Echoes for 15 Years', *Guardian*, 08.07.99.

67 Odom (NSA) daily log, 7.04.86, File 7, Box 25, Odom papers, LC.

68 Aid, *Secret Sentry*, pp.186–7.

69 K. Schemeri, 'We Saved Gaddafi, Not Craxi – Mifsud Bonnici', *Malta Today on Sunday*, 02.11.08.

70 Some have insisted that there is evidence that the Lockerbie attack was perpetrated by the Iranians in retaliation for the mistaken shootdown of an Iranian airliner by the USS *Valdez* in the Gulf in July 1987.

71 One of these seems to have been the reading of the communications traffic of the East German foreign intelligence service. Odom (NSA) daily log, Box 25, Odom papers, LC

72 Lanning and Norton-Taylor, *Conflict of Loyalties*, pp.24–6.

73 GCHQ Working Group, CCSU, 'Pay Claim 1985 – The Communications Science and Technology Class GCHQ', GCHQ 87/95, 15.04.85, GCHQ-UR, MSS.384/3/38, WMRC.

74 'Andrew Saunders', Odom (NSA) daily log, 21.02.86, File 7, Box 25, Odom papers, LC.

75 'Len Nuuno', Odom (NSA) daily log, 18.04.86, File 7, Box 25, Odom papers, LC.

76 Gill, "Allo, 'Allo, 'Allo', pp.189–201.

77 Weatherill to Clerk of the House, 09.02.87, WEA/PP E144, Weatherill papers, Scarman Library, University of Canterbury.

78 Schlesinger, *Putting 'Reality' Together*, p.xxvi.

79 Raymond (Bondman and Partners) to GCHQ Trade Unions, 'Police Investigation Re: Duncan Campbell', 10.03.87, MSS.384/3/27, GCHQ-UR, WMRC.

80 Lawson, *The View From No.11*, p.314.

81 For example, Frank Cooper was now

against it. See Healey, *Time of My Life*, p.570.

82 'Marychurch', Odom (NSA) daily log, 01.05.87, File 1, Box 26, Odom papers, LC.

83 Urban, *UK Eyes Alpha*, pp.62–4.

84 Harvey, *Europe's Space Programme*, p.103.

AFTER 1989: GCHQ GOES GLOBAL

Chapter 23: From Cold War to Hot Peace – The Gulf War and Bosnia

1 Stankovic, *Trusted Mole*, p.251.

2 Urban, *UK Eyes Alpha*, pp.288–9.

3 Garton Ash, *The Polish Revolution*, pp.276, 301.

4 Loehnis comments at JIC (65) 3rd mtg (9), 21.01.65, CAB159/31. On the wider issues see Mobley, 'Deterring Iraq: The UK Experience'.

5 Trend (CS) to Wilson (PM), 16.11.64, discussing JIC (64) 81, 'UK Intelligence Operations of a Special Nature', DEFE 13/404.

6 Urban, *UK Eyes Alpha*, pp.143–8.

7 C. Powell, 'Reading Behind the Lines', *Spectator*, 02.03.02.

8 Andrew, *President's Eyes Only*, pp.518–20; Aid, *Secret Sentry*, pp.192–3.

9 Freedman, *A Choice of Enemies*, p.219.

10 J. Fullerton, 'British Ruse Held Iraqis' Attention While Real Invasion Came Elsewhere', *Philadelphia Inquirer*, 03.03.91.

11 R. Atkinson, 'Iraqis Called Vulnerable to Land Attack', *Washington Post*, 15.02.91.

12 Falconer, *First into Action*, pp.413–14.

13 D. Leigh and R. Evans, 'How £1bn was Lost When Thatcher Propped Up Saddam', *Guardian*, 28.02.03.

14 Aid, *Secret Sentry*, p.194.

15 A. Cordesman, 'The Intelligence Lessons of the Iraq Wars', 06.08.04, http://csis.org/files/media/csis/pubs.

16 T. Burchill, 'GCHQ Spoof Letter Hoax', *Gloucestershire Echo*, 31.08.90.

17 T.W. Lippman and B. Gellman, 'US Says it Collected Iraq Intelligence via UNSCOM', *Washington Post*, 08.01.99. See also J. Hyland, 'MI6 Involved in Spying Against Iraq Through UNSCOM', *Independent*, 26.01.99.

18 Ritter, *Iraq Confidential*, pp.212–16.

19 'Admoni, head of MOSSAD', Odom (NSA) daily log, 18.11.87, File 1, Box 26, Odom papers, LC.

20 R.J. Aldrich, 'America Used Islamist to Arm the Bosnian Muslims', *Guardian*, 22.04.02.

21 Wiebes, *Intelligence and the War in Bosnia*, pp.258–63.

22 J.T. Kuhner, 'Tribunal Probes US Aid to Croatia', *Washington Times*, 06.12.02.

23 *Nacional Issue* (291) – 14.6.01 http://www.nacional.hr/htm/291052.en.htm Also private information.

24 Stankovic, *Trusted Mole*, pp.250–2

25 Ibid. p.368.

26 McPeek, 'Electronic Warfare: British Style', pp.23–7.

27 Lake, 'Nimrod R.1', pp.29–35.

28 Wiebes, *Intelligence and the War in Bosnia*, pp.262–3.

29 FCO Defence Dept, 'Management Review of MoD: Illustrations for Use in Discussion with Review Team', 01.10.75, FCO46/1246.

30 Sims (GCHQ) to Lovegrove (PSA), 'CHK Planning: Antenna Maintenance Complex', F/6025/6002/4/20, 20.11.78, CM 6/3; Earwood, 'CSOS, Chum Hom Kok, Hong Kong', 08.78, CM 6/5. The American liaison officer during construction was 'Mr Tuboric'.

31 Its Australian code name was 'Kittiwake'. See Ball, 'Over and Out', pp.485–9.

32 Lee (GCHQ) to Hopewell (PSA), 'Siting of Antennas/Building at CHK', EOD/0738/2005/51/2, 27.11.78, CM 6/3.

33 Sims (GCHQ) to Lovegrove (PSA), 'Chum Hom Kok: Layout of Main Building', F/0037/6002/4/20, 12.01.79, ibid.

34 Chiverton (GCHQ) to PSA, F/3299GA/6002/4/20, 24.09.81, CM 6/234.

35 Rodgers (Lockheed) to PSA, 'Subsystem Design Review', 23.10.81, ibid.

36 PSA Chum Hom Kok Site to Hopewell (Demos-4), 14.08.81, ibid.

37 Adye (GCHQ) to Robbins (Demos-4), F/0371FP/6002/4/20, 15.12.81, ibid. In 1981 John Adye was Head of F Division.

38 Urban, *UK Eyes Alpha*, p.297.

39 'Hong Kong', Odom (NSA) daily log, 16.06.86, File 7, Box 25, Odom papers, LC.

40 Odom (NSA) daily log, 08.07.86, File 7, Box 25, Odom papers, LC.

41 Urban, *UK Eyes Alpha*, p.244.

42 Smith, *Spying Game*, pp.255–6.

43 Conversation with a commercial shipping entrepreneur in Shanghai in 1998.

44 Odom (NSA) daily log, 09.03.82, File 3, Box 20, Odom papers, LC

45 Urban, *UK Eyes Alpha*, p.263.

46 Tomlinson, *The Big Breach*, pp.115–17.

47 S. Boggan, 'Bugging: Can You Hear Me Darling?', *Independent on Sunday*, 17.01.93.

48 Butler (Cab Sec) to Whitmore (HO), 'Review of Security Arrangements for Public Figures', AO90/2395, 12.10.90, CM 44/34; Home Office, 'Review of Security Arrangements for Public Figures', section on 'Technical Protection', pp.30–41, 10.90, ibid.

49 R. Edwards, 'Home Secretary "blocked Diana Squidgygate inquiry" ', Telegraph, 12.02.08.

50 D. Goodin, 'UK Spooks Deliberately Leaked "Squidgygate" Tapes', The Register, 09.01.08.

51 AO93/192, Note for the Record, mtg between Butler (Cab Sec), Rimington (MI5), Adye (GCHQ) and an unnamed SIS officer, 23.01.93, Scott-Baker Inquiry, http://www.scottbaker-inquesrs.gov.uk/evidence/docs.INQ00606 96.pdf

52 Kevin Sullivan, 'British Police Conclude Diana's Death an Accident', Washington Post, 15.12.06.

53 N. Allen and G. Rayner, 'Diana's Squidgygate Tapes "leaked by GCHQ"', Telegraph, 10.01.08.

54 Robertson, 'Recent Reform of Intelligence in the UK', pp.144–58.

55 Ibid.

56 HL Deb 528, 1-12, 09.12.93, col.1039–40.

Chapter 24: The New Age of Ubiquitous Computing

1 Statement for the Record by Lieutenant General Michael V. Hayden, USAF Director, NSA Before the Joint Inquiry of the Senate Select Committee on Intelligence and The House Permanent Select Committee on Intelligence 17.10.02, para.20.

2 P. Kaihla, 'The Technology Secrets of Cocaine Inc.', Business2.com, July 2002, http://www.business2.com/articles/mag/print/0,1643,41206,FF.html

3 Cobb, 'Thinking About the Unthinkable', pp.1–2

4 Insight Team, 'Secret DTI Inquiry Into Cyber Terror', Sunday Times, 09.06.96.

5 Robertson, 'Recent Reform of Intelligence in the UK', pp.148–9

6 Johnson, American Cryptology, Vol.3, pp.233–4, 236.

7 'Quadripartite mtg London', Odom (NSA) daily log, 06.06.85, File 5, Box 25, Odom papers, LC

8 Levy, Crypto, pp.26–8; Singh, The Code Book, pp.256–9.

9 House of Commons, Select Committee on Trade and Industry, Examination of Witnesses (Questions 72–82), Sir Brian Tovey, 10.11.98.

10 NPL Report CTU 1, Davies, Price and Parkin, 'An Evaluation of Public Key Cryptosystems', 03.79, DSIR32/295.

11 Singh, The Code Book, pp.286–9; D. Campbell, 'Great Idea – Hide It', Guardian, 06.05.99.

12 OH–375, Interview with Martin Hellman, 22.11.04, Charles Babbage Institute Center for the History of Information Technology, University of Minnesota, pp.52–3.

13 Urban, UK Eyes Alpha, pp.251–3.

14 Singh, The Code Book, pp.279–92.

15 Seymour M. Hersh, 'The Intelligence Gap: How the Digital Age Left Our Spies out in the Cold', New Yorker, 06.12.99, pp.58–76.

16 Lustgarten and Leigh, In From the Cold, pp.393–4.

17 Report by Sir Michael Quinlan, 'Review of Intelligence Requirements and Resources, Part 1: Processes for Handling', 23.11.93. Professor Peter Hennessy obtained this document under FOIA, and I am most indebted to him for sight of it.

18 GCSF Annual Report 2005, pp.24–5, GCHQ-UR, MSS.384/3/37, WMRC. See also Urban, UK Eyes Alpha, pp.258–9. Even the tame Government Communications Staff Federation was moved to remark that management had 'completely fouled up' the redundancy process.

19 In reality, taking into account hidden costs and additional areas such as Defence Intelligence Staff, the real spend was probably over £2 billion at this point.

20 Aitken, Pride and Perjury, pp.4–7

21 GCSF Annual Report 1995, pp.27–8, GCHQ-UR, MSS.384/3/37, WMRC.

22 Aitken, Pride and Perjury, pp.4–7.

23 GCSF Annual Report 1995, pp.27–8, GCHQ-UR, MSS.384/3/37, WMRC.

24 Aitken, Pride and Perjury, pp.4–7.

25 New divisions like Q, U and W began to sprout. GCSF Annual Report 1995, pp.27–8, GCHQ-UR, MSS.384/3/37, WMRC.

26 Ibid., pp.30–1.

27 Downing Street press release, 'Appointment of Security and Intelligence Coordinator and Permanent Secretary, Cabinet Office', 20.06.02, http://www.number10.gov.uk/Page2583

28 GCHQ TU, Mins of Campaign Team, 20.03.95, GCHQ-UR, MSS.384/1/4/3, WMRC.

29 GCSF Annual Report 1995, p.32, GCHQ-UR, MSS.384/3/37, WMRC.

30 Clarke, 'Effective Implementation', p.46
31 In fact, towards the end of John Adye's tenure, GCHQ had brought forward plans for a large new building called 'O Block' on the eastern side of the Oakley site, absorbing the helipad. This was to be a fairly large conventional modern office building of thirteen thousand square metres, three storeys high, with a curved roof and clad in white metal panels that improved its comsec performance. The project got as far as the planning stage, and received reluctant permission from the local council. However, the review halted it. Moreover, local planners did not like its semi-rural setting, and clearly preferred to see the redevelopment of the Benhall site. K. Richardson, 'New GCHQ Building "a Carbuncle" ', *Gloucestershire Echo*, 10.01.94.
32 This included the long-overdue provision of a flat for the GCHQ Director to stay in when in London. Details from Westminster Council planning request for new air-conditioning systems.
33 It was envisaged that by 2003 staff would number about 4,500.
34 R.D. Cole, 'GCHQ: A Doughnut on the Landscape', *Eye Spy*, 1 (2001): 91–2; R. Norton-Taylor, 'GCHQ to Get New Headquarters for £800 m', *Guardian*, 07.03.00; M. Evans, 'Spies Pack Their Tea-Chests for £300m Move', *The Times*, 07.03.00; M. Evans, 'Spy HQ Bill Overshoots by £227m', *The Times*, 26.11.99.
35 Lanning and Norton-Taylor, *Conflict of Loyalties*, p.204
36 Grindley (GCHQ TU) to Blair, 28.07.92, MSS.384/3/49, GCHQ-UR, WMRC; Blair to Grindley, 14.10.92, ibid.
37 Brown to Grindley (GCHQ TU), 18.06.92 and 19.08.92, MSS.384/3/49, GCHQ-UR, WMRC.
38 Jowell to Grindley (GCHQ TU), 17.06.92, MSS.384/3/49, GCHQ-UR, WMRC; Mandelson to Grindley, 04.06.92, ibid.
39 Appendix: Examples of Labour Party Leadership Pledges on GCHQ, Grindley (Chair GCHQ TUs) to Brett (IPMS), 02.04.96, MSS.384/3/20, GCHQ-UR, WMRC.
40 Grindley (GCHQ TU) to Cook (FCO), 22.04.97, MSS.384/3/55, GCHQ-UR, WMRC.
41 Although downsizing was over by the later 1990s, there remained significant issues to deal with. One of the first prob-lems addressed by the restored unions was damage to the hearing of Radio Operators. Poor headphones combined with opera-tors' tendency to turn the volume up to catch crackly transmissions had left some of them with a form of progressive deaf-ness termed 'Noise Induced Hearing Loss'. About a hundred specialist staff received initial compensation payments totalling £500,000. J. Berry and C. Hastings, 'GCHQ Eavesdroppers "Are Going Deaf" ', *Sunday Telegraph*, 09.04.00.
42 P. Lashmar, 'A Province that is Full of Spies and Their Gadgets', *Independent*, 09.12.99; Wilkinson, *Secrecy and the Media*, p.366.
43 Ibid.
44 Entry for 31.03.99, Campbell, *The Blair Years*, p.375.
45 In 2003 Liam Clarke, a journalist on the *Sunday Times*, was arrested after he included transcripts from a bugging operation code-named 'Narcotic1' in a biography of Martin McGuinness. 'Editor Arrested Over "Phone Tap"', *Sunday Times*, 01.05.03.
46 'How Britain Eavesdropped on Dublin', *Independent*, 16.07.99.
47 A. Palmer, 'Omagh Bombing: Details from Phone Taps "Not Passed On"', *Telegraph*, 14.09.08; Robert Booth, ' "Bombers" Were Tracked Across Border by GCHQ on Their Way to Omagh', *Guardian*, 15.09.08.
48 Sir Peter Gibson, *Review of Intercepted Intelligence in Relation to the Omagh Bombing of 15 August 1998*, 16.01.09, para 23 http://www.nio.gov.uk/review_of_inter-cepted_intelligence_in_relation_to_the_omagh_bombing_of_15_august_1998.pdf Gibson,
49 BBC *Panorama* response to the Review of intercepted intelligence in relation to the Omagh bombing by Sir Peter Gibson arising from transmission of *Panorama: Omagh – What the Police were Never Told*, p.20. http://news.bbc.co.uk/1/shared/bsp/hi/pdfs/12_02_09_panoramagibsonresponse.pdf
50 Gibson, para 4.30.
51 BBC *Panorama* response.
52 Machon, *Spies, Lies and Whistleblowers*, pp.299–301.
53 N.Rufford, 'Blair's Spy Summit on Red Mafia', *Sunday Times*, 05.12.99.
54 Barnett, *Britain Unwrapped*, pp.366–7.
55 *ISC Annual Report, 1999–2000*, HMSO, 08.00, para 106.
56 K. Sengupta and P. Lashmar, 'How Noye was Caught', *Independent*, 14.04.00; K. Sengupta and P.Lashmar, 'Noye's Tangled

Web of Corruption', *Independent*, 14.04.00;
R. Evans and D. Hencke, 'Gag on Spies'
Role in Noye Case', *Guardian*, 22.07.00.
57 D.Sapsted, 'Witness at Noye Trial Shot
Dead in his Car', *Telegraph*, 19.06.01.
58 G. McLagan, 'Journalists Caught on Tape
in Police Bugging', *Guardian*, 21.09.02; G.
McLagan, 'Fraudster Squad', *Guardian*,
21.09.02.
59 J. Werran, 'The Home Office's Policy on
E-security 1999 Part 1: From Escrow To
Where?', 13.12.99, http://www.thesour-
cepublishing.co.uk/indexf.html?00389
60 Charles Clarke, the new Home Secretary,
insisted that the new Bill would not usher
in 'an Orwellian nightmare of unfettered
mass surveillance' that some had
predicted. An Open Letter from Charles
Clarke (13.03.00), *The Source*.
61 R. Reeves, 'E-Squad Launched to Crack
Criminal Codes on the Net', *Guardian*,
05.09.99; Peter Soomer, 'Protection or
Persuasion?', *Guardian*, 30.03.00.
62 Government had already addressed the
hacking problem by creating the National
Infrastructure Security Coordinating
Centre (NISCC), an alliance of security
departments working under Cabinet
Office leadership to address anxieties
about IT attacks.
63 Comments of Brian Paterson at Cityforum
2000, Conference Transcripts, 'Strategies
to Defeat Crime Cybercrime – Can
Governments Respond Adequately?'
64 GTAC was later called NTAC. Margaret
Beckett, Ministerial Statement, 31.10.06,
Hansard, Written Ministerial Statements,
Column 11WS.
65 Statement for the Record by Lieutenant
General Michael V. Hayden, USAF
Director, NSA Before the Joint Inquiry of
the Senate Select Committee on
Intelligence and the House Permanent
Select Committee on Intelligence
17.10.02, para.20.
66 Hersh, 'The Intelligence Gap: How the
Digital Age Left Our Spies out in the Cold',
New Yorker, 06.12.99, pp.58–76.
67 Ibid.

Chapter 25: The 9/11 Attacks and the Iraq War
1 Aid, *Secret Sentry*, p.216.
2 Seldon, *Blair Unbound*, pp.2–13.
3 Paul Vallely, 'Eliza Manningham-Buller:
Spying Dame', *Independent*, 11.11.06; *ISC
Annual Report 2000–1*, Cm. 5542, HMSO,
Aug 2002.

4 Blunkett, *The Blunkett Tapes*, p.301.
5 W. Pincus, 'NSA Intercepted Warnings on
Eve of Attacks', *Washington Post*, 19.06.02.
6 Aid, *Secret Sentry*, p.205.
7 *ISC Annual Report 2000–1*, Cmnd.5542,
HMSO, 08.02.
8 Bamford, *The Shadow Factory*, pp.56–7; Aid,
Secret Sentry, pp.213–15.
9 *ISC Report*, 'Rendition', Cmnd.7171,
HMSO, 07.07.
10 J. Risen and D. Johnston, 'Agency is
Under Scrutiny for Overlooked Messages',
New York Times, 20.06.02.
11 *ISC Annual Report*, 1999–2000, HMSO,
08.00, para.66
12 Aid, *Secret Sentry*, p.207.
13 *ISC Annual Report*, 1999–2000, HMSO,
Aug. 2000, para.29.
14 S. Shane, 'Excessive Caution Kept NSA
Passive', *Baltimore Sun National Staff*,
23.07.04; D. Campbell, 'How the Plotters
Slipped US Net', *Guardian*, 27.09.01.
15 Omand, 'Intelligence Secrets and Media
Spotlights', p.34.
16 S. Stellin, 'Terror's Confounding Online
Trail', *New York Times*, 28.03.02.
17 M. Lane, 'How terror talk is tracked', *BBC
News Online*, 21.05.03 http://news.
bbc.co.uk/go/em/fr//2/hi/uk_news/30411
51.stm ; P. Kaihla, 'In the Company of
Spies', *Business2 Magazine*, 05.03,
http://www.business2.com/articles/mag/p
rint/0,1643,49068,00.html
18 Andrew, *Defence of the Realm*, p.803.
19 N. Fielding, 'Phone Call Gave Away al
Qaida Hideout', *Sunday Times*, 15.09.02.
20 N. Fielding, 'War on Terror: Knocking on
al-Qaeda's Door', *Sunday Times*, 22.09.02.
21 M. Lane, 'How Terror Talk is Tracked', *BBC
News Online*, 21.05.03. http://news.bbc.
co.uk/go/em/fr/-/2/hi/uk_news/
3041151.stm; P. Kaihla, 'In the Company
of Spies', Business2 Magazine, 05.03,
http://www.business2.com/articles/mag/p
rint/0,1643,49068,00.html
22 S. Shane, 'Inside a 9/11 Mastermind's
Interrogation', *New York Times*, 22.06.08.
23 ISC Report, 'Rendition', Cmnd.7171,
HMSO, Jul. 2007.
24 S. Shane, 'Inside a 9/11 Mastermind's
Interrogation', *New York Times*, 22.06.08.
25 The failure to secure convictions remains
troubling in this case.
26 D. Bamber, O. Craig and F. Elliott, 'Blair
Sent in Tanks After "Chilling" Threat',
Sunday Telegraph, 16.02.03.
27 *ISC Annual Report 2003–4*, Cmnd.6240,
06.04, paras 48, 67.

28 Aldrich, 'The UK and Iraq'. SIS fairly quickly discounted the defector held by the Germans and code-named 'Curveball'.

29 'US Plan to Bug Security Council: The Text', *Observer*, 02.03.03; M. Bright, 'GCHQ Arrest Over *Observer* Spying Report', *Observer*, 09.03.03.

30 Svendsen, *Intelligence Cooperation and the War on Terror*, pp.132–3.

31 S. Schlesinger, 'Cryptanalysis for Peacetime', pp.217–35.

32 S. Shane and A. Sabar, 'Alleged NSA Memo Details US Eavesdropping at UN', *Baltimore Sun*, 04.03.03.

33 Entry for 07.03.03, Campbell, *The Blair Years*, p.672.

34 The nature of the coup is still disputed. See Gustafson, *Chile*.

35 M. Bright, E. Vulliamy and P. Beaumont, 'UN Launches Inquiry into American Spying', *Observer*, 09.03.03.

36 M. Bright, P. Beaumont and J. Tuckman, 'British Spy Op Wrecked Peace Move', 15.02.04.

37 Blix, *Disarming Iraq*, p.128.

38 M. Bright, 'GCHQ Arrest Over Observer Spying Report', *Observer*, 09.03.03.

39 Arguably, Jock Kane had tried in 1984 with his banned book, *GCHQ: The Negative Asset*.

40 M. and T. Mitchell, *The Spy Who Tried to Stop a War*, pp.6–7.

41 BBC Radio 4, *Saturday Live*, interview with Katharine Gun, 11.02.09.

42 Ibid.

43 Blunkett, *The Blunkett Tapes*, pp.457–8.

44 Ibid. See also Wilkinson, 'Balancing National Security and the Media', pp.147–8.

45 Bamford, *Pretext for War*, p.362.

46 Aid, *Secret Sentry*, p.249.

47 Short, *An Honourable Deception?*, pp.242–3

48 N. Watt, 'Top Civil Servant Tells Short to Shut Up', *Guardian*, 01.03.04.

49 'How GCHQ Spies Cracked Saddam's Top-Secret Codes', *Western Daily Press*, 09.04.03.

50 J. Borger and S. Millar, '2pm: Saddam is Spotted. 2.48pm: Pilots Get Their Orders. 3pm: 60ft Crater at Target', *Guardian*, 09.04.03.

51 L. Cpl. Hark, 'Y Troop' at http://www.onceamarinealwaysamarine.co.uk/3cdobdetelic.htm

52 Ibid.

53 Aid, *Secret Sentry*, p.254.

54 This was especially true of the CIA, which was prescient about the insurgency.

55 R. Norton-Taylor, 'IT Expert Named as New Head of GCHQ', *Guardian*, 01.02.03.

56 J. Gerard, 'All Systems Glow at Spook Central', *Sunday Times*, 31.08.03; *ISC Annual Report 2003–4*, Cmnd 6240, HMSO, 06.04, para.54.

57 Allen et al., *Working Without Walls*, p.16; Graham, 'Giving the Information Message Traction: Embedding Knowledge Sharing at GCHQ', pp.25–30.

58 David Pepper, Select Committee on Public Accounts, Minutes of Evidence, Examination of Witnesses (Questions 1–19), 01.12.03.

59 Public Accounts Committee, *Government Communications Headquarters New Accommodation Programme*, 23rd Report of Session 2003–4, HC 65, HMSO, 05.05.04.

60 The ventilation shaft for this secret Cold War bunker complex was hidden within the southern light-well of the Ministry of Defence main building, Johnston (PSA) to Chope (PSA), 'Project Pindar', 11.11.86, CM 46/26.

61 Fensome (PSA) to Hawtin (T), 'Project Pindar', and enclosure DCA/SRA 17469/01, 19.04.85, ibid.

62 PSA to Hawtin (T), 'Project Pindar', 30.04.87, ibid.; PSA to Bevan (MoD), 'Pindar', 19.02.87, ibid.

63 'The Spies' Biggest Secret', *Punch*, Issue 134, 04–17.07.01.

64 'GCHQ Criticised for Huge Move Overspend', BBC News, 16.07.03, http://news.bbc.co.uk/go/pr/fr/-/2/hi/uk_news/england/gloucestershire/3069501.stm

65 Andrew, *Defence of the Realm*, p.793.

66 *ISC Annual Report 2002–3*, Cm. 5837, 06.03, para 23. http://www.cabinetoffice.gov.uk/intelligence/annual_reports.aspx

67 F. Elliott, 'Millions Wasted on Faulty GCHQ Signals System', *Telegraph*, 15.06.03.

68 *ISC Annual Report, 1999–2000*, HMSO, 2002, para 14. See also S. Fidler and M. Huband, 'A Special Relationship?', *Financial Times*, 06.07.04.

69 D.R. Nicoll, 'Knowledge of Intelligence Analysts Under Examination', *The Times*, 06.02.04.

70 Aldrich, 'Four Enquiries', pp.74–7.

71 CBS *60 Minutes* Transcript, Interview with Drumheller, http:/thinkprogress.org/60-minutes-42306.

72 Aldrich, 'Four Enquiries', pp.73–5, 81.

73 Seldon, *Blair Unbound*, p.140. Butler was more forthright in his interview with Seldon than in his own report.

74 Butler Report, 'Review of Intelligence and Weapons of Mass Destruction', Cmnd. 898, 14.07.04, para 427.
75 Entry for 03.09.02, Campbell, *The Blair Years*, p.577.
76 Conversation with Peter Freeman.
77 Butler Report, 'Review of Intelligence and Weapons of Mass Destruction', Cmnd.898, 14.07.04. Beginning in 1990, the report avoided looking at the failure of the Foreign Office to take any notice of intelligence specialists, who were warning them loudly that the Russians were cheating on their arms control treaties and running a vast and terrifying biological weapons programme in the 1980s.
78 Jervis, 'Reports, Politics and Intelligence Failures', pp.3–52.

Chapter 26: From Bletchley Park to a Brave New World?

1 D. Leppard, 'Internet Firms Resist Minister's Plan to Spy on Every E-Mail', *Sunday Times*, 02.08.09.
2 Seldon, *Blair Unbound*, pp.372–8.
3 Hoffman, 'The Global Terrorist Threat', p.49.
4 Van der Reijn, 'Germany and the Netherlands', pp.223–4.
5 Primarily from 226 Squadron.
6 'Lightweight Emitter Acquisition, Recording and Analysis System (LEARAS) (Project Scarus) (UK), Intelligence system – Signals Intelligence', *Jane's C4I Systems*.
7 UK AOC Newsletter ,10.07, http://www.ukaoc.org/newsletters/oct07.htm
8 N. Britten and J. Petrie, 'Proud to be a Muslim, a Soldier and British', *Telegraph*, 04.07.06.
9 'GCHQ Staff Spend Christmas in Afghanistan', *Cheltenham Citizen*, 23.12.08.
10 Aid, *Secret Sentry*, p.282.
11 UK AOC Newsletter, 01.09, http://www.ukaoc.org/newsletters/jan09.htm
12 G. Adams et al., 'Bridging the Gap: European C4ISR Capabilities and Transatlantic Interoperability', National Defence University, 2004, p.38.
13 M. Evans, 'Biggest Military Loss Since Start of Afghanistan War is a Terrible Accident', *Sunday Times*, 3.10.06.
14 N. Allen and J. Kirkup, 'Royal Marine Killed on Christmas Eve in Afghanistan', *Telegraph*, 25.12.08.
15 J. Lewis, 'Spy-in-Sky Patrols Over British Cities in Hunt for Taliban Fighters', *Mail on Sunday*, 03.08.08.
16 Wright, *Spycatcher*, p.108.

17 N. Tweedie and D Gardham, 'A Hole in the Road Here Means MI5', *Telegraph*, 01.05.09.
18 P. Kaihla, 'Weapons of the Secret War', *Business2.com*, 11.01.
19 *ISC Annual Report 2005–6*, Cmnd.6864, HMSO, 06.06, paras 57–8.
20 *ISC Annual Report 2006–7*, Cmnd.7299, HMSO, 01.08, paras 47, 54.
21 ISC Report. 'Rendition', Cm.7171, HMSO, 07.07.
22 J. Risen and D. Johnston, 'Agency is Under Scrutiny for Overlooked Messages', *New York Times*, 20.06.02.
23 K. Ahmed, 'Police to Spy on all Emails: Fury Over Europe's Secret Plan to Access Computer and Phone Data', *Guardian*, 08.06.02.
24 S. Millar, 'Internet Providers Say No to Blunkett', *Guardian*, 22.10.02.
25 *ISC Annual Report, 2004–5*, Cmnd.6510, HMSO, Apr. 2005, paras 93–4.
26 D. Rose, 'Juries "Should Hear Phone Taps" to Nail Crime Gangs', *Observer*, 08.09.02.
27 *ISC Annual Report 2006–7*, Cmnd.7299 HMSO, 01.08, paras 113–14.
28 Sean O'Neill, Daniel McGrory and Philip Webster, 'Police had Hamza "Murder Evidence" 7 Years Ago: Phone-Tap Record Inadmissible in UK Will be Used by Americans', *The Times*, 09.02.06
29 *ISC Annual Report 2007–8*, Cmnd.7542 HMSO, Mar. 2009, para.171.
30 Evidence by Ken Macdonald and Keir Starmer to Home Affairs Select Committee Inquiry into Home Office Counter-Terrorism, 10.11.09.
31 R. Verkaik and N. Morris, 'Exclusive: Storm Over Big Brother Database', *Independent*, 15.10.08.
32 C. Williams, 'Spy Chiefs Plot £12bn IT Spree for Comms Überdatabase', *The Register*, 07.10.08, http://www.theregister.co.uk/2008/10/07/detica_interception_modernisation/
33 Sommer and Hosein, *Briefing on the Internet Modernisation Programme*, pp.18–19.
34 D. Leppard, 'Internet Firms Resist Minister's Plan to Spy on Every E-Mail', *Sunday Times*, 02.08.09.
35 B. Waterfield, 'Claims of Big Brother Surveillance at Google', *Age*, 27.05.07.
36 J. Bamford, 'Who's in Big Brother's Database?', *New York Review of Books*, 56/17, 05.11.09.
37 David Leppard and Chris Williams, 'Jacqui Smith's Secret Plan to Carry on Snooping', *Sunday Times*, 03.05.09.

38 Gandy, 'Data Mining, Surveillance, and Discrimination', pp.163–84

39 Jobs at Government Communications Headquarters – GCHQ Lead Researcher – Stream Data Mining, 21/01/2009. CommsRD/1/08(9). https://www11.i-grasp.com/fe/tpl_gchq01ssl.asp?s=raCzFK hUsJVaXxJsp&newlang=1&jobid=26073, 1251216561&key=3153107&c=40727254 3425&pagestamp=dblmimnuarjgycsxay.

40 Sir Ken Macdonald QC, CPS Lecture – 'Coming Out of the Shadows', 20.10.08, http:/www.cps.gov.uk/news/national-news.comi.

41 'Surveillance is a distinctive product of the modern world. Indeed, surveillance helps to constitute the world as modern.' Lyon, 'Surveillance Technology and Surveillance Society', p.161.

Bibliography

All books referred to in the bibliography are published in London unless otherwise stated. All references to primary documents in the endnotes are to the UK National Archives unless otherwise stated.

Major Repositories of Unpublished Documents
British Telecom Archives, Holborn, London (BT)
Canadian National Archives (CNA)
Firestone Library, Princeton University (PU)
Howard Gotlieb Archival Research Center, University of Boston (HGARC)
India Office Records, British Library (IO)
Library and Archives of Canada (LAC)
Modern Records Centre, University of Warwick (MRC)
National Archive for the History of Computing, University of Manchester (NAHC)
The National Archives, formerly the Public Record Office, Kew Gardens, Surrey (TNA)
National Archives of Australia (NAA)
Royal Navy Submarines Museum, Gosport (RNSM)
US National Archives, College Park, Maryland (NARA)
US Naval Operational Archives Branch, Navy Yard, Washington DC (USNOAB)

Private Papers
I. Great Britain
Lord Avon, Foreign Secretary (PRO and BUL)
Tony Beasley (LHCMA)
Patrick Beesly and other Ultra historians (CCC)
Sir Frederick Brundrett (CCC)
Sir Winston Churchill (CCC)
Arthur Cooper (in private hands)
Dr Alan Crick (LHCMA)

Sir Andrew Cunningham (BL)
Alec Douglas-Home (Scottish Record Office)
M.J. Hurley (RNSM)
General Sir Hastings Ismay (LHCMA)
Admiral Louis Le Bailly (CCC)
Selwyn Lloyd (CCC)
Stuart Milner-Barry (CCC)
Sir Walter Monckton (BOD)
Field Marshal Lord Montgomery of Alamein (IWM)
Admiral Lord Mountbatten (HL)
Admiral William Parry (IWM)
Major General Sir William Penney (LHCMA)
Commander Alfred Roake (RNSM)
Vice Admiral Gerard Rushbrooke (IWM)
Duncan Sandys (CCC)
Air Commodore Colin Simpson (LHCMA)
Lord Strang (CCC)
George Strauss (CCC)
Lord Swinton (CCC)
Lord Weatherill (Templeman Library, University of Kent at Canterbury)
Solly Zuckerman (University of East Anglia)

II. United States
Stewart Alsop (HGARC)
Henry Brandon (LC)
William Bundy (PU)
General Charles Cabell (BAFB)
William Colby (PU)
Charles H. Donnelly (USMHI)
Allen Dulles (PU)
Dwight D. Eisenhower (DDEL)
Foreign Affairs Oral History Program (LL)
General A.M. Gruenther (DDEL)
C.D. Jackson (DDEL)
Lyndon B. Johnson (LBJL)
Philip M. Kaiser (HSTL)
George Lardner (LC)
Admiral William D. Leahy (OAB, WNY)
Clare Booth Luce (LC)
John McCone (DDEL)
Cord Meyer (LC)
General William Odom (LC)

General Samuel Phillips (LC)
General Walter Bedell Smith (DDEL)
Harry S. Truman (HSTL)

Published Documents, Reports, Diaries and Autobiographies

Aitken, J., *Pride and Perjury* (HarperCollins, 2000)

Barker, N., *Beyond Endurance: An Epic of Whitehall and South Atlantic Conflict* (Barnsley: Leo Cooper, 2002)

Bearden, M. and Risen, J., *The Main Enemy: The Inside Story of the CIA's Final Showdown with the KGB* (NY: Random House, 2003)

Benjamin, R., *Five Lives in One: An Insider's View of the Defence and Intelligence World* (Tunbridge Wells: Parapress, 1996)

Benn, T., *Out of the Wilderness, Diaries 1963–67* (Hutchinson, 1987)

— *Office Without Power, Diaries 1968–72* (Hutchinson, 1988)

Benson, R.L. and Warner, R., *Venona: Soviet Espionage and the American Response, 1939–57* (Menlo Park, CA: Aegean Park Press, 1997)

Bilton, M. and Kosminksy, P., *Speaking Out: Untold Stories from the Falklands War* (Grafton, 1987)

Blake, G., *No Other Choice* (Jonathan Cape, 1990)

Blix, H., *Disarming Iraq* (NY: Pantheon, 2004)

Blunkett, D., *The Blunkett Tapes: My Life in the Bear Pit* (Bloomsbury, 2006)

Borovik, G., *The Philby Files* (Little, Brown, 1995)

Bryant, T., *Dog Days at the White House: The Outrageous Story of a Presidential Kennel Keeper* (NY: Macmillan, 1975)

Callaghan, J., *Time and Chance* (Collins, 1987)

Calvocoressi, P., *Threading My Way* (Duckworth, 1994)

Campbell, A., *The Blair Years: Extracts From the Alastair Campbell Diaries* (Hutchinson, 2007)

Carrington, Lord, *Reflections on Things Past: The Memoirs of Lord Carrington* (Collins, 1988)

Castle, B., *The Castle Diaries 1964–70* (Weidenfeld and Nicolson, 1984)

Cavendish, A., *Inside Intelligence* (Collins, 1990)

Cherkashin, V., *Spy Handler: Memoir of a KGB Officer* (NY: Basic 2005)

Clark, A., *Diaries: Into Politics* (Weidenfeld and Nicolson, 2000)

Clayton, A., *The Enemy is Listening: The Story of the Y Service* (Hutchinson, 1980)

Cole, D.J., *Geoffrey Prime: The Imperfect Spy* (Robert Hale, 1998)

Colville, J., *The Fringes of Power* (Hodder and Stoughton, 1985)

Comptroller and Auditor General, *Government Communications Headquarters (GCHQ): New Accommodation Programme* (The Stationery Office HC 955, 2003)

Coote, J., *Submariner* (NY: Norton, 1992)

Cradock, P., *Experiences of China* (John Murray, 1994)

de la Mare, A., *A Jersey Farmer's Son in the Diplomatic Service* (Jersey: La Haule Books, 1994)

de Silva, P., *Sub Rosa: The CIA and the Use of Intelligence* (NY: Times Books, 1978)

Donoughue, B., *Downing Street Diary: With Harold Wilson in No.10* (Pimlico, 2006)

Elliott, G. and Shukman, H., *Secret Classrooms: An Untold Story of the Cold War* (St Ermin's, 2002)

Evans, H., *Good Times, Bad Times* (Weidenfeld and Nicolson, 1983)

Fahey, J.A., *Licensed to Spy* (Annapolis: Naval Institute Press, 2002)

Falconer, D., *First Into Action: A Dramatic Personal Account of Life in the SBS* (Little, Brown, 2001)

Flicke, W.F., *War Secrets of the Ether* (Laguna Hills CA: Aegean Park Press, 1994)

Frost, M., *Spyworld: Inside the Canadian and American Intelligence Establishments* (Toronto: Doubleday, 1994)

Garner, J.R., *Codename Copperhead: My True Life Exploits as a Special Forces Soldier* (NY: Simon and Schuster, 1994)

Gibson, S., *The Last Mission* (Stroud: Sutton, 2005)

Gilchrist, A., *Cod Wars and How to Lose Them* (Edinburgh: Q Press, 1978)

Haines, J., *Glimmers of Twilight* (Politico's, 2003)

Hampshire, S., *Innocence and Experience* (Allen Lane, 1989)

Harvey-Jones, J., *Getting It Together* (Heinemann, 1991)

Healey, D., *The Time of My Life* (Michael Joseph, 1989)

Heath, E., *The Course of My Life: The Autobiography of Edward Heath* (Hodder and Stoughton, 1998)

Heseltine, M., *Life in the Jungle: My Autobiography* (Hodder and Stoughton, 2000)

Howe, G., *Conflict of Loyalty* (Macmillan, 1994)

Hunt, R., Russell, G. and Scott, K, *Mandarin Blue: RAF Chinese Linguists – 1951 to 1962 – in the Cold War* (Oxford: Hurusco Books, 2008)

Ingham, B., *Kill the Messenger* (HarperCollins, 1991)

Jenkins, R., *Life at the Centre* (Macmillan, 1991)

Joint Technical Language Service, *Arabic Personal Names: JTLS Working Aid 97(E)/93* (Cheltenham: GCHQ, 1993)

Jones, R.V., *Most Secret War* (Hamish Hamilton, 1978)

— *Reflections on Intelligence* (Heinemann, 1989)

Kalugin, O. and Montaigne, F., *The First Directorate: My First 32 Years in Intelligence and Espionage Against the West – The Ultimate Memoirs of a Master Spy* (NY: St Martin's Press, 1994)

King, C.H., *The Cecil King Diaries, 1965–1970* (Jonathan Cape, 1972)

Kot, S., *Conversations with the Kremlin and Dispatches from Russia* (Oxford: Oxford UP, 1963)

Lamphere, R.J. and Shachtman, T., *The FBI-KGB War: A Special Agent's Story* (W.H. Allen, 1986)

Lawson, N., *The View From No.11: Memoirs of a Tory Radical* (Heinemann, 1992)

Lederer, W., *The Last Cruise: The Sinking of the Submarine USS Cochino* (William Sloane, 1950)

Leutze, J. (ed.), *The London Observer: The Journal of General Raymond E. Lee, 1940–1941* (Hutchinson, 1972)

McGehee, R.W., *Deadly Deceits: My 25 Years in the CIA* (NY: Sheridan Square, 1983)

McManners, H., *Falklands Commando* (William Kimber, 1984)

— *Forgotten Voices of the Falklands: The Real Story of the Falklands War* (Ebury, 2008)

Machon, A., *Spies, Lies and Whistleblowers: MI5, MI6 and the Shayler Affair* (Lewes: The Book Guild, 2005)

Major, J., *The Autobiography* (HarperCollins, 1999)

Mathams, R.H., *Sub-Rosa; Memoirs of an Australian Intelligence Analyst* (Sydney: Allen and Unwin, 1982)

Mendez, A. and J., *Spy Dust: Two Masters of Disguise Reveal the Tools and Operations that Helped Win the Cold War* (NY: Atria Books, 2002)

Mills, D., *My Life as a Coder (Special), D/MX 919781, 1952–54* (Branston, Lincs: privately published, 2005)

Modin, Y., *My Five Cambridge Friends* (Headline, 1994)

Nott, J., *Here Today Gone Tomorrow: Recollections of an Errant Politician* (Politico's, 2002)

Owen, D., *Time to Declare* (Michael Joseph, 1991)

Patten, C., *Not Quite the Diplomat: Home Truths About World Affairs* (Allen Lane, 2005)

Pavlov, V., *Memoirs of a Spymaster: My Fifty Years in the KGB* (NY: Carroll and Graf, 1994)

Philby, K., *My Silent War* (MacGibbon and Key, 1968)

Prime, R., *Time of Trial: The Personal Story Behind the Cheltenham Spy Scandal* (Hodder and Stoughton, 1984)

Prior, J., *A Balance of Power* (Hamish Hamilton, 1986)

Putney, D. (ed.), *Ultra and the Army Air Forces in World War II: An Interview with Associate Justice of the US Supreme Court Lewis F. Powell Jr.* (Washington DC: Office of Air Force History, 1987)

Ratcliffe, P., *Eye of the Storm: Twenty-Five Years in Action with the SAS* (Michael O'Mara, 2000)

Reeve, J., *Cocktails, Crisis and Cockroaches: A Diplomatic Trail* (Radcliffe Press, 1999)

Report of the Security Commission, May 1983, Cmnd 8876 (HMSO, 1983)

Report of the Security Commission, October 1986, Cmnd 9923 (HMSO, 1986)

Robertson, G., *The Justice Game* (Chatto and Windus, 1998)

Russell, S., *Sheridan's Story: Sheridan Russell 1900–1991* (Privately published, 1993)

Sawatsky, M., *For Services Rendered* (Markham, Ontario: Penguin Books, 1983)

Short, C., *An Honourable Deception?: New Labour, Iraq and the Abuse of Power* (NY: Free Press, 2004)

Sly, K., *Horse Grows Horns: An Autobiography* (Hartwell, Victoria: Temple House, 2006)

Smith, K., *Inside Time* (Harrap, 1989)

Sommer, P. and Hosein, G., *Briefing on the Internet Modernisation Programme* (LSE Policy Engagement Network, 2009)

Stankovic, M., *Trusted Mole: A Soldier's Journey into Bosnia's Heart of Darkness* (HarperCollins, 2000)

Stripp, A.J., *Code-breaker in the Far East* (Frank Cass, 1989)

Sudoplatov, P., *Special Tasks: The Memoirs of an Unwanted Witness – A Soviet Spymaster* (Little, Brown, 1994)

Thatcher, M., *The Downing Street Years* (HarperCollins, 1993)

Thomas, T., *Signal Success* (Lewes: Book Guild, 1995)

Tomlinson, R., *The Big Breach: From Top Secret to Maximum Security* (Edinburgh: Cutting Edge, 2001)

Walden, G., *Lucky George: Memoirs of an Anti-Politician* (Penguin, 1999)

Wilson, H., *The Labour Government 1964–1970: A Personal Record* (Michael Joseph, 1971)

Winterbotham, F., *The Ultra Secret* (Weidenfeld and Nicolson, 1974)

Woodhead, L., *My Life as a Spy* (Macmillan, 2005)

Woodward, S., *One Hundred Days: The Memoirs of the Falklands Battle Group Commander* (HarperCollins, 1992)

Wright, P., *Spycatcher: The Candid Autobiography of a Senior Intelligence Officer* (NY: Viking, 1987)

Secondary Works: Books and Theses

Adams, T.W. and Cottrell, A.J., *Cyprus Between East and West* (Baltimore: The Johns Hopkins Press, 1968)

Aid, M., *Secret Sentry: The Untold History of the National Security Agency* (NY: Bloomsbury, 2009)

Aid, M. and Wiebes, C. (eds), *Secrets of Signals Intelligence During the Cold War and Beyond* (Frank Cass, 2001)

Albright, J. and Kunstel, M., *Bombshell: The Secret Story of America's Unknown Atomic Spy Conspiracy* (NY: Time Books, 1997)

Aldrich, R.J. (ed.), *British Intelligence, Strategy and the Cold War, 1945–51* (Routledge, 1992)

— (ed.), *Espionage, Security and Intelligence in Britain, 1945–70* (Manchester: Manchester UP, 1998)

— *Intelligence and the War Against Japan: Britain, America and the Politics of Secret Service* (Cambridge: Cambridge UP, 1999)

— *The Hidden Hand: Britain, America and Cold War Secret Intelligence* (John Murray, 2001)

Aldrich, R.J. and Hopkins, M.F. (eds), *Intelligence, Defence and Diplomacy: British Policy in the Post-War World* (Frank Cass, 1994)

Aldrich, R.J., Rawnsley, G. and Rawnsley, M.Y. (eds), *The Clandestine Cold War in Asia, 1945–65* (Frank Cass, 1999)

Allen, T. et al., *Working Without Walls: An Insight into the Transforming Government Workplace* (Office of Government Commerce, 2004)

Andrew, C.M., *Secret Service: The Making of the British Intelligence Community* (Heinemann, 1985)

— *For the President's Eyes Only: Secret Intelligence and the American Presidency from Washington to Bush* (HarperCollins, 1995)

— *Defence of the Realm: The Official History of the Security Service* (Allen Lane, 2009)

Andrew, C.M. and Dilks, D. (eds), *The Missing Dimension: Governments and Intelligence Communities in the Twentieth Century* (Macmillan, 1982)

Andrew, C.M. and Gordievsky, O., *KGB: The Inside Story* (Hodder and Stoughton, 1990)

Andrew, C.M. and Mitrokhin, V., *The Sword and the Shield: The Mitrokhin Archive and the Secret History of the KGB* (NY: Basic, 1999)

Anton, B. and Pemrobuch, A., *Radioespionage* (Moscow: Mezhdchnarode, 1996)

Ball, D. and Horner, D., *Breaking the Code: Australia's KGB Network* (Sydney: Allen and Unwin, 1988)

Bamford, J., *The Puzzle Palace: America's National Security Agency and Its Special Relationship with GCHQ* (Sidgwick and Jackson, 1983)

— *Body of Secrets: How NSA and Britain's GCHQ Eavesdrop on the World* (NY: Doubleday, 2001)

— *The Shadow Factory: The Ultra-Secret NSA from 9/11 to Eavesdropping on America* (NY: Doubleday, 2008)

Barnett, H., *Britain Unwrapped: Government and Constitution Explained* (Penguin, 2002)

Baumann, C., *Diplomatic Kidnappings: A Revolutionary Tactic* (The Hague: Nijhof, 1973)

Bennett, G., *Churchill's Man of Mystery: Desmond Morton and the World of Intelligence* (Routledge, 2007)

Bennett, R., *Ultra in the West: The Normandy Campaign of 1944–45* (Hutchinson, 1979)

— *Behind the Battle: Intelligence in the War with Germany* (Sinclair Stevenson, 1994)

Bergman, R. and Meltzer, G., *Yom Kippur War, Real Time: The Updated Edition* (Tel Aviv: Hemed Books, 2004)

Bertrand, G., *Enigma, ou la plus grande énigme de la guerre 1939–1945* (Paris: Librairie Plon, 1973)

Beschloss, M.R., *Mayday: Eisenhower, Khrushchev and the U-2 Affair* (NY: Harper and Row, 1986)

Best, A., *British Intelligence and the Japanese Challenge in Asia, 1914–1941* (Routledge, 2002)

Bicheno, H., *Razor's Edge: The Unofficial History of the Falklands War* (Weidenfeld and Nicolson, 2006)

Blaxland, J., *Signals Swift and Sure: A History of the Royal Australian Corps of Signals, 1947 to 1972* (Sydney: Royal Australian Signals Corps Committee, 1998)

Bower, T., *The Perfect English Spy* (William Heinemann, 1995)

Bracken, P.J., *The Command and Control of Nuclear Forces* (New Haven: Yale UP, 1983)

Breindel, E. and Romerstein, H., *The Venona Secrets: The Soviet Union's War II Espionage Campaign Against the United States and How America Fought Back* (NY: Basic Books, 2000)

Bryden, J., *Best Kept Secret: Canadian Intelligence in the Second World War* (Toronto: Lester Publishing, 1993)

Budiansky, S., *Battle of Wits: The Complete Story of Code-breaking in World War II* (NY: Free Press, 2000)

Burrows, W.E., *By Any Means Necessary: America's Secret Air War* (Hutchinson, 2001)

Calvocoressi, P., *Top Secret Ultra* (Cassell, 1980)

Campbell, D., *The Unsinkable Aircraft Carrier* (Michael Joseph, 1984)

— *Surveillance électronique planétaire* (Paris: Editions Allia, 2001)

— *Interception Capabilities 2000* (European Parliament, STOA, 2000)

Clark, R.W., *The Man Who Broke Purple: The Life of the World's Greatest Cryptologist, Colonel William F. Friedman* (Weidenfield and Nicolson, 1977)

Clarke, A., 'Effective Implementation of Management Information Systems within a GCHQ Technical Domain', M.Sc. thesis, Faculty of Engineering, Bristol University, 2000

Cloake, J., *Templer, Tiger of Malaya: The Life of Field Marshal Sir Gerald Templer* (Harrap, 1985)

Cole, D.J., *Geoffrey Prime: The Imperfect Spy* (Robert Hale, 1998)

Collacott, P.J., 'Organisational and Cultural Change at CESG, Cheltenham', MBA thesis, Imperial College London, 1997

Cook, P.M., 'The Application of User Surveys and Their Role in Improving the Profile of Special Libraries in the UK with Particular Reference to GCHQ', M.Lib. dissertation, University of Wales, 1990

Cooley, J.K., *Unholy Wars* (Chicago: Uni. of Michigan Press, 2000)

Copeland, B.J., *Colossus: The Secrets of Bletchley Park's Code-Breaking Computers* (Oxford: Oxford UP, 2006)

Cristol, A.J., *The Liberty Incident: The 1967 Israeli Attack on the US Navy Spy Ship* (Washington: Brassey's, 2002)

Daalder, I.H., *The Nature and Practice of Flexible Response: NATO Strategy and Theater Nuclear Forces since 1967* (NY: Columbia UP, 1991)

Davies, P.H.P., *MI6 and the Machinery of Spying* (Frank Cass, 2004)

Deighton, A., *The Impossible Peace: Germany* (Oxford: Clarendon Press, 1988)

Deletant, D., *Ceausescu and the Securitate: Coercion and Dissent in Romania, 1965–89* (Hurst, 1995)

Denniston, R., *Churchill's Secret War: Diplomatic Decrypts, The Foreign Office and Turkey, 1942–44* (Stroud: Alan Sutton, 1997)

— *Thirty Secret Years: A.G. Denniston's Work in Signals Intelligence, 1914–1944* (Polperro Heritage Press, 2007)

Dickens, P., *SAS: The Jungle Frontier- 22 Special Air Service Regiment in the Borneo Campaign, 1963–1966* (Arms and Armour Press, 1983)

Diffie, W. and Landau, S., *Privacy on the Line: The Politics of Wiretapping and Encryption* (Cambridge, Mass: MIT Press, 2nd edn, 2010)

Dorril, S., *MI6: Fifty Years of Special Operations* (4th Estate, 2000)

Dover, R. and Goodman, M. (eds), *Spinning Intelligence: Why Intelligence Needs the Media, Why the Media Needs Intelligence* (NY: Columbia UP, 2009)

Drewry, G. and Butcher, T., *The Civil Service Today* (Oxford: Blackwell, 1988)

Dumbrell, J., *Special Relationship: Anglo–American Relations from the Cold War to Iraq* (Palgrave, 2006)

Easter, D., *Britain and the Confrontation with Indonesia, 1960–66* (IB Tauris, 2004)

Fitzgerald, P. and Leopold, M., *Strangers on the Line: A Secret History of Phone-tapping* (The Bodley Head, 1987)

Freedman, L., *Britain and Nuclear Weapons* (RIIA, 1980)

— *The Official History of the Falklands Campaign*, Vols 1 and 2 (Routledge, 2005)

— *A Choice of Enemies: America Confronts the Middle East* (Oxford: Oxford UP, 2008)

Freedman, L. and Gamba-Stonehouse, V., *Signals of War: The Falklands Conflict of 1982* (Princeton: Princeton UP, 1991)

Freeman, P., *How GCHQ Came to Cheltenham* (Cheltenham: GCHQ, 2002)

— *GCHQ Buildings Since 1914* (Cheltenham: GCHQ, 2006)

Friedman, N., *The Fifty-Year War: Conflict and Strategy in the Cold War* (Annapolis MD: Naval Institute Press, 2007)

Garbett, M. and Goulding, B., *The Lincoln at War, 1944–1966* (Ian Allen, 1979)

Garton Ash, T., *The Polish Revolution: Solidarity* (NY: Scribner's, 1984)

Gerraghty, T., *Beyond the Front Line: The Untold Exploits of Britain's Most Daring Spy Mission* (HarperCollins, 1996)

Goodman, M.S., *Spying on the Nuclear Bear: Anglo–American Intelligence and the Soviet Bomb* (Stanford: Stanford UP, 2007)

Gorodetsky, G., *Grand Delusion: Stalin and the German Invasion of Russia* (Yale UP, 2001)

Grayson, W.C., *Chicksands: A Millennium of History* (Shefford: Shefford Press, 1992)

Gustafson, K., *Hostile Intent: US Covert Operations in Chile, 1964–1974* (Washington DC: Potomac Books, 2007)

Hager, N., *Secret Power* (Auckland: Craig Potton, 1996)

Harvey, B., *Europe's Space Programme: To Ariane and Beyond* (NY: Springer, 2003)

Hastings, M. and Jenkins, S., *The Battle for the Falklands* (Pan, 1997)

Haynes, J.E. and Klehr, H., *Venona: Decoding Soviet Espionage in America* (New Haven: Yale UP, 1999)

Hennessy, P., *Whitehall* (NY: The Free Press, 1989)

— *Never Again: Britain, 1945–51* (Vintage, 1993)

— *The New Protective State* (Continuum, 2007)

— *The Secret State: Whitehall and the Cold War* (Penguin, 2001)

Herman, M., *Intelligence Power in Peace and War* (Cambridge: Cambridge UP, 1992)

— *Intelligence Services in the Information Age* (Cass, 2001)

Hinsley, F.H. et al., *British Intelligence in the Second World War*, Vols 1–4 (HMSO, 1979–83)

Hinsley, F.H. and Stripp, A. (eds), *Code-Breakers: The Inside Story of Bletchley Park* (Oxford: Oxford UP, 1993)

Hitchcock, W.T. (ed.), *The Intelligence Revolution in Historical Perspective* (Washington DC: US Air Force Academy, 1991)

Holland, R., *Emergencies and Disorder in the European Empires after 1945* (Frank Cass, 1994)

— *Britain and the Revolt in Cyprus* (Oxford: Oxford UP, 1998)

Horner, D., *SAS: Phantoms of War, A History of the Special Air Service* (Sydney: Allen and Unwin, 2002)

Hyam, R., *Britain's Declining Empire: The Road to Decolonisation, 1918–68* (Cambridge: Cambridge UP, 2003)

Jackson, P., *Hambuhren, Lower Saxony: A Military History, 1939–1999* (Wheatley, Oxford, privately published, 2001)

Jeffreys-Jones, R., *The CIA and American Democracy* (New Haven: Yale UP, 1991)

Jensen, K., *Cautious Beginnings: Canadian Foreign Intelligence, 1939–51* (Toronto: UBC Press, 2008)

Johnson, T.R., *American Cryptology During the Cold War, 1945–1989*, Vols 1–4 (NSA, declassified 2009)

Jones, C., *Britain and the Yemen Civil War, 1962–1965: Ministers, Mercenaries and Mandarins: Foreign Policy and the Limits of Covert Action* (Brighton: Sussex Academic Press, 2004)

Kahn, D., *The Code-breakers* (NY: Scribner's, 2nd edn. 1996)

— *The Reader of Gentlemen's Mail: Herbert O. Yardley and the Birth of American Code-Breaking* (New Haven: Yale UP, 2004)

Keefe, P., *Chatter: Dispatches from the Secret World of Eavesdropping* (NY: Random House, 2005)

Keegan, J., *Intelligence in War: Knowledge of the Enemy from Napoleon to Al-Qaeda* (NY: Knopf, 2003)

Kennedy-Pipe, C., *Stalin's Cold War: Soviet Strategies in Europe* (Manchester: Manchester UP, 1995)

Knightley, P. and Kennedy, C., *An Affair of State: The Profumo Case and the Framing of Stephen Ward* (Cape, 1987)

Kyle, K., *Suez* (Weidenfeld and Nicolson, 1991)

Kyriakides, K.A., 'British Cold War Strategy and the Struggle to Maintain Military bases in Cyprus', Ph.D., U. of Cambridge, 1997

Lacey, N., *A Life of H.L.A. Hart: The Nightmare and the Dream* (Oxford: Oxford UP, 2004)

Ladd, J., *SBS: The Invisible Raiders. The History of the Special Boat Squadron from World War Two to the Present* (Arms and Armour Press, 1983)

Lanning, H. and Norton-Taylor, R., *Conflict of Loyalties* (Cheltenham: New Clarion Press, 1994)

Lashmar, P., *Spy-Flights of the Cold War* (Stroud: Sutton, 1996)

Lashmar, P. and Oliver, J., *Britain's Secret Propaganda War: The Foreign Office and the Cold War, 1948–1977* (Stroud: Sutton, 1998)

Lerner, M.B., *The Pueblo Incident: A Spy Ship and the Failure of American Foreign Policy* (Lawrence: UP of Kansas, 2002)

Levy, S., *Crypto: Secrecy and Privacy in the New Code War* (Allen Lane, 2001)

Lewin, R., *Ultra Goes to War: The Secret Story* (Hutchinson, 1978)

Lewis, J., *Changing Direction: British Military Planning for Post-War Strategic Defence, 1942–7* (Frank Cass, 2nd edn, 2003)

Long, P, *'In Support of So Many'. Royal Air Force Station Watton 1945–2000* (Privately published, 2001)

Lucas, W.S., *Divided We Stand: Britain, the US and the Suez Crisis* (Hodder and Stoughton, 1991)

Lustgarten, L. and Leigh, I., *In from the Cold: National Security and Democracy* (Oxford: Oxford UP, 1994)

McKnight, D., *Australia's Spies and their Secrets* (U. College London Press, 1994)

McLachlan, D., *Room 39: Naval Intelligence in Action 1939–45* (Weidenfeld and Nicolson, 1968)

Maddrell, P., *Spying on Science: Western Intelligence in Divided Germany, 1945–61* (Oxford: Oxford UP, 2006)

Mango, A., *Turkey and the War on Terror: 'For Forty Years We Fought Alone'* (Routledge, 2005)

Mastny, V., *A Cardboard Castle: An Inside History of the Warsaw Pact, 1955–91* (Budapest: Central European UP, 2005)

Middlebrook, M., *The Fight for the 'Malvinas': The Argentine Forces and the Falklands War* (Viking, 1989)

Mikesh, R.C., *B-57: Canberra at War* (Ian Allan, 1980)

Mitchell, M. and T., *The Spy Who Tried to Stop a War: Katharine Gun and the Secret Plot to Sanction the Iraq Invasion* (PoliPointPress, 2008)

Montgomery Hyde, H., *George Blake: Superspy* (Futura, 1987)

Murphy, D.E., Kondrashev, S.A. and Bailey, G., *Battleground Berlin: CIA vs KGB in the Cold War* (New Haven: Yale UP, 1997)

Norton-Taylor, R. and Lanning, H., *A Conflict of Loyalties: GCHQ 1977–91* (Cheltenham: New Clarion Press, 1991)

O'Malley, B. and Craig, I., *The Cyprus Conspiracy: America, Espionage and the Turkish Invasion* (IB Tauris, 2001)

Packard, W., *A Century of Naval Intelligence* (Washington DC: Office of Naval Intelligence, 1996)

Parrish, T., *The Ultra Americans: The US Role in Breaking Nazi Codes* (NY: Stein and Day, 1986)

Paterson, M., *Voices of the Code-breakers: Personal Accounts of the Secret Heroes of World War II* (Newton Abbot: David and Charles, 2007)

Pedlow, G.W. and Welzenbach, D.E., *The CIA and the U-2 Program, 1954–1974* (Washington, DC: Central Intelligence Agency, 1998)

Perrett, B., *Weapons of the Falklands Conflict* (Poole: Blandford Press, 1982)

Pidgeon, G., *The Secret Wireless War* (UPSO, 2003)

Pilger, J., *Freedom Next Time* (Random House, 2006)

Pimlott, B., *Harold Wilson* (HarperCollins, 1992)

Pincher, C., *Too Secret Too Long* (Sidgwick and Jackson, 1984)

— *Traitors; Labyrinths of Treason* (Sidgwick and Jackson, 1987)

Pocock, C., *The U-2 Spyplane: Toward the Unknown* (Atglen PA: Schiffer Military History, 2000)

Powers, T., *The Man Who Kept the Secrets: Richard Helms and the CIA* (Weidenfeld and Nicolson, 1979)

Ranelagh, J., *The Agency: The Rise and Decline of the CIA* (NY: Simon and Schuster, 1986)

Ratcliff, R.A., *Delusions of Intelligence: Enigma, Ultra and the End of Secure Ciphers* (NY: Cambridge UP, 2006)

Reefe, P.K., *Chatter: Dispatches from the Secret World of Global Eavesdropping* (NY: Random House, 2005)

Rees, J., *Looking for Mr Nobody: The Secret Life of Goronwy Rees* (Weidenfeld and Nicolson, 1994)

Richelson, J., *A Century of Spies: Intelligence in the Twentieth Century* (NY: Oxford UP, 1995)

— *The US Intelligence Community* (NY: Ballinger, 1989)

— *The Wizards of Langley: Inside the CIA's Directorate of Science and Technology* (Boulder CO: Westview, 2001)

Richelson, J. and Ball, D., *Ties that Bind: Intelligence Cooperation between the UKUSA Countries* (Boston: Allen and Unwin, 1985)

Riste, O., *The Norwegian Intelligence Service, 1945–70* (Frank Cass, 1999)

Ritter, S., *Iraq Confidential: The Untold Story of America's Intelligence Conspiracy* (IB Tauris, 2005)

Schecter, J.L. and Deriabin, P.S., *The Spy Who Saved the World* (NY: Charles Scribner's, 1992)

Schwartz, D.N., *NATO's Nuclear Dilemmas* (Washington DC: Brookings, 1983)

Scott, L.V., *Macmillan, Kennedy and the Cuban Missile Crisis: Political, Military and Intelligence Aspects* (Macmillan, 1999)

Scott, L.V. and Twigge, S., *Planning Armageddon: Britain, the United States and the Command and Control of Western Nuclear Forces, 1945–64* (Harwood, 2000)

Sebag-Montefiore, H., *Enigma: The Battle for the Code* (Weidenfeld and Nicolson, 2000)

Seldon, A., *Blair Unbound* (Simon and Schuster, 2008)

Short, A., *The Communist Insurrection in Malaya, 1948–1960* (Muller, 1975)

Singh, S., *The Code Book* (4th Estate, 1999)

Siniver, A., *Nixon, Kissinger and US Foreign Policy Making: The Machinery of Crisis* (Cambridge: Cambridge UP, 2008)

Smith, B.F., *The Ultra-Magic Deals and the Most Secret Special Relationship, 1940–1946* (Shrewsbury: Airlife Publishing, 1993)

— *Sharing Secrets with Stalin: How the Allies Traded Intelligence, 1941–45* (Kansas: U. of Kansas Press, 1996)

Smith, M., *New Cloak, Old Dagger: How Britain's Spies Came in from the Cold* (Victor Gollancz, 1996)

— *Station X: The Code-Breakers of Bletchley Park* (Channel 4 Books, 1998)

— *The Emperor's Codes: Bletchley Park and the Breaking of Japan's Secret Ciphers* (Bantam, 2000)

— *The Spying Game: A Secret History of British Espionage* (Politico's, 2003)

— *Killer Elite: The Inside Story of America's Most Secret Special Operations Team* (NY: St Martin's Press, 2007)

Smith, M. and Erskine, R. (eds), *Action This Day: Bletchley Park from the Breaking of the Enigma Code to the Birth of the Modern Computer* (Bantam, 2001)

Sontag, S. and Drew, C., *Blind Man's Buff: The Untold Story of American Submarine Espionage* (NY: Public Affairs, 1998)

Stacy, W.W., *US Army Border Operations in Germany, 1945–1983* (Headquarters US Army, Europe and 7th Army, Military History Office, 1984)

Stafford, D., *Spies Beneath Berlin* (John Murray, 2nd edn, 2002)

Stares, P.B., *Command Performance: The Neglected Dimension of European Security* (Washington DC: The Brookings Institution, 1991)

Strehle, R., *Verschlüsselt* [Encrypted]: *Der Fall Hans Bühler* (Zurich: Werd Verlag, 1993)

Stromseth, J.E., *The Origins of Flexible Response: NATO's Debate over Strategy in the 1960s* (NY: St Martin's, 1987)

Svendsen, A., *Intelligence Cooperation and the War on Terror: Anglo–American Security Relations after 9/11* (Routledge, 2009)

Tamnes, R., *The United States and the Cold War in the High North* (Aldershot: Dartmouth, 1991)

Tantin, K., *Revolt in Paradise* (Heinemann, 1960)

Thomas, R., *Espionage and Secrecy: The Official Secrets Acts 1911–1989 of the United Kingdom* (Routledge, 1991)

Thorne, C., *Allies of a Kind* (Hamish Hamilton, 1979)

Urban, M., *UK Eyes Alpha: The Inside Story of British Intelligence* (Faber and Faber, 1996)

Van der Art, D., *Aerial Espionage: Secret Intelligence Flights by East and West* (Shrewsbury: Airlife, 1986)

Van der Bijl, N., *Nine Battles to Stanley* (Leo Cooper, 1999)

— *Confrontation: The War with Indonesia, 1962–1966* (Leo Cooper, 2006)

Vincent, J., *The Culture of Secrecy: Britain 1832–1988* (Oxford: Oxford UP, 1998)

Weadon, P.D., *The Sigsaly Story* (Fort Meade: NSA Center for Cryptologic History, 2009)

Weinstein, A. and Vassiliev, A., *The Haunted Wood: Soviet Espionage in America* (NY: Random House, 1999)

West, N., *A Matter of Trust: MI5, 1945–72* (Weidenfeld and Nicolson, 1982)

— *GCHQ: The Secret Wireless War, 1900–86* (Weidenfeld and Nicolson, 1986)

— *The Secret War for the Falklands* (Little, Brown, 1997)

— *Venona* (HarperCollins, 1999)

Westlake, M., *Kinnock: The Biography* (Little, Brown, 2001)

Whaley, B., *Codeword Barbarossa* (Boston: MIT Press, 1973)

Wilkinson, N., *Secrecy and the Media: The Official History of the UK's D-Notice System* (Routledge, 2009)

Winterbotham, F.W., *The Ultra Secret* (Weidenfeld and Nicolson, 1974)

Wylde, N. (ed.), *The Story of Brixmis, 1946–1990* (Arundel: Brixmis Association, 1993)

Young, J and Kent, J., *International Relations Since 1945* (Oxford: Oxford UP, 2004)

Young, J.W., *The Labour Governments, 1964–1970: International Policy* (Manchester: Manchester UP, 2003)

Ziegler, P., *Wilson: The Authorised Life* (Weidenfeld and Nicolson, 1993)

Zubok, V. and Pleshakov, C., *Inside the Kremlin's Cold War from Stalin to Khrushchev* (Cambridge: Harvard UP, 1997)

Secondary Works: Articles and Papers

Aid, M., 'Relations with Allies', unpublished paper

— 'The Russian Target: The UK–US Cryptologic Effort Against the Soviet Union, 1945–1950', Paper to the Annual Conference of the Society for Historians of American Foreign Relations, June 2003

— 'US Humint and Comint in the Korean War: From the Approach of War to the Chinese Intervention', *I&NS*, 14/4 (1999): 17–63

— 'US Comint in the Korean War (Part II): From the Chinese Intervention to the Armistice', *I&NS*, 15/1 (2000): 14–49

Aldrich, R.J., 'Secret Intelligence for a Post War World', in Aldrich, *British Intelligence, Strategy and the Cold War*: 15–49

— 'GCHQ and Sigint in the Early Cold War 1945–70', *I&NS*, 16/1 (2001): 67–96

— 'British Intelligence, Security and Western Cooperation in Cold War Germany: The Ostpolitik Years', in Beatrice de Graaf, Ben de Jong, Wies Platje (eds), *Battlegound Western Europe: Intelligence Operations in Germany and the Netherlands in the Twentieth Century* (Amsterdam: Uitgeverij Het Spinhuis, 2007)

— 'Whitehall and the Iraq War: The UK's Four Intelligence Enquiries', *Irish Studies in International Affairs*, 16/1 (2005): 73–88

— 'The US–UK Intelligence Alliance in 1975: Economies, Evaluations and Explanations', *I&NS* 21/4 (2006): 557–67

Aldrich, R.J. and Coleman, M., 'The Cold War, the JIC and British Signals Intelligence, 1948', *I&NS*, 4/3 (1989): 535–49

Alvarez, D., 'Behind Venona: American Signals Intelligence in the Early Cold War', *I&NS*, 14/2 (1999): 179–86

Anderson, R. and Roe, M., 'The GCHQ Protocol and its Problems', *Lecture Notes in Computer Science*, Issue 1233 (1997): 134–48

Andrew, C.M., 'Gordon Welchman, Sir Peter Marychurch and the "Birth of Ultra" ', *I&NS*, 1/2 (1986): 277–81

— 'The Growth of Intelligence Collaboration in the English-Speaking World', *Wilson Center Working Paper*, 83 (November 1987)

— 'Churchill and Intelligence', *I&NS*, 3/3 (1988): 181–94

— 'The Growth of the Australian Intelligence Community and the Anglo–American Connection', *I&NS*, 4/2 (1989): 213–57

— 'Intelligence Collaboration between Britain and the United States During The Second World War', in Hitchcock, W.T. (ed.), *The Intelligence Revolution: A Historical Perspective* (Washington DC: US Air Force Academy, 1991): 111–23

— 'The Making of the Anglo–American SIGINT Alliance', in Peake and Halperin, *In the Name of Intelligence*: 95–109

— 'The Venona Secret', in Robertson, K. (ed.), *War, Diplomacy and Intelligence* (Macmillan, 2002): 203–25

— 'Intelligence and International Relations in the Early Cold War', *Review of International Studies*, 24/3 (1998): 321–30

Andrew, C.M. and Aldrich, R.J. (eds), 'Intelligence Services in the Second World War', *Contemporary British History*, 13/4 (1999): 130–69

Andronov, A., 'American Geosynchronous Sigint Satellites', *Zarubezhnoye Voyennoye Obozreniye*, 12 (1993): 37–43

Anonymous, 'Wyton's Cold War Spyplanes/No.51 Squadron Canberras', *International Air Power Review* (2001): 130–7

Anonymous, 'RAF Nimrod R.1.', *AIR International*, July 2001: 29–35

Ball, D., 'Controlling Theatre Nuclear War', *British Journal of Political Science*, 19/3 (1989): 303–27

Ball, D.J., 'Allied Intelligence Cooperation Involving Australia During World War II', *Australian Outlook*, 32 (1978): 299–309

— 'Over and Out: Signals Intelligence (Sigint) in Hong Kong', *I&NS*, 11/3 (1996): 474–96

Barker, G., 'The Mystery Boats', *Australian Financial Review*, 28 November 2003: 16–18

Baylis, J., 'British Nuclear Doctrine: The "Moscow Criterion" and the Polaris Improvement Programme', *Contemporary British History*, 19/1 (2005): 53–65

Bonsall, A., 'Bletchley Park and the RAF Y Service: Some Recollections', *I&NS*, 23/6 (2008): 827–41

Brown, K., 'Intelligence and the Decision to Collect it: Churchill's Wartime American Diplomatic Signals Intelligence', *I&NS*, 10/3 (1995): 449–67

— 'The Interplay of Information and Mind in Decision-Making: Signals Intelligence and Franklin D. Roosevelt's Policy-shift on Indochina', *I&NS* 13/1 (1998): 109–31

Brugioni, D.A., 'The Effects of Aerial and Satellite Imagery on the 1973 New Yom Kippur War', *Air Power History*, Fall 2004: 1–14

Budiansky, S., 'Bletchley Park and the Birth of the Special Relationship', in M. Smith and R. Erskine (eds), *Action This Day*, pp.211–36

Cain, F., 'An Aspect of Postwar Relations with the UK and the US: Missiles, Spies and Disharmony', *Australian Historical Studies*, 23/92 (1989): 186–203

— 'Venona in Australia and its Long-term Ramifications', *Journal of Contemporary History*, 35/2 (2000): 211–48

Calvert, R.J., '39 Steps', *Aircraft Illustrated*, 29/5 (1996): 76–81

Campbell, D., 'Official Secrecy and British Libertarianism', *Socialist Register*, 1979

— 'Phone Tappers and the State', *New Statesman*, 1981: 54–5

— 'The Parliamentary Bypass Operation', *New Statesman*, 23 January 1987: 8–12

Clarke, W.F., 'Post-War Organisation', *Cryptologia*, 13/2 (1989): 118–22

Clement, B., 'GCHQ and the Unions: The Fight is not Over', *New Statesman*, 9/419 (1996): 23

Cole, R.D., 'GCHQ: A Doughnut on the Landscape', *Eye Spy*, 1 (2001): 91–2

Constance, J., 'How Jim Bamford Probed the NSA', *Cryptologia*, 21/1 (1977): 71–4

Corby, S., 'The GCHQ Union Ban, 1984–1997: The Unions' Strategy and the Outcome', *Labour History Review*, 65/3 (Winter 2000): 317–32

Cranston, A., 'US Signals Intelligence to New Zealand Blocked', *Jane's Defence Weekly* 3 (16 February 1985): 243

Creevy, M., 'A Critical Review of the Wilson Government's Handling of the D-Notice Affair in 1967', *I∂NS*, 14/3 (1999): 209–27

Croft, J., 'Reminiscences of GCHQ and GCB, 1942–5', *I∂NS*, 13/4 (1998): 133–43

Davies, P.J., 'Organizational Politics and the Development of British Intelligence Producer/Consumer Interfaces', *I∂NS*, 10/4 (1995): 113–32

Denham, H., 'Bedford–Bletchley–Kilindi–Colombo', in Hinsley and Stripp (eds), *Code-Breakers*, 265–81

Denniston, A.G., 'The Government Code and Cypher School Between the Wars', *I∂NS*, 1/1 (1986): 48–70

Donini, L., 'The Cryptographic Services of the Royal (British) and Italian Navies: A Comparative Analysis of Their Activities in World War II', *Cryptologia*, 14/3 (1990): 97–127

Drewry, G., 'The GCHQ Case: A Failure of Government Communications', *Parliamentary Affairs*, 38 (1985): 371–86

Easter, D., 'GCHQ and British External Policy in the 1960s', *I∂NS*, 23/5 (2008): 681–706

Edwards, G., 'Europe and the Falklands Crisis', *Journal of Common Market Studies*, 22/4 (1984): 295–313

Erskine, R., 'Anglo–US Cryptological Cooperation', paper to the Fifth Annual Meeting of the International Intelligence History Study Group, Tutzing, Bavaria, June 1999

— 'When a Purple Machine Went Missing: How Japan nearly Discovered America's Greatest Secret', *I∂NS*, 12/3 (1997): 185–9

— 'The Holden Agreement on Naval Sigint: The First BRUSA?', *I∂NS*, 14/2 (Summer 1999): 187–97

— 'The Admiralty and Cipher Machines During the Second World War: Not so Stupid After All', *Journal of Intelligence History*, 2/2 (Winter 2002): 49–68

— 'Churchill and the Start of the Ultra-Magic Deals', *IJICI*, 10/1 (1997): 57–74

Erskine, R. and Freeman, P., 'Brigadier John Tiltman: One of Britain's Finest Cryptologists', *Cryptologia*, 27/4 (2003): 289–318

Ferris, J., 'From Broadway House to Bletchley Park: The Diary of Captain Malcolm Kennedy, 1934–46', *I∂NS*, 4/3 (1989): 421–51

— 'Coming in from the Cold: The Historiography of American Intelligence, 1945–1990', *DH*, 10/1 (1995): 87–116

Forster, A., 'No Entry: Britain and the EEC in the 1960s?', *Contemporary British History*, 12/3 (1998): 139–46

Gaddis, J.L., 'Intelligence, Espionage and Cold War Origins', *Diplomatic History*, 13/2 (1989): 191–213

Gandy, Oscar H. Jr, 'Data Mining, Surveillance, and Discrimination in the Post-9/11 Environment', in K. Haggerty and R. Ericson (eds), *The New Politics of Surveillance and Visibility* (Toronto: University of Toronto Press, 2006): 363–84

Garthoff, R.L., 'Estimating Soviet Military Force: Some Light From the Past', *International Security*, 14/4 (1990): 93–116

Gill, P., "Allo, 'Allo, 'Allo, Who's in Charge Here Then?', *Liverpool Law Review*, 9/2 (1987): 189–201

Goodman, M., 'The Dog that Didn't Bark: The Joint Intelligence Committee and the Warning of Aggression', *Cold War History*, 7/4 (2007): 38–42

— 'The Tentacles of Failure: British Intelligence, Whitehall and the Buster Crabb Affair', *International Historical Review*, 30/4 (2008): 768–84

Graham, K., 'Giving the Information Message Traction: Embedding Knowledge Sharing at GCHQ', *Network*, 2 (Autumn 2006): 25–30

Grey, C. and Sturdy, A., 'The 1942 Reorganization of the Government Code and Cypher School', *Cryptologia*, 32/4 (2008): 311–33.

— 'A Chaos that Worked: Organizing Bletchley Park', *Public Policy and Administration*, 25/1 (2010): 47–68

Hamilton, K., 'Britain, France and America's Year of Europe, 1973', *Diplomacy and Statecraft*, 17/4 (2006): 871–95

Hanyok, R.J., 'Soviet Comint During the Cold War', *Cryptologia*, 23/2 (1999): 168–70

Harrison, E.D.R., 'Some Reflections on Kim Philby's *My Silent War* as a Historical Source', in Aldrich, R.J. and Hopkins, M. (eds), *Intelligence, Defence and Diplomacy* (Frank Cass, 1994): 205–25

— 'More Thoughts on Kim Philby's *My Silent War*', *I&NS*, 10/3 (1995): 514–26

Hennessey, P. and Brownfeld, G., 'Britain's Cold War Security Purge: The Origins of Positive Vetting', *Historical Journal*, 25/4 (1982): 965–73

Herman, M., 'Up from the Country: Cabinet Office Impressions 1972–75', *Contemporary British History*, 11/1 (1997): 83–97

— 'The Cold War: Did Intelligence Make a Difference?', in *Intelligence Service in the Information Age* (Frank Cass, 2001): 159–63

— 'Sir Leonard Hooper', *New Dictionary of National Biography*

Hinsley, F.H., 'British Intelligence and Barbarossa', in Erickson and Dilks (eds), *Barbarossa*: 43–75

Hoffman, B., 'The Global Terrorist Threat: Is Al Qaeda on the Run or on the March?', *Middle East Policy*, 14/2 (2007): 44–58

Hughes, G., 'Britain, the Transatlantic Alliance and the Arab–Israeli War of 1973, *Journal of Cold War Studies*, 10/2 (2008): 3–40

Huntington, T., 'The Berlin Spy Tunnel', *American Heritage of Invention and Technology*, 10 (1995): 44–52

Jervis, R., 'Reports, Politics and Intelligence Failures: The Case of Iraq', *Journal of Strategic Studies*, 29/1 (2002): 3–52

Kahn, D., 'Code-Breaking in World War I and II: The Major Successes and Failures, Their Causes and Their Effects', *Historical Journal*, 23/3 (1980): 617–39

— 'Soviet Comint in the Cold War', *Cryptologia*, 22/1 (1998): 1–24

Kerr, S., 'The Secret Hotline to Moscow: Donald Maclean and the Berlin Crisis of 1948', in Deighton (ed.), *Britain and the First Cold War*: 71–87

Kipling, R., 'Wireless', in *Traffics and Discoveries* (Macmillan, 1904): 213–39

Kiralfy, R.J.C., 'Current Issues for RAF Oakhanger and Number 1001 Signals Unit', IEE Colloquium on Military Satellite Communications II (Ref. No: 1997/322), 18 November 1997, Vol.5, pp.1–6

Krahenbuhl, M., 'The Turkish Communists: Schism Instead of Conciliation', *Studies in Comparative Communism*, 6/4 (Winter 1973): 405–13

Lake, J., 'Nimrod R.1: The RAF's Sigint Platform Extraordinaire', *Air International*, July 2001: 29–35

Lashmar, P., 'Canberras over the USSR', *Aeroplane Monthly*, 23/2 (1995): 32–5

Lavington, S., 'In the Footsteps of Colossus: A Description of Oedipus', *IEEE Annals of Computing* (2006): 44–55

Leary, B., 'George Blake and the Berlin Tunnel: Success or Failure?', paper to the Fifth Annual Meeting of the International Intelligence History Study Group, Tutzing, Bavaria, June 1999

Lombardo, J.R., 'American Consulate in Hong Kong, 1949–1964: A Mission of Espionage, Intelligence Gathering and Psychological Operations', *I&NS*, 14/4 (1999): 64–81

Lyon, D., 'Surveillance Technology and Surveillance Society', in Misa, T.J., Brey, P. and Feenberg, A. (eds), *Modernity and Technology* (Mass: MIT Press, 2004): 161–80

McKay, C.G., 'British SIGINT and the Bear, 1919–41: Some Discoveries in the GC&CS Archive', *Kungl Krigsvetenskapsakademiens Handlingar Och Tidskrift*, 2 Haftet 1997: 81–96

McPeek, R.L., 'Electronic Warfare: British Style', *Military Intelligence Professional Bulletin*, January–March 1996: 23–7

Maddrell, P., 'British-American Scientific Intelligence Cooperation during the Occupation of Germany', *I&NS*, 15/2 (2000): 74–95

— 'The Western Secret Services, the East German Ministry of State Security and the Building of the Berlin Wall', *I&NS*, 21/5 (2006): 829–47

—'Operation "Matchbox" and the Scientific Containment of the USSR', in Jackson, P. and Siegel, J. (eds), *Intelligence and Statecraft: The Use and Limits of Intelligence in International Society* (Westport CT: Praeger, 2005): 173–206

Madsen, W., 'Crypto AG: The NSA's Trojan Whore?', *Covert Action Quarterly*, No.63 (Winter 1998): 36–42

Mallinson, W., 'US Interests, British Acquiescence and the Invasion of Cyprus', *British Journal of Politics and International Relations*, 9/3 (2007): 494–508

Marsh, S., 'Technological Influences on Globalisation and Fragmentation: The Demise of the Nation-State?', *RUSI Journal*, June 1996: 44–50

Milner-Barry, S., ' "Action This Day": The Letter from Bletchley Park Cryptanalysts to the Prime Minister, 21 October 1941', *I&NS*, 1/2 (1986): 272–6

Mobley, R., 'Deterring Iraq: The UK Experience', *I&NS*, 16/2 (2001): 55–82

Murray, W.A.S., 'Radar Tracking at R.R.E., Malvern', *Philosophical Transactions of the Royal Society of London. Series A: Mathematical and Physical Sciences*, 262/1124, 'A Discussion on Orbital Analysis' (13 July 1967): 41–5

Nicholls, J., 'Unattended Ground Sensors', *Field Artilleryman*, March 1971: 6–11

Omand, D., 'Intelligence Secrets and Media Spotlights: Balancing Illumination and Dark Corners', in Dover and Goodman (eds), *Spinning Intelligence*: 37–56

Pepper, D., 'The Business of Sigint: The Role of Modern Management in the Transformation of GCHQ', *Public Policy and Administration*, 25/1 (2010): 85–99

Porritt, V.L., 'Tim Hardy: Special Branch, Sarawak, December 1961–March 1968', *Borneo Research Bulletin* (2006): 1–18

Price, E., 'Interview Lord Carrington', *Country Life*, 30 August 2007

Rawnsley, G.D., 'Cold War Radio in Crisis: The BBC Overseas Service, the Suez Crisis and the Hungarian Uprising, 1956', *Historical Journal of Film, Radio and Television*, 15/2–3 (1995): 197–217

— 'Overt and Covert: The Voice of Britain and Black Radio Broadcasting in the Suez Crisis, 1956', *I&NS*, 11/3 (1996): 497–522

Robertson, K.G., 'Recent Reform of Intelligence in the UK: Democratisation or Risk Management?', *I&NS*, 13/2 (1988): 144–58

Rudner, M., 'Britain Betwixt and Between: UK Sigint Alliance Strategy's Transatlantic and European Connections', *I&NS*, 19/4 (2004): 571–609

Samin, A., 'The Tragedy of the Turkish Left', *New Left Review* (March–April 1981)

Schlesinger, S., 'Cryptanalysis for Peacetime and the Birth of the Structure of the United Nations', *Cryptologia*, 19/2 (1995): 217–35

Scott, L., 'Espionage and the Cold War: Oleg Penkovsky and the Cuban Missile Crisis', *I&NS*, 14/4 (1999): 23–48

Shapiro, S., 'Intelligence Services and Foreign Policy: German–Israeli Intelligence and Military Cooperation', *German Politics*, 11/1 (2002): 33–4

Stafford, D., 'The British Foreign Office and the Intelligence Struggle in Germany During the 1960s: A Personal Perspective', paper to the Fifth

Annual Meeting of the International Intelligence History Study Group, Tutzing, Bavaria, June 1999

Streetly, M., 'The Intelligence War: Vital Role of SIGINT in the Battle for Baghdad Cannot be Overstated', *Jane's Defence Weekly*, 39/12 (2003): 23–7

Stripp, A.J., 'Breaking Japanese Codes', *I&NS*, 2/4 (1987): 135–50

Syari, S., 'The Terrorist Movement in Turkey: Social Composition and Generational Changes', *Conflict Quarterly* (Winter 1987): 21–33

Tamkin, N., 'Diplomatic Sigint and the British Official Mind During the Second World War: Soviet Claims on Turkey, 1940–45', *I&NS*, 23/6 (2008): 749–66

Taylor, T., 'Anglo–American Signals Intelligence Cooperation', in Hinsley and Stripp (eds), *Code-Breakers*: 71–3

Thomas, A., 'British Signals Intelligence After the Second World War', *I&NS*, 3/4 (1988): 103–10

Thomas, M., 'France in British Signals Intelligence', *French History*, 14/1 (2000): 41–66

Toms, S., 'Enigma and the Eastcote Connection', *Ruislip, Northwood and Eastcote Local History Society Journal*, February 2005

Tow, W.T., 'The ANZUS Alliance and United States Security Interests', in Berkovitch, J. (ed.), 'ANZUS in Crisis: Alliance Management in International Affairs' (Macmillan, 1988): 61–6

Van der Meulen, M., 'German Air Force Signal Intelligence 1956: A Museum of COMINT and SIGINT', *Cryptologia*, 23/3 (1999): 240–56

— 'Cryptologic Services of the Federal Republic After 1945', paper to the Fifth Annual Meeting of the International Intelligence History Study Group, Tutzing, Bavaria, June 1999

Van der Reijn, J., 'Germany and the Netherlands in the Headquarters of the International Security Assistance Force in Afghanistan (ISAF): An Intelligence Perspective', in de Graaf, B., de Jong, B. and Platje, W. (eds), *Battleground Western Europe: Intelligence Operations in Germany and the Netherlands in the Twentieth Century* (Amsterdam: Uitgeverij Het Spinhuis, 2007): 217–36

Voltaggio, F., 'Out in the Cold: Early ELINT Activities of Strategic Air Command', *Journal of Electronic Defence*, 10, 2 (1984): 127–40

Walker, W., 'Borneo', *British Army Review*, August 1969: 7–15

Wark, W.K., 'In Never Never Land? The British Archives on Intelligence', *Historical Journal*, 35/1 (1992): 196–203

— 'Cryptographic Innocence: The Origins of Signals Intelligence in Canada in the Second World War', *Journal of Contemporary History*, 22/3 (1997): 639–65

Wentz, L. and Hingorani, G., 'NATO Communications in Transition', *IEEE Transactions on Communications*, 28/9 (1980): 1524–39

Westerfield, H.B., 'America and the World of Intelligence Liaison', *I&NS*, 11/3 (1996): 523–60

Whitaker, P. and Kruh, L., 'From Bletchley Park to the Berchtesgaden', *Cryptologia*, 11/3 (1987): 129–41

Wiebes, C., 'Dutch Sigint During the Cold War, 1945–94', *I&NS*, 16/1 (2001)

Wilkinson, N., 'Balancing National Security and the Media', in Dover and Goodman (eds), *Spinning Intelligence*: 133–50

Winter, P., 'A Higher Form of Intelligence: Hugh Trevor-Roper and Wartime British Secret Service', *I&NS*, 22/6 (2007): 847–80

Wright, J., Wilkin, D., and Newton, N., 'GCHQ: Managing the Matrix', *Engineering Management Journal* (February 2004): 5–10

Young, J.W., 'George Wigg, the Wilson Government and the 1966 Report into Security in the Diplomatic Service and GCHQ', *I&NS*, 14/3 (1999): 198–209

Index

Sykes, Richard 297, 298, 335, 593
Syria 156, 157, 271, 291, 300, 301–2, 304, 308, 336, 344

Tai Mo Shan (New Territories) 154
Taipei 195
Taiwan 152, 195, 323
Taliban 535, 537
Tanzania 511
Taper (Soviet cypher traffic) 54, 108
Tartus (Syria) 331
TASS News Agency 190
Taylor, Telford 43
Tebbit, Kevin 498, 504
Technical Committee of London Signals Intelligence Committee 267
Technical Radio Interception Committee 131
Tedder, Lord 5
Tel Aviv 157–8, 180
telephone tapping and intercepts 170–6, 180, 244–5, 299, 340, 341–6, 376, 377, 474–5, 479–83, 486, 499, 500–1, 523, 541–5
Tempest (radiation/emanation phenomenon) 209, 215–18
Templer, Sir Gerald 150, 219
terrorists, terrorism 9, 168, 277, 307, 320–1, 452, 531; and 9/11 509–15; domestic 539; and Heathrow plot (2003) 515–16; and IRA 498–503; Libyan 455–8; see also kidnapping and hostage-taking
Teufelsberg (Germany) 478
Thatcher, Margaret 8; and Falklands conflict 298, 396, 400, 403–4; and mole-mania 363, 367; 1987 general election 433; obsession with secrecy 492; and polygraph 434; and removal of trade unions from GCHQ 415, 416–17, 423, 425, 426, 427, 428, 429, 430–1, 435; and tightening of the

Official Secrets Act 363; and Zircon project 442, 460
Third World 203, 259, 334
Thistlethwaite, Dick 255
Thomas, Richard 544
Thomas, Teddy 234
Thompson, Julian 402, 410–12
Thompson, Ralph 94
Thompson-CSF (arms company) 489
Thomson, Mike 131
Thorneycroft, Peter 163
Thorpe, Peter 535
Tiananmen Square massacre (1989) 476
Tickell, Crispin 290
TICOM (Target Intelligence Committee) teams 48–56, 76, 78
Tiltman, John 19, 31–2, 42, 44, 67, 78, 79, 96, 213
Tirpitz (German battleship) 35
Titchner, Lambert 186
Tito, Josip 4
Tomlinson, Richard 521
Tonkin, Derek 330, 333
Tornado Multi-Role Combat Aircraft 345
Toumlin, George 432
Tovey, Brian 167, 414, 415, 421–2, 423, 424, 428, 433, 442, 448, 461, 490
trade unions 317, 368, 389, 416–36, 497–8
Trades Union Congress (TUC) 416, 417, 419, 426, 427, 509
Travis, Edward 27, 28, 36, 43, 48, 49, 53, 56, 60, 67–9, 69, 92, 94, 101, 121
Trawlerman (DIS computer scheme) 527–8
Trend, Burke 221, 240, 241, 242, 269–70, 288, 322–3, 354, 364
Trevor-Roper, Hugh 221
Tromsø 134
Truman, Harry S. 73, 85, 91, 101, 108, 109, 116